The Declaration of Independence

The Declaration of Independence

America's First Founding Document in U.S. History and Culture

JOHN R. VILE

An Imprint of ABC-CLIO, LLC
Santa Barbara, California • Denver, Colorado

Library of Congress Cataloging-in-Publication Data

Names: Vile, John R., author.
Title: The Declaration of Independence : America's first founding document in U.S. history and culture / John R. Vile.
Description: Santa Barbara, California : ABC-CLIO, 2019. | Includes bibliographical references and index.
Identifiers: LCCN 2018018947 (print) | LCCN 2018025767 (ebook) | ISBN 9781440863035 (eBook) | ISBN 9781440863028 (hardcopy : alk. paper)
Subjects: LCSH: United States. Declaration of Independence—Encyclopedias. | United States—Politics and government—1775-1783—Encyclopedias.
Classification: LCC E221 (ebook) | LCC E221 .V46 2019 (print) | DDC 973.3/13—dc23
LC record available at https://lccn.loc.gov/2018018947

ISBN: 978-1-4408-6302-8 (print)
978-1-4408-6303-5 (ebook)

23 22 21 20 19 1 2 3 4 5

This book is also available as an eBook.

ABC-CLIO
An Imprint of ABC-CLIO, LLC

ABC-CLIO, LLC
130 Cremona Drive, P.O. Box 1911
Santa Barbara, California 93116-1911
www.abc-clio.com

This book is printed on acid-free paper ∞

Manufactured in the United States of America

Dedicated with appreciation and with recollections of happy memories to my two alma maters: the College of William and Mary, which educated Jefferson, and the University of Virginia, which Jefferson founded, and which is celebrating its bicentennial in 2019.

Contents

Topical List of Entries

Documents, Models, Predecessors, and Sources of Declaration

Engravings, Printings, and Memorials

Forms of Government

Minority Groups

Miscellaneous

Movements, Documents, and Individuals Inspired by, or Opposed to, Declaration

Speeches

States and Their Signers

Stylistic Qualities

Words and Phrases within Declaration [Also see Charges against the King and Glossary]

Writing of the Declaration

Preface

American laws require parents to complete birth certificates for newborns. The document that comes closest to a birth certificate for the United States, and apparently the first government document officially to use the name the United States of America, is the Declaration of Independence. Largely written by Thomas Jefferson before being debated and revised in the Second Continental Congress, it was adopted on July 4, 1776 (two days after the Continental Congress had adopted a resolution declaring independence), which continues to be recognized as Independence Day.

Except for the elegance of its language, the Declaration is written much like a legal indictment, with the majority of the document detailing the reasons that the colonies were renouncing the authority of the British king to assume their own equal station in the world. The opening paragraphs explain that in doing so, the one-time colonies were affirming the God-given rights to "life, liberty, and the pursuit of happiness," not only of the American people, but of all mankind. These evocations of equality and liberty have been constant sources of inspiration and controversy throughout American history. The document has been so fundamental, and its ideas so seminal, that it is altogether fitting to devote an encyclopedia to it. As I will attempt to explain next, I think it is also particularly fitting that I have had the opportunity to write it.

I have quoted throughout this book from *A Declaration by the Representatives of the United States of America, In General Congress Assembled* (Philadelphia: John Dunlap, July 4, 1776). Readers may find this full text in the appendix to this volume. I would encourage readers to begin by reading this Declaration prior to looking at individual entries. Throughout this book, I also refer often to passages that were modified, added, and omitted from Jefferson's initial draft. A copy of the transcript with Congress's edits can be found on the Thomas Jefferson Monticello website: "Transcript of the Declaration of Independence (Rough Draft)" (1950. Boyd, J. P. et al., eds. *The Papers of Thomas Jefferson.* Vol. 1. Princeton, NJ: Princeton University Press, p. 426. https://www.monticello.org/site/jefferson/transcript-declaration-independence-rough-draft).

The "Necessity" of Writing This Book: A Personal Journey

According to my mother, when I was in the sixth grade, my teacher told us to learn what we could about Thomas Jefferson in preparation for writing about him during a class period. Like others of my age, I enjoyed recess, but on that day, I asked if I could use my recess in order to continue writing. I simply could not conceive of how I could tell all that I knew about Jefferson in a single class period!

Fifty some years later, I find myself writing an introduction to an encyclopedia not on Jefferson's life but on a single one of his works, the Declaration of Independence. Just as Jefferson viewed the Declaration as both a choice and a necessity, so too, writing this encyclopedia is both something that I gladly chose to do and something that I seem to have been fated to do.

I had the good fortune of being raised and educated in the Commonwealth of Virginia, and although I have not lived there since graduate school, I return as often as I can. I even used a recent spring break to take students on a pilgrimage to historic sites there and in the nation's capital. I have commented elsewhere, with only a touch of hyperbole, that it was not until our own daughters got married and began spending their holidays at beaches that I realized that most families do not regularly plan their vacations (and, in my case, part of a honeymoon) around historic sites. I now recognize that some of the textbook history I learned as a child was designed to justify Virginia's continuing opposition to racial integration. I can still remember uncritical praise of "Carry Me Back to Old Virginia," which then served as the state song. I also recall historical interpretations that elevated the dignity of the "Lost Cause" over the rights of man (I still remember asking a teacher why, if the slaves had been so happy, they joyfully greeted Lincoln as a liberator when he visited Richmond). Despite such flaws, the subjects that stirred my greatest interest in elementary school were my fourth- and seventh-grade Virginia history classes. Each devoted prominent attention to the lives and deed of great Virginia statesmen, although as I grew older, it was difficult not to notice that most were from previous centuries.

Given such a background, it was almost as though I was fated to attend the College of William and Mary in Colonial Williamsburg, where we had taken a number of trips during my childhood. When I was in college, the musical *1776* was about as popular as today's *Hamilton*. It was good to be on a campus where my friends, many of whom were drawn to the college by the same considerations that drew me to it, celebrated the musical, too. As the dedication of this book reveals, I deeply appreciate my undergraduate education at William and Mary, where Jefferson had attended first as an undergraduate and then by reading law under George Wythe. When I read the Declaration and compare Jefferson's elegant prose to my own less polished efforts, however, I often recall a conversation that I had with one of our daughters after listening to her play the piano: "What did you do with the money?" "What money?" "The money we spent on your piano lessons!" In defense of both the college and me, I can report that my own professors were quite devoted to their jobs, and that I studied quite hard. As I ruminate on the differences between Jefferson and myself, I can only conclude that I did not arrive to the college with the same native abilities or preparation as my esteemed predecessor had and that the colonial classical curriculum might also have proved better than some of its modern alternatives at teaching the foundations of rhetoric. Still, I remain awed by the felicity of expression of a 33-year old graduate of the same college that I attended and feel a deep obligation to present his views and those of an emerging nation in as clear a manner as I can.

In continuing to reflect upon the relationship between choice and necessity, I further recognize that my wife's parents also mixed family vacations with historic exploration. Even though my wife was from New Jersey, William and Mary exerted the same gravitational pull on her as it did on me. We got married on the weekend before the bicentennial of American independence, persuaded that the following weekend would inconvenience friends who might have had already made plans for that celebration. Almost as if to confirm the role of fate, my wife discovered at a recent high school reunion that the first boy she had ever dated was now teaching constitutional law at a prestigious college in her home state.

I went from undergraduate classes at William and Mary to graduate classes at the University of Virginia. Mr. Jefferson played a role in founding the university, and he asked for this role to be one of three achievements listed on his tombstone. He has an even more ubiquitous spiritual presence at the University of Virginia than at William and Mary. The first question I remember when I was defending my dissertation on the philosophy of William James (why I did not choose to write about a Founding Father remains a mystery to me) in a room in the magnificent rotunda that he had designed to cap off his famous lawn with faculty and student housing was what Jefferson would have thought about James. Not surprisingly, one of my summer jobs was serving as a guide of what was then thought to have been James Monroe's "summer cottage," now believed to have been his guesthouse, which is not far from Jefferson's own Monticello.

I have been interested in politics at least since the presidential election of 1960, and so it almost also seemed a matter of necessity that I would major in political science, or "government," as both institutions I attended preferred to call the discipline. I have now spent almost 40 years teaching and writing about this subject, often giving particular attention to the statesmen from my home state. To this point, I have generally devoted greater attention to James Madison than to Jefferson, his closest political friend and ally, apart perhaps from Madison's wife, Dolley.

In addition to other works, I have written an encyclopedia about the Constitutional Convention of 1787, which was recently republished in a new edition. I have authored a separate book on the delegates to the convention and on the deliberations of the convention as well as multiple works, including encyclopedias, on the U.S. Constitution and various amendments to it. I have also completed four volumes annotating documents from the Founding period through the Civil War. Although a number of these books have touched on the subject, I have never before written extensively on the Declaration of Independence.

The idea for this present work grew from one of my more recent encyclopedic treatments of the U.S. flag, which I also wrote for ABC-CLIO. I enjoyed the project so much that even before I completed it, I began looking for a topic of similar breadth and consequence. Absent an encyclopedic treatment on the Bible, which I am not professionally qualified to write, I could not find any document that I thought had been more influential, or could hold my attention as long, as the

Declaration of Independence. I am pleased to report that the experience has been both intellectually and emotionally rewarding.

With the assistance of Middle Tennessee State University's (MTSU's) interlibrary loan office, J-STOR, Lexis-Nexis, and a host of other search engines and sources, I was constantly able to find new topics related to the document and new sources for these topics. In a home library that is otherwise becoming something of a growing albatross to house and organize, I have also discovered, and rediscovered, numerous books and essays, most of which I originally purchased for other purposes but that contain vital information about the Declaration. I owe special thanks to my wife, who has remained understanding as our library and credit card expenditures on books have continued to expand during my research.

Need for This Book

I would like to think that everyone has similar interests to my own, but I know that everyone does not, and that such diversity undoubtedly contributes to a better world. As an educator who believes that knowledge is essential to democracy, however, I do worry that many contemporary citizens know far more about contemporary pop culture than they do about their own heritage. This seemed confirmed when just prior to Independence Day in 2017, the National Public Radio Network tweeted out 113 consecutive posts of the Declaration of Independence only to be accused of having distributed "spam," "trash," "propaganda," and the like (reported in an article in the *Washington Post* on July 5, 2017, by Amy B. Wang, entitled "Some Trump Supporters Thought NPR Tweeted 'Propaganda.' It Was the Declaration of Independence"). There may be serious cause for concern when a large number of citizens cannot recognize such a fundamental document. Not knowing about the Declaration is a bit like not knowing about one's own birth.

Organization of This Book

Because it is an encyclopedia, I have arranged this book in a standard A to Z (or, in this case, A to W) format with a fair number of cross-references for topics that one might seek to find under different titles. Each entry references one or more additional entries that contain related information, as well as suggestions for further reading and research. Readers should know that apart from some key delegates to the Second Continental Congress like Jefferson, Adams, and Franklin (who not only signed the Document but were particularly influential in writing it or contributing to debates on the subject), I have not, as in my earlier encyclopedia of the Constitutional Convention, written individual essays on each signer, most of whose lives are fairly extensively documented elsewhere. This prompted a colleague to suggest that I had a fairly exclusive encyclopedia if even the signers did not warrant their own essays! Partly in answer to this critique, I have included short biographies of each signer in the entries that describe incidents and sentiments within each state that led up to its ratification. Thus, for example, the entry on Massachusetts and its signers includes a short biography about Elbridge Gerry, and the essay on New York and its signers includes information about Alexander Hamilton.

Key Topics

In addition to entries on each of the 13 states, I have written at least one entry on each sentence in the Declaration. Just as I have covered the lives of the signers within essays on individual states, so too I have often grouped topics that the Declaration treats in a single sentence such as "life, liberty, and the pursuit of happiness" and "our lives, our fortunes, and our sacred honor" into a single essay.

Most commentary on the Declaration has focused on its opening sentences, and the noble philosophy they embody, and I have tried to give them their due. The great bulk of the Declaration is a list of 28 accusations, however, written much like a legal indictment, against the king and his associates. I find them particularly important. Not only do they illumine the history of the period, but by describing institutions and policies that the colonists believed were dysfunctional, they also pointed to the kind of representative institutions that they favored and according to which they would pattern the constitutional documents they wrote. I have accordingly included individual entries on each of these charges. The topical table of contents lists these under Charges Against the King in the order in which Jefferson made them, typically using a phrase or key word from each of the accusations.

Although my primary focus is on the Declaration that the Continental Congress debated, revised, and printed, I have also included entries on the major revisions and deletions that Congress chose to make in the document. Unlike some writers, I have not done so because I think that Jefferson's draft was superior to the one that Congress adopted. Although I do not generally recommend editing by committee, I believe that almost anyone can use a good set of editors. Instead, I believe we understand the document not only by what it said but by what delegates decided to exclude.

Given the breadth of sources with which the Founding Fathers were familiar, the list of potential influences on the Declaration are virtually endless. Without delving too deeply into debates about which influence was the greatest, I have included entries on key theorists and movements such as John Locke, the Scottish Enlightenment, natural law theorists, and Whig political thought, whose overlapping perspectives influenced the Declaration. I have also included entries on contemporary documents such as Thomas Paine's *Common Sense*, the Virginia Declaration of Rights, the Declaration of Sentiments, the Declaration on Taking Up Arms, Richard Henry Lee's Resolution for Independence, John Dickinson's speech cautioning against proceeding with independence too quickly, and other relevant works.

I have made particular efforts to include contemporary criticisms of the Declaration, particularly as they relate to the charges against the King. I expect readers to draw their own conclusions, but—making some allowance for hyperbole and the fact that fighting, and the accompanying fog of war, had already bred considerable mistrust and ill will between the colonies and the mother country—I find that all the accusations are grounded in facts. This did not mean that denizens on opposite sides of the Atlantic (or even on one side or the other) would necessarily draw the same conclusions, either in 1776 or today, but were they willing to listen, they might at least agree on the central points of dispute. Not all will do so. David A. Randall, who specialized in collecting early American manuscripts, thus reports in his essay "Dukedom Large Enough" that a British citizen once plaintively queried him "as to why Jefferson so disliked the English. 'Good God,' I remarked, 'haven't you ever read the Declaration of Independence?' And she blandly replied that she hadn't and furthermore had no intention of doing so!" (Randall, David A. 1962. "'Duketon Large Enough': III. Thomas Jefferson and the Declaration of Independence." *Papers of the Bibliographical Society of America* 45: 472–480.)

One could undoubtedly write an entire book on interpretations of the Declaration throughout U.S. history. Although I have included essays on John C. Calhoun, Abraham Lincoln, and a number of other statesmen who have had a major impact on how their contemporaries understood the document, I have not sought to include everyone who has made such observations. I have included essays on congressional and presidential references to and U.S. Supreme Court interpretations of the Declaration as well as on the continuing influence that the Declaration has had on constitutional interpretation, one of my own academic areas of interest, throughout our history.

Like the U.S. flag, the Declaration has become a cultural icon. Again recognizing that even an encyclopedic treatment will not be exhaustive, I have tried to identify key monuments, paintings, coins, stamps, and other artifacts that have helped shape many of our understandings of the document. There are far too many printings of the document to include them all, but I have identified early printings that were especially significant and that treasure hunters would want to retain should they find one in a colonial attic.

I have included numerous other essays on miscellaneous matter. I regret that I do not have a specific entry on humor and the Declaration, but one rather informal measure of its influence is that it is not unusual to see cartoons or hear jokes that refer directly or indirectly to the document. In a cartoon labeled "Great Presidential Writings Throughout History," cartoonist Stephen Pastis (*Pearls Before Swine*) recently quoted three presidents and an unnamed figure he labels as President Rat. Pastis quoted Jefferson as writing "That all men are created equal"; Lincoln as saying, "Four score and seven years ago"; Franklin Roosevelt as observing that we have "nothing to fear but fear itself"; and President Rat as tweeting "illegal to punch journalists in the head. Sad!" More recently, a posting "Under Men's Humor," which adheres more closely to the language of the Virginia Declaration of Rights than to the Declaration of Independence, observed that "all men are born free and equal. If they go and get married, that's their own fault." Yet another web posting entitled "Hilarious Kid Answers to Test Questions" reported that when asked "Where was the Declaration of Independence signed," a student responded, "At the bottom."

Navigating This Book

In addition to cross references and citations of sources, this book included both a conventional table of contents and a topical table of contents. An appendix includes the text of the Declaration of Independence with notations of additions and deletions to which readers may want to refer. For those who want to track specific phrases and sentences within the document, I have further added footnotes to direct readers to specific entries related to each of them. As one who often turns first to a book's bibliography, I have included most references in a separate bibliography, which is divided into two parts. One focuses on articles, chapters, and pamphlets, and the other identifies key books. The book also includes an index, for which I gratefully credit Larry Baker, and which I always find indispensable in my own research. I owe special thanks to Jane Glenn, the development editor at ABC-CLIO, as well as to Ellen Rasmussen, media editor, who helped secure the art.

I have included three other aids. One is a timeline that highlights key dates. The second is a set of interesting facts that might be of special interest to school students and their teachers. A third is an extensive glossary that attempts to tease out some of the nuances of the words that the Declaration employed that might otherwise be lost after more than 240 years.

Audience for This Book

Although this book does not have the word "encyclopedia" in its title, this book is effectively organized as such a work. Although I anticipate that its chief use will be for individuals seeking specific answers to immediate questions, I hope there are at least some readers who will more fully immerse themselves in the entries. I believe that this book will be most helpful to librarians in high schools, colleges, law schools, and public libraries. I also hope that some of my professorial colleagues, with interest in America's founding documents, may find it useful enough to purchase for their own use.

Although I have added some entries on topics such as moral virtue and the treatment of human nature within the Declaration, on which I could not locate similar books or articles, this work is not designed to provide a pathbreaking new interpretation but to summarize existing scholarship. In this respect, I have designed this book to resemble the Declaration itself, which Jefferson said he had not designed to articulate new principles but to present the common sense of the subject in understandable prose.

Interpreting the Document

After studying the Declaration for more than 40 years and immersing myself (consistent with my Baptist heritage) in the topic for many months, I have discovered both a pet peeve and a source of considerable confusion and speculation in reading existing interpretations of the document: that is what I consider to be the mistake of seeking to understand the document through a single phrase or through the single perspective of Jefferson and/or one of the philosophies that may have influenced him and his contemporaries. Much as I respect many aspects of the man whom commentator George Will designated as the "Person of the Millennium" in an editorial that he published in the *Washington Post* on December 16, 1990, I believe that the Declaration is a public document. As such, I believe that it should be interpreted by what it said rather than by what Jefferson, or any of his colleagues, may have privately thought. Such private thoughts are undoubtedly valuable in their own right, but the document speaks in its own public language, and I have attempted to focus on it rather than on any merely personal or esoteric meaning.

Recognizing that there may be some fortuity in the phrasing of the document, I believe that Jefferson and those who revised the document were thoughtful men who chose their words, especially their public expressions, with care. I was thus somewhat dismayed to hear a proponent of human rights being interviewed on November 25, 2017, on National Public Radio refer to rights "that our founders accidentally put down." Not everyone will be consoled by my own belief that the Framers did not always live up to their own principles and that they could sometimes be hypocritical in identifying the motes in the king's eyes without calling attention to the log of slavery in their own. I think there are cases, however, where it is more accurate to recognize that the Founders could sometimes act hypocritically than to accuse them of loose, or "accidental," thinking, especially at such a time of national peril.

The opening verse of the gospel of John observes that "in the beginning was the Word." As a scholar, I prize thoughts and the words with which we express them. I realize that words can be catalysts to actions and that, however they may sometimes serve similar purposes, they are more than mere beaks and claws (Thomas Hobbes) or (as Hume described Reason) mere slaves of passion. Knowing that individuals can employ words both to denigrate and to inspire, I especially value words such as those within the Declaration of Independence that kindle noble thoughts and inspire great deeds. I believe that America has been at its best when it has sought to live up to the principles of the Declaration of Independence, and I hope that readers will not lose sight of the Declaration's ideals and principles amid the welter of individual entries.

John R. Vile
Middle Tennessee State University
In the two thousand and eighteenth year of our Lord and
in the two hundred and forty-second year of the
independence of the United States of America

Introduction

Lest readers become lost amid the approximately 200 individual entries in this volume, I am providing this brief introductory history of the adoption and significance of the Declaration of Independence. The Declaration both profits and suffers from the fact that many people know, or think they know, about it. Indeed, it is common to find articles, especially around Independence Day, that begin by refuting the most common myths that surround it, including when it was signed, what it actually did (and did not do), and when it became unanimous.

Colonial Background

The United States of America began as 13 colonies, most of which were initially planted by, and all of which became subject to, Great Britain. Some, like Delaware, Pennsylvania, and Maryland, were ruled by proprietors. Others (most notably Connecticut and Rhode Island) chiefly relied on charters. Still others, which constituted a majority, were ruled by governors appointed by the British king.

The colonies were founded and settled before the British Parliament had gained its current legal ascendancy, or sovereignty, within Britain, which had previously been regarded largely as having a mixed constitution balancing monarchy (the king or queen), aristocracy (the House of Lords), and democracy (the House of Commons). In the meantime, American colonies developed their own representative institutions (the Virginia House of Burgesses first met in 1619), which with respect to internal affairs, they regarded as parliamentary equals. Colonists, who believed they had brought their treasured rights of Englishmen with them to the newly discovered continent, increasingly began to see themselves, much like Scotland or contemporary nations in the British Commonwealth of Nations, as politically bound to Britain largely through allegiance to a common king. They also recognized this common history, adherence to English common law, and what the Declaration referred to as ties of consanguinity, or kinship, as binding them to the mother country.

In early years, American colonists, who, like their British forebears, were predominately Protestants, looked warily at perceived dangers from French Catholics to the north, Native American "savages" (for such most colonists conceived them) to the west, and Spanish Catholics to the south. Just as today's Americans look to the president as commander in chief of the nation's armed forces, colonial Americans expected that the king, who had issued their charters and appointed their governors, would protect them against such potential foes.

Americans, including George Washington, actually helped trigger the conflict that enmeshed them with the British in a war against France and its Native American Indian allies. The success of this endeavor led to the transfer of French possessions in Canada from France to Great Britain. Ironically, this loosened ties between Britain and the 13 colonies by relieving them of a major threat against which they needed British protection. As a result of the war, Britain faced massive debt and rising taxes, the burdens of which it thought that the colonies should share.

The End of the French and Indian War

At about the same time, Britain and other empires were seeking to consolidate their power over their possessions. Whereas Britain had previously largely viewed the colonies, whose trade it had restricted, as trading partners, and exercised what Edmund Burke described as a "wise and salutary neglect" over other matters, its leaders began increasingly to regard them as revenue sources. To achieve this end, the king and his royal governors began taking an increased role in the colonies, which often prompted resistance among colonial legislatures.

Deeply cognizant of the rights of Englishmen, colonists could cite the Magna Carta (1215), the English Bill of Rights (1689), and other documents for the principle of "no taxation without representation." From the emerging colonial perspective, because representatives in Britain could not feel the effects of taxation that they imposed in the colonies, they had no right to enact them. From the British perspective, members of Parliament represented all Englishmen at home and abroad (so-called virtual representation) and those who shared in the benefits of British citizenship were obligated to share in the burdens.

Beginning with the adoption of the Sugar Act in 1764 and the Stamp Act in 1765, Parliament began to devise ways to impose taxes that it had a reasonable chance of collecting in the colonies. After this second act led to significant opposition, evident in the calling of a colonial Stamp Act Congress, which representatives of 12 of the 13 colonies attended, Parliament repealed the tax. It adopted a Declaratory Act the following year, however, which affirmed that it still had the right to enact similar measures. The colonists, who were ever jealous of their rights, and whose favorite political theorists had cautioned them to resist the first signs of arbitrary power, pushed back, even in the face of the Townshend Duties (taxes) on glass, lead, and other commodities of 1767. These, in turn, like the 1773 imposition of a tax on tea, led to the arrival of English troops to quell colonial disturbances and multiplied the occasions for negative interactions, like the so-called Boston Massacre of 1770, the colonial torching of the HMS *Gaspee* in 1772, and the Boston Tea Party of 1773.

This latter expression of colonial disdain for British policies in turn provoked the British to adopt the Coercive, or Intolerable, Acts, which were designed to punish Boston. Their most important effect was to strengthen colonial resolve as expressed in the calling of the First Continental Congress in 1774, which adopted a boycott of British imports.

The Second Continental Congress

The Second Continental Congress, which met not long after British attempts to confiscate colonial arms led to the Battles of Lexington and Concord in April 1775, resulted in the adoption of the Declaration of Independence. Even after the colonies appointed George Washington to lead a continental army and engage the British just outside Boston in the pitched battle known as Bunker Hill, a majority of colonists continued to hope for reconciliation. Colonial theoreticians and apologists had continued to profess loyalty to the English king while rejecting parliamentary power. Working through committees, the Continental Congress assumed most legislative and executive powers on behalf of the colonies.

When the Second Continental Congress convened in May of 1775, delegates were divided as to how to proceed. An increasing number of delegates were beginning to talk about independence, but the majority were still convinced that the problems the colonists had encountered were the result of parliamentary actions or bad advice from the king's counselors rather than of the king himself. Initially, Washington's troops saw themselves as fighting against parliamentary forces, rather than against the king. This position became more difficult to sustain after the king proclaimed on August 23, 1775 that the colonists were in "open and avowed" rebellion, after he refused even to receive the "Olive Branch" petition, and after he began recruiting foreign troops, which the colonists derisively described as "mercenaries," to enforce his will in America.

Against this background, Thomas Paine, who had newly immigrated to America from Britain, published *Common Sense* in January 1776. Although it must have been shocking for many readers to see him identify kingship so unequivocally with corruption, war, and oppression, Paine made a strong case, especially against the institution of hereditary succession. His work, and the king's own continuing actions, turned the negative sentiments that the colonist had been directing against the authority of the Parliament to the king, who became the primary target of the Declaration of Independence.

As winter turned to spring, states began sending authorizations to their delegates to vote for independence. As governors dismissed state legislatures and governments disintegrated in the colonies, John Adams and Richard Henry Lee introduced resolutions encouraging states to adopt new constitutions. Adams was among those who thought that the adoption of this resolution in May 1776 came close to declaring independence. If the colonists were to create their own governments, what need would there be for a king?

In Virginia, Governor Dunmore (John Murray) had dissolved the legislature and was attempting to govern from a ship, from which he was promising freedom to slaves who would join his cause. On May 15, 1776, a convention in Virginia accordingly adopted a resolution for independence. Richard Henry Lee introduced this resolution in Congress on June 7, along with other resolutions proposing that the Congress seek foreign allies and begin formulating another government. Thankfully, scholars are increasingly pointing to the way that these resolutions were related and how the Declaration rightly pointed not only to the equality of men but also to the equality of nations and peoples.

Initial debate demonstrated that the time was not quite ripe for an affirmative vote. Although the northeastern and southern states largely agreed on the need for independence, opinion lagged in the less homogenous middle states. Although most were not opposed in principle to independence, they were unsure that the times was ripe. They were also divided about whether a formal declaration would, as its proponents argued, encourage foreign aid, or whether opposition to a king might stir unease among other monarchs who would otherwise welcome the opportunity to decrease British power.

The committee to write the Declaration consisted of delegates from all three regions of the nation. Its members were Thomas Jefferson (VA), John Adams (MA), Benjamin Franklin (PA), Roger Sherman (CT), and Robert Livingston (NY). The Committee agreed that Jefferson, who had already drafted a list of indictments against the king and was known to have a felicitous pen, would write the rough draft, to which Franklin and Adams made a number of relatively inconsequential emendations, prior to its submission to Congress. There would, however, be no need of a document declaring independence unless and until Congress decided to declare it.

On July 1, a Committee of the Whole in the Continental Congress took a vote. It showed 9 states ready to support independence, with Pennsylvania, Delaware, and South Carolina split and the delegates from New York still without official authorization to vote for independence. By the next day, Caesar Rodney had made a feverish ride from Delaware to break his state's tie, and Edward Rutledge was ready to put South Carolina in the yes column. Likewise, Robert Morris and John Dickinson either stayed home or abstained from voting, so that Pennsylvania could give its approval for independence. John Adams was convinced that the nation would thenceforth celebrate this date as Independence Day.

This honor went instead to July 4. It marks the day that the Continental Congress, after two additional days of debate, accepted the Declaration of Independence as its formal justification of its decision to separate from Britain. The debates over the Declaration had been quite painful for the young Jefferson (Franklin had sought to console him with an amusing anecdote) as he silently watched Congress modify or delete key phrases and sections. Today, however, there is general scholarly agreement that most of the changes strengthened the document. It announced independence, proclaimed ringing philosophical principles, and listed multiple grievances designed, much like a legal indictment, to show that the King was attempting to govern the colonies despotically. It ended with a mutual pledge among the delegates to support the resolution for independence. The Declaration never even mentioned the British Parliament by name, since Americans had long since rejected its authority.

John Dunlap first printed the Declaration on the night of July 4 with the printed signature of John Hancock, the president of the Congress, and Charles Thomson, the secretary. John Hancock, the president of the Continental Congress, sent the document throughout the states for proclamation and it provoked fairly widespread celebration. Some Tories remained critical of independence, but for the *most* part, they laid low. Sometimes they were encouraged to do so due to the knowledge that Patriots sometimes tarred and feathered those who disagreed with them. Only after Congress received word on July 19 that New York agreed to make state consent unanimous, did Congress order the document to be engrossed by Timothy Matlack on the parchment copy that was signed on August 2, and days following. After an early period of relative neglect, the Declaration is now reverently displayed in the National Archives along with the U.S. Constitution and the proposals that eventually became the Bill of Rights.

After the Document Was Signed

Although the Declaration served its purpose in mobilizing both internal and external constituencies, attention quickly turned to the day-to-day waging of war, to drafting the Articles of Confederation, and to the task of securing allies. Once Congress declared independence, there was little need to reiterate past grievances, except perhaps to motivate those engaged in the fight. For many years, Jefferson's role as chief author of the document was largely unknown and unheralded, and by the time his role became known, his name was so associated with the Democratic-Republican Party that the Declaration and its celebration became more of a partisan rallying point than a national one.

Jealousy also seemed to play a part. There was little doubt that John Adams had carried much of the burden in the fight for independence, but in time his work seemed less important than Jefferson's words and the actions of men in the field like George Washington. Adams would later complain that "In Virginia . . . all geese are swans." Adams tried to gain some credit for having insisted (for so he remembered) that Jefferson serve as the primary author, but he and Federalist colleagues could not help but quibble that the work was not particularly original and may have even been plagiarized from John Locke and others. Jefferson willingly acknowledged that he had not sought to be original but that he had aimed at expressing common colonial sentiments. Still, he remained proud enough of this achievement that he asked that it be the first of three to be listed on his tombstone, and in one of his final letters, he described its purpose as that of sounding the death knell to hereditary privilege and oppression.

As much as any event, the deaths of Jefferson and Adams fifty years to the day that the Continental Congress had approved the Document, helped heal some of the partisan divisions that had plagued earlier Independence Day celebrations and redirected attention to the document. These deaths further redirected attention to the values expressed in the Declaration.

The conflict over Missouri's admission into the Union as a slave state in 1820 (resolved by also admitting Maine as a free state) had demonstrated that the nation was split on whether African Americans should have liberty to earn bread by the sweat of their own brows and by claims of John C. Calhoun and others that the equality announced in the Declaration was a palpable lie. In the *Dred Scott* decision of 1857, which declared that the Missouri Compromise and other attempts to exclude slavery from federal territories had been unconstitutional, Chief Justice Roger Taney agreed that the Constitution applied only to "white men." Abraham Lincoln, who described the Declaration of Independence as the "apple of gold" that animated the constitutional frame of silver, came down firmly on the side of those who believed that the announcement of equal rights should apply to all. Lincoln's election, and the Southern response to it, prompted the Civil War that ended slavery and resulted in the incorporation of an "equal protection" clause within the Fourteenth Amendment to the U.S. Constitution.

As much as the principles of the Declaration had fueled the struggle for emancipation, new generations arose to question the whole idea of self-evidence, of inalienability, and even the concept of human rights themselves. U.S. senator (MA) Rufus Choate once derisively referred to the principles of the Declaration as a set of "glittering generalities." Social Darwinists questioned whether human nature was fixed and sought scientific justifications for theories that some races might be more evolved, and thus superior to, others. Some Populist and Progressive spokespersons further questioned principles like separation of powers and checks and balances and sought to replace representative institutions with more democratic mechanisms or with what they thought would be less partisan rule by bureaucratic elites.

The Declaration Today

In addition to its role in inspiring nationalist movements abroad, advocates of women's rights, the rights of African Americans, LGBTQ rights, rights of the handicapped, immigrant rights, rights of the unborn, and others have subsequently appealed to the principles of the Declaration with varying degrees of success. In the process, they have often highlighted the gaps between the principles that America's Founders—especially those who bought, sold, and owned slaves—professed and the degrees to which they were able to implement them.

I certainly recognize the Founders' failure to live up to all of their own ideals. Still, amid a world of despotism and cynicism, I remain grateful that Jefferson and his colleagues chose to highlight such enduring values as truth, equality of rights, liberty, and representative government based on consent. I believe, with the poet Robert Browning, that "a man's reach should exceed his grasp." I further believe that the elegant words and high ideals of the Declaration not only provided inspiration for the immediate occasion and guidance for the establishment of new government but that they should continue to challenge us to achieve new heights.

Timeline

1215	Magna Carta establishes principle of "no taxation without representation."
1606	James I grants charters to the London Company and the Plymouth Company to settle in America.
1689	British Declaration of Rights outlines principles by which William and Mary agree to govern.
1696	The king establishes a Board of Trade to help administer overseas dominions.
1733	Britain enacted the Molasses Act, but it was poorly enforced and collected little revenue.
1755–1763	The French and Indian War, which pitted France and its Indian allies against Britain and the 13 colonies, results in a win for Britain and the transfer of Canada to Britain. The British Parliament subsequently ends its policy of "salutary neglect" and seeks to tax the colonists.
1759	The British capture Quebec.
1760	George III ascends to the English throne at the age of 22.
1761	James Otis argues against British Writs of Assistance.
October 7, 1763	British proclamation seeks to reserve lands beyond the Appalachian Mountains for Native Americans.
April 4, 1764	Parliament adopts the Sugar Act.
March 22, 1765	Parliament adopts the Stamp Act.
May 1765	Parliament adopts Quartering Act.
October 7–25, 1765	Meeting of the Stamp Act Congress takes place in New York City.
March 18, 1766	Parliament repeals the Stamp Act while adopting the Declaratory Act.
1767	Parliament adopts the Townshend Revenue Acts.
January 1770	Frederic North becomes British prime minister.
March 5, 1770	Five people are killed in the so-called Boston Massacre, which was popularized in a contemporary print produced by Paul Revere.

November 1772	First Committee of Correspondence is formed in Boston, largely at the urging of Samuel Adams.
1773	Virginia takes the lead in setting up committees of correspondence.
May 10, 1773	Parliament adopts the Tea Act.
December 16, 1773	Patriots throw tea from British ships into the Boston Harbor.
1774	James Wilson publishes *Considerations on the Nature and Extent of the Legislative Authority of the British Parliament.*
	Thomas Jefferson's *A Summary View of the Rights of British America* is published.
March 28, 1774	British adopt the Coercive (Intolerable) Acts.
May 20, 1774	British adopt the Administration of Justice Act.
May 24, 1774	Jefferson drafts a Virginia Resolution calling for a Day of Fasting, Humiliation, and Prayer for June 1, 1774.
May 27, 1774	Virginia delegates call for a Continental Congress.
June 22, 1774	British adopt the Quebec Act.
September 5, 1774	The First Continental Congress begins meeting in Philadelphia and decides to meet in Carpenters' Hall.
September 6, 1774	Congress agrees that each state will have a single vote.
September 17, 1774	Congress adopts the Suffolk Resolves in protest against the Coercive Acts.
September 28, 1774	Joseph Galloway introduces a plan of union designed to prevent war, but it was not adopted.
October 14, 1774	Congress adopts its Declaration and Resolves.
October 20, 1774	Congress adopts the Articles of Association, proposing a boycott of the import and export of goods with Britain to begin on December 1.
October 26, 1774	The First Continental Congress adjourns.
November 24, 1774	The king issues a royal instruction prohibiting assent to any colonial naturalization acts.
December 15, 1774	Patriots attack Fort William and Mary in New Hampshire and capture arms and ammunition.
April 1775	The lord mayor of London sends a petition to the king, effectively taking the side of the colonists in the dispute.
April 19, 1775	Fighting breaks out between the British and Americans in Lexington and Concord, Massachusetts.
May 5, 1775	The Second Continental Congress convenes in Philadelphia.

June 14, 1775	Congress adopts a resolution that creates the Continental Army.
June 15, 1775	Congress appoints George Washington to lead the Continental Army.
June 17, 1775	The Battle of Bunker Hill, north of Boston, resulted in a costly British victory.
July 6, 1775	Congress adopts the Declaration on the Causes and Necessity of Taking Up Arms.
July 8, 1775	The Continental Congress adopts the Olive Branch Petition to send to George III.
July 16, 1775	The Second Continental Congress adopts its Declaration on Taking Up Arms.
July 31, 1775	Congress rejects Lord North's Conciliatory Proposal, which would have let the colonists tax themselves at a rate similar to that in England.
August 23, 1775	George III proclaims the colonists to be in "open and avowed" rebellion.
October 1775	The Continental Congress authorizes the creation of the U.S. Navy.
October 18, 1775	British warships bombard and destroy the town of Falmouth, Massachusetts.
October 27, 1775	George III gives another speech to Parliament identifying colonial leaders as conspirators.
November 3, 1775	Congress recommends that New Hampshire establish a new elected government.
November 4, 1775	Congress recommends that South Carolina adopt a new government
November 7, 1775	Governor Dunmore of Virginia declares martial law and offers freedom to slaves who join the British military.
November 29, 1775	Congress creates a Committee of Secret Correspondence in attempts to gain foreign allies.
December 4, 1775	Congress recommends that Virginia hold new elections and reorganize its government.
December 22, 1775	Parliament adopts the Prohibitory Act, granting British ships the right to seize all American ships and to impress their crews for military service.
1776	John Lind publishes *An Answer to the Declaration of the American Congress.*
	Thomas Hutchinson publishes his *Strictures upon the Declaration of Independence.*

January 1, 1776	British ships fire on Norfolk, Virginia. Patriots take advantage of the situation to torch Tory property.
January 8, 1776	Second Continental Congress gets George III's Speech to Parliament of October 26, 1775.
March 29, 1776	Congress instructs emissaries to urge Canada to join the 13 colonies and adopt a new constitution.
April 5, 1776	The Georgia legislature authorizes its delegates to the Continental Congress to exercise their judgment with respect to independence.
April 6, 1776	Congress opens all ports to international trade, thus nullifying English Acts of Trade and Navigation.
April 12, 1776	The North Carolina Provincial Congress unanimously authorizes its representatives to vote for independence.
May 4, 1776	Rhode Island authorized its delegates to vote for independence but did not specifically use the word.
May 10, 1776	John Adams and Richard Henry Lee introduce a resolution encouraging states to adopt new governments.
May 14, 1776	Congress approves the Adams/Lee resolution encouraging states to adopt new governments.
	Jefferson arrives in Philadelphia as a delegate to Congress from Virginia.
May 15, 1776	The Convention that met in Williamsburg to approve the Virginia Constitution and Declaration of Rights adopts a resolution asking the Continental Congress to declare the colonies to be free from both the British Crown and Parliament.
	Maryland delegates walk out of the Continental Congress.
	Congress votes to add the Preamble to its resolution on May 10.
May 17, 1776	Congress declares a day of "fasting, humiliation, and prayer."
June 7, 1776	Richard Henry Lee introduces resolution in Second Continental Congress for Independence. He also proposes arrangements for foreign alliances and for a new government.
June 10, 1776	The Continental Congress votes to table Lee's motion for three weeks as it waits for wavering colonies to agree to independence, but it also creates a committee to prepare a declaration of independence.
	The newly elected Provincial Congress of New Jersey voted to form a new government.
June 11, 1776	Congress appoints Thomas Jefferson, John Adams, Benjamin Franklin, Roger Sherman, and Robert Livingston to

	a Committee to draft a declaration of independence and resolves to create committees to seek treaties and draft a new government.
June 12, 1776	Congress appoints John Adams, Ben Franklin, John Dickinson, Benjamin Harrison, and Robert Morris to draft a plan for treaties with foreign governments and a committee of 13 delegates to draw up a new government.
June 15, 1776	Delaware allows delegates to promote "the liberty, safety, and interests of America."
June 19, 1776	The Virginia Convention approves a new state constitution.
June 20, 1776	Lord Richard Howe, commander of the British navy in North America, issued a declaration stating his authority to issue pardons and restore trade with American colonies who agreed to accept his authority.
June 23, 1776	New Jersey authorizes its delegates to vote for independence.
June 24, 1776	The Provincial Conference of Pennsylvania, which had effectively usurped the regular legislature, conveys its willingness to endorse independence.
June 25, 1776	The New Hampshire House of Representatives instructs its delegates to Congress to vote for independence.
June 28, 1776	Thomas Jefferson submits the draft he has written, and which John Adams and Benjamin Franklin had lightly revised, to the Committee of the Whole of the Second Continental Congress.
	Maryland changes its delegates' instructions so that they can vote for independence.
June 29, 1776	Thousands of British and Hessian troops arrive on Staten Island, New York.
July 1, 1776	Congress meets as a Committee of the Whole to discuss the proposed Declaration of Independence, but only 9 of 13 states are ready to declare independence, with Delaware split and New York still awaiting instructions.
July 2, 1776	The Second Continental Congress adopts the resolution for independence by a vote of 12–0 (New York abstaining) that Virginia's Richard Henry Lee introduced on June 7 and resolves itself as a Committee of the Whole for further discussion of the Declaration.
	General Sir William Howe lands 10,000 British troops on Staten Island.
July 4, 1776	After meeting yet again as a Committee of the Whole, the Second Continental Congress adopts a revised version of

	the Declaration of Independence that Thomas Jefferson authored.
	The Continental Congress appoints Franklin, Adams, and Jefferson to a Committee to devise a seal for the United States.
July 4–5, 1776	John Dunlap prints the first broadside of the Declaration of Independence.
July 6, 1776	First official printing of the Declaration of Independence by the *Pennsylvania Evening Post*.
July 8, 1776	The Declaration of Independence was publicly proclaimed in the State House Yard in Philadelphia.
July 9, 1776	New York approves the Declaration of Independence, so it now has unanimous consent of the states.
	New York City residents pulled down the statute of George III on Bowling Green Park in Manhattan to melt down for bullets.
July 15, 1776	Congress receives word that New York has approved the Declaration, thus making state consent unanimous.
July 19, 1776	Congress orders that the Declaration be engrossed on parchment, which is done by Timothy Matlack.
August 2, 1776	Delegates begin signing the Declaration of Independence.
August 16, 1776	First date under which Declaration of Independence is printed (*London Chronicle*) in Great Britain.
October 31, 1776	George III responds to Declaration of Independence in speech to Parliament.
December 26, 1776	Revolutionary forces win battle in Trenton, New Jersey.
January 3, 1777	Revolutionary forces capture Princeton, New Jersey.
January 18, 1777	Congress orders copies of Declaration of Independence be printed with names of signers.
1778	David Ramsey of South Carolina delivers what is believed to be the first Independence Day Address.
1781	Maryland is the last state to ratify the Articles of Confederation.
1783	Ezra Stiles, the president of Yale, gives a sermon, subsequently issued as a pamphlet, that identified Thomas Jefferson as the primary author of the Declaration of Independence.
September 3, 1783	Diplomats sign the Treaty of Paris, officially providing British recognition of the United States as a new state.
1787	Fifty-five delegates meet in Philadelphia to draft the U.S. Constitution.

July 13, 1787	Congress adopts the Northwest Ordinance.
1789	The government under the new U.S. Constitution goes into effect.
	The French Constituent Assembly adopts the Declaration of the Rights of Man and of Citizen.
1791	States ratify the Bill of Rights, which includes the Fifth Amendment, which prohibits deprivations of "life, liberty, or property" without due process of law.
1814	Facing British invasion, the Declaration was moved from the War Office Building to the house of a clergyman in Leesville, Virginia.
1818	Benjamin Owen Tyler publishes an engraved copy of the Declaration of Independence.
1819	John Binn publishes a decorated copy of the Declaration of Independence.
April 30, 1819	The *Raleigh Register and North Carolina Gazette* publishes an article by Dr. Joseph McKnitt Alexander discussing the Mecklenburg Declaration of Independence, now generally regarded as spurious.
1820	The Declaration is moved to the Department of State.
July 4, 1821	Secretary of State John Quincy Adams reads the Declaration of Independence to the U.S. House of Representatives and extolls the document in a speech.
July 4, 1823	Timothy Pickering, an ardent Federalist, gave a speech in which he attempted to minimize Jefferson's role with respect to the Declaration of Independence.
1823	Secretary of State John Quincy Adams authorized a facsimile of the Declaration, which was made by William J. Stone, and Congress distributes it.
1823–1827	Joseph M. Sanderson publishes a nine-volume *Biography of the Signers of the Declaration of Independence*.
July 4, 1826	Thomas Jefferson and John Adams die on the 50th anniversary of the adoption of the Declaration of Independence.
1829	Charles A. Goodrich publishes one-volume *Lives of the Signers to the Declaration of Independence*.
July 4, 1831	James Monroe, one of the last of the Founding Fathers, dies.
1841	Secretary of State Daniel Webster orders the Declaration to be moved from the Department of State to the new Patent Office.
1848	The Seneca Falls Convention, which advocates women's suffrage, patterns its Declaration of Sentiments on the Declaration of Independence.

1854	The adoption of the Kansas-Nebraska Act reopens the issue of slavery in the territories.
1860	Abraham Lincoln is elected president, prompting many Southern states to secede.
1861	The Civil War begins.
1863	Union forces defeat Confederate forces at the Battle of Gettysburg. Lincoln's Gettysburg Address ties the Union cause to the Declaration.
1864	Congress specifies that the constitutions of new states admitted to the Union must adhere to the principles of the Declaration of Independence.
1865	The Civil War ends with Lee's surrender at Appomattox.
	President Lincoln is assassinated.
	The Thirteenth Amendment eliminates involuntary servitude.
1868	States ratify Fourteenth Amendment, which guarantees "equal protection of the laws" and protects against "life, liberty, or property" without "due process of law."
1870	Independence Day is proclaimed to be a national holiday.
1876	The nation celebrates the centennial of the Declaration.
1904	Herbert Friedenwald publishes *The Declaration of Independence: An Interpretation and an Analysis*.
1920	The Nineteenth Amendment prohibits the use of sex as a condition for voting.
September 30, 1921	The Engrossed Manuscript of the Declaration is transferred to the Library of Congress.
1922	Carl L. Becker publishes *The Declaration of Independence: A Study in the History of Political Ideas*.
1941	The Declaration of Independence and other historic documents were moved to Fort Knox, Kentucky, for greater protection during World War II.
1943	Dedication of the Jefferson Memorial in Washington, D.C., with statue of Jefferson and engravings of words from the Declaration of Independence.
	Julian Boyd publishes *The Declaration of Independence: The Evolution of the Text as Shown in Facsimiles of Various Drafts by its Author, Thomas Jefferson*.
October 1, 1944	The Declaration is displayed again at the shrine of the Library of Congress.

1946	Ho Chi Minh uses the Declaration of Independence as a model when declaring Vietnam's independence from France.
1950	Edward Dumbauld publishes *The Declaration of Independence and What It Means Today*.
December 13, 1952	The Declaration is transferred to the National Archives Building.
1963	Dr. Martin Luther King Jr. delivers his "I Have a Dream" speech at the March on Washington, D.C.
July 2, 1964	Congress adopts the Civil Rights Act of 1964, banning discrimination in most places of public accommodation.
1964	David Freeman Hawke publishes *A Transaction of Free Men: The Birth and Course of the Declaration of Independence*.
1967	Robert Ginsberg publishes *A Casebook on The Declaration of Independence*.
1974	President Richard Nixon resigns from office in the face of the Watergate scandal and possible impeachment, demonstrating that American presidents remain subject to law.
1976	The nation celebrates the bicentennial.
1978	Garry Wills publishes *Inventing America: Jefferson's Declaration of Independence*.
1997	Pauline Maier publishes *American Scripture: Making the Declaration of Independence*.
1998	Allen Jayne publishes *Jefferson's Declaration of Independence*.
July 5, 2001	The engrossed Declaration is removed from public viewing at the National Archives so the display can be renovated over the next two year.
	Hans L. Eicholz publishes *Harmonizing Sentiments: The Declaration of Independence and the Jeffersonian Idea of Self-Government*.
2002	Scott Douglas Gerber publishes *The Declaration of Independence: Origins and Impact*.
2012	Alexander Tsesis publishes *For Liberty and Equality*.
2014	Barry Shain publishes *The Declaration of Independence in Historical Context*.
2017	Tim Patrick publishes *Self-Evident*.
2026	The nation will celebrate the sestercentennial (250th) anniversary of the Declaration.

Interesting Facts

The Second Continental Congress actually voted for independence from Great Britain on July 2, 1776. July 4 was the date on which it adopted the Declaration of Independence as an explanation of its prior action. John Adams was among those who thought that Independence Day would be celebrated on July 2.

Aside from the president of the Congress (John Hancock) and its secretary (Charles Thomson), the delegates did not sign the Declaration prior to August 2, and then not all at the same time.

Jefferson received relatively little recognition for writing the Declaration of Independence in the early years, when it was generally regarded as more of a collective project and in which his initial authorship was relatively unknown.

Many towns and cities had drafted instructions calling upon their delegates to the Continental Congress to declare independence prior to its actual decision to do so.

Contrary to stories that George III wrote that "Nothing of importance happened today" on July 4, 1776, he did not keep a diary.

Thomas Jefferson and John Adams both died on the 50th anniversary of July 4, 1776. James Monroe died on July 4, 1831. President Calvin Coolidge was born on July 4, 1872.

The Declaration was unanimous only in that it was approved by a majority of each of the state delegations that were present in Philadelphia.

Although the building where the Declaration of Independence was signed is typically called Independence Hall, in 1776 it was known as the Pennsylvania State House because it served as the seat of government in Pennsylvania. The building was also the site of the Constitutional Convention of 1787.

Writing the Declaration of Independence is the first of three achievements that Thomas Jefferson asked to be recorded on his epitaph. The other two achievements for which he asked to be remembered were writing the Virginia Statute for Religious Liberty and founding the University of Virginia.

The Declaration of Independence was one of only three documents that members of the Second Continental Congress individually signed.

Thomas McKean was the last individual who signed the Declaration of Independence, which he did sometime in January 1777 or thereafter.

George Read is the only individual known to have voted against independence who nonetheless signed the Declaration.

The paper on which the first broadsides of the Declaration of Independence were printed contained Dutch watermarks, which included a crown in the design.

The Declaration of Independence appears to be the first document that refers to the "United States of America," previously generally referred to as the "United Colonies."

On the morning of July 4, 1776, Jefferson went shopping and bought a new thermometer and seven pairs of women's gloves.

After the Declaration of Independence was read in New York, a mob tore down a statute of King George III in the Bowling Green Park in Manhattan. The metal was subsequently melted down into 42,088 bullets for Revolutionary soldiers.

In writing the *Dred Scott* decision in 1857, Chief Justice Roger Taney interpreted the provision stating that "all men are created equal" to apply only to white men. Abraham Lincoln, who would soon be elected president, took quite a different view.

During World War II, the Declaration of Independence was moved to Ft. Knox, Kentucky, for safekeeping.

Although the Declaration of Independence listed King George III as the subject of most of its grievances, up until 1776, the colonists had leveled most of their complaints, particularly with respect to "taxation without representation" against the British Parliament. The publication of Thomas Paine's *Common Sense* is one of the factors that may have turned popular sentiment against kingship in general and George III in particular.

Jefferson's original draft of the Declaration of Independence had accused the king of introducing slavery into the colonies and of refusing to allow them to stop the slave trade. Congress deleted this accusation, probably considering it to be somewhat hypocritical.

Benjamin Franklin was the oldest delegate at both the Second Continental Congress, which proposed the Declaration of Independence, and at the Constitutional Convention of 1787 and therefore also the oldest person to sign each of these documents.

Although Thomas Jefferson is widely celebrated for his felicity of expression, he often omitted capitalizing the first words of sentences and had similar quirks when it came to punctuation.

The words of the Declaration of Independence on the inside wall of the Jefferson Memorial in Washington, DC, omit some key portions of the document, including the people's right "to alter or abolish" governments that do not secure the rights of their people.

When critics accused Thomas Jefferson of having plagiarized some portions of the Declaration of Independence, he said that it was not intended to be original but to be "an expression of the American mind."

Although Abigail Adams has asked her husband to "Remember the Ladies," the Declaration was phrased in terms of the equality of men (a term, which can, however, be interpreted to mean mankind).

John Witherspoon, the president of the College of New Jersey (today's Princeton), was the only active clergyman to sign the Declaration of Independence.

At least 22 of the 56 men who signed the Declaration of Independence were lawyers, making this the best-represented profession.

More than half the men who signed the Declaration of Independence were members of the Anglican Church, the official Church of England and the established church within a number of colonies. Anglican clergymen had signed oaths to support king and country, and quite a number therefore continued to support the Loyalist cause.

The debates over the Declaration took place in a Committee of the Whole and were secret. Fortunately, we have numerous letters from delegates to the Congress, indicating various arguments they made.

The Declaration of Independence is largely written in the form of a legal indictment, albeit without many of the "whereases" and "wherefores" that one might otherwise expect in such a document. Jefferson was a lawyer, but fortunately, he also knew how to write for a public audience!

When members of the Continental Congress signed the Declaration of Independence, they realized that if they were captured, they could be tried for treason against the king and be executed. Many states also adopted laws making opposition to the Declaration treason within their jurisdictions.

The Declaration of Independence contains just over 1,300 words.

Benjamin Rush, a delegate from Pennsylvania, composed short biographies of almost all the signers of the Declaration of Independence, which he included in an autobiography that was not, however, published until 1905.

Although they joined together in the cause of Revolution, John Adams and Thomas Jefferson later became members of rival political parties and were so alienated that outgoing president Adams did not stay for Jefferson's presidential inauguration. Benjamin Rush later helped them to reconcile, and they resumed a fruitful correspondence.

Delegates are believed to have drawn ink from the same silver inkwell in writing both the Declaration of Independence and the U.S. Constitution.

A

ABDICATION OF GOVERNMENT (CHARGE #23)

Although scholars and laypersons typically devote far more attention to the broad statements of principle in the opening paragraphs of the Declaration of Independence, the central part of the document consists of a series of accusations against Britain's King George III and against the king and "others" (largely a veiled reference to Parliament). These accusations end by describing a number of warlike actions that the British had taken against the colonists since fighting broke out at Lexington and Concord in April 1775.

The first of these war-related charges accused the king of having "abdicated Government here, by declaring us out of his Protection and waging War against us." Thomas Jefferson's original proposal also had accused the king of "withdrawing his governors" (three of whom had tried to govern from ships), but Congress had deleted this accusation, perhaps recognizing that the colonies had a part in driving some of the governors away. Whereas Jefferson had said that the king had declared the colonies "out of his allegiance and protection," Congress deleted the reference to allegiance.

The second paragraph of the Declaration had declared that government rested upon "the consent of the governed." A king who resorted to force necessarily had abandoned the search for such consent. He had thus "abdicated," or abandoned, his governance of the colonies as effectively as if he had "abdicated" his throne in Britain by stepping down from his kingly role or fleeing as James II of England had done in 1688. George III may have remained on the throne with regard to his subjects in Britain, but the colonists thought he had betrayed them when he ceased protecting them and declared war against them.

The accusation against the king was related both to his proclamation of August 23, 1775, and to a subsequent speech he delivered on October 27, 1775. The Proclamation of Rebellion had been designed to squelch the "open and avowed rebellion" that the king thought had been "much promoted and encouraged by the traitorous correspondence, counsels and comfort of divers [various] wicked and desperate persons within this realm." To this end, it had charged military and civilian officials as well as "all subjects" "to disclose and make known all traitorous conspiracies and attempts against us, our crown and dignity," so that they could be punished for their "traitorous designs" (George III, 1775a).

In his subsequent speech to both houses of Parliament on October 26, the king had questioned the good faith of members of the Continental Congress and made it clear that he supported the authority of Parliament, which the colonists had disputed. He had further expressed his wishes for "the re-establishment of order and tranquility through the several parts of my dominions, in a close connection and constitutional dependence."

It is not surprising that in defending the king, John Lind observed that the king had the right to withdraw his protection from individuals who were in rebellion against him. As Lind put it, "The Americans have only to return to their allegiance; and by that very return they are reinstated under the protection of the King" (1776, 94).

See also Dissolution of Government; George III, Speech to Parliament (October 27, 1775); George III, Speech to Parliament (October 31, 1776)

Further Reading

George III. 1775a. "His Majesty's Most Gracious Speech to Both Houses of Parliament," Friday, October 27, 1775. Philadelphia. Library of Congress. http://www.loc.gov/resource/rbpe.1440150a.

George III. 1775b. "Proclamation of Rebellion," August 23, 1775. Sources of British History. http://www.britannia.com/history/docs/procreb.html.

Lind, John. 1776. *An Answer to the Declaration of the American Congress*. London: J. Walter, Charing-Cross and T. Sewell.

ABOLISHING THE FREE SYSTEM OF ENGLISH LAWS

See Quebec Act of 1774 (Charge #20)

ABOLITIONISM

Although the Declaration of Independence had proclaimed that government rested upon the "consent of the governed," that "all men are created equal," and that government should be based upon consent, many African American men and women remained enslaved. Even slaveholders such as Thomas Jefferson, who considered slavery to be morally wrong and who sought to ban it from the Northwest Territory, saw whites and blacks as different people and could not envision a world in which former slaves and their masters could live in harmony with one another (Jefferson [1785] 1964, 132–133). To the extent that such individuals considered emancipation, it was often in conjunction with attempts to recolonize slaves in Africa or elsewhere.

The Declaration of Independence nonetheless served, along with "the Constitution, Christianity, and belief in the right to self-ownership" (Bean 2009, 13), to inspire the antislavery movement (as it would, as well, for the woman's suffrage movement). It grew in strength as Northern states, often influenced by the Declaration, began freeing their slaves and as Congress eliminated the slave trade in 1808. Pauline Maier observed that "the most important statement of rights for early nineteenth century Americans—particularly those who opposed slavery—was not what we call the Bill of Rights but the Declaration of Independence" (2017, 503). Noting that the statements of equality and of unalienable rights "were conspicuously absent in the Federal Constitution and its first ten amendments," Maier observed that "Americans liked to see their basic rights confirmed on parchment, and the only parchment that served that purpose for the nation as a whole was the Declaration of Independence" (2017, 503).

James Forten (1766–1842), a free black in Philadelphia, thus observed that "one of the most prominent features in the Declaration of Independence" was the statement "that God created all men equal" (Bean 2009, 15). David Walker (1796?–1830), who authored his *Appeal to the Colored Citizens of the World* (1829), further cited the Declaration not only for the principle of equal rights, but also for the legitimacy of revolting against governments that did not secure such rights (Bean 2009, 24). Lysander Spooner (1808–1887) argued that natural law was opposed to slavery. He said that if the Declaration of Independence "were the law of the country even for a day, it freed every slave in the country . . . and the burden would then be upon the slaveholder to show that slavery had since been constitutionally established" (Bean 2009, 36).

Focusing on debates from 1819 to 1821 over whether to admit Missouri as a slave state, Alexander Tsesis observes that "the Declaration of Independence played a central role" (2012, 73). This debate, which eventually resulted in the admission of Missouri as a slave state and Maine as a free one, hardened racial attitudes on both sides of the Mason-Dixon Line. Attitudes against slavery strengthened in the North, and Southerners increasingly argued that slavery was not simply a necessary evil but also a positive good.

Editor, orator, and abolitionist Frederick Douglass was the foremost African American leader of the 19th century. He gave a speech in 1852 entitled "What to the Slave is the Fourth of July?" in which he pointed out the disparity between the ideals of the Declaration of Independence and the reality of American slavery. (National Archives)

William Lloyd Garrison (1805–1879), who is often considered to be the father of the abolitionist movement, published the first issue of the *Liberator* on January 1, 1831. He announced there that "assenting to the 'self-evident truth' maintained in the American Declaration of Independence, 'that all men are created equal, and endowed by their Creator with certain inalienable rights—among which are life, liberty and the pursuit of happiness,' I shall strenuously contend for the immediate enfranchisement of our slave population" (Vile 2017, 37).

Frederick Douglass (1818–1895), a former slave best known for his *Narrative of the Life of Frederick Douglass, an American Slave* (1845), delivered a memorable Independence Day address in 1852 entitled "What to the Slave Is the Fourth of July?" Beginning with praise for the bravery of the men who signed the Declaration of Independence, Douglass went on to point to the wide disparity between the whites in his audience and fellow African Americans and him. He observed that "whether we turn to the declarations of the past, or to the professions of the present, the conduct of the nation seems equally hideous and revolting. America is false to the past, false to the present, and solemnly binds herself to be false to the future" (Vile 2017, 173). Undoubtedly with a view to the Declaration's statement that "all men are created equal," Douglass observed that slaves were men and were therefore entitled to equal treatment. He continued to hope that the ideals of the Declaration and its principles would eventually bring about a year of jubilee in which slaves would be freed.

Accepting the fact that the Constitution had left slavery in place within existing states, Abraham Lincoln cited the Declaration to argue against the expansion of slavery within the territories. Initially proclaiming that the Civil War was being fought to preserve the Union, in time, Lincoln would tie in his Gettysburg Address the success of the war to vindicating the "proposition that all men are created equal."

In 1865, the same year that the Civil War ended and Lincoln was assassinated, the nation adopted the Thirteenth Amendment, which eliminated slavery. The Fourteenth Amendment (1868) further identified all persons "born or naturalized in the United States" as citizens and extended to them the "equal protection of the laws."

Racial segregation was sanctioned by the U.S. Supreme Court in *Plessy v. Ferguson* (1896) and remained the law of the land until the Court's decision in *Brown v. Board of Education* (1954). This was one of the factors that sparked a civil rights movement that led to the Civil Rights Act of 1964 and the Voting Rights Act of 1965. Martin Luther King Jr. evoked the power of the Declaration in his "I Have a Dream" speech of 1963, saying that his dream included seeing the United States "live out the true meaning of its creed: 'We hold these truths to be self-evident, that all men are created equal.'"

See also Consent of the Governed; Equality; Lincoln, Abraham; Northwest Ordinance of 1787; Slavery

Further Reading

Bay, Mia. 2006. "See Your Declaration Americans!!! Abolitionism, Americanism, and the Revolutionary Tradition in Free Black Politics." In *Americanism: New Perspectives on the History of an Ideal*, edited by Michael Kazin and Joseph A. McCartin, 25–52. Chapel Hill: University of North Carolina Press

Bean, Jonathan, ed. 2009. *Race and Liberty in America: The Essential Reader*. Lexington: University Press of Kentucky.

Jefferson, Thomas. (1785) 1964. *Notes on the State of Virginia*. New York: Harper and Row.
King, Martin Luther, Jr. 1963. "I Have a Dream . . ." Speech presented at the March on Washington, Washington, DC. August 28. National Archives, accessed March 27, 2018. https://www.archives.gov/files/press/exhibits/dream-speech.pdf.
Maier, Pauline. 2017. "The Strange History of the Bill of Rights." *Georgetown Journal of Law and Public Policy* 15 (Summer): 497–511.
Tsesis, Alexander. 2012. *For Liberty and Equality: The Life and Times of The Declaration of Independence*. New York: Oxford University Press.
Vile, John R. 2017. *The Jacksonian and Antebellum Eras: Documents Decoded*. Santa Barbara, CA: ABC-CLIO.

ABUSES AND USURPATIONS

In the second paragraph of the Declaration of Independence, Thomas Jefferson says that individuals have a right to revolt when they face "a long train of abuses and usurpations."

Much of the Declaration accordingly outlines various grievances that the colonies have against the king and others in Britain. Hans L. Eicholz has suggested that it is useful to divide these charges into the two broad categories Jefferson identified. As Eicholz understands the former, "an abuse of power can be within the letter of constitutional authority, but in violation of the principle of an equal or impartial application of the laws. It is, in other words a misuse of power" (2001, 51). He cites some of the initial charges where the Declaration accuses the king of refusing assent to laws that benefit the colonies, suspending laws, and the like. By contrast, Eicholz says that "usurpations . . . referred to an application of power not sanctioned by any constitutional provision" (2001, 51). The most obvious would be the king's cooperation with Parliament in taxing colonists who were not represented in that body.

Eicholz believes that in crafting the Declaration, Jefferson largely began with abuses and then worked up to usurpations. The final charges, of course, relate to war atrocities.

See also Charges against the King and Others

Further Reading

Barnett, Randy. 2017. "What the Declaration of Independence Said and Meant." *Washington Post*, July 4.
Eicholz, Hans L. 2001. *Harmonizing Sentiments: The Declaration of Independence and the Jeffersonian Idea of Self-Government*. New York: Peter Lang.

ACT OF ABJURATION (*PLAKKAAT VAN VERLATINGE*, 1581)

Scholars continue to look for documents upon which Thomas Jefferson might have modeled the Declaration of Independence. One possibility is the *Plakkaat van Verlatinge*, or Act of Abjuration, which the Low Countries (Holland) issued on July 26, 1581, in announcing that they would no longer accept the authority of King Philip II of Spain.

The document began with the words "as 'tis apparent to all," which seem to parallel the Declaration's idea of "self-evident truths." Using a scriptural analogy, the document further accuses the king of violating a contract with the people by refusing to "Shepherd his sheep." It points to the "humble Petitions and Remonstrances" of the people and the king's "tyrannical Proceedings," which violated the "Law of Nature" (Lucas 1998, 162). Much as the body of the U.S. Declaration of Independence consists in a list of charges against George III, so too, 68 percent of the Dutch text consists of a set of specific grievances against King Philip II (Lucas 1998, 163) and ends with a renunciation of "Allegiance" to him and a unanimous declaration that he has therefore forfeited his authority.

In a famous charge to a grand jury in Charleston, South Carolina, that he gave on October 14, 1776, Judge William Henry Drayton (1742–1779) drew parallels between the American cause and that of the Dutch. He observed that "the inhabitants of that speck of earth compelled the master of dominions so extensive that it was boasted the sun was never absent, to treat with them as a free and independent people!" (1776, 2:1052).

Parallels do not, of course, necessarily provenance. There is evidence that many of the American Founders were familiar with Dutch history and precedents (Riker 1957). Moreover, it is possible that the central means of influence was not direct but through the Plakkaat's influence on the English Declaration of Rights, which is believed to be another possible model for the American document ("The Act of Abjuration").

See also Charges against the King and Others; English Declaration of Rights; Self-Evident Truths

Further Reading

"The Act of Abjuration and the Declaration of Independence." 2018. https://www.newnetherlandinstitute.org/history-and-heritage/additional-resources/dutch-treats/the-act-of-abjuration/.

Drayton, William Henry. 1776. "Judge Drayton's Charge to the Grand Jury of Charleston." American Archives, Documents of the American Revolutionary Period, 1774–1776. 2:1047–1058. http://amarch.lib.niu.edu/islandora/object/niu-amarch%3A100837.

Lucas, Stephen E. 1998. "The Rhetorical Ancestry of the Declaration of Independence," *Rhetoric and Public Affairs* 1 (Summer): 143–184.

Nordholt, J. W. Schulte. 1982. *The Dutch Republican and American Independence*. Translated by Herbert H. Rowen. Chapel Hill: University of North Carolina Press.

Parker, Geoffrey. 1981. "July 26, 1581: The Dutch 'Declaration of Independence.'" *History Today* 31 (July): 3–6.

Riker, William H. 1957. "Dutch and American Federalism." *Journal of the History of Ideas* 18 (October): 495–521.

ADAMS, JOHN

Few, if any, individuals worked harder or longer for American independence than John Adams (1735–1826). Born in Braintree, Massachusetts, near Boston in 1735—where both the home of his birth and the home where he and his wife lived are now open to the public—Adams attended Harvard, taught school, studied for the bar, and earned a reputation as a practicing lawyer. One of his most storied cases was his successful defense of the British soldiers who had been charged with murder in the so-called Boston Massacre.

Portrait of John Adams, by Gilbert Stuart, ca. 1821. John Adams was a prominent member of the Continental Congress and a member of the committee to draft the Declaration of Independence. He was elected the second president of the United States in 1796. (National Gallery of Art)

Adams had been fired up by James Otis's opposition to Writs of Assistance and often claimed that the real revolution in popular sentiment had begun far earlier than the American Revolution. In a series of letters written under the name of Novanglus, which appeared in the *Boston Gazette* from January to April 1775, Adams outlined a view of American/British relations that was similar to the later British Commonwealth of Nations. Robert J. Taylor believes, however, that sometime in the summer or fall of 1775, Adams had come to the conclusion that independence was necessary (1977, 67).

Adams represented a state that felt the brunt of British reprisals resulting from the Boston Tea Party and was the site of the first conflict with British troops in April 1775. His second cousin, Samuel Adams, who was another delegate to the Continental Congress, was often portrayed, not altogether correctly, as a kind of one-man provocateur of the Revolution (Raphael 2004, 45-63), but he worked largely behind the scenes. By contrast, John was much more vocal in public debates and was particularly impatient with delegates like John Dickinson, who favored further petitions to the king.

Adams introduced a resolution on May 10, 1776, authorizing colonies whose royal governors had abandoned them "to adopt such governments as shall, in the opinion of the representatives of the people, best conduce to the happiness and safety of their constituents in particular, and America in general" (Shain 2014, 441). He subsequently helped draft a preamble to this resolution that condemned the king for ignoring colonial petitions and for making war on the colonies.

After Richard Henry Lee introduced a resolution for independence on June 7, 1776, Adams was one of five men appointed to the committee to write a justification for such action in the anticipated event that it would be ratified. The others were Thomas Jefferson, Benjamin Franklin, Roger Sherman, and Robert Livingston.

Just as Adams had nominated George Washington as commander in chief of U.S. military forces (some think that fellow state delegate John Hancock had coveted the job), so, too, Adams insisted that Jefferson write the preliminary draft. He did so in part by flattering him for his writing skills and in part by suggesting that the text would be far more likely to be received if it were written by a Virginian than by someone from Massachusetts. He and Franklin made some minor suggestions for revision of the document before it was debated at the Second Continental Congress.

When the Declaration of Independence was debated on July 1, John Dickinson of Pennsylvania gave a long speech opposing the resolution. Adams gave what was generally conceded to be a powerful speech on behalf of those who thought the time was now ripe for doing so. He was apparently asked to repeat this speech when the New Jersey delegation arrived. Adams seemed to have a clear-eyed view of the challenges that awaited. Adams wrote the following to Samuel Chase on July 1:

> If you imagine that I expect this Declaration will ward off, Calamities from this Country, you are much mistaken. A bloody Conflict We are destined to endure. This has been my opinion, from the Beginning. You will certainly remember, my decided opinion was, at the first Congress, when We found, that We could not agree upon an immediate Non Exportation, that the Contest, should not be Settled without Bloodshed, and that, if Hostilities Should once commence, they would terminate in an incurable Animosity, between the two Countries. Every political Event, Since the Nineteenth of April 1775 has confirmed me in this opinion. (Burnett 1921)

Adams was delighted when the Congress finally voted for independence on July 2, but incorrectly thought that that day, rather than July 4, which marked the actual adoption of the document, would subsequently be celebrated as Independence Day. Adams thus observed that:

> The second day of July, 1776, will be the most memorable epocha in the history of America. I am apt to believe that it will be celebrated by succeeding generations as the great anniversary festival. It ought to be commemorated as the day of deliverance, by solemn acts of devotion to God almighty. It ought to be solemnized with pomp and parade, with shows, games, sports, guns, bells, bonfires, and illuminations, from one end of this continent to the others, from this time forward evermore. (Zall 2004, 76)

In a letter that he wrote to his wife, Abigail, on July 3, Adams indicated his frustration with how long the process was taking. He thus noted that "had a Declaration of Independency been made seven Months ago, it would have been attended with many great and glorious Effects." He observed, "We might before this Hour, have formed Alliances with foreign States.—We should have mastered Quebec and been in Possession of Canada." Having expressed such regret, Adams also recognized some benefits:

> The Hopes of Reconciliation, which were fondly entertained by Multitudes of honest and well meaning tho weak and mistaken People have been gradually and at last totally extinguished.—Time has been given for the whole People, maturely to consider the great Question of Independence and to ripen their judgments, dissipate their Fears, and allure their Hopes, by discussing it in News Papers and Pamphletts, by debating it, in Assemblies, Conventions, Committees of Safety and Inspection, in Town and county Meetings, as well as in private Conversations, so that the whole People in every Colony of the 13, have now adopted it, as their own Acts.—This will cement the Union, and avoid those Heats and perhaps convulsions which might have been occasioned, by such a Declaration Six Months ago. (Adams 2018)

In contrast to some revolutionaries like Thomas Paine, Adams thought that governmental forms, including a bicameral legislature and separation of powers, were quite important. Adams was the primary author of the Massachusetts Constitution of 1780, which became something of a model for the U.S. Constitution (Peters 1978).

Although he was often separated from her by governmental business in the United States and by diplomatic assignments abroad, Adams had a remarkable relationship with his wife, Abigail, who reminded him to "remember the ladies" while securing independence for men. Although Adams treated her suggestion as something of a joke, he recognized that the declaration had stirred wider aspirations for liberty.

Adams spent much of the Revolutionary War seeking foreign support. Paired for a time with Benjamin Franklin in France, Adams was jealous of Franklin's public adulation and repulsed by his love of luxury and public praise. Adams did help to negotiate the Treaty of Paris, which ended the war. Polling second behind George Washington, Adams became the first vice president, in which capacity he presided over the Senate but was mocked for supporting high titles, which Congress rejected, for the president.

Adams gravitated toward the Federalist Party, which put him at odds with Thomas Jefferson. Elected to the presidency in 1796, after Washington retired, Adams remained largely estranged from Jefferson, who was elected as his vice president, as well as from Alexander Hamilton and much of the cabinet that Adams had inherited from Washington. Adams's presidency, during which there was an undeclared war with France, which he succeeded in keeping from flaring into full conflict, was marred by the passage of the Alien and Sedition Acts of 1798, which Democratic Republicans considered to violate the First Amendment. When Jefferson subsequently succeeded him, Adams did not stay for his inauguration.

As Jefferson's reputation for writing the Declaration grew, Adams became increasingly resentful of the accolades, in part because he believed that he had been the real workhorse behind the movement for independence. Adams joined those who questioned the originality of the Declaration, which prompted Jefferson to say that originality had never been his intention. Benjamin Rush eventually got Adams and Jefferson corresponding again, and they became even more firmly joined in popular memory when both died on July 4, 1826. Prior to his death, Adams did see his son, John Quincy Adams, elected to the presidency. When he was serving as secretary of state in the Monroe Administration, John Quincy Adams delivered a notable speech on the Declaration to Congress in 1821.

See also Committee Responsible for Writing the Declaration of Independence; Dickinson (John) Speech Opposing the Declaration of Independence; Franklin, Benjamin; Jefferson, Thomas; Massachusetts and Its Signers

Further Reading

Adams, John. 1979. *Papers of John Adams*. Vol. 4, *February–August 1776*, edited by Robert J. Taylor. Cambridge, MA: Belknap Press of Harvard University Press.

Adams, John. 2018. John Adams to Abigail Adams, July 3, 1776. "Had a Declaration . . ." [electronic edition]. *Adams Family Papers: An Electronic Archive*. Massachusetts Historical Society. http://www.masshist.org/digitaladams/.

Burnett, Edmund C., ed. 1921. *Letters of Members of the Continental Congress*. Washington, DC: Carnegie Institution of Washington.

Ellis, Joseph J. 1993. *Passionate Sage: The Character and Legacy of John Adams*. New York: W. W. Norton.

Ferling, John. 1992. *John Adams: A Life*. New York: Henry Holt.

McCullough, David. 2002. *John Adams*. New York: Simon and Schuster.

McGlone, Robert E. 1998. "Deciphering Memory: John Adams and the Authorship of the Declaration of Independence." *Journal of American History* 85 (September): 411–438.

Peters, Ronald M., Jr. 1978. *The Massachusetts Constitution of 1780: A Social Compact*. Amherst: University of Massachusetts Press.

Raphael, Ray. 2004. *Founding Myths: Stories That Hide Our Patriotic Past*. New York: MJF Books.

Shain, Barry Alan, ed. 2014. *The Declaration of Independence in Historical Context*. Indianapolis: Liberty Fund.

Taylor, Robert J. 1977. "John Adams: Legalist as Revolutionist." *Proceedings of the Massachusetts Historical Society*. 3rd ser., 89:55–71.

Zall, Paul M. 2004. *Adams on Adams*. Lexington: University Press of Kentucky.

ADAMS, JOHN QUINCY, INDEPENDENCE DAY ADDRESS (JULY 4, 1821)

Although he was only a boy during the American Revolution, it is not surprising that John Quincy Adams (1767–1848) would have been justly proud of the accomplishments of his father, who had served on the committee that the Second Continental Congress had commissioned to write the Declaration of Independence or that he would have wanted to perpetuate his legacy.

In his youth, Adams had accompanied his father on a number of diplomatic missions. Before becoming the sixth president of the United States, John Quincy Adams served as secretary of state under President James Monroe. In this capacity, he was a major architect of the Monroe Doctrine, which proclaimed that the United States would look with disfavor upon any further interference by European powers in the affairs of the Western Hemisphere.

In 1810, Adams commissioned William J. Stone to create a facsimile of the Matlack engrossing of the Declaration of Independence, including the signatures of the delegates. On July 4, 1821, the 45th anniversary of the adoption of the Declaration of Independence, Adams brought the original Matlack Declaration, which he read to the House of Representatives. He did this in conjunction with a speech that remains one of the most memorable and laudatory of the many such speeches that had already become a tradition in U.S. history.

Adams portrayed the revolutionary conflict between the American colonies and Britain as one "between the oppressions of power and the claims of right." He further viewed the conflict as the triumph of "reason" over both political and ecclesiastical oppression, thus linking the American Revolution with the previous work of the Protestant Reformation. He lauded the American revolutionaries for standing true to their original charters and for replacing a social compact based on force with one based upon consent.

After reading the Declaration to the House, Adams observed in his Independence Day speech that "it is not the long enumeration of intolerable wrongs concentrated in this declaration; it is not the melancholy catalogue of alternate oppression and entreaty, of reciprocated indignity and remonstrance, upon which, in the celebration of this anniversary, your memory delights to dwell." Instead, its primary interest lies "in the principles which it proclaims." He continued:

> It was the first solemn declaration by a nation of the only legitimate foundation of civil government. It was the corner stone of a new fabric, destined to cover the surface of the globe. It demolished at a stroke the lawfulness of all governments founded upon conquest. It swept away all the rubbish of accumulated centuries of servitude. It announced in practical form to the world the transcendent truth of the unalienable sovereignty of the people.

As if harkening back to the Pilgrim image of the city on a hill, Adams lauded the Declaration as a singular achievement:

> It stands, and must forever stand alone, a beacon on the summit of the mountain, to which all the inhabitants of the earth may turn their eyes for a genial and saving light, till time shall be lost in eternity, and this globe itself dissolve, nor leave a wreck behind. It stands forever, a light of admonition to the rules of men; a light of salvation and redemption to the oppressed.

Adams observed that the Declaration had not resulted in "anarchy," but that the people had remained bound together by law, and they had created institutions "to cement and prepare for perpetuity their common union," "to erect and organize civil and municipal governments in their respective states," and "to form connexions of friendship and commerce with foreign nations." He attributed these successes to the fact that "Our manners, our habits, our feelings, are all republican."

Rhetorically asking "what has America done for the benefit of mankind?"—a question reinforced later in the speech by outlining the many scientific achievements for which the mother country was known—Adams answered that America had "proclaimed to mankind the inextinguishable rights of human nature, and the only lawful foundations of government." Arguably ignoring that fact that American success had relied in large part on the help of foreign allies, Adams proceeded to use the Declaration to vindicate the principle (similar to that of George Washington's

Farewell Address and in the Monroe Doctrine), that the United States would lead by example rather than by interfering in the affairs of other nations. He thus noted:

> Wherever the standard of freedom and independence has been or shall be unfurled, there will her heart, her benedictions and her prayers be. But she goes not abroad in search of monsters to destroy. She is the will-wisher to the freedom and independence of all. She is the champion and vindicator only of her own. She will recommend the general cause, by the countenance of her voice, and the benignant sympathy of her example. She well knows that by once enlisting under other banners than her own, were they even the banners of foreign independence, she would involve herself, beyond the power of extrication, in all the wars of interest and intrigue, of individual avarice, envy, and ambition, which assume the colors and usurp the standard of freedom.

In the penultimate paragraph of the speech, Adams further observed that "Her glory is not dominion, but liberty. Her march is the march of mind. She has a spear and a shield; but the motto upon her shield is Freedom, Independence, Peace. This has been her declaration: this has been, as far as her necessary intercourse with the rest of mankind would permit, her practice."

After he left the presidency, Adams went on to a long and distinguished career in the U.S. House of Representatives. His service was most notable for his opposition to slavery and to gag orders that Southern congressmen had introduced to table any motions that arrived in advocacy of this position.

See also Adams, John; Dunlap Broadside Printing of the Declaration of Independence; Engrossed Declaration of Independence (Matlack)

Further Reading

Adams, John Quincy. "Speech on Independence Day." TeachingAmericanHistory.org. http://teachingamericanhistory.org/library/document/speech-on-independence-day/.

Engels, Jeremy. 2010. *Enemyship: Democracy and Counter-Revolution in the Early Republic.* East Lansing: Michigan State University Press.

Puleo, Stephen. 2016. *American Treasures: The Secret Efforts to Save the Declaration of Independence, the Constitution, and the Gettysburg Address.* New York: St. Martin's

ADDRESS TO THE INHABITANTS OF THE COLONIES (WILSON)

Although never issued to its intended audience, an address that James Wilson drafted as part of a committee that included John Dickinson, James Duane, and William Hooper and presented to Congress on February 19, 1776, gives considerable insight into the development of sentiments for revolution and provides some parallels to the later Declaration of Independence. Wilson appeared to be attempting to show fellow colonists how events were pushing them toward independence, but how they would much prefer to remain part of the English empire, with their own rights properly understood and defended.

Drawing from the British constitution, Wilson began with fundamental principles that are quite similar to those of the second paragraph of the Declaration of

Independence. Wilson summarized: "That all Power was originally in the People—that all the Powers of Government are derived from them—that all Power, which they have not disposed of, still continues theirs" (2007, 4:135).

Wilson reasoned that because colonists had already vested their individual legislatures with the power of taxation, and they were unrepresented in Parliament, only colonial legislatures could tax them. Parliamentary attempts to tax and legislation for the colonies posed threats to "Your Fortunes, your Liberties, your Reputation, [and] your Lives" (4:136).

Defending Congress as a legal body justified by English precedents, Wilson took serious umbrage to the king's belief that protestations of allegiance had only been attended to divert and amuse the English people while the colonists prepared for revolt. Wilson defended colonial petitions as legitimate exercises of their rights "as Men and as British Subjects" (4:139). He used a similar defense for their taking up arms to defend themselves. Wilson said that the intention of the colonies was "the Defence and the Re-establishment of the constitutional Rights of the Colonies" (4:141).

Wilson said that the connections between the colonies and Britain were firmly based on mutual benefits: "upon Religion, Laws, Manners, Customs and Habits common to both Countries" (4:144). Wilson further claimed that "we are too much attached to the English Laws and Constitution, and know too well their happy Tendency to diffuse Freedom, Prosperity and Peace wherever they prevail, to desire an independent Empire" (4:145).

Whereas the Declaration of Independence would blame the king, Wilson laid the blame clearly on Parliament and, specifically, on the House of Commons. Showing that he understood how Whig theory diverged in Great Britain and the colonies, he said that "the same Principles, which directed *your Ancestors* to oppose the exorbitant and dangerous Pretensions of the crown, should direct *you* to oppose the no less exorbitant and dangerous Claims of the House of Commons" (4:145).

Wilson thus observed, "We are *desirous* to continue Subjects: But we are *determined* to continue Freemen" (4:146). He concluded by observing that the first wish of the colonies is "that America may be free" (4:146).

Jack Rakove believes that the address, despite some memorable lines, had literary flaws. More fundamentally, he thinks that its "central defect" lay "in its awkward attempt to straggle the widening gap between the original goals of resistance and the growing likelihood of independence" (1979, 90).

See also Address to the Inhabitants of the Colonies (Wilson); George III, Speech to Parliament (October 27, 1775); Pennsylvania and Its Signers

Further Reading

Bailyn, Bernard. 1967. *The Ideological Origins of the American Revolution*. Cambridge, MA: Belknap Press of Harvard University Press.

Journals of the Continental Congress, 1774–1789. 1906. Vol. 4, *January 1–June 4, 1776*. Washington, DC: Government Printing Office.

Rakove, Jack N. 1979. *The Beginnings of National Politics: An Interpretive History of the Continental Congress*. New York: Alfred A. Knopf.

ADDRESS TO THE PEOPLE OF GREAT BRITAIN (OCTOBER 21, 1774)

Although it is not as well known as the Declaration and Resolves that the First Continental Congress adopted on October 14, the Address to the People of Great Britain that the Congress adopted on October 21, 1774, provides another window on colonial thought of the time. The Declaration of Independence later repeated a number of the grievances that it outlined.

Largely authored by John Jay of New York, this address, listed under the names of each of the 12 colonies at the Continental Congress (all but Georgia) addressed the British as "friends and fellow-subjects." It nonetheless expressed concern that the British nation had either "ceased to be virtuous, or been extremely negligent in the appointment of her Rulers."

Asserting that the colonists "are and ought to be as free as our fellow-subjects in *Britain*, and that no power on earth has a right to take our property from us without our consent," the document went on to claim the right of "Trial by Jury," to protest the power of the Courts of Admiralty, and to bemoan the heavy hand that the British had exerted since the French and Indian War. The address condemned Britain for punishing all the people of Boston for the Boston Tea Party without trying to distinguish the guilty from the innocent. It cited British attempts to alter the royal charter that it had given Massachusetts. It was also highly critical of British recognition of the Roman Catholic Church in Canada, noting that this religion "has deluged your Island in blood, and dispersed impiety, bigotry, persecution, murder, and rebellion, through every part of the world." Believing that "there is yet much virtue, much justice, and much publick spirit in the *English* Nation," it suggested that British leaders were attempting to reduce the colonists to slaves—"to be hewers of wood or drawers of water."

The final paragraph expressed the hope "that the magnanimity and justice of the *British* Nation will furnish a Parliament of such wisdom, independence, and publick spirit, as may save the violated rights of the whole Empire from the devices of wicked Ministers and evil Counsellors."

In completing the indictment against Britain in the Declaration, Jefferson noted, "We have warned them from time to time of attempts by their legislature to extend an unwarrantable jurisdiction over us" and "have appealed to their native justice and magnanimity."

See also Declaration and Resolves of the First Continental Congress (1774); New York and Its Signers; Nor Have We Been Wanting in Attention to Our English Brethren

Further Reading

"Address to the People of Great Britain." *American Archives*. 4th ser., 1:917–921. http://amarch.lib.niu.edu/islandora/object/niu-amarch%3A97565.

Klein, Milton M. 2000. "John Jay and the Revolution." *New York History* 81 (January): 19–30.

ALBERT H. SMALL DECLARATION OF INDEPENDENCE COLLECTION

The world's most comprehensive collection of materials connected to the Declaration of Independence is found in Charlottesville on the campus of the University of Virginia, which Thomas Jefferson founded in 1819.

Contributed by Albert H. Small, a real estate developer who received his undergraduate degree from the university in 1948, and his wife Shirley, the collection is housed near the university's Alderman Library. It consists of millions of documents, including signatures of each of the 56 signers, a letter by Caesar Rodney describing his ride to Philadelphia through a thunderstorm to cast his vote for independence, Benjamin Owen Tyler's manuscript subscription book for his facsimile Declaration of Independence (the first three signatures were Thomas Jefferson, James Madison, and John Quincy Adams), a John Binns engraving of the Declaration, and numerous others.

The collection, which is housed underground, includes displays of early printings of the Declaration of Independence and related documents and artifacts. The collection is open to the public, and to scholars seeking to do research, most days other than Sundays. The collection is described in an essay by Christian Y. Dupont in a beautifully illustrated book that features pictures of some of the printings and engravings of the Declaration of Independence (2008, 72–81).

See also Binns Engraving of the Declaration of Independence; Tyler Engraving of the Declaration of Independence

Further Reading

Dupont, Christian Y., and Peter S. Onuf, eds. 2008. *Declaring Independence: The Origin and Influence of America's Founding Document*. Charlottesville: University of Virginia Library.

ALL MEN ARE CREATED EQUAL

See Equality

AMBITION

Thomas Jefferson's original rough draft of the Declaration, which he revised possibly at the suggestion of fellow committee members before submitting it to Congress, was considerably different from the current document. Opening with the familiar "When in the course of human events," it had gone on to say "it becomes necessary for a people to advance from that subordination in which they have hitherto remained, & to assume among the powers of the earth the equal & independent station to which the laws of nature and of nature's god entitle them" (King 2013, 171).

In reviewing this language, William Casey King argues that the original version was more melodious, pointing out that "in Jefferson's original 'subordination' rhymes with 'station' and 'remained' and 'change' form approximate rhymes, while repeated 'which' clauses create a further rhetorical parallel" (2013, 173). He further believes that "advance from that subordination" does not contain the same rhetorical "gap" as the phrase "connected them with another" (2013, 175).

Seeking to account for a change that he thinks is rhetorically inferior to the original, King believes that the answer may lie in the desire by Patriots to avoid accusations that they were motivated by ambition, which was often then associated, especially in theology, with vice and rebellion (2013, 185). Such motivation may also have guided the decision by Congress to delete a section from Jefferson's penultimate paragraph of the Declaration that observed that "we [Americans and British] might have been a free & a great people together, but a communication of grandeur and of freedom, it seems, is below their dignity. Be it so, since they will have it. The road to happiness and to glory is open to us too; we will climb it apart from them."

King points out that by 1777, John Adams was arguing that "Ambition in a Republic, is a great Virtue, for it is nothing more than a Desire, to Serve the Public, to Promote the Happiness of the People, to increase the Wealth, the Grandeur, and Prosperity of the Community. This, Ambition is but another Name for public Virtue, and public Spirit" (2013, 187). In a similar fashion, other American Framers would attempt to distinguish between the desire for "fame" as opposed to simple "notoriety" or "popularity" (Adair 1974).

See also Adams, John; Style of the Declaration of Independence

Further Reading

Adair, Douglass. 1974. "Fame and the Founding Fathers." In *Fame and the Founding Fathers: Essays*, edited by Trevor Colbourn, 3–26. New York: Norton.

King, William Casey. 2013. *Ambition, a History: From Vice to Virtue*. New Haven, CT: Yale University Press.

AN ANSWER TO THE DECLARATION OF THE AMERICAN CONGRESS (LIND)

One of the most extensive responses by the British to the Declaration of Independence was the anonymously publish book entitled *An Answer to the Declaration of the American Colonies*. The author was John Lind, an Oxford graduate, who had served abroad in British courts, had studied law, and had written two previous pamphlets (Peckham 1976, 399). Lord Frederick North (1732–1792), who served as British prime minister from 1770 to 1782 and consistently took a hard line against the colonists, had recruited Lind for the job.

Although George III had not addressed colonial grievances in depth, Lind's work came to 117 pages. Lind indicated that one of his reasons for publishing the work was that it would be beneath the king's dignity to do so (1776, 5). Lind's rhetoric did not approach the style of Thomas Jefferson, but his work remains notable for examining each of the Declaration's 28 charges against the king and attempting to refute them. It is likely that the length of Lind's work probably made it less accessible than the much shorter pamphlet by former Massachusetts governor Thomas Hutchinson entitled *Strictures upon the Declaration of Independence*.

Many of the refutations focused on common themes. Lind correctly perceived that the colonists' central grievances were not with the king but with parliamentary authority. Lind pointed to the irony of upbraiding the king for failing to assent to some acts of colonial legislation while urging him to disregard the laws of Parliament with respect to the colonies. He further showed that many of the Declaration's complaints dated back to policies that had been enforced and accepted long before George III had become king. Lind pointed to the irony of colonies rebelling against the king and then claiming that he was waging war against them. In similar fashion, Lind showed the contradiction between arguing that all men were created equal and then condemning the king for seeking to free them (1776, 107).

Like George III, Lind expressed skepticism about colonial motives and about their reasonableness. He ended his narrative (1776, 117) by observing, "Had an Angel descended from Heaven with terms of accommodation, which offered less than independence, they would have driven him back with hostile scorn" (1776, 117).

Lind's essay was paired with another essay, the "Short Review of the Declaration," which is now known to have been authored by Jeremy Bentham, the English utilitarian thinker and a friend of Lind's. Unlike Lind, Bentham directed most of his attack on the opening paragraphs of the Declaration and their advocacy of natural rights.

See also Bentham's Short Review of the Declaration of Independence; George III, Speech to Parliament (October 31, 1776); *Strictures upon the Declaration of Independence* (Hutchinson)

Further Reading

Avery, Margaret. 1978. "Toryism in the Age of the American Revolution: John Lind and John Shebbeare." *Historical Studies* 18:24–36.

Capansky, Trisha. 2011. "The Declaration of Independence: A New Genre in Political Discourse or Mixed Genres in an Unlikely Medium?" PhD diss., East Carolina University.

Lind, John. 1776. *An Answer to the Declaration of the American Congress*. London: J. Walter, Charing-Cross and T. Sewell.

Peckham, Howard H. 1975. "Independence: The View from Britain." *Proceedings of the American Antiquarian Society* 85 (October): 387–403. www.americanantiquarian.org /proceedings/44498108.pdf.

York, Neil L. 2017. "Natural Rights Dissected and Rejected: John Lind's Counter to the Declaration of Independence." *Law and History Review* 35 (August): 563–593.

ATTESTATION CLAUSES

One difference between the Declaration of Independence and some other founding documents, including the Articles of Confederation and the U.S. Constitution, is the clause immediately before the signatures, often called an attestation clause.

The signatures that follow the Declaration of Independence are recorded after the concluding sentence: "And for the support of this Declaration, with a firm reliance on the Protection of Divine Providence, we mutually pledge to each other our lives, our Fortunes and our sacred Honor" (Vile 2015, 290). Donald S. Lutz observes that "any document calling on God as a witness would technically be a covenant," although he believes the Declaration might also be described as a contract (1990, 145). Likely because the document is intended to be the first official document formally separating the colonies from Great Britain, it does not contain any reference to antecedents.

By contrast, the signatures on the Articles of Confederation, which Congress proposed in 1777, sent to the states in 1778, and ratified by the required number of states in 1781, are prefaced differently. It is as follows: "In Witness whereof we have hereunto set our hands in congress, Done at Philadelphia in the state of Pennsylvania the ninth Day of July in the Year of our Lord one Thousand seven Hundred and Seventy-eight, and in the third year of the independence of America" (Vile 2015, 297).

The U.S. Constitution has a similar preface to the signatures of its 39 delegates. It is as follows: "Done in Convention by the Unanimous Consent of the States present the Seventeenth Day of September in the Year of our Lord one thousand seven hundred and Eighty seven and of the Independence of the United States of America the Twelfth In Witness whereof We have here unto subscribed our Names" (Vile 2015, 278). The Constitution's Framers wanted to emphasize that their document furthered the goals of the Declaration. Michael Coenen has noted that "the sheer number of signatures that appeared on the Constitution would have reminded ratifiers of the Declaration, one of the few well-known national documents to display a comparably large number of names" (2010, 1000).

Some scholars have used the attestation clause of the U.S. Constitution as a way of suggesting that its authors intended to incorporate the principles of the Declaration (and perhaps its references to the Deity) into its understanding and interpretation. This argument is somewhat undercut by the fact that the form appears to follow that established by other domestic and international documents, which typically included both the "regnal year" (the year of the existing monarch's reign) and the "year of grace" (or year of our Lord) (Cross 2012, 1251).

Just as the Declaration declared independence from the British monarch, so too, the attestation clauses of the Articles and the Constitution highlight the continuing absence of such a crowned sovereign.

See also God; Signing of the Declaration of Independence; U.S. Constitution and the Declaration of Independence

Further Reading

Coenen, Michael. 2010. "The Significance of the Signatures: Why the Framers Signed the Constitution and What They Meant by Doing So." *Yale Law Journal* 119 (March): 966–1010.

Lutz, Donald S. 1990. "The Declaration of Independence, 1776: Commentary." In *Roots of the Republic: American Founding Documents Interpreted*, edited by Stephen L. Schechter, 1138–1145. Madison, WI: Madison House.

Ross, Jesse. 2012. "'Done in Convention': The Attestation Clause and the Declaration of Independence." *Yale Law Journal* 121 (March): 1236–1249.

Vile, John R. 2015. *A Companion to the United States Constitution and Its Amendments*. 6th ed. Santa Barbara, CA: Praeger.

AUDIENCES FOR THE DECLARATION OF INDEPENDENCE

The opening paragraph of the Declaration of Independence refers to "the opinions of mankind." As the Document introduces colonial grievances, it submits them "to a candid [unbiased] world." Immediately after approving the document, however, delegates to the Second Continental Congress voted to send copies "to the several assemblies, conventions and committees, or councils of safety, and to the several commanding officers of the continental troops; that it be proclaimed in each of the United States, and at the head of the army" (Maier 1997, 130). This had led Pauline Maier to observe that the document "was designed first and foremost for domestic consumption" (1997, 131); one of its tasks would be to convince those who had previously supported the king and Parliament (Davidson and Lytle 1982, 80). Thomas Jefferson's concern for how the document would sound when read (Fliegelman 1993) also appears to have put far greater concern with its reception by domestic than foreign audiences (in the latter of which it would often first have to be translated).

Delegates to the Continental Congress undoubtedly anticipated that declaring independence would make it easier to solicit foreign allies. Still, it is doubtful that the kings of France or Spain would be particularly convinced by the Declaration's social contract philosophy. Indeed, Howard Mumford Jones thus observed that Jefferson's demonization of George III both outraged British public opinion and "did not precisely hearten other monarchies, where heads of state, not averse to seeing Britain humbled, were extremely hesitant about supporting wild-eyed American radicals" (1976, 61).

By couching its rhetoric in philosophical terms, the Declaration was appealing to the intellectual elite. As Jones so colorfully put it, when those who read Jefferson's appeal to "the opinions of mankind," they did "not think that Jefferson was aiming at the Japanese or the Hottentots or the Highlanders or the Algerians; he was talking to that elite group, limited in number but admirable in brain power, which made the high culture of the eighteenth century the great thing it truly was" (1976, 71). David Armitage (2007) has demonstrated that the document has had a major influence on subsequent documents throughout the world.

See also International Law; Reason

Further Reading

Armitage, David. 2007. *The Declaration of Independence: A Global History*. Cambridge, MA: Harvard University Press.

Davidson, James West, and Mark Hamilton Lytle. 1982. *After the Fact: The Art of Historical Detection*. New York: Alfred A. Knopf.

Fliegelman, Jay. 1993. *Declaring Independence: Jefferson, Natural Language, and the Culture of Performance*. Stanford, CA: Stanford University Press.

Jones, Howard Mumford. 1976. "The Declaration of Independence: A Critique." *Proceedings of the American Antiquarian Society*, 55–72. www.americanantiquarian.org/proceedings/4449897.pdf.

Maier, Pauline 1997. *American Scripture: Making the Declaration of Independence*. New York: Alfred A. Knopf.

B

BENTHAM'S SHORT REVIEW OF THE DECLARATION OF INDEPENDENCE

The same book that included John Lind's 117-page attempted refutation of the charges in the Declaration of Independence also includes a "Short Review of the Declaration," which is even more hard-hitting. It is now known to have been authored by Jeremy Bentham (1748–1821), the English utilitarian philosopher. Whereas Lind had concentrated on the accusations against the king, Bentham focused on the philosophy of the Declaration in the preamble, which he observes deserves "little notice" and which he compares to "witchcraft" (1776, 119).

A forceful and prodigious writer who identified himself as a utilitarian, Jeremy Bentham exercised an enormous influence on British law, administration, and politics in the early 19th century. He critiqued the idea of natural rights as a form of "rhetorical nonsense." (Library of Congress)

Bentham described its "theory of Government" as "absurd and visionary" and its prescriptions as "nefarious" (1776, 119). In referencing the doctrine of natural rights, Bentham observed that "they perceive not, or will not seem to perceive, that nothing which can be called Government ever was, or ever could be, in any influence, exercised, but at the expense of one or other of those rights" (1776, 120). Comparing American revolutionaries to earlier "German Anabaptists" (1776, 121), he further accused the philosophy of the Declaration of putting "the axe to the root of all Government" (1776, 122). Bentham observed that the colonists' chief grievance was not that "they were actually taxed more than they could bear . . . but that they were *liable* to be so taxed" because it would be "*possible*" that Parliament might do so (1776, 122). Bentham further echoed Lind's arguments that many of the charges directed against King George III could just as accurately have been lodged against his predecessors. He thought that many of these actions had long ago been sanctioned by "tacit consent and approbation" (1776, 124) and still others by express consent. Bentham believed, "If the exercise of powers, thus established by usage, thus recognized by express declarations, thus sanctified by their beneficial effects, can justify rebellion, there is not that subject in the world, but who has, ever has had, and ever must have, reason sufficient to rebel" (1776, 126). The acts the Declaration had identified were neither acts of "*tyranny*" nor "*usurpation*" (1776, 126). Not surprisingly, Bentham interpreted what the Declaration identified as war atrocities as legitimate acts of "self-defense, exercised in *consequence* in resistance already shewn" (1776, 128).

Bentham hoped that publication of the Declaration would finally alert fellow Britons to the conspiratorial designs of American leaders and unite them in opposition to them. He further observed that "it is one thing for them to *say*, the connection, which bound them to us, is *dissolved*, another to *dissolve* it" and that "to *accomplish* their *independence* is not quite so easy as to *declare* it" (1776, 131).

Bentham continued to criticize the ideas in the Declaration of Independence, the Virginia Declaration of Rights, and the French Declaration of the Rights of Man and Citizen until the end of his life. He considered the doctrine of natural rights to be "rhetorical nonsense, nonsense upon stilts" (Armitage, 2007, 80).

See also *An Answer to the Declaration of the American Congress* (Lind); *Strictures upon the Declaration of Independence* (Hutchinson)

Further Reading

Armitage, David. 2007. *The Declaration of Independence: A Global History*. Cambridge, MA: Harvard University Press.

[Bentham, Jeremy]. 1776. "Short Review of the Declaration." In *An Answer to the Declaration of the American Congress*, 119–132. London: J. Walter, Charing-Cross and T. Sewell.

BILL OF EQUITY

See Legal Form of Declaration of Independence

BILL OF RIGHTS

Early declarations of bills of rights were often based on the English Declaration of Rights (1689). They typically began with a set of grievances, often against the king (sometimes in alliance with judges) and with statements of abstract principles. They were also usually phrased in terms of "oughts" rather than in terms of the "shalls" that dominate the first ten amendments to the U.S. Constitution, which are today typically known as the national Bill of Rights.

In a recent book on the Bill of Rights, however, Gerard N. Magiocca (2018) has pointed out that designating the first ten amendments, which include the First Amendment protections for freedom of speech (which have been held to include the right to burn the flag in symbolic protest), as the Bill of Rights did not become widespread practice until after the Spanish-American War of 1898. Then, as in the subsequent New Deal period, leaders used this designation to reassure individuals that even though Congress was assuming greater powers, it would continue to honor their rights, which the judiciary would continue to enforce. During World War II and the Cold War, American leaders further highlighted the first ten amendments as a way of contrasting American democratic values with those of repressive foreign totalitarian regimes.

Prior to this time, individuals sometimes referred to the Declaration and Resolves of the First Continental Congress (October 14, 1774), the provisions within Article I, Sections 9 and 10 of the Constitution (which respectively limited Congress and the states), and the Declaration of Independence as the American Bill of Rights, with the latter designation being the most frequent. Magiocca observes that "the case for treating the Declaration of Independence as the national Bill of Rights was compelling. Not only was that statement modeled on the 1689 English Declaration of Rights, but the 1776 Declaration contained all the ringing philosophical statements that Americans expected in a bill of rights" (2018, 58). One advantage for abolitionists that the Declaration of Independence had over the first ten amendments was that the Declaration specifically emphasized human equality, which Congress subsequently incorporated into the Fourteenth Amendment (1868).

See also Declaration (Meaning of Term); English Declaration of Rights

Further Reading

Amar, Akhil Reed. 1998. *The Bill of Rights: Creation and Reconstruction*. New Haven, CT: Yale University Press.

Magliocca, Gerard N. 2018. *The Heart of the Constitution: How the Bill of Rights Became the Bill of Rights*. New York: Oxford University Press.

Maier, Pauline. 1999. "The Strange History of 'All Men Are Created Equal.'" *Washington and Lee Law Review* 56 (Summer): 873–888.

Maier, Pauline. 2017. "The Strange History of the Bill of Rights." *Georgetown Journal of Law and Public Policy* 15 (Summer): 497–511.

BINNS ENGRAVING OF THE DECLARATION OF INDEPENDENCE

Shortly after the Second Continental Congress commissioned John Dunlap to print a one-page broadside, a large paper printed on one side that was used like a contemporary poster, of the Declaration of Independence, it also commissioned Timothy Matlack to prepare an engrossed (handwritten) copy, which the delegates subsequently signed. In 1777, Congress commissioned Mary Katherine Goddard to print the Declaration with the names of the signers, which had previously been secret.

Until 1818, there was no print or engraving of the Declaration of Independence in Matlack's hand available to the public. Perhaps because of patriotic sentiment stirred by the War of 1812, two engravers, John Binns and Benjamin Owen Tyler, both began the task. Although Binns started first (selling subscriptions to his project), Tyler finished first, with an unornamented print that he published in April 1818, including facsimile signatures. Tyler dedicated the work to Thomas Jefferson.

Engraving of the Declaration of Independence by John Binns, published in 1819. The print shows a facsimile of the Declaration of Independence in an ornamental oval frame with medallions of seals of the 13 original colonies, and medallion portraits of John Hancock, George Washington, and Thomas Jefferson. Above is an eagle with shield, olive branch, and arrows, holding a streamer reading *E Pluribus Unum*. (Library of Congress)

Although Binns (1772–1860), the publisher of a partisan newspaper the *Democratic Press*, did not publish his own print until 1819, it was much more elaborate, and was reduced in size so that it could be printed within an oval cartouche that featured a picture of George Washington, flanked by John Hancock and Thomas Jefferson and the seals of each of the 13 original states. He had to rearrange the signatures to fit within the cartouche (Puleo 2016, 239). Binns dedicated his work, which measured 35-5/16-by-24 inches, to the people of the United States.

In 1820, then Secretary of State John Quincy Adams commissioned a facsimile of the Declaration by William J. Stone, which he completed in 1823, and which became recognized as the official copy.

See also Dunlap Broadside Printing of the Declaration of Independence; Engravings and Printings of the Declaration of Independence; Goddard Printing of the Declaration of Independence; Stone Engraving of the Declaration of Independence

Further Reading

"Declaration of Independence by Binns (Engraving)." Thomas Jefferson's Monticello. https://www.monticello.org/site/house-and-gardens/declaration-independence-binns/engraving.

Puleo, Stephen. 2016. *American Treasures: The Secret Efforts to Save the Declaration of Independence, the Constitution, and the Gettysburg Address*. New York: St. Martin's.

BRITISH CONSTITUTION

When it drafted its Declaration and Resolves in 1774, the First Continental Congress based its arguments on three sources. They were the laws of nature, "the principles of the English Constitution," and the colonial compacts.

When the Second Continental Congress drafted the Declaration of Independence, it relied chiefly on the doctrine of natural rights. It did so because, by proclaiming themselves to be a separate people, Americans could no longer claim the protection of the English Constitution.

By contrast to the Constitution that delegates to the Constitutional Convention of 1787 would draft, the English Constitution is an "unwritten Constitution," which consists of a series of documents (for example, the Magna Carta and the English Bill of Rights) and practices that go back hundreds of years. The British Constitution was often identified as a "mixed government," because it was thought to combine three classes (the king, the aristocracy, and the people) respectively in the monarchy, the House of Lords, and the House of Commons. British rights were further protected by a system of judge-issued law known as the common law and based on precedents that included the development of the jury system.

Over time, within Britain, the Parliament had acquired primary sovereignty, with the king retaining some powers but serving chiefly as head of state rather than as head of government. Although the idea that Parliament was sovereign had become commonplace in Britain, Americans adhered to an older conception, often associated with Lord Edward Coke (1552–1634), which subjected the king and Parliament to natural law principles. Moreover, Americans interpreted the Magna Carta and other British documents as prohibiting the taxation of populations who were not physically represented there (known as actual representation). By contrast, the Parliament believed that it represented, and could thus legislate for, all Englishmen, whether they resided within Britain or the colonies (known as virtual representation).

In the initial conflict between Britain and the American colonies, the colonies attempted to appeal to the British king against the British Parliament, albeit ultimately without success. The king thought that the adoption of the Declaratory Act in 1766 had definitively established the right of Parliament to legislation in all matters for the colonies.

Although repudiating the power of both the Parliament and the king, Americans recognized that they would need to establish their own forms of government, which already had a firm foundation within colonial assemblies and would grow with united actions by the First and Second Congresses. Although Thomas Paine's *Common Sense* appeared to convince most of the colonists that kingship led to war and corruption, Americans remained strongly committed to representative institutions and to an independent judiciary. Moreover, the later creation of the presidency would indicate that they also recognized the need for executive power, albeit not based on heredity.

In time, the American conception of an empire bound together by adherence to a common monarch and through common trade was partially vindicated by the creation of the British Commonwealth of Nations.

See also *Common Sense* (Paine); Declaratory Act of 1766; Declaration and Resolves of the First Continental Congress (1774); Laws of Nature and of Nature's God

Further Reading

Sadosky, Leonard J. 2009. *Revolutionary Negotiations: Indians, Empires, and Diplomats in the Founding of America.* Charlottesville: University of Virginia Press.

BRITISH CROWN

The closing paragraph of the Declaration of Independence announces that the representatives of America considered themselves "absolved from all allegiance to the British Crown." This phrase came from the Resolutions that Richard Henry Lee had introduced in Congress on behalf of Virginia on June 7, 1776.

British monarchs (whether kings or queens) are entitled to wear a crown as a symbol of their authority and do so when addressing Parliament. Contemporary visitors to England may visit the Tower of London to see the royal crowns and other jewels. The British Crown thus arguably refers to the British monarch. On the surface, it might therefore appear that the Declaration was only severing its connection with that institution. Significantly, most of the grievances that the Declaration cites are directed at the king ("He has . . ."), although at times the document also accuses him of having "combined with others."

It is clear, however, that the colonists had, as in their opposition to parliamentary taxes and in the Declaration and Resolves of the First Continental Congress (1774), already indicated that they thought the British Parliament had no sovereignty, or power, over them—the Declaratory Act of 1766 had shown that Parliament disagreed. Almost as if anticipating the later British Commonwealth of Nations, colonial spokesmen had initially maintained that while repudiating parliamentary claims to legislate on their behalf, they still retained their loyalty to the British nation through their allegiance to a common king, who in turn had rebuffed their petitions. As the opening paragraph of the Declaration makes clear, by announcing their separation from the English Crown, the colonies thought they were separating from not only the English king but from the English people as a whole.

When Parliament adopts laws, it does so under the authority of "The King (or Queen) in Parliament," thus merging the two institutions. Similarly, American laws require the consent of both legislative and executive branches or, in cases of a presidential veto, a supermajority of both houses of the former. Whereas the United States unites the role of head of government and head of state in one person, Britain separates them into the monarch and the prime minister. As head of state, the ruling monarch (who is frequently pictured on stamps and coins) is a symbol of the entire realm.

This strongly suggests that the reference to the "British Crown" in the Declaration did not simply mean the king but included any other governmental authorities within England who might seek to assert control over the one-time colonies. As the remainder of Lee's resolution, which the Declaration quotes, declares, Americans were asserting that "all political connection between them and the state of Great Britain is & ought to be totally dissolved." The United States recognized neither the continuing authority of the English Parliament nor that of the English king but sought to make its own way in the world as an independent member of the family of nations.

See also Charges against the King and Others; Declaration and Resolves of the First Continental Congress (1774); Declaratory Act of 1766; People

Further Reading

Fisher, Sydney George. 1907. "The Twenty-Eight Charges against the King in the Declaration of Independence." *Pennsylvania Magazine of History and Biography* 31:247–303.

McKee, Mary. 2017. "British Reaction to America's Declaration of Independence." British Newspaper Archive, https://blog.britishnewspaperarchive.co.uk/2017/07/04/british-reaction-to-americas-declaration-of-independence/.

BRITISH DEPOSITION APOLOGIAS

In seeking to identify models for the Declaration of Independence, Stephen E. Lucas observed that from the time of the Norman conquest until the Declaration, seven English monarchs had been deposed. They were: "Edward II, in 1327; Richard II, in 1399; Henry VI, in 1460; Edward V, in 1483; Richard III, in 1485; Charles I, in 1649; and James II, in 1689" (1998, 152).

Lucas further observed that the documents announcing their departures shared a number of features, which the Declaration emulated. First, Lucas said that "they assign all responsibility for the wretched state of affairs to the king" (1998, 152). Second, they "do not indict the king for petty mistakes in policy, but for a deliberate assault on the constitution" (1998, 153). Third they "typically contain a bill of particulars spelling out the kings' crimes" (1998, 154). Lucas sees a particular affinity between the Declaration of Independence and the English Declaration of Rights of 1689.

William Huse Dunham Jr. and Charles Wood have shown how depositions "contributed greatly to Englishmen's understanding of the authorities by which they were ruled" (1976, 760). They observed, "Under normal circumstances their governance was primarily regal, but in the process of removing unsatisfactory kings, men of politics and law gradually set limits beyond which a reigning monarch could not safely go" (1976, 760). They further noted that some depositions were based on the Idea of "the Bad King (one who had violated England's law, custom, and morality)," whereas others centered on "The Useless King (the incompetent executive and inept politician who had not mastered the art of handling men)" (1976, 760). By arguing that George III was a "tyrant," the Declaration clearly placed him in the former category.

See also English Declaration of Rights; Tyranny

Further Reading

Dunham, William Huse, Jr., and Charles T. Wood. 1976. "The Right to Rule in England: Depositions and the Kingdom's Authority, 1327–1485." *American Historical Review* 81 (October): 738–761.

Lucas, Stephen E. 1998. "The Rhetorical Ancestry of the Declaration of Independence." *Rhetoric and Public Affairs* 1 (Summer): 143–184.

C

CALHOUN, JOHN C.

John C. Calhoun (1782–1850), of South Carolina, who respectively served in the U.S. House of Representatives, as secretary of war, as vice president, as secretary of state, and as U.S. senator, is often ranked with Daniel Webster and Henry Clay as one of the nineteenth-century giants of the U.S. Senate. A strong nationalist, Calhoun became increasingly concerned that the numerical majority might one day use the constitutional amending process to abolish slavery, and he developed the idea of nullification (allowing individual states to invalidate federal laws) and secession as a way of protecting this institution.

John C. Calhoun was a political philosopher and statesman who defended the institution of slavery as a positive good and was an ardent proponent of states' rights during the early 19th century. He opposed the Declaration's assertion that "all men are created equal." (Library of Congress)

A man of considerable intellect, Calhoun fashioned the idea of concurrent majorities, which would give each major interest (including slaveholders) a veto on policy innovations (Lerner 1963). In contrast to Founding Fathers, who had viewed slavery as at best a necessary evil, Calhoun argued that the institution benefited both whites and blacks (the latter of whom he thought were incapable of governing themselves), and he argued vigorously for the expansion of slavery at a time when Northerners were increasingly attempting to stop its spread into new states and territories.

Perhaps recognizing the way that abolitionists were evoking the principles of the Declaration of Independence to further their cause, Calhoun not only denied that the words of the Declaration of Independence applied to nonwhites but argued that they were palpably false. His most vigorous statement of this doctrine is found in a speech that he delivered in Congress on June 17, 1848, on a bill that would have excluded slavery from the Oregon Territory.

Fearing that the exclusion of slavery might eventually dissolve the Union, Calhoun traced the practice to the Northwest Ordinance of 1787 and the Missouri Compromise of 1820. Lying behind both was what Calhoun identified as "a proposition which originated in a hypothetical truism, but which, as now expressed and now understood, is the most false and dangerous of all political errors." He further observed that "the proposition to which I allude, has become an axiom in the minds of a vast majority on both sides of the Atlantic, and is repeated daily from tongue to tongue, as an established and incontrovertible truth; it is, that 'all men are born free and equal.'"

Calhoun launched a major, if perhaps somewhat over literalistic, critique of this philosophy:

> Taking the proposition literally (it is in that sense it is understood), there is not a word of truth in it. It beings with "all men are born," which is utterly untrue. Men are not born. Infants are born. They grow to be men. And concludes with asserting that they are born "free and equal," which is not less false. They are not born free. While infants they are incapable of freedom, being destitute alike of the capacity of thinking and acting, without which there can be no freedom. Besides, they are necessarily born subject to their parents, and remain so among all people, savage and civilized, until the development of their intellect and physical capacity enables them to take care of themselves. They grow to all the freedom of which the condition in which they were born permits, by growing to be men. Nor is it less false than they are born "equal." They are not so in any sense in which it can be regarded; and thus, as I have asserted, there is not a word of truth in the whole proposition, as expressed and generally understood. (1854, 507)

Acknowledging that the "proposition" is "differently expressed in the Declaration of Independence, as 'all men are created equal,'" Calhoun subjected it to similar criticism: "The form of expression, though less dangerous, is not less erroneous. All men are not created. According to the Bible, only two, a man and a woman, ever were, and of these one was pronounced subordinate to the other." In a statement with which Abraham Lincoln would agree, but from which he would draw very different consequences, Calhoun observed that:

> It was inserted into our Declaration of Independence without any necessity. It made no necessary part of our justification in separating from the parent country, and declaring ourselves independent. Breach of our chartered privileges, and lawless encroachment on our acknowledged and well-established rights by the parent country, were the real causes, and of themselves sufficient, without resorting to any other, to justify the step. Nor had it any weight in constructing the government which were substituted in the place of the colonial. (1848)

Calhoun believed that the Declaration had taken the phrase from John Locke and Algernon Sydney, who had said that "all men in the state of nature were free and equal." Calhoun observed, however, that because men were naturally social and political, the state of nature was "purely hypothetical." Thus, "when we say all men are free and equal in it, we announce a mere hypothetical truism; that is, a truism resting on a mere supposition that cannot exist, and of course one of little or no practical value."

Almost as if to anticipate the maximum that George Orwell made famous in *Animal Farm* ("all animals are equal, but some animals are more equal than others"), Calhoun then sought to differentiate among different peoples:

> Instead, then, of all men having the same right to liberty and equality, as is claimed by those who hold that they are all born free and equal, liberty is the noble and highest reward bestowed on mental and moral development, combined with favorable circumstances. Instead, then, of liberty and equality being born with man; instead of all men and all classes and descriptions being equally entitled to them, they are high prizes to be won, and are in their most perfect state, not only the highest reward that can be bestowed on our race, but the most difficult to be won—and when won, the most difficult to be preserved. (1854, 511)

Calhoun said that "we now begin to experience the danger of admitting so great an error to have a place in the declaration of independence. For a long time it lay dormant; but in the process of time it began to germinate, and produce its poisonous fruits" (1854). He traced these from Thomas Jefferson, to the Northwest Ordinance of 1787, and to the entire country.

Abraham Lincoln saw such words as an indication of how far the nation had strayed from founding principles. He agreed with Calhoun that the statement of human equality had been unnecessary to the formulation of the Declaration, but thought that it had value as an aspiration, which the Constitution should embody.

See also Abolitionism; Equality; Lincoln, Abraham; Northwest Ordinance of 1787; People; Slavery

Further Reading

Calhoun, John C. 1848. "Speech on the Oregon Bill." June 27. TeachingAmericanHistory.org/ http://teachingamericanhistory.org/library/document/oregon-bill-speech/. In *Union and Liberty: The Political Philosophy of John C. Calhoun*, edited by Ross M. Lence. Indianapolis: Liberty Fund, 1992.

Calhoun, John C. 1854. *The Works of John C. Calhoun*. Vol. 4. New York: D. Appleton.

Lerner, Ralph. "Calhoun's New Science of Politics." *American Political Science Review* 57 (December): 918–932.

CALLED TOGETHER LEGISLATIVE BODIES UNUSUALLY (CHARGE #4)

The fourth charge that the Declaration of Independence lodged against the king was that "he has called together legislative bodies at places unusual, uncomfortable, & distance from the depository of their public records, for the sole purpose of fatiguing them into compliance with his measures." Originating on a separate slip of paper, this complaint may have been added by John Adams (Dumbauld 1950, 100).

Professor Herbert Friedenwald says that this charge refers to the removal of the Massachusetts Assembly from Boston to Cambridge from 1769 to 1772 and the removal of the South Carolina capital from Charleston to Beauford in 1772 (1904, 225). According to Sydney George Fisher, the first was occasioned when Massachusetts legislators objected to holding sessions while being surrounded by troops; the second was in the aftermath of disturbances related to the Stamp Act (1907, 273). Professor Dumbauld further notes that when Thomas Jefferson was a member of the Virginia House of Burgesses in 1775, Lord Dunmore, the governor, took refuge on a warship named the *Fowey* and extended an invitation for the legislature to meet him there, thus perhaps accounting for the accusation's references to "unusual" and "uncomfortable" (1950, 101–102).

Former Massachusetts governor Thomas Hutchinson, who played a major role in moving the Massachusetts General Court (its legislature) from Boston to Cambridge, observed that, far from being unusual, the Massachusetts legislature had previously met in Cambridge during a smallpox scare and that being only four miles away, it was "less *distant* than any other Town fit for the purpose" (1776). John Lind further observed that by moving the Massachusetts legislature, the king was actually responding to their concerns about meeting in a city where they were surrounded by troops (1776, 30–31).

These responses failed to grasp the way in which Massachusetts had regarded the removal of its legislature as an improper exercise of governmental prerogative that also threatened other liberties. Two scholars of the subject observed that the debate in Massachusetts had raised questions about "the extent of parliamentary power" and that "the removal controversy reinforced the predisposition among public men in pre-Revolutionary Massachusetts—and during a period of constitutional strife—to conceive of institutions as players in a moral drama" (Lord and Calhoon 1969, 754).

See also Charges against the King and Others

Further Reading

Dumbauld, Edward. 1950. *The Declaration of Independence and What It Means Today*. Norman: University of Oklahoma Press.

Fisher, Sydney George. 1907. "The Twenty-Eight Charges against the King in the Declaration of Independence." *Pennsylvania Magazine of History and Biography* 31:257–303.

Friedenwald, Herbert. 1904. *The Declaration of Independence: An Interpretation and an Analysis*. New York: Macmillan.

Hutchinson, Thomas. 1776. "1776: Hutchinson, Strictures upon the Declaration of Independence." Online Library of Liberty. http://oll.libertyfund.org/pages/1776-hutchinson-strictures-upon-the-declaration-of-independence.

Lind, John. 1776. *An Answer to the Declaration of the American Congress*. London: J. Walter, Charing-Cross and T. Sewell.

Lord, Donald C., and Robert M. Calhoon. 1969. "The Removal of the Massachusetts General Court from Boston, 1769–1772." *Journal of American History* 55 (March): 735–755.

CAPITALIZATION AND PUNCTUATION IN THE DECLARATION OF INDEPENDENCE

Eighteenth-century grammatical conventions differed from those of today. For example, it is common to see the word "it's" used as a possessive rather than, as in current usage, as a contraction for "it is" (with the word "its" being possessive). Similarly, the rules of capitalization also differed, although in the case of the Declaration, these rules vary between the so-called Dunlap broadside, the first to be printed for public inspection, and the later parchment copy engrossed by Timothy Matlack, which was not printed until after the New York delegation gave its consent.

James Munves observes that at the time the Declaration was written, "Nouns were capitalized haphazardly for emphasis" (1978, 120). He observed, however, that Thomas

> Jefferson went to the other extreme and used capital letters very sparingly—only at the beginnings of paragraphs and in the names of nations (Great Britain) or peoples (Indians). He used even fewer capital letters than we do today (leaving even *god* in lowercase). With all this, his style was closer to what came later than that of his contemporaries (1978, 120).

Richard Wendorf is unsure whether Jefferson's sparing use of capitals was prompted by his "desire to increase the manual speed or an authorial hand constantly in motion" or "as a visual reflection of his democratic social and political beliefs" (2014, 308). Wendorf notes that Jefferson's draft of the Declaration did capitalize "MEN" when blaming the king for the slave trade while underscoring the words "infidel" and speaking of the "Christian" king of Great Britain (2014, 311). In addition to capitalizing words that begin sentences, the Dunlap copy, with only a few exceptions, appears to capitalize nouns, but not adjectives or pronouns (Larson, 2001, 738–739). Pointing to this usage, Carlton Larson observes that in a number of phrases, like "United Colonies" and "Free and Independent States," the capitalization of the initial adjectives suggest that the terms are "complete noun phrases" signifying a collective national entity rather than 13 individual states. This is consistent with his larger argument that the Declaration represented the creation of a new nation rather than signaling the independence of the 13 former colonies from one another. Because the Dunlap manuscript departed so significantly from Jefferson's own style, it is difficult to know what, if any, significance to attach to Larson's observation, especially since the engrossed Matlack manuscript is titled "The Unanimous Declaration of the thirteen united States of America" and follows neither the capitalization style of Jefferson nor of the Dunlap printing.

In recent years, Danielle Allen, a Harvard professor who has written on the Declaration, has argued that the official transcript of the Declaration produced by the National Archives and Records Administration has mistaken an errant ink mark for a period after "the pursuit of happiness." She believes that Jefferson intended instead for his self-evident truths to include the assertion that governments derive their just powers from "the consent of the governed" (Schuessler 2014).

See also Captions of the Declaration of Independence

Further Reading

Larson, Carlton F. W. 2001. "The Declaration of Independence: A 225th Anniversary Re-interpretation." *Washington Law Review* 76 (July): 701–791.

Munves, James. 1978. *Thomas Jefferson and the Declaration of Independence: The Writing and Editing of the Document that Marked the Birth of the United States of America*. New York: Charles Scribner's Sons.

Schuessler, Jennifer. 2014. "If Only Thomas Jefferson Could Settle the Issue." *New York Times*. July 2. https://www.nytimes.com/2014/07/03/us/politics/a-period-is-questioned-in-the-declaration-of-independence.html?_r=0.

Wendorf, Richard. 2014. "Declaring, Drafting, and Composing American Independence." *Bibliographical Society of America* 108:307–324.

CAPTIONS OF THE DECLARATION OF INDEPENDENCE

The most common way to refer to the document that the Continental Congress approved on July 4, 1776, is to call it the Declaration of Independence. This usage, which this book emulates, has the advantages of both brevity and specificity. Such an appellation is about as common as those used for the U.S. Constitution or the Gettysburg Address.

The "Declaration of Independence" is, in fact, the way the document is listed in the *Journals of the Continental Congress* (5:491), which are taken from drafts in the handwriting of John Adams and from the document held by the Department of State and reproduced in facsimile. Immediately below this title, however, the manuscript reports to be "a Declaration by the Representatives of the United States of America, in general Congress assembled."

In the first printed edition of the Declaration of Independence, executed by John Dunlap, the document is headed by five lines as follows:

> IN CONGRESS, JULY 4, 1776
> A DECLARATION
> BY THE REPRESENTATIVES OF THE
> UNITED STATES OF AMERICA,
> IN GENERAL CONGRESS ASSEMBLED.
> (Ford 1893, 42)

Dennis Mahoney observes that this heading "emphasizes the representative character of the Declaration" (1987, 57).

After New York approved of independence on July 18, 1776, however, Congress sent the document to Timothy Matlack, to be engrossed, or converted to calligraphy, on animal skin. Perhaps in part to leave room for the signers, Matlack covered the five-line title to two, the second indicating state unanimity, as follows:

> IN CONGRESS, JULY 4, 1776,
> THE unanimous Declaration of the thirteen united States of America.
> (Ford 1893, 42)

See also Dunlap Broadside Printing of the Declaration of Independence; Engrossed Declaration of Independence (Matlack)

Further Reading

Ford, Paul Leicester, ed. 1893. *The Writings of Thomas Jefferson*. Vol. 2, *1776–1781*. New York: G. P. Putnam's Sons.

Journals of the Continental Congress, 1774–1789. 1906. Edited from the Original Records in the Library of Congress by Worthington Chauncey Ford. Vol. 5. *1776 (June 5–October 8)*. Washington, DC: Government Printing Office.

Mahoney, Dennis J. 1987. "The Declaration of Independence as a Constitutional Document." In *The Framing and Ratification of the Constitution*, edited by Leonard W. Levy and Dennis J. Mahoney, 54–68. New York: Macmillan.

CHARGES AGAINST THE KING AND OTHERS

Although most contemporary commentary focuses on the first two paragraphs of the Declaration of Independence, a majority of the document is devoted to charges against the English king, whom the document does not mention by name.

These accusations might have been somewhat disorienting to those who had followed the emerging conflict between the American colonies and Britain. Up to the adoption of the Coercive Acts, the fighting at Lexington and Concord, the king's rejection of colonial petitions, and the publication of Thomas Paine's *Common Sense*, dissenting colonists had placed most of the blame either on the British Parliament or the king's ministers. By contrast, they had shared an exalted view of George III, likening him to a "patriot king" as described by Henry St. John, Viscount Bolingbroke (1678–1751), in his essay "The Idea of a Patriot King" (Liddle 1979, 953). Even after fighting began, George Washington and troops fighting under his command typically referred to British troops as "the Ministerial Troops" rather than associating them directly with the king (Liddle 1969, 965). As it became increasingly apparent that the king was going to side with Parliament rather than with the colonies, Americans approached the realization that the king was not taking their side with a combination of "sorrow and perplexity" or "indignation and resentment" (Liddle 1969, 967).

Phrased much like a legal brief, or bill of equity, the charges are collectively designed to show the king's desire to establish "an absolute tyranny over these states." Robert Grudin believes that Thomas Jefferson may further have been using a literary device, borrowed in part from Cicero, known as "copia," "which normally consists of an eloquent piling up of diverse details that all related to a central topic or theme" (2010, 118). Few of the charges were new. Donald S. Lutz observes that "this list surprised no one. Americans had been producing similar lists of abuses in their newspapers since the infamous Stamp Act more than a decade earlier" (1989, 47; see also Duff 1949). What made the charges unique was that they were now directed at the king rather than at Parliament or the king's ministers.

In contrast to some of these earlier documents, Jefferson did not cite specific dates, making it more difficult for modern readers to identify the specific incidents, which sometimes applied only to a single colony and sometimes to the colonies collectively. William Smith thus notes that the "facts" that the Declaration of Independence cited "have not the concreteness of events. They are facts abstracted" (1965). Howard Mumford Jones observes that Jefferson was "[a] master of propaganda," who often "translated into a general statement covering all the colonies, what had happened in two or three of them" (1976, 7). Jones further observes that "the eighteenth-century habit of writing in general terms made this an easy thing to do" (1976, 7–8).

As the Second Continental Congress likely viewed the situation, it has previously cited specific dates, only to be ignored. The British had had sufficient occasion to seek to remedy the injustices. It was therefore appropriate for the Declaration of Independence to state, but unnecessary to defend, or document, the charges.

In comparing the Declaration of Independence to previous documents in the same genre, Hans L. Eicholz further notes that "the intention" of these documents was different (2001, 45). Both the English Declaration of Right and many state declarations sought not only to justify what they were doing but also to set the framework for the government to follow. By contrast, the Declaration of Independence sought simply to announce the reasons for independence and left it to another document to outline how a new government would operate.

The first 12 accusations all begin with the words "he has," with the word "he" referring specifically to George III. Jefferson took most of these from the preamble to the Virginia Constitution, which he had also written. The first seven of these accusations centered on the king's actions with regard to colonial legislatures and the legislation they had adopted; the next two dealt with his interference with the administration of justices; the next dealt with bureaucracies he had created; and the last two dealt with military forces he had sent and how they were governed.

The second set of 10 charges begin with the words "he has combined with others." The "others" in question refer to the two houses of Parliament, which the Declaration consciously refused to recognize. Indeed, the first such phrase refer to "their acts of pretended legislation." Each of these remaining charges is further followed by the preposition "for" and a present progressive verb as in "for quartering," "for protection," "for cutting off," and the like.

The last set of five accusations returned to the "he has" construction of the first set. These charges dealt specifically with war atrocities that the declaration attributed to the king. The charges seem to gain momentum throughout the manuscript, "starting softly, building to a dramatic crescendo" with the final charges using verbs that "are more evocative and stirring than the previous ones" (Parkinson 2016, 251–252).

Ross M. Lence further associated the first 13 charges with: "injuries," or abuses of constitutional power; sections 14 through 22 with "grievances associated with the 'usurpations,' or the exercise of power that others have a right to"; and charges 23–27 with "capricious and barbarous acts of George III which shock all contemporary canons of decency and are the very markings of a tyrant" (1986, 36). Alternatively, Lence suggests that one can view the first 7 charges as: "interference with colonial representative institutions"; charges 8 through 12 with "Violations of the principles of separation of powers, at least as the colonists understood that concept"; charges 13 through 22 as "Instances of 'pretended acts of legislation'"; and charges 23 to 27 as "instances of tyrannical, pernicious acts of the king" (1984, 36).

These charges are followed by a description of prior colonial petitions and their rejection by the king, the Parliament, and the English people. This is, in turn, followed by the actual proclamation of independence and the delegates' mutual pledge to one another in the last paragraph.

Arguing that "the gravamen of colonial complaints was not against the king but against Parliament or the ministry or both," Howard Mumford Jones believes that in terms of propaganda, "it is wiser to concentrate your venom on a person than on an impersonal institution" (1976, 8). He observes, however, that this may have resulted in three negative consequences. First, he notes that "it outraged British public opinion so that the war in America became known as the King's War." Second, he thinks it may have stirred fears in other monarchs who might otherwise want to strike a blow at Britain. Third, he thinks it further split American public opinion (1976, 9).

Two contemporaries, former Massachusetts governor Thomas Hutchinson and John Lind, published pamphlets designed to refute the Declaration's charges. Others have sought to explain and defend (Friedenwald 1904, 208–259) or analyze them. In an unusually harsh analysis, a contemporary U.S. historian has identified the Declaration as "America's first proclamation of victimology." As he explained, "Instead of admitting that they simply had no desire to cough up taxes, even to pay for a war that drove the French out of North America and thus made possible a situation where settlers were now secure enough to demand self-government, the colonists blamed King George for every outrage conceivable" (Diggins 1995, A15).

All the charges had a basis in fact, but all were filtered from the colonial perspective, which regarded parliamentary sovereignty as limited and the refusal of the king to invalid such actions as indications of his own perfidy. In later years, the British would seek to retain the benefits of being a mother country by recognizing a commonwealth system, in which both mother country and colonies were bound under the authority of the monarch, but this model was not at the time available to either side, who thus went to war.

See also Virginia Constitution of 1776

Further Reading

Charles, Patrick J. 2008. *Irreconcilable Grievances: The Events That Shaped the Declaration of Independence*. Westminster, MD: Heritage Books.

Diggins, John Patrick. 1995. "The Pursuit of Whining." *New York Times*, September 25, A15.

Duff, Stella F. 1949. "The Case against the King: The Virginia Gazettes Indict George III." *William and Mary Quarterly* 6 (July): 383–397.

Eicholz, Hans L. 2001. *Harmonizing Sentiments: The Declaration of Independence and the Jeffersonian Idea of Self-Government*. New York: Peter Lang.

Fisher, Sydney George. 1907. "The Twenty-Eight Charges against the King in the Declaration of Independence." *Pennsylvania Magazine of History and Biography* 31:247–303.

Friedenwald, Herbert. 1904. *The Declaration of Independence: An Interpretation and an Analysis*. New York: Macmillan.

Grudin, Robert. 2010. *Design and Truth*. New Haven, CT: Yale University Press.

Hutchinson, Thomas. 1776. "1776: Hutchinson, Strictures upon the Declaration of Independence." Online Library of Liberty. http://oll.libertyfund.org/pages/1776-hutchinson-strictures-upon-the-declaration-of-independence.

Jones, Howard Mumford. 1976. "The Declaration of Independence: A Critique." In *The Declaration of Independence: Two Essays by Howard Mumford Jones and Howard H. Peckham*, 3–20. Worcester, MA: American Antiquarian Society.

Lence, Ross M. 1986. "The American Declaration of Independence: The Majority and the Right of Political Power." In *Founding Principles of American Government: Two Hundred Years of Democracy on Trial,* rev. ed., edited by George J. Graham Jr. and Scarlett G. Graham, 29–59. Chatham, NJ: Chatham House Publishers.

Liddle, William D. 1979. "'A Patriot King or None': Lord Bolingbroke and the American Renunciation of George III." *Journal of American History* 65 (March): 951–970.

Lind, John. 1776 *An Answer to the Declaration of the American Congress*. London: J. Walter, Charing-Cross and T. Sewell.

Lossing, B. J. 1848. *Biographical Sketches of the Signers of the Declaration of American Independence; The Declaration Historical Considered; and a Sketch of the Leading Events Connected with the Adoption of the Articles of Confederation and of the Federal Constitution*. New York: George F. Cooledge and Brothers.

Lutz, Donald S. 1989. "The Declaration of Independence as Part of an American National Compact." *Publius* 19 (Winter): 41–58.

Parkinson, Robert G. 2016. *The Common Cause: Creating Race and Nation in the American Revolution*. Chapel Hill: University of North Carolina Press.

Patrick, Tim. 2017. *Self-Evident: Discovering the Ideas and Events That Made the Declaration of Independence Possible*. Seattle, WA: Owani Press.

Peckham, Howard H. 1976. "Independence: The View from Britain." *Proceedings of the American Antiquarian Society* 85:387–403. www.americanantiquarian.org/proceedings/44498108.pdf.

Smith, William Raymond. 1965. "The Rhetoric of the Declaration of Independence." *College English* 26 (January): 306–309.

Zetterberg, Hans L. 2010. "A Vocabulary Justifying Revolutions." *Sociologisk Forskning* 47:75–81.

CIRCUMSTANCES OF OUR EMIGRATION AND SETTLEMENT

The settlement and protection of America looked quite different from two sides of the Atlantic. From the British perspective, such settlement would not have been possible without British help, which brought with it obligation to the British Parliament. From the colonial perspective, the colonists had largely shouldered the burdens of colonization, and the primary tie that they had maintained up to the Declaration of Independence had been to the British king.

After noting that Americans had not "been wanting [lacking] in attentions to our English brethren" and warning against "attempts by their legislature to extend an unwarrantable jurisdiction over us," the Declaration observed that "we have reminded them of the circumstances of our emigration and settlement here." The Declaration, however, deleted Thomas Jefferson's longer explanation, which further observed that:

> No one of which could warrant so strange a pretension: that these were effected at the expense of our own blood and treasure; unassisted by the wealth or the strength of Great Britain: that In constituting indeed our several forms of government, we had adopted one common king; thereby laying a foundation for perpetual league and

> amity with them: but that submission to their parliament was no part of our constitution, or ever in idea, if history may be credited. (Jefferson 1893, 55)

There are at least three possible reasons for this omission. First, it would have specifically mentioned Parliament, which the Declaration had previously omitted. Second, it might have provided an opportunity for factual disputes about the respective contributions of Britain and the colonists to settlement. Third, even if colonists were now agreed upon "a perpetual league," there would be little reason to seek such a relationship simultaneous to independence.

In his *Summary View of the Rights of British America* as well as in his "Refutation of the Argument that the Colonies Were Established at the Expense of the British Nation" (Jefferson 1950, 1:277–284), Jefferson had outlined his view that those who came to America had done so at their own expense and had established independent sovereignties, bound only by allegiance to the king. John Quincy Adams criticized this view in 1831, when he noted

> The argument of Mr. Jefferson that the emigration of the first colonists from Great Britain which came to America was an expatriation, dissolving their allegiance and constituting them independent sovereignties, was doubtful in theory and unfounded in fact. The original colonists came out with charters from the King, with the rights and duties of British subjects. They were entitled to the protection of the British King, and owed him allegiance." (Wills 1977, 84, quoting Adams's *Memoirs*)

See also *A Summary View of the Rights of British America* (Jefferson)

Further Reading

Jefferson, Thomas. 1893. *The Writings of Thomas Jefferson*. Vol. 2, edited by Paul Leicester Ford. New York: G. P. Putnam's Sons.

Jefferson, Thomas. 1950. *The Papers of Thomas Jefferson,* edited by Julian P. Boyd. Vol. 1, *1760–1776*. Princeton, NJ: Princeton University Press.

Lewis, Anthony M. 1948. "Jefferson's Summary View as a Chart of Political Union." *William and Mary Quarterly* 5 (January): 34–51.

Wills, Garry. 1978. *Inventing America: Jefferson's Declaration of Independence*. Garden City, NY: Doubleday.

CIVILIAN CONTROL OF THE MILITARY (CHARGE #12)

One of the most succinct charges that the Declaration of Independence lodged against George III was that "he has affected to render the military independent of, & superior to, the civilian power." This charge immediately followed the related charge that the king had allowed for standing armies in the colonies without the colonists' consent.

The use of the word "affected" in this passage, which is somewhat archaic, means "sought" but probably also suggests that what the king was doing was to pretend to exercise powers contrary to republican principles. Notably, the very next accusation says that the king had given his assent to Parliament's "acts of pretended legislation."

After questioning the right of the king to send any troops to America without the consent of colonial legislatures, in *A Summary View of the Rights of British America*, Thomas Jefferson had made a similar point. There he had said that "to render these proceedings still more criminal against our laws, instead of subjecting the military to the civil powers, his majesty has expressly made the civil subordinate to the military" (Jefferson 1774).

The specific accusation is usually traced to the Massachusetts Government Act of 1774, which was adopted in reaction to the Boston Tea Party. This law, which was one of the Coercive, or Intolerable, Acts, had appointed General Thomas Gage, who headed British military forces in America, as governor of that colony. Jack Sosin has argued that the aims of the Massachusetts Acts of 1774 "were limited: legally to put down what appeared a revolutionary movement aimed at overthrowing its authority" (1963, 250). Denying that the ministers had attempted to render the military independent of civilian authority, Sosin believed that the British "merely sought to arrest a revolutionary challenge through legally constituted civil officers" (1963, 250). He does not, however appear to deny that Howe was actually wielding both civilian and military authority with little accountability to the people of Massachusetts.

It is possible that this accusation against the king may also have been designed to encompass actions by British military authorities in the colonies. During the French and Indian War, they had sometimes asserted that they had the right to quarter troops in private homes without local colonial assent (Rogers 1970).

Emphasis on civilian control of the military was not new to the Declaration. Dr. Joseph Warren had thus observed that "The sword should, in all free States, be subservient to the civil powers . . . we tremble at having an Army (although consisting of our own countrymen) established here without a civil power to provide for and control them" (Unger 2000, 209). George Washington had affirmed civilian control over the military by accepting the authority of the Second Continental Congress over his command. Under the Articles of Confederation, Congress continued to exercise direct control over the military. The Constitutional Convention of 1787 sought to continue civilian control of the military by providing that only Congress could declare war but also specifying that the president would be the commander in chief of the military.

See also Quartering Troops (Charge #14); Standing Armies (Charge #11); *A Summary View of the Rights of British America* (Jefferson)

Further Reading

Jefferson, Thomas. 1774. *A Summary View of the Rights of British America*. Colonial Williamsburg. www.history.org/almanack/life/politics/sumview.cfm. Accessed July 8, 2017.

Rogers, J. Alan. 1970. "Colonial Opposition to the Quartering of Troops during the French and Indian War." *Military Affairs* 34 (February): 7–11.

Sosin, Jack M. 1963. "The Massachusetts Acts of 1774: Coercive or Preventive?" *Huntington Library Quarterly* 26 (May): 235–252.

Unger, Harlow Giles. 2000. *John Hancock: Merchant King and American Patriot*. New York: John Wiley and Sons.

COINS AND STAMPS DEPICTING THE DECLARATION OF INDEPENDENCE

Numerous coins have been minted and stamps have been printed commemorating the Declaration of Independence. As might be expected, anniversaries of the American Independence have been the most popular times for such issues, some of which have been printed by foreign countries.

Depictions of the signing of the Declaration or of Independence Hall are often issued along with depictions of other revolutionary events like the Boston Massacre, the Boston Tea Party, or military victories. Pictures of Thomas Jefferson, the chief author of the document, are, of course, portrayed on the nickel, on the front of the two-dollar bill, and on numerous stamps. Since the bicentennial, the two-dollar bill has included a cropped picture of John Trumbull's painting, which is displayed in the rotunda of the U.S. Capitol Building, on the reverse side; a hundred-dollar bank note issued in 1869 had a similar depiction. Benjamin Franklin is on the hundred-dollar bill, which features an engraving of Independence Hall on the back.

There is a certain irony in recalling that one of the incidents that led to the Declaration was the Stamp Act of 1765. The stamps in question were not postage stamps, which had yet to be invented, but dies embossed on specified documents.

The first stamp specifically to commemorate the Declaration was a 24-cent stamp first published in 1869 with an engraved vignette by James Smillie (1807–1843) based on John Trumbull's famous painting. This painting was also used for four stamps, each with a different cartouche from that painting. Another set of four related 10-cent stamps issued during the bicentennial featured depictions of Carpenters' Hall, a quotation from the First Continental Congress, a quotation from the Declaration ("Deriving their Just Powers from the Consent of the Governed"), and Independence Hall. Quarters issued for the bicentennial were also altered so that the front side picturing the bust of George Washington listed both 1776 and 1976, and the obverse side contained a picture of a drummer boy rather than the traditional American eagle.

Numerous decorative prints have featured the Declaration with borders embroidered with historic scenes or engravings of the Founding Fathers. These were particularly common during centennial celebrations, which often featured scenes designed to show a reunited North and South and depictions that contrasted earlier days to modern technology (trains, steamships and the like). It is common to see replicas of the Declaration of Independence and other formative documents, typically on paper made to resemble that of the original documents, for sale at historic sites

See also Franklin, Benjamin; Independence Hall; Jefferson, Thomas; Trumbull, John (Paintings)

Further Reading

"American Declaration of Independence." Mintage World: Online Museum and Collectorspedia. https://www.mintageworld.com/blog/american-declaration-of-independence/.

"Stamp for Independence: A Brief Philatelic Tour of the Declaration of Independence." http://blogs.bl.uk/americas/2017/06/stamp-for-independence-a-brief-philatelic-tour-of-the-declaration-of-independence.html.

COMMITTEE RESPONSIBLE FOR WRITING THE DECLARATION OF INDEPENDENCE

Although Thomas Jefferson is known to have been the primary author of the Declaration of Independence, the proposed document was actually recommended by a committee of five delegates. In addition to Jefferson, they included the following: John Adams, often called the "Atlas" of the Revolution for his passionate advocacy; Benjamin Franklin, a printer and the committee's only nonlawyer; Connecticut's Roger Sherman, a largely-self-taught almanac writer and judge; and New York's Robert Livingston. Of these, Livingston is the only member whose previous support of such a Declaration has been questioned, and he may have been chosen to serve on the committee as a way of swaying fellow conservatives to the cause (Ferling 2011, 294).

The committee was drawn primarily from the most populous eastern (northern) states and from Virginia, which were generally the most favorable for immediate independence. Just as the committee had selected George Washington as commander in chief of revolutionary forces in part because he was from Virginia, which was the largest and most populous state, so too, it was no mistake that the delegates headed the committee with a Virginian. Adams observed that "Mr. Jefferson came into Congress in June 1775, and brought with him a reputation for literature, science, and a happy talent of composition. Writings of his were handed about remarkable for the peculiar felicity of expression. Though a silent member in Congress, he was so prompt, frank, explicit and decisive upon committees and in conversation . . . that he soon seized upon my heart" (Boyd 1999, 21).

Adams recalled that a subcommittee had selected Jefferson to do the writing, but Jefferson did not recall one. Although it seems likely that the Congress intended for Jefferson to do the writing, Adams later claimed that he had been the one who encouraged Jefferson to do so and offered reasons to overcome what might otherwise have been Jefferson's deference to an older man. According to Adams, he offered three reasons: "Reason first—You are a Virginian, and a Virginian ought to appear at the head of this business. Reason second—I am obnoxious, suspect, and unpopular. You are very much otherwise. Reason third—You can write ten times better than I can" (Zall 2004, 75–76).

The last of these arguments reinforces the idea that Jefferson's felicity of expression was already well known in the colonies for his authorship of the *Summary View of the Rights of British America*.

After accepting the task, Jefferson presented the document both to Adams and Franklin, who made minor emendations before they sent the document to the Continental Congress. Congress debated the Declaration on July 3 and 4, in what proved to be an excruciating experience for the primary author. Jefferson reported that Franklin helped console him as the Congress made extensive changes, mostly deletions, by telling him the story of John Thompson, a former apprentice who was about to open his own shop. He composed a sign with a picture of a hat saying "John Thompson, Hatter, makes and sells hats for ready money." After being told that the word "hatter" was tautologous, that customers would not care who made the hat, that "for ready money" was unnecessary, and that the word "sells" could be omitted since no one expected him to give them away, he ended up with a sign with a figure of a hat and the name "John Thompson" (Jefferson 1974, 1:65–66).

Congress added a number of phrases to Jefferson's reference to "nature's god" that further acknowledged the deity. It deleted what would have been Jefferson's only direct mention of Parliament, excised his extensive condemnation of slavery and the king's putative role in promoting it in the colonies, and incorporated the specific wording of Richard Henry Lee's Resolution for Independence. Although Jefferson continued to believe that his own creation was superior to the final product, these changes were sufficient to assure that the document was, as Jefferson would describe it to be, "an expression of the American mind" (Smith 2011) rather than of a single individual or even a single committee.

See also Adams, John; Franklin, Benjamin; Jefferson, Thomas; Originality of the Declaration of Independence; *A Summary View of the Rights of British America* (Jefferson)

Further Reading

Boyd, Julian P. 1999. *The Declaration of Independence: The Evolution of the Text*. Rev. ed. Washington, DC: Library of Congress in association with the Thomas Jefferson Memorial Foundation.

Ferling, John. 2011. "'The Character of a Fine Writer': Thomas Jefferson and the Drafting of the Declaration of Independence." In *Independence: The Struggle to Set America Free,* 294–317. New York: Bloomsbury Press.

Jefferson, Thomas. 1974. *Thomas Jefferson: A Biography in His Own Words*. 2 vols. New York: Newsweek.

McGlone, Robert. 1998. "Deciphering Memory: John Adams and the Authorship of the Declaration of Independence." *Journal of American History* 85 (September): 411–438.

Renker, Elizabeth M. 1989. "'Declaration-Men' and the Rhetoric of Self-Presentation." *Early American Literature* 24:129–134.

Smith, George H. 2011. "Was Thomas Jefferson a Plagiarist?" Libertanism.org. https://www.libertarianism.org/publications/essays/excursions/was-thomas-jefferson-plagiarist.

Zall, Paul M. 2004. *Adams on Adams*. Lexington: University Press of Kentucky.

COMMON SENSE (PAINE)

One of the publications that appears most influential in persuading the public that the time had come for independence from Great Britain was *Common Sense*. It was anonymously published in January 1776 by Thomas Paine (1737–1809), a recent immigrant from England who was close friends with Benjamin Franklin and Benjamin Rush. In America, *Common Sense* ranks with Harriet Beecher Stowe's *Uncle Tom's Cabin* in mobilizing public opinion.

Prior to the publication of this work, the Second Continental Congress had sought to deny the power of the English Parliament in the colonies while maintaining their allegiance to the English king, to whom they appealed to redress their grievances. Most colonists seemed to have general affection for the king, who had been on the throne since 1760 and whose birthday was widely celebrated in the colonies. Many colonists would further have lauded the British system of government, which was generally regarded as a "mixed" form of government that combined elements of monarchy (the king), aristocracy (the House of Lords), and the people (the House of Commons).

Paine's role was to call the authority of the king, and the principle of hereditary succession by which successors were chosen, into question and to argue that the time was propitious for the separation that the Declaration of Independence would later announce. Notably, the Declaration of Independence directed almost all its indictments against the king.

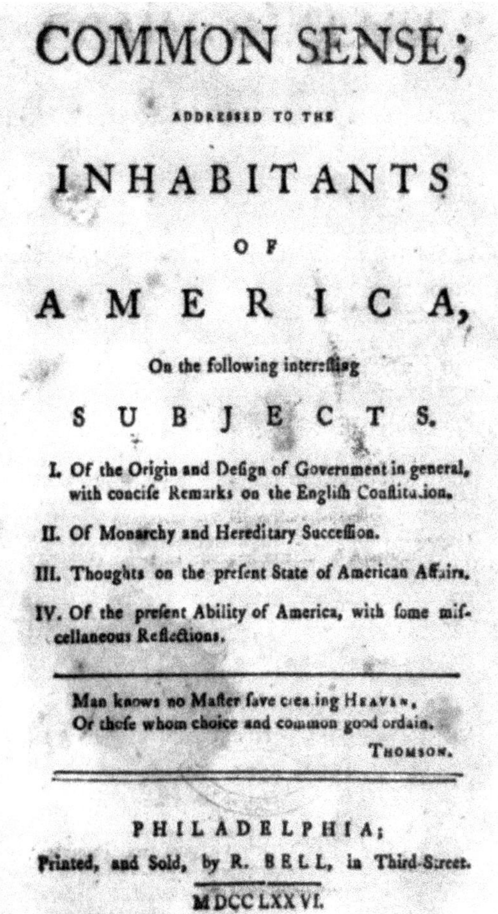

COMMON SENSE;

ADDRESSED TO THE

INHABITANTS

OF

AMERICA,

On the following interesting

SUBJECTS.

I. Of the Origin and Design of Government in general, with concise Remarks on the English Constitution.

II. Of Monarchy and Hereditary Succession.

III. Thoughts on the present State of American Affairs.

IV. Of the present Ability of America, with some miscellaneous Reflections.

Man knows no Master save creating Heaven,
Or those whom choice and common good ordain.
Thomson.

PHILADELPHIA;
Printed, and Sold, by R. Bell, in Third-Street.
MDCCLXXVI.

Title page of Thomas Paine's influential *Common Sense*, published in 1776. This volume convinced many people that monarchy, and hereditary succession, were undesirable and that the time for independence had arrived. (Library of Congress)

Paine, who would rely heavily on conceptions of an original state of nature, began by distinguishing society from government: the first was "produced by our wants"; the second was by "our wickedness." Man's social nature forced men to come together, whereas men created governments "to supply the defect of moral virtue." Paine believed that the simpler government remained, the better it would be. In contrast to those, including John Adams, who would later laud separation of powers (Kenyon 1951), Paine observed that "the constitution of England is so exceedingly complex, that the nation may suffer for years together without being able to discover in which part the fault lies." The mixed government of Britain consisted not of a careful balance but of "The remains of monarchical tyranny in the person," "The remains of aristocratical tyranny in the persons of the peers," and "The new republican materials, in the persons of the commons" (Paine 1776, 267–269). Moreover, Paine believed that the king used his power of appointment to corrupt the other two branches, and was restrained less by the two houses of Parliament than by the character of the English people.

Foreshadowing the Declaration's appeal to human equality, Paine argued that "Mankind being originally equals in the order of creation," the distinction between kings and commoners had no grounding in nature: "Male and female are the distinctions of nature, good and bad are the distinctions of heaven; but how a race of men came into the world so exalted above the rest, and distinguished like some new species, is worthy inquiring into." Paine observed that "all men being originally equals, no *one* by *birth* could have a right to set up his family in perpetual preference to all others for ever" (Paine 1776, 270–272).

Paine, who would later be known for his skepticism of Scripture, launched into an extended discussion of how God had warned the Israelites against establishing kingship, and about how nations led by kings were much more likely to go to war than republics. Paine connected the formation of kingship to "priest-craft" and observed that "monarchy in every instance is the Popery of government" (1776, 272). Paine further launched into an extended attack on hereditary succession, observing that one generation's consent to such an institution could hardly bind succeeding generations, and he pointed out how successors often lacked the abilities of their predecessors.

In reflecting on the current state of affairs in America, Paine argued that "Now is the seed time of continental union, faith and honour" ([1776] 2007, 274). Britain's interest in the colonies had been for "the sake of trade and dominion" ([1776] 2007, 275). As to claims that Britain was the mother, or parent country, what parent would treat her children in such a fashion? Given British deprecations, it was "our duty to mankind at large, as well as to ourselves . . . to renounce the alliance" (1776, 275).

Paine proceeded to outline his own plan for a continental assembly of at least 390 representatives who would be required to gain three-fifths of greater majorities to carry out policies. Asking "But where say some is the King of America?" Paine responded that it should be God. He thus noted: "Yet that we may not appear to be defective even in earthly honours, let a day be solemnly set apart for proclaiming the charter; let it be brought forth placed on the divine law, the word of God; let a crown be placed thereon, by which the world may know, that so far as we approve of monarchy, that in America THE LAW IS KING" ([1776] 2007, 277–278).

Further arguing that America had sufficient strength to be able to achieve its independence, Paine ended with arguments designed "to shew, that nothing can settle our affairs so expeditiously as an open and determined declaration of independence" ([1776] 2007, 280). He put particular emphasis on the way that other nations would be more willing to help the American cause if they thought Americans were separating than if they thought "we mean only to make use of that assistance for the purpose of repairing the breach, and strengthening the connection between Britain and America" (1776, 180). Paine argued that "such a memorial would produce more good effects to this Continent, than if a ship were freighted with petitions to Britain" ([1776] 2007, 280).

In addition to influencing the movement for independence in America, Paine also influenced government in Pennsylvania by directing it in a more populist direction (Rosenfeld 2011). Samuel Adams wrote an essay, signed "Candidus," on February 3, 1776, in which he too argued for independence. Arguing that even if it were possible to return to relations with Britain prior to 1763 "vague and uncertain laws, and more especially constitutions, are the very instruments of slavery," Adams believed that a declaration of independence would make foreign aid more likely. As he explained that "while we profess ourselves the subjects of Great Britain, and yet hold arms against her, they have a right to treat us as rebels, and that, according to the laws of nature and nations, no other state has a right to interfere in the dispute." By contrast, "on our declaration, the maritime states, at least, will find it their interest (which always secures the question of inclination) to protect a people who can be so advantageous to them" (Adams 1907, 3:177).

James Chalmers, also writing under the name Candidus, authored a reply called *Plain Truth*, but it did not have nearly the impact of Paine's own work.

Paine would later seek to raise flagging American morale with the publication of *The Crisis*, but his later works were better known for their religious skepticism and were less favorably received in America. Whereas Paine denigrated all kings, the Declaration focused on George III. In 1876, Robert Ingersoll gave a speech on the Declaration of Independence, which arguably comes closer to praising the ideals of Paine's *Common Sense* than of the Declaration. Ironically, Joseph Lewis published a book in 1947 that was designed to show that Paine had authored the Declaration of Independence, but the argument has not been accepted by those who have otherwise traced the history of that document, whose authorship Thomas Jefferson rightly claimed.

See also Adams, John; Franklin, Benjamin; Kingship

Further Reading

Adams, Samuel. 1907. *The Writings of Samuel Adams*. Vol. 3, *1773–1777*. Edited by Harry Alonzo Cushing. New York: G. P. Putnam's Sons.

Candidus [Chalmers, James]. 1776. *Plain Truth: Addressed to the Inhabitants of American, Containing Remarks on a Late Pamphlet, Intitled Common Sense*. 2nd ed. Philadelphia.

Ingersoll, Robert G. 1924. "Declaration of Independence." In *44 Complete Lectures*. Chicago: M. A. Donohue. Accessible at https://lectures-by-ingersoll.blogspot.com/2012/04/declaration-of-independence.html

Jordan, Winthrop D. 1973. "Familial Politics: Thomas Paine and the Killing of the King, 1776." *Journal of American History* 60 (September): 294–308.

Kenyon, Cecelia M. 1951. "Where Paine Went Wrong." *American Political Science Review* 45 (December): 1086–1099.

Lewis, Joseph. *Thomas Paine, Author of the Declaration of Independence*. New York: Freethought Press Association.

Lucas, Stephen E. 1976. *Portents of Rebellion: Rhetoric and Revolution in Philadelphia, 1765–1776*. Philadelphia: Temple University Press.

Paine, Thomas. *Common Sense*. (1776) 2007. In *Classics of American Political and Constitutional Thought*, vol. 1, *Origins through the Civil War*, edited by Scott J. Hammond, Kevin R. Hardwick, and Howard L. Lubert, 267–280. Indianapolis, IN: Hackett.

Rosenfeld, Sophia. 2008. "Tom Paine's *Common Sense* and Ours." *William and Mary Quarterly*, 3rd ser. 65 (October): 633–668.

Rosenfeld, Sophia. 2011. *Common Sense*. Cambridge, MA: Harvard University Press.

CONGRESS VOTING INDEPENDENCE (PAINTING BY SAVAGE)

Although the most iconic painting associated with the Declaration of Independence is that of John Trumbull, his depiction of the room was based on recollections by Thomas Jefferson rather than on Trumbull's own observations, and the painting is thus a better depiction of the participants than of the setting. The painting that best appears to reflect this setting is entitled *The Congress Voting Independence* and was first discovered by Charles Henry Hart, in what he described as "a dark corner of the old Boston Museum, on Tremont Street (Hart 1905, 2).

Hart was convinced that the painting had been begun by Robert Edge Pine (1730–1799), an immigrant from England who had been given access to the Assembly Room in Independence Hall, where the Declaration had been debated and signed, and finished by Edward Savage (1761–1817), an American-born artist and engraver. A more recent article, while agreeing that the painting is a better depiction of the room where the Declaration was signed, believes it is more likely that the painting was done by Savage, possibly relying in part on a larger painting that Pine had done.

The Second Continental Congress votes for independence in 1776 in Philadelphia in the painting *Congress Voting Independence*, by Robert Edge Pine and Edward Savage, ca. 1788. The Congress, which also called for creation of the Articles of Confederation, served as the colonial government during most of the American Revolution. The painting shows Thomas Jefferson setting the Declaration of Independence on the table. Benjamin Franklin sits to his right, and John Hancock sits behind the table. Also shown are fellow Declaration committee members (standing just left of Jefferson, from left to right) John Adams, Roger Sherman, and Robert R. Livingston. (Library of Congress)

Scholars have not been able definitively to identify all the figures in the painting, which is displayed in the Hall of the Pennsylvania Historical Society

See also Independence Hall; Trumbull, John (Painting)

Further Reading

Hart, Charles Henry. 1905. "*The Congress Voting Independence*: A Painting by Robert Edge Pine and Edward Savage in the Hall of the Historical Society of Pennsylvania." *Pennsylvania Magazine of History and Biography* 29:1–14.

Mulcahy, James M. 1956. "*Congress Voting Independence*: The Trumbull and Pine-Savage Paintings." *Pennsylvania Magazine of History and Biography* 80 (January): 74–91.

CONGRESSIONAL AND PRESIDENTIAL REFERENCES TO THE DECLARATION OF INDEPENDENCE

As a seminal founding document, it is not surprising to find that American elected officials have often cited its principles and grappled with its meaning. Although these references do not appear to have been as well studied as those of the Supreme Court, they are nonetheless important.

In part because its most important function was the immediate one of justifying America's split with Great Britain, the Declaration was not the subject of much debate during its first 25 years or so (Detweiler 1962). One of the causes for revived interest in the document was its association with Thomas Jefferson, one of the founders of the Democratic-Republican Party, which used the document to highlight its own ideals and cast their opponents as Tories and monarchists (Kromkowski 2002, 104).

The first major debate over the Declaration of Independence in Congress began in 1819 and centered on whether to admit Missouri as a slave state. Those who opposed this move, which was eventually accomplished by simultaneously admitting Maine as a free state and thus maintaining the slave/free state balance in the U.S. Senate, believed that it was inconsistent with the Declaration's commitment to equality. Those favoring the move argued that because slaves were "property," the right to own them was also protected. Some slave spokesmen denigrated the Declaration's assertion that "all men are created equal" either by restricting its use to white men or by ridiculing it as too abstract, if not ridiculous. Philip Detweiler observed that the implications of the Declaration were debated so extensively and with such contrary conclusions, that in the end, the debate became stale (1948). To some degree, members of Congress who opposed slavery were using the Declaration to correct deficiencies they perceived within the text of the Constitution.

In time, advocates of slavery further focused on the notion that as entities that had entered the Union as "free and independent states," slave states had the right to withdraw from the national contract if they thought that their right to perpetuate slavery was in jeopardy. Presidents Franklin Pierce and James Buchanan, who preceded Lincoln in the White House, both accepted this contract theory (Kromkowski 2002, 128–129).

Both as a candidate and as president, Abraham Lincoln took quite a different view. Believing that the union of states had preceded the Constitution, Lincoln denied the right of secession and was determined to prevent the further expansion of slavery in U.S. territories. Claiming in a speech at Independence Hall on February 22, 1861, that "I have never had a feeling politically that did not spring from the sentiments embodied in the Declaration of Independence," Lincoln had previously asserted in his "Fragment on the Constitution and Union" that the principle of "Liberty to all" with the Declaration was the "apple of god," with the Constitution serving as "*the picture of sliver*, subsequently framed around it" (Gerber 2002, 240). As he explained "The *picture* was made for the apple—*not* the apple for the picture" (Gerber 2002, 240). In the Gettysburg Address, Lincoln further dated the birth of the nation to the Declaration rather than to the Constitution that followed.

At the end of the war, the nation adopted three constitutional amendments with the intent of overturning the *Dred Scott* decision of 1857 and providing "equal protection of the law" to all. In time, however, the due process clause became the primary vehicle by which courts would apply most of the provisions of the Bill of Rights (beginning with protections for private property) to the states.

In early American history, politicians sometimes used the Declaration to argue for liberal immigration policies. As American policies became more restrictive, particularly with respect to Japanese and Chinese, advocates of such policies interpreted the Declaration more restrictively, often questioning whether members of these races were equipped for citizenship. After America acquired foreign colonies after the Spanish-American War, critics charged that it was betraying the anticolonial sentiments that the Declaration had articulated.

Presidents Woodrow Wilson and Calvin Coolidge often cited the Declaration, the former in hopes of spreading U.S. ideals abroad and the latter in stressing American individualism and the importance of spiritual over material values. Advocates of women's suffrage also used the principle of equality in arguing for the Nineteenth Amendment.

Faced with the Great Depression, President Franklin D. Roosevelt suggested that the negative rights that were articulated within the Declaration and the Bill of Rights needed to be supplemented with "a second Bill of Rights" that would include social and economic rights. Most New Deal programs were designed with such needs in mind. In a speech that he delivered at the Lincoln Memorial in 1947, Roosevelt's successor, Harry S. Truman, evoked the Declaration of Independence for the cause of racial equality. Dr. Martin Luther King Jr., President Lyndon Johnson, and other advocates of the Civil Rights Act of 1964 followed a similar strategy.

See also Lincoln, Abraham; Slavery; Supreme Court and the Declaration of Independence

Further Reading

Detweiler, Philip F. 1958. "Congressional Debate on Slavery and the Declaration of Independence, 1819–1821." *American Historical Review* 63:598–616.

Detweiler, Philip. 1962. "The Changing Reputation of the Declaration of Independence: The First Fifty Years." *William and Mary Quarterly*, 3rd ser. 29:557–574.

Gerber, Scott Douglas, ed. 2002. *The Declaration of Independence: Origins and Impact*. Washington, DC: CQ Press.

Kromkowski, Charles A. 2002. "The Declaration of Independence, Congress, and Presidents of the United States." In *The Declaration of Independence: Origins and Impact*, edited by Scott Douglas Gerber, 118–141. Washington, DC: CQ Press.

CONGRESSIONAL RESPONSE TO LORD NORTH'S CONCILIATORY RESOLUTION

On February 20, 1775, Lord North proposed a conciliatory plan. It provided that Parliament would suspend the tax on any of the colonies, acting individually or collectively, that agreed to contribute their proper portion of the general defense and the administration of government.

Individual states drafted answers to this proposal, which were then sent to the First Continental Congress. Thomas Jefferson had a primary hand both in drafting the response of the Virginia General Assembly and that of the First Continental Congress.

The penultimate paragraph of the latter document, dated July 31, 1775, is especially important because it lists a number of grievances that the colonies had against Britain that would later be repeated or refined in the Declaration of Independence. Jefferson thus argued for rejection of this proposal:

> Because too it does not propose to repeal the several Acts of Parliament passed for the purposes of restraining the trade and altering the form of government of one of our colonies; extending the boundaries and changing the government of Quebec; enlarging the jurisdiction of the courts of Admiralty and Vice Admiralty; taking from us the rights of trial by Jury of the vicinage in cases affecting both life and property; transporting us into other countries to be tried for criminal offenses; exempting by mock-trial the murderers of Colonists from punishment; and quartering soldiers on us in times of profound peace. ("Resolution of Congress")

The response further noted, "Nor do they renounce the power of suspending our own Legislatures, and of legislating for us in all cases whatsoever" ("Resolution of Congress").

Jefferson's authorship of this document, as well as of *A Summary View of the Rights of British Americans*, contributed to his reputation for writing and probably influenced his selection to serve on the committee to write the Declaration of Independence.

See also Charges against the King and Others; Jefferson, Thomas; *A Summary View of the Rights of British America* (Jefferson)

Further Reading

Charles, Patrick J. 2008. *Irreconcilable Grievances: The Events That Shaped the Declaration of Independence*. Westminster, MD: Heritage Books.

"Resolutions of Congress on Lord North's Conciliatory Proposal." 1775. Avalon Project. http://avalon.law.yale.edu/18th_century/jeffnort.asp. Accessed March 19, 2018.

"Virginia Resolutions on Lord North's Conciliatory Proposal, 10 June 1775." Founders Online. https://founders.archives.gov/documents/Jefferson/01-01-02-0106.

CONNECTICUT AND ITS SIGNERS

Connecticut was one of the northeast states that supported independence from a fairly early date. This resulted in part because of its historic ties to neighboring Massachusetts, against which Britain had directed its infamous Coercive (Intolerable) Acts. It is the home of Yale University.

Like nearby Rhode Island, Connecticut was a charter colony. The charter that Charles II granted to it in 1662 essentially reiterated the Fundamental Orders of Connecticut and was so prized that the state continued to be governed by it until 1818. Strongly influenced by the congregational model of government, the state was fond of frequent elections, while managing to keep most authority concentrated in a few ruling families.

Although the state appears to have profited from the Revolutionary War (Gipson 1931), it relied heavily on commerce. Four Connecticut delegates signed the Declaration of Independence. They were Samuel Huntington, Roger Sherman, William Williams, and Oliver Wolcott. When Patrick Henry asked Sherman why the people of his state were so jealous for liberty, he reportedly responded, "Because we have more to lose than any of them" (Collier 1988, 93).

Samuel Huntington (1731–1796) had been apprenticed to a barrel maker prior to reading law, serving as a king's attorney, serving in the Connecticut legislature, becoming a judge, and being elected to the Continental Congress. He was president during the period when the Articles of Confederation were ratified. He was selected first as lieutenant governor and then as governor of the state.

Roger Sherman (1721–1793) was arguably the most prominent of the Connecticut delegates. He was the only delegate not only to serve on the Committee to Write the Declaration but also to sign the Articles of Confederation and the U.S. Constitution. Trained as a cobbler, Sherman later published almanacs, studied law, became a legislator, a judge, a member of the Governor's Council, and the treasurer of Yale. Sherman was one of the most influential delegates at the Constitutional Convention of 1787 and was a leading force behind the so-called Connecticut (or Great) Compromise, which guaranteed small states like his own equal representation in the Senate (Boyd 1932). In the first Congress that met after adoption of the U.S. Constitution, Sherman played a major role in seeing that constitutional amendments were appended to the end of the document rather than being incorporated within the text. Sherman is often considered to be one of Congress's greatest exemplars of Puritan values (Hall 2009).

William Williams (1731–1811) was educated at Harvard, served in the militia during the French and Indian War, and was very active in the revolutionary movement. He penned a satirical essay in response to the Coercive Acts in 1774 but was not actually elected to Congress until July 11 as a replacement for Oliver Wolcott.

Oliver Wolcott (1726–1797) was another soldier-statesman. A graduate of Yale, he served as a major general in the Connecticut Militia and fought at the Battle of Saratoga. Present in New York City when a mob overturned the lead statute of George III in Bowling Green, Wolcott shipped the fallen statue to Connecticut, where it was melted into bullets. Wolcott signed the Articles of Confederation and later served as lieutenant governor and as governor of Connecticut, succeeding Samuel Huntington to the post.

See also Committee Responsible for Writing the Declaration of Independence; Covenants and Compacts

Further Reading

Boyd, Julian P. 1932. "Roger Sherman: Portrait of a Cordwainer Statesman." *New England Quarterly* 5 (April): 221–236.

Collier, Christopher. 1988. "Sovereignty Finessed: Roger Sherman, Oliver Ellsworth, and the Ratification of the Constitution in Connecticut." In *The Constitution and the States: The Role of the Original Thirteen in the Framing and Adoption of the Federal Constitution*, edited by Patrick T. Conley and John P. Kaminski, 93–112. Madison, WI: Madison House.

Gipson, Lawrence H. 1931. "Connecticut Taxation and Parliamentary Aid Preceding the Revolutionary War." *American Historical Review* 36 (July): 721–739.

Hall, David D. 2011. *A Reforming People: Puritanism and the Transformation of Public Life in New England.* Chapel Hill: University of North Carolina Press.

Hall, Mark David. 2009. "Roger Sherman: An Old Puritan in a New Nation." In *The Forgotten Founders on Religion and Public Life*, edited by Daniel L. Dreisbach, Mark David Hall, and Jeffrey H. Morrison 248–277. Notre Dame, IN: University of Notre Dame Press.

CONSENT OF THE GOVERNED

One of the most distinctive aspects of the Declaration of Independence is its attempt to ground government in "the consent of the governed." Indeed, the Declaration argued that governments are illegitimate unless they secure unalienable rights and unless they rest on such consent.

The second paragraph of the Declaration specifically said that governments derive "their just powers from the consent of the governed." It further declared that when governments no longer have such consent, the people have the right "to institute new government" in according with "such principles" "as to them shall seem most likely to effect their safety and happiness."

One of the primary causes of the American Revolution was the colonial claim, based on the Magna Carta (1215) and the English Bill of Rights (1689), that Parliament had no right to tax the colonists because they were not represented in that body. In its eleventh accusation against the king, the Declaration charged him with keeping "standing armies" among them "without the consent of our legislatures." After later charging that the king had "combined with others" in "giving his *assent* [a term it had previously used a number of times] to their [Parliament's] acts of pretended legislation," the Declaration thus faulted them "for imposing taxes on us without our *consent* [both italics mine]" (West 2003, 123).

Although its purpose was not to establish a new form of government, but to separate from an existing one, the Declaration frequently tied the idea of consent to representation. Congress drafted the Articles of Confederation, to which state legislatures gave consent, but the United States used special conventions both to propose and to ratify the current U.S. Constitution, thus attempting to achieve consent in "establishing government" (West 2003, 120). Consent to the "operation" of government (West 2003, 120) is provided through elections and other democratic mechanisms.

See also Majority Rule and Unanimity; Representative (Republican) Government; Revolution; Taxes (Charge #17)

Further Reading

Cassinelli, C. W. 1959. "The 'Consent' of the Governed." *Western Political Quarterly* 12 (June): 391–409.

Dunn, John. 1967. "Consent in the Political Theory of John Locke." *Historical Journal* 10:153–182.

West, Thomas G. 2003. "The Political Theory of the Declaration of Independence." In *The American Founding and the Social Compact*, edited by Ronald J. Pestritto and Thomas G. West, 95–146. Lanham, MD: Lexington Books.

Wilhoite, Fred H., Jr. 1965. "'The Consent of the Governed' in Two Traditions of Political Thought." *Southwestern Social Science Quarterly* 46 (June): 59–66.

CONSIDERATIONS ON THE NATURE AND EXTENT OF LEGISLATIVE AUTHORITY OF THE BRITISH PARLIAMENT (WILSON)

In 1774, James Wilson published a pamphlet, previously written in 1768, entitled *Considerations on the Nature and Extent of the Legislative Authority of the British Parliament*. This work was authored by an individual who served in the Continental Congress and signed the Declaration of Independence, who was later influential at the Constitutional Convention of 1787, and who went on to become a Supreme Court justice. The pamphlet is important in understanding why the colonists denied the right of the English Parliament to legislate on their behalf. The document also uses language that is similar to that Thomas Jefferson later employed in the Declaration of Independence.

Noting that Americans, like British subjects, were proud of their status as freemen, Wilson observed, in arguments that are repeated in the Declaration, that "All men are, by nature, equal and free: no one has a right to any authority over another without his consent: all lawful government is founded on the consent of those who are subject to it: such consent was given with a view to ensure and to increase the happiness of the governed above what they could enjoy in an independent and unconnected state of nature (1774, 4–5).

Acknowledging that Parliament was recognized as sovereign within Britain (1774, 4), Wilson observed that the importance of this doctrine "is derived from its tendency to promote the ultimate end of all government" (1774, 4). "Parliaments are not infallible: they are not always just" (1774, 5). He pointed out, however, that members of the House of Commons were frequently elected from among the people of England, that they were aware of their circumstances, and that they were subject to the laws that they adopted. By contrast, Americans were not represented in that body whose representatives might well gain an advantage by seeking to tax them without their consent.

Wilson repeated the claim that individuals who migrated to America contained their rights as "freemen." As a lawyer, Wilson cited court decisions relating to Ireland and Jamaica that he believed further buttressed his argument.

Acknowledging that Americans were still members of colonies, Wilson proceeded to argue that the common bond was not the authority of Parliament but that of the king, whose continuing protection the colonists enjoyed. He concluded: "The connexion and harmony between Great Britain and us, which is her interest and ours mutually to cultivate, and on which her prosperity, as well as ours, so materially depends, will be better preserved by the operation of the legal prerogatives of the crown, than by the exertion of an unlimited authority by parliament" (1774, 30).

Holding premises similar to those of Wilson, Jefferson did not specifically mention Parliament in the Declaration but directed his attention to describing why the colonies were now dissolving their final ties to the king.

See also Address to the Inhabitants of the Colonies (Wilson)

Further Reading

Jezierski, John V. 1971. "Parliament or People: James Wilson and Blackstone on the Nature and Location of Sovereignty." *Journal of the History of Ideas* 32 (January–March): 95–106.

Wilson, James. 2007. "Considerations on the Nature and Extent of the Legislative Authority of the British Parliament, 1774." In *Collected Works of James Wilson*, edited by Kermit L. Hall and Mark David Hall, 2:3–30. Indianapolis, IN: Liberty Fund.

Wood, Gordon S. 2011. "The Problem of Sovereignty." *William and Mary Quarterly* 68 (October): 573–577.

CONSPIRACY

One of the more problematic elements about the Declaration of Independence is that it embodied a conspiratorial view of British actions. This view, combined with charges that at times seem overblown and at other times overly vague, somewhat detract from the persuasiveness of the document.

The Declaration expressed the view that Americans had faced "a long train of abuses and usurpations, pursuing invariably the same object" that "evinces a design to reduce them under absolute despotism." It further characterized the king's actions as "having in direct object the establishment of an absolute tyranny over these states."

Contemporary descriptions of George III hardly seem to put him into the same category as modern dictators (Thomas 1985). These descriptions further highlight what appears to be the exaggerated nature of Thomas Jefferson's claims.

Historian Bernard Bailyn (1976) notes that this view was reflected in a variety of contemporary colonial documents, but that they in turn reflected fears by British Whigs that the king had used corruption to bend Parliament to his will (also see York 2009, 446). Stephen E. Lucas believes British policies toward the colonies were "marked more by confusion than by consistency" and were too diffuse to constitute a genuine conspiracy (1976, 104–105). He thinks, however, that the conspiracy narrative helped explain British polices that the colonists otherwise found incomprehensible and provided a narrative that eventually left the colonies with little choice but to revolt.

Perhaps as importantly, Bailyn shows that George III had a similarly conspiratorial view of American leaders, regarding most of their early protestations of loyalty as duplicitous attempts to hide their true motives (1976; Labaree 1970). Thus, in his speech to Parliament on October 27, 1775, the king said of the Continental Congress that "They meant only to amuse by expressions of attachment to the Parent State, and the strongest protestations of loyalty to me whilst they were preparing for a general revolt." Similarly, in his speech to Parliament on October 31, 1776, he charged that the object of the leaders of the Revolution had "always been Dominion and Power."

T. H. Breen says that quite apart from their grievances over British governmental actions, Americans had begun to feel that the citizens of England were treating them as second-class citizens. Arthur Lee thus complained that Virginians "are treated, not as the fellow-subjects but as the servants of Britain" (Breen 1997, 30). In an essay in the *Boston Gazette* under the pseudonym "Humphry Ploughjogger," which he wrote in 1765 (while colonists were still quite loyal to England), John Adams complained, in racist language, that he and his fellows were not "their Negroes" and that God had "never intended us for slaves" (Breen 1997, 29).

In like manner, former Massachusetts governor Thomas Hutchinson observed in his *Strictures upon the Declaration of Independence* that even had Parliament ceased from taxing the colonies, "other pretenses would have been found for exception to the authority of Parliament."

Perhaps in part because British law (especially common law) rests so strongly on precedents, the colonies responded as strongly to the possibility that assertions of power could eventuate in colonial oppression as to what they perceived to be actual examples of such actions. Similarly, knowing how the colonists capitalized on the manner in which Britain had, prior to the French and Indian War, exercised "salutary neglect" over the colonies, the king was as wary as Parliament of appearing to show weakness.

With defenders of the king believing that they were upholding the rights of Parliament over the entire empire (with the Declaratory Act essentially defining this relationship) and with defenders of American patriots refusing to accept the authority of a legislative body in which they had not sent delegates, it was difficult for partisans on either side to concede to the others. The geographic distance between Britain and the colonies further highlighted mutual differences.

In addition to charging the king with conspiracy, the Declaration further indicated that necessity pushed them on a course counter to their continuing mutual friendship and consanguinity. Seeking to defend American revolutionaries against charges that they overestimated British intentions, Harvey C. Mansfield Jr. argued that a prudent people must "anticipate necessity," "extrapolate from ambiguous signs," and "read intent into mistake" (1976, 156). Since "necessity must be seen before it actually exists," "it might therefore make more sense to explain the ideology of conspiracy by the American Revolution, rather than the other way round" (1976, 156).

See also Declaratory Act of 1766; George III, Speech to Parliament (October 27, 1775); George III, Speech to Parliament (October 31, 1776); Necessity; *Strictures upon the Declaration of Independence* (Hutchinson)

Further Reading

Bailyn, Bernard. 1976. *The Ideological Origins of the American Revolution*. Cambridge, MA: Belknap Press of Harvard University Press.

Breen, T. H. 1997. "Ideology and Nationalism on the Eve of the American Revolution: Revisions Once More in Need of Revising." *Journal of American History* 84 (June): 13–39.

Labaree, Benjamin W. 1970. "The Idea of American Independence: The British View, 1774–1776." *Proceedings of the Massachusetts Historical Society*, 3rd Ser. 83:3–20.

Lucas, Stephen E. 1976. *Portents of Rebellion: Rhetoric and Revolution in Philadelphia, 1765–1776*. Philadelphia: Temple University Press.

Mansfield, Harvey C., Jr. 1976. "The Right of Revolution." *Daedalus* 105 (Fall): 151–162.

Thomas, P. D. G. 1985. "George III and the American Revolution." *History* 70 (February): 16–31.

York, Neil. 2009. "George III, Tyrant: 'The Crisis' as Critics of Empire, 1775–1776," *History* 94 (October): 434–460.

CONSTITUTION

See U.S. Constitution and the Declaration of Independence

CONSTRAINED OUR FELLOW CITIZENS TAKEN CAPTIVE ON THE HIGH SEAS (CHARGE #26)

The United States of America has engaged in two wars with Great Britain, one to secure American Independence and the other largely in reaction to British impressment of American seamen. Those familiar with the later controversy (the War of 1812), may be surprised to find that the controversy actually dated back to revolutionary days.

In listing the war atrocities that the British had committed, the Declaration of Independence noted that "he has constrained our fellow citizens taken captive on the high seas to bear arms against their country, to become the executioners of their friends & brethren, or to fall themselves by their hands."

This is often taken to be a reference to the Prohibitory Act, which Parliament had enacted on December 22, 1775, in reaction to American attempts to boycott British goods and to seek other trading partners. However, Denver Brunsman has pointed out that Royal Navy officers had long impressed Americans and British civilians into naval service, and that such actions, which had often caused riots in the colonies, such as the Boston Liberty Riot of June 1768, had largely taken place on the seas (2013, 241–242). Brunsman further notes that Benjamin Franklin had critiqued a leading British case, *Rex v. Broadfoot* (1743), which had upheld the practice of impressment, suggesting at one point that such impressment should be applied to judges and even to the king (2013, 243). English Whigs were sharply critical of impressment (Sainsbury 1978, 442).

The Prohibitory Act would have brought past grievances to mind. The law allowed British ships to capture American ships "as if the same were the ships and effects of open enemies," to confiscate their cargoes, and "to enter the names of such of the said mariners and crews, upon the book or books of his Majesty's said ships or vessels, as they . . . shall . . . think fit." British sailors who deserted were subject to punishment by death , thus, as Jefferson noted, forcing any of them who might be deployed in America of having to choose between seeking to preserve their own lives or fighting against fellow countrymen (Dumbauld 1950, 144–145).

Under British law, subjects of Britain always remained subjects thereof (Vile 2016, xxiv). As Jefferson had explained in his *Summary View of the Rights of British America*, Americans initially took the position that they carried their full rights of English citizens (including the prohibition of taxation without representation) to the New World. In issuing a Declaration of Independence, Americans could claim that they were no longer British subjects, eligible for such impressment.

In answering this charge, John Lind observed that the individuals that Jefferson was calling "fellow citizens" were actual "Rebels," who deserved "Death, forfeiture of goods, [and] corruption of blood" (1776, 105). Lind further compared such forceful impressment to the "zeal" that "agents of the Colonists have, of late years, been employed inveighing citizens and labourers to go to America" (1776, 105).

See also Franklin, Benjamin; *A Summary View of the Rights of British America* (Jefferson)

Further Reading

Brunsman, Denver. 2013. *The Evil Necessity: British Naval Impressment in the Eighteenth-Century Atlantic World*. Charlottesville: University of Virginia Press.

Dumbauld, Edward. 1950. *The Declaration of Independence and What It Means Today*. Norman: University of Oklahoma Press.

Lind, John. 1776. *An Answer to the Declaration of the American Congress*. London: J. Walter, Charing-Cross and T. Sewell.

Sainsbury, John. 1978. "The Pro-Americans of London, 1769 to 1782." *William and Mary Quarterly* 35 (July): 423–454.

Vile, John R. 2016. *American Immigration and Citizenship: A Documentary History*. Lanham, MD: Rowman and Littlefield.

COVENANTS AND COMPACTS

It is common to explain the philosophy of the Declaration of Independence in terms of English Social Contract theory as reflected in the respective works of Thomas Hobbes and John Locke. This theory sought to understand government by imagining a prepolitical "state of nature" in which there was no government. Although Hobbes and Locke portrayed such a state of nature somewhat differently, both agreed that individuals would exercise equal authority with respect to one another. As Locke described the situation, laws would not be "established, settled, or known," there would be no impartial judge to determine questions of right and right, and there would be no impartial executive to enforce such judgments even if they were made (Locke 1924, 180).

In such a situation, Locke hypothesized that men would unanimously decide to create a civil society, deciding by majority vote what kind of government could best protect their lives, liberties, and property. They could in turn alter such governments if they found that they no longer served the purposes for which they were established.

Although not identical, this theory resembled ideas, taken from Old Testament scriptures, that the people of Israel had entered into a "covenant" with God that he would be their God, and that they would be his people and follow his laws. When Puritans settled in America, they thus entered into a mutual compact with one another known as the Mayflower Compact (see Vile 2015, 11–12). Settlers looked to the charters that the king had given them (much as we today might look to the U.S. Constitution) to establish their rights in relation to him. The Declaration and Resolves of the First Continental Congress (1774) cited these charters as one of three bases for its rights (the others being the laws of nature and the English constitution). At the outbreak of the U.S. Constitution, individual states created constitutions to serve similar purposes. One of the charges that the Declaration of Independence leveled against the king and Parliament was that of "taking away our charters abolishing our most valuable laws, and altering fundamentally the forms of our government."

Donald S. Lutz has argued that Americans viewed the Declaration as representing a new social contract that served, with the U.S. Constitution, to create a new people. He thus believes that the documents are inexorably connected to one another, much as state constitutions were preceded by bills or declarations of rights. Noting that the Declaration cites both "Nature" and "Nature's God," Lutz says that "the Declaration of Independence may well be part of a national covenant. It is definitely part of a national compact" (1989, 58).

Approaching this from a somewhat different angle, Rabbi Lord Jonathan Sacs says that "the social contract creates a state but the social covenant creates a society." He thus observes that just as ancient Israel traced its founding both to the Ten Commandments and the occupation of the Promised Land, so it the United States "had its social covenant in the Declaration of Independence in 1776 and its social contract in the Constitution in 1787" (2017).

Michael Zuckert (2004) finds greater discontinuity than some scholars between early Pilgrim covenants and the Declaration of Independence and other more secular documents.

See also Declaration and Resolves of the First Continental Congress (1774); Locke, John

Further Reading

Locke, John. (1690) 1924. *Two Treatises of Government*. London: Dent, Everyman's Library.

Lutz, Donald S. 1989. "The Declaration of Independence as Part of an American National Compact." *Publius* 19 (Winter): 41–58.

Sacks, Jonathan. 2017. "2017 Irving Kristol Award Recipient Rabbi Lord Jonathan Sacks' Remarks." ADI. https://www.aei.org/publication/2017-irving-kristol-award-recipient-rabbi-lord-jonathan-sacks-remarks/.

Vile, John R. 2015. *Founding Documents of America: America Decoded*. Santa Barbara, CA: ABC-CLIO.

Zuckert, Michael P. 2004. "Natural Rights and Protestant Politics." In *Protestantism and the American Founding*, edited by Thomas S. Engeman and Michael P. Zuckert, 21–76. Notre Dame, IN: University of Notre Dame Press.

CREATION OF NEW STATE GOVERNMENTS

Prior to independence, the thirteen colonies had been divided into three types. Rhode Island and Connecticut were charter colonies, which were considered to be largely self-governing. Delaware, Maryland, and Pennsylvania were proprietary colonies, which were under the directorship of a proprietor (or his heirs) who had been given territory by the king. By far, the greatest number of colonies were royal colonies. These included New Hampshire, Massachusetts, New York, New Jersey, North Carolina, South Carolina, and Virginia. This latter classification, combined with the fact that each colony had its own legislature, particularly helps to explain why the colonies did not readily accept the authority of the British Parliament over them. Each colony did, however, have a governor, who in royal colonies was appointed directly by the Crown.

Although most colonies continued to cherish their ties to the king through early 1776, once fighting had broken out between colonial and royal forces, a number of states faced governors who had dissolved the legislatures and who in some case had fled to the safety of British ships, where they began to direct military action against the colonies. Just as the states sent representatives to two Continental Congresses, which had no legal sanction under British law, so too a number had called unconventional legislative bodies together and had petitioned Congress with guidance as to what to do.

John Adams was among those who appears to have had a conscious strategy of encouraging such colonies to set up new governments. As he explained in a letter to Patrick Henry dated June 3, 1776:

> It has ever appeared to me that the natural course and order of things was this; for every colony to institute a government; for all the colonies to confederate, and define the limits of the continental Constitution; then to declare the colonies a sovereign state, or a number of confederated sovereign states; and last of all, to form treaties with foreign powers. (Adams 2001, 48)

Responding to a query from Massachusetts as to what it should do after the king had sought to revoke its charter, in June 1775, it counseled that the colony should consider the offices of governor and lieutenant governor vacant and hold new legislative elections until such time as a royal governor was willing to honor its charter (Adams 2001, 52). Resisting suggestions that it should draw up a model constitution for state governments to follow, Congress responded to a query from New Hampshire by recommending that it "call a full and free representation of the People, and that the Representatives if they think it necessary, establish such a form of Government as in their Judgment will best produce the happiness of the People" (Adams 2001, 56). It provided similar instructions to South Carolina on November 4, 1775, and Virginia on December 4, 1774, and urged Canadians to do the same and join them on March 20, 1776 (Adams 2001, 57–58).

On May 10, 1776, Congress adopted a resolution. It provided that "where no government sufficient to the exigencies of their affairs have been hitherto established," the states should "adopt such government as shall . . . best conduce to the happiness and safety of their constituents" ("Preamble to Resolution . . ."). Five days later, Congress adopted a preamble to this resolution, which was authored by John Adams and designed to nudge the colonies closer to independence. After pointing to Britain's exclusion of the colonies from its protection, its refusal to answer colonial petitions, and its efforts to recruit foreign missionaries, it read as follows:

> And whereas, it appears absolutely irreconcileable to reason and good Conscience, for the people of these colonies now to take the oaths and affirmations necessary for the support of any government under the crown of Great Britain, and it is necessary that the exercise of every kind of authority under the said crown should be totally suppressed, and all the powers of government exerted, under the authority of the people of the colonies, for the preservation of internal peace, virtue, and good order, as well as for the defense of their lives, liberties, and properties, against the hostile invasions and cruel depredations of their enemies; therefore, resolved, &c. (Preamble 1776)

In describing this event to his wife in a letter that he sent on May 17, 1776, John Adams observed:

> Great Britain has at last driven America to the last step, a complete separation from her; a total absolute independence, not only of her Parliament, but of her crown, for such is the amount of the resolve of the 15th. Confederation among ourselves, or alliances with foreign nations are not necessary to a perfect separation from Britain. That is effected by extinguishing all authority under the crown, Parliament, and nation, as the resolution for instituting government has done, to all intents and purposes. (*Letters of Members of the Continental Congress*, 1:453)

Apparently responding to an observation by Landon Carter, who believed that the resolution was similar to a declaration of independence, Carter Braxton, writing on the same day as Adams, observed that "It was not so understood by Congress, but I find those out of doors on both sides [of] the question construe it in that manner" (*Letters of Members of the Continental Congress* 1:453–454). Similarly, Caesar Rodney observed in a letter, also dated May 17, that "Most of those here who are termed the Cool Considerate Men think it amounts to a declaration of Independence. It certainly savours of it, but you will see and Judge for Your Self" (*Letters of Members of the Continental Congress* 1:455).

By comparison to the Declaration, the preamble that Adams wrote and that Congress adopted to the Resolution on Independent Governments focused chiefly on British rejection of colonial petitions and its decision to use force. Similarly, the three repetitions of "whereas" give the document a much more prosaic and legalistic flavor than the language of the Declaration, with its evocation of human equality and human rights in its second paragraph.

John Adams, Richard Henry Lee, Thomas Jefferson, George Wythe, and George Mason were among those who later sought to influence the construction of state constitutions (Selby 1976).

See also Adams, John

Further Reading

Adams, William Paul. 2001. *The First American Constitutions: Republican Ideology and the Making of the State Constitutions in the Revolutionary Era.* Lanham, MD: Rowman and Littlefield.

Letters of Members of the Continental Congress. 1921. Edited by Edmund C. Burnett. Vol. 1, *August 29, 1774 to July 4, 1776.* Washington, DC: Carnegie Institute.

"Preamble to Resolution on Independent Governments, 15 May 1776," Founders Online. https://founders.archives.gov/documents/Adams/06-04-02-0001-0006.

Selby, John E. 1976. "Richard Henry Lee, John Adams, and the Virginia Constitution of 1776." *Virginia Magazine of History and Biography* 84 (October): 387–400.

"The States and the Congress Move toward Independence, 1775–1776." *Publius* 6 (Winter): 135–143.

CREED/SCRIPTURES

Religions are often based on common understandings of revealed texts, or scriptures. Adherents may further frame their beliefs in the forms of creeds to which its members commit themselves.

Similarly, the Declaration of Independence is often described as a national creed or scripture. Indeed, the title of one of the best treatments of the Declaration is *American Scripture*, in which the author likens the Declaration and other Founding Documents on display at the National Archives to Lenin's body in the Kremlin (1997, xiii). Alexander Tsesis has argued for the importance of interpreting the document as "a statement of a living creed" rather than as "a lustrous artifact of U.S. history (2012, 5).

In an article titled "The American Creed," David Fellman claims that "the real bond of union is a body of ideas and ideals, which we may call the American Creed" (1947, 231). He includes "our great public documents, such as the Declaration of Independence, the Constitution of the United States, the state constitutions, and notable papers of leading statesmen, judges and publicists" (1947, 231). He further claims, "In no other country is there such an endless repetition of general ideas about right and justice, freedom and democracy" (1947, 231). Joaquin Trujillo argues that the ideas of "equality, freedom, and self-government" in the Declaration of Independence and Lincoln 's Gettysburg and Second Inaugural addresses, "form the basis of the American Creed: the body of political, economic, and religious ideas that define American identity, unify Americans as a nation, and have been 'broadly supported by most elements in American society' since the late eighteenth century" (2011,1).

Although the Declaration was largely ignored as a document during its early years (Detweiler 1962), Jefferson claimed that he had not intended for it to declare new principles but to be "an expression of the American mind." Thus, concepts of liberty, equality, and human rights were already integral to America's self-understanding even before the document became the source of arguments for abolitionists, advocates of woman's suffrage, and other causes.

Cal Jillson observes that G. K. Chesterton of Britain said that "America is the only nation in the world that is founded on a creed. That creed is set forth with . . . theological lucidity in the Declaration of Independence." Similarly Gunnar Myrdal, who would make important contributions to America's understanding of race, observed that America's creed was based on "the essential dignity of the individual human being, of the fundamental equality of all men, and of certain inalienable rights to freedom, justice, and a fair opportunity" (2016, 3).

Some scholars have likened the Declaration to a covenant that helped create a people even before those people created a state (see, for example, Sacks 2017). Notably, Abraham Lincoln referred in his Gettysburg Address to the need for the nation to rededicate itself to "a new birth of freedom," much as leaders in ancient Israel often urged their countrymen to recommit themselves to the covenant. Sacks is among those who fear that this sense of community is being undermined by identity politics and what he calls "a politics of anger."

Although some Muslims are apparently adverse to translating the Koran, it is common for Christians from St. Jerome to Martin Luther to present-day theologians to issue translations of scriptures. An attempt to provide "the Declaration of Independence in Modern English," while chiefly designed as a learning tool for modern kids who are unfamiliar with eighteenth-century English nonetheless further highlights the role that the Declaration plays in modern discourse.

See also Covenants and Compacts; Lincoln, Abraham; U.S. Constitution and the Declaration of Independence

Further Reading

Azerrad, David. 2017, July 3. "The Declaration of Independence and the American Creed." Heritage Foundation. https://www.heritage.org/political-process/commentary/the-declaration-independence-and-the-american-creed.

"The Declaration of Independence in Modern English." Surfnetkids. Feldman Publishing. https://www.surfnetkids.com/independenceday/267/the-declaration-of-independence-in-modern-english/.

Detweiler, Philip F. 1962. "The Changing Reputation of the Declaration of Independence: The First Fifty Years." *William and Mary Quarterly* 19 (October): 557–574.

Fellman, David. 1947. "The American Creed." *Prairie Schooner* 21 (Summer): 231–243.

Jillson, Cal. 2016. *The American Dream: In History, Politics, and Fiction*. Lawrence: University Press of Kansas.

Maier, Pauline. 1997. *American Scripture: Making the Declaration of Independence*. New York: Alfred A. Knopf.

Sacks, Jonathan. 2017. "2017 Irving Kristol Award Recipient Rabbi Lord Jonathan Sacks' Remarks." ADI. https://www.aei.org/publication/2017-irving-kristol-award-recipient-rabbi-lord-jonathan-sacks-remarks/.
Trujillo, Joaquin. 2011. "The American Appropriation of God in Select Foundational Documents of the United States." *Analecta Hermeneutica* 3:1–15.
Tsesis, Alexander. 2012. *For Liberty and Equality: The Life and Times of the Declaration of Independence*. New York: Oxford University Press.

CRITICISMS OF THE BRITISH PEOPLE

See Nor Have We Been Wanting in Attention to Our English Brethren; We Have Appealed to Their Native Justice & Magnanimity

D

DEBATES OVER THE DECLARATION OF INDEPENDENCE

On November 9, 1775, the Second Continental Congress strengthened a resolution of the previous September by adopting a resolution. It provided:

> That every member of this Congress considers himself under the ties of virtue, honor and love of his Country not to divulge directly or indirectly any manner or thing agitated or debated on Congress before the same shall have been determined, without leave of the Congress; nor any matter or thing determined in Congress which a majority of the Congress shall order to be kept secret and that if any member shall violate this agreement he shall be expelled [from] this congress and deemed an enemy to the liberties of America & liable to be treated as such and that every member signify his consent of this agreement by signing the same. (Ritz 1986, 185)

All but five members who signed the Declaration subscribed to this resolution (Ritz 1986, 185).

This secrecy does not mean, however, that modern scholars are unaware of the events that transpired in the Congress. There are several factors that aid the study of this period. First, although the proceedings were not conducted publicly, secret journals were kept, and these have since been published. Thomas Jefferson did a particularly good job of summarizing the arguments for and against the Declaration of Independence, which are covered in a separate entry, and he circulated copies of his original draft, thus giving historians a point of comparison. Richard Smith, a delegate to Congress from New Jersey, kept a diary of events that transpired from September 12 to October 1, 1775, and from December 12, 1775, to March 30, 1776 (Diary 1896).

Second, as Jefferson's notes reveal, it seems unlikely that debates within Congress were much different than those among members of the general population, and these had been fermenting at least since the end of the French and Indian War. Works by John Adams, Thomas Jefferson, Benjamin Franklin, James Wilson, John Dickinson, and Thomas Paine all provide insights into the colonists' developing views. It is clear from these works that the colonies consistently resisted the authority, or sovereignty, of Parliament (especially in taxation), believing that only their locally elected representatives had such a right. British documents, most notably the Declaratory Act of 1766, and various speeches by George III, make it equally clear that British authorities insisted that they thought that parliamentary authority and taxation extended to America. Long into the crisis, the colonists continued to seek connection to Britain through allegiance to the British king, but he sided with Parliament, and once fighting broke out between the two sides, reconciliation become more and more difficult.

Third, in addition to other records, the Journals of the Continental Congress provide the wording of an increasing number of resolutions from the states either authorizing, and in some cases imploring, their delegations to vote for independence.

Fourth, we have contemporary letters from delegates to the convention as well as recollections from a number of participants, most notably John Adams and Thomas Jefferson, that further illumine the debates.

Fifth, the Declaration of Independence itself gives insight into the debates that preceded it. In arguing for the right of revolution, the Declaration of Independence thus stressed the need for prudence. Consistent with what we know from other sources as well as the time it took to get from the introduction of Richard Henry Lee's resolution to the actual adoption of the Declaration of Independence, it seems reasonable to assume that many of the delegates who thought an eventual break with Britain was almost inevitable (after all, fighting had broken out between British and American forces in April 1775, and the king had since declared the colonists to be outside his protection and had begun warring against them) either doubted the capacity of the colonies to fight what was then the world's largest empire or were looking for a better time. The opening words of the Declaration—"When in the course of human events"—focus on timing. Moreover, by delineating more than 25 grievances against the king and his allies, the Declaration attempted to show that this time had arrived. There thus seems to have been tension between delegates like John Dickinson, James Wilson, and John Rutledge, who wanted to secure foreign allies before taking such a step, and those like John Adams, Thomas Jefferson, and George Wythe, who thought that a firm declaration was necessary to secure such aid.

Sixth, reactions to the Declaration of Independence, especially Thomas Hutchinson's *Strictures upon the Declaration of Independence* and John Lind's *An Answer to the Declaration of the American Congress*, further indicate that not everyone was persuaded by the Declaration's arguments. These arguments were ultimately settled through war.

See also Address to the Inhabitants of the Colonies (Wilson); *An Answer to the Declaration of the American Congress* (Lind); *Common Sense* (Paine); *Considerations on the Nature and Extent of Legislative Authority of the British Parliament* (Wilson); Declaration on the Causes and Necessity of Taking Up Arms; Dickinson (John) Opposing Speech Opposing the Declaration of Independence; George III, Speech to Parliament (October 27, 1775); Jefferson's Notes on Debates over Independence; Secrecy; *Strictures upon the Declaration of Independence* (Hutchinson); *A Summary View of the Rights of British America* (Jefferson); Timing of the Declaration of Independence; Vote for Independence

Further Reading

Burnett, Edmund C. 1964. *The Continental Congress*. New York: W. W. Norton.

Ginsberg, Robert, ed. 1967. *A Casebook on the Declaration of Independence*. New York: Thomas Y. Crowell.

Journals of the Continental Congress, 1774–1789. 1906b. Vol. 5, *1776* (June 5–October 8). Washington, DC: Government Printing Office.

Lengyel, Cornel. 1958. *Four Days in July*. Garden City, NY: Doubleday.
Ritz, Wilfred J. 1986. "The Authentication of the Engrossed Declaration of Independence on July 4, 1776." *Law and History Review* 4 (Spring): 179–204.
Smith, Richard. 1896. "Diary of Richard Smith in the Continental Congress, 1775–1776." *American Historical Review* 1 (January): 288–310 and 1 (April): 493–516.

DECLARATION (MEANING OF TERM)

Although Danielle Allen has described the Declaration of Independence as "just an ordinary memo" (2014, 85), it is better understood, consistent with its most common title, as a Declaration.

According to Professor David Armitage, the term "declaration" historically referred to "a public document issued by a representative body such as Parliament" (2007, 30). Professor Pauline Maier describes a declaration as "a particularly emphatic pronouncement or proclamation that was often explanatory" (1997, 51). She further links it to "the fourteenth century declaration," which "implied 'making clear' or 'telling" (1997, 51). A scholar of the English Declaration of Rights, who also says that the word means "'making clear' or 'telling,'" believes that the term was stronger than either "petition" or "address" (Schwoerer 1981, 16). Under English law, as articulated by the great jurist William Blackstone, "the *declaration*, *narration*, or *count*" was also the form "in which the plaintiff sets forth his cause of complaint at length" (Armitage 2007, 31). Contemporaries also sometimes applied the term as well to "a formal international announcement by an official body," which might take the form of a "general manifesto," as in a declaration of war (Armitage 2007, 31; also see Armitage 2002, 45).

Stephen E. Lucas has distinguished "declaration" from "proclamations, petitions, memorials, remonstrances, messages, [and] addresses" (1998, 146). He further argued that the term was the most appropriate (1998, 148). Lucas observes that the Declaration of Independence followed a form similar to earlier parliamentary declarations:

They typically begin with introductory remarks stating the purpose of the declaration, the audience to whom it is addressed, and the major claim it intends to prove. Up to 75 percent of the text is devoted to providing a mass of evidence in proof of the major claim. The evidence is usually presented chronologically in narrative; occasionally it is presented topically without regard to chronology. Most of the declarations have brief conclusions, often containing the word "therefore," that recapitulate the major claim and reaffirm the commitment of the declarants to their cause. In addition, many of the declarations identify the audience not just as interested parties in England but as "the world" or "the whole world," charge the king and/or his evil counselors with conspiring to alter the constitution and destroy the liberties of the people, proclaim that the declarants are acting with clear consciences out of a commitment only to the public good, pledge to continue the struggle even at the cost of the declarants' "lives and fortunes," and appeal to the aid and protection of almighty God for ultimate success and vindication. (1998, 150–151).

Congress had already *declared* independence when it voted to accept Richard Henry Lee's Resolution "That these United Colonies are, and of right ought to be, free and independent states" on July 2 (Lence 1976, 5). The very first paragraph of the Declaration of Independence thus explained its title by stating that its purpose was to "declare the causes" that impelled the colonies toward separation. Lucas thinks that by using this expression, the document "purports to do no more than a natural philosopher would do in reporting the causes of any physical event." He further notes that "the issue, it implies, is not one of interpretation but of observation" (1990).

The declaration from English history with which the colonists would have been most familiar was the Declaration of Rights of 1689, whereby the Parliament ended the rule of James II, who had fled the country, and accepted that of William and Mary. Cotton Mather had issued a similar declaration, *The Declaration of the Gentlemen, Merchants and Inhabitants of Boston, and the Country Adjacent* (April 18, 1689), against the rule of Governor Edmund Andros (Levin 1977). Parliament later reenacted the 1689 Declaration as the Bill of Rights (Maier 1997, 53). In writing the preamble to the Constitution for Virginia, Thomas Jefferson, who was in Philadelphia at the time and had sent his draft via his former teacher, George Wythe, drew from the opening section of the English Declaration of Rights (Maier 1997, 55). Maier has found about 90 declarations that states and localities directed to Congress, most authorizing or calling for independence, in the months leading up to the adoption of the Declaration of Independence.

Prior to the Declaration of Independence, the only such declarations that the Continental Congresses had issued were the Declaration and Resolves of the First Continental Congress of October 14, 1774, and the Declaration on the Causes and Necessity of Taking Up Arms of July 6, 1775 (in 1642, the English Parliament had issued a Declaration to Justify Their Proceedings and Resolutions to Take Up Arms against Charles I), not long after conflict between British troops and American minutemen had broken out at Lexington and Concord in Massachusetts. A number of states, most notably Virginia, had also issued their own Declarations of Rights. In issuing its prior declarations, the Continental Congresses were asserting their authority to speak on behalf of the united colonies.

See also Declaration and Resolves of the First Continental Congress; Declaration on the Causes and Necessity of Taking Up Arms; English Declaration of Rights; Howe's Circular Letter (1776); Virginia Declaration of Rights

Further Reading

Allen, Danielle. 2016. *Our Declaration: A Reading of the Declaration of Independence in Defense of Equality*. New York: W. W. Norton.

Armitage, David. 2002. "The Declaration of Independence and International Law." *William and Mary Quarterly* 59 (January): 39–64.

Armitage, David. 2007. *The Declaration of Independence: A Global History*. Cambridge, MA: Harvard University Press.

Lence, Ross. 1976. "Thomas Jefferson and the American Declaration of Independence: The Power and Natural Rights of a Free People." *Political Science Reviewer* 6 (Fall): 1–31.

Levin, David. 1977. "Cotton Mather's Declaration of Gentlemen and Thomas Jefferson's Declaration of Independence." *New England Quarterly* 50 (September): 509–514.

Lucas, Stephen. 1990, Spring. "The Stylistic Artistry of the Declaration of Independence." *Prologue: Quarterly of the National Archives and Records Administration*. https://www.archives.gov/founding-docs/stylistic-artistry-of-the-declaration.

Lucas, Stephen. 1998. "The Rhetorical Ancestry of the Declaration of Independence," *Rhetoric and Public Affairs* 1 (Summer): 143–184.

Maier, Pauline. 1997. *American Scripture: Making the Declaration of Independence*. New York: Alfred A. Knopf.

Schwoerer, Lois G. 1981. *The Declaration of Rights, 1689*. Baltimore: Johns Hopkins University Press.

DECLARATION AND RESOLVES OF THE FIRST CONTINENTAL CONGRESS (1774)

The First Continental Congress, which met from September 5 to October 26, 1774, adopted its Declaration and Resolves on October 14, 1774. A committee consisting of 2 delegates from each of the 12 states attending, with Thomas Cushing (MA), Patrick Henry (VA), and Thomas Mifflin (PA) being added later (York 1998, 358–359), formulated them. The Declaration and Resolves were enacted in response to the Coercive Acts (colonists called them the Intolerable Acts), which the British Parliament had adopted to punish Boston and its colony for the Tea Party and other acts considered treasonous.

Only one of three documents adopted by the Continental Congresses with the term "Declaration" in its title, the document is most notable for relying on three sources for American rights, namely, "the immutable laws of nature, the principles of the English constitution, and the several charters or compacts" ("Declaration and Resolves," 77). Nineteenth-century texts often referred to this document, rather than the first 10 amendments to the U.S. Constitution, as the Bill, or Declaration, of Rights ("Declaration and Resolves," 75), and the document is both a precursor to these amendments and to the earlier Declaration of Independence.

The document begins with a series of four paragraphs, each introduced by a "whereas." They respectively pointed to the claims of the British Parliament to tax Americans and to extend the courts of admiralty to the New World, to the manner in which judges were beholden to the king, to the three Intolerable Acts that Parliament had adopted, and to the proroguing of colonial assemblies and the rejection of colonial petitions.

Listing the 12 English colonies south of Canada then attending (all but Georgia), the document proceeded to list the 3 previously mentioned sources of rights before introducing a series of 10 resolutions.

The first, later echoed but slightly altered, by the Declaration of Independence, asserted colonial rights to "life, liberty and property." The second and third said that those who immigrated to America had brought these rights with them from England, undiminished "as their local and other circumstances enable them to exercise and enjoy" ("Declaration and Resolves," 77). This was a common understanding of the application of English common law in the colonies.

The 4th resolution, authored by John Adams (Karsch n.d.) outlined an idea, elsewhere largely attributed to the Magna Carta. It was that the people had a right to participate in their legislative councils and that, as a body where colonists were unrepresented, the British Parliament therefore had no right to enact taxes, albeit conceding some control over their "external commerce" ("Declaration and Resolves," 78).

The 5th resolution further associated British common law with the right to trial by "their peers of the vicinage" ("Declaration and Resolves," 78). The 6th focused on the colonists' right to be protected by existing British statutes.

The 7th resolution, which would find echoes in both Article IV and the Fourteenth Amendment of the U.S. Constitution, referred to "the immunities and privileges" (the Constitutional provisions will reverse this order) "granted and confirmed to them by royal charters or secured by their several codes of provincial laws" ("Declaration and Resolves," 79). The 8th resolution refers specifically to the "right peaceably to assemble, consider of their grievances, and petition the king" (provisions later echoed in the First Amendment to the U.S. Constitution) ("Declaration and Resolves," 79)

The ninth resolution argued that it was illegal for Britain to maintain a "standing army" in the colonies without their consent. The 10th cited "the English constitution" as guaranteeing the independence of both legislative branches and those as invalidating the British practice of allowing the king to appoint a council ("Declaration and Resolves," 79).

Claiming that such parliamentary acts "demonstrate a system to enslave America" ("Declaration and Resolves," 80), the document proceeded to denounce each of the Intolerable Acts. One provision also denounced a recent law establishing the Roman Catholic Church in Canada, which particularly irritated Protestants in the 13 colonies.

The final paragraph announced that the colonies were taking three actions. These were: "1. To enter into a non-importation, non-consumption, and non exportation agreement or association. 2. To prepare an address to the people of Great-Britain, and a memorial to the inhabitants of British America: and 3. To prepare a loyal address to his majesty agreeable to resolutions already entered into" ("Declaration and Resolves," 80).

All but the 4th and 6th resolutions were listed as "N.C.D." This was for the Latin "nemine contra dicente," which means "no one contradicting."

Joseph Galloway, who also proposed a plan of union designed to secure continuing colonial allegiance to Britain, provided counterarguments to the Declaration and Resolves in *A Candid Examination of the Mutual Claims of Great Britain, and the Colonies: With a Plan of Accommodation, on Constitution Principles* (1775). It stressed that colonial rights also brought duties with them.

The Non-Importation Agreement, which the colonists subsequently adopted on October 20, 1774, reflects the style of the Declaration of Independence in that it is followed by the signature of the president of the Congress, Peyton Randolph, and then by those of delegates listed by colonies from North to South. The Petition to the King, which was adopted on October 25, was also signed by individual delegates.

See also Address to the People of Great Britain (October 21, 1774); Laws of Nature and of Nature's God; Parliament; Petition to King George III (1774)

Further Reading

Ammerman, David. 1974. *In the Common Cause: American Response to the Coercive Acts of 1775.* Charlottesville: University Press of Virginia.

"Declaration and Resolves of the First Continental Congress." (1774) 2015. In *Founding Document of America: Documents Decoded*, edited by John R. Vile, 75–80. Santa Barbara, CA: ABC-CLIO.

Galloway, Joseph. 1775. *A Candid Examination of the Mutual Claims of Great-Britain and the Colonies, with a Plan of Accommodation, on Constitutional Principles.* New York: James Rivington.

Karsch, Carl G. n.d. "The First Continental Congress: A Dangerous Journey Begins." Carpenters' Hall. Accessed March 27, 2018. http://www.ushistory.org/carpentershall/history/congress.htm

York, Neil L. 1998. "The First Continental Congress and the Problem of American Rights." *Pennsylvania Magazine of History and Biography* 122 (October): 353–383.

DECLARATION HOUSE

One tourist site connected to the Declaration of Independence is the Declaration House. It is located on the corner of Seventh and Market Streets in Philadelphia, not far from Independence Hall.

A three-story house that was originally constructed by Jacob Graff, a bricklayer, in 1775, it was torn down in 1883, but replicated for the bicentennial celebrations in 1976, based in part on photographs that had been taken before the original building had been demolished. The second story of the original house, consisting of a bedroom, a parlor, and stairs, served as Thomas Jefferson's residence during the time when he wrote the draft of the Declaration of Independence while he served in the Second Continental Congress. Graff, his wife, and an infant son lived on the first floor.

Located at the corner of 7th and Market streets in Philadelphia, this is a re-creation of the house in which Thomas Jefferson lodged when he wrote the first draft of the Declaration of Independence. (Alexandre Fagundes De Fagundes/Dreamstime.com)

On previous trips to Philadelphia, Jefferson had lodged closer to the city's population center at the home of Benjamin Randolph, near Second and Walnut Streets. Randolph was a cabinetmaker, who had the distinction of crafting the desk on which

Jefferson would draft the Declaration. Jefferson had chosen the Graff House when he returned to Philadelphia because it was then in a more rural setting with more freely circulating air.

The house, which is open to the public during limited times, features exhibits related to the Declaration on the first floor and period furniture on the second.

See also Declaration of Independence Desk

Further Reading

Constitutional Walking Tour. "The Declaration House (Graff House)." 2015. http://www.theconstitutional.com/blog/2014/08/18/declaration-house-graff-house.

Donaldson, Thomas. 1898. *The House in Which Thomas Jefferson wrote the Declaration of Independence*. Philadelphia: Avil Printing Company.

Enjoying Philadelphia. n.d. "Declaration House—An Exact Replica of Where Thomas Jefferson Stayed in 1776." Accessed March 27, 2018. http://www.enjoyingphiladelphia.com/declaration_house.html.

DECLARATION OF INDEPENDENCE DESK

Important historical events are often associated with key artifacts and symbols. The portable desk on which Thomas Jefferson composed the Declaration of Independence is among these.

Thomas Jefferson was among the individuals who recognized its value and made sure it was preserved for posterity. Jefferson had commissioned the desk after his arrival at the Second Continental Congress from Benjamin Randolph, a prominent cabinetmaker from whom he had procured lodging before moving farther away from the city at the house of Jacob Graff Jr. Much like an architect's drafting table, the mahogany desk of 9-3/4-by-14-3/4-by-3-1/4 inches ("Declaration of Independence Desk") was adjustable and could be folded out to double its size for both reading and writing. It contained a drawer with a metal handle and a number of compartments for paper, an inkwell, and other writing supplies (Bedini 1981, 2–6).

On May 27, 1825, Eleanora Wayles Randolph, one of Jefferson's favorite grandchildren, became engaged to Joseph Coolidge Jr., a Bostonian and Harvard graduate who had visited Jefferson at Monticello. Jefferson had one of his African American carpenters, John Hemings, design a beautiful desk for the couple, which was, however, lost at sea along with a number of letters from Jefferson that his granddaughter had saved. After ascertaining that Hemings would be unable to design another, Jefferson decided to send the new couple the desk on which he had written the Declaration of Independence.

Although Jefferson was near bankruptcy, he recognized that the desk he was sending was priceless, as he explained at considerable length. Indeed, he compared the desk to a religious relic:

> If these things acquire a superstitious value, because of their connection with particular persons, surely a connection with the greater Charter of our Independence may give a value to what has been associated with that; and such was the idea of the enquirers after the room in which it was written. Now I happen still to possess the writing box on which it was written. It was made from a drawing of my own by

> Ben Randall [*sic*], a cabinet-maker in whose house I took my first lodgings on my arrival in Philadelphia in May, 1776, and I have used it ever since. It claims no merit of particular beauty. It is plain, neat, convenient, and asking no more room on the writing table than a moderate 4 degree volume, it yet displays itself sufficiently for any writing. Mr. Coolidge must do me the favor of accepting this. Its imaginary value will increase with years, and if he lives to my age, or another half-century, he may see it carried in the procession of our nation's birthday, as the relics of the Saints are in those of the Church. (Bedini 1981, 34–35)

Jefferson accompanied the gift with an affidavit, which, after being revised, reads as follows:

> Th. Jefferson gives this Writing Desk to Joseph Coolidge, Jr. as a memorial of affection. It was made from a drawing of his own, by Ben. Randall, cabinet maker of Philadelphia, with whom he first lodged on his arrival in that city in May 1776 and is the identical one on which he wrote the Declaration of Independence. Politics as well as Religion has its superstitions. These, gaining strength with time, may, one day, give imaginary value to this relic, for its association with the birth of the Great Charter of our Independence. Monticello, Nov. 18, 1825. (Bedini 1981, 36)

Ellen Coolidge died on April 30, 1876, and her husband on December 15, 1879. Working with Robert C. Winthrop, the family presented this relic to President Rutherford B. Hayes at the White House on April 15, 1880, who presented it to Congress on April 22 (Bedini 1981, 44–46). Congress had a broadside printed for the occasion. Initially displayed at the Department of State, the desk was subsequently turned over to the Smithsonian Institution, where it has been displayed in the National Museum of American History since January 23, 1964, only occasionally being lent out for special occasions.

Although the Smithsonian had a clear line of provenance, it began to receive reports from individuals that they too had Jefferson's original writing desk. Extensive investigations indicated that a number of copies had been made along with a facsimile of Jefferson's original letter, but the relic in the Smithsonian is the original (Bedini 1981, 86–88).

Although the desk has received the majority of attention, Jefferson is also believed to have written the Declaration while sitting on a rotating Windsor Chair, which he had commissioned. He later took the chair back to Monticello, where it was modified by replacing the original legs with bamboo and adding a writing surface to one of the arms (Eltringham 2016).

See also Declaration House

Further Reading

Bedini, Silvio A. 1981. *Declaration of Independence Desk: Relic of Revolution*. Washington, DC: Smithsonian Institution Press.

"Declaration of Independence Desk." http://americanhistory.si.edu/collections/search/object/nmah_513641. Accessed August 20, 2017.

Eltringham, Mark. 2016. "How Thomas Jefferson Came to Invent the Swivel Chair and Laptop." http://workplaceinsight.net/thomas-jefferson-came-invent-swivel-chair-laptop/.

DECLARATION OF SENTIMENTS (1848)

Although Abigail Adams had urged her husband to "remember the ladies" when drawing up a new form of government, states continued to deny women the right to vote and other rights well into the late-nineteenth century. Seeking redress for this and other grievances, the Seneca Falls Convention, which met in New York on July 19 and 20, 1848, adopted a Declaration of Sentiments (Berhard and Fox-Genovese 1995; Tetrault 2014), which delegates patterned after the Declaration of Independence.

Chiefly called by Elizabeth Cady Stanton and Lucretia Mott, the convention, which consisted of about 300 delegates, highlighted the manner in which women had been denied full social and political rights. The first two paragraphs of the document that the convention adopted echoed the language of the Declaration of Independence. Whereas the Declaration of Independence had referred to two peoples (British and American), the Declaration of Sentiments referred to "the family of man." Whereas the Declaration of Independence had affirmed that "all men are created equal," the Declaration of Sentiments affirmed that "all men and women are created equal."

Reflecting the argument of the first document, the second observed, "The history of mankind is a history of repeated injuries and usurpations on the part of man toward woman, having in direct object the establishment of an absolute tyranny over her." Like the earlier document, it then proceeded to list a series of grievances (14 in all), each of which began with the word "he," which was used to refer collectively to men.

The first, which was considered to be the most radical, condemned men for never permitting women "to exercise her inalienable right to the elective franchise." Other grievances focused on laws related to property and divorce, on unequal job opportunities and educational facilities, and on lessening women's self-respect "to make her willing to lead a dependent and abject life." Contrasting the plight of women to others, the Declaration of Sentiments observed at one point that "He has withheld from her rights which are given to the most ignorant and degraded men—both natives and foreigners."

Lacking the rhetorical flourish of the final words of the Declaration of Independence, the document concluded with the insistence that women "have immediate admission to all the rights and privileges which belong to them as citizens of the United States."

Although many American women were at the forefront of the abolitionist movement, the Fourteenth Amendment (1868) specifically focused on the rights of males, while the Fifteenth Amendment (1870) prohibited discrimination on the basis of race but not of sex. It was not until 1920 that the Nineteenth Amendment prohibited discrimination in voting on the basis of sex.

See also Remember the Ladies

Further Reading

Bernhard, Virginia, and Elizabeth Fox-Genovese, eds. 1995. *The Birth of American Feminism: The Seneca Falls Woman's Convention of 1848*. St. James, NY: Brandywine Press.

Stanton, Elizabeth Cady. "The Declaration of Sentiments." Seneca Falls Women's Convention, 1848. http://coursesite.uhcl.edu/hsh/whitec/litr/4232/research/pritexts/stantonsentiments.htm.

Tetrault, Lisa. 2014. *The Myth of Seneca Falls: Memory and the Woman's Suffrage Movement, 1848–1898*. Chapel Hill: University of North Carolina Press.

DECLARATION ON THE CAUSES AND NECESSITY OF TAKING UP ARMS

Prior to the Declaration of Independence, the Continental Congresses issued only two documents labeled as "declarations." They were the "Declaration and Resolves," which it issued on October 14, 1774, and the "Declaration on the Causes and Necessity of Taking Up Taking Arms," which it adopted on July 6, 1775.

John Dickinson was the chief author of the final document, which had emerged from an original committee consisting of John Rutledge (SC), William Livingston (NJ), John Jay (NY), Thomas Johnson (MD), and Benjamin Franklin (PA). After discontent was expressed with Rutledge's first draft of the document, Dickinson and Thomas Jefferson were added to the committee (Shain 2014, 274–275).

The document was not only a chronological, but also an ideological, precursor to the Declaration of Independence. The First Continental Congress issued the second of these declarations on behalf of "the Representatives of the United Colonies of North America" (1775, 277). The first paragraph arguably set up American slaveholders to charges of hypocrisy when it said that reasonable men could not believe, in reference to colonial relations with Britain, that "the Divine Author of our existence intended a part of the human race to hold an absolute property in, and an unbounded power over others" (1775, 277).

In arguments that the Declaration of Independence would later echo, the paragraph further argued that the purpose of government was "to promote the welfare of mankind," for whose benefit it should be administered (1775, 278). Like the later Declaration of Independence, it also referenced the need to proclaim its concerns "to the rest of the world" (1775, 278).

The next paragraph echoed arguments that Thomas Jefferson had articulated the previous year in *A Summary View of the Rights of British America*. This paragraph linked the settlement of America "then filled with numerous and warlike nations of barbarians" (1775, 278), to the blood, wealth, and toil of American settlers.

The following paragraphs observed how British policies toward the colonies had changed after the French and Indian War and how Great Britain had engaged in a series of provocations. In addition to seeking "to give and grant our money without our consent" (1775, 278), the document listed several other offenses. These included the trials of Americans, British suspension of colonial legislatures, and quartering soldiers among them. Portraying themselves as "freemen" seeking to resist such violations of their rights, the document proceeded to describe the battles that had subsequently arisen between British and colonial forces intent on avoiding "voluntary slavery" (1775, 281).

In the final three paragraphs, the document departed from the Declaration that would follow by indicating that "we mean not to dissolve that Union which so long and so happily subsisted between us, and which we sincerely wish to see restored" (1775, 281). Indeed, in a passage that William Casey King has highlighted in a recent book, which discusses the way that the term "ambition" changed in the years leading up to the American Revolution (2013, 168–190), the document disclaimed that it was raising armies "with ambitious designs of separating from Great Britain, and establishing independent states" or "for glory or conquest" (1775, 282).

The document concluded with an expression of confidence "in the mercies of the supreme and impartial Judge and Ruler of the universe" (1775, 282). It further expressed the hope that the colonial show of force would lead to reconciliation with the mother country.

See also Ambition; Dickinson (John) Speech Opposing the Declaration of Independence; Jefferson, Thomas; *A Summary View of the Rights of British America* (Jefferson)

Further Reading

Boyd, Julian P. 1950. "The Disputed Authorship of the Declaration on the Causes and Necessity of Taking up Arms, 1774." *Pennsylvania Magazine of History and Biography* 74 (January): 51–73.

"Declaration on Taking Arms." (July 6, 1775) 2014. In *The Declaration of Independence in Historical Context: American State Papers, Petitions, Proclamations, and Letters of the Delegates to the First National Congresses*, compiled and edited by Barry Alan Shain, 277–282. Indianapolis, IN: Liberty Fund.

King, William Casey. 2013. *Ambition: A History*. New Haven, CT: Yale University Press.

DECLARATORY ACT OF 1766

Most of the criticisms of Great Britain that the Declaration of Independence articulated were directed against the British king. This was not because the colonies accepted the authority of the British Parliament. To the contrary, almost from the imposition of the Stamp Act in 1765, many colonial representatives had denied the power of the Parliament over the colonies, particularly with respect to internal taxation (some thought that Parliament had the right to enact some imposts as part of its trade regulations).

One of the reasons that the colonies and the English seemed to talk past one another throughout most of this controversy is that Parliament, which considered itself to be sovereign, thought that it had settled the matter with the adoption of the Declaration Act of March 18, 1766. Described as "An act for the better securing the dependency of his majesty's dominions in American upon the crown and parliament of Great Britain," the law specifically responded to colonial claims that only their local assemblies had the right to tax them. Whereas colonists attempted to distinguish between their loyalty to the king versus their unwillingness to accept parliamentary taxation, the Declaratory Act specifically proclaimed:

> That the said colonies . . . and are of right ought to be, subordinate unto, and dependent upon the imperial crown and parliament of Great Britain; and that the King's

> majesty, by and with the advice and consent of the lords spiritual and temporal, and commons of Great Britain, in parliament assembled, had, hath, and of right ought to have, full power and authority to make laws and statutes of sufficient force and validity to bind the colonies and people of America, subjects of the crown of Great Britain, in all cases whatsoever.

The law did not specifically refer to taxation, but this power was clearly embraced by the phrase "in all cases whatsoever" (Morgan 1968, 168–169).

The second section of the law declared that all colonial "resolutions, votes, orders, and proceedings . . . whereby the power and authority of the parliament of Great Britain, to make laws and statutes as aforesaid, is denied, or drawn into question, are, and are hereby declared to be, utterly null and void to all in purposes whatsoever." This explains why the king essentially refused to consider future colonial petitions questioning parliamentary power (Chaffin 1974, 18).

The same day that Parliament adopted the Declaratory Act, it also repealed the Stamp Act. Although the two appeared to be directed to different ends, Professor Robert Chaffin does not believe that the Declaratory Act was actually responsible for the repeal of the Stamp Act (1974, 24).

John Dickinson wrote an *Essay on the Constitutional Power of Great Britain* (1774) in which he opposed the Declaratory Act. James Wilson made similar arguments in *Considerations on the Nature and Extent of Legislative Authority of the British Parliament* (1774) as did John Adams in *Novanglus* (1775). The First Continental Congress also disputed this Act in its "Declaration and Resolves."

On June 7, 1776, Richard Henry Lee of Virginia introduced a resolution for independence before the Second Continental Congress on June 7, 1776, which "Resolved that these United Colonies are, and of right ought to be, free and independent States, that they are absolved from all allegiance to the British Crown." In doing so, he therefore directly contradicted, and arguably mocked (Munves 1978, 9), the language of the Declaratory Act.

See also Declaration and Resolves of the First Continental Congress (1774); Resolutions Introduced by Richard Henry Lee (June 7, 1776)

Further Reading

Chaffin, Robert J. 1974. "The Declaratory Act of 1766: A Reappraisal." *Historian* 37 (November): 5–25.

"The Declaratory Act." https://uwmadison.app.box.com/s/5zwbnxqdcehyr534fsfgzuyyj1tmepqy.

Morgan, Edmund S. 1968. "Colonial Ideas of Parliamentary Power, 1764–1766." In *The Reinterpretation of the American Revolution, 1763–1789*, edited by Jack P. Greene, 151–180. New York: Harper and Row.

Munves, James. 1978. *Thomas Jefferson and the Declaration of Independence: The Writing and Editing of the Document That Marked the Birth of the United States of America*. New York: Charles Scribner's Sons.

Reid, John Philip. 1991. *Constitutional History of the American Revolution: The Authority to Legislate*. Madison: University of Wisconsin Press.

DELAWARE AND ITS SIGNERS

Although Swedes and Dutch were the first Europeans to populate Delaware, the British eventually gained title and allowed it to serve as a proprietary colony under William Penn. Closely connected to Pennsylvania from the outset, the small colony was politically divided into upper counties, more closely associated with New York, and lower counties, which were more closely associated with Pennsylvania, but which eventually sent representatives to New Castle (Bower and Ratledge 2009, 3). Because Delaware did not have to submit its legislation to the English for approval, it exercised a degree of self-government similar to that of Connecticut and Rhode Island (Bower and Ratledge 2009, 3).

Delaware was a small state that often had difficulty finding able individuals to serve or to attend Congress (Munroe 1952). Like other Middle Colonies, the state was divided between Whigs, who favored independence, and Tories, who either opposed independence or thought that it should wait. Delaware's instructions to its delegates, which sentiment it repeated on at least two occasions, had emphasized the need to avoid "everything disrespectful or offensive to our most gracious sovereign, or . . . any measure evasive of his just rights and prerogatives," and Delaware's vote for independence may well have been ahead of majority sentiment within the state (Rowe 1971, 238, 243).

Nowhere was the division of sentiment more evident than on July 1, 1776, when it became clear that the two Delaware delegates who were present, George Read and Thomas McKean, were divided with Read not yet ready to approve of independence but with McKean favoring the measure. The musical *1776* is among the works of art that celebrate the fact that McKean sent a rider informing Caesar Rodney of his need to arrive and how he rode through the night covering approximately 70 miles to get there in time for the vote on July 2. Although Rodney did have face cancer, which he covered with a green handkerchief, he was not, as the musical implies, near death, and he lived an additional eight years.

Although George Read opposed independence on July 2, he later signed the document. While Thomas McKean voted for independence, he is believed to be the last individual to sign the Declaration, possibly as late of 1782.

Thomas McKean (1735–1817) had been born in Pennsylvania and educated at Francis Alison's New London Academy before moving to Delaware, where he studied law under a cousin, David Finney. He represented Delaware in the Continental Congress for every year but one between 1774 and 1783, despite the fact that he lived most of this time in Pennsylvania, where he also served as chief justice. Even though he lived in a neighboring state, he participated in almost 75 percent of the congressional votes, often being its only representative present (Rowe 1971, 229). He encountered considerable opposition for attempting to wear two hats, but managed to hang on to both, at one time even serving as president of Congress. McKean was allied fairly early on with those who sought independence, and he had favored the creation of new state governments to replace royal authority even prior to adoption of the Declaration of Independence. Remaining committed to the revolutionary cause after Lord North attempted reconciliation with the colonies in 1778, McKean indicated that "I am determined never to give up on the Independence of the United States after so much expense of blood and treasure, whilst I have a breath to draw" (Rowe 1971, 247).

Explaining why he signed later than others, McKean wrote in later years that "I was not in Congress after the 4th. For some months, having marched with my regiment of associators of this city, as Colonel, to support General Washington." He further observed that "I have been told that a resolve had been passed a few days after [Congress had ordered the Declaration to be engrossed] and was entered on the secret journal, that no person should have a seat in congress, during that year until he should have signed the declaration, or order (as I have been given to understand) to prevent traitors or spies from worming themselves amongst us" (Letters of Members of the Continental Congress, 1:535).

George Read (1733–1798), the son of Irish immigrants, had been born in Maryland, had (like McKean) attended Alison's Academy, and had read law before being admitted to the bar in Pennsylvania and Delaware. Although he sided with John Dickinson in opposing the adoption of the Declaration of Independence, he nonetheless decided to sign it. He would later sign the U.S. Constitution, not only on his own behalf, but as a proxy for Dickinson. Read had served both as Delaware's attorney general and as a colonial legislator prior to being selected as a delegate to the Continental Congress, and he served as the state's president from 1777 to 1778.

Caesar Rodney (1728–1784), who made his grand entrance at the Congress after receiving news from Stockton that his vote was needed to break the state's tie, had been born in Delaware and attended the Latin School in Philadelphia before becoming an attorney and politician. A lifelong bachelor known for his good humor, he served in the militia during the French and Indian War and again during the Revolutionary War. Like his fellow delegates from Delaware, he had been a delegate to the Stamp Act Congress, and he would serve as the president of Delaware from 1778 to 1781.

Delaware is called "the First State" because it became the first to ratify the U.S. Constitution. It undoubtedly recognized that it needed a stronger national government if it were to preserve its own existence.

See also Musical Play *1776*; Vote for Independence

Further Reading

Boyer, William W., and Edward C. Ratledge. 2009. *Delaware Politics and Government*. Lincoln: University of Nebraska Press.

Letters of Members of the Continental Congress. 1921. Edited By Edmund C. Burnett. Vol. 1, *August 29, 1774, to July 4, 1776*. Washington, DC: Carnegie Institute.

Munroe, John A. 1952. "Nonresident Representation in the Continental Congress: The Delaware Delegation of 1782." *William and Mary Quarterly*, 3rd ser. 9 (April): 166–190.

Rodney, Caesar A., and Thomas McKean. 1915. "Caesar Rodney's Ride, July 1776." *Pennsylvania Magazine of History and Biography* 39:454–461.

Rowe, G. S. 1971. "A Valuable Acquisition in Congress; Thomas McKean, Delegate from Delaware to the Continental Congress, 1774–1783." *Pennsylvania History: A Journal of Mid-Atlantic Studies* 38 (July): 225–264.

Tiedemann, Joseph S. 2010. "A Tumultuous People: The Rage for Liberty and the Ambiance of Violence in the Middle Colonies in the Years Preceding the American Revolution." *Pennsylvania History: A Journal of Mid-Atlantic Studies* 77 (Autumn): 387–431.

DEMOCRACY

It is perhaps natural to associate the Declaration of Independence with a commitment to democracy, or government by the people, but the document does not mention this specific word. The opening paragraph does identify as self-evident the principles that "all men are created equal" and that they are entitled to certain "unalienable rights." It further says that government should rest on "the consent of the governed" and declares that the governed have the right to overturn governments that do not provide for liberty. As much as its indictments against the current British king might have pointed in the direction of representative democracy and as much as many of the newly minted state constitutions may have been democratic, the purpose of the Declaration was not, like that of the Articles of Confederation and the Constitution, to prescribe a particular form of government. Instead, its purpose was to justify the colonial decision to seek independence from Great Britain.

According to the Declaration, the primary purpose of government was to secure liberty. Many of the Founders would have commended the mixed form of government (which included a king) for securing such liberties in Great Britain, while arguing that, without representation of the colonies in the British Parliament, their own liberties were in jeopardy. After observing that the Declaration does not mention the word "democracy," Paul Eidelberg observes that "what the Declaration emphasizes is not the forms but the ends of government" (1974, 447). Such ends would obviously preclude subjecting one's country to tyranny, or modern totalitarianism, while still leaving a number of forms, such as constitutional monarchy, that might preserve liberty.

When delegates gathered in Philadelphia to write the Constitution, they created a system in which states were represented according to population in the House of Representatives, whose members served short, two-year terms. They provided longer terms for senators, who were initially elected by state legislatures, and they created an indirect system of election for the U.S. president. Significantly, this constitution abolished titles of nobility, which, like hereditary monarchy, suggested that some families were more entitled to rule than others. The document further relied on mechanisms like bicameralism, separation of powers, checks and balances, federalism, and judicial review to temper direct democracy so as to avoid tyrannical majorities (Diamond 1976).

In time, the principle of equality led to increased democratization, which included women, African Americans, and others. Moreover, the Fourteenth Amendment embodied the protection of equal protection that the Declaration had previously articulated. As Abraham Lincoln had indicated, the Declaration proclaimed the goals of liberty and equality, which were to be worked out in practice by future generations (Balkin 1999).

See also Consent of the Governed; Equality; Lincoln, Abraham; Majority Rule and Unanimity; Representative (Republican) Government; State Constitutions and the Declaration of the Independence; U.S. Constitution and the Declaration of Independence

Further Reading

Balkin, J. M. "The Declaration and the Promise of a Democratic Culture." *Widener Law Symposium Journal* 4:167–180.

Diamond, Martin. 1976. "The American Idea of Equality: The View from the Founding." *Review of Politics* 38 (July): 313–331.
Eidelberg, Paul. 1974. *A Discourse on Statesmanship: The Design and Transformation of the American Polity*. Urbana: University of Illinois Press.

DICKINSON (JOHN) SPEECH OPPOSING THE DECLARATION OF INDEPENDENCE

One of the individuals who participated in debates over the Declaration of Independence and did not sign was John Dickinson of Pennsylvania. Although the official notes of these debates are fairly skimpy, historians have discovered the notes that Dickinson used in a speech that he delivered on July 1, 1776, the day before the Congress adopted Richard Henry Lee's resolution for independence, which the Declaration of Independence then sought to justify.

Although Dickinson had delineated colonial arguments with great effectiveness, as in his *Letters from a Farmer in Pennsylvania*, he had long struggled for reconciliation with Britain and was the chief author of the Olive Branch Petition. Frustrated by what he considered to be Dickinson's excessive timidity, John Adams had once derisively referred to him as a man of "Great Fortune and piddling Genius" (Knollenberg 1963, 141). By contrast, Adams would later admit that "In a speech of great length, and with all his eloquence . . . combined together all that that had been written in pamphlets and newspapers, and all that had from time to time been said in Congress by himself and others. He conducted the debate not only with great ingenuity and eloquence, but with equal politeness and candour, and was answered in the same spirit" (Powell 1950, 55).

John Dickinson, who authored the Olive Branch Petition, delivered a speech to the Second Continental Congress in which he argued that independence was premature. Although he did not sign the document, he fought on behalf of independence and later served at the Constitutional Convention of 1787 where he signed the Constitution by proxy. (Chaiba Media)

Dickinson recognized that he was swimming against the tide of opinion within Congress. At the beginning of his speech, Dickinson accordingly acknowledged that his opposition to independence would likely diminish his popularity. He nonetheless felt compelled to express his opinion. Invoking "Almighty God" (Powell 1941, 469), Dickinson fretted that

"Resentment of the Injuries offered to their Country, may irritate them [his fellow countrymen] to Counsels & to Actions that may be detrimental to the Cause, they would dye to advance" (Powell 1941, 470).

In surveying the anticipated advantages of declaring independence, Dickinson indicated that he did not think the people needed such a declaration to rally them, and that military victory would do more to win foreign allies than any such declaration (Powell 1941, 471). Moreover, it would be better to consult with them in advance of such a declaration than to present them with a fait accompli (Powell 1941, 472). Dickinson further argued that the colonies should establish a common government prior to declaring independence rather than afterward.

Dickinson thought that it was in the colonies' interest for the British to believe that they favored reconciliation for as long as possible (Powell 1941, 475). He feared that, especially if the military conflict took a bad turn, the people would blame Congress for "our Rashness" (Powell 1941, 476). Further fearing that a declaration could lead to a partition of the states, Dickinson said that declaring independence was like destroying a house prior to building a new one (Powell 1941, 478).

Dickinson observed that declaring independence might foreclose the possibility that Britain might come to better terms with the colonies with respect to their existing commercial regulations. He also repeated his concern that a Declaration might further rend the current union of the states (Powell 1941, 480).

John Adams appears to have responded to this speech, partly at the request of newly arrived delegates from New Jersey, who wanted a recapitulation of the arguments they had missed. Although Adams's speech is generally acknowledged to have been a tour de force, no similar outline is known to exist.

Although Dickinson's reputation suffered for his decision not to sign the Declaration, Dickinson supported the Patriot side during the Revolution and had a major role in drawing up the Articles of Confederation. He later participated in the Constitutional Convention of 1787 and signed the document by proxy.

See also Adams, John; Debates over the Declaration of Independence; Olive Branch Petition; Pennsylvania and Its Signers

Further Reading

Calvert, Jane E. 2008. *Quaker Constitutionalism and the Political Thought of John Dickinson*. Cambridge: Cambridge University Press.

Colburn, H. Trevor. 1959. "John Dickinson, Historical Revolutionary." *Pennsylvania Magazine of History and Biography* 83 (July): 271–292.

Head, John M. 1968. *A Time to Rend: An Essay on the Decision for American Independence*. Madison: State Historical Society of Wisconsin.

Knollenberg, Bernhard. 1963. "John Dickinson vs. John Adams, 1774–1776." *Proceedings of the American Philosophical Society* 107 (April 15): 138–144.

Powell, John H. 1941. "Notes and Documents, Speech of John Dickinson Opposing the Declaration of Independence, 1 July 1776." *Pennsylvania Magazine of History and Biography* 65 (October): 458–481.

Powell, John H. 1950. "The Debate on American Independence: July 1, 1776." *Delaware Notes* 23:37–62.

Rakove, Jack. 2010. "The Patriot Who Refused to Sign the Declaration of Independence." http://www.historynet.com/the-patriot-who-refused-to-sign-the-declaration-of-independence.htm.

DISSOLUTION OF GOVERNMENT

The opening paragraph of the Declaration of Independence refers to the necessity of dissolving the "political bands" between the American colonies and the mother country. Similarly, the last chapter of John Locke's *Second Treatise on Government* devoted itself to "the dissolution of governments." Locke began by distinguishing the "dissolution of the society," which usually occurs through foreign invasion, and "the dissolution of the government" ([1690] 1924, 224). This distinction enabled Locke, like Jefferson, to believe that it was possible to dissolve the agreement that an existing people have with those who govern without therefore dissolving the bonds of society.

Locke argued that governments can be "dissolved from within" ([1690] 1924, 225) "when the legislature is altered" or when the executive refused to execute the laws ([1690] 1924, 227). Focusing on the first situation in a case like Britain, which combined a hereditary monarch with an assembly of Lords and Commons, Locke further described four situations where dissolutions can occur. The first was "when such a single person or prince sets up his own arbitrary will in place of the laws which are the will of the society declared by the legislative [body]" ([1690] 1924, 226). The second occurs "when the prince hinders the legislative from assembling in its due time, or from acting freely, pursuant to those ends for which it was constituted" ([1690] 1924, 226). The third happens when elections "are altered without the consent and contrary to the common interest of the people" ([1690] 1924, 226). The fourth occurs when a king delivers a people into the hands of a foreign power. Locke observed that "when the government is dissolved, the people are at liberty to provide for themselves" by creating new governments ([1690] 1924, 228).

Edward Dumbauld (1950, 76) and Allen Jayne (1998, 45) have observed that the Declaration of Independence charges the king with almost all of these offenses that Locke listed.

See also Charges against the King and Others; Dissolved Representative Houses (Charge #5); Locke, John

Further Reading

Dumbauld, Edward. 1950. *The Declaration of Independence and What It Means Today.* Norman: University of Oklahoma Press.

Jayne, Allen. 1998. *Jefferson's Declaration of Independence.* Lexington: University Press of Kentucky.

Locke, John. (1690) 1924. *Two Treatises of Government.* London: Dent, Everyman's Library.

DISSOLVED REPRESENTATIVE HOUSES (CHARGE #5)

The fifth accusation that the Declaration of Independence leveled against George III was that "he has dissolved Representatives houses repeatedly for opposing with manly firmness his invasions on the rights of the people." Like each of the first seven accusations, this focused on the king's conduct with respect to the legislative branches.

Herbert Friedenwald says that the king had twice dissolved the Virginia Assembly (1904, 225–226). He had done so in 1765 after it had adopted four resolutions, proposed by Patrick Henry, opposing parliamentary taxation of the colonies ("Virginia Stamp Act Resolutions") and again in 1769 after it adopted resolutions against reviving a statute of Henry VIII permitting the transportation to England to try individuals accused of treason. Similarly, the king had dissolved the Massachusetts legislature in 1768 after it overwhelmingly refused to revoke the Circular Letter that it had sent to the other colonies denying parliamentary authority to adopt the Townshend Acts imposing duties on a variety of items, including tea (See "Massachusetts Circular Letter"). Sydney George Fisher said that this suspension also applied to the Virginia and South Carolina legislatures (1907, 274).

Herbert Friedenwald further observed that when colonists called the First Continental Congress together in 1774, "all but three of the colonies had to elect delegates by means of provincial conventions or committees of correspondence, because their assemblies had been dissolved by the governors" (1904, 226).

In assessing these charges, British apologist John Lind observed that the charge "amounts to nothing" because "It states only, that his Majesty has exercised a power, which has always been considered as inherent in the crown" (1776, 31–32). In Lind's view, it was just as "manly" for the King to protect his prerogatives as it was for the colonies to question them.

In summarizing these conflicting views, Hans L. Eicholz has observed that the king symbolically called and ended parliamentary sessions in England, but these were "purely symbolic performances" (2001, 58). By contrast, colonial legislatures had been established under the king's authority. Eicholz observes that "for patriots, this proved that their governments had a direct relationship with the monarch that admitted of no interference by Parliament." Eicholz goes on to observe that, contrariwise, "for loyalists, the fact that the King possessed real executive power in America was fully consistent with his role as the keeper of the laws of the empire, in which his authority was subsumed by Parliament and designated by the term, 'King-in-Parliament'" (2001, 59).

See also Charges against the King and Others; Representative (Republican) Government

Further Reading

Bradford, Alden. 1818. "Massachusetts Circular Letter to the Colonial Legislatures; February 11, 1768." *Speeches of the Governors of Massachusetts from 1765 to 1775*. Boston: Russell and Gardner.

Colonial Williamsburg. n.d. "Virginia Stamp Act Resolutions." Accessed March 27, 2018. http://www.history.org/history/teaching/tchcrvar.cfm.

Eicholz, Hans L. 2001. *Harmonizing Sentiments: The Declaration of Independence and the Jeffersonian Idea of Self-Government*. New York: Peter Lang.
Fisher, Sydney George. 1907. "The Twenty-Eight Charges against the King in the Declaration of Independence." *Pennsylvania Magazine of History and Biography* 31:257–303.
Friedenwald, Herbert. 1904. *The Declaration of Independence: An Interpretation and an Analysis*. New York: Macmillan.
Lind, John. 1776. *An Answer to the Declaration of the American Congress*. London: J. Walter, Charing-Cross and T. Sewell.

DUNLAP BROADSIDE PRINTING OF THE DECLARATION OF INDEPENDENCE

The first copies of the Declaration of Independence to be distributed to the public do not visually resemble the document engrossed in calligraphy (handwriting) by Timothy Matlack on parchment that is preserved and displayed at the National Archives. Instead, they were printed as one-page broadsides by John Dunlap (1747–1812), an Irish-born Philadelphia publisher who (with his partner, David Claypoole) was later also entrusted with the task of printing the U.S. Constitution. The broadside measured approximately 18-3/8-by-12-3/8 inches (Capansky 2011, 134; for variations, see Goff 1976, 13). Because the signers' names remained secret, the broadsides did not include written signatures like the later engrossed document.

As the chief author, Thomas Jefferson wrote the first four-page copy of the Declaration by hand. John Adams and Benjamin Franklin made corrections on this draft, which was, much to Jefferson's chagrin, further amended and considerably shortened after debates in Congress. Jefferson would later mail friends copies of his own original.

Because It was common for printers to begin with a complete copy in calligraphy before they put manuscripts in print, it seems likely that someone, probably Jefferson, would have handwritten a corrected document from which Dunlap would have worked. If such a copy were made, it is missing and may have been cut into pieces for the ease of the printer (Boyd 1976). Moreover, it is possible that Congress had previously authorized Dunlap to print Jefferson's rough draft for members so they could more readily debate it (Ritz 1992).

The heading of the Dunlap printing encompasses five lines and says:

> In CONGRESS, July 4, 1776,
> A DECLARATION
> By THE REPRESENTATITVES OF THE
> UNITED STATES OF AMERICA,
> IN GENERAL CONGRESS ASSEMBLED.

The largest printing was used for "A DECLARATION" with the words "CONGRESS" and "UNITED STATES OF AMERICA" in the next largest print (see picture in Malone 1954, 78).

In 1975, Frederick R. Goff worked with the Library of Congress to gather 17 Dunlap broadsides for comparison. The copy owned by the Historical Society of Pennsylvania, and believed to be a proof copy, had a series of quotation marks—or possibly diacritical accents that Jefferson had inserted for possible public readings

IN CONGRESS, JULY 4, 1776.

A DECLARATION

BY THE REPRESENTATIVES OF THE

UNITED STATES OF AMERICA,

IN GENERAL CONGRESS ASSEMBLED.

WHEN in the Course of human Events, it becomes necessary for one People to dissolve the Political Bands which have connected them with another, and to assume among the Powers of the Earth, the separate and equal Station to which the Laws of Nature and of Nature's God entitle them, a decent Respect to the Opinions of Mankind requires that they should declare the causes which impel them to the Separation.

WE hold these Truths to be self-evident, that all Men are created equal, that they are endowed by their Creator with certain unalienable Rights, that among these are Life, Liberty, and the Pursuit of Happiness—That to secure these Rights, Governments are instituted among Men, deriving their just Powers from the Consent of the Governed, that whenever any Form of Government becomes destructive of these Ends, it is the Right of the People to alter or to abolish it, and to institute new Government, laying its Foundation on such Principles, and organizing its Powers in such Form, as to them shall seem most likely to effect their Safety and Happiness. Prudence, indeed, will dictate that Governments long established should not be changed for light and transient Causes; and accordingly all Experience hath shewn, that Mankind are more disposed to suffer, while Evils are sufferable, than to right themselves by abolishing the Forms to which they are accustomed. But when a long Train of Abuses and Usurpations, pursuing invariably the same Object, evinces a Design to reduce them under absolute Despotism, it is their Right, it is their Duty, to throw off such Government, and to provide new Guards for their future Security. Such has been the patient Sufferance of these Colonies; and such is now the Necessity which constrains them to alter their former Systems of Government. The History of the present King of Great-Britain is a History of repeated Injuries and Usurpations, all having in direct Object the Establishment of an absolute Tyranny over these States. To prove this, let Facts be submitted to a candid World.

HE has refused his Assent to Laws, the most wholesome and necessary for the public Good.

HE has forbidden his Governors to pass Laws of immediate and pressing Importance, unless suspended in their Operation till his Assent should be obtained; and when so suspended, he has utterly neglected to attend to them.

HE has refused to pass other Laws for the Accommodation of large Districts of People, unless those People would relinquish the Right of Representation in the Legislature, a Right inestimable to them, and formidable to Tyrants only.

HE has called together Legislative Bodies at Places unusual, uncomfortable, and distant from the Depository of their public Records, for the sole Purpose of fatiguing them into Compliance with his Measures.

HE has dissolved Representative Houses repeatedly, for opposing with manly Firmness his Invasions on the Rights of the People.

HE has refused for a long Time, after such Dissolutions, to cause others to be elected; whereby the Legislative Powers, incapable of Annihilation, have returned to the People at large for their exercise; the State remaining in the mean time exposed to all the Dangers of Invasion from without, and Convulsions within.

HE has endeavoured to prevent the Population of these States; for that Purpose obstructing the Laws for Naturalization of Foreigners; refusing to pass others to encourage their Migrations hither, and raising the Conditions of new Appropriations of Lands.

HE has obstructed the Administration of Justice, by refusing his Assent to Laws for establishing Judiciary Powers.

HE has made Judges dependent on his Will alone, for the Tenure of their Offices, and the Amount and Payment of their Salaries.

HE has erected a Multitude of new Offices, and sent hither Swarms of Officers to harrass our People, and eat out their Substance.

HE has kept among us, in Times of Peace, Standing Armies, without the consent of our Legislatures.

HE has affected to render the Military independent of and superior to the Civil Power.

HE has combined with others to subject us to a Jurisdiction foreign to our Constitution, and unacknowledged by our Laws; giving his Assent to their Acts of pretended Legislation:

FOR quartering large Bodies of Armed Troops among us:

FOR protecting them, by a mock Trial, from Punishment for any Murders which they should commit on the Inhabitants of these States:

FOR cutting off our Trade with all Parts of the World:

FOR imposing Taxes on us without our Consent:

FOR depriving us, in many Cases, of the Benefits of Trial by Jury:

FOR transporting us beyond Seas to be tried for pretended Offences:

FOR abolishing the free System of English Laws in a neighbouring Province, establishing therein an arbitrary Government, and enlarging its Boundaries, so as to render it at once an Example and fit Instrument for introducing the same absolute Rule into these Colonies:

FOR taking away our Charters, abolishing our most valuable Laws, and altering fundamentally the Forms of our Governments:

FOR suspending our own Legislatures, and declaring themselves invested with Power to legislate for us in all Cases whatsoever.

HE has abdicated Government here, by declaring us out of his Protection and waging War against us.

HE has plundered our Seas, ravaged our Coasts, burnt our Towns, and destroyed the Lives of our People.

HE is, at this Time, transporting large Armies of foreign Mercenaries to compleat the Works of Death, Desolation, and Tyranny, already begun with circumstances of Cruelty and Perfidy, scarcely paralleled in the most barbarous Ages, and totally unworthy the Head of a civilized Nation.

HE has constrained our fellow Citizens taken Captive on the high Seas to bear Arms against their Country, to become the Executioners of their Friends and Brethren, or to fall themselves by their Hands.

HE has excited domestic Insurrections amongst us, and has endeavoured to bring on the Inhabitants of our Frontiers, the merciless Indian Savages, whose known Rule of Warfare, is an undistinguished Destruction, of all Ages, Sexes and Conditions.

IN every stage of these Oppressions we have Petitioned for Redress in the most humble Terms: Our repeated Petitions have been answered only by repeated Injury. A Prince, whose Character is thus marked by every act which may define a Tyrant, is unfit to be the Ruler of a free People.

NOR have we been wanting in Attentions to our British Brethren. We have warned them from Time to Time of Attempts by their Legislature to extend an unwarrantable Jurisdiction over us. We have reminded them of the Circumstances of our Emigration and Settlement here. We have appealed to their native Justice and Magnanimity, and we have conjured them by the Ties of our common Kindred to disavow these Usurpations, which, would inevitably interrupt our Connections and Correspondence. They too have been deaf to the Voice of Justice and of Consanguinity. We must, therefore, acquiesce in the Necessity, which denounces our Separation, and hold them, as we hold the rest of Mankind, Enemies in War, in Peace, Friends.

WE, therefore, the Representatives of the UNITED STATES OF AMERICA, in GENERAL CONGRESS, Assembled, appealing to the Supreme Judge of the World for the Rectitude of our Intentions, do, in the Name, and by Authority of the good People of these Colonies, solemnly Publish and Declare, That these United Colonies are, and of Right ought to be, FREE AND INDEPENDENT STATES; that they are absolved from all Allegiance to the British Crown, and that all political Connection between them and the State of Great-Britain, is and ought to be totally dissolved; and that as FREE AND INDEPENDENT STATES, they have full Power to levy War, conclude Peace, contract Alliances, establish Commerce, and to do all other Acts and Things which INDEPENDENT STATES may of right do. And for the support of this Declaration, with a firm Reliance on the Protection of divine Providence, we mutually pledge to each other our Lives, our Fortunes, and our sacred Honor.

Signed by ORDER *and in* BEHALF *of the* CONGRESS,

JOHN HANCOCK, PRESIDENT.

ATTEST.
CHARLES THOMSON, SECRETARY.

PHILADELPHIA: PRINTED BY JOHN DUNLAP.

The Declaration of Independence broadside first printed by John Dunlap on the evening of July 4, 1776. A later, final copy of the Declaration was signed by delegates to the Second Continental Congress. (Library of Congress)

(Fliegelman 1993, 5)—that were missing for the other copies. These appear, in turn, to have been printed in "two distinct states," which are distinguishable by the placement of Thomson's name (Goff 1976, 7).

Twelve copies had distinctive Dutch watermarks, some of which ironically include a crown (Goff 1976, 9). The chain lines in the copies "are not quite parallel to the printed text," indicating that the paper may have been set on the press "slightly askew" (Goff 1976, 11). Moreover, some of the copies appear to have been folded before the ink on the upper portion was dry (Goff 1976, 11), another possible sign of haste.

The American Philosophical Society has a vellum edition of the Dunlap Broadside with 70, rather than 76 lines, of printed text (Goff 1976, 12).

There are a number of other known early broadside printings of the Declaration of Independence. These include one that Ezekiel Russell at Salem, Massachusetts, printed, another from the Boston press of "John Gill, and Powars and Willis, in Queen-Street," and yet another that was probably printed in Exeter, New Hampshire (see Goff 1947, 12, 13, 15).

When Congress sent the Dunlap Broadsides to the states, John Hancock, the president of the Congress, included the following note:

> I do myself the honour to enclose, in obedience to the commands of Congress, a copy of the Declaration of Independence, which you will please to have proclaimed in your Colony, in such way and manner as you shall judge best. The important consequences resulting to the American States from this Declaration of Independence, considered as the ground and foundation of a future government, will naturally suggest the propriety of proclaiming it in such a mode that the people may be universally informed of it. (Desbler 1892, 166)

Hancock's use of the word "colony" suggests that old habits may have been hard to break. Hancock's letter to General George Washington was more precise: "The Congress have judged it necessary to dissolve the connexion between Great Britain and the American Colonies, and to declare them free and independent States, as you will perceive by the enclosed Declaration, which I am directed to transmit to you, and to request you will have it proclaimed at the head of the army, in the way you shall think most proper" (Desbler 1892, 166)

See also Engravings and Printings of the Declaration of Independence; Engrossed Declaration of Independence (Matlack); Hancock's Letter Accompanying the Declaration of Independence

Further Reading

Boyd, Julian P. 1976. "The Declaration of Independence: The Mystery of the Lost Original." *Pennsylvania Magazine of History and Biography* 100 (October): 438–467.

Capansky, Trisha. 2011. "The Declaration of Independence: A New Genre in Political Discourse or Mixed Genres in an Unlikely Medium?" PhD diss., East Carolina University.

Desbler, Charles D. 1892. "How the Declaration Was Received in the Old Thirteen." *Harper's New Monthly Magazine* 85 (July): 165–187.

Fliegelman, Jay. 1993. *Declaring Independence: Jefferson, Natural Language, and the Culture of Performance*. Stanford, CA: Stanford University Press.

Goff, Frederick R. 1947. "A Contemporary Broadside Printing of the Declaration of Independence." *Quarterly Journal of Current Acquisitions* 5 (November): 12–16.

Goff, Frederick R. 1976. *The John Dunlap Broadside: The First Printing of the Declaration of Independence*. Washington, DC: Library of Congress.

Hays, Minis. 1900. "A Contribution to the Bibliography of the Declaration of Independence." *Proceedings of the American Philosophical Society* 39 (January): 69–78.

Malone, Dumas. 1954. *The Story of the Declaration of Independence*. New York: Oxford University Press.

Ritz, Wilfred J. 1992. "From the Here of Jefferson's Handwritten Rough Draft of the Declaration of Independence to the There of the Printed Dunlap Broadside." *Pennsylvania Magazine of History and Biography* 116 (October): 499–512.

E

ENDEAVORED TO PREVENT THE POPULATION (CHARGE #7)

The seventh accusation that the Declaration of Independence made against the king was that "He has endeavored to prevent the population of these states; for that purpose obstructing the laws for naturalization of foreigners; refusing to pass others to encourage their migrations hither; & raising the conditions of new appropriations of lands." The term "prevent" as used in this passage essentially means stop, reduce, or check.

This charge is often analyzed in two parts. A number of scholars believe that the initial statement is intended to refer to the Royal Proclamation of October 7, 1763. In addition to providing government for Canada and seeking to define the boundaries of East and West Florida, this proclamation sought in the aftermath of the French and Indian War to reserve the land between the Appalachian Mountain Range and the Mississippi River for Native American Indian tribes ("The Royal Proclamation"), who were not general objects of favor in the colonies. Although the law, which appears to be the primary work of William Petty, the earl of Shelburne (Humphreys 1934), did have a significant effect on the ability of land companies to settle in this area, it was generally regarded as a temporary measure (Papa 1975).

The statements regarding naturalization and immigration reflect similar concerns in Thomas Jefferson's *A Summary View of the Rights of British America*. After noting that American immigrants had been "farmers, not lawyers," Jefferson had observed that:

> The fictitious principle that all lands belong originally to the king, they were early persuaded to believe real; and accordingly took grants of their own lands from the crown. And while the crown continued to grant for small sums, and on reasonable rents; there was no inducement to arrest the error, and lay it open to public view. But his majesty has lately taken on him to advance the terms of purchase, and of holding to the double of what they were, by which means the acquisition of lands being rendered difficult, the population of our country is likely to be checked.

The Declaration, however, seems more concerned with issues of naturalization, attitudes about which differed significantly in Great Britain, where individuals born under the king's sovereignty were considered permanent subjects, and America, where ideas of naturalization were considerably more fluid (Carpenter 1904). America was so situated that it needed many immigrants, but one difficulty that colonies had in luring them was that each individual colony could offer citizenship only to immigrants within that colony, although many did so on fairly generous terms. In 1772, the king had disallowed a North Carolina law, adopted the previous year, in which North Carolina had exempted immigrants from taxation for four years; in November, the king prohibited all the colonies from naturalizing any aliens (Friedenwald 1904, 229). In 1767, the king had also disallowed a Georgia law offering tax incentives to encourage immigrants (Dumbauld 1950, 105; see also Totten 2008). Steve Pincus believes that British attempts to restrict colonial immigration were tied to larger commercial policies that were partly based on fears that the British Isles were being depopulated (2016b, 118–121)

In examining charges relating to population, John Lind charged that the Declaration was being inconsistent in accusing the king of vetoing colonial laws and then expecting him to veto laws of Parliament. Lind further asked, "How comes it, that local, subordinate legislatures should assume the power of making laws for naturalization? Of what country are persons thus naturalized to be reputed natural-born subjects? Is it of the whole British Empire at large? And is the jurisdiction of these local legislatures so extensive! The idea is too ridiculous to be admitted."

See also Charges against the King and Others; *A Summary View of the Rights of British America* (Jefferson)

Further Reading

Carpenter, A. H. 1904. "Naturalization in England and the American Colonies." *American Historical Review* 9 (January): 288–303.

Dumbauld, Edward. 1950. *The Declaration of Independence and What It Means Today*. Norman: University of Oklahoma Press.

Friedenwald, Herbert. 1904. *The Declaration of Independence: An Interpretation and an Analysis*. New York: Macmillan.

Humphreys, R. A. 1934. "Lord Shelburne and the Proclamation of 1763." *English Historical Review* 49 (April): 241–264.

Jefferson, Thomas. 1774. *A Summary View of the Rights of British America*. Colonial Williamsburg. www.history.org/almanack/life/politics/sumview.cfm. Accessed July 8, 2017.

Lind, John. 1776. *An Answer to the Declaration of the American Congress*. London: J. Walter, Charing-Cross and T. Sewell.

Papa, Eugene M. Del. 1975. "The Royal Proclamation of 1763: Its Effect upon Virginia Land Companies." *Virginia Magazine of History and Biography* 83 (October): 406–411.

Pincus, Steve. 2016a. "America's Declaration of Independence was Pro-immigrant." Aeon Ideas. https://aeon.co/ideas/america-s-declaration-of-independence-was-pro-immigrant.

Pincus, Steve. 2016b. *The Heart of the Declaration: The Founders' Case for an Activist Government*. New Haven, CT: Yale University Press.

"The Royal Proclamation—October 7, 1763," Avalon Project. http://avalon.law.yale.edu/18th)_century/proc1763.asp.

Totten, Robbie. 2008. "National Security and U.S. Immigration Policy, 1776–1790." *Journal of Interdisciplinary History* 39 (Summer): 37–64.

ENGLISH DECLARATION OF RIGHTS

One of the ironies of the Declaration of Independence is that in declaring colonial independence from Great Britain, it followed, in form and substance, a number of models that were firmly grounded in English history.

One of these documents was the English Bill of Rights, which was adopted in 1689 by the House of Commons and phrased as a declaration. In the document, Parliament invited William and Mary to replace James II, who had attempted to exercise executive prerogatives before fleeing to France. The first line of the Bill refers to itself as "An Act Declaring the Rights and Liberties of the Subject and Settling the Succession of the Crown" (Vile 2015, 44).

Starting somewhat more legalistically than the Declaration of Independence, with two statements beginning with "Whereas," the document had proceeded to list a series of accusations against James II, and how he "did endeavor to subvert and extirpate the Protestant religion and the laws and liberties of this kingdom," each beginning with the word "By" (Vile 2015, 44–45). Most of the accusations come closer to charges that the king had denied rights later articulated in the U.S. Bill of Rights (the first ten amendments to the U.S. Constitution), but some are almost identical to those in the Declaration. Thus, for example, the English Bill of Rights accused James II of "raising and keeping a standing army within this kingdom in time of peace without consent of Parliament, and quartering soldiers contrary to law" (Vile 2015, 45). The document also referred to "the pretended power of dispensing with laws or the execution of laws by regal authority" (Vile 2015, 47) and accused the king of failing to heed petitions for redress and the like.

Whereas the English Bill of Rights turned the executive authority over to another hereditary ruler, the Declaration of Independence left the disposition of the new government to Congress to propose. It settled first on the Articles of Confederation, with no independent executive, and then through a Constitutional Convention on an executive who was chosen by the people rather than passed down through a royal line of hereditary succession.

See also Charges against the King and Others; Declaration (Meaning of Term); Petitions for Redress Ignored (Charge #28); Quartering Troops (Charge #14); Standing Armies (Charge #11)

Further Reading

Barone, Michael. 2007. *Our First Revolution: The Remarkable British Upheaval That Inspired America's Founding Fathers*. New York: Crown Publishers.

Charles, Patrick J. 2008. *Irreconcilable Grievances: The Events That Shaped the Declaration of Independence*. Westminster, MD: Heritage Books.

Schwoerer, Lois G. 1981. *The Declaration of Rights, 1689*. Baltimore: Johns Hopkins University Press.

Vile, John R. 2015. *Founding Documents of America: Documents Decoded*. Santa Barbara, CA; ABC-CLIO.

ENGRAVINGS AND PRINTINGS OF THE DECLARATION OF INDEPENDENCE

In addition to a work of statesmanship, the Declaration of Independence is also a historical artifact. Like the U.S. Constitution, which has the disadvantage of being much longer and thus less suitable for such displays, the Declaration is often displayed as a work of art not only in government buildings but also in private homes and businesses.

John Dunlap, the official printer for the Continental Congress, published the first copy of the Declaration that would appear publicly as a broadside in block print with the name of John Hancock, the convention president, and Dunlap's own, at the bottom. It was reprinted in a number of newspapers, often with some emendations. John Holt, a Manhattan printer, published 500 copies, one of which was to be auctioned on November 11, 2017, for an estimated one-half million to one million dollars (Kahn 2017).

Timothy Matlack is believed to have printed the engrossed copy of the Declaration, currently displayed at the National Archives, which has 56 signatures. They were added on August 2 and the months following. This parchment would have been made of animal skin. Mary Katharine Goddard of Baltimore, Maryland, published the first printed copy of the Declaration with the signers' names in January 1777.

Benjamin Owen Tyler and John Binns published ornamented script copies of the Declaration in 1818 as did William Woodruff in 1819. Woodruff's copy had calligraphic signatures. Whereas the Woodruff copy had an oval picture of George Washington at the top, flanked by Thomas Jefferson and John Adams, the Binns copy featured Washington in the company of John Hancock and Jefferson.

All these commercial endeavors faced competition when then–secretary of state John Quincy Adams commissioned William Stone to print a replica of the Engrossed Declaration. Two hundred copies were printed on vellum in 1823 ("The History"). Peter Force, who later claimed to have discovered the Mecklenburg Declaration of Independence, printed more copies, which were again reprinted in 1942 by lithographer Theodore Ohman. Other copies include a print by Thomas Morrison of Philadelphia, which was copyrighted in 1832 and which contains a bust of George Washington.

Like engravings and prints of paintings by John Trumbull and others of the Declaration, numerous printings of the Declaration have been made for various anniversaries of the Declaration, particularly the centennial and bicentennial. Although many are profusely illustrated with portraits and pictures, many are simply facsimiles of the Matlack Document made on brown parchment paper, sometimes falsely leading people who find them in relatives' belongings to believe that they own a manuscript that is 200 years old.

Original printings, especially within the first 50 years of the Declaration, often fetch impressive prices. Thus, an original Dunlap printing of the Declaration found folded in a picture frame bought at a flea market for $4, fetched $2.42 million at an auction at Sotheby's on June 13, 1991 (Blau 1991). Similarly, a William Stone engraving sold for $477,000 after being purchased in a Nashville, Tennessee, thrift shop in 2006 for $2.48.

Much paper printed at the time of the Declaration contained hemp (the primary component in most rope of the day, which contains significantly less THC than marijuana). The Dutch paper on which Jefferson wrote his original drafts were more likely made from flax or linen rags ("Declaration of Independence Paper").

See also Binns Engraving of the Declaration of Independence; Dunlap Broadside Printing of the Declaration of Independence; Engrossed Declaration of Independence (Matlack); Goddard Printing of the Declaration of Independence; Mecklenburg Declaration of Independence; Signing of the Declaration of Independence; Stone Engraving of the Declaration of Independence

Further Reading

Blau, Eleanor. June 14, 1991. "Declaration of Independence Sells for $2.4 Million." *New York Times*. http://www.nytimes.com/1991/06/14/arts/declaration-of-independence-sells-for-2.4-million.html.

Kahn, Eve M. October 5, 2017. "Newly Discovered Copy of Declaration of Independence Will Be Auctioned." New York Times. https://www.nytimes.com/2017/10/05/arts/design/declaration-of-independence-holt-broadside-auction.html.

Monticello. n.d. "Declaration of Independence Paper." Thomas Jefferson Encyclopedia. Accessed March 27, 2018. https://www.monticello.org/site/jefferson/declaration-independence-paper.

ENGROSSED DECLARATION OF INDEPENDENCE (MATLACK)

The image of the Declaration of Independence that is most familiar to most Americans is the one written in calligraphy, which has been frequently copied and which is on display at the National Archives. Congress voted to engross the Document on July 19, 1776, and delegates began signing it on August 2.

There is a general consensus that this document was prepared by Timothy Matlack (1736–1826), who had been born in Haddonfield, New Jersey, and was a clerk to the Continental Congresses. He was a fervent democrat who was engaged both in liberalizing the Pennsylvania state constitution and in the movement for independence. He was also a brewer whose love of cockfighting and racing, as well as his service in the revolutionary militia, contributed to his expulsion from his Quaker congregation.

One of the anomalies of the Declaration is that whereas some important congressional documents began as handwritten documents and were then printed, the Declaration began its public career in print (quite obviously Thomas Jefferson had an original handwritten draft, which was amended in the course of congressional debates) before being "transmogrified into an artifact" (Starr 2002, 154).

Whereas the title of the original Dunlap Broadside, which was printed on the evening of July 4, consisted of five lines, Matlack's engrossed version had only two. It seems likely that he conflated the lines so as to save room for delegates' signatures at the bottom (Coelho 2013, 60). Because New York had given its approval, Matlack was able to label the document as "The unanimous Declaration of the thirteen united States of America."

The names of the actual signers of the Matlack manuscript were not printed until January 18, 1777. At that time, they were published in Baltimore by Mary Katharine Goddard.

In 1821, then–secretary of state John Quincy Adams commissioned William J. Stone to do a copper engraving of the document, which has been the source of subsequent printings.

The Museum of Fine Arts in Boston displays a portrait of Matlack that was painted by Charles Willson Peale and that includes a picture of the seal of Pennsylvania and the state constitution that he helped to draft as well as a Bible and some lawbooks. Peale apparently painted at least two other pictures of Matlack, one in about 1779, and the other, which portrays Matlack with a beard, that is displayed at the Independence National Historical Park, in 1826 (Sellers and Peale 1952, 140). Rembrandt Peale painted another image of Matlack, which pictures him writing at a desk.

See also Adams, John Quincy, Independence Day Address (July 4, 1821); Dunlap Broadside Printing of the Declaration of Independence; Goddard Printing of the Declaration of Independence; Signing of the Declaration of Independence; Stone Engraving of the Declaration of Independence

Further Reading

Coelho, Chris. 2013. *Timothy Matlack: Scribe of the Declaration of Independence*. Jefferson, NC: McFarland.

Sellers, Charles Coleman, and Charles Willson Peale. 1952. "Portraits and Miniatures by Charles Willson Peale." *Transactions of the American Philosophical Society* 42:1–369.

Starr, Thomas. 2002. "Separated at Birth: Text and Context of the Declaration of Independence." *Proceedings of the American Antiquarian Society*. http://www.americanantiquarian.org/proceedings/44539508.pdf.

EQUALITY

One of the most quoted phrases from the Preamble of the Declaration of Independence proclaims that "all men are created equal." It further ties this equality to the fact that "they are endowed by their Creator with certain inalienable rights." Previously, colonists had often phrased their claims as claims for their rights as Englishmen, but in severing ties to Britain and in appealing to foreign audiences, they now stated their rights more universally (Brown 2017, 2).

The same paragraph of the Declaration that speaks of human equality also speaks of another kind of equality, namely that of peoples, who are entitled to "the equal station to which the laws of nature and of nature's god entitle them." The concluding paragraph further stresses that that the former colonies are now "free & independent states," with "full power to levy war, conclude peace, contract alliances, establish commerce," and the like. In social contract theory, which appears to have influenced the Declaration, people in a prepolitical state of nature, like independent nations that live independently in a world with no common sovereign, were regarded as having equal rights to secure their existence, their possessions, and their happiness. David S. Lovejoy (1959) has demonstrated how differing jurisdictions of admiralty courts in Britain and American highlighted colonial perceptions that they had been denied their equal rights as Englishmen.

An unnamed critic, adding notes under the title of "An Englishman" to a printing of the Declaration in *The Scots Magazine* of Edinburg in August 1776 questioned the connection between a belief in equality and the proclamation of independence. He observed, "All men, it is true, are equally created: but what is this to the purpose? It certainly is no reason why the Americans should turn rebels, because the people of G. Britain are their fellow-creatures, i.e. are created as well as themselves. It may be a reason why they should not rebel, but most indisputably is none why they should" (1776).

The statement declaring all men to be created equal may be at least an indirect attack on hereditary succession, which Thomas Paine so successfully criticized in *Common Sense,* where he had observed that there was no justification for the division of humans into "Kings" and "Subjects" (See Adams 2001, 169). This practice, which passed down the British throne on the basis of birth, suggested that some ("blue bloods") were born entitled to more privileges than others. Thomas Jefferson, who had opposed the practice of primogeniture in Virginia (the practice of giving firstborn sons all or a larger share of inheritances), thus noted in a famous letter to Roger Weightman of June 24, 1826, that the Declaration had highlighted "the rights of man." He further observed "that the mass of mankind has not been born with saddles on their backs, nor a favored few booted and spurred, ready to ride them legitimately, by the grace of god." Notably, in an effort to further republicanism, the U.S. Constitution later prohibited titles of nobility.

Danielle Allen rightly emphasizes that there is a difference between being "equal" and being the "same." The Declaration does not require individuals (indeed, how could it?) to be equally talented, handsome, wealthy, or otherwise advantaged to share in the right to make their own decisions any more than nations must be equal in size or power to govern their own affairs. Similarly, the Declaration does not guarantee that individuals will be equally happy but that they have an equal right to pursue such happiness.

Allen further ties human equality to an equality "in sharing a status as rights-bearing creatures, a status that flows from the fact that we are also equal in being political creatures, a status that requires for its realization that we all have equal access to the tools of government" (2014, 184). Republican governments, like those that the former colonies were establishing, did not recognize hereditary privilege and titles of nobility, which were thought to assume the control of some families over others. The Declaration did not describe George III as a monarch by divine right but subjected all governments to the test of consent based on whether they were promoting human safety and happiness.

Although women, Native Americans, and African Americans were not accorded equal status in 1776, Abraham Lincoln was among those who regarded the Declaration's statement of equality as aspirational. Lincoln used syllogistic reasoning, much like that in the Declaration, to show that once the nation accepted the fact that African Americans were men, they were therefore compelled to recognize their rights. M. E. Bradford (1979, 29–58) criticizes Lincoln for what Bradford believes was a too-abstract view of equality, and yet Lincoln frequently indicated that he did not believe that recognition of equal rights would necessarily lead to equal social status.

Interestingly, Thomas Jefferson's original draft of the Declaration of Independence accused the king of waging "cruel war against human nature itself, violating it's most sacred rights of life & liberty in the persons of a distinct people, who never offended him, capitating and carrying them into slavery in another hemisphere" thus keeping "open a market where MEN should be bought & sold." Even though he was a slaveholder, he thus recognized the humanity of the slaves.

By contrast, in the *Dred Scott* decision of 1857, which declared that Africans were not and could never be citizens, Chief Justice Roger Taney read the Declaration to say that "all white men are created equal." Similarly, leaders of the Confederate States of America later critiqued the U.S. government for being based on the principle of human equality rather than on what they believed to be clear racial differences.

In 1868, the requisite number of states ratified the Fourteenth Amendment. It prohibited states from denying to any person the "equal protection of the laws." This liberty would in time extend to women, Native Americans, and member of the LBGTQ community. Pauline Maier has argued that we have found it "easier to reconcile ourselves to change" by conceiving of it as working out a pre-established plan" (1999, 888). She notes, however, that "by attributing to Jefferson and the Founders a knowledge of the future that they did not claim, we underplay the astounding achievements of those later generations who saved the Declaration of Independence from oblivion, made it into a quasi-legal bill of rights to compensate for the failure of the eighteenth century to supply a more appropriate document, and then discovered a way to read its principles into the Constitution" (1998, 888).

Legal equality rarely leads to complete economic equality. In arguing In Federalist No. 10 on behalf of a representative government over a large land area like that of the United States, James Madison thus observed that:

> The most common and durable source of factions has been the various and unequal distribution of property. Those who hold and those who are without property have ever formed distinct interests in society. Those who are creditors, and those who are debtors fall under a like discrimination. A landed interest, a manufacturing interest, a mercantile interest, a moneyed interest, with many lesser interests, grow up of necessity in civilized nations, and divide them into different classes, actuated by different sentiments and views. ([1787–1788] 1961, 79)

Madison went on to say that "The regulation of these various and interfering interests forms the principal task of modern legislation and involves the spirit of party and faction in the necessary and ordinary operations of government" ([1787–1788] 1961, 79).

See also *Common Sense* (Paine); Human Nature and the Declaration of Independence; Jefferson, Thomas; Locke, John; People; Slavery

Further Reading

Adams, William Paul. 2001. *The First American Constitutions: Republican Ideology and the Making of the State Constitutions in the Revolutionary Era*. Lanham, MD: Rowman and Littlefield.

Allen, Danielle. 2014. *Our Declaration: A Reading of the Declaration of Independence in Defense of Equality*. New York: W. W. Norton.

Bradford, M. E. 1979. *A Better Guide Than Reason: Studies in the American Revolution*. La Salle, IL: Sherwood Sugden.

Brown, Richard D. 2017. *Self-Evident Truths: Contesting Equal Rights from the Revolution to the Civil War*. New Haven, CT: Yale University Press.

Diamond, Martin. 1976. "The American Idea of Equality: The View from the Founding." *Review of Politics* 38 (July): 313–331.

"An Englishman." 1776. Notes accompanying printing of the Declaration of Independence. *The Scots Magazine* 38 (August): 433–434.

Hamilton, Alexander, James Madison, and John Jay. (1787–1788) 1961. *The Federalist Papers*. New York: New American Library.

Huston, James L. *The American and British Debate over Equality, 1776–1920*. Baton Rouge: Louisiana State University Press.

Jefferson, Thomas. 1826. "Thomas Jefferson to Roger Weightman." Library of Congress. https://www.loc.gov/exhibits/jefferson/214.html.

Lovejoy, David S. 1959. "Rights Imply Equality: The Case against Admiralty Jurisdiction in America, 1764–1776." *William and Mary Quarterly* 16 (October): 459–484.

Maier, Pauline. 1999. "The Strange History of 'All Men Are Created Equal.'" *Washington and Lee Law Review* 56 (Summer): 873–888.

ERECTED A MULTITUDE OF NEW OFFICES (CHARGE #10)

The 10th accusation that the Declaration of Independence lodged against the king was that "he has erected a multitude of new offices & sent hither swarms of officers to harass our people, and eat out their substance."

In hyperbolic form, this is a charge that may well be lodged against almost any government. This is among the most emotionally evocative of the charges, in part because it sounds much like a biblical plague of locusts, which were known for eating everything in their paths.

Most taxes must be enforced. With colonial opposition to any taxes imposed by Parliament ("no taxation without representation"), the Townshend Acts had authorized the king to appoint customs commissioners, who, in turn, had power to appoint subordinates (Friedenwald 1904, 236). Since they were paid from revenues collected, they had a special incentive to do their jobs.

On a related note, in 1764, Britain had authorized the admiral in charge of the North American coast to seize any illegal trade, much of which had previously been unregulated. This trade, though illegal, had been one of the few sources of colonial currency. Admiralty courts had been established as early as 1764 (one in Halifax) for this purpose (Friedenwald 1904, 237).

In its Declaration and Resolves of 1774, the First Continental Congress had accused Britain of having "established a board of commissioners with unconstitutional powers." It further accused it of having "extended the jurisdiction of courts of admiralty, not only for collecting the said duties, but for the trial of causes merely arising within the body of a county" ("Declaration and Resolves," 75).

In responding to this, John Lind observed that the king had not demanded that the colonies pay the salaries of these officials. He further claimed that Britain had set up admiralty courts so that Americans would not have to go to Britain for redress (1776, 49).

See also Declaration and Resolves of the First Continental Congress (1774); Taxes (Charge #17)

Further Reading

"Declaration and Resolves of the First Continental Congress." 2015. In *Founding Document of America: Documents Decoded*, edited by John R. Vile, 75–80. Santa Barbara, CA: ABC-CLIO.

Friedenwald, Herbert. 1904. *The Declaration of Independence: An Interpretation and an Analysis*. New York: Macmillan.

Lind, John. 1776. *An Answer to the Declaration of the American Congress*. London: J. Walter, Charing-Cross and T. Sewell.

EVOLUTION OF THE TEXT

One can view the evolution of the Declaration either in terms of its manuscript predecessors and philosophical influences, of which there are many, or in terms of how the document came to be composed.

Richard Henry Lee of Virginia had introduced the resolution for independence in Congress on June 7, 1776. Congress subsequently delayed debates until July 1, but appointed a committee of five men, consisting of Thomas Jefferson, John Adams, Benjamin Franklin, Roger Sherman, and Robert Livingston, to draft a justification for such an action. Largely because of Jefferson's reputation as a writer, the committee appears to have agreed that he should draw up the first draft of the document; Jefferson specifically contested Adams's suggestion that a subcommittee had made this recommendation (Boyd 1999, 22).

The word "Declaration" that was used to classify the document was generally reserved for fairly formal governmental pronouncements. In terms of purpose, the document was not designed to announce the decision, which had been formally done on July 2, but to explain these reasons to both internal and external audiences. There were numerous previous lists of grievances, including a list that Jefferson had drawn up to preface the Virginia Declaration of Rights, numerous local petitions for independence, and prior congressional works, many of which drew from Whig political thought, Scottish Common Sense philosophy, and other sources.

The writing appears to have proceeded in three major stages. Jefferson wrote the rough draft, which may well have gone through a number of drafts before he presented it to the committee. At least two committee members (John Adams and Benjamin Franklin) made some emendations during the second stage. This amended draft was then presented to the Continental Congress during the third phase. Congress made a substantial number of changes, including adding references to God, deleting an explicit reference to Parliament and another to Scottish mercenaries, and eliminating a long passage accusing the king of having encouraged both the slave trade and revolts by slaves against their masters.

The best work on the subject observes that "both numerically and quantitatively, Congress eliminated more and added fewer words to the Declaration than any or all of the Committee of Five" (Boyd 1999, 36). It further notes that "in the first stage of the progress of the Declaration, fifteen alterations were made; in the second thirty-two; and in the third, thirty-nine" (Boyd 1999, 36). Although Jefferson found it difficult to sit through congressional debates and thought that his own manuscript was better, there is general agreement among scholars that the changes that resulted from congressional debate made the document more acceptable throughout the former colonies.

The Declaration was printed on the evening of July 4 and possibly the morning of the fifth. After New York added its affirmation to make voting on the Declaration unanimous, it was then ordered to be engrossed on July 19, and it was signed on August 2 and days following.

The first printing of the Declaration with the names of the signers took place on January 18, 1777.

See also Committee Responsible for Writing the Declaration of Independence; Declaration (Meaning of Term); Dunlap Broadside Printing of the Declaration of Independence; Engrossed Declaration of Independence (Matlack); Jefferson, Thomas

Further Reading

Boyd, Julian P. 1999. *The Declaration of Independence: The Evolution of the Text*. Rev. ed. Washington, DC: Library of Congress in association with the Thomas Jefferson Memorial Foundation.

Jefferson, Thomas. 1950. *The Papers of Thomas Jefferson*. Edited by Julian P. Boyd. *Vol 1: 1760–1776*. Princeton. NJ: Princeton University Press.

F

FACTS

The Declaration of Independence prefaces its numerous indictments against the king as a set of "facts." Although today this term almost always refers to matters that are true and well established, the Declaration appears to be using them in the legal sense of occurrences or actions. Although he cannot be positive that the authors of the Declaration had this particular meaning in mind, Stephen E. Lucas further ties the term to "an evil deed or crime," as in "accessories after the fact [crime]" or in sentencing an individual "for the 'fact' of horse stealing" (1990).

The law continues to distinguish between facts, which are usually committed to the judgment of jurors (as in the audience reading the Declaration) and issues of law, which may remain for judges. Similarly, jurists continue to distinguish, as in civil rights cases, between de facto (in practice or fact) and de jure (mandated by law).

Dispute continues to swirl about the objectivity or trustworthiness of many of the specific charges that Thomas Jefferson leveled against the king (this part of the Declaration resembles a legal brief or indictment). However, the central "fact," or truth, that the Declaration sought to establish was that the king's actions constituted a despotic pattern that evidenced a desire to take away colonial liberties.

Congress undoubtedly thought that it contributed to its credibility when it deleted "for the truth of which we pledge a faith yet unsullied by falsehood" immediately after saying "let facts be submitted to a candid world" (Hawke 1964, 189).

See also Charges against the King and Others

Further Reading

Hawke, David Freeman. 1964. *A Transaction of Free Men: The Birth and Course of the Declaration of Independence*. New York: Charles Scribner's Sons.

Lucas, Stephen E. Spring, 1990. "The Stylistic Artistry of the Declaration of Independence." *Prologue: Quarterly of the National Archives and Records Administration*. https://www.archives.gov/founding-docs/stylistic-artistry-of-the-declaration.

FAMILY

One implication of arguing that the Declaration of Independence was based largely on liberal Lockean theory is that this philosophy is often interpreted as being highly individualistic. Although the Declaration clearly refers to the rights of individuals, it also refers to individual peoples, most notably Americans, British, Native Americans, and African Americans.

Throughout U.S. history, the principle of equality that the Declaration articulated has been applied to an increasing number of groups. It served as a basis for equalizing the rights of African Americans, of women, of members of the LGBTQ community, and others. Moreover, Norma Basch has observed that "The words 'brethren,' 'consanguinity,' and 'kindred' in the Declaration not only exemplify the easy interchangeability of family and state in Enlightenment thinking but also mark their transfiguration. Severing the bonds of empire entailed the radical separation of two peoples who were as intimately related as the members of one family" (2003, 36–37).

James Stoner (2005), however, has questioned the degree to which the Declaration adequately accounts for the origin of society and the degree to which it is able to explain hierarchical structures that may remain within societies. Stoner points out that classical political philosophers built their philosophy of government from the ground up, beginning with the family, and then describing the transition to the village and polis (city-state). It the polis were, as Plato asserted, "man writ large," then it would stand to reason that the polity might mirror relationships in families where fathers were generally regarded as rulers and children enter without their consent (although most such philosophers did not advocate kingship, which would be the nearest parallel).

Even if one accepted the more egalitarian approach that husbands and wives were equal, they would still exercise authority over their children in a manner that one would not expect a government to rule over its people. As Stoner expresses it, according to the Founding Fathers, "the patriarchal state had to go because it makes children of real fathers, refusing to allow them the manly responsibility of governing themselves and those with whose care they are charged" (2005).

Stoner believes that the way out of this dilemma is to interpret the Declaration in light of common law principles. By this understanding, although "the principles of the Declaration" are "constitutive of our fundamental law," they are inadequate "to every exigency in our personal, our religious, or even our political lives" (2005). David Azerrad thus points out that the Declaration "doesn't speak of friendship, family, and music, for example, not because it denies their importance, but because they fall outside its properly defined political purpose" (2013).

Even in the political realm, children are not accorded equal political rights, and governments generally interfere relatively reluctantly in matters of family relations. Moreover, the Declaration nowhere asserts the equality of children and parents, specifically referring to the rights of "men," which is generally interpreted to include women but is limited to adults.

See also Abolitionism; Consent of the Governed; Equality; Locke, John; People; Remember the Ladies

Further Reading

Azerrad, David. July 3, 2017. "The Declaration of Independence and the American Creed." The Heritage Foundation. https://www.heritage.org/political-process/commentary/the-declaration-independence-and-the-american-creed.

Basch, Norma. 2003. "Declarations of Independence: Women and Divorce in the Early Republic." *Women and the U.S. Constitution*, 3rd ed., edited by Sibyl A. Schwarzenbach and Patricia Smith, 34–44. New York: Columbia University Press.
Stoner, James. 2005. "Is There a Political Philosophy in the Declaration of Independence?" https://home.isi.org/there-political-philosophy-declaration-independence.

FAULKNER, BARRY (PAINTING)

One of the most striking depictions of the origins of the Declaration of Independence is a large 14-by-37.5-foot mural in the National Archives. It complements a second mural of a similar size on the Constitution. Both documents, as well as the Bill of Rights, are currently housed between the two murals. Although these documents were not moved until 1952, the murals were installed by October 15, 1936, and the public was able to view them that November (Gorelic 2014, 53).

The murals were actually commissioned prior to the documents being moved from the Library of Congress to the Archives. The artist was Barry Faulkner (1881–1966) a New Hampshire–born artist who had already established a reputation as a muralist. Faulkner had mapped out a number of sketches, some of which were rejected, prior to getting approval.

Whereas most other depictions of both events are indoor scenes, this one is set outdoors on a series of steps amid Greek columns designed to represent the "pillars of democracy." Relying in part on advice from historian J. Franklin Jameson, who was then employed by the Library of Congress, the mural of the Declaration portrays 33 men. Whereas George Washington is clearly in the middle of the painting on the Constitution (with James Madison holding a copy of the document on his left), the Declaration mural does not have as clear a focus. To the right is a depiction of the five men on the committee who wrote the Declaration, with Thomas Jefferson holding the document, which he is presenting to John Hancock, the congressional president, who is flanked by a number of other congressmen. Richard Henry Lee and Benjamin Harrison stand under a

Photograph of the mural *The Declaration of Independence*, by Barry Faulkner, in the National Archives. The mural represents Thomas Jefferson and his committee, Benjamin Franklin, John Adams, Roger Sherman, and Robert R. Livingston, submitting the Declaration of Independence to the presiding officer, John Hancock. (National Archives)

group of flags on the right of the picture, where prominent delegates to the left of Hancock's group include Samuel Hopkins, Charles Carroll, and Robert Morris. Faulkner used differing colors to highlight "the contrasting puritan and cavalier [northern and southern] strains" (Gorelic 2014, 51). He also made a point of including at least one delegate from each colony.

Dark clouds in the background, some in the shape of Abraham Lincoln's face on its side, are designed to associate the Declaration with war. The more placid sky in the other painting is designed to associate the Constitution with peace.

Faulkner assembled the murals in a studio above New York's Grand Central Station, then rolled them up on wooden drums before they were shipped to the Archives, installed, and varnished. In part due to crumbling plaster, the work had to be restored from 1999 to 2002, during which time the Archives were closed.

See also Preserving the Declaration of Independence; U.S. Constitution and the Declaration of Independence

Further Reading

Gorelic, Lester S. 2014: "Depicting the Creation of a Nation: The Story behind the Murals about Our Founding Documents. *Prologue* (Spring): 44–54.

New England Historical Society. 2016. "The Faulkner Murals Come to Life after Three Long Years." October 5, 2016. http://www.newenglandhistoricalsociety.com/faulkner-murals-come-life-three-long-years/.

FEDERALISM

One of the enduring issues of American politics involves the respective relationship between the United States of America as a collective entity and the individual fifty states.

In the years leading up to the Declaration of Independence, states claimed to be joined by their common loyalty to the king, but this loyalty arguably tied themselves as much to the English people in Great Britain as it did to one another. The Stamp Act Congress and the First and Second Continental Congresses, in turn, resulted in increasingly closer ties among the 13 colonies as they found themselves in opposition to policies of the mother country. The failure of the colonists on the periphery and the English at the center of an empire to come to a mutual understanding of their relationship ultimately led to the Declaration of Independence (Greene 2000).

When it came time to declare independence from the mother country, it was not always clear whether the states were doing so collectively or on an individual basis. Whereas the original John Dunlap printing of the Declaration of Independence, which Congress commissioned on July 4, 1776, thus capitalized "UNITED STATES OF AMERICA," Timothy Matlack's embossed printing was titled *The Unanimous Declaration of the Thirteen United States of America*, with the words "States of America" written in larger print but the word "United" not so (compare facsimiles in Malone 1954 at 78 and 87) .

In examining the evidence within the Declaration, Donald S. Lutz observed that "from the very beginning, the document begs the important question of whether this is an agreement among the states, and thus among thirteen separate peoples, or whether it is an agreement creating one united people on a national scale" (1989, 50). He observes that while the document initially talks about "one people" dissolving their political bonds "with another," it ends by affirming that "these united colonies are and of right ought to be free and independent states" (1989, 50).

Although delegates signed the embossed Declaration in groups by states, the original Matlack edition did not list the states by name.

The United States has never adopted a unitary government but has always had a system whereby individuals were typically citizens both of the nation and of an individual state. There is general consensus that the first form of government proposed by the Second Continental Congress, but not ratified until almost the end of the Revolutionary War, created a confederal government, in which primary sovereignty in almost all matters not directly related to international affairs rested in the individual states. When that government proved too weak, delegates met at the Constitutional Convention of 1787 to create a federal government that more equally divided power between the national government and the states. During the Civil War, Southern states attempted to revive the confederal form, while the adoption of the Fourteenth Amendment after the War (1868) gave Congress greater power to enforce individual rights against state abuses.

The primary purpose of the Declaration of Independence was not, of course, to outline the specific form that continental government would take, but it reflected the ambiguity that very much remains part of the systems of government that replaced British rule.

See also Dunlap Broadside Printing of the Declaration of Independence; Engrossed Declaration of Independence (Matlack); People

Further Reading

Greene, Jack P. 2000. "The American Revolution." *American Historical Review* 105 (February): 93–102.

Lutz, Donald S. 1989. "The Declaration of Independence as Part of an American National Compact." *Publius* 19 (Winter): 41–58.

Malone, Dumas. 1954. *The Story of the Declaration of Independence*. New York: Oxford University Press.

Van Tyne. Claude H. 1907. "Sovereignty in the American Revolution: An Historical Study." *American Historical Review* 12 (April): 529–545.

FORBIDDING GOVERNORS FROM PASSING LAWS (CHARGE #2)

The Declaration of Independence's second accusation against George III was that "he has forbidden his governors to pass laws of immediate & pressing importance unless suspended in their operation till his assent should be obtained; and when so suspended, he has utterly neglected to attend to them." This charge is similar to the first, which accused him of having "refused his assent to laws the most wholesome and necessary for the public good." This charge was also similar to one that Thomas Jefferson had articulated in his *Summary View of the Rights of British America*.

B. J. Lossing tied this accusation to the king's disallowance of a New York measure to placate the Six Nations Indian Tribes and to a similar disallowance of a Massachusetts law taxing customs commissioners the same as other citizens (1848, 271–271). Professor Herbert Friedenwald cited a number of examples where Britain had utilized this policy. In 1759, it had instructed the New York governor to suspend laws that empowered justices of the peace with power to try minor cases unless they contained a suspending clause (1904, 219). In 1769, it had attached a similar restriction to colonial lotteries in New York and in 1776 in Virginia (1904, 220). Focusing on the second part of the accusation, Friedenwald pointed to four laws that Virginia adopted in 1770 that took almost three years for the Lords Commissioners for Trade and Plantations to consider and one of which they set aside until receiving further information. Friedenwald further tied this charge to what he described as "the opposition created by the increase, after 1770, in the number of royal instructions issued to the governors" (1904, 221).

In seeking to refute this charge, or set of charges, John Lind observed that the power of allowing the king to examine extraordinary laws before governors consented to them was not novel but was begun by Queen Anne in 1708, thus undermining Jefferson's argument that George III was acting as a despot. Lind observed that the rules applied specifically to laws "affecting the trade and shipping of Great Britain; the prerogatives of the Crown, and the property of the subjects of the empire in general" (1776, 17). Lind thus portrayed such restrictions as a way of protecting the empire as a whole against acts by single parties. Moreover, Lind observed that when Massachusetts appealed to the House of Commons in 1733 against the king, Parliament considered its complaint to be trivial. Moreover, again, in 1740, the House of Commons had insisted that the king include a clause suspending certain laws until he had given his consent (1776, 20–21), which the king had implemented by a royal instruction in March 1752 (Friedenwald 1904, 219).

After noting that the British continued such policies in other colonies after the American Revolution, Sydney George Fisher concluded that disallowances and suspensions worked "more smoothly in Canada and Australia." He believed this was "because the people have been of a milder temper than ourselves and so scattered and insignificant in numbers compared with England, that complete control of them was comparatively easy in spite of their remote situation" (1907, 268).

See also *A Summary View of the Rights of British America* (Jefferson)

Further Reading

Fisher, Sydney George. 1907. "The Twenty-Eight Charges against the King in the Declaration of Independence." *Pennsylvania Magazine of History and Biography* 31:247–303.

Friedenwald, Herbert. 1904. *The Declaration of Independence: An Interpretation and an Analysis*. New York: Macmillan.

Greene, Evarts B. 1917. "American Opinion on the Imperial Review of Provincial Legislation, 1776–1787." *American Historical Review* 23 (October): 104–107.

Hutchinson, Thomas. 1776. "1776: Hutchinson, Strictures upon the Declaration of Independence." Online Library of Liberty. http://oll.libertyfund.org/pages/1776-hutchinson-strictures-upon-the-decvlaration-of-independence.

Jefferson, Thomas. 1774. *A Summary View of the Rights of British America.* Williamsburg, VA: Clementina Rind. Reprint, with an introduction by Paul Leicester Ford. New York: Historical Printing Club, 1892.

Lind, John. 1776 *An Answer to the Declaration of the American Congress.* London: J. Walter, Charing-Cross and T. Sewell.

Lossing, B. J. 1848. *Biographical Sketches of the Signers of the Declaration of American Independence; The Declaration Historical Considered; and a Sketch of the Leading Events Connected with the Adoption of the Articles of Confederation and of the Federal Constitution.* New York: George F. Cooledge Brothers.

FRANKLIN, BENJAMIN

Benjamin Franklin (1706–1790) was one of the most prominent individuals who served in the Second Continental Congress and who voted for independence. At the age of 70, he was its oldest member. Born in Boston in 1706, Franklin had left Boston for Philadelphia where he established himself as an author and printer. Largely self-educated, Franklin detailed his rise in his *Autobiography*, which remains widely read today.

Benjamin Franklin achieved worldwide renown as a writer, scientist, statesman, and diplomat. He was a member of the Committee to draft the Declaration of Independence and sought to console Thomas Jefferson as the Congress made changes to Jefferson's original draft. (National Gallery of Art/Gift of Adele Lewisohn Lehman)

Franklin spent the years immediately before the Continental Congress where he represented a number of colonies and simultaneously served as deputy postmaster for the colonies. In 1754, Franklin had proposed the Albany Plan of Union, which he partly patterned on the earlier New England Confederation, but it had been rejected (Matthews 1913; Olson 1960). Franklin also sought to convert Pennsylvania from a proprietary to a royal colony.

Franklin enjoyed his role representing American interests in Britain (the house where he stayed in London is open to the public) but was caught in the crosswinds after he took responsibility for leaking private papers from Governor Thomas Hutchinson to British authorities that cast doubt on the governor's good faith after the British received word of the Boston Tea Party. After Franklin was publicly humiliated before Parliament and stripped of his postmaster position (Penegar 2011), he returned to Philadelphia.

Although delegates were initially unsure where he stood, he soon revealed that he supported independence, and Congress appointed him to committees to check on American forces under George Washington and to assess the situation in Canada. Franklin had been influential in helping Thomas Paine, the author of the provocative *Common Sense*, to immigrate to America from Britain. After Richard Henry Lee submitted resolutions for independence on June 7, 1776, Franklin was appointed, along with Thomas Jefferson, John Adams, Roger Sherman, and Robert Livingston, to the committee to draft the Declaration of Independence. Franklin and Adams made some emendations before Jefferson introduced the document in Congress.

During the debates, Franklin consoled the thin-skinned Jefferson regarding the changes that the Congress was making by telling him the story about another man named Thompson whose suggestions were subject to group correction. After Thompson accepted these suggestions, a sign that he had contemplated saying "John Thompson, hatter, makes and sells hats for ready money" and a picture of a hat was pared to "John Thompson" and the picture of the hat (Isaacson 2003, 313).

Franklin voted for independence and went on to serve as a diplomat to France where, as in England, he was exceedingly popular and where he helped secure finances for the Revolution (one of the goals of adopting a formal declaration of independence). He helped negotiate the Treaty of Paris that ended the Revolutionary War and returned to Philadelphia, where he was elected as president of Pennsylvania and as a delegate to the Constitutional Convention of 1787, where again he was the oldest delegate.

As he had during the debates in the Second Continental Congress, Franklin sought to play the role of mediator at the Convention, and he signed the document. After observing the sun painted on the back of the president's chair, Franklin expressed his confidence that it was rising on a new and better day for America.

One of the saddest consequences of the Revolution was that it resulted in estranging Franklin from his son, William, who was the Loyalist governor of New Jersey. Franklin never subsequently reconciled with him.

See also Committee Responsible for Writing the Declaration of Independence; *Common Sense* (Paine); Resolutions Introduced by Richard Henry Lee (June 7, 1776)

Further Reading

Greene, Jack P. 1976. "The Alienation of Benjamin Franklin—British American." *Journal of the Royal Society of Arts* 124 (January): 52–73.

Isaacson, Walter. 2003. *Benjamin Franklin: An American Life*. New York: Simon and Schuster.

Matthews, L. L. 1914. "Benjamin Franklin's Plans for a Colonial Union, 1750–1775." *American Political Science Review* 8 (August): 393–412.

Olson, Alison Gilbert. 1960. "The British Government and Colonial Union, 1754." *William and Mary Quarterly*, 3rd ser. 17 (January): 22–34.

Penegar, Kenneth Lawing. 2011. *The Political Trial of Benjamin Franklin: A Prelude to the American Revolution*. New York: Algora Publishing.
Wood, Gordon S. 2004. *The Americanization of Benjamin Franklin*. New York: Penguin Press.

FRIENDS AND ENEMIES

After citing the way that English citizens had rejected American petitions, the penultimate paragraph of the Declaration of Independence proclaimed that Americans would "acquiesce in the necessity which denounces our separation and hold them [the English people], as we hold the rest of mankind, enemies in war, in peace friends."

Rhetorically, this phrase employs the form of a chiasmus. That is, rather than saying "enemies in war, friends in peace," the document inverts the words "friends" and "peace" as to "slow the text" forcing listeners "to concentrate on the message" (Memmott 2015).

The language of friends and enemies was originally part of a large passage that Congress excised. It had stated that "we might have been a free & a great people together; but a communication of grandeur and freedom, it seems, is below their dignity. Be it so since they will have it. The road to happiness and glory is open to us too; we will climb it apart from them." It is possible that members of Congress thought that the references to "grandeur" and "glory" were more likely to be associated with individuals seeking to establish an empire than for a "free people."

This language of friendship and enmity is the language of both personal and national relations. It serves as a reminder that the Declaration of Independence might well be considered to be the equivalent of a declaration of war. The language also points back to the second paragraph of the Declaration, with its likeness to a Lockean state of nature, where, in the absence of a law that is established, settled, and known, an impartial judge to judge between individuals, or an impartial executive, one-time friends may become enemies, and enemies may one day become friends.

In contrast to Thomas Hobbes, who described individuals within the state of nature, like nations in the international realm, as in a constant state of war, the Declaration does not assume that nations that are not bound together by common ties must necessarily be enemies. In light of the war atrocities that it has listed, however, it would be difficult to imagine that reconciliation would come about other than by a military victory by one or the other side.

Although the Declaration does not elaborate on the matter, one might even assume that once the political bands connecting England and the colonies have been dissolved, they might still be expected to live in relative peace with one another after the war ended. Such peace would rest on shared history, kinship, and similarity of domestic forms of government. Although the respective citizens of the two nations might no longer consider themselves "brethren," as they were referred to earlier in the document, they might still be "friends" (Mahoney 1987, 61). In point of fact, they remain close allies.

See also International Law; Locke, John; Style of the Declaration of Independence

Further Reading

Mahoney, Dennis J. 1987. "The Declaration of Independence as a Constitutional Document." In *The Framing and Ratification of the Constitution*, edited by Leonard W. Levy and Dennis J. Mahoney, 54–68. New York: Macmillan.

Masters, Roger D. 1967. "The Lockean Tradition in American Foreign Policy." *Journal of International Affairs* 21:253–277.

Memmott, Mark. July 4, 2015. "Just a Few Important Words about the Declaration of Independence." NPR. http://www.npr.org/sections/thetwo-way/2015/07/04/419243874/just-a-few-important-words-about-the-declaration-of-independence.

G

GEORGE III, PROCLAMATION OF REBELLION (AUGUST 23, 1775)

George III had refused to accept the Olive Branch Petition from the colonies because he thought that the Declaratory Act had settled the authority of Parliament that the colonists were asking him to question. He also issued a Proclamation of Rebellion on August 23, 1775. This proclamation did much to weaken the hands of moderates within the colonies who still thought that reconciliation with Britain was possible even after fighting had broken out between Americans and the British.

George III believed that his "subjects" had been "misled by dangerous and ill designing men," and that they had forgotten "the allegiance which they owe to the power that has protected and supported them." Pointing to "various disorderly acts committed in disturbance of the publick peace," he accused them of being in "open and avowed rebellion." He therefore called upon all civil and military officials to help "suppress such rebellion, and to bring the traitors to justice" so that they could be punished.

The typical punishment for treason against the realm was death.

See also Olive Branch Petition; Treason

Further Reading

Britannia Historical Documents. n.d. "Proclamation of Rebellion." August 23, 1775. http://www.britannia.com/history/docs/procreb.html.

"Continental Congress Responds to King George III's Proclamation of Rebellion, December 6, 1775." Library of Congress, Accessed March 27, 2018. https://www.loc.gov/teachers/classroommaterials/presentationsandactivities/presentations/timeline/amrev/shots/responds.html.

Maier, Pauline. 1997. *American Scripture: Making the Declaration of Independence*. New York: Knopf.

GEORGE III, SPEECH TO PARLIAMENT (OCTOBER 27, 1775)

The period between fighting between American and British troops on April 19, 1775, and the American adoption of the Declaration of Independence on July 4, 1776, was quite consequential. At least until the publication of Thomas Paine's *Common Sense* in January 1776, most of the colonists continued to profess loyalty to the king, to whom they looked for redress against what they considered to be illegal parliamentary taxation.

George III (1738–1820), king of Great Britain and Ireland. Although he appears to have been loved by many of his British subjects, the 13 colonies considered his actions toward them to be tyrannical. The Declaration of Independence levied most of its charges directly against him. (The New York Public Library)

One of the events that led to increased disillusionment with the king was the speech that he delivered to both houses of the British Parliament on Friday, October 27, 1775 (George III, His Majesty's Most Gracious Speech). This speech made it clear that he was in accord with the punitive measures that Parliament had taken in response to the Boston Tea Party and other signs of colonial dissatisfaction, and that he was unwilling to accept the theory that he had a right to withstand Parliament on behalf of colonial grievances.

Although the speech referred a number of times to "my people in America," he believed that their leaders were openly avowing "their revolt, hostility and rebellion," as manifested by their action in raising troops. Moreover, the king viewed prior actions of the Continental Congress as part of a "desperate conspiracy." As the king viewed such documents, "They meant only to amuse by expressions of attachment to the Parent State, and the strongest protestations of loyalty to me whilst they were preparing for a general revolt." Claiming that the British had attempted "rather to reclaim than to subdue," and that they had adopted mild measures designed to prevent "the effusion of the blood of my subjects; and the calamities which are inseparable from a state of war," he charged that America's revolutionary leaders sought to establish "an independent empire."

In his *Summary of the Rights of British Americans*, Thomas Jefferson had argued that the colonists had settled America through their own sweat and tears. George III had a much different view. He said that the British had planted such colonies "with great industry, nursed with great tenderness, encouraged with many commercial advantages, and protected and defended at much expense of blood and treasure."

His answer to colonial intransigence was twofold. He sent military forces while authorizing certain emissaries to "grant general or particular pardons and indemnities" to calm the rebellion and restore peace to colonies willing to express their allegiance.

Near the end of his speech, the king assured Parliament that "The constant employment of my thoughts, and the most earnest wishes of my heart, tend wholly to the safety and happiness of all my people, and to the re-establishment of order and tranquility through the several parts of my dominions, in a close connection and constitutional dependence."

James Wilson headed a committee that also included John Dickinson, James Duane, and William Hooper, to draft an address to the American people apparently designed to point to the necessity of independence while denying the king's accusations that they intended to set up an independent empire. Congress tabled the address on February 13, 1776.

In the Declaration of Independence, the united colonies proclaimed that while governments were established to promote the safety and happiness of the people, the British government had failed in this endeavor. This was their basis for claiming that they had to revolt against the current government and replace it with one that would better secure human rights.

See also George III, Proclamation of Rebellion (August 23, 1775); George III, Speech to Parliament (October 31, 1776); *A Summary View of the Rights of British America* (Jefferson)

Further Reading

Black, Jeremy. 2006. *George III: America's Last King*. New Haven, CT: Yale University Press.

George III. "His Majesty's Most Gracious Speech to Both Houses of Parliament, on Friday, October 27, 1775." Philadelphia. Library of Congress. http://www.loc.gov/resource/rbpe.1440150a.

GEORGE III, SPEECH TO PARLIAMENT (OCTOBER 31, 1776)

George III's first official response to the Declaration of Independence was his speech to both houses of Parliament dated October 31, 1776 (George III, "His Majesty's Most Gracious Speech"). More than any previous document, the Declaration had been aimed directly at him and his administration, because the colonists had previously rejected the authority of Parliament to enact taxes.

As in his earlier response to the Olive Branch Petition, the king continued to blame the Declaration on the "Delusion" brought about by "Leaders, whose Object has always been Dominion and Power." Labeling this action as "Treason," the King said that if such treason were allowed "to take Root," then "much Mischief must grow from it, to the Safety of My loyal Colonies, to the Commerce of My Kingdoms, and indeed to the present System of all Europe." This latter phrase may well have been designed to give pause to other colonial powers considering giving aid to American rebels.

The king was heartened by recent military victories that his forces had won, and, as if responding to the Declaration's claim that Americans had a right to adopt a government that would promote their happiness, the king observed that "No people ever enjoyed more Happiness, or lived under a milder Government, than those now revolted Provinces." He further expressed the desire, which was also a response to the Declaration's claim that he was a "tyrant," "to restore to them the Blessings of Law and Liberty, equally enjoyed by every British Subject, which they have fatally and desperately exchanged for all the calamities of War, and the arbitrary Tyranny of their Chiefs."

See also George III, Proclamation of Rebellion (August 23, 1775); George III, Speech to Parliament (October 27, 1775); Life, Liberty, and the Pursuit of Happiness; Olive Branch Petition

Further Reading

George III. 1776. "His Majesty's Most Gracious Speech to Both Houses of Parliament on Thursday, October 31, 1776." London: Charles Eyre and William Strahan.

Harvard University. 2016. "September Highlight: Extravagant and Inadmissible Claim of Independency." September 4, 2016. https://declaration.fas.harvard.edu/blog/september-kings-speech.

GEORGIA AND ITS SIGNERS

Three Georgians, all of whom had been born outside the state, signed the Declaration of Independence. They were Lyman Hall, George Walton, and Button Gwinnett. The state straggled behind most of the other southern states in the movement for independence, in part perhaps it was quite sparsely populated and because it continued to face threats not only from Native Americans but also from Spanish neighbors to the south. John W. Blassingame observes that "the young, sparsely settled colony of Georgia, heavily dependent for its protection and economic welfare on the crown and ruled by one of the most popular royal governors in the colonies, probably had the largest proportion of people who remained loyal to England" (1968, 73).

Eunice Perkins cites an earlier writer, who observed that "but for the efforts of the three Georgia signers of the Declaration, the 'baby of the colonial family group might have been left a foundling on the doorstep of the British'" (1933, 261). The remains of all three signers have been reinterred beneath a signers' monument in Augusta, Georgia, which was dedicated in 1886.

Although some Georgians had protested the Stamp Act, the royal governor succeeded in seeing that the colony was the only one of the 13 that did not send representatives to the Stamp Act Congress or to the First Continental Congress. The movement for independence is often traced to a meeting held at Tondee's Tavern in Savannah on July 22, 1774. This, in turn, led to the convening of a provincial congress on January 18, 1775.

Although this congress appointed Noble Wymberley Jones, Archibald Bulloch, and John Houstoun to serve in the Second Continental Congress before being adjourned by the governor, they represented only five parishes and did not accordingly attend. St. John's Parish appointed Dr. Lyman Hall, who participated as a nonvoting member (Perkins 267). When the Provincial Congress chose Noble Wymberley Jones, Archibald Bulloch, Reverend John Jubly, John Houstoun, and Lyman Hall in July, they were prevented from attending because of fears of a Native American uprising. Georgia did not instruct the delegates to support independence but apparently gave them leeway to do so.

Lyman Hall (1724–1790) was a Connecticut-born, Yale-educated pastor, who after a contentious pastorate, switched his vocation to medicine and moved first to South Carolina and then to Georgia. He later served as state governor and helped establish Franklin College, which became the University of Georgia.

George Walton (ca. 1749–1804), had been born in Virginia, orphaned at a young age, and eventually taught himself enough to be admitted to the bar. Walton was wounded during service during the Revolutionary War and held prisoner for about a year. He later held office as the state's chief justice, governor, and as a U.S. senator. He was outspoken as chief justice and was particularly critical of Governor John Houstoun (Lamplugh 1981).

Button Gwinnett (ca. 1735–1777) had been born in England and was a merchant and planter. In addition to signing the Declaration, Gwinnett helped write Georgia's first constitution. Appointed as the state's first acting governor, he became involved in a bitter dispute with Colonel Lachlan McIntosh, who taunted him into a duel, in which both were wounded, but from which only Gwinnett died. Gwinnett's signatures are quite rare and have fetched high auction prices (Robertson 1946).

Thomas Jefferson would attribute the demise of his condemnation of slavery within the Declaration to delegates from South Carolina and Georgia. They further supported slavery at the Constitutional Convention of 1787, where concessions on this issue to their liking and their continuing need for a strong union against Native Americans led to prompt ratification of that document.

See also Native American Indians (Charge #27); Signing of the Declaration of Independence; Slavery

Further Reading

Blassingame, John W. 1968. "American Nationalism and Other Loyalties in the Southern Colonies, 1763–1775." *Journal of Southern History* 334 (February): 50–75.

Coleman, Kenneth. 1958. *The American Revolution in Georgia, 1763–1789*. Athens: University of Georgia Press.

Johnson, Amanda. 1932. "Georgia: From Colony to Commonwealth, 1774–1774." *Georgia Historical Quarterly* 16 (December): 253–273.

Kiernan, Denise, and Joseph D'Agnese. 2009. *Signing Their Lives Away: The Fame and Misfortune of the Men Who Signed the Declaration of Independence*. Philadelphia: Quirk Books.

Lamplugh, George R. 1981. "George Walton, Chief Justice of Georgia, 1783–1785." *Georgia Historical Quarterly* 65 (Summer): 82–91.

Perkins, Eunice Ross. 1933. "The Progress of the Revolution in Georgia." *Georgia Historical Quarterly* 17 (December): 259–275.

Robertson, William J. 1946. "Rare Button Gwinnett." *Georgia Historical Quarterly* 30 (December): 297–307.

GOD

There is sharp conflict, some based on interpretation of the Declaration of Independence, about the degree to which the U.S. people or government are Christian, or religious.

In contrast to the U.S. Constitution, which does not mention God, the Declaration references God on four occasions. Early in the document, there are references to "nature and of nature's god" and to the "Creator." The other references to the "Supreme Judge of the world" and "divine Providence" are near the end of the manuscript and were added during congressional debates. The reference to "sacred honor" in the last sentence of the document was also penned by Thomas Jefferson, who had originally classified the "truths" that it asserted as "sacred and undeniable" rather than "self-evident" (Holland 2007, 102). The term "sacred" is typically connected to the Deity and is often contrasted with the secular.

Jefferson's personal views are known to be theologically unorthodox, sometimes classified as Deist and sometimes as Unitarian (Dershowitz 2003, 33). The views of John Adams were similar. Of the remaining members of the committee that was assigned the task of writing the Declaration, only Roger Sherman, or "Father Sherman" as he was sometimes called, appeared to reflect Calvinist Protestant orthodoxy (Davis 2000, 96–99).

The personal views of committee members are not, however, a sure guide to the words of the Declaration, both because it was a public document designed to reflect the American mind and because, as indicated above, it was modified in debate. Citing other contemporary documents that outlined colonial grievances against Britain, John Alvis thus observes that "the Congress and conventions in the colonies made clear from the outset their expectation of a document friendly to scriptural religion from whoever should compose a statement of the colonies' separation from the parent country" (1998, 369). Alvis, who believes John Locke's own references to God are unnecessary to his arguments, believes that the Declaration is more similar, in this respect, to the writings of John Milton, who in his *Pro Populo*, which argued against Claude Salmasius's arguments for absolutism, responded that those who had sought the overthrown of Charles I had done so "by the law of God and Nature" (1998, 370; see also Waites 1903).

Professor Derek H. Davis observes that the only reference to God in Jefferson's original draft of the Declaration was to "Nature's God" (1994, 472), although Holland also notes that he had also made a "sneering reference to King George as 'the Christian king of Great Britain" who had upheld the slave trade (Holland 2007, 101). Davis further observes that it was Benjamin Franklin who suggested altering Jefferson's wording "that from that equal creation—they derive rights inherent and inalienable" to "they are endowed by their Creator with certain unalienable rights" (1994, 472). Elsewhere, Davis observes "that a majority of the American people would never have endorsed a colonial separation from the mother country unless they believed it had God's sanction" (2000, 95).

Owen Anderson argues persuasively that the idea of human rights rests solidly on the idea that God created humans equal (2017, 14–15). Davis, however, stresses the manner in which the rhetoric of natural rights that the Declaration of Independence employed was designed to unite both religious and secular thinkers. Contrasting what he calls the "theistic" framework of the Declaration of Independence to the "deistic" worldview (which rejected special revelation in scripture including miracles) that Thomas Jefferson and some other leading Founders embraced and the "Christian" viewpoint that may well have been held by most citizens (and would have included belief in scripture, including miracles), Davis argues that the document "appealed to both" (1994, 479). Steven Waldman (2008, 89) takes a similar view.

R. L. Bruckberger observes that by placing man within a nature ordered by God, the Declaration avoids the idolatry of the state that he associated with the French Revolution and others that followed (1959, 86). Bruckberger believes that "the greatest luck of all for the Declaration was precisely the divergence and the compromise between the Puritan tradition and what Jefferson wrote" (1949, 93). He explains that "had the Declaration been written in the strictly Puritan tradition it would probably not have managed to avoid an aftertaste of theocracy and religious fanaticism. Had it been written from the standpoint of the lax philosophy of that day, it would have been a-religious, if not actually offensive to Christians" (1959, 93). Rather counterintuitively, Bruckberger concludes that "the Declaration itself is superior to the men who signed it," much as "prophecy is always superior to the prophet" (1959, 99).

Bruckberger observes that one concept that the Declaration clearly rejected was that of "divine right." Bruckberger argues that early Western thought had understood that while God established right and justice, the people were responsible for creating political sovereignty and thus capable of creating kings. He therefore thinks that "the American Declaration restored and solemnly reaffirmed the earlier chain of political succession: God, the people and the people subject to the laws they made and government protecting these laws" (1959, 102).

The First Amendment to the U.S. Constitution prohibited the "establishment" of religion and guaranteed its "free exercise." In 1954, Congress added the words "under God" to the Pledge of Allegiance to the U.S. flag, largely as a way of contrasting what it perceived to be America's religious values against those of godless communism embraced by America's Cold War enemies. This specific term, however, derived from a speech by Abraham Lincoln rather than from the Declaration of Independence.

See also Franklin, Benjamin; Jefferson, Thomas; Laws of Nature and of Nature's God

Further Reading

Alvis, John. 1998. "Milton and the Declaration of Independence." *Interpretation* 25 (Spring):367–405.

Anderson, Owen. 2017. *The Declaration of Independence and God: Self-Evident Truths in American Law*. New York: Cambridge University Press.

Bruckberger, R. L. 1959. *Image of America*. New York: Viking Press.

Davis, Derek H. 1994. "Religious Dimensions of the Declaration of Independence: Fact and Fiction." *Journal of Church and State* 36 (Summer): 469–482.

Davis, Derek H. 2000. *Religion and the Continental Congress, 1774–1789: Contributions to Original Intent*. New York: Oxford University Press.

Dershowitz, Alan. 2003. *America Declares Independence*. Hoboken, NJ: John Wiley and Sons.

Hall, Mark David. 2011. "Did American Have a Christian Founding?" *Faculty Publications—Department of History, Politics, and International Studies*. Paper 53. http//digitalcommons.georgefox.edu/hist_fac/53.

Holland, Matthew S. 2007. *Bonds of Affection: Civil Charity and the Making of America—Winthrop, Jefferson, and Lincoln*. Washington, DC: Georgetown University Press.

Lawler, Peter Augustine. 2010. *Modern and American Dignity: Who We Are as Persons, and What That Means for Our Future*. Wilmington, DE: ISI Books.

McKenna, George. 2007. *The Puritan Origins of American Patriotism*. New Haven, CT: Yale University Press.
Stewart, Matthew. 2014. *Nature's God: The Heretical Origins of the American Republic*. New York: Norton.
Waites, Alfred. 1903. *A Brief Account of John Milton and His Declaration of Independence*. Worcester, MA: Gilbert G. Davis.
Waldman, Steven. 2008. *Founding Faith: Providence, Politics, and the Birth of Religious Freedom in America*. New York: Random House.

GODDARD PRINTING OF THE DECLARATION OF INDEPENDENCE

Although the Declaration was originally printed as a broadside by John Dunlap on the evening of July 4, 1776, Congress subsequently ordered it to be engrossed on vellum. It assigned this task to Timothy Matlack. The delegates subsequently signed this document from August 2 through the next few months.

The Dunlap broadside contained only the names of John Hancock, the president of the Congress, of Charles Thomson, the secretary, and of Dunlap as printer. Waiting until news of American victories at Trenton and Princeton, New Jersey, on January 18, 1777, Congress ordered a second official printing, which would include the signers' names. It gave this job to Mary Katherine Goddard (1738–1816), a Connecticut-born postmistress, printer, and newspaper publisher in Baltimore. She had been the first woman to print the text of the Declaration, which she had done in the July 10 issue of the *Maryland Journal*, which she edited ("March Highlight: Mary Katherine Goddard").

Although she divided the document into two columns, Goddard replicated the Dunlap printing of the Declaration with the printed names of the signers in italics and added the names of the states that they represented. In the process, she reduced the number of columns of names from six to four and reordered the arrangement of states, which she had read from right to left so that the signatures from Georgia now appeared on the top right (rather than on the bottom right) and those from Connecticut on the bottom right. Goddard's copy does not include the name of Thomas McKean, who had probably not yet signed the document. On the bottom of the broadside, she further added "BALTIMORE, IN MARYLAND: PRINTED BY MARY KATHERINE GODDARD."

Only 11 known printings of this document are known to remain ("March Highlight").

See also Dunlap Broadside Printing of the Declaration of Independence; Engravings and Printings of the Declaration of Independence; Engrossed Declaration of Independence (Matlack)

Further Reading

Dvorak, Petula. July 3, 2017. "This Woman's Name Appears on the Declaration of Independence. So Why Don't We Know Her Story?" *Washington Post*. https://www.washingtonpost.com/local/this-womans-name-appears-on-the-declaration-of-independence-so-why-dont-we-know-her-story/2017/07/03/ce86bf2e-5ff1-11e7-84a1-a26b75ad39fe_story.html?utm_term=.

"March Highlight: Mary Katherine Goddard." Declaration Resource Project. https://declaration.fas.harvard.edu/blog/march-goddard.

Puleo, Stephen. 2016. *American Treasures: The Secret Efforts to Save the Declaration of Independence, the Constitution, and the Gettysburg Address*. New York: St. Martin's Press.

Walker, Gay. 1987. "Women Printers in Early American Printing History." *Yale University Library Gazette* 61 (April): 116–124.

GRAFF HOUSE

See Declaration House

H

HANCOCK'S LETTERS ACCOMPANYING THE DECLARATION OF INDEPENDENCE

The Second Continental Congress tasked John Hancock of Massachusetts, as president of the Congress, with sending copies of the Dunlap Broadside to military forces and to all thirteen states.

George Washington had been a member of the Continental Congress, which had appointed him as commander in chief of colonial forces. In a letter to Washington, Hancock began with a sentence that noted, "The Congress, for some Time past, have had their Attention occupied by one of the most interesting and important Subjects, that could possibly come before them, or any other Assembly of Men" (Hancock 1776).

The patriot leader John Hancock, president of the Continental Congress, signed his name to the Declaration of Independence with such exceptional size and clarity that today his name is used informally to mean a person's signature. This picture portrays Hancock penning letters to accompany copies of the Declaration of Independence to the states and military leaders. (New York Public Library)

Hancock then proceeded with a sentence that began the letters he sent to the states. Just as the Declaration itself had fluctuated between descriptions of the Declaration as a "necessity" and descriptions of the Declaration as an act of will, or "consent," so too Hancock balanced both views with a reference to God. He thus wrote, "Altho it is not possible to foresee the Consequences of Human Actions, yet it is nevertheless a Duty we owe ourselves and Posterity, in all our public Counsels, to decide in the best Manner we are able, and to leave the Event to that Being who controls both Causes and Events to bring about his own Determinations."

In the next sentence, Hancock summarized the Declaration: "Impressed with this Sentiment, and at the same Time fully convinced that our Affairs may take a more favourable Turn, the Congress have judged it necessary to dissolve the Connection between Great Britain and the American Colonies, and to declare them free & independent States."

Hancock's letter to Washington suggested that the Declaration be proclaimed to the army, whereas the letter to the states observes in its last paragraph that "The important Consequences to the American States from this Declaration of Independence, considered as the Ground and Foundation of a future Government" suggests the propriety of disseminating the document within the colonies. Dennis J. Mahoney has argued that Hancock's statement about "the Ground and Foundation of future Government" provides warrant for accepting "the constitutional status of the Declaration of Independence" (1987, 55).

See also God; Necessity; Proclamation, Reading, and Reception of the Declaration of Independence; U.S. Constitution and the Declaration of Independence

Further Reading

Hancock. John. 1776. "To George Washington from John Hancock, 6 July 1776." Founders Online. https://founders.archives.gov/documents/Washington/03-05-02-0153.

Hancock, John. 1865. "A Relic of the Revolution; Letter from John Hancock to the Convention of North Carolina." https://www.nytimes.com/1865/08/13/news/relic-revolution-letter-john-hancock-convention-north-carolina.html.

Mahoney, Dennis J. 1987. "The Declaration of Independence as a Constitutional Document." In *The Framing and Ratification of the Constitution*, edited by Leonard W. Levy and Dennis J. Mahoney, 54–68. New York: Macmillan.

HAPPINESS

See Life, Liberty, and the Pursuit of Happiness

HE HAS COMBINED WITH OTHERS (CHARGE #13)

Almost without exception, those who have studied the origins of the Revolutionary War have suggested that many of the controversies that led to this conflict centered on differing conceptions of empire (Blumrosen and Blumrosen 2005, 107–109). The British thought that their Parliament had the right to enact legislation for the colonies, including the right of taxation. The British Parliament had affirmed this right in the Declaratory Act of 1766, and because Parliament considered itself to be the sovereign lawmaking authority for the empire, Parliament thought this effectively settled the matter.

The colonists, who relied on the principle of "no taxation without representation," which they had gleaned from the Magna Carta and other documents, denied this power. Prior to the Declaration of Independence, they acknowledged that they were bound to the English people by a common king but argued that the only bodies with the power to tax them were their own legislatures.

As Edward Dumbauld explains, "The difficulty which led to misunderstanding was that in England the body which represented the people and protected them against tyrannical exercise of power by the crown was Parliament, whereas in America the body which represented the people was each colony's local assembly" (1950, 123).

Recognizing that the colonies had already denied parliamentary authority and that the one legal tie that remained to the British Empire was that of a common king, the Declaration of Independence directed its primary attention toward the abuses they thought he had perpetuated, which justified revolution. The first 13 accusations in the Declaration thus all begin with the words "he has," with the word "he" specifically referring to the unnamed George III.

By 1776, the British Parliament had significantly cabined the king's authority. Blaming the king for acts of parliament would be roughly equivalent to blaming a modern president for acts of legislation that might have fallen far short of the president's own desires.

In thereby attempting to widen the remaining charges, the Declaration uses the words "he has combined with others." This phrase transitions from acts that it could justifiably attribute to the king to acts of Parliament—unnamed, presumably as a way of further denying its jurisdiction within the colonies—in which the king had concurred, much as some earlier accusations had accused him of failing to veto acts of Parliament that were inimical to colonial interests. Just as the first 12 accusations began with the words "he has," so too, the next 9 accusations all begin with the word "for," as in "for quartering large bodies of armed troops among us." Beginning with the charge that "he has abdicated government here," the document reverted to the "he has" construction for the remaining charges, which it directed more particularly against the king.

The remaining language of this charge further expands the Declaration's critique. It accuses the king of combining with others "to subject us to a jurisdiction foreign to our constitution and unacknowledged by our laws; giving his assent to their acts of pretended legislation." This more clearly highlights the way in which the colonists considered parliamentary legislation to be "foreign," and thus "unconstitutional" (the colonies had not adopted a common written constitution, like the Articles of Confederation, so it used the term to refer to accepted customs and usages, thus posing a colonial counterpart to the "British Constitution") within the colonies. Although Parliament might "pretend," or falsely assert, its authority to legislate on behalf of the colonies, the king should have refused assent to such lawmaking, which in the Declaration's view, colonial legislatures retained. This charge looked to a time when the king was thought to have far more power over Parliament than he did in 1776. Eric Nelson thus observes that "only because patriots remained convinced that the king possessed a constitutional prerogative power to 'refuse his assent' to parliamentary bills could they indict him for having refused to wield it on behalf of the colonies" (2014, 65).

Rhetorically, this charge is 13th of 27 or 28 (if one counts rejection of colonial petitions) charges, after Congress deleted 2, which puts this charge roughly in the middle. That fact, with the transitional phrase accusing the king of "combining with others," may have been a rhetorical way of highlighting the importance of the unstated principle of "no taxation without representation," which had so dominated much of the prior debate.

See also British Constitution; Charges against the King and Others; Declaratory Act of 1766

Further Reading

Blumrosen, Alfred W., and Ruth G. Blumrosen. 2005. *Slave Nation: How Slavery United the Colonies and Sparked the American Revolution*. Naperville, IL: Sourcebooks, Inc.

Dumbauld, Edward. 1950. *The Declaration of Independence and What It Means Today*. Norman: University of Oklahoma Press.

Nelson, Eric. 2014. *The Royalist Revolution: Monarchy and the American Founding*. Cambridge, MA: Harvard University Press.

Palmer, R. R. 2014. *The Age of the Democratic Revolution: A Political History of Europe and America, 1760–1800*. Princeton, NJ: Princeton University Press.

HOWE'S CIRCULAR LETTER (1776)

Shortly before the adoption of the Declaration of Independence, George III authorized Lord Richard Howe to issue a declaration, undoubtedly offered in hopes of dividing the colonies, offering a pardon to those individuals and colonies who were willing "by a speedy return to their duty, to reap the benefits of the Royal favour" (Shain 2015, 545). Dated June 20, 1776, this declaration proclaimed that Howe had the authority "to declare any Colony or Province, Colonies or Provinces, to be at the peace of his Majesty" (Shain 2015, 545).

When George Washington asked Congress how he should respond, Congress said that it would make appropriate arrangements to receive peace commissioners if they applied for entry. The majority of colonists appeared to take the attitude of Benjamin Franklin, who responded to Howe on July 20, 1776, by noting that "Directing Pardons to be offered the Colonies, who are the very Parties injured, expresses indeed that Opinion of our Ignorance, Baseness, & Insensibility which your uninform'd and proud Nation has long been pleased to entertain of us" (Shain 2015, 550).

See also Declaration (Meaning of Term); Franklin, Benjamin

Further Reading

Gruber, Ira D. 1972. *The Howe Brothers and the American Revolution*. Chapel Hill: University of North Carolina Press.

Shain, Barry Alan, ed. 2015. *The Declaration of Independence in Historical Context: American State Papers, Petitions, Proclamations, and Letters of the Delegates to the First National Congresses*. Reprint edition. Indianapolis, IN: Liberty Fund.

HUMAN NATURE AND THE DECLARATION OF INDEPENDENCE

The opening sentence of the Declaration of Independence refers to "human events," and the document makes a number of pronouncements and assumptions about human nature that sometimes go unexamined.

Scholars have examined the claims that "all men are created equal" and that they are therefore entitled to "life, liberty, and the pursuit of happiness." Moreover, Thomas Jefferson's original draft accused the king of waging "cruel war against human nature itself, violating it's most sacred rights of life & liberty in the persons of a distinct people, who never offended him." The idea that men are "created" and subsequent references to God as the "Supreme Judge of the world" and to "divine Providence" suggest that human beings are necessarily limited. As humans, they have no right, or ability, to act as gods. Although men are subject to passions, they are also capable of reason, which gives them access to the laws of nature, and which would set them apart from other animals. The Declaration thus respectfully appeals to "the opinions of mankind."

The Declaration featured a unique interplay between human will and necessity that played upon man's role as a reasonable but limited creation. The very first sentence suggested that it was "necessary" to dissolve the political bands that have connected America to Britain. Other parts of the document referenced a similar necessity. God, as theologians usually describe him, is not subject to such necessity, except perhaps to be true to his own natural goodness. Men, by contrast, can act like "tyrants" in seeking to dominate others or as "good people" seeking to uphold their God-given freedom.

The idea of human equality means that some are not born to rule and others to be ruled, as in a hereditary system or one in which individuals are born with titles. The delineation of the right to life means that individuals have the right of self-preservation. The right to liberty indicates that humans have the right to seek to chart the course of their lives. The pursuit of happiness suggests that they may further choose what gives them the greatest satisfaction.

The Declaration indicated that humans are moral creatures by appealing to a number of moral virtues. These included the public-spiritedness associated with patriotism, prudence (which involves the wise use of reason), courage, humility, justice, magnanimity, and friendship. Humans have mutual duties as well as mutual rights. They are bound to others by ties of kinship and history.

As described in the Declaration, men are divided into different peoples. In at least some cases (African Americans and Native American Indians), the Declaration appeared to delineate these groups by race. Although all are people, some such groups, as well as the tyrants who appeal to them, are "uncivilized" in part because they do not appear to distinguish among "ages, sexes, and conditions," who are presumably owed special treatment because they are more vulnerable than others.

Human beings have the moral capacity to choose the governments that can best protect their liberties and provide for their future happiness. Psychologically, however, people are generally "disposed to suffer, while evils are sufferable, than to right themselves by abolishing the forms to which they are accustomed." Such reluctance can be overcome, however, when people sense "a design to reduce them under absolute despotism" and recognize their duty to overthrow tyrants.

However equal men may be created, if given the opportunity, some men will clearly seek to dominate their peers, perhaps in part to gain their property. Human institutions and actions can be despotic in and of themselves or because they have a tendency to despotism. Thus, the Declaration criticizes the merger of military and civilian power, the presence of standing armies, and the absence or corruption of representative institutions. While leaving the form of government to replace British rule to the people, it is clear that whatever form is chosen should rest upon popular consent and be accountable to the people.

In defending and explicating the U.S. Constitution, James Madison later observed that "If men were angels, no government would be necessary" (Hamilton, Madison, and Jay ([1788] 1961, 322). He further observed that "In framing a government which is to be administered by men over men," it was necessary first to "enable the government to control the governed" and second to "oblige it to control itself" ([1788] 1961, 322). He thought this required both "[a] dependence on the people" and "the necessity of auxiliary precautions" ([1788] 1961, 322), most notably separation of powers and checks and balances.

See also Equality; God; Life, Liberty, and the Pursuit of Happiness; Moral Virtues in the Declaration of Independence; Necessity

Further Reading

Hamilton, Alexander, James Madison, and John Jay. (1788) 1961. *The Federalist Papers*. Reprint. New York: New American Library. Citations refer to the New American Library edition.

Kmiec, Douglas W. 2005. "The Human Nature of Freedom and Identity—We Hold More than Random Thoughts." *Harvard Journal of Law and Public Policy* 29:33–52.

I

INDEPENDENCE

"Independence" is a synonym for freedom and contrasts to dependence, or reliance. As 13 colonies, Americans had depended on Great Britain. Even after they had repudiated the right of the British Parliament to tax them, they believed they retained a tie with the English people through the English king until they repudiated this too in the Declaration of Independence.

Just as the Dutch had, in an earlier century, abjured their allegiance to Philip II, so too, in proclaiming their independence from Great Britain, the Declaration of Independence asserted that Americans now considered themselves to be a distinct people. They therefore dissolved the "political bands" that had previously connected them to the British Empire.

Just as children generally assume adult status when they reach the age of 18 or 21, so too, countries that have been settled by others get to the point where they find it more efficient and more conducive to their own interest to run their own affairs rather than having another government do this for them. Winning the Revolutionary War was one indication that America now had the capacity to govern itself.

American independence became the harbinger of other independence movements throughout Latin American in the nineteenth century, and in Africa and Asia in the twentieth and twenty-first centuries. Some of these nations have patterned their own declarations of independence on the U.S. model.

It is important to recognize that in declaring their independence from Britain, the colonies were not declaring a belief in domestic anarchy. Thus, the same document that declared independence proclaimed the right of the people to set up new governments that would secure their rights to life, liberty, and the pursuit of happiness.

Just as adults expect to be able to exercise rights equal to those of other adults, so too, American Founders anticipated that the American people would assume their "equal station" in international affairs. Many Founders anticipated that other nations would be more likely to come to their aid if they were asserting an equal status with other nations rather than engaging in a civil war with the mother country.

Although America became a colonial power during the Spanish-American War at the end of the nineteenth century, acquiring foreign territories through such conquest is arguably at odds with the spirit of the Declaration of Independence. In part because of this, America has freed a number of its former colonies, including the Philippines, and incorporated both Alaska (which it purchased from Russia in 1867) and Hawaii (which it annexed in 1898), into the Union. America's largest former colony, Puerto Rico, is a commonwealth, which, depending on the wishes of its own people, might also one day become a state or an independent nation.

See also Act of Abjuration (*Plakkaat van Verlatinge*, 1581); International Law; People

Further Reading

Armitage, David. 2007. *The Declaration of Independence: A Global History*. Cambridge, MA: Harvard University Press.

Morgan, Edmund S. 1976. *The Meaning of Independence: John Adams, Thomas Jefferson, George Washington*. New York: Norton.

Rachum, Illan. 1993. "From 'American Independence' to the 'American Revolution.'" *Journal of American Studies* 27 (April): 73–81.

INDEPENDENCE DAY

Americans celebrate Independence Day on July 4. However, delegates to the Second Continental Congress had actually approved the resolution for independence that Richard Henry Lee of Virginia had introduced on June 7, 1776, on July 2, and John Adams was among those who thought that this day, rather than July 4, would be the day that the nation chose to celebrate the occasion.

Although the adoption of the resolution on July 2 would certainly have been a sufficient indication that America intended to become a separate nation, the written Declaration not only sought to articulate the reasons for such separation but pointed to the principles to which the new nation was committed, even before it adopted a written constitution. These principles, which are sometimes likened to an American creed, continue to resonate long after many of the specific reasons for independence from Britain have been largely forgotten.

Although this event was celebrated in the years immediately after the approval of the Declaration, from 1788 and throughout the early years of the republic, the event took on a distinctly partisan cast, initially dividing Federalists supporters of the proposed Constitution against Anti-Federalist opponents, and later pitting Federalist Party members against Democratic-Republicans (Warren 1945). Charles Warren noted that "by 1798, partisan controversies had grown so heated that the two parties could not unite in celebrating the Fourth and they held separate processions, dinners and orations" (1945, 261). He observed that one of the reported toasts from the Boston celebration of 1798 was "John Adams—may he like Sampson slay thousands of Frenchmen with the jawbone of Jefferson" (1945, 261). The party controversy was, however, partly responsible for spreading public knowledge that Thomas Jefferson had been the primary author of the Declaration.

By 1826, much of the early rancor had died down as the nation prepared to celebrate fifty years of independence. The deaths of both John Adams and Thomas Jefferson on Independence Day did much to further solidify and hallow this date in the American mind (Burstein 2001). James Monroe died five years later on the same day. Although Congress did not declare July 4 to be a national holiday until 1870, many states had already done so.

In 1852, Frederick Douglass, a former slave and prominent abolitionist, gave a speech in which he asked, "What to the Slave Is the Fourth of July?" In the speech, he pointed to the disparity between the aspirations of the Declaration of Independence celebrated on Independence Day and slavery (Vile 2017, 171–176). Reflecting such sentiments, some African Americans celebrated July 5 as a form of protest (Kammen 2003, 190). African Americans have increasingly participated in traditional Independence Day celebrations since the adoption of the Thirteenth Amendment, which abolished involuntary servitude—although many preferred to celebrate Emancipation Day instead (O'Leary 1999, 114). Initially tepid toward Independence Day celebrations, former Southern states, which had fought under a rival banner during the war, also joined in the celebrations after the Civil War.

American history has witnessed numerous speeches on Independence Day, many of which focused on the meaning of the Declaration of Independence. The Missouri Digital Heritage site at http://laurel.lso.missouri.edu/search/?searchtype=a&SORT=D&searcharg=Fourth+of+July+Orations+Collection+%28University+of+Missouri+Digital+Library%29&searchscope=8 contains a good number of such orations.

See also Adams, John; Creed/Scriptures; Jefferson, Thomas; Reputation of the Declaration of Independence

Further Reading

Bolla, Peter de. 2007. *The Fourth of July and the Founding of America*. Woodstock, NY: Overlook Press.

Burstein, Andrew. 2001. *America's Jubilee: How in 1826 a Generation Remembered Fifty Years of Independence*. New York: Alfred A. Knopf

Kammen, Michael. 2003. "Commemoration and Contestation in American Culture: Historical Perspectives." *Amerikastudien/American Studies* 48, no. 2: 185–205.

O'Leary, Cecilia Elizabeth. 1999. *To Die For: The Paradox of American Patriotism*. Princeton, NJ: Princeton University Press.

Smelser, Marshall. 1970. "The Glorious Fourth—or, Glorious Second? Or Eighth?" *History Teacher* 3 (January): 25–30.

Traves, Len. 1997. *Celebrating the Fourth: Independence Day and the Rites of Nationalism in the Early Republic*. Amherst: University of Massachusetts Press.

Vile, John R. 2017. *The Jacksonian and Antebellum Eras: Documents Decoded*. Santa Barbara, CA: ABC-CLIO.

Warren, Charles. 1945. "Fourth of July Myths." *William and Mary Quarterly* 2 (July): 237–272.

INDEPENDENCE HALL

Because it hosted the Second Continental Congress (the first had met in Carpenter's Hall), Independence Hall, long known as the Pennsylvania State House, was the site of the original signing of the Declaration of Independence, which took place on August 2 and the months that followed. This red brick building also witnessed the signing of the Articles of Confederation (America's first government after the end of British rule) and of the U.S. Constitution. In addition, the building had been

The Pennsylvania State House was the site of the meeting of the Second Continental Congress that approved the Declaration of Independence and proposed the Articles of Confederation. It also served as the site of the Constitutional Convention of 1787. (Alexandre Fagundes De Fagundes/Dreamstime.com)

the site where the Continental Congress had approved the appointment of George Washington as commander in chief and where delegates had signed the Olive Branch Petition to the King.

The Pennsylvania Assembly authorized the construction of the building, which is located on Chestnut Street between Fifth and Sixth Streets, in 1729. The Assembly speaker, Andrew Hamilton, who had a prominent role in designing the building, had been the attorney in the historic Peter Zenger case, which had helped to establish freedom of the press in the colonies. Architecturally, the building was influenced by the Italian Andrea Palladio, who also had a major influence on Thomas Jefferson. The room would have contained round tables covered in green velour and surrounded by Windsor chairs. Delegates are known to have dipped their quills into a silver inkstand designed by Philip Syng Jr. (1703–1789) of Philadelphia in 1752.

The Georgia-style building had two floors. The delegates to the Second Continental Congress, like those at the Constitutional Convention of 1787, would have met in the East Room, or Assembly Room, on the first floor. It was just across from a room on the other side that served as a provincial courtroom. The upstairs contained an additional lengthwise long room and a series of chambers for committee meetings (Mires 1999, 8).

By the time of the writing of the Declaration of Independence, the distinctive steeple had replaced the original cupola, and housed the Liberty Bell, which had prophetically borne the words from Leviticus 25:10: "Proclaim liberty throughout all the land to all the inhabitants thereof." This relic is now displayed in a special center outside the building. On the evening after the Declaration of Independence was read from Independence Hall, someone took down the king's coat of arms, which had been displayed over the king's courts in the building and burned it to the delight of those assembled (Desbler 1892, 166–167).

Independence Hall has been a popular site for commemorations marking various anniversaries of both the Declaration of Independence and the Constitution. In 1824, the building was used to welcome Marquis de Lafayette; Abraham Lincoln raised a flag at Independence Hall on the way to his first presidential inauguration. In 1901, Philadelphia constructed a new city hall, leaving Independence Hall simply as a historic site (Mires 1999, 53). In 1951, Philadelphia turned the building over to the National Park Service (Mires 1999, 58), which continues to administer it to this day. In 2003, the National Constitution Center opened on Independence Mall, facing the building.

See also Lincoln, Abraham; Olive Branch Petition; Philadelphia; Syng Inkstand; U.S. Constitution and the Declaration of Independence

Further Reading

Desbler, Charles D. 1892. "How the Declaration Was Received in the Old Thirteen." *Harper's New Monthly Magazine* 85 (July): 165–187.

Lukacs, John. 1987. "Unexpected Philadelphia." *American Heritage* (May–June): 72–81.

Mires, Charlene. 1999. "In the Shadow of Independence Hall: Vernacular Activities and the Meanings of Historic Places." *Public Historian* 21 (Spring): 49–64.

Mires, Charlene. 2013. *Independence Hall in American Memory*. Philadelphia: University of Pennsylvania Press.

National Park Service. n.d. "Assembly Room of Independence Hall." Accessed March 27, 2018. https://www.nps.gov/inde/learn/historyculture/places-independencehall-assemblyroom.htm.

Riley, Edward M. 1953. "The Independence Hall Group." *Transactions of the American Philosophical Society* 43:7–42.

INDIANS

See Native American Indians (Charge #27)

INDICTMENT

See Legal Form of the Declaration of Independence

INTERNATIONAL LAW

Although Americans typically focus on the second paragraph of the Declaration of Independence, with its evocation of natural rights, the central aim of the Declaration was not to articulate a national creed but to declare its independence as a separate nation. Without such a status, any hope for obtaining help from foreign allies would be unlikely, as international norms generally preclude interference in civil wars—why Abraham Lincoln would later call the conflict from 1861 to 1865 a civil war, whereas rebels called it the War between the States. Notably, when proposing independence, Richard Henry Lee had also introduced resolutions to seek the help of foreign allies and to settle on a more permanent government for the colonies as a whole.

The Declaration serves as an important document in international law. It is a clear assertion of American sovereignty (Sims 1991). One of its models appears to have been the Dutch Act of Abjuration, which had, in 1581, announced its renunciation of the rule of Philip II of Spain. David Armitage has persuasively argued that in 1776, international law was considered to be a combination of both natural (unwritten) law, like that evoked in the second paragraph of the Declaration, and of positive law, which consisted of international agreements and norms. Like natural laws within the state of nature, such international norms may not have been enforceable, and thus called for national self-help, since states had no common sovereign over them.

The Declaration raises the same dilemma as that of deciding whether the chicken or the egg came first. The one-time colonists had to consider themselves to be independent in order to give such notice to others, and yet it would be recognition by others, first in the form of alliances (as with France), and then by the mother country in the Treaty of Paris, that recognized true independence.

As relates to international law, the first paragraph of the Declaration of Independence declares that the thirteen colonists are now a separate "people," who are assuming (undoubtedly in hopes of recognition by other peoples) "the separate and equal station to which the laws of nature and of nature's god entitle them." By further evoking "the opinions of mankind," the Declaration is further appealing to those beyond its own borders.

Similarly, the last paragraph of the document proclaims, in the language of Richard Henry Lee's Resolution of June 7, 1776, "that these united colonies are and of right ought to be free and independent states." The paragraph further declares that "as free & independent states, they have full power to levy war, conclude peace, contract alliances, establish commerce, & to do all other acts and things which independent states may of right do."

After noting "the difference between de facto and de jure independence" (2002, 61), Armitage regards the Declaration as proclaiming "statehood in the international order" rather than true nationhood, which is understood to rest on "shared history, traditions, and institutions," which he thinks came later (2002, 61). One might, however, note both that the Declaration of Independence preceded the creation of the Articles of Confederation or the Constitution of 1787 and that the term "people," which the Declaration employed, comes closer to the idea of a nation than an international state.

In declaring independence from Britain, the Declaration of Independence arguably differed from the French Revolution that followed. Armitage thus notes that the aims of the American Revolution "were more limited, and its maxims not so plainly destructive to the law of nations, because the Americans had requested admission to the international order with their Declaration of Independence rather than threatened its overthrow" (2002, 64).

See also Act of Abjuration (*Plakkaat van Verlatinge*, 1581); Independence; Laws of Nature and of Nature's God; People; Resolutions Introduced by Richard Henry Lee (June 7, 1776)

Further Reading

Armitage, David. 2002. "The Declaration of Independence and International Law." *William and Mary Quarterly* 59 (January): 39–64.

Armitage, David. 2007. *The Declaration of Independence: A Global History*. Cambridge, MA: Harvard University Press.

Masters, Roger D. 1967. "The Lockean Tradition in American Foreign Policy." *Journal of International Affairs* 21:253–277.

Onuf, Peter S. 1998. "A Declaration of Independence for Diplomatic Historians." *Diplomatic History* 22 (Winter): 71–83.

Sims, Kevin F. 1991. *The Defense of American Sovereignty: The Declaration of Independence as a Foreign Policy Statements*. PhD diss., Claremont Graduate School.

INTERPRETING THE DECLARATION OF INDEPENDENCE

Most interpretations of the Declaration of Independence focus on the first and second paragraphs rather than on the main body of the document, which listed grievances against the English king and Parliament—the latter of which it never directly named.

It seems clear that the central purpose of the document was to proclaim the reasons that Americans were announcing their separation from Great Britain and thereby to establish their equal standing in the world—whether as a single nation or a series of united states is not always clear. The document also contains more universalistic statements that apply to all men, however—a term, that itself requires the determination of whether it is limited to males or refers to all humans. The assertion that "all men are created equal" and that they are endowed with certain "unalienable rights," would appear to challenge not only hereditary kingship or similar systems based on the notion that certain "bluebloods" have a God-given right to rule over others. It can also be understood to condemn the system of chattel slavery that remained in the majority of the colonies when it was made.

Numerous historians and political scientists have sought to tease out the origins of the Declaration of Independence. Some trace its origins chiefly to state and local declarations (Maier 1997), some to early state constitutions (Lutz 1989), some to Lockean liberalism (Becker 1970), some to civic republicanism, and some to natural law and religious truths (Anderson 2015), with most commentators recognizing that there were multiple influences, many of which had multiple strains. Because Thomas Jefferson was the primary author of the document, it is also common to assume that the document should be interpreted through the eyes of his own complex philosophy.

When criticized for having plagiarized the Declaration from other sources, however, Jefferson responded that "Neither aiming at originality of principle or sentiment, nor yet copied from any particular and previous writing, it was intended to be an expression of the American mind, and to give to that expression the proper tone and spirit called for by the occasion" (Smith 2011). This indicates that Jefferson clearly knew the difference between his own philosophic reflections and expressions of public sentiment. Thus establishing that Jefferson may have been a Deist, a slaveholder, or an agrarian does not therefore establish that the document, fellow delegates, or the American people as a whole fell into the same categories.

As the Declaration's emphasis on prudence, or practical wisdom, might suggest, neither Jefferson nor other members of the committee that drafted the Declaration or the Congress that proposed it were mere theoretical philosophers but practical statesmen facing concrete issues. In reflecting on how to interpret the Declaration, Donald S. Lutz thus wisely distinguishes between public documents and more philosophic counterparts:

> Unlike political treatises written by political philosophers, which can contain a hidden or esoteric meaning, public documents that are the basis for common commitments must, when being subjected to close textual analysis, be read for public meaning. If the meaning is not apparent to the average reader, then the document ceases to perform the function for which it was written. Those writing political tracts must be well aware of the nature of their audience. Novelty will be accepted only if it is based upon what is already understood and approved. The rhetoric and symbols must be familiar and widely shared. We are speaking here of a document whose very purpose is to elicit approval; therefore, we will not be inclined to accept interpretations of the Declaration that would be at variance with how it was generally read at the time it was written. (Lutz 1989, 45)

Combined with the knowledge that the Second Continental Congress made fairly extensive alterations in the Declaration, this observation would caution against reading the Declaration as a mere private reflection or reflexively equating it with Jefferson's overall thought. Thus, Mark David Hall has observed "that documents created by representatives acting in their official capacities, especially 'organic' documents such as the Declaration, better reflect the national purpose than private sentiments (including private comments of individuals involved in making the organic documents" (2002, 151). John Phillip Reid observes that Jefferson's perceptions of other philosophers "are relevant to the meaning of the document only to the extent his congressional colleagues knew of these perceptions and endorsed them with their votes" (1981, 83).

Once the principles of the Declaration of Independence are identified, they still need to be applied to concrete circumstances. If one, for example, believes that the Declaration articulated the idea of universal human freedoms, one will still have to determine which institutions are most responsible for securing and enhancing such freedoms.

One of the goals of those who wrote the U.S. Constitution was to translate the broad ideals of the Declaration into concrete institutions. Those who struggled with wording subsequent amendments, particularly those adopted in the aftermath of the U.S. Civil War, faced similar challenges. This challenge continues to this day.

See also Audiences for the Declaration of Independence; Originality of the Declaration; Prudence; U.S. Constitution and Declaration.

Further Reading

Anderson, Owen. 2015. *The Declaration of Independence and God: Self-Evident Truths in American Law*. New York: Cambridge University Press.

Becker, Carl. 1970. *The Declaration of Independence: A Study in the History of Political Ideas*. New York: Vintage Books.

Cosgrove, Charles H. 1998. "The Declaration of Independence in Constitutional Interpretation: A Selective History and Analysis." *University of Richmond Law Review* 32 (January): 107–164.

Hall, Mark David. 2002. "The Declaration of Independence in the Supreme Court." *The Declaration of Independence: Origins and Impact*, edited by Scott Douglas Gerber, 142–160. Washington, DC: CQ Press.

Lutz, Donald S. 1989. "The Declaration of Independence as Part of an American National Compact." *Publius* 19 (Winter): 41–58.

Maier, Pauline. 1997. *American Scripture: Making the Declaration of Independence*. New York: Alfred A. Knopf.

Reid, John Phillip. 1981. "The Irrelevance of the Declaration." In *Law in the American Revolution and the Revolution in the Law*, edited by Hendrik Hartog, 46–89. New York: New York University Press.

Smith, George H. 2011. "Was Thomas Jefferson a Plagiarist?" Libertanism.org. https://www.libertarianism.org/publications/essays/excursions/was-thomas-jefferson-plagiarist.

Strang, Lee J. 2006. "Originalism, the Declaration of Independence, and the Constitution: A Unique role in Constitutional Interpretation?" *Penn State Law Review* 111 (Fall): 413–479.

Wills, Garry. 1978. *Inventing America: Jefferson's Declaration of Independence*. Garden City, NY: Doubleday.

J

JEFFERSON, THOMAS

Thomas Jefferson (1743–1826) was the primary author of the Declaration of Independence, having been appointed to a Committee of Five, which vested him with primary authority to do the writing. Fellow committee members Benjamin Franklin and John Adams made a few changes before Jefferson's draft was debated in the Second Continental Congress, where it underwent substantial changes, most notably deletions of Jefferson's condemnation of the king for perpetuating slavery in the colonies and colonial governors for encouraging slave revolts.

Jefferson, age 33, was one of the younger members of the Congress but one of the most talented. He was known for his authorship of a *Summary View of the Rights of British America*, for authoring resolutions on Lord North's Conciliatory Proposals, and for an early version of the Declaration of Taking Up Arms (the final version appears to owe more to the more conservative John Dickinson). Given Virginia's position as the most populous state, it was fairly important to have a Virginian on the committee to write the Declaration, and the most obvious candidate, Richard Henry Lee, who had introduced the resolution for independence on June 7, was heading home. Jefferson himself might have preferred to have gone back to Virginia to help draft a constitution (he sent proposals for this document via George Wythe), but he stayed, and John Adams offered several reasons why he should draft the document, including what he considered to be Jefferson's ability to write.

Jefferson was born in Shadwell, Virginia, near Charlottesville, not far from which Jefferson would construct his famed home, Monticello, which is now a world heritage site. He attended the College of William and Mary, where he had stayed to study law under George Wythe, who would later be named the first professor of law in the United States. Jefferson was a bibliophile with a large personal library, which the Library of Congress later purchased. As a lawyer, Jefferson would have been familiar with legal forms and documents appropriate for the occasion as well as leading Enlightenment thinkers. A masterful penman, Jefferson was active on committees at the Second Continental Congress but was not a gifted orator and rarely spoke before the entire assembly.

When he wrote the Declaration, Jefferson was staying at a house constructed by Jacob Graff, not far from the Pennsylvania State House (Independence Hall), where the Declaration was approved. Both the desk on which Jefferson wrote and the chair on which he is believed to have composed the document have achieved iconic status. In bequeathing his desk to a granddaughter, Jefferson later anticipated that it might one day be "carried in the procession of our nation's birthday, as the

Portrait of Thomas Jefferson, third president of the United States during 1801–1809. Jefferson was the chief author of the Declaration of Independence, who stressed that he intended for it to be "an expression of the American mind." (BiographicalImages.com)

relics of the Saints are in those of the Church" (Bedini 1981, 35).

Jefferson, who kept very helpful notes on debates over the Declaration, found it excruciating to sit through the debates on the Declaration and had to be consoled by Benjamin Franklin. Jefferson remained convinced that his original document was better than the one that the Continental Congress produced, but most scholars believe otherwise.

Although the initial two paragraphs articulating a philosophy of government (and of rebellion in appropriate circumstances), to which Congress made relatively few emendations, are the best known, the main body of the document consists of 28 charges against the king. Jefferson knew that the colonies had long denied that the British Parliament had authority to legislate for the colonies and that colonists had, prior to the Declaration, largely affirmed their loyalty to the king, so it made sense to explain why the time had come to renounce this tie. Similarly, although many of the grievances that Jefferson listed were expectations created by British customs and usages, Jefferson chose to ground the philosophy of the Declaration in "the laws of nature and of nature's God," which he thought would have more international appeal, and knowing that it would be contradictory to assert purely British rights while declaring independence.

Many scholars have sought to explore Jefferson's rich reading and writings in order to understand the Declaration and the intellectual influences on Jefferson (Wills 1978; Jayne 1998), but it is important to recognize that he was writing a public document rather than the expression of his personal philosophy. When in later life Timothy Pickering (1745–1829), a Massachusetts Federalist, accused Jefferson of having copied the Declaration from John Locke and from James Otis, Jefferson claimed to have turned to neither. He observed that "I know only that I turned to neither book nor pamphlet while writing it. I did not consider it as any part of my charge to invent new ideas altogether, and to offer no sentiment which had ever been expressed before." In another letter, which he wrote in 1825, he observed, "Neither aiming at originality of principle or sentiment, nor yet copied from any particular and previous writing, it was intended to be an expression of the American mind, and to give to that expression the proper tone and spirit called for by the occasion" (Smith 2011).

Although it appears to have been well received, the initial printed copy of the Declaration, which Jefferson may have helped to oversee, contained only the names of John Hancock (congressional president), Charles Thomson (congressional secretary), and John Dunlap (the printer). By contrast, the engrossed copy recorded the signatures, but by states in a way that did not highlight Jefferson's role. As Jefferson rose to head the Democratic Republican Party, his role became better known, so much so that the Fourth of July was often celebrated in partisan fashion. In time, Jefferson's authorship became a matter for envy, with Adams, Pickering, and others seeking to minimize the contribution that the Declaration had made and with Jefferson explaining that he had not aimed to produce an original work but to express general sentiments.

During the Revolution, Jefferson served for a time as governor of Virginia (during which the British nearly captured him) and was appointed as a minister to France, where he was serving during the Constitutional Convention of 1787, where his friend James Madison played such an important role. Unlike many of the Framers of this document, Jefferson professed to be little concerned with Shay's Rebellion in Massachusetts, noting that "I hold it that a little rebellion now and then is a good thing, and as necessary in the political world as storms in the physical" (Koch 1950, 45). Although generally pleased with the work of the Constitutional Convention, Jefferson wrote to Madison advocating the addition of a Bill of Rights—a task that Madison spearheaded in the first Congress.

Jefferson was called back to serve as the first secretary of state under President George Washington. In this post, he ended up in frequent conflict with secretary of the treasury Alexander Hamilton, whose vision for a strong national government that encouraged the growth of commerce and industry conflicted with Jefferson's narrower construction of the Constitution and his vision of a nation populated by independent farmers.

By virtue of coming in second to John Adams in the election of 1796, Jefferson served as vice president. Jefferson defeated Adams in the next election and served two terms as president from 1801 to 1809. He was followed in this office by his secretary of state and fellow Virginian, James Madison, who was in turn succeeded by James Monroe, another Jefferson friend and fellow Democratic Republican. Jefferson's term in office coincided with a war against north African pirates, the purchase of the Louisiana Territory from France, the explorations of Lewis and Clark, and an unpopular embargo against Great Britain that did not succeed in preventing war during his successor's presidency. In retirement, Jefferson helped found the University of Virginia and was reconciled with John Adams, with whom he resumed a lively correspondence.

In debt and declining health that prevented him from attending jubilee celebrations of the Declaration of Independence, Jefferson penned a letter to the mayor of Washington, D.C., expressing his regrets. Echoing the words of a former English revolutionary, Jefferson observed, "All eyes are opened, or opening, to the rights of man. The general spread of the light of science has already laid open to every view the palpable truth, that the mass of mankind has not been born with saddles on their backs, nor a favored few booted and spurred, ready to ride them legitimately, by the grace of God" (Adair 1952).

When both Jefferson and Adams died on July 4, 1826, their deaths seemed to confirm God's blessing on the event that this day commemorated. Jefferson asked that his tombstone list his authorship of the Declaration and of the Statute of Virginia for Religious Freedom and his role as the father of the University of Virginia. He omitted his service as U.S. president (Cogliano 2006, 137).

As one of four presidents whose face is carved on Mt. Rushmore, Jefferson remains a vital symbol of American values who was commemorated by the Jefferson Memorial, which was completed in Washington, D.C., in 1943. It includes a large statue of him amid a classical revival domed marble structure with columns and walls engraved with words from the Declaration.

In more recent times, scholars have explored Jefferson's view of race and his apparent relationship with Sally Hemings, one of his slaves and half-sister to his wife who had died, and their children. Jefferson seemingly understood that the institution of slavery—which he had tried to limit in his youth and in the Ordinance of 1784, which served as a model for the Northwest Ordinance—was immoral but believed that it would be impossible for former slaves and masters to live peacefully together if both were free (Jefferson 1950).

See also Charges against the King and Others; Committee Responsible for Writing the Declaration of Independence; Declaration House; Declaration of Independence Desk; Jefferson Memorial; Jefferson's Last Words on the Declaration of Independence; Jefferson's Notes on Debates over Independence; Jefferson's Resolutions on Lord North's Conciliatory Proposal; Resolutions Introduced by Richard Henry Lee (June 7, 1776); Signing of the Declaration of Independence; Slavery; *A Summary Views of the Rights of British America* (Jefferson); Virginia and Its Signers

Further Reading

Adair, Douglass. 1952. "Rumbold's Dying Speech, 1685, and Jefferson's Last Words on Democracy, 1826." *William and Mary Quarterly* 9 (October): 521–531.

Bedini, Silvio A. 1981. *Declaration of Independence Desk: Relic of Revolution*. Washington, DC: Smithsonian Institution Press.

Cogliano, Francis D. 2006. *Thomas Jefferson: Reputation and Legacy*. Edinburgh: Edinburgh University Press.

Cunningham, Noble E. 1987. *The Pursuit of Reason: The Life of Thomas Jefferson*. Baton Rouge: Louisiana State University Press.

Jayne, Allen. 1998. *Jefferson's Declaration of Independence*. Lexington: University Press of Kentucky.

Jefferson, Thomas. 1950. "Notes of Proceedings in the Continental Congress, 7 June to 1 August 1776." In *The Papers of Thomas Jefferson*, edited by Julian Boyd, vol. 1, *1760–1776*. Princeton, NJ: Princeton University Press.

Jefferson, Thomas. 1964. *Notes on the State of Virginia*. New York: Harper and Row.

Koch, Adrienne. 1950. *Jefferson and Madison: The Great Collaboration*. New York: Oxford University Press.

Malone, Dumas. 1948–1977. *Jefferson and His Time*. 6 vols. Boston: Little, Brown.
McDonald, Robert M. S. 1999. "Thomas Jefferson's Changing Reputation as Author of the Declaration of Independence: The First Fifty Years." *Journal of the Early Republic* 19 (Summer): 169–195.
Meacham, Jon. 2012. *Thomas Jefferson: The Art of Power*. New York: Random House.
Smith, George H. "Was Thomas Jefferson a Plagiarist?" Libertanism.org. https://www.libertarianism.org/publications/essays/excursions/was-thomas-jefferson-plagiarist.
Wills, Garry. 1978. *Inventing America: Jefferson's Declaration of Independence*. Garden City, NY: Doubleday.

JEFFERSON MEMORIAL

With the possible exception of the home he designed and where he lived and the university he founded, the most beautiful memorial to Thomas Jefferson is probably the Jefferson Memorial in Washington, D.C. It is located in West Potomac Park, beside the Potomac River Tidal Basin.

Constructed during World War II when Nazism threatened American ideals, the memorial was begun in 1939 and completed in 1943. In 1947, a bronze statue of Jefferson, designed by Rudulph Evans, was added to the classical revival domed-and-columned marble structure, which is managed by the National Park Service.

The Jefferson Memorial might be thought to balance the Lincoln Memorial in that Jefferson is often considered to be the father of the Democrats and Abraham

View of the Jefferson Memorial at the Tidal Basin in Washington, D.C. It was begun in 1939 and completed in 1943 when the United States was at war with Nazism, which threatened American ideals. (E. M. Kaplin/Dreamstime.com)

Lincoln of the Republicans. Lincoln, however, professed that his own ideas had been built on those of the Declaration.

The inside walls of the memorial contain a number of quotations, among them some from the Declaration of Independence. Although faithful to Jefferson's original preference for the word "inalienable" over the "unalienable" that ended up on the engrossed copy of the Declaration, Frank Fetter has criticized the engraving for omitting some individual words, changing its punctuation, and excising key passages. These include the statement that governments derive "their just powers from the consent of the governed" and that they have a right "to alter or abolish" governments that do not secure their citizens' rights (Fetter 1974).

See also Lincoln, Abraham

Further Reading

Fetter, Frank Whitson. 1974. "The Revision of the Declaration of Independence in 1941." *William and Mary Quarterly* 31 (January): 133–138.

Monticello. n.d. "Quotations on the Jefferson Memorial." Accessed March 27, 2018. https://www.monticello.org/site/jefferson/quotations-jefferson-memorial.

National Park Service. n.d. "Thomas Jefferson Memorial Features." Accessed March 27, 2018. https://www.nps.gov/thje/learn/historyculture/memorialfeatures.htm.

JEFFERSON'S EPITAPH

Thomas Jefferson's grave is on his estate Monticello, just outside Charlottesville, Virginia, which houses the University of Virginia that he founded. Consistent with Jefferson's written wishes, the six-foot obelisk above his grave, which is part of a larger family cemetery, has the following epitaph:

> Here was buried Thomas Jefferson
> Author of the Declaration of Independence
> Of the Statute of Virginia for Religious Freedom
> & the Father of the University of Virginia
> (Cogliano 2006, 137)

The original obelisk was destroyed by weather and relic hunters (Donaldson 1898, 11). The site is now surrounded by an iron fence, the gate to which reads:

> Ab Eo Libertas,
> A Quo Spiritus

An inscription taken from a coat of arms that Jefferson sometimes used, this can be translated as "The spirit (comes) from him from whom liberty comes," or "He who gives life gives liberty" ("Coat of Arms.")

As an individual whose letters and other writings fill numerous volumes and whose offices included that of serving as a member of Congress, governor of Virginia, minister to France, secretary of state and two-term president of the United States, Jefferson had many achievements from which he could have chosen. His inclusion of his authorship of the Declaration of Independence, and the fact that he listed it first, indicates that he thought this work was one of his highest achievements.

Jefferson may have intended for his epitaph to counter those who had questioned his role in the writing of the document (his primary authorship was not widely recognized until almost 15 years after he wrote it) or the significance of its sentiments. Pairing this achievement with the Virginia Statute for Religious Freedom emphasized how he favored both liberty against oppressive government and against established religion. Pairing the Declaration with his founding of the University of Virginia further emphasized the importance he believed that education played in the formation of good citizens.

There is evidence that Jefferson believed that the Declaration that he had presented to the Second Continental Congress was superior to the document that the Congress adopted, although some scholars dispute this (see Maier 1997). Although Jefferson's role was paramount, Congress made substantial changes (especially deletions), and Jefferson had himself emphasized the manner in which he had not written the document in order to express new sentiments but to give expression to the American mind of the time.

See also Jefferson, Thomas; Jefferson's Last Words on the Declaration of Independence

Further Reading

Cogliano, Francis D. 2006. *Thomas Jefferson: Reputation and Legacy*. Edinburgh: Edinburgh University Press.

Detweiler, Philip F. 1962. "The Changing Reputation of the Declaration of Independence: The First Fifty Years." *William and Mary Quarterly,* 3rd ser. 19 (October): 557–574.

Maier, Pauline. 1997. *American Scripture: Making the Declaration of Independence*. New York: Alfred A. Knopf.

Monticello. n.d. "Coat of Arms." Accessed March 27, 2018. https://www.monticello.org/site/research-and-collections/coat-arms.

JEFFERSON'S LAST WORDS ON THE DECLARATION OF INDEPENDENCE

Roger C. Weightman, the mayor of Washington, D.C., invited Thomas Jefferson to the 50th anniversary celebrations of the Declaration of Independence that were to take place in his city on July 4, 1826. Knowing that he was too feeble to attend, Jefferson wrote a letter dated June 24, 1826, in which he attempted to describe the significance of the document of which he had been the primary author. He appears to have written at least two other letters before his death, both of which deal with fairly mundane matters (Looney 2004).

Jefferson observed that he and his compatriots had made a choice "between submission or the sword," and he expressed gratitude that "our fellow citizens, after half a century of experience and prosperity, continue to approve the choice we made" ("Letter") Jefferson further expressed the hope that it "May be to the world, what I believe it will be, (to some parts sooner, to others later, but finally to all), the signal of arousing men to burst the chains under which monkish ignorance and superstition had persuaded them to bind themselves, and to assume the blessings and security of self-government." He further noted that "That form which we have substituted, restores the free right to the unbounded exercise of reason and freedom of opinion." He followed with his most memorable lines:

> All eyes are opened, or opening, to the rights of man. The general spread of the light of science has already laid open to every view the palpable truth, that the mass of mankind has not been born with saddles on their backs, nor a favored few booted and spurred, ready to ride them legitimately, by the grace of God.

What is fascinating about this quotation, especially in light of criticisms that he had largely copied the Declaration of Independence from John Locke, is that Jefferson appears to have appropriated his central analogy from the speech that Colonel Richard Rumbold of England (a former member of Oliver Cromwell's army) had delivered on June 26, 1685, before being executed for his alleged participation in the Rye House Plot. In that speech, after referring to the manner in which "*Popery* and *Slavery*" had been "riding" on the people, he said that "I am sure there was no Man born marked of God above another; for none comes into the World with a Saddle on his Back, neither any Booted and spurr'd to Ride him" (Adair 1952, 530).

In his speech, Rumbold stressed his own adherence to "the *True Protestant Religion*" (Adair 1952, 530) whereas in his letter, Jefferson emphasized his belief in the power of reason to lead to further progress. Both affirmed that men were not created to be tyrannized by another.

Jefferson's words achieve special poignancy when both John Adams and he died on July 4, 1826.

See also Equality; Jefferson, Thomas; Jefferson's Epitaph; Life, Liberty, and the Pursuit of Happiness; Originality of the Declaration of Independence; Treason

Further Reading

Adair, Douglass. 1952. "Rumbold's Dying Speech, 1685, and Jefferson's Last Words on Democracy, 1826." *William and Mary Quarterly* 9 (October): 521–531.

Butterfield, L. H. 1953. "The Jubilee of Independence, July 4, 1826." *Virginia Magazine of History and Biography* 61 (April): 119–140.

Jefferson, Thomas. 1826. "Letter to Roger C. Weightman." June 24, 1826. Teaching American History.org. http://teachingamericanhistory.org/library/document/letter-to-roger-c-weightman/.

Looney, J. Jefferson. 2004. "Thomas Jefferson's Last Letter." *Virginia Magazine of History and Biography* 112:178–184.

JEFFERSON'S NOTES ON DEBATES OVER INDEPENDENCE

The most complete account of the debates that transpired in the Second Continental Congress over the Declaration of Independence are found in notes that Thomas

Jefferson took for the period from June 7 to August 1, which he later included in his autobiography. The editor of Jefferson's papers believes he completed the notes sometime prior to June 1, 1783 (Boyd 1950, 1:305).

Jefferson groups arguments from James Wilson, Robert Livingston, John and Edward Rutledge, John Dickinson, and unnamed "others" together, on one side, against arguments that he attributes to John Adams, Richard Henry Lee, George Wythe, and "others" on the other side, but he describes both in fairly impartial terms. Lawyers are often encouraged to learn their opponents' side as well as their own, and Jefferson's notes would indicate that he had such knowledge. Interestingly, however, he portrays most of the arguments against the Declaration as arguments for delay rather than arguments on behalf of the actions of the British government. Although this does not necessarily indicate that the nation was unified, it suggests that most delegates to the Congress had already concluded that separation would occur and chiefly differed on the timing.

The lead argument that Jefferson cites on behalf of those who wanted to delay independence was "That tho' they were friends to the measures themselves, and saw the impossibility that we should ever again be united with Gr. Britain, yet they were against adopting them at th[at] time" (Jefferson 1950, 1:309). These arguments were reinforced with arguments that Congress should wait on the expression of "the voice of the people" (1950, 1:309); that opinion was still quite uncertain in "the middle colonies" where, however, opinion against Britain was "ripening"; and that this had been demonstrated by those colonies' reaction to the May 15 Resolution encouraging colonies to create their own governments. Jefferson further observed that some states had either "expressly forbidden" their delegates from voting for independence or that they had "given no instruction" (1950, 1:310); that one set of colonies could not make the decision on behalf of others; and that Pennsylvania, New Jersey, and Delaware were in the process of providing such permission. This was further linked to the possibly that states that had not yet "ripened" might "secede from the Union," thus weakening it and jeopardizing the prospect of help from foreign allies (1950, 1:310).

Jefferson also cited arguments that "we had little reason to expect an alliance"; that "France & Spain had reason to be jealous" of America's rising power; that there was a prospect that foreign intrigue could result in "a partition of our territories, restoring Canada to France, & the Floridas to Spain" (1950, 1:310); that the colonies should await news from France, and that, by waiting, the colonies might "expect an alliance on better terms" (1950, 1:310). Opponents had further argued that "it was prudent to fix among ourselves the terms on which we would form alliance, before we declared" and that when agreed upon, our ambassador could take such terms to Europe.

As with the arguments against independence, Jefferson's arguments for independence rested as much on timing as on substance. Indeed, Jefferson's opening summary was that "no gentleman had argued against the policy or the right of separation from Britain, nor had supposed it possible we should ever renew our connection: that they had only opposed it's being now declared" (1950, 1:311).

As if contemplating the opening sentence of his Declaration—"When in the course of human events"—Jefferson next observed that the real question was "not whether, by a declaration of independence, we should make ourselves what we are not; but whether we should declare a fact which already exists" (1950, 1:311).

Whereas the Declaration focused specifically on ties to the king, Jefferson's summary includes opposition to Parliament. Proponents of independence had observed that parliamentary "restraints on our trade" had existed only "from our acquiescence only & not from any rights they possessed of imposing them" and that this "federal" arrangement had been "dissolved by the commencement of hostilities" (1950, 1:311). Similarly, proponents of independence had argued that any ties to the king were "now dissolved by his assent to the late acts of parliament" (1950, 1:311). This was coupled with the observation "that allegiance & protection are reciprocal, the one ceasing when the other is withdrawn" (1950, 1:311).

Further arguments rested on parallels between George III and James II (whom Parliament had replaced in the Glorious Revolution of 1688), and on the belief that "No delegates . . . can be denied, or ever want, a power of declaring an existent truth" (1950, 1:311). Others argued that Delaware was in fact ready to vote for independence and that instructions from Pennsylvania and Maryland had not prohibited such a vote but only reserved the right to reject it.

Opponents cited the king's response to the petition from the lord mayor of London as an indication "that Britain was determined to accept nothing less than a carte blanche" (1950, 1:312). They also argued that it was time to lead the people, who were ready for independence, even if not all of their representatives were. Countering those who cited negative responses to the congressional resolution of May 15 calling upon states to create their own governments, proponents of the Declaration believed that the majority of the people in the contested middle states had actually supported them. Attitudes among elites in Pennsylvania and Maryland might be attributed to "the influence of proprietary power & connections, & partly to their having not yet been attacked by the enemy," neither of which was likely to change (1950, 1:312).

Others questioned whether unanimity would be possible on such a momentous measure, where some colonies might be purposely holding back in order to avoid taking the brunt of British retaliatory actions. Proponents further cited the success of the Dutch Revolution and argued that a Declaration would be needed to render the situation "consistent with European delicacy for European powers to treat with us, or even to receive an Ambassador from us" (1950, 1:312). This would also make it more likely that such powers would receive American ships and accept the result of American courts of admiralty.

Proponents countered arguments that France and Spain would be jealous by arguing that they would see America as less formidable when detached from the British Empire. Proponents further argued that it would be "idle to lose time in settling the terms of alliance"; that trade was needed more immediately; and that the nation had already lost time by not entering into an alliance with France six months earlier. They claimed that at that time French troops might have "marched an army into Germany and prevented the petty princes there from selling their unhappy subjects to subdue us" (1950, 1:313)—a clear reference to German mercenaries.

After summarizing the arguments on both sides, Jefferson proceeded to detail the voting on independence. In describing debates on July 2, he observed that:

> The pusillanimous idea that we had friends in England worth keeping terms with, still haunted the minds of man, for this reason those passage which conveyed censures on the people of England were struck out, lest they should give them offense. The clause too, reprobating the enslaving the inhabitants of Africa, was struck out in complaisance to South Carolina & Georgia, who had never attempted to restrain the importation of slaves, and who on the contrary still wished to continue it. (1950, 1:314)

He noted, however that these southern states had some support among northern merchants.

Although Jefferson's notes are quite valuable, they are not flawless. After reporting that debates were closed on July 4, Jefferson indicates that it was "signed by every member present, except Mr. Dickinson" whereas it is now believed that the Document was not printed until the evening of July 4 or the morning of July 5 and that individual delegates did not sign until August 2 and thereafter ("Unsullied by Falsehood").

See also Debates over the Declaration of Independence; Jefferson, Thomas; Signing of the Declaration of Independence; Slavery

Further Reading

Harvard University. 2016. "Unsullied by Falsehood: The Signing." Course of Human Events. https://declaration.fas.harvard.edu/blog/signing.

Jefferson, Thomas. 1950. "Notes of Proceedings in the Continental Congress 7 June to 1 August 1776]." In *The Papers of Thomas Jefferson*, vol. 1, *1760–1776*, edited by Julian Boyd. Princeton, NJ: Princeton University Press.

JEFFERSON'S RESOLUTIONS ON LORD NORTH'S CONCILIATORY PROPOSAL

Because so much of the Declaration of Independence focuses on colonial grievances against the king, scholars continue to look for earlier iterations of these complaints.

One such source is found in a series of resolutions that Thomas Jefferson drew up for Virginia and for Congress in 1775 in response to a conciliatory proposal by Britain's Lord North. North's proposal would have assessed taxes on the colonies but let the colonial legislatures decide how they would be raised.

Jefferson served as the primary author both of the Virginia legislative response and of the congressional response to this resolution. Indeed, Garry Wills believes that this work, more than his *Summary View of the Rights of British America*, may have been the primary reason that Jefferson was selected to write the Declaration of Independence (1978, 77).

The Virginia Resolutions were adopted on June 10, 1775, and focus chiefly on denying parliamentary claims to assess or raise taxes in America. In the process, however, the resolutions list a number of more general accusations, most of which would later find their way into the Declaration of Independence: These include:

> still leaving unrepealed their several Acts passed for the purposes of restraining the trade and altering the form of Government of the Eastern Colonies; extending the boundaries and changing the Government and Religion of; enlarging the jurisdiction of the Courts of Admiralty, and taking from us the right of trial by jury; and transporting us into other Countries to be tried for criminal Offences. Standing armies too are still to be kept among us, and the other numerous grievances of which ourselves and sister Colonies separately and by our representatives in General Congress have so often complained, are still to continue without redress. (Jefferson 1950, 1:172).

This report, which was adopted on July 31, 1775, reiterated many of these same themes. It thus says that Lord North's proposal was inadequate:

> Because too it does not propose to repeal the several Acts of Parliament passed for the purposes of restraining the trade and altering the form of government of one of our Colonies; extending the boundaries and changing the government of Quebec; enlarging the jurisdiction of the Courts of Admiralty and Vice Admiralty; taking from us the rights of trial by a Jury of the vicinage in cases affecting both life and property; transporting us into other countries to be tried for criminal offenses; exempting by mock-trial the murderers of Colonists from punishment; and quartering soldiers on us in times of profound peace. Nor do they renounce the power of suspending our own Legislatures, and of legislating for us themselves in all cases whatsoever. (Jefferson 1950, 1:233)

The final paragraph of the Document further notes that the British continued "to claim a right to alter our Charters and established laws, and leave us without any security for our Lives or Liberties" (Jefferson 1950, 1:233). The resolution is more specific than the Declaration of Independence in directly mentioning "their treatment of Boston, and burning of Charlestown" and "the great armaments with which they have invaded us, and the circumstances of cruelty with which these have commenced and prosecuted hostilities" (1950, 1:233).

See also Charges against the King and Others; Jefferson, Thomas; *A Summary View of the Rights of British America* (Jefferson)

Further Reading

Burnett, Edmund Cody. 1941. *The Continental Congress*. New York: Macmillan.

Jefferson, Thomas. 1950. *The Papers of Thomas Jefferson*. Vol. 1, *1760–1776*., edited by Julian P. Boyd. Princeton, NJ: Princeton University Press.

Marsh, Esbon R. 1941. "The First Session of the Second Continental Congress." *Historian* 3 (Spring): 187–194.

Wills, Garry. 1978. *Inventing America: Jefferson's Declaration of Independence*. Garden City, NY: Doubleday.

JEFFERSON'S SPEECH TO JEAN BAPTISTE DUCOIGNE (1781)

It is common to attempt to simplify the sentiments within the Declaration of Independence so as to explain the causes of the American Revolution.

Thomas Jefferson, the chief author of the document, did so himself in June 1781, as he was getting ready to leave the governorship of Virginia. His audience was Brother Jean Baptiste Ducoigne, who had not only paid him a visit but smoked a peace pipe with him and left him with animal hides with Native American drawings. Ducoigne was chief of the Kaskaskia nation.

Jefferson observed that:

> You find us, brother, engaged in war with a powerful nation. Our forefathers were Englishmen, inhabitants of a little island beyond the great water, and, being distressed for land, they came and settled here. As long as we were young and weak, the English whom we had left behind, made us carry all our wealth to their country, to enrich them; and, not satisfied with this, they at length began to say we were their slaves, and should do whatever they ordered us. We were now grown up and felt ourselves strong; we knew we were free as they were, that we came here of our own accord and not at their biddance, and were determined to be free as long as we should exists. For this reason they made war on us. (Jefferson 1781)

After further observing, "This quarrel, when it first began, was a family quarrel between us and the English, who were then our brothers," Jefferson (who had accused the English within the Declaration of enlisting "the merciless Indian savages") went on to recommend against Indian intervention on either side. He did note, however, that if the English had attacked the Indians, then, "you have a right to go to war with them, and revenge the injury, and we have none to restrain you" (Jefferson 1781).

Although the tenor of this speech is paternalistic, it echoes the theme, within the Declaration of Independence, that portrayed the Revolution as a struggle of the American people against attempts by the English king to subject them to slavery (Gittleman 1974).

See also Native American Indians (Charge #27); Slavery

Further Reading

Gittleman, Edwin. 1974. "Jefferson's 'Slave Narrative': The Declaration of Independence as a Literary Text." *Early American Literature* 8 (Winter): 239–256.

Jefferson, Thomas. 1781. "Speech to Jean Baptiste Ducoigne [CA. 1] June 1781. Founders Online. https://founders.archives.gov/documents/Jefferson/01-06-02-0059

Onuf, Peter S. 1999. "'We Shall All Be Americans': Thomas Jefferson and the Indians." *Indiana Magazine of History* 95 (June): 103–141.

JUSTICE

Justice is generally defined as fairness. It is associated both with the content of laws and with their administration. Judges thus sometimes distinguish between substantive and procedural due process.

Justice necessarily presupposes that there are certain moral laws or standards. The Declaration of Independence bases such standards on "the laws of nature and of nature's God," which it believes are accessible to all mankind. It further presupposes that governments are designed to secure the rights of "life, liberty, and the pursuit of happiness," and that when government fails to do so, the people are justified in replacing it with another.

The second paragraph of the Declaration of Independence affirms that governments derive "their just powers from the consent of the governed." The Declaration's eighth accusation against the king specifically associates proper "administration of justice" with the establishment of "judiciary powers." All the accusations are based on the idea that there are just ways of dealing with people, which the British repeatedly transgressed.

After citing a litany of injustices of which the Declaration believes the king and those associated with him have engaged, the Declaration says that Americans have appealed to the British people's "native [meaning inborn, or innate, sense of] justice & magnanimity," but they "have been deaf to the voice of justice and of consanguinity [common ancestry]."

Garry Wills is among those who believe that Thomas Jefferson was deeply influenced by Scottish Common Sense Philosophy (1978). One way of interpreting this phrase is through this lens, which posited a universal "moral sense," akin to conscience, that was as accessible to human beings as were the rational laws of nature (Nicgorski 1976, 170). It would be consistent with the notion that conscience is a kind of inner voice or guide to just conduct. This would give special validity to the idea that the rights that Americans considered to be "self-evident" would also appeal to "the opinions of mankind."

See also Audiences for the Declaration of Independence; Consent of the Governed; Laws of Nature and of Nature's God; Life, Liberty, and the Pursuit of Happiness

Further Reading

Nicgorski, Walter. 1976. "The Significance of the Non-Lockean Heritage of the Declaration of Independence." *American Journal of Jurisprudence* 21:156–177.

Wills, Garry. 1978. *Inventing America: Jefferson's Declaration of Independence*. Garden City, NY: Doubleday.

KINGSHIP

One of the striking features of the Declaration of Independence is that it does not directly mention the British Parliament, whose taxes the colonists had resisted, but focuses instead on the grievances Americans had against the king, whom it also accused of having combined with unnamed "others." This strong indictment might suggest that the document precluded subsequent American adoption of kingship as a form of government or even a component of it.

Such a conclusion is unwarranted. Unlike Thomas Paine's *Common Sense*, which indicted kingship in general and hereditary succession in particular, the Declaration of Independence focuses on a particular king and his alleged abuses just as it focuses on the reason for changing an existing government rather than governments in general. In examining the phrase "A Prince, whose Character is thus marked by every act which may define a Tyrant, is unfit to be the Ruler of a Free people," Dan Himmelfarb thus observed that "'Prince' and 'Tyrant,' apparently, are not equivalent" (1990, 176).

Although the Declaration specifically identifies "the right of representation in the legislature" as an "inestimable" right, its purpose was not to create a new form of government but to explain the one-time colonists' reason for severing the ties to the government of Great Britain. The second paragraph of the Declaration of Independence indicates that governments "derive their just powers from the consent of the governed," that people have the right "to institute new government laying it's foundation on such principles, and organizing it's powers in such form as to them shall seem most likely to effect their safety and happiness," and that they have the right "to provide new guards for their future security." It does not, however, seek to delineate what this form shall be.

Although not necessarily indicting the general institution of kingship (especially as part of a mixed or balanced government), the Declaration of Independence would likely caution against selecting such kings, or any other rulers, through hereditary succession. That is because the second paragraph of the Declaration claims that "that all men are created equal." If men are equal, then there would be no reason to prefer one bloodline for ruling over another.

The example of George III certainly served as a warning to Americans of the harms that an abusive king could inflict. George Washington's later renunciation of the idea of kingship in America also played an important role in seeing that the institution did not take root here.

See also *Common Sense* (Paine); Equality; Representative (Republican) Government; U.S. Constitution and the Declaration of Independence

Further Reading

Himmelfarb, Dan. 1990. "The Constitutional Relevance of the Second Sentence of the Declaration of Independence." *Yale Law Journal* 100 (October): 169–187.

Paine, Thomas. (1776) 2010. *Common Sense*. Reprint with an introduction by Alan Taylor. Cambridge: Harvard University Press.

L

LAWS OF NATURE AND OF NATURE'S GOD

When the Continental Congress drew up its Declaration and Resolves on October 14, 1774, which was often described as a bill of rights, they appealed to "the immutable laws of nature, the principles of the English constitution, and the several charters or compacts." In proclaiming that the colonists were severing the bonds to Britain and declaring Americans to be a separate "people," the Declaration of Independence could no longer appeal to their rights as Englishmen, and since the king had issued their charters, they were likewise of limited argumentative use.

In the circumstances, the colonies appealed to "the laws of nature and of nature's god." In so doing, they were tapping into a political tradition that dated, in one form or another, to classical political philosophy and that was often echoed in early American history. James Otis had referred to "the natural, inherent, and inseparable rights of men and citizens" in arguing against British Writs of Assistance (Kauper 1976, 43). Alexander Hamilton would claim that "the sacred rights of mankind . . . are written, as with a sunbeam, in the whole volume of human nature, by the hand of the divinity itself, and can never be erased or obscured by mortal power" (Kauper 1976, 44). In preparing his farewell to the army in 1783, George Washington further observed that:

> The foundation of our Empire was not laid in the gloomy age of Ignorance and Superstition, but at an Epocha when the rights of mankind were better understood and more clearly defined, than at any former period, the researches of the human mind, after social happiness, have been carried to a great extent, the Treasures of knowledge, acquired by the labours of Philosophers, Sages and Legislatures, through a long succession of years, are laid open for our use, and their collected wisdom may be happily applied in the Establishment of our forms of Government. ("Washington's Circular Letter" 1783)

In articulating his moral and political thought, the Greek philosopher Aristotle sought to ground his thought on what was right by nature. Recognizing that cultures had widely different laws and customs, he, like Socrates and Plato before him, sought to articulate principles that would transcend such cultures.

This philosophy was then taken embraced by Stoic Roman philosophers, most notably Cicero, and eventually incorporated into Christian doctrine. Writing in the Middle Ages, St. Thomas Aquinas distinguished among four types of law—the eternal, natural, human, and divine. Eternal law was God's governance of the universe, not unlike what Thomas Jefferson and other Enlightenment thinkers might describe as the laws of nature. Divine law is revealed in the Bible, and contains knowledge—for example, of the Trinity—that mankind might not be able to ascertain by the mere use of reason. Human law is positive, or enacted law, and may or may not reflect the natural law, or the law accessible, without revelation, to individuals who genuinely seek to determine what is right or wrong through the exercise of reason and conscience. Natural law would strongly suggest that individuals, not wishing to be murdered, to be stolen from, to be cheated on, would not themselves engage in murder, theft, or adultery. Natural law thus was often tied not only to the concept of rights but also to duties. Richard Hooker applied doctrines similar to those of Aquinas to the Anglican Church in his *Laws of Ecclesiastical Polity.*

Early social contract thinkers secularized natural law and tended to emphasize natural rights over natural duties (Oswald 2008; McClellan 2000). Thomas Hobbes described the state of nature as a harsh environment in which even the weakest of individuals would have the power to kill the strongest (perhaps when they were asleep) and where chaos and violence would therefore predominate. His primary understanding of a law of nature was that of self-defense. His only solution to the chaos of the state of nature was to set up a supreme sovereign who could arbitrate among men, but in so raising up the sovereign, he left the people vulnerable to his will even if (as Jefferson would say of George III) he became a tyrant.

John Locke tamed his description of the state of nature by suggesting that people would be able to recognize the differences between right and wrong. Still, he acknowledged that without a law that was established, settled, and known, without impartial judges, and without an administrator, life in the state of nature would leave the security of one's rights, liberties, and property in danger. He suggested that once people had covenanted together to leave the state of nature and move into a state of society, they could then choose rules to protect rights that had previously been insecure, with the understanding that they could depose rulers and dissolve governments in cases where they betrayed this trust.

Natural law thinking was also reflected in the idea of a law of nations that applied to nations that, like prepolitical individuals, were otherwise in something of a state of nature with respect to one another. Hugo Grotius of Holland (1583–1645), Samuel von Pufendorf of Germany (1632–1694), Jean Jacques Burlamaqui of Switzerland (1694–1748), and other thinkers thus emphasized the equality of nations. Similarly, the Declaration claimed America's right as a "free and independent state" with "full power to levy war, conclude peace, contract alliances, establish commerce, & to do all other acts and things which independent states may of right do."

By appealing both to the existence of "unalienable rights" and to laws of nature, Jefferson appealed over the authority of the king and Parliament to fundamental principles. He based this appeal on reason and on premises about human equality. In a letter to Richard Henry Lee dated May 8, 1825, Jefferson said that he had intended for the Declaration of Independence to be "an expression of the American mind." He further indicated that "all its authority rests then on the harmonizing sentiments of the day, whether expressed in conversations, in letters, printed essays or in the elementary books of public rights, as Aristotle, Cicero, Locke, Sidney &c." (Ginsberg 1967, 33). All these individuals had articulated philosophies of natural law or natural rights. Moreover, English common law, which the colonists highly prized, was the result of thousands of court decisions recognizing fundamental rights including trial by jury, which "was widely thought to be the product of equivalent of natural law" (Bradburn 2009, 30).

Many modern philosophers scoff at the idea of natural law, some because they believe it is too vague and others, because they believe that all law is positive law. Even such philosophers might articulate principles—for example, "the greatest good for the greatest number"—that could themselves become standards against which to judge existing regimes (see, however, Seagrave 2011).

Natural law provides a standard against which to measure existing laws. While a racist living in America prior to the Civil War might claim that slavery was legal, someone like Abraham Lincoln, who believed that the Declaration of Independence was correct when it said that all men are created equal, could claim that slavery nonetheless violated natural, or higher law. Similarly, prior to the Supreme Court's decision in *Brown v. Board of Education* (1954), while many might urge obedience to laws mandating racial segregation, advocates of natural law such as Dr. Martin Luther King Jr. could urge that the law was unnatural and unjust because it did not treat individuals equally.

Scholars debate the degree to which the natural law principles of the Declaration of Independence may also be embodied in the Constitution and/or should be enforced by courts (compare Gerber 1995 and Hamburger 1993).

John Phillip Reid has added additional nuances by arguing that most of the Declaration's concrete accusations against the king had far more to do with English customs and usages than with natural law (1981, 48). He also argues that many contemporaries associated the British constitution, including the system of common law, with natural law (1981, 67–69; see also Grey 1978).

Jefferson had a lifelong interest in the natural sciences, so another way of interpreting the laws of nature would be that of associating them with physical laws, such as Isaac Newton (one of Jefferson's heroes) had discovered. After reviewing Jefferson's scientific views, however, Keith Thomson has concluded that Jefferson's references within the Declaration refer "neither to science in general nor to Newton in particular" but to "moral law" that "entailed the natural rights of equality and freedom" (2012, 258).

See also Declaration and Resolves of the First Continental Congress (1774); Human Nature and the Declaration of Independence; Lincoln, Abraham; Locke, John; Reason; Revolution

Further Reading

Amos, Gary T. 1989. *Defending the Declaration: How the Bible and Christianity Influenced the Writing of the Declaration of Independence*. Charlottesville, VA: Providence Foundation.

Bradburn, Douglas. 2009. *The Citizenship Revolution: Politics and the Creation of the American Union, 1774–1804*. Charlottesville: University of Virginia Press.

Fairbanks, Rick. 1994–1995. "The Laws of Nature and of Nature's God: The Role of Theological Claims in the Argument of the Declaration of Independence." *Journal of Law and Religion* 11:551–589.

Finnis, John. 2011. *Natural Law and Natural Rights*. New York: Oxford University Press.

Gerber, Scott Douglas. 1995. *To Secure These Rights: The Declaration of Independence and Constitutional Interpretation*. New York: New York University Press.
Ginsberg, Robert. 1967. *A Casebook on the Declaration of Independence*. New York: Thomas Y. Crowell.
Grey, Thomas C. 1978. "Origins of the Unwritten Constitution: Fundamental Law in American Revolutionary Thought." *Stanford Law Review* 30 (May): 843–893.
Hamburger, Philip A. 1993. "Natural Rights, Natural Law, and the American Constitutions." *Yale Law Journal* 102 (January): 907–960.
Kauper, Paul G. 1976. "The Higher Law and the Rights of Man in a Revolutionary Society." In *American's Continuing Revolution*, 41–68. New York: Anchor Press.
McClellan, James. 2000. *Liberty, Order, and Justice: An Introduction to the Constitutional Principles of American Government*. 3rd ed. Indianapolis, IN: Liberty Fund.
Ostwald, Martin. 2009. *Language and History in Ancient Greek Culture*. Philadelphia: University of Pennsylvania Press.
Reid, John Phillip. 1981. "The Irrelevance of the Declaration." In *Law in the American Revolution and the Revolution in the Law*, edited by Hendrik Hartog, 47–89. New York: New York University Press.
Seagrave, Adam. 2011. "Darwin and the Declaration." *Politics and the Life Sciences* 30 (Spring) 2–16.
Stewart, Matthew. 2014. *Nature's God: The Heretical Origins of the American Republic*. New York: Norton.
Strauss. Leo. 1999. *Natural Rights and History*. Rev. ed. Chicago: University of Chicago Press.
Thomson, Keith. 2012. *Jefferson's Shadow: The Story of His Science*. New Haven, CT: Yale University Press.
Valsania, Maurizio. 2013. *Nature's Man: Thomas Jefferson's Philosophical Anthropology*. Charlottesville: University of Virginia Press.
Washington, George. June 8, 1783. "Washington's Circular Letter of Farewell to the Army." http://www.loc.govve/teachers/classroommaterials/presentationsandactivities/presentations/timeline/amrev/peace/circular.html.
White, Morton. 1978. *The Philosophy of the American Revolution*. New York: Oxford University Press.
Wolfe, Christopher. 2004. "Thomistic Natural Law and the American Natural Law Tradition." In *St. Thomas Aquinas and the Natural Law Tradition: Contemporary Perspectives*, edited by John Gotette et al., 197–228. Washington, DC: Catholic University of America Press.
Zuckert, Michael P. 2004. "Natural Rights and Protestant Politics." *Protestantism and the American Founding*, edited by Thomas S. Engeman and Michael P. Zuckert, 21–76. Notre Dame, IN: University of Notre Dame Press.

LEGAL FORM OF THE DECLARATION OF INDEPENDENCE

Like other members of the Second Continental Congress, Thomas Jefferson was an attorney. One way of understanding the Declaration of Independence is as a legal brief, or indictment, against the king. As in a brief, the most extensive portion of the Declaration consists of a list of 28 charges against the king and his allies. As in some prosecutions, these facts together provided evidence of a conspiracy on the part of the king to take away popular liberties through despotic actions. Arguing that too many commentators on the Declaration have overly focused on the preamble of the Declaration, John Phillip Reid observes that commentators "must realize it is an indictment they are reading" (1981, 84).

Pursuing this thought somewhat further, Peter Hoffer has argued that Jefferson designed the Declaration like a bill in equity. Hoffer points out that Jefferson was trained in equity law and that he shared this interest with his teacher, George Wythe (1989, 191). By way of explanation, the English designed the law of "equity" to provide remedies where regular common law procedures failed to do so. Instead of simply dishing out punishments, equity law could issue injunctions and other remedies, prior to the infliction of further harm.

Hoffer believes that the Declaration incorporates a number of features of a bill of equity. Such bills typically included up to nine parts, including a statement of grievances, an accusation of conspiracy, a discussion of the need to resort to equity, a statement of the equity sought, and an oath (1989, 197). The greatest difficulty with such a form is that equity courts had originally been established by the monarch. Jefferson thus had to appeal beyond the king to natural law, but he could justify such an appeal on the basis that the king had failed to honor the trust that the people had placed in him (Hoffer 1989, 201).

David J. Shestokas has also identified six elements that the Declaration shares in common with a legal complaint. They are a statement, typically begun with "whereas," explaining the document's purpose; a statement of the relevant law; a description of the defendant's conduct; a description of the plaintiff's conduct; a conclusion that presents a remedy; and the plaintiff's signature (2017, 109).

See also Jefferson, Thomas; Laws of Nature and of Nature's God

Further Reading

Hoffer, Peter Charles. 1989. "The Declaration of Independence as a Bill in Equity." In *The Law in America, 1607–1861*, edited by William Pencak and Wythe W. Holt Jr. 186–209. New York: New York Historical Society.

Reid, John Phillip. 1981. "The Irrelevance of the Declaration." In *Law in the American Revolution and the Revolution in the Law*, edited by Hendrik Hartog, 47–89. New York: New York University Press.

Shestokas, David J. 2017. *Creating the Declaration of Independence*. Lemont, IL: Constitutionally Speaking.

LENGTH OF THE DECLARATION OF INDEPENDENCE

One of the reasons that the Declaration of Independence remains so accessible is that it can be read in a single sitting. In this respect, it is similar to Abraham Lincoln's First Inaugural Address and his Gettysburg Address. Howard Mumford Jones has observed that, excluding the title (and presumably the accompanying signatures), the document consists of only 1,310 words—perhaps because she includes the title, Allen says it has 1,337 (2014, 33). Jones notes that the "most familiar paragraph" of the Declaration "runs to 267 words and is nine words shorter than the

Gettysburg Address," but, as if by way of defense, he immediately adds that "the Gettysburg Address does not set forth a theory of political philosophy" (1976).

Because the document was written, and can be printed, on a single page, it is much more suitable for framing than is the Constitution of 1787. It is thus more commonly displayed in American homes, offices, and businesses than is the Constitution, which generally requires four pages.

Further Reading

Allen, Danielle. 2014. *Our Declaration: A Reading of the Declaration of Independence in Defense of Equality*. New York: Norton.

Jones, Howard Mumford. 1976. "The Declaration of Independence: A Critique." In *The Declaration of Independence: Two Essays,* by Howard Mumford Jones and Howard H. Peckham, 3–20. Worcester, MA: American Antiquarian Society.

LIBERTY

See Life, Liberty, and the Pursuit of Happiness

LIBERTY BELL

See Independence Hall

LIFE, LIBERTY, AND THE PURSUIT OF HAPPINESS

Of all the phrases in the Declaration of Independence, few are more memorable or more quoted than the proclamation in its second paragraph that individuals have the unalienable rights of "life, liberty, and the pursuit of happiness."

The idea that such rights are unalienable, which is treated in a separate essay, was Jefferson's way of indicating that human nature is so constituted that individuals are naturally inclined to protect them. Absent the kind of mental disorientation that might lead to suicide or the extraordinary altruism that might compel others to risk or sacrifice their lives or liberties for another, as in serving in the military, it is difficult to imagine individuals turning themselves over voluntarily to be killed or enslaved. Such a renunciation would effectively transfer their own pursuit of happiness to the direction of another. Moreover, few would be likely to blame individuals who sought to regain control over their lives by escaping from slavery.

The Declaration arguably listed rights in their order of importance. Without life, one cannot have liberty. Without liberty, one cannot organize one's own pursuits for happiness or any other goal. Notably, the term "among these" indicates that the Declaration did not describe these three rights as the only rights, or even the only unalienable rights. The charges against the king thus describe "the right of representation in the legislature" as "a right inestimable to them, & formidable to tyrants."

In addition to its alliterative qualities, Thomas Jefferson probably chose the word "liberty" over "freedom" because the former term generally denotes what Matthew Spalding describes as "the rightful exercise of freedom, the balancing of rights and responsibilities" (2009, 9). Spalding further believes that liberty "is an inherently *human word*," indicating that "while we say man has liberty or is at liberty to do something, we do not say the same of animals, because animals lack a rational capacity to choose their own actions" (2009, 9).

Although the idea of the pursuit of happiness will probably always be especially tied to Thomas Jefferson, a number of classical European and colonial writers had previously expressed the idea that government was designed to provide for the happiness of the people (Ganter 1936a,b). Patrick J. Charles identifies the phrase "life, liberty, and the pursuit of happiness" with "a well-established political, constitutional, and legal idea that government is established for the public or common good" (2011, 471). Classical philosophers had generally agreed that men sought happiness, while recognizing that for some this might involve the pursuit of pleasure, for others fame, for others virtue, and, for still others, the hope of eternal bliss. Classical philosophers often associated true happiness with philosophical reflection and intellectual attainments, much on the order of a Renaissance Man such as Thomas Jefferson or Benjamin Franklin.

Two issues seem most prominent in debates over this phrase. One, which stems from John Locke's virtual preoccupation with property, is intent on discovering whether Jefferson intended to distance himself from Locke's philosophy or to send some other message, by citing the pursuit of happiness rather than property.

Jefferson's language differed from the Declaration and Resolves of the First Continental Congress, which had referred specifically to "life, liberty and property" (Vile 2015, 77). Moreover, Jefferson later suggested to Lafayette that the French Declaration of Rights of Man should omit the word "property" from its list of inalienable rights (Haske 1964, 149).

It seems unlikely that someone like Jefferson, who had praised those who owned and worked the land as God's "chosen people" (Jefferson 1964) and who had elsewhere said that "The End of Government would be defeated by the British Parliament exercising a Powers over the Lives, the Property, and the Liberty of the American Subject" (Smith 2017, 125), would have undervalued property rights. He might, however, have thought that property, or at least a certain kind of property, was "alienable," in a way that life and liberty were not (Gerber 1993, 216). Contemporary philosophers argued that individuals had "property" in their lives and their liberties, but there is a substantial difference between selling one's house or giving up one's life or selling one's self into slavery! More generally, Jefferson may have thought that happiness was a more embracive term that could include the possession of property, without being identical to it.

Another possibility, which is consistent with the U.S. Constitution's later omission of the word "slavery," is that Jefferson substituted the pursuit of happiness for property because in his day, some individuals would have interpreted the right of property to include the right to hold slaves, while Jefferson appears to have looked forward to slavery's eventual extinction. Alfred W. Blumrosen and Ruth G. Blumrosen thus believe that "by using the more abstract term 'pursuit of happiness,' he did not embed slavery in the document expressing our national raison d'etre" (2005, 138). Because some people within the former colonies were "born" into slavery, the Blumrosens also believe that this alteration helps, at least in part, account for why the document chose to say that men were "created equal"

(2005, 132–33). Henry Alonzo Myers believes that the Declaration may have avoided the term "property" both because this helped them avoid the issue of slavery and because "their intention to confiscate the large Tory estates implied a distinction between the rights of loyalists and the rights of patriots which could not be honestly described as self-evident and natural" (1955, 129).

A second discussion that Jefferson's phraseology triggers is why he chose to describe "the pursuit of happiness," rather than its attainment, as a right. It seems logical to assume that he recognized that people were largely responsible for seeking to obtain their own happiness, and that while government could facilitate this quest, it could never guarantee it, especially to those who sought happiness in the hereafter. Indeed, in Aristotelian philosophy, one could not fully declare a man to have led a happy life until after he were dead, because only then did one know its outcome. As Willmore Kendall and George W. Carey have observed, the authors of the Declaration "do not claim that any new government which might result from the Declaration will provide for the 'Safety and Happiness' of the constituents but it will be one that 'shall seem' to the people 'most likely to effect their Safety and Happiness'" (1970, 82).

The Declaration of Independence was arguably more concerned with the collective right of the former colonies to pursue their happiness through their own self-governance and the exercise of their individual freedoms than it was concerned with an individual right to happiness. Independence was no guarantee that the new nation would gain such happiness but only that it would be able to pursue it on its own terms. Caroline Robbins notes that although Jefferson sometimes claimed to be an Epicurean (a philosophy that emphasized the pursuit of pleasure), he thought the Epicureans had not fully understood their obligation to others. As Robbins summarized the Declaration, "Happiness meant public happiness" (1976, 133). Darrin McMahon observes that Jefferson had observed, in a letter of 1763, that "the most fortunate of us, in our journey through life, frequently meet with calamities and misfortunes which may greatly afflict us" (1976, 68).

The Virginia Declaration of Rights, which George Mason largely authored, had referred to "the enjoyment of life and liberty, with the means of acquiring and possessing property, and pursuing and obtaining happiness and safety" (Vile 2015, 96). Historian Arthur M. Schlesinger believes that Jefferson, who was known for his conciseness, may have simply cut the words "obtaining happiness and safety" as a matter of style (1965, 327).

Having proclaimed the right to three unalienable rights, the Declaration attempted to show how the colonists' relationship to Britain threatened them. Thus, the 24th charge against the king accused him of having engaged in war measures that "destroyed the lives of our people." Similarly, the next observed that he was attempting "to complete the works of death" by sending over foreign mercenaries, and the one after that observed that the king was aiding Native Americans who engaged in "an indistinguished destruction of all ages, sexes, & conditions." By classifying the king as a tyrant, the Declaration further indicated that he was jeopardizing the rights of Americans, which would surely undermine their collective happiness (Ginsberg 1984, 32–33).

The Fifth Amendment of the U.S. Constitution, which is part of the Bill of Rights, which the states ratified in 1791, subsequently guaranteed that the national government should not deprive anyone "of life, liberty, or property, without due process of law." The Fourteenth Amendment added a similar provision against state action in 1868.

See also Declaration and Resolves of the First Continental Congress (1774); Jefferson, Thomas; Locke, John; Slavery; Unalienable Rights; Virginia Declaration of Rights

Further Reading

Blumrosen, Alfred W., and Ruth G. Blumrosen. 2005. *Slave Nation: How Slavery United the Colonies and Sparked the American Revolution*. Naperville, IL: Sourcebooks.

Ford, John C. 1951. "Natural Law and the Pursuit of Happiness." Notre Dame Law Review 26:429–461.

Ganter, Herbert Lawrence. 1936a. "Jefferson's 'Pursuit of Happiness' and Some Forgotten Men." *William and Mary Quarterly* 16 (July): 422–434.

Ganter, Herbert Lawrence. 1936b. "Jefferson's 'Pursuit of Happiness' and Some Forgotten Men." *William and Mary Quarterly* 16 (October): 558–585.

Gerber, Scott D. 1993. "Whatever Happened to the Declaration of Independence? A Commentary on the Republican Revisionism in the Political Thought of the American Revolution. *Polity* 26 (Winter): 207–231.

Ginsberg, Robert. 1984. "Suppose that Jefferson's Rough Draft of the Declaration of Independence Is a Work of Political Philosophy." *Eighteenth Century* 25 (Winter): 25–43.

Hawke, David Freeman. 1964. *A Transaction of Free Men: The Birth and Course of the Declaration of Independence*. New York: Charles Scribner's Sons.

Jefferson, Thomas. (1785). 1964. *Notes on the State of Virginia*. New York: Harper and Row.

Jones, Howard Mumford. 1953. *The Pursuit of Happiness*. Ithaca, NY: Cornell University Press.

Kendall, Willmoore, and George W. Carey. 1970. *The Basic Symbols of the American Political Tradition*. Baton Rouge: Louisiana State University Press.

McMahon, Darrin M. 2004. "From the Happiness of Virtue to the Virtue of Happiness: 400 B.C.–A.D. 1780." 133 *Daedalus* (Spring): 5–17.

McMahon, Darrin M. 2005. "The Quest for Happiness." *Wilson Quarterly* 29 (Winter): 62–71.

Myers, Henry Alonzo. 1955. *Are Men Equal? An Inquiry into the Meaning of American Democracy*. Ithaca, NY: Great Seal Books of Cornell University Press.

Patrick, Charles J. 2011. "Restoring 'Life, Liberty, and the Pursuit of Happiness' in Our Constitutional Jurisprudence: An Exercise in Legal History." *William and Mary Bill of Rights Journal* 20 (December) 457–532.

Robbins, Caroline. 1976. "The Pursuit of Happiness." In *America's Continuing Revolution: Eighteen Distinguished Americans Discuss Our Revolutionary Heritage*, 115–136. New York: Anchor Press.

Schlesinger, Arthur M. 1964. "The Lost Meaning of 'The Pursuit of Happiness.'" *William and Mary Quarterly* 21 (July): 325–327.

Smith, George H. 2017. *The American Revolution and the Declaration of Independence*. Washington, DC: Cato Institute.

Spalding, Matthew. 2009. *We Still Hold These Truths: Rediscovering Our Principles, Reclaiming Our Future*. Wilmington, DE: ISI Books.

Vile, John R. 2015. *Founding Documents of America: Documents Decoded*. Santa Barbara, CA: ABC-CLIO.

LINCOLN, ABRAHAM

Few, if any, individuals have highlighted the Declaration of Independence in their rhetoric and made it a more vital part of their philosophy than Abraham Lincoln (1809–1865), the Kentucky-born lawyer who became a U.S. representative and the first Republican to become president of the United States. He served during the tumultuous years of the Civil War, which led to the abolition of slavery, soon after which he was assassinated.

In his famous Gettysburg Address, which he delivered on November 19, 1863, Lincoln dated the foundation of the nation ("four score and seven years ago") back to the Declaration of Independence. Looking back on this event, he claimed that American's Founders had "created a new nation, conceived in Liberty, and dedicated to the proposition that all men are created equal."

In a speech that he delivered at Independence Hall on the way to his inauguration as the nation's 16th president, Lincoln said that "I have never had a feeling politically that did not spring from the sentiments embodied in the Declaration of Independence" (Lincoln 1953, 4:240). He went on to say, "It was not the mere matter of the separation of the colonies from the mother land; but something in that Declaration giving liberty, not alone to the people of this country, but hope to the world for all future time. It was that which gave promise that in due time the weights should be lifted from the shoulders of all men, and that all should have an equal chance." (4:240). In this same speech, he said that he would rather be assassinated than surrender its principles.

President Abraham Lincoln, 1864. Lincoln, who was the first Republican president, often referred back to the Declaration's statement that "all men are created equal" and converted the Civil War to a war to save the Union and to eliminate slavery. (BiographicalImages.com)

Lincoln had expressed his commitment to the Declaration in his Address before the Young Men's Lyceum of Springfield, Illinois, on January 27, 1838, where he had expressed concern over mob violence. There he had urged his audience to "Let every American, every lover of liberty, every well wisher to his posterity, swear by the blood of the Revolution, never to violate in the least particular, the laws of the country; and never to tolerate their violation by others. As the patriots of seventy-six did to the support of the Declaration of

Independence, so to the support of the Constitution and Laws, let every American pledge his life, his property, and his sacred honor" (1953, 1:112).

As a member of the emerging Republican Party, which originated in opposition to the expansion of slavery, Lincoln increasingly relied on the Declaration for support. Lincoln was particularly opposed to the doctrine of popular sovereignty, advocated by Senator Stephen A. Douglas, which would have enabled each new state to decide for itself whether it wanted to allow slavery.

In a speech that he gave in Peoria, Illinois, on October 16, 1854, Lincoln observed that the author of the Declaration had also drafted the Northwest Ordinance to exclude slavery from the Northwest Territory. Saying that "no man is good enough to govern another man, *without that other's consent*," Lincoln identified this principle, which he associated with the Declaration of Independence, as "the sheet anchor of American republicanism" (2:266). Noting in a speech of October 27, 1854, in Chicago that a certain politician had called the Declaration "a 'self-evident lie,'" Lincoln claimed that had this politician said this in Independence Hall: "The door-keeper would have taken him by the throat and stopped his rascally breath awhile, and then have hurled him into the street" (1953, 2:284).

Especially during his famed debate with Stephen A. Douglas, Lincoln took particular aim at Chief Justice Roger Taney's decision in *Dred Scott v. Sandford* (1857) where Taney had argued that while the words of the Declaration appeared to apply to all men, they really applied only to white men. In his speech at Springfield, Illinois, of June 26, 1857, Lincoln sided with the dissenting justices, who observed that some states that had ratified the U.S. Constitution had included free blacks as citizens. He observed that "the authors of that notable instrument intended to include *all* men, but they did not intend to declare all men equal in *all respects*. They did not mean to say all were equal in color, size, intellect, moral developments, or social capacity. They defined with tolerable distinctness, in what respects they did consider all men created equal—equal in 'certain inalienable rights, among which are life, liberty, and the pursuit of happiness'" (1953, 2:405–406).

Lincoln put particular emphasis on the right of individuals, regardless of color, to work for themselves. Noting that just because he did not favor keeping a black woman as a slave did not mean that he would want to marry her, Lincoln said that "In some respects she certainly is not my equal; but in her natural right to eat the bread she earns with her own hands without asking leave of any one else, she is my equal, and the equal of all others" (1953, 3:405). Lincoln offered an extended explanation as to how some Framers could have endorsed the Declaration while retaining their slaves:

> They did not mean to assert the obvious untruth, that all were then actually enjoying that equality, nor yet that they were about to confer it immediately upon them. In fact they had no power to confer such a boon. They meant simply to declare the *right*, so that the *enforcement* of it might follow as fast as circumstances should permit. They meant to set up a standard maxim for free society, which should be familiar to all, and revered by all; constantly looked to, constantly labored for, and even though never perfectly attained, constantly approximated, and thereby constantly spreading and deepening its influence, and augmenting the happiness and value of life to all

> people of all colors everywhere. The assertion that "all men are created equal" was of no practical use in effecting our separation from Great Britain; and it was placed in the Declaration, not for that, but for future use. (1953, 2:406)

In this same speech, Lincoln said that "the Declaration contemplated the progressive improvement in the condition of all men everywhere" (1953, 2:407).

Lincoln wrote in a similar vein in a widely published letter to Henry L. Pierce dated April 6, 1859. Associating Jefferson and the Declaration with putting a priority on "the *personal* rights of men" over "the rights of *property*," Lincoln identified "The principles of Jefferson" with "the definitions and axioms of free society" (1953, 3:375). Noting that "he who would be no slave, must consent to have no slave," Lincoln continued with a tribute to the Declaration's author: "All honor to Jefferson—to the man who, in the concrete pressure of a struggle for national independence by a single people, had the coolness, forecast, and capacity to introduce into a merely revolutionary document, an abstract truth, applicable to all men and all times, and so to embalm it there, that today, and in all coming days, it shall be a rebuke and a stumbling-block to the very harbingers of re-appearing tyranny and oppression" (1953, 3:376).

In a "Fragment on the Constitution and Union," which he penned in January 1861, Lincoln described the principles of the Declaration as being at the heart of the Constitution. Referring to the principle of "Liberty to all," Lincoln observed that:

> The *expression* of that principle, in our Declaration of Independence, was most happy, and fortunate. *Without* this, as well as *with* it, we could have declared our independence of Great Britain; but *without* it, we could not, I think, have secured our free government, and consequent prosperity. No oppressed, people will *fight,* and *endure*, as our fathers did, without the promise of something better, than a mere change of masters. (1953, 4:169)

Continuing with a biblical analogy, Lincoln said that:

> The assertion of that *principle*, at *that time*, was the word, "*fitly spoken*" which has proved an "apple of gold" to us. The *Union*, and the *Constitution*, are the *picture* of *silver*, subsequently framed around it. The picture was made, nor to *conceal*, or *destroy* the apple; but to *adorn*, and *preserve* it. The picture was made *for* the apple—*not* the apple for the picture. So let us act, that neither *picture*, or *apple* shall ever be blurred, or bruised or broken. (1953, 4:169).

There has been considerable discussion about Lincoln's commitment to constitutionalism, in part because of his strong reliance on the Declaration and in part on his strong exertions of executive power to preserve the Union. Herman Belz has concluded that "Lincoln viewed the Declaration of Independence as the nation's primary constitutive document, and as the source of the substantive principles of the Constitution. The Declaration created the Union, making liberty, equality and consent the fundamental principles of republican government. The Constitution in turn was written in order to make a more perfect Union that would preserve these principles" (1988, 181).

The Fourteenth Amendment to the U.S. Constitution, which was ratified in 1868, overturned the *Dred Scott* decision by declaring in its first section that all persons "born or naturalized in the United States" were citizens protected against state deprivation of their rights. One of these rights, with a clear lineage to the Declaration, was "the equal protection of the laws."

See also Consent of the Governed; Equality; Life, Liberty, and the Pursuit of Happiness; Northwest Ordinance of 1787; Slavery; U.S. Constitution and the Declaration of Independence

Further Reading

Abbott, Philip. 1997. The Declaration of Independence: From Philadelphia to Gettysburg to Birmingham." *Amerikastudien / American Studies* 42:451–469.

Belz, Herman. 1988. "Abraham Lincoln and American Constitutionalism." *Review of Politics* 50 (Spring): 169–197.

Burt, John. 2009. "Lincoln's Dred Scott: Contesting the Declaration of Independence." *American Literary History* 21 (Winter): 730–751.

Jacobsohn, Gary Jeffrey. 1993. *Apple of Gold: Constitutionalism in Israel and the United States*. Princeton, NJ: Princeton University Press.

King, Willard L., and Allan Nevins. 1959. "The Constitution and Declaration of Independence as Issues in the Lincoln-Douglas Debates." *Journal of the Illinois State Historical Society* 52 (Spring): 7–32.

Lightner, David. 1982. "Abraham Lincoln and the Ideal of Equality." *Journal of the Illinois State Historical Society* 75 (Winter): 289–308.

Lincoln, Abraham. 1953. *The Collected Works of Abraham Lincoln*. Edited by Roy P. Basler. 9 vols. New Brunswick, NJ: Rutgers University Press.

LIST OF INFRINGEMENTS AND VIOLATIONS OF RIGHTS (WARREN)

The Declaration of Independence largely consists of a list of grievances against the king and his associates. Scholars still debate whether Thomas Jefferson, who had previously composed similar lists of his own, consulted other sources when compiling his own list for the Declaration. Had he done so, one source that he might have consulted or that other delegates (particularly John Adams) on the Committee appointed to write the Declaration might have known was a list that Dr. Joseph Warren (1741–1774) had composed.

Warren, a physician who had played a leading part in the events leading up to the Revolution prior to his own death at the Battle of Bunker Hill, which is celebrated in the painter John Trumbull's *Death of Major General Joseph Warren at the Battle of Bunker's Hill*, had entitled his essay "A List of Infringements and Violations of Rights." It had been published by the Boston Committee of Correspondence in 1772 as part of the Boston Pamphlet. It consisted of an introductory essay, "The Rights of the Colonies," composed by Samuel Adams, and a concluding essay entitled "A Letter of Correspondence to the Other Towns," by Dr. Benjamin Church (Warner 2009).

Just as the Declaration of Independence is addressed to "a candid world," so the opening paragraph of Warren's essay refers to "every candid Person." Unlike the Declaration of Independence, which was announcing the colonial decision to declare independence in the face of repeated British refusals to remedy perceived abuses, Warren's stated purpose was "to obtain a Redress of the Grievances under which we labor." It appears to be addressed chiefly to other colonists.

By the time Jefferson wrote, the colonies were ready to renounce allegiance to George III, but writing in 1772, Warren did not identify the king as a tyrant and blamed most of the colony's woes on the British Parliament. The first of his 12 accusations (considerably fewer than those of the Declaration) therefore accused the Parliament of having "assumed the Power to Legislate for the Colonists in all Cases whatsoever without obtaining the Consent of the Inhabitants." The second accusation specifically addressed the assertion of Parliament's right to tax the colonies without their consent.

Warren's third and fourth grievances were that Britain had appointed "[a] Number of new Officers" unknown to the colony's charter and commissioned them with unconstitutional powers. He devoted particular attention to their right to search under authority of general warrants, which was a grievance especially felt in Boston and the subject of legal actions by James Otis, who was part of its Committee of Correspondence.

Warren's fifth accusations blames Britain for using "Fleets and Armies" to support such officers. Like the later Declaration of Independence, it complains about the use of standing armies and quartering them among the people.

The sixth accusation accuses Britain of upsetting the "Equilibrium" by providing salaries to the governor, lieutenant governor, and judges to make them independent of the colonial legislature. Warren feared that this could "complete our Slavery."

The seventh accusation, which is paralleled by similar accusations within the Declaration, accuses English authorities of making the legislature "merely a ministerial Engine." Warren observed that the governor had "called and adjourned our General Assemblies to a place highly inconvenient to the Members," as well as proroguing and dissolving them.

As in the latter Declaration, Warren's eighth complaint objects to vice admiralty courts and trials without benefit of juries. The ninth complaint, in turn, goes into much greater detail than the latter Declaration by pointing to British trade legislation that prevented the erection of mills and restraining the manufacture of hats and the transportation of wool.

The 10th accusation focused on British legislation designed to allow the transport of colonists accused of destroying British vessels to Britain where they might again be subject to trial without juries of their peers.

The 11th accusation, not later mentioned in the Declaration of Independence, expresses concern over Britain's alleged desire to establish "an American Episcopate." Warren feared that such an establishment would interfere with the "free exercise of their Religion."

Finally, Warren pointed to British alterations in the boundaries of the Colonies, and granting lands that settlers had already cleared and settled to others.

Lacking the rhetorical flourishes of the Declaration and more directed to the woes that had befallen a single colony, Warren's list demonstrates that Jefferson had many such stated grievances from which to borrow when he composed his Document.

See also Charges against the King and Others; Erected a Multitude of New Offices (Charge #10); Made Judges Dependent on His Will (Charge #9); Massachusetts and Its Signers; Quartering Troops (Charge #14); Standing Armies (Charge #11); Suspending Legislatures (Charge #22); Taxes (Charge #17); Trade (Charge #16); Transporting Us beyond Seas (Charge #19); Trial by Jury (Charge #18)

Further Reading

Boston Committee of Correspondence. 1772. Document known as the "Boston Pamphlet." http://americainclass.org/sources/makingrevolution/crisis/text6/bostonpamphlet.pdf.

Forman, Samuel A. 2011. *Dr. Joseph Warren: The Boston Tea Party, Bunker Hill, and the Birth of American Liberty*. Gretna, LA: Pelican Publishing.

Warner, William B. 2009. "The Invention of a Public Machine for Revolutionary Sentiment: The Boston Committee of Correspondence." *Eighteenth Century* 40 (Summer/Fall): 145–164.

LOCKE, JOHN

John Locke (1632–1704) was an English philosopher and physician who disputed the theory of divine right of kings. Both building upon and revising Thomas Hobbes's theory of a state of nature, Locke developed a social contract theory that lies at the basis of classical liberalism and served as the justification for deposing James II in England. Many classical interpretations of the opening paragraphs of the Declaration of Independence have attempted to show how Thomas Jefferson, who in justifying independence was no longer able to appeal to the rights of Englishmen, built instead on the natural rights philosophy that Locke had articulated in his *Second Treatise of Government*.

In describing the prepolitical state of nature, which he largely seems to have used as a heuristic device, Locke said that it was a state of equality and liberty. Whereas Thomas Hobbes had described such a state as a war of all against all (Downes 2012), Locke had argued that "though this be a state of liberty, yet it is not a state of licence" ([1690] 1924, 119). He explained that "The state of Nature has a law of Nature to govern it, which obliges every one, and reason, which is that law, teaches all mankind who will but consult it, that being all equal and independent, no one ought to harm another in his life, health, liberty or possessions" ([1690] 1924, 119).

As men labor, they create wealth, which the invention of money helped them to accumulate, the security of which remains insecure in the state of nature. This led to the formation of government. As Locke explains in chapter 9 of his *Second Treatise*: "though in the state of Nature he hath such a right, yet the enjoyment of it is very uncertain and constantly exposed to the invasion of others; for all being kings as much as he, every man his equal, and the greater part no strict observers of equity and justice, the enjoyment of the property he has in this state is very

John Locke was a 17th-century English political philosopher who help created the groundwork for classical liberal theories of government. Locke posited that individuals in a stateless "state of nature" would find their lives, liberties, and property threatened and would enter into a social contract to protect their rights. He believed that if government failed to secure such rights, the people could create a new government that did so. (Library of Congress)

unsafe, very insecure" ([1690] 1924, 179).

Explaining that the chief end of man is "the preservation of their property" ([1690] 1924, 180), which he defined quite broadly, Locke identified three problems with doing so in the state of nature.

First, he noted that the law of nature is not "established, settled, [or] known," that is, universally recognized. Second, there was not "a known an indifferent Judge, with authority to determine all differences according to the established law." Third, there was no one to execute such judgments ([1690] 1924, 180). Men are accordingly "quickly driven into society" ([1690] 1924, 180). After coming together in community, humans then create legislative, executive, and federative (largely dealing with foreign policy) powers to secure their rights.

Because the people have instituted such governments to protect their lives, liberties, and property, rather than rules being imposed by divine right, the people have the right to dissolve governments that do not accomplish these goals, especially in cases where rules usurp powers or rule tyrannically. Denying that such a doctrine erodes the foundations of government by laying "a ferment for frequent rebellion" ([1690] 1924, 230), Locke says that the people generally bear misadministration but that "if a long train of abuses, prevarications, and artifices, all tending the same way, make the design visible to the people . . . it is not to be wondered that they should then rouse themselves, and endeavor to put the rule into such hands which may secure to them the ends for which government was at first erected" ([1690] 1924, 231).

Parallels between the Declaration and Locke should be obvious and have been outlined elsewhere (see especially Sheldon 1991, 45–48; Becker 1970). The Declaration describes men as being free and equal. The Declaration outlines similar aims for government (the protection of "life, liberty, and the pursuit of happiness"). The Declaration seeks to ground government in consent. The Declaration argues that revolution is acceptable under extreme circumstances. The Declaration, which is itself issued by a body that is exercising governmental power in America, does not anticipate that changing government will result in a resumption of a state of nature but will leave a society, or people, who will be free to form a new government (Becker 1970). Notably, the Declaration ascribes the equality to peoples (Americans and British) that Locke had ascribed to individuals within the state of nature.

In explaining his contributions to the Declaration, Jefferson did not, of course, claim to be presenting the philosophy of John Locke but to be expressing the American mind, and he listed several philosophers who had influenced him. Other scholars have thus found elements of classical republicanism (which tended to stress the role of civic virtue), the philosophy of the Old Whigs, Scottish Common Sense philosophy (see Wills 1978), Protestantism, and numerous other elements that may have influenced Jefferson and the other founders who contributed to the document (Nicgorski 1976). Many of these thinkers in turn influenced one another sometimes, thus making it almost impossible to know with certainty which individually had the most significant influence on Jefferson or on the Declaration of Independence.

See also Dissolution of Government; Laws of Nature and Nature's God; Revolution

Further Reading

Downes, Paul. 2012. "Does the Declaration of Independence Declare a State of Emergency?" *Canadian Review of American Studies* 42:7–20.

Gerber, Scott D. 1993. "Whatever Happened to the Declaration of Independence? A Commentary on the Republican Revisionism in the Political Thought of the American Revolution." *Polity* 26 (Winter): 207–231.

Locke, John. (1690) 1924. *Two Treatises of Government*. London: Dent, Everyman's Library.

Mishra, Pramod K. 2002. "[A]ll the World Was America": The Transatlantic (Post) Coloniality of John Locke, William Bartram, and the Declaration of Independence. *New Centennial Review* 2 (Spring): 213–258.

Nicgorski, Walter. 1976. "The Significance of the Non-Lockean Heritage of the Declaration of Independence." *American Journal of Jurisprudence* 21:156–177.

Pangle, Thomas L. 1988. *The Spirit of Modern Republicanism: The Moral Vision of the American Founders and the Philosophy of Locke*. Chicago, IL: University of Chicago Press.

Sheldon, Garrett Ward. 1991. *The Political Philosophy of Thomas Jefferson*. Baltimore, MD: Johns Hopkins University Press.

Wills, Garry. 1978. *Inventing America: Jefferson's Declaration of Independence*. Garden City, NY: Doubleday.

Yolton, John W., ed. 1969. *John Locke: Problems and Perspectives*. Cambridge: Cambridge University Press.

LOYALISTS

See Tories

MADE JUDGES DEPENDENT ON HIS WILL (CHARGE #9)

The ninth accusation that the Declaration of Independence makes against King George III is that "he has made judges dependent on his will alone, for the tenure of their offices, and the amount & payment of their salaries." This is the second accusation that the Declaration directed against the king's policies respecting the judiciary, the first having charged that the king had refused "his assent to laws for establishing judiciary powers."

In governments that employ a system of separation of powers in order to protect liberty, it is a fundamental assumption that the institution that provides salaries may influence decision making (Kaufman 1980). Under the current U.S. Constitution, Congress appropriates money for federal judges, but it is prevented from lowering such salaries lest this power be used to exert undue influence (Vile 2015, 81). Judges further serve "during good behavior," which means that they remain in their positions until they die, resign, or are impeached and convicted of designated crimes.

New Jersey had been the site of a dispute between the colonies and the justices as to tenure of one of its members, which had actually resulted in the dismissal of a state governor in 1762 (Dumbauld 1950, 113–114). Other conflicts had arisen in New York and Massachusetts. In these colonies, the king insisted that he would pay the judges and that, as of 1761, he could also remove them. This was contrary to the policy toward English judges (Friedenwald 1904, 233). The hated Townshend Act arguably had rubbed salt into this wound when it stated that it was designed to make "a more certain and adequate Provision for defraying the Charge of the Administration of Justice and the Support of Civil Government, in such provinces as it shall be found necessary" (Friedenwald 1904, 234).

Governor Thomas Hutchinson, whose salary the king paid, further aggravated his relations with Massachusetts when in February 1773, he announced that the king would henceforth provide the salaries for superior court justices. This seemed to pose a further threat to judicial independence. The Massachusetts legislature thus impeached its chief justice by a vote of 96–9, although the governor had refused to remove him (Lossing 1848, 282).

Acknowledging that "There has been a change in the constitution of England in respect of the tenure of the office of the Judges," Hutchinson asked, "How does this give a claim to America?" (1776). In his view, this was an issue for the king to decide. As to salaries, he pointed out that "they are fixed and do not depend upon the behavior of the Judges, nor have there ever been any instances of salaries being withheld" (1776). John Lind charged that the colonies had sought to retain control by refusing to provide permanent salaries for either governors or judges refused to provide. He thus observed that "the dependence of the Judges on the Crown is infinitely less entire, and less likely to be abused, than that dependence on the people we have above described" (1776, 47).

See also Charges against the King and Others; Obstructed the Administration of Justice (Charge #8)

Further Reading

Dumbauld, Edward. 1950. *The Declaration of Independence and What It Means Today*. Norman: University of Oklahoma Press.

Friedenwald, Herbert. 1904. *The Declaration of Independence, An Interpretation and an Analysis*. New York: Macmillan.

Hutchinson, Thomas. 1776. "1776: Hutchinson, Strictures upon the Declaration of Independence." Online Library of Liberty. http://oll.libertyfund.org/pages/1776-hutchinson-strictures-upon-the-declaration-of-independence.

Kaufman, Irving R. 1980. "The Essence of Judicial Independence." *Columbia Law Review* 80 (May): 671–701.

Lind, John. 1776 *An Answer to the Declaration of the American Congress*. London: J. Walter, Charing-Cross and T. Sewell.

Lossing, B. J. 1848. *Biographical Sketches of the Signers of the Declaration of American Independence; The Declaration Historical Considered; and a Sketch of the Leading Events Connected with the Adoption of the Articles of Confederation and of the Federal Constitution*. New York: George F. Cooledge and Brothers.

Vile, John R. 2015. *A Companion to the United States Constitution and Its Amendments*. 6th ed. Santa Barbara, CA: Praeger.

MAJORITY RULE AND UNANIMITY

The Declaration of Independence that is displayed at the National Archives is labeled "The unanimous Declaration of the thirteen united States of America." This caption was made possible by the belated authorization of the Document by New York's delegation to the Second Continental Congress, but, when the actual vote had been taken on the Declaration on July 4, only 12 states had given their consent. Moreover, there were citizens within each of the states who wished to remain loyal to Great Britain.

The second paragraph of the Declaration refers to "the consent of the governed," but it does not directly specify how such consent should be ascertained. The Declaration does make it clear that it is the product of representatives, and the initial adoption of the Declaration without New York's authorization indicates that these representatives did not think that unanimity would be required. Ross Lence observes that absent unanimity, the only two possibilities by which the people could act were through a majority or a minority (1986, 42). He says that "the conclusion that for the purposes of the dissolution of government the framers of the Declaration understood the people to mean a majority of the community is also consistent with the antecedent thought of the colonists to be found in the political pamphlets which circulated in the colonies in the years immediately preceding the proclamation of independence" (1986, 43). Lence observes that the Virginia Declaration of Rights had specifically noted that "a majority of the community hath an indubitable, inalienable, in indefeasible right to reform, alter or abolish it [government]" (1986, 45).

See also Captions of the Declaration of Independence; Consent of the Governed; Democracy; People

Further Reading

Lence, Ross M. 1986. "The American Declaration of Independence: The Majority and the Right of Political Power." In *Founding Principles of American Government: Two Hundred Years of Democracy on Trial,* rev. ed., edited by George J. Graham Jr. and Scarlett G. Graham, 29–59. Chatham, NJ: Chatham House

MANKIND

See Remember the Ladies

MARTIN LUTHER KING JR. LEGISLATION

Dr. Martin Luther King Jr. was among modern leaders who put special emphasis on the Declaration of Independence and its assertion that "all men are created equal." On November 2, 1983, the third Monday in January was proclaimed a national holiday in his honor.

In extending the Martin Luther King Jr. Federal Holiday Commission on May 17, 1989, Congress made three observations that epitomize the place that the Declaration retains. It observed that:

(1) The ideas expressed in the Declaration of Independence have inspired freedom-loving people throughout the world.
(2) The eloquent language of the Declaration of Independence has stirred the hearts of the American people.
(3) The Declaration of Independence ranks as one of the greatest documents in human history. (Section 8)

The law accordingly mandated that a bronze replica of the Declaration that had been presented for display in the Capitol Rotunda on July 2, 1952, and subsequently had been moved to the small House Rotunda between the Capitol Rotunda and Statuary Hall and been replaced by a bust of King, be "returned to a place of prominence in the Rotunda of the United States Capitol where it shall remain on permanent display."

The Capitol Rotunda also displays a massive painting by John Trumbull of the writing of the Declaration of Independence.

See also Trumbull, John (Paintings)

Further Reading

Martin Luther King Jr., Federal Holiday Commission Extension Act, H.R. 1385 https://www.congress.gov/bill/101st-congress/house-bill/1385/text.

MARYLAND AND ITS SIGNERS

Maryland had a unique political history that began when Cecil Calvert, the Second Lord Baltimore, landed in 1634 under authority of a royal grant that was later extended under Charles I, to "Terra Maria," or Mary's Land (Smith and Willis 2012, 18). The grant specified that that Calvert would have broad rights "to be had, exercised, used, and enjoyed, as any Bishop of Durham, within the Bishopric or County Palatine of Durham, in our Kingdom of England, ever heretofore hath had, held, used, or enjoyed, or of right could, or ought to have, hold, use, or enjoy" (Martinez 2008–2010, 308). A palatinate was essentially a feudal arrangement whereby the proprietor's full authority was recognized within a realm in return for the palatine's support. This grant included a specific clause against parliamentary taxation (Martinez 2008–2010, 323).

Unable to secure an adequate number of Catholics to settle the colony, Baltimore had offered religious toleration to Protestants. In time, however, the Anglican Church became the established church of the colony. The colony had a number of border disputes with others that eventually resulted in the drawing of the historic Mason-Dixon Line in 1767, which was subsequently seen as the boundary between Northern and Southern states.

Albert J. Martinez Jr. has documented how the king's grant did little to quell a constant struggle between Calvert and his successors on the one hand and the colonial assembly on the other for power, in which both attempted to claim broad jurisdiction, free even from parliamentary control even after Parliament successfully claimed power over the Durham Palatinate within Britain. Alexander Hamilton observed in 1775 that Maryland's charter "contains such ample and exalted privileges, that no man in his senses can read it, without being convinced it is repugnant to every idea of dependence on Parliament" (Martinez 2002–2019, 324).

Marylanders were relatively united in their opposition to the British Stamp Act, William Paca and Samuel Chase, both of whom would sign the Declaration of Independence, formed chapters of the Sons of Liberty in Baltimore (the nation's third largest port after Philadelphia and New York) and Annapolis (Smith and Willis 2012, 21). Moreover, the adoption of the Tea Act of 1774 led to the torching of the *Peggy Stewart*, whose owner had otherwise been threatened with tarring and feathering (Smith and Willis 2012, 21).

Tidewater planters, who relied chiefly on tobacco and on foreign trade, sought, however, to maintain relations with the king while opposing parliamentary taxes as long as they could. News authorizing Maryland delegates to vote for independence did not arrive until July 1, 1776. Chase and Charles Carroll of Carrollton had actually returned to the state to lobby for such authority.

Maryland, which would play such a celebrated role in the War of 1812 (Francis Scott Key wrote "The Star-Spangled Banner" after Baltimore successfully resisted a British attack that followed on the burning of the U.S. Capitol), remained relatively unscathed during the Revolutionary War. The state may be best known for withholding its approval of the Articles of Confederation until 1781, after the last of the large states had given up their western land claims.

Maryland's four signers included Charles Carroll of Carrolton, Samuel Chase, William Paca, and Thomas Stone. Only Paca, Stone, and John Rogers (who subsequently left Congress before delegates had a chance to sign the Declaration) were present on July 4, 1776.

Born of a common-law relationship (later legitimized), Charles Carroll of Carrollton (1737–1832) was a wealthy planter who had studied in France and England and owned many slaves. The first cousin of John Carroll, the first Catholic bishop of America, Charles is chiefly known as the only Roman Catholic to sign the Declaration, but he had been a stalwart supporter of the cause. In 1773, he had written four essays under the title of "First Citizen," opposing British fees on tobacco (Curran 2014, 236). Because of his religion, he had been selected by Congress even before being elected as a delegate to join the unsuccessful efforts to persuade Canada, which was generally pleased with the Quebec Act of 1774, in which Britain had acknowledged the right of Canadian Catholics to worship as they pleased, to join the other 13 colonies in opposing England. Carroll, who helped draft Maryland's Declaration of Rights, was not elected until July 4, 1776, to Congress but later included his signature on the Declaration of Independence. It was reported that when asked to sign, he responded, "Most willingly," and that a bystander, reflecting on Carroll's vast wealth, observed that "There go a few millions" (Birzer 2010, 115). Writing in 1829, Carroll stated, "When I signed the Declaration of Independence, I had in view not only our Independence of England but the toleration of all Sects, professing the Christian Religion, and communicating to them all great rights" (Bitzer 2010, 116). Charles's cousin, Daniel Carroll, attended the Constitutional Convention of 1787 and signed the resulting document. Charles served for three years in the U.S. Senate. Although the deaths of John Adams and Thomas Jefferson on July 4, 1826, are better known, Carroll was actually the last of the signers of the Declaration of Independence to die.

Samuel Chase (1741–1811) was one of the more irascible members of the Continental Congress. Chase had studied law under attorney John Hall and practiced in Annapolis, where he got the unflattering name of "Old Bacon Face." An early leader in the revolutionary movement, Chase was not present when Congress signed the Declaration but did later sign his name. He later opposed the adoption of the U.S. Constitution before turning into a militant member of the Federalist Party. After he had served as chief justice of the District Criminal Court in Baltimore and later of the Maryland General Court, George Washington appointed Chase to the Supreme Court in 1796. Chase's intemperate remarks on the court resulted in his impeachment by his Democratic-Republican rivals, although the Senate failed to convict him and remove him from office.

William Paca (1749–1799), another early advocate of independence, studied law at London's Middle Temple and was good friends with Chase. Paca had attended the College of Philadelphia before reading law and beginning his practice. He had served as a member of the Maryland Committee of Correspondence before being selected to the Continental Congress. He would later serve as governor of Maryland and as a member of the U.S. District Court for Maryland. Paca spent considerable personal money in support of continental soldiers during the Revolutionary War. He is believed to have been of Italian ancestry (Belfiglio 1976, 7–12). A full-length painting by Charles Willson Peale portrayed Paca situated between a bust on the Roman statesman Cicero (who was murdered for his political stances) on his right and his gardens on the left. Peale thereby sought to portray a life that alternated between what Joseph Manca (2003, 69) describes as "public engagement" (Cicero) on one hand and "private satisfaction" on the other. Paca's house and garden in Annapolis constitute a national historic landmark.

Thomas Stone (1743–1787) read law before entering private practice. Elected to the Continental Congress by the Maryland legislature in which he had served, Stone seems to have signed the Declaration largely because other Maryland delegates had done so. He later served on the committee that drafted the Articles of Confederation.

See also Quebec Act of 1774 (Charge #20); Signers, Collective Portrait

Further Reading

Belfigio, Valentine J. 1976. "Italians and the American Revolution." *Italian Americana* 3 (Autumn): 1–17.

Birzer, Bradley J. 2010. *American Cicero: The Life of Charles Carroll*. Wilmington, DE: ISI Books.

Curran, Robert Emmett. 2014. *Papist Devils*. Washington, DC: Catholic University of America Press.

Manca, Joseph. 2003. "Cicero in America: Civic Duty and Private Happiness in Charles Willson Peale's Portrait of William Paca." *American Art* 17 (Spring): 68–89.

Martinez, Albert J., Jr. 2008–2010. "The Palatinate Clause of the Maryland Charter, 1632–1776: From Independent Jurisdiction to Independence." *American Journal of Legal History* 50 (July): 305–325.

Smith, Herbert C., and John T. Willis. 2012. *Maryland Politics and Government*. Lincoln: University of Nebraska Press.

MASSACHUSETTS AND ITS SIGNERS

With the possible exception of Virginia, Massachusetts was the leading state in pushing the movement for independence from Great Britain. Founded largely by Puritan dissenters from the English Church who had landed in 1620 and signed the famed Mayflower Compact, Massachusetts had been granted a charter by the British king but also had a royal governor, with whom it came into increasing conflict in the time leading up to the American Revolution. Massachusetts was the home of Harvard University, the oldest such institution of higher learning in the 13 English colonies.

As a coastal state, Massachusetts particularly depended on trade in the Boston Harbor, and prior to the adoption of the Sugar Act, the colony had largely succeeded in evading British custom duties. When the British began to crack down on such smuggling, they did so both through the use of writs of assistance, which combined with general warrants, led to great concern over privacy rights, which was argued to great effect by attorney James Otis.

Britain sent troops to Boston to enforce regulations while increasing the possibility for incidents with locals, most evident in the so-called Boston Massacre in 1770 and the Boston Tea Party in 1773. Britain, which had long regarded Massachusetts as a hotbed of revolution (Higginbotham 1994), subsequently adopted the Coercive Acts (what the colonists called the Intolerable Acts) and sent additional troops, whose attempts to secure colonial weapons and arrest John Hancock and Samuel Adams led to the battles at Lexington and Concord in April 1775. The Suffolk Resolves protesting the Coercive Acts originated in Massachusetts.

Because they were so directly involved, and because they were considered by other colonists to be impatient, Massachusetts delegates at the Constitutional Convention sometimes had to lie low. John Adams thus nominated George Washington, rather than John Hancock, to lead colonial forces, and was later equally insistent that Thomas Jefferson of Virginia should take the lead in authoring the Declaration of Independence.

Five delegates from Massachusetts signed the Declaration of Independence: John Adams, Samuel Adams, Elbridge Gerry, John Hancock, and Robert Treat Paine.

None of the delegates was better known that John Adams (1735–1826), to whom this book devotes a longer entry. Educated at Harvard, Adams began as a schoolteacher before studying law. Although he opposed the Stamp Act, he successfully defended the British soldiers who were ensnared in the Boston Massacre. A member of both the First and Second Continental Congresses, Adams authored his *Thoughts on Government* in 1776. Appointed to the five-member committee to write the Declaration of Independence, he was content to let Jefferson do most of the writing. He may have thought that his own speech in defense of independence (answering an earlier speech by John Dickinson opposing it) and the earlier resolution that Adams had introduced in May authorizing states to create their own governments might ultimately be judged the more important historical document. Adams served as a diplomat to France and other European nations during most of the war (he was there during the Constitutional Convention of 1787) and helped negotiate the Treaty of Paris that ended the war. He was subsequently elected as the nation's first vice president and served a single term as president, before being defeated by Jefferson. After partisanship interrupted his prior friendship with Jefferson, the two resumed correspondence in their later years, and both died on July 4, 1826, 50 years to the day that Congress had approved of the Declaration of Independence. Adams's son, John Quincy Adams, became president, making them one of two father/son teams (the other being George H. W. and George W. Bush) to have this distinction.

Samuel Adams (1722–1803), a cousin of John Adams, was one of the patriots' most effective propagandists and organizers, for which he earned the unremitting enmity of Massachusetts governor Thomas Hutchinson, who blamed him for much of the opposition to his policies. The British mission to capture Adams and John Hancock and to seize colonial weapons led to the battles at Lexington and Concord in April of 1775. Born in Boston and educated at Harvard, Adams was not very successful as a tax collector, a businessman, or a brewer (Sam Adams remains the name of a famous beer) but had a knack for organizing opposition to British policies, which he thought threatened individual rights. He served as a clerk to the Massachusetts Assembly and helped issue the call for the Continental Congress, where he was one of the most ardent in calling for independence. He later served both as lieutenant governor and as governor of his state.

Elbridge Gerry (1744–1814) was a merchant who had been born in Marblehead and educated at Harvard. An early opponent of British policy, Gerry, a friend of Samuel Adams, helped create a committee of correspondence for the town of his birth but encountered opposition for establishing a hospital to give smallpox vaccinations, which made him wary of popular government. Elected to the colonial legislature, Gerry served for five years in the Continental Congress, where he signed both the Declaration of Independence and the Articles of Confederation. Although he also attended the Constitutional Convention of 1787, he was one of three delegates who stayed to the end of the meeting but refused to sign the document. Nonetheless, he later served two terms in the U.S. House of Representatives and as vice president under James Madison. During the Adams Administration, Gerry was one of three delegates who was sent to France to help the country avoid war and was caught up in the so-called XYZ Affairs, in which French officials attempted to extort a bribe in order to participate in negotiations. Gerry may be best known for approving an oddly shaped Massachusetts district in order to give Democratic-Republicans an electoral advantage. This practice is today known as gerrymandering. John Adams once commented in a letter to James Warren that Gerry was "a man of immense worth." He went on to say that "If every man here was a Gerry, the liberties of America would be safe against the Gates of Earth and Hell" (Morison 1929, 14). The monument to Gerry at the DC Congressional Cemetery quotes Gerry as saying: "It is the duty of every man, though he may have but one day to live, to devote that day to the good of his country" (Bradsher 2006, 30).

John Hancock (1737–1793) is probably best known for his bold signature on the Declaration, which he signed in his capacity as president of the Continental Congress. Hancock's father died when his son was still young, and he was therefore sent to live with a wealthy uncle, who saw that he received an education in Harvard and visited England, where he witnessed the coronation of George III. Hancock subsequently inherited his uncle's estate and became one of the wealthiest individuals in Massachusetts. Hancock, whose businesses included smuggling, was deeply concerned about the Sugar Act, the Stamp Act, and other taxes and became part of the boycott of British goods. Largely as a result of the ill will that his stance had generated, the British confiscated his ship, *Liberty*, and it was subsequently burned. Hancock was a vain man who dressed sharply but was known for his generosity. He did not embrace the cause of independence as quickly as John Adams and Samuel Adams may have wanted, but he is credited with seeking the consensus within the Continental Congress that eventually made independence possible. Although he did not attend the Constitutional Convention of 1787, Hancock did preside over his state's ratifying convention. Hancock served as governor for close to ten years and was honored with a lavish funeral.

Robert Treat Paine (1731–1814) was born in Boston and educated at Harvard, after which he tried a number of careers before taking up law. He was one of the prosecutors in the Boston Massacre Case and later against leaders of Shay's Rebellion. Paine served both on the Massachusetts General Court and the Provincial Congress before being elected to the Continental Congress, where he supported the Olive Branch Petition and other moderate measures before signing the Declaration. He served as a justice on the Massachusetts Supreme Court from 1790 to 1804.

The Massachusetts Constitution of 1780, largely the work of John Adams, was formally the product of a convention, the work of which a convention then ratified. This set a pattern for popular constitution making that the U.S. Constitution would follow. The taxpayer revolt known as Shay's Rebellion, which took place in the winter of 1786–1787, led to concerns that the nation was unable to protect states against domestic insurrection and provided an impetus for the Constitutional Convention of 1787.

See also Adams, John; Committee Responsible for Writing the Declaration of Independence; Suffolk Resolves of 1774

Further Reading

Billias, George Athan. 1976. *Elbridge Gerry: Founding Father and Republican Statesman*. New York: McGraw-Hill.

Bradsher, Greg. 2006. "A Founding Father in Dissent." *Prologue* 38 (Spring): 30–35.

Higginbotham, Don. 1994. "Fomenters of Revolution: Massachusetts and South Carolina." *Journal of the Early Republic* 14 (Spring): 1–33.

Maier, Pauline. 1976. "Coming to Terms with Samuel Adams." *American Historical Review* 81 (February): 12–37.

Morison, S. E. 1929. "Elbridge Gerry, Gentleman-Democrat." *New England Quarterly* 2 (January): 6033.

Proctor, Donald J. 1977. "John Hancock: New Soundings on an Old Barrel." *Journal of American History* 64 (December): 652–677.

Stoll, Ira. 2008. *Samuel Adams, A Life*. New York: Free Press.

Unger, Harlow Giles. 2000. *John Hancock: Merchant King and American Patriot*. New York; John Wiley and Sons.

MATLACK, TIMOTHY

See Engrossed Declaration of Independence (Matlack)

MECKLENBURG DECLARATION OF INDEPENDENCE

As the reputation of the Declaration of Independence grew, so did attempts to find antecedents. One of the strangest claims to provenance was made in an article first published in the *Raleigh Register* and *North Carolina Gazette* on April 30, 1819, when Dr. Joseph McKnitt Alexander alleged that representatives of the Mecklenburg County militia met on May 20, 1775, and drew up a Declaration that served as a template for that adopted on July 4. The document contained a number of phrases like "the inherent and inalienable rights of man," "political bands," and "our lives, our fortunes, and our most sacred honor," which were found within the latter document (Maier 1997, 172–173).

John Adams, who was jealous of the increasing attention that Thomas Jefferson was receiving for his primary authorship of the Declaration, believed the report to be true, and Jefferson was equally sure that it was not. His reservations were not, however, known until after the publication of his letters in 1829. This led to an initial round of responses, mostly by North Carolinians, defending the authenticity of the Mecklenburg Declaration, and then by more measured scholarly studies.

Over time, subsequent investigations revealed that the words did not come from the original document, purportedly destroyed in a fire, but from later recollections of the document, which could easily have mixed recollections of both. Moreover, a resolution from Mecklenburg discovered from May 31, 1775, was to stay in force only until Britain should "resign its unjust and arbitrary pretensions with respect to America" (Current 1977, 174).

The Mecklenburg document remained a source of local pride, with the date May 20, 1775, even finding its way onto the state flag adopted on May 20, 1861, the date that a North Carolina convention passed an ordinance of secession (Current 1977, 176). The tide of scholarship gradually turned against the authenticity of the document, which, however, remained enshrined in North Carolina legend for many years.

See also Adams, John; Jefferson, Thomas; North Carolina and Its Signers

Further Reading

Current, Richard N. 1977. "That Other Declaration, May 20, 1775–May 20, 1975." *North Carolina Historical Review* 54 (April): 169–191.

Faulkner, Ronnie W. 2006. "Mecklenburg Declaration of Independence." Encyclopedia of North Carolina. http://www.ncpedia.org/mecklenburg-declaration.

Maier, Pauline. 1997. *American Scripture: Making the Declaration of Independence*. New York: Alfred A. Knopf.

MEMORIAL TO THE 56 SIGNERS OF THE DECLARATION OF INDEPENDENCE

One of the lesser-known memorials in Washington, D.C., is the Memorial to the 56 Signers of the Declaration of Independence. It is located in Constitutional Gardens on the National Mall, not far from the Vietnam Veterans Memorial.

The memorial, which was created by Public Law 95 in 1978 and dedicated on July 2, 1984, consists of 56 stone markers. Each replicates the signature and identifies the profession and hometown of each of those signed the document. To get to it, one crosses a bridge to an island within a small lake.

See also Jefferson Memorial

Further Reading

City Walking Guide. n.d. "56 Signers of the Declaration of Independence Memorial." https://www.citywalkingguide.com/westnationalmall/56-signers-of-the-declaration-of-independence-memorial.

Harvard University. n.d. "Memorial to the 56 Signers of the Declaration of Independence." https://declaration.fas.harvard.edu/resources/destinations/memorial-56.

MERCENARIES

See Transporting Large Armies of Foreign Mercenaries (Charge #25)

MORAL VIRTUES IN THE DECLARATION OF INDEPENDENCE

As America's own fascination with its Pilgrim forebears suggests, many nations pride themselves on the beginnings. Most further seek to establish the legitimacy of such origins. In commenting on the Declaration of Independence, Harvey C. Mansfield Jr. observed that in making the claim for government by consent, Thomas Jefferson attempted to demonstrate "a measure of moderation and wisdom in those consenting" (1983, 27). The document contains other virtues as well.

The four classical cardinal (most important) virtues were temperance, prudence, courage, and justice. Christian theologians, in turn, identified seven primary virtues, some of which, dealing chiefly with private affairs, would not have been directly applicable to a document like the Declaration. They were chastity, temperance, charity, diligence, patience, kindness, and humility and were often contrasted with seven equally specific deadly sins. Neither list was, of course, exclusive.

All these virtues were unique to human beings (or gods) in that they required that human will be subservient to the faculty of *reason*, which could weigh options and steer individuals to long-term happiness, which might, at times, be inconsistent with short-term pleasures. By appealing to the "opinions of mankind" and by listing specific grievances against the king, the Declaration attempted to justify the course that the one-time colonies had chosen. Although military force would determine the outcome of individual battles, reason might be just as important in mobilizing opinion within the colonies and soliciting foreign allies. The notion of reason was often tied to the idea that all individuals possessed a "moral sense," to which rational appeals could be made. This was, in turn, sometimes associated with the existence of a universal "natural law" (Darsey 1997, 53).

Classical republican thinkers stressed *public-spiritedness* and *patriotism*, which could involve public service (as on juries or in public affairs) and militia participation on behalf of one's nation, which would reduce the need for standing armies, which the Declaration criticized. In the years leading up to the Revolution, Americans had often sacrificed by boycotting British goods and refusing to export to Britain, while opinion makers had often attributed the actions of the British government to "corruption" and had encouraged public-spiritedness (Agresto 1977). The delegates who participated in the Second Continental Congress were engaging in public service, with all the delegates except for those who lived in Philadelphia or its vicinity having to leave their homes and families, perhaps at the sacrifice of their full-time occupations or vocations. Although the central focus of the Declaration remained that of vindicating colonial rights, the document referred at one point to the "duty" of throwing off despotic government, which would require the kind of moral "manliness" mentioned elsewhere in the document.

The Declaration arguably represents a unique blend of *prudence* and courage. Much of the power of the document rests on its argument that the colonists have exercised considerable *patience*, or *moderation*, in the face of an overwhelming set of grievances on the part of the king and those with whom he was associated. In justifying revolution, the Declaration stressed that "Prudence, indeed, will dictate that governments long established should not be changed for light and transient causes." The second paragraph of the Declaration refers to "the patient sufferance of these colonies."

The fact that Congress waited until it received the consent of an overwhelming majority of the colonies (with New York later adding its approval to make state consent unanimous) further highlights the delegates' prudence. Even in the face of multiple kingly grievances, it would have been imprudent to proceed prior to persuading fellow colonists of the dangers they posed, and of the need for unity if there were to be any chance of military success against the world's largest empire.

Even with the possibility of collective victory, delegates, some of whom would risk their lives on battlefields, recognized that they could individually be tried for treason and executed. Their action in drafting, and signing, the document was therefore an act of collective *courage*. This was evident when, in the final sentence, the delegates mutually pledged their lives, their fortunes, and their sacred honor. Paul Eidelberg ties this courage to what he calls "an abiding commitment to reason and truth," which he further ties to "civility" (1974, 449). He also identifies what he describes as "a decent respect, but never subservience, to prevailing opinion" (1974, 449).

Honor was, of course, associated with mutual respect and admiration. It, and courage, may further be associated with Jefferson's claims that the colonists had opposed "with manly firmness" the king's "invasions on the rights of the people." It may also be associated with the "decent respect to the opinions of mankind," which the Declaration's first paragraph highlighted.

This, as well as the Declaration's argument that "all men are created equal," arguably also represents *humility*. Although the colonies were not debasing themselves below others, they were not claiming superiority but merely asking for their "equal status" among other nations of the earth. The document thus observed that "we have petitioned for redress in the most humble terms."

The document as a whole is, of course, a plea for *justice*, or fair treatment, which it associates with "the consent of the governed." Justice, like humility, is tied to the perception that the human beings who occupy the former 13 colonies are equal to those, including a king who claimed hereditary rights, who have sought to rule over them from afar. One obstacle to the American claim was that they themselves kept slaves. Jefferson had attempted to blunt such criticism by blaming the slave trade on the English king, but, when combined with the fact that this king was now encouraging slaves to seek their freedom, this accusation appeared hypocritical and was rejected by the Continental Congress during debates over the document.

Virtuous men and women obey laws. Although the Declaration is renouncing rule by the British, it is affirming its own *adherence to the rule of law*, in its general appeal to "the laws of nature and of nature's god," its criticism of the king for departing from established legal norms, and its expressed intention of creating a new government that would secure rights. One of the charges that the Declaration levels against the king is that of "taking away our charters and altering fundamentally the forms of our government." Therefore commentators often identify the American Revolution as a conservative event rather than as a call for future anarchy.

Although scholars will continue to debate the degree to which the God of nature (and of Jefferson's conceptions) was similar to or different from the Christian God of Creation and Redemption, the specific pronouncements of the document, especially as revised by the Congress, also evidence *piety*, or proper acknowledgment of God. Not only does the Declaration acknowledge that men are created beings, but it also appeals to God as "The Supreme Judge of the World," and professes "a firm reliance on the protection of divine providence."

The Declaration reports that the colonists have appealed to the "native justice and *magnanimity* [another classical virtue tied to greatness of spirit]" as well as to common "*consanguinity*" of the colonists' English "brethren" ("common kindred"). In so doing, it thereby affirms values of *friendship* (essential to classical notions of virtue) to which it hopes the nation might return after the conflict.

In most ethical systems, virtues involve not only right actions but also *pure intentions*. The concluding paragraph of the Declaration accordingly appeals to God "for the rectitude [rightness] of our intentions." This is designed to allay fears that the delegates were seeking private glory over public interests. Ultimately, only the One who knows human hearts could affirm such rectitude, which delegates hoped to display through their actions, or verify that the colonists were "the good people" that the Declaration proclaimed them to be.

See also Ambition; Equality; God; Human Nature and the Declaration of Independence; Our Lives, Our Fortunes, and Our Sacred Honor; Prudence; Revolution; Scottish Enlightenment; Slavery; Standing Armies (Charge #11); Treason

Further Reading

Agresto, John T. 1977. "Liberty, Virtue, and Republicanism, 1776–1787." *Review of Politics* 39 (October): 473–504.

Darsey, James. 1997. *The Prophetic Tradition and Radical Rhetoric in America*. New York: New York University Press.

Eidelberg, Paul. 1974. *A Discourse on Statesmanship: The Design and Transformation of the American Polity*. Urbana: University of Illinois Press.

Mansfield, Harvey C., Jr. 1983. "Thomas Jefferson." In *American Political Thought: The Philosophic Dimension of American Statesmanship*, edited by Morton J. Frisch and Richard G. Stevens, 23–50. Itasca, IL: F. E. Peacock,

MUSICAL PLAY *1776*

One reason that the signing of the Declaration of Independence is among the better-known events in U.S. history is that it has been celebrated in a musical play entitled *1776*. It debuted on Broadway on March 16, 1969, and ran for 1,217 consecutive performances during the next three years. It has subsequently been produced as a movie directed by Peter H. Hunt in 1972 and performed as a musical in many other venues (Rubin 2013).

Written by Sherman Edwards (1919–1981), a former pianist and history teacher, and assisted by Peter Stone (1930–2003), the musical features two acts with seven scenes involving 26 cast members, most representing delegates to the Second Continental Congress. Lead roles went to individuals playing John Adams, Benjamin Franklin, Thomas Jefferson, and John Dickinson. The only musical ever performed at the White House (during the Nixon administration), the musical has been described as "a one-of-a-kind work of sophistication without irony, corn without camp, and history without apology" (Galati 2013, 10).

The play effectively portrays the conflict between those like John Adams, who were impatient for revolution, and those like John Dickinson, who feared that the nation was moving too quickly. In the process, it also highlights the way that Congress debated the Declaration deleting, among other sections, Jefferson's condemnation of slavery.

The authors took a few liberties with the facts, including a visit to Philadelphia by Martha Jefferson, the presence of a large ledger recording the votes of states, and a signing on July 4, rather than on August 2 and days following. It successfully

Scene from the Broadway musical *1776*. Conceptualized by songwriter and former history teacher Sherman Edwards, the musical dramatizes the debates of the Second Continental Congress over the adoption of the Declaration of Independence during the American Revolution. *1776* was the recipient of three Tony Awards, including the award for Best Musical in 1969. (Photofest)

conveyed that the individuals who voted for the document were not cardboard figures and that the events in which they participated were significant.

See also Adams, John; Franklin, Benjamin; Jefferson, Thomas; Signing of the Declaration of Independence; Slavery

Further Reading

Galati, Frank. 2013. "1776 at A.C.T.: A Director's Introduction: *1776, A Musical Play*." Edited by Dan Rubin. Play Program, Geary Theater. Presented by The American Conservatory Theater.

Kare, Jeffrey. 2016. "The Making of America's Musical, *1776*: The Story behind the Story." July 4, 2016. https://www.broadwayworld.com/article/The-Making-of-Americas-Musical—1776-The-Story-Behind-the-Story-20160704.

N

NATIONAL ARCHIVES

See Preserving the Declaration of Independence

NATIVE AMERICAN INDIANS (CHARGE #27)

When Bostonians sought to express their disdain for British attempts to collect customs on tea, they dressed as Mohawk Indians (partly as a way of concealing their identities) and threw barrels of tea into the city harbor. Although some Native Americans (Squanto in Massachusetts and Pocahontas in Virginia) had certainly been friendly to European settlers, such relations had often been hostile, with Native Americans fearing both European diseases and encroachments on their lands and white settlers fearing Indian attacks, and especially their use of tomahawks.

In declaring that it was time for one "people" to dissolve the "political bands" that had bound them to the mother-country, the Declaration arguably excluded both African Americans and Native American Indians. Colonists held the former as slaves and regarded the latter as uncivilized.

The former were held as slaves in many of the states, while the Indians' land had been taken during the process of colonization. In accusing the king of having endeavored "to prevent the population of the states," the Declaration was criticizing the Royal Proclamation of October 7, 1763, which had sought to stop further white immigration across the Appalachian Mountains, which had been a primary cause of friction between whites and Native Americans. After accusing the king of having "excited domestic insurrections amongst us," a reference to efforts by Virginia's governor, Lord Dunmore, to encourage slave revolts (Kaplan 1976), the Declaration had further charged that he has "endeavored to bring on the inhabitants of our frontiers the merciless Indian savages, whose known rule of warfare is an undistinguished destruction of all ages, sexes & conditions."

In the French and Indian War, the 13 colonies had often faced Native American warriors who had been allied with France. As the Revolutionary War approached, both sides sought to recruit such fighters to their side, but there were constant rumors leading up to the Declaration of Independence not only of the king's efforts to recruit foreign mercenaries but also of atrocities by Native Americans against Patriot troops, especially those that had been fighting in Canada (Parkinson 2016, 236ff). Indeed, Thomas Jefferson had served on a committee in the Second Continental Congress to investigate Indian mistreatment of Patriots who had surrendered to Native Americans in Canada (Parkinson 2016, 243). Although many Native Americans regarded the conflict between the English and Americans as a family quarrel, Americans sought either to encourage them to stay neutral or to enlist them on their side.

Linking Native Americans to slaves and referring to them as "merciless Indian savages" who engaged in uncivilized warfare was hardly designed to encourage alliances with them or to recognize them as part of the American people who had appropriated their lands. For their part, Native Americans sometimes professed to be baffled by the war. While Americans might consider themselves to be a different "people" from those of Britain, an Oneida leader told Connecticut governor John Trumbull that "We cannot intermeddle in this dispute between two brothers. The quarrel seems to be unnatural. You are *two brothers of one blood*" (Wunder 2000/2001, 67).

Native Americans had not been treated well by either "people." It is hardly surprising that Native Americans often, in turn, referred to Americans as "Ecunnaunuxulgee," or "people greedily grasping after the lands of red people" (Wunder 2000/2001, 66).

John Wunder has observed that the Declaration of Independence has been used in three ways with respect to Native Americans: "as a document of colonialism in the century of its creation; as a document used as a basis for assimilation and the forced alteration of nineteenth-century cultures; and as a twentieth-century document turned on its head in the fight for the restoration of Native sovereignty" (2000/2001, 66). Wunder notes that in recent years, Native Americans have looked to the Declaration of Independence as a way of articulating their own grievances against the U.S. government. Vine Deloria Jr. has thus published a book entitled *Behind the Trail of Broken Treaties: An Indian Declaration of Independence* (1985).

Native Americans were not granted citizenship until 1924, long after the Fourteenth Amendment had extended such citizenship to African Americans in 1868. Native Americans had to wait even later in some states to gain the right to vote. Most Supreme Court decisions have declared them to be "domestic dependent nations," leaving them in a status not unlike that which the colonies once felt themselves with relation to Great Britain.

See also Endeavored to Prevent the Population (Charge #7); Jefferson's Speech to Jean Baptiste Ducoigne; People; Slavery; Transporting Large Armies of Foreign Mercenaries

Further Reading

Charles, Patrick J. 2008. *Irreconcilable Grievances: The Events That Shaped the Declaration of Independence*. Westminster, MD: Heritage Books.

Deloria, Vine, Jr. (1974) 1985. *Behind the Trail of Broken Treaties: An Indian Declaration of Independence*. El Paso: University of Texas Press.

Hamer, Phillip M. 1930. "John Stuart's Indian Policy during the Early Months of the American Revolution." *Mississippi Valley Historical Review* 17 (December): 351–366.

Kaplan, Sidney. 1976. "The 'Domestic Insurrections' of the Declaration of Independence." *Journal of Negro History* 61 (July): 243–255.

Parkinson, Robert G. 2016. *The Common Cause: Creating Race and Nation in the American Revolution*. Chapel Hill: University of North Carolina Press.

Sadosky, Leonard J. 2009. *Revolutionary Negotiations: Indians, Empires, and Diplomats in the Founding of America*. Charlottesville: University of Virginia Press.

Wunder, John R. 2000/2001. "'Merciless Indian Savages' and the Declaration of Independence: Native Americans Translate the Ecunnaunuxulgee Document." *American Indian Law Review* 25: 65–92.

NATURAL LAW AND NATURAL RIGHTS

See Laws of Nature and of Nature's God

NATURE'S GOD

See God

NECESSITY

The opening sentence of the Declaration of Independence proclaimed that it had become "necessary" for the erstwhile colonies "to dissolve the political bands which have connected them with another."

Somewhat later, the document referenced "the necessity which constrains them [one-time colonies] to alter their former systems of government." Again, in the penultimate paragraph, the Declaration stated the need "to acquiesce in the necessity, which denounces [proclaims] our own Separation." Such references necessarily provoke reflections, which have long challenged human beings, to sort out the degree to which they take fate into their own hands and the degree to which they are influenced, or compelled, by circumstances beyond their own control.

Mortimer J. Adler and William Gorman argue that the necessity that the Declaration identifies "is not physical necessity" but "moral necessity—necessity in the order of freedom and obligation" (1975, 23). This would explain why the Declaration proclaims that an oppressed people have not only the "right" but also the "duty" to throw off their government. The term "necessity" might also have pointed to the role of independence in securing other goals, such as securing foreign alliances. In a letter that he wrote to Landon Carter on June 2, 1776, Richard Henry Lee had thus observed that "It is not choice . . . but necessity that calls for independence as the only means by which foreign alliance can be obtained and a proper confederation by which internal peace and union may be secured" (Unger 2017, 108).

The theme of necessity further helped transition to "the Laws of Nature and of Nature's God," which were thought to be orderly and changeless, and may further have foreshadowed the idea of national destiny. As Stephen E. Lucas has so elegantly suggested:

> Characterizing the Revolution as necessary suggested that it resulted from constraints that operated with lawlike force throughout the material universe and within the sphere of human action. The Revolution was not merely preferable, defensible, or justifiable. It was as inescapable, as inevitable, as unavoidable within the course of human events as the motions of the tides or the changing of the seasons within the course of natural events. (Lucas 1990)

In using the language of necessity, Thomas Jefferson was echoing two earlier documents, which were also called Declarations. One was known as the "Necessity to Take Up Arms," which the English Parliament had issued in explaining its opposition to Charles I in 1642 at the beginning of the English Civil War. The other was the "Declaration on the Causes and Necessity of Taking Up Arms," which the Second Continental Congress had adopted on July 6, 1775.

As Lucas observes, describing a war or rebellion as a necessity further added to its moral force because it is difficult to fault individuals or peoples for simply acting as necessity dictates. Indeed, in social contract thinking, the inconveniences of the state of nature almost necessitated that people would form governments to protect their lives, liberties, and properties.

Not all invocations of necessity, of course, prove accurate. The philosophy of Karl Marx, which called for class warfare that was very much at odds with that of the Declaration of Independence, was later based on so-called inexorable laws of history that he mistakenly thought would inevitably bring about the rule of the proletariat.

See also Declaration (Meaning of Term); Declaration on the Causes and Necessity of Taking Up Arms; Laws of Nature and of Nature's God

Further Reading

Adler, Mortimer J., and William Gorman. 1975. *The American Testament*. New York: Praeger.

Lucas, Stephen E. 1990. "The Stylistic Artistry of the Declaration of Independence." *Prologue: Quarterly of the National Archives and Records Administration* (Spring). https://www.archives.gov/founding-docs/stylistic-artistry-of-the-declaration.

Unger, Harlow Giles. 2017. *First Founding Father: Richard Henry Lee and the Call to Independence*. New York: Da Capo Press.

NEW HAMPSHIRE AND ITS SIGNERS

New Hampshire was the northernmost of the 13 colonies. It consisted of three sections, which corresponded to three watersheds. The Piscataqua watershed was near the coast and included cities like Portsmouth and Exeter that thrived on trade. The Merrimack watershed included the central part of the state, while the Connecticut watershed included those in the west, which, like those in the central area, sometimes felt neglected by the state legislature (Daniel 1988, 182). New Hampshire was the first state to adopt a constitution to replace royal rule.

New Hampshire had three delegates at the Second Continental Congress. They were Josiah Bartlett, Matthew Thornton, and William Whipple. All of them signed the Declaration, but Thornton was not appointed until September 1776 and did not sign until November of that year. Whereas the signatures of Bartlett and Whipple are at the top right of the signature spaces, Thornton's is at the bottom of this line, indicating that delegates from Massachusetts, who signed immediately below, had not left adequate space and may not have anticipated his later arrival.

Josiah Bartlett (1729–1795) had learned medicine under a local doctor and served as a member of the New Hampshire legislature and would serve as a physician to members of the New Hampshire militia. In addition to signing the Declaration, he also signed the Articles of Confederation. He later served as chief justice of the New Hampshire superior court, as state president, and as state governor. As a judge, he was influential in the ratification of the U.S. Constitution.

Matthew Thornton (ca. 1714–1803), whose parents had immigrated to America from Scotland when he was four years old, also became a medical doctor by studying under a local physician. He also had served in the colonial legislature as well as a local Committee of Safety, became New Hampshire's first president, and helped to write the New Hampshire constitution even before independence was declared. Toward the end of his life, Thornton authored an essay entitled "Paradise Lost: or the Origin of the Evil called Sin examined; or how it ever did or ever can come to pass, that a creature should or could do anything unfit or improper for the creature to do; or how it ever did, or ever can come to pass, that a creature should or could omit, or leave undone what the creature ought to have done, or was fit and proper for that creature to do; or how it ever was, or can be possible for a creature to displease the Creator in Thought, Word, or Action" (Wrenn 1969, 32). Fortunately, the epithet on his tombstone is much simpler: "An Honest Man."

William Whipple (1730–1785), who was born in Maine, went to sea, and became a ship's captain by the age of 21, had been able to retire at the age of 45. He went on to fight in a number of Revolutionary War battles. Like Bartlett, he also served for a time as a state judge.

See also Signers, Collective Portrait

Further Reading

Daniell, Jere. 1988. "Ideology and Hardball: Ratification of the Federal Constitution in New Hampshire." In *The Constitution and the States: The Role of the Original Thirteen in the Framing and Adoption of the Federal Constitution*, edited by Patrick T. Conley and John P. Kaminski, 181–200. Madison, WI: Madison House.

Kiernan, Denise, and Joseph D'Agnese. 2009. *Signing Their Lives Away: The Fame and Misfortune of the Men Who Signed the Declaration of Independence*. Philadelphia: Quirk Books.

Wrenn, Tony P. 1969. "The Honest Man—Matthew Thornton of New Hampshire." *Pioneer America* 1 (July): 30–39.

NEW JERSEY AND ITS SIGNERS

Although originally settled by immigrants from Sweden and Holland, New Jersey had been governed by Britain since 1664. Its jurisdiction had not prevented political conflict between the East, which had closer ties to New York, and the West, which was more closely tied to Pennsylvania (Vile 2016, 2:589). Largely an agricultural state, New Jersey was one of the middle colonies where sentiment about declaring independence, like the state itself, was extremely divided. The months leading up to the Declaration led to increased dissatisfaction with Governor William Franklin, the son of Benjamin Franklin, who was eventually arrested and sent to Connecticut. It was not until June 2 that the Provincial Congress of New Jersey resolved "That a government be formed for the regulating the internal police of this Colony, pursuant to the recommendation of the Continental Congress of the fifteenth of May last" (Gerlach 1976, 336).

Because the New Jersey delegation to the Continental Congress had largely opposed this measure and had largely through resignations fallen below the three required to transact business there, the provincial assembly appointed five men on June 22, 1776, to replace them. There were Abraham Clark, John Hart, Francis

Hopkinson, Richard Stockton, and John Witherspoon. All but John Hart, the only Baptist in the Second Continental Congress, were Presbyterians. Because Hopkinson, who had arrived on June 28, was the only delegate to arrive prior to July 1, the New Jersey delegation asked for a recapitulation of arguments for independence. This led to a highly praised, but unrecorded, speech by John Adams detailing the case for separation from Britain.

Abraham Clark (1726–1794) had been born in Elizabethtown, New Jersey, and was from a modest background but learned surveying and the rudiments of law and had held local offices. On July 4, Clark wrote a letter to Colonel Elias Dayton in which, expecting the Declaration to be approved, he observed that "We are now, Sir, embarked on a most Tempestuous Sea; Life very uncertain, seeming dangers scattered thick around us. Plots against the military and it is whispered against the Senate; let us prepare for the Worst. We can Die here but once. May all our Business, all our purposes and pursuits tend to fit us for that important event" (Buffett 1877, 446). On August 6, after he had signed the document, Clark continued with a sense of foreboding in another letter to Dayton:

> As to my title, I know not yet whether it will be honourable or dishonourable; the issue of the war must settle it. Perhaps our Congress will be exalted on a high gallows. We were truly brought to the case of the three lepers [a biblical allusion]; If we continued in the state we were in, it was evident we must perish; if we declared Independence we might be saved—we could but perish. I assure you, Sir, I see, I feel, the danger we are in. I am far from exulting in our imaginary happiness; nothing short of the almighty power of God can save us. It is not in our numbers, our union, our valour, I dare trust. I think an interposing Providence hath been evident in all the events that necessarily led us to what we are—I mean independent States; but for what purpose, whether to make us a great empire to make our ruin more complete, the issue can only determine. (Buffett 1877, 447)

Clark spent most of the remainder of his life serving either in Congress or the state legislature. The British captured two of Clark's sons during the war. Ruth Bogin, who described him as a "radical Republican," notes that he "feared the concentration of power at a distance from the voters" (1978, 109). Clark introduced antislavery legislation in New Jersey and favored allowing individuals to use paper money to repay debts (Cassell 2011, 6). He expressed his views in a pamphlet entitled *The True Policy of New Jersey*, and he opposed ratification of the new U.S. Constitution without the adoption of a Bill of Rights.

John Hart (ca. 1711–1779) was another farmer. He was born in Connecticut. He also owned some saw- and gristmills and had served on a Committee of Correspondence and a Committee of Safety. He did not arrive in Philadelphia until July 4. Soon after signing the Declaration, he became speaker of the New Jersey legislature, where he served until his death in 1779, the same year that his wife died. Hart had to flee from the British during their military foray through the state.

Although he does not appear to have played a large part in the proceedings of the Second Continental Congress, Francis Hopkinson (1737–1791) would have lent luster to almost any gathering. A lawyer whose father had immigrated from England, Hopkinson had been born in Philadelphia and graduated from the

College of Philadelphia before moving to Bordentown. He was a true Renaissance Man, a musician, composer, and humorist and, like his father, a friend of Benjamin Franklin. Trained in the law, Hopkinson had a part in designing the Great Seal of the United States and the American Flag. During the Revolutionary War, Hopkinson had used his literary skills on behalf of the Patriot cause (Wilkinson 1941).

Richard Stockton (1730–1781) has the notorious distinction of being the only signer of the Declaration who, after being captured by the British, signed allegiance to the king in return for being allowed to depart for his house in New Jersey, which until 1981 would serve as the governor's mansion. A lawyer, educated at the College of New Jersey, he helped recruit John Witherspoon as its president and served as a trustee. Stockton admired the British constitution and had been skittish about the Declaration from the beginning, He was the father of six children, the oldest of whom was married to Benjamin Rush, a fellow signer from Pennsylvania. Rush was impressed when she had complimented the preaching of John Witherspoon, who later married them. After a tie vote for governor, that was resolved in favor of William Livingston, Stockton had become chief justice of the state's new supreme court, but obviously lost favor after pledging loyalty to the king.

With the possible exception of Hopkinson, John Witherspoon (1723–1794) is probably the best known of the New Jersey signers. Born in Scotland and educated at the University of Edinburgh, Witherspoon became a Presbyterian minister, the only active pastor to sign the Declaration. A noted writer, who was lured by Richard Stockton to come to America and to head the University of New Jersey (today's Princeton), Witherspoon was responsible for educating many of America's founding fathers, including James Madison. Witherspoon had written an essay in 1774 entitled "Thoughts on American Liberty," in which he had said, "We are firmly determined never to submit to, and do deliberately prefer war with all its horrors and even extermination itself, to slavery riveted upon us and our posterity" (Kimball 2006). In May 1776, he had preached a sermon, "Dominion of Providence over the Passions of Men," in which he had argued that "There is not a single instance in history, in which civil liberty was lost, and religious liberty preserved entire" (Kimball 2006). Witherspoon is probably best known in the Second Continental Congress for responding to arguments that independence needed further time to "ripen," by responding that "In my judgement the country is not only ripe for the measure, but in danger of becoming rotten for the want of it" (Kimball 2006). During the Revolutionary War, one of his sons was killed during the Battle of Germantown, and the British burned most of Witherspoon's books when they ransacked his college.

As Witherspoon's loss of a son suggests, New Jersey was a prime battlefield during the Revolutionary War. The state adopted a new constitution in 1776, which largely followed the pattern of other early state constitutions (Gerlach 1976, 343) and was especially notable for granting widespread suffrage.

See also Franklin, Benjamin; Signers, Collective Portrait; Treason

Further Reading

Bogin, Ruth. "New Jersey's True Policy: The Radical Republican Vision of Abraham Clark." *William and Mary Quarterly* 35 (January): 100–109.

Buffett, E. P. 1877. "Abraham Clark." *Pennsylvania Magazine of History and Biography* 1:445–448.
Cassell, Melissa. 2011. *Abraham Clark*. n.p.: Infinity Publishing.
Gerlach, Larry R. 1976. *Prologue to Independence: New Jersey in the Coming of the American Revolution*. New Brunswick, NJ: Rutgers University Press.
Hammond, Cleon E. 1977. *John Hart: The Biography of a Signer of the Declaration of Independence*. Newfane, VT: Pioneer.
Hastings, George E. 1926. *The Life and Work of Francis Hopkinson*. Chicago: University of Chicago Press.
Kimball, Roger. November 2006. "The Forgotten Founder: John Witherspoon." *New Criterion*. https://www.newcriterion.com/issues/2006/6/the-forgotten-founder-john-witherspoon.
Mailer, Gideon. *John Witherspoon's American Revolution: Enlightenment and Religion from the Creation of Britain to the Founding of the United States*. Chapel Hill: University of North Carolina Press.
Miller, Thomas P., ed. 2015. *The Selected Writings of John Witherspoon*. Landmarks in Rhetoric and Public Address. Carbondale: Southern Illinois University Press.
Miller, William B. 1958. "Presbyterian Signers of the Declaration of Independence." *Journal of the Presbyterian Historical Society* 36 (September): 139–179.
Morrison, Jeffry H. 2007. *John Witherspoon and the Founding of the American Republic*. Notre Dame, IN: University of Notre Dame Press.
Tiedemann, Joseph S. 2010. "A Tumultuous People: The Rage for Liberty and the Ambiance of Violence in the Middle Colonies in the Years Preceding the American Revolution." *Pennsylvania History: A Journal of Mid-Atlantic Studies* 77 (Autumn): 387–431.
Vile, John R. 2016. *The Constitutional Convention of 1787: A Comprehensive Encyclopedia of America's Founding*, Rev. 2nd ed. 2 vols. Clark, NJ: Talbot Publishing.
Wilkinson, Norman B. 1941. "Francis Hopkinson: Humor Propagandist of the American Revolution." *Historian* 4 (Autumn): 5–33.

NEW YORK AND ITS SIGNERS

New York was among the middle colonies that, despite a number of conflicts with its colonial governors, was somewhat reluctant to embrace independence. Indeed, while other states voted for independence on July 2, 1776, New York did not authorize its delegates to do so for another two weeks.

New York had originally been settled by the Dutch before falling under British rule. It included both the bustling port city of New York and the manorial estates of the Hudson Valley. New York City was the site of King's University, today's Columbia. Although its administrators were Tories, it produced a number of revolutionaries, including Alexander Hamilton (1755–1804), who wrote pamphlets, including *A Full Vindication of the Measures of Congress* and *The Farmer Refuted*, advocating independence. He later served under Washington during the Revolutionary War, attended the Constitutional Convention of 1787, and defended the new document in *The Federalist*, served as the nation's first secretary of the treasury, was one of the founders of the Federalist Party, and is the subject of a modern Broadway musical.

New York was also the home of Gouverneur Morris (1752–1816), another supporter of the Revolutionary cause, who represented Pennsylvania at the Constitutional Convention of 1787, where he was one of the most influential members.

Still later, he served as an ambassador to France, a U.S. senator, and chairman of the Erie Canal Commission.

John Jay was also from New York. He established himself as a diplomat (he helped negotiate the Treaty of Paris that ended the Revolutionary War) and as the third author of *The Federalist* in support of ratification of the U.S. Constitution. Although he was considered a moderate, he supported the Declaration of Independence but was not on hand to sign it. George Washington appointed him as the first chief justice of the U.S. Supreme Court, but he resigned this position in order to become governor of New York.

Four delegates from New York signed the Declaration of Independence. They were as follows: William Floyd, Francis Lewis, Philip Livingston, and Lewis Morris. In addition, Robert Livingston served on the Committee to write the document.

Robert Livingston (1746–1813), a cousin of Philip Livingston, was a graduate of King's College, who, like Philip, served both in the New York state legislature and at the Continental Congress. Although present for the vote on the Declaration, Robert was back at the state legislature when the Declaration was signed. He would serve as New York's first chancellor (its highest judicial office), in which capacity he later administered the oath of office to President George Washington. Livingston also served as a minister to France during the Jefferson administration.

William Floyd (1734–1821), who managed the family farm after the early death of his father, served in the state militia. He was elected to the Continental Congress for three years and for more than ten years in the New York Senate. He was a presidential elector for Thomas Jefferson in the elections of 1800 and 1804.

Francis Lewis (1713–1802) was born in Wales, raised largely by an aunt, and immigrated to the United States, where he was a merchant. Captured and imprisoned while fighting for the British in the French and Indian War, Lewis served as a delegate to the Stamp Act Congress and was a member of the Sons of Liberty before being elected to the Continental Congress. In addition to signing the Declaration, he also signed the Articles of Confederation. His home was ransacked by the British during the Revolutionary War, and his wife was imprisoned.

Philip Livingston (1716–1778) was a member of one of New York's most prominent families. He became a merchant in New York City after graduating from Yale. He served for nine years as a New York alderman after which he served in the colonial General Assembly, where he served for a time as speaker. He was also a delegate to the Stamp Act Congress. Livingston was a member of a number of important committees at the Continental Congress. After signing the Declaration, Livingston was a member of the convention that wrote the state constitution, and after being reelected to the Continental Congress, he died while serving there.

Lewis Morris (1726–1798), a half-brother to Gouverneur Morris, was a wealthy planter who was educated at Yale and had served as a judge of the admiralty court and as a member of the provincial assembly before being selected to the Continental Congress. Although he was commanding militia when Congress voted for independence, he returned to sign the document. Moore subsequently served as a county judge, as a member of the New York senate, and as a member of the New York convention to ratify the U.S. Constitution.

New York was the site of considerable fighting during the Revolutionary War. Its constitution of 1777 was something of a model for the U.S. Constitution. The New York delegation to the Constitutional Convention of 1787 was divided, and it had relatively little influence there. The state, which had taxed goods coming into its ports from other states, was one of the last to ratify the document, but after a long debate, it gave its consent.

Every Fourth of July, the *New York Times*, one of the nation's leading newspapers, publishes the Declaration of Independence.

See also Committee Responsible for Writing the Declaration of Independence; Signing of the Declaration of Independence

Further Reading

Anthony, Robert W. 1924. "Philip Livingston—A Tribute." *Quarterly Journal of the New York State Historical Association* 5 (October): 311–316.

Becker, Carl. 1903a. "Election of Delegates from New York to the Second Continental Congress." *American Historical Review* 9 (October): 66–85.

Becker, Carl. 1903b. "The Nomination and Election of Delegates from New York to the First Continental Congress, 1774." *Political Science Quarterly* 18 (March): 17–46.

Brookhiser, Richard. 2003. *Gentleman Revolutionary: Gouverneur Morris, the Rake Who Wrote the Constitution*. New York: Free Press.

Champagne, Roger J. 1964. "New York's Radicals and the Coming of Independence." *Journal of American History* 51 (June): 21–40.

Chernow, Ron. 2004. *Alexander Hamilton*. New York: Penguin Press.

Hess, Stephen. 2016. *America's Political Dynasties*. Washington, DC: Brookings Institution Press.

Ketcham, Richard M. 2002. *Divided Loyalties: How the American Revolution Came to New York*. New York: Henry Holt.

Stahr, Walter. 2005. *John Jay: Founding Father*. New York: Bloomsbury.

NOR HAVE WE BEEN WANTING IN ATTENTION TO OUR ENGLISH BRETHREN

An accusation that the Declaration of Independence directed to the king (sometimes acting in conjunction "with others") was that he had ignored the petitions that the colonists had directed to him. He had thereby shown himself to be a tyrant "unfit to be the ruler of a free people."

Almost as if to suggest that the king's rule within England might be more subject to popular control, and thus less tyrannical, than his rule over the colonies, the Declaration immediately continued by commenting that "Nor have we been wanting in attention to our English brethren." It elaborated by observing that "we have warned them from time to time of attempts by their legislature to extend an unwarrantable jurisdiction over us." It further said that "we have reminded them of the circumstances of our emigration and settlement here" and that "we have appealed to their native justice & magnanimity, and we have conjured them by the types of our common kindred, to disavow these usurpations, which would inevitably interrupt our connections & correspondence," only to find that "they too have been deaf to the voice of justice and of consanguinity."

Because individuals within Great Britain (including Scotland) were represented within the Parliament that was seeking to tax the colonists, it was logical for the colonists to have appealed to them for help. These people, of course, would have personal incentives to transfer some of their tax burden to the colonies, whom they had sought to defend during the French and Indian War and other conflicts.

Perhaps anticipating such a justification (the other side of which would be that the king had drawn the 13 colonies into his wars with other European powers), the Declaration immediately sought to remind the English people "of the circumstances of our emigration and settlement here." At this point, Congress chose to strike out Thomas Jefferson's longer explanation, which he had outlined at even great length in his *Summary View of the Rights of British America*. Reminding British kin that none of the circumstances of the settlement of America "Could warrant so strange a pretention [to parliamentary taxation in America]," Jefferson had asserted that "these were effected at the expence of our own blood and treasure, unassisted by the wealth or the strength of Great Britain."

Perhaps because the delegates no longer thought that, with independence, their own view of what the British empire should have been particularly germane, Congress also deleted Jefferson's explanation that "in constituting indeed our several forms of government, we had adopted one common king, thereby laying a foundation for perpetual league and amity with them: but that submission to their parliament was no part of our constitution, or ever in idea, if history and be credited." By making this deletion, Congress was also able to delete a specific reference to Parliament, which Jefferson had studiously avoided to this point, thus underlining the manner in which the colonists had conclusively rejected its authority.

Jefferson continued this indictment of the English people by observing their inactions to appeals to their "native justice & magnanimity." As explained in another essay, Congress made even more extensive deletions to this section. By tempering its criticism of the British people, Congress may have been anticipating that the end of the war would bring resumption of trade with Britain (Hawke 1964, 197).

See also Petitions for Redress Ignored (Charge #28); *A Summary View of the Rights of British America* (Jefferson); We Have Appealed to their Native Justice & Magnanimity

Further Reading

Hawke, David Freeman. 1964. *A Transaction of Free Men: The Birth and Course of the Declaration of Independence*. New York: Charles Scribner's Sons.

Hedges, William L. 1987. "Telling off the King: Jefferson's 'Summary View' as American Fantasy. Early American Literature." *Politics as Art, Art as Politics: Literature of the Early Republic, 1760–1820* 22 (Fall): 166–174.

Sainsbury, John "The Pro-Americans of London, 1769 to 1762." *William and Mary Quarterly* 35 (July): 423–454.

NORTH CAROLINA AND ITS SIGNERS

In 1776, North Carolina was deeply divided. John M. Head has thus observed that "Eastern North Carolina opponents of Parliament divided nearly equally on the question of independence, while backcountry men armed and fought for England"

(1968, 115). By contrast, the state has long been associated with the Mecklenburg Declaration of Independence, which, while now discredited, was supposed to have been drawn up by militiamen more than a month before the document that was adopted in Philadelphia on July 4 and that appeared to have echoed its language. Committees of safety appear to have played a major role in stifling Tory dissent and in mobilizing opinion on behalf of revolution (Watson 1996).

Three delegates to the Continental Congress, none of whom had been born in the state, represented North Carolina, which at the time included the current state of Tennessee. Two of the delegates were on hand to vote for the document, which all three signed. They were Joseph Hewes, William Hooper, and John Penn. The Provincial Congress of the state had authorized them to vote for independence on April 12, 1776.

William Hooper (1742–1790) was the son of a Boston minister. Hooper had graduated from Harvard and studied under James Otis before moving south to practice law. He was a gifted orator and appears to have been the leader of the North Carolina delegation. He had served in the First Continental Congress with Joseph Hewes and Richard Caswell, a Maryland-born planter and legislator, who had resigned in September 1775 after being named treasurer of the southern district of the state, after which he was replaced by John Penn. Although Hooper had opposed the Regulator Movement within his state, which some scholars believe was a precursor to the Revolution (Sadler 2012), he had written a letter to James Iredell on April 26, 1774, in which he indicated that the colonies were "striding fast to independence" and that they could "build an empire upon the ruins of Great Britain" and "adopt its constitution purged of its impurities" (Morgan and Schmidt 1975, 215). In 1774, Hooper noted that "A much greater man than I am once gloried that he was born a Briton; with as much pride I boast myself an American" (Blassingame 1968, 66). Hooper was away on business when the Declaration was adopted, faced the loss of two homes during the Revolution, and contracted malaria while on the run from the British (Kiernen and D'Agnese 2001, 201). After resigning from Congress, he served several terms in the North Carolina general assembly and established a thriving legal practice in Hillsborough (Morgan and Schmidt 1976, 32).

Joseph Hewes (1730–1779) was a merchant who had been born in Princeton, New Jersey, where he had attended college before joining a merchant in Philadelphia and then moving to North Carolina. He was one of two bachelors who signed the Declaration. Hewes initially opposed Lee's Resolution for Independence both because he held the British political system in high esteem and because he feared that a lengthy war would disrupt trade (Morgan and Schmidt 1975, 227). However, on June 18, Hewes wrote a letter to James Iredell in which he observed that "On Monday the great question of independence and total separation from all political intercourse with Great Britain will come on. It will be carried, I expect, by a great majority, and then, I suppose we shall take upon us a new name" (McCurry 1963, 463). John Adams believed that he may have been won over by one of his speeches, but in a letter to Samuel Johnson dated June 28, 1776, Hewes referenced debates over creating a federation and securing foreign allies and observed that "These two capital points ought to have been settled before our declaration of Independence went forth to the world. This was my opinion long ago and every days experience serves to confirm me in that point" (McCurry 1963, 463). Hewes appears to have been able to serve the Revolutionary cause as well as lining up profitable contracts during the Revolutionary War (Morgan & Schmidt 1976, 27). After serving in the North Carolina legislature, Hewes had returned to Congress, where he put in long hours and died.

John Penn (1740–1788) had been born in Fredericksburg, Virginia, and largely through self-instruction and work under Edmund Pendleton had educated himself in the law and practiced in Virginia before moving to North Carolina. An early advocate of independence, he had written a letter on February 12, 1776, to Brigadier General Thomas Person saying: "For God's sake my Good Sir, encourage our People, animate them to dare even to die for their country. Our struggle I hope will not continue long—may unanimity and success crown your endeavors" (Kiernan and D'Agnese 2001, 203). He and Hewes were present for the vote on independence and joined Hooper in signing the document on their state's behalf. Penn also signed the Articles of Confederation.

See also Mecklenburg Declaration of Independence; Signers, Collective Profile; Signing of the Declaration of Independence

Further Reading

Blassingame, John W. 1968. "American Nationalism and Other Loyalties in the Southern Colonies, 1763–1775." *Journal of Southern History* 334 (February): 50–75.

Head, John M. 1968. *A Time to Rend: An Essay on the Decision for American Independence*. Madison: State Historical Society of Wisconsin.

Kiernan, Denise, and Joseph D'Agnese. 2009. *Signing Their Lives Away: The Fame and Misfortune of the Men Who Signed the Declaration of Independence*. Philadelphia: Quirk Books.

McCurry, Allan J. 1963. "Joseph Hewes and Independence: A Suggestion." *North Carolina Historical Review* 40 (October): 455–464.

Morgan, David T., and William J. Schmidt. 1975. "From Economic Sanctions to Political Separation: The North Carolina Delegation to the Continental Congress, 1774–1776." *North Carolina Historical Review* 52 (July): 215–234.

Morgan, David T., and William J. Schmidt. 1976. *North Carolinians in the Continental Congress*. Winston-Salem, NC: John F. Blair.

Sadler, Sarah. 2012. "Prelude to the American Revolution? The War of Regulation: A Revolutionary Reaction for Reform." *History Teacher* 46 (November): 97–126.

Watson, Alan D. 1996. "The Committees of Safety and the Coming of the American Revolution in North Carolina, 1776–1776." *North Carolina Historical Review* 73 (April): 131–155.

NORTHWEST ORDINANCE OF 1787

Of all the laws adopted in American history, few arguably come closer to embodying the ideals of the Declaration of Independence than the Northwest Ordinance of 1787. The law was adopted in New York on July 13, 1787, by the Congress under the Articles of Confederation while delegates were formulating the Constitution in Philadelphia.

Just as the Declaration had declared that the one-time colonies were "free & independent states," so too, the Northwest Ordinance, like the Constitution itself, provided that new states would enter the Union on an equal basis with those that were already there. Applying to territory that would eventually become the states of Ohio, Indiana, Illinois, Michigan, and Wisconsin, the law provided that " the States so formed shall be distinct republican States, and admitted members of the Federal Union, having the same rights of sovereignty, freedom, and independence as the other States" (Eastman 2002, 103). This principle became known as "the Equal Footing Doctrine" (Eastman 2002, 103).

The ordinance, largely attributed to Nathan Dane of Massachusetts, was based on an earlier ordinance of 1784, chiefly penned by Thomas Jefferson, which had not been put into effect. Just as the Declaration of Independence had declared that "all men are created equal," so too, article 6 of the ordinance provided that "There shall be neither slavery nor involuntary servitude in the said territory, otherwise than in the punishment of crime, whereof the party shall have been duly convicted" (Eastman 2002, 103). New states, like Tennessee, Alabama, and Mississippi, which would be formed to the south of this territory, subsequently entered the Union, like the states from which they had been formed, as slave states, whereas those formed from free states generally entered as free.

George Anastaplo notes that "the Congress demonstrated in its 1787 provisions for the Northwest Territory how Parliament should have dealt with its American territories well before Independence" (2007, 38). Robert Remini has observed that the Northwest Ordinance was largely responsible for preventing the American republic from "collapsing immediately into an empire . . . by providing . . . a new concept of Union" (1988, 16). By limiting the time that western territories would be governed by officials appointed by the national government and allowing new states to enter on an equal basis with the old, the law thus helped avoid the kind of colonial domination that the British had sought to exercise in the original 13 colonies and that had led to the Declaration.

Drawing from state bills and declarations of rights, the ordinance further provided for the protection of civil rights and liberties (Baxter 1987), albeit omitting freedom of speech and press, unless they are considered to have been implied (Anastaplo 2007, 41). The ordinance further provided that "Religion, morality and knowledge being necessary to good government and the happiness of mankind, schools and the means of education shall forever be encouraged" (Hill 1988, 50).

See also Jefferson, Thomas; Representative (Republican) Government; Slavery

Further Reading

Anastaplo, George. 2007. *Reflections on Freedom of Speech and the First Amendment.* Lexington: University Press of Kentucky.

Baxter, Maurice. 1987. "The Northwest Ordinance—Our First National Bill of Rights." *OAH Magazine of History* 2 (Fall): 13–14, 18.

Eastman, John C. 2002. "The Declaration of Independence as Viewed from the States." In *The Declaration of Independence: Origins and Impact*, edited by Scott Douglas Gerber, 96–117. Washington, DC: CQ Press.

Hill, Robert S. 1988. "Federalism, Republicanism, and the Northwest Ordinance." *Publius* 18 (Autumn): 41–52.

Remini, Robert V. 1988. "The Northwest Ordinance of 1787: Bulwark of the Republic." *Indiana Magazine of History* 84 (March): 15–24.

O

OBSTRUCTED THE ADMINISTRATION OF JUSTICE (CHARGE #8)

Whereas the first seven accusations in the Declaration of Independence outlined ways in which the king had interfered with or obstructed legislative processes in the colonies, the next two accusations focused specifically on the judiciary. The first charged that "he has obstructed the administration of justice by refusing his assent to laws for establishing judiciary powers." Thomas Jefferson's original version was somewhat stronger, specifically saying that "he has suffered [permitted] the administration of justice totally to cease in some of these states."

Herbert Friedenwald believes that this charge originated in a controversy that began in North Carolina in January 1768, when the governor signed a law establishing superior courts, which the British asked the colony to amend because it permitted creditors to attach the property of debtors who had never been in the colony, even though this was in tension with British laws (1904, 231). After the legislature readopted this law over the king's objection, the king disallowed it. When the king attempted to establish courts on his own, the assembly refused to appropriate salaries for them. The North Carolina assembly subsequently dissolved, effectively leaving the state without such courts until 1776.

Given that this charge seems to implicate both the North Carolina legislature and the king, it is not surprising that Thomas Hutchinson observed "that the transaction, referred to, is a reproach upon the Colony, which the Congress have most wickedly perverted to cast reproach upon the King" (1776).

See also Charges against the King and Others; North Carolina and Its Signers

Further Reading

Friedenwald, Herbert. 1904. *The Declaration of Independence: An Interpretation and an Analysis*. New York: Macmillan.

Hutchinson, Thomas. 1776. "1776: Hutchinson, Strictures upon the Declaration of Independence." Online Library of Liberty. http://oll.libertyfund.org/pages/1776-hutchinson-strictures-upon-the-declaration-of-independence.

OLIVE BRANCH PETITION

After stating its quarrels with George III, the Declaration of Independence noted that "In every stage of these oppressions, we have petitioned for redress in the most humble terms; our repeated petitions have been answered only by repeated injury."

One of the petitions that Jefferson undoubtedly had in mind was the so-called Olive Branch petition, which the Second Continental Congress adopted on July 5, 1775, and signed on July 8. The document was authored by John Dickinson, the so-called Penman of the Revolution, who was known for his political moderation and for his desire to avoid conflict with Great Britain. The document is called the "Olive Branch" Petition because the olive branch was traditionally a sign of peace and reconciliation, and Dickinson wrote the petition at a time when members of Congress continued to hope that the king would intervene on the colonists' behalf against taxation by Parliament that the colonists believed to be unconstitutional ("no taxation without representation").

The petition was phrased in very deferential language. The opening lines referred to "the King's most excellent Majesty" and addressed him as "Most Gracious Sovereign."

Listing each of the colonies separately, the document recognized that "The union between our Mother country and these colonies, and the energy of mild and just government, produced benefits so remarkably important" that they were envied by other countries. The document went on to describe how, after the late war with France, the colonies had expected "to share in the blessings of peace, and the emoluments of victory and conquest" in which they had participated but that they had instead faced "a new system of statutes and regulations adopted for the administration of the colonies."

In contrast to the Declaration of Independence, but not unlike the petition that the First Continental Congress had issued in 1774, the Olive Branch Petition declined "the ungrateful task of describing the irksome varieties of artifices, practiced by many of your Majesty's Ministers, the delusive presences, fruitless terrors, and unavailing severities, that have, from time to time, been dealt out by them." In so phrasing the grievances, the petition was based on the premise that "the king can do no wrong," and that any offenses that had proceeded from his office must have been the result of bad advice from his ministers. Dickinson further attributed the colonists' decision to arm themselves as a result of "Your Majesty's Ministers, persevering in their measures."

Citing "obligations to Almighty God, to your Majesty, to our fellow subjects, and to ourselves," the petition was an attempt "to use all the means in our power, not incompatible with our safety, for stopping the further effusion [outpouring] of blood, and for averting the impending calamities that threaten the British Empire." It thus appealed to the king's "royal magnanimity and benevolence" in bringing about reconciliation.

Avoiding any statements of recognizing parliamentary sovereignty over the colonies, the petition assured the king that the colonies continued to be "Attached to your Majesty's person, family, and government, with all devotion that principle and affection can inspire," and they they "ardently desire the former harmony . . . may be restored." It further assured the king that despite their sufferings, the colonies "retain too tender a regard for the kingdom from which we derive our origin, to request such a reconciliation as might in any manner be inconsistent with her dignity or her welfare."

The petition then asked "that your royal authority and influence may be graciously interposed to procure us relief from our afflicting fears and jealousies, occasioned by the system before mentioned, and to settle peace through every part of your dominions."

Whereas Thomas Paine would soon question the institution of hereditary succession (passing the throne to a monarch's children) in his *Common Sense*, this document specifically ended with the wish that "your Majesty may enjoy a long and prosperous reign, and that your descendants may govern your dominions with honor to themselves and happiness to their subjects."

This is one of only three documents (the Declaration of Independence and the Articles of Confederation were the other two) that delegates signed.

The document was given to the king on September 1, 1775, but he refused to receive it because he believed that the Declaratory Act that Parliament had adopted in 1765 had legally established the right of Parliament to tax the colonies, and he believed that the British Constitution did not give him the power to overrule such acts.

Although phrased in a conciliatory form and for a conciliatory purpose, the ultimate effect of the petition, and its rejection by the king, thus actually undercut the power of those moderates, like Dickinson, in the Second Continental Congress who were seeking a compromise that would avoid conflict.

See also *Common Sense* (Paine); Declaratory Act of 1776; Dickinson (John) Speech Opposing the Declaration of Independence; Petition to King George III (1774)

Further Reading

"Petition to the King, July 8, 1775." 1775. *Journals of the Continental Congress, 1774–1789.* Vol. II. Edited from the original records in the Library of Congress by Worthington Chauncey Ford; Chief Division of Manuscripts. Washington, DC: Government Printing Office, 1905. Accessed at http://avalon.law.yale.edu/18th_century/contcong_07-08-75.asp.

ORIGINALITY OF THE DECLARATION OF INDEPENDENCE

Perhaps in part out of jealousy over the praise that Thomas Jefferson had received for being the chief author of the Declaration of Independence, in 1822 John Adams wrote a letter to Thomas Pickering, his former secretary of state, questioning the document's originality. Adams noted that:

> As you justly observe, there is not an idea in it but what had been hackneyed in Congress for two years before. The substance of it is contained in the declaration of rights and the violation of those rights in the Journals of Congress in 1774. Indeed, the essence of it is contained in a pamphlet, voted and printed by the town of Boston, before the first congress met, composed by James Otis . . . and pruned and polished by Samuel Adams." (Smith 2011)

Richard Henry Lee had further accused Jefferson of having largely copied the introductory paragraphs of the Declaration from John Locke's *Second Treatise on Government*.

Writing to his friend James Madison, Jefferson agreed that the sentiments he expressed were not new, but he denied having seen Otis's pamphlet. He continued: "I know only that I turned to neither book nor pamphlet while writing it. I did not consider it as any part of my charge to invent new ideas altogether, and to offer no sentiment which had ever been expressed before" (Smith 2011).

In another letter in 1825, Jefferson said:

> Neither aiming at originality of principle or sentiment, nor yet copied from any particular and previous writing, it was intended to be an expression of the American mind, and to give to that expression the proper tone and spirit called for by the occasion. All its authority rests then on the harmonizing sentiments of the day, whether expressed in conversation, letters printed essays, or in the elementary books of public right, as Aristotle, Cicero, Locke, Sidney, etc. (Smith 2011)

It is important to remember that Jefferson was writing a document for a legislative body where originality would not be valued nearly so highly as an ability to state felicitously sentiments that were shared by fellow delegates, who are known to have deleted major portions of Jefferson's original to which they could not agree. Moses Coit Tyler thus observed that "for such a paper as Jefferson was commissioned to write, the one quality which it could not properly have had, the one quality which would have been fatal to its acceptance either by the American Congress or by the American people—is originality" (1896, 7). As William Huntting Howell observes in an article that centers on David Rittenhouse's orreries (models of the solar system), "the proper duty of the natural philosopher was to discover and translate the laws of nature and nature's God as accurately as possible—to limn a more perfect copy of the principles that govern the universe—not to create the world anew (Howell 2007, 758).

It is also important to remember that the largest segment of the Declaration consisted of colonial grievances. While Jefferson transformed most of these grievances by laying responsibility at the door of the English king, rather than at the Parliament whose sovereignty the colonies had rejected, and by attempting to show that collectively they showed the king's intent to govern like a tyrant, these grievances had long before been accepted by the colonies as "facts." Many of these charges had been previously stated in the Virginia Declaration of Rights and in the Declaration on the Causes and Necessity of Taking Up Arms.

See also Adams, John; Declaration on the Causes and Necessity of Taking Up Arms; Jefferson, Thomas; Locke, John; Style of the Declaration of Independence; Virginia Declaration of Rights

Further Reading

Becker, Carl L. 1970. *The Declaration of Independence: A Study in the History of Political Ideas*. New York: Vintage Books.

Howell, William Huntting. 2007. "A More Perfect Copy: David Rittenhouse and the Reproduction of Republican Virtue." *William and Mary Quarterly*, 3rd ser. 64 (October): 757–790.

Smith, George H. 2011. "Was Thomas Jefferson a Plagiarist?" Libertarianism.org. November 15, 2011. https://www.libertarianism.org/publications/essays/excursions/was-thomas-jefferson-plagiarist.

Tyler, Moses Coit. 1896. "The Declaration of Independence in the Light of Modern Criticism." *North American Review* 163 (July): 1–16.

OUR LIVES, OUR FORTUNES, AND OUR SACRED HONOR

One of the most ringing phrases of the Declaration of Independence, which is highlighted in the title of an important book on the American Revolution (Beeman 2013), is the concluding sentence. There the delegates mutually pledged "to each other our lives, our fortunes, and our sacred honor." The solemnity of this phrase, accented by the reference to "sacred," was arguably further highlighted when congressional delegates subsequently signed the Declaration.

Stephen E. Lucas says that the term "'Lives and fortunes' was one of the most hackneyed phrases of eighteenth-century Anglo-American political discourse" (National Archives). He observes that "what marks [Thomas] Jefferson's 'happy talent for composition' in this case is the coupling of 'our sacred Honor' with 'our Lives" and 'our Fortunes' to create the eloquent trilogy that closes the Declaration." He observes that "the concept of honor (and its cognates fame and glory) exerted a powerful hold on the eighteenth-century mind." As he explains, "The cult of honor was so strong that in English judicial proceedings a peer of the realm did not answer to bills in chancery or give a verdict 'upon oath, like an ordinary juryman, but upon his honor'" (National Archives).

This complete phrase seems to be a logical complement to an earlier triad within the Declaration that refers to the "unalienable rights" of "life, liberty, and the pursuit of happiness." The only difference between the first two words of each phrase is that the one is generally singular (albeit not necessarily as initially used in the Declaration) and the other plural.

By contrast, the term "fortunes," if understood as an indirect reference to property (which was omitted from the original triad), is related to liberty only in the sense that such wealth might be a consequence of being able to pursue one's affairs freely as in a free enterprise system. It might also, or alternatively, refer to an unknown common fate or destiny, which could result either in eventual victory and the securing of jeopardized rights or in trials for treason. Such fortune arguably contrasts with the necessity that the first paragraph of the Declaration references. If the Declaration intends to convey this latter meaning, the delegates would be pledging to continue on a common course and share in any common punishments rather than seeking individual pardons like those that the king had authorized General William Howe to give in his Circular Letter.

The term "sacred honor" seems to be an unlikely complement to "the pursuit of happiness," since it emphasizes an element of elevated character rather than the routine pursuit of one's well-being. This might show that the document did not intend for the two phrases to be parallel. Alternatively, in context, the reference to "sacred honor" term might be intended to suggest that such a pursuit finds higher fulfillment in public service than in the mere private pursuit of pleasure. The phrase ties to the Declaration's earlier claim that the colonies not only had the "right" but also to "duty" to throw off the British government (Webking 1988, 108).

Commentators on the Declaration often quote Benjamin Franklin's reputed quip that after the Declaration, the colonists must either "hang together, or hang separately" from the ends of British nooses. This sentiment may very well have been inspired by the last sentence, since, as Pauline Maier has observed, "In British law, death and the forfeiture of estate were the punishment for treason" (1997, 59).

See also Franklin, Benjamin; Howe's Circular Letter (1776); Life, Liberty, and the Pursuit of Happiness; Necessity; Signing of the Declaration of Independence; Treason

Further Reading

Beeman, Richard R. 2013. *Our Lives, Our Fortunes, and Our Sacred Honor: The Forging of American Independence, 1774–1776*. New York: Basic Books.

Gregory, Tappan. 1948. "The Annual Address: 'Our Lives, Our Fortunes, and Our Sacred Honor.'" *American Bar Association Journal* 34 (October): 874–876, 969–974.

Maier, Pauline. 1997. *American Scripture: Making the Declaration of Independence*. New York: Alfred A. Knopf.

Lucas, Stephen E. "The Stylistic Artistry of the Declaration of Independence." National Archives. https://www.archives.gov/founding-docs/stylistic-artistry-of-the-declaration.

Webking, Robert H. 1988. *The American Revolution and the Politics of Liberty*. Baton Rouge: Louisiana State University Press.

OUTLINE AND ORGANIZATION OF THE DECLARATION OF INDEPENDENCE

The Declaration of Independence falls into a number of distinct parts. There are a number of ways of describing them. Howard Mumford Jones says, "Its form is that of a classical oration in five parts" (1976, 3). He explains that it includes "an exordium; the statement of a general political theory to which appeal is made; an indictment of the king in twenty-six counts; a resume of the legal recourse the colonists have vainly employed for redress of grievances; and a peroration stating what Congress had done and appealing to Divine Providence because of the rectitude of those making the appeal" (1976, 3).

The first two paragraphs (sometimes identified as the preamble) explain the purpose of the document and outline a set of principles to which Americans are committed. This includes an assertion of the people's right to dissolve a government that is not serving its purposes and to replace it with another.

The body of the document outlines a series of "abuses and usurpations" of the English king and other authorities, which is meant to prove that these actions are designed to take away American liberties. These accusations can, in turn, be subdivided into those directed specifically against the king's administration, those associating his actions with "others" (the Parliament), and those that delineated war atrocities.

The last two paragraphs explained how the colonists had previously petitioned the English government. It concluded with the resolution for independence that Richard Henry Lee had introduced and with a mutual commitment of the members of the Continental Congress to the cause.

In common with some other important documents of the day, the engrossed copy, which was commissioned after New York's approval of the document, achieved state unanimity, further included the signatures of the delegates.

Scholars have noted that the document is based on syllogistic reasoning, with major premises leading to logical conclusions (Lucas 1990). Focusing on the main elements of the document, Ross Lence has further observed that "the format of the Declaration seems to parallel the three parts of any traditional essay (an introduction, a body, and a conclusion)" (1976, 5–6).

This suggests that the Declaration is "a coherent whole" (Lence 1976, 6) and that interpreters should approach it accordingly. It should further be recognized that the Declaration is a public document that was revised during debate in the Second Continental Congress and that it is thus not simply the personal views of the primary author, or authors, but of the Congress, and the people they represent, as a whole.

Unlike the U.S. Constitution, which is somewhat longer, the Declaration is not divided into articles and sections. In addition to varying the print in the heading of the Document, the printed Dunlap version does, however, use paragraph divisions to set off the accusations against the king and others.

See also Charges against the King and Others; Interpreting the Declaration of Independence; Legal Form of the Declaration of Independence; Resolutions Introduced by Richard Henry Lee (June 7, 1776); Signing of the Declaration of Independence

Further Reading

Jones, Howard Mumford. 1976. "The Declaration of Independence: A Critique." In *The Declaration of Independence: Two Essays by Howard Mumford Jones and Howard H. Peckham*, 3–20. Worcester, MA: American Antiquarian Society.

Lence, Ross. 1976. "Thomas Jefferson and the American Declaration of Independence: The Power and Natural Rights of a Free People." *Political Science Reviewer* 6 (Fall): 1–31.

Lucas, Stephen E. 1990. "The Stylistic Artistry of the Declaration of Independence." *Prologue: Quarterly of the National Archives and Records Administration*. https://www.archives.gov/founding-docs/stylistic-artistry-of-the-declaration.

P

PENNSYLVANIA AND ITS SIGNERS

Even though it provided the site for the writing of the Declaration of Independence, Pennsylvania was (like most of the middle colonies) one of the more reluctant colonies to approve of the decision for independence. Nonetheless, more delegates from this state signed the document than any other. Moreover, one of these delegates (Benjamin Franklin) served on the committee to write the Declaration. Yet another delegate (John Dickinson), who did not sign the document, made major contributions to debates leading up to independence and fought for the cause, where one of the delegates who did sign (Robert Morris) had joined Dickinson in absenting himself from the Continental Congress to allow a majority to approve. Pennsylvania was also serving as home to Thomas Paine, whose publication of *Common Sense* helped spur the decision to cut ties to the English king.

Pennsylvania had been a proprietary colony (William Penn was the original proprietor), and conflict over whether to vote for independence became entwined in the decision as to whether to keep the propriety government or adopt a more democratic document. In November 1775, the Assembly of Pennsylvania had chosen the following to represent the colony in Congress: Andrew Allen, Edward Biddle, John Dickinson, Benjamin Franklin, Charles Humphreys, Robert Morris, Thomas Willing, and James Wilson (Stille 1890, 385). That same month, it had instructed them to seek redress with Britain "and utterly reject any proposition (should such be made) that may cause or lead to a separation from the mother-country, or a change in the form of this government" (Stille 1889, 386). The legislature balked when the Continental Congress voted in May of 1776 that colonies should adopt new governments.

Thereafter a Whig party arose in the colony. It called for the establishment of a new, more democratic, government. Members of this party boycotted the colonial assembly, which was then unable to operate; created a provincial constitutional convention, and appointed a Council of Safety to govern until the new constitution was formulated (Doutrich 1988, 39). The assembly elected the men who would sign the document. Meanwhile, on July 2, Franklin, John Morton, and Wilson voted on Pennsylvania's behalf for independence, whereas Humphreys and Willing voted against it, and Dickinson and Morris either absented themselves or abstained (Doutrich 1988, 39).

George Clymer (1739–1813) was a Philadelphia merchant with lots of public service. Prior to serving in the Continental Congress from 1776 to 1777 and again from 1780 to 1782, he had been a member of the Philadelphia Common Council, a justice of the Court of Quarter Sessions, and a member of the Committee of

Correspondence and the Pennsylvania Council of Safety (Mohr 1938, 282–283). He later served in the state legislature and as a delegate to the Constitutional Convention of 1787, as well as a member of the House of Representatives. He also served both as a trustee of the University of Pennsylvania and as the president of the Pennsylvania Academy of Fine Arts.

None of the Pennsylvania signers was more recognized than Benjamin Franklin (1706–1790). The oldest member of the Continental Congress, Franklin had served as postmaster general and as the colonial representative for the colonies in Britain before being humiliated before Parliament (he had taken responsibility for leaking incriminating letters of Massachusetts governor Thomas Hutchinson) and returning home. Franklin, a printer, whose scientific discoveries were internationally known, had helped persuade Thomas Paine to immigrate to the United States. Franklin was one of five members who served on the committee to write the Declaration, and he and John Adams of Massachusetts made minor, mostly stylistic, changes in the document before Congress debated it. Franklin helped console Thomas Jefferson during debates, which Jefferson thought were marring his handiwork. Franklin went on to play a major role in securing foreign aid for the Revolutionary cause, and he represented Pennsylvania at the Constitutional Convention of 1787, where he argued that it was the best document that such a diverse group could have formulated. Franklin's son William was deposed as the royal governor of New Jersey, and father and son became alienated and never reconciled.

Although Robert Morris (1734–1806) did not vote for the Declaration of Independence, he later signed the document and subsequently said that he thought his failure to vote for it on July 2 had been a mistake. A merchant who had been born in England, he was one of the richest men in the colonies. He later signed both the Articles of Confederation and the U.S. Constitution. From 1781 to 1783, he was superintendent of finance for the nation. He later served in the U.S. Senate. His involvement in western land speculation plunged him into bankruptcy and led to a stint in debtors' prison.

John Morton (ca. 1724–1777) was a farmer and surveyor of Finnish/Swedish ancestry who had served as a justice of the peace and as a sheriff. A delegate to the Stamp Act Congress of 1765, an associate justice of the state supreme court, and a member of the provincial assembly, Morton died within a year after signing the Declaration. One of the sides of the nine-foot monument above Morton's grave notes that his vote broke the tie in the Pennsylvania delegation on behalf of independence. Another side observes: "John Morton being censured by some of his friends for his boldness in giving his casting vote for the Declaration of Independence, his prophetic spirit dictated from his deathbed the following message to them: 'Tell them they will live to see the hour when they shall acknowledge it to have been the most glorious service I ever rendered to my country'" (St. Paul's Burying Ground).

George Ross (1739–1779) was a successful lawyer who had until 1775 largely sided with Tories. He became judge of the admiralty court under the Articles of Confederation. Ross was the uncle of John Ross, the husband of Betsy Ross, a Philadelphia flag maker to whom the making of the first U.S. flag has been incorrectly attributed.

Benjamin Rush (1746–1813) was a medical doctor who had studied in Scotland and was one of the most educated members of the Continental Congress. He may be best known for character sketches that he wrote of fellow delegates. A deeply religious man who cared a great deal for his patients, Rush was strongly convinced of the efficacy of bleeding patients to cure them. Rush published a book entitled *Medical Inquiries and Observations upon Diseases of the Mind*, which has given him the title of the Father of American Psychiatry. A friend of both John Adams and Thomas Jefferson, he was instrumental in getting them to renew their friendship and resume their correspondence in their later years. On July 16, 1776, Rush wrote a letter to Patrick Henry celebrating "the declaration of the freedom & independence of the American colonies." He observed that "Such inestimable blessings cannot be too joyfully received, nor purchased at too high a price. They would [be] cheaply bought at the loss of all thye towns & of every fourth, or even third man in America" (Butterfield 1951, 251). He also suggested that Virginia had made a mistake in excluding clergymen from being able to serve in the state legislature.

James Smith (1719–1806) was an Irish immigrant who was both a lawyer and a surveyor and also owned a local forge. In 1774 he wrote a piece, "Essay on the Constitutional Power of Great Britain over the Colonies in America," proposing a boycott of British goods. He was not elected to Congress until after it had endorsed the Declaration of Independence, but he was in place in time to sign it.

George Taylor (ca. 1716–1791) was another working man who had been born in Ireland and came to America as an indentured servant to an ironmaster. When the ironmaster died, Taylor married his widow. Taylor was subsequently elected to the provincial assembly and participated in the Committee of Correspondence and a Committee of Safety. After serving in Congress, he served briefly as a member of the Pennsylvania Supreme Council.

James Wilson (1741–1798) had been born and educated in Scotland before coming to America to teach at the College of Philadelphia and study law under John Dickinson. A strong proponent of colonial rights, he authored "Considerations on the Nature and Extent of the Legislative Authority of the British Parliament" but was generally considered to be a moderate. He would oppose the democracy of the state's 1776 constitution, although he was among the most democratically inclined members who would later attend the Constitutional Convention of 1787 and sign the document. Appointed as an associate justice to the U.S. Supreme Court by George Washington, Wilson became enmeshed in land speculation and was being hounded by his creditors at his death.

In addition to the Pennsylvania delegates who signed the Declaration, it is important to recall that Charles Thomson (1729–1824), whose name was printed along with John Hancock's in the first printing of the Declaration and who was often called "the Sam Adams of Philadelphia" (Zimmerman 1958), served during the entire Continental Congress as secretary. Orphaned at the age of 10, he fled a possible indenture to a blacksmith, was befriended by a woman after he told her he wanted to become a scholar, and received a classical education (Grobel 1943, 145). Fred Rolater argues that toward the end of the Articles of Confederation, Thomson served as a virtual "prime minister" of the United States (1977). An immigrant from Ireland, Thomson was a member of Philadelphia's Sons of Liberty and helped design the Great Seal of the United States. A gifted man, Thomson devoted his later years to translating the Septuagint version of the bible from Greek into English.

Pennsylvania was the home both of John Dunlap, who printed the first broadside of the Declaration of Independence. It was also home to Timothy Matlack, who was the first to engross the document that is now displayed at the National Archives.

Pennsylvania's Independence Hall was also the site of the Constitutional Convention of 1787. Its members were among the most influential in that body. Shortly thereafter, the state adopted a new constitution, which more closely followed the new national model, including a bicameral legislature.

See also *Common Sense* (Paine); Committee Responsible for Writing the Declaration of Independence; Dickinson (John) Speech Opposing the Declaration of Independence; Dunlap Broadside Printing of the Declaration of Independence; Engrossed Declaration of Independence (Matlack); Franklin, Benjamin; Independence Hall; Philadelphia; Second Continental Congress

Further Reading

Alkana, Joseph. 1992. "Spiritual and Rational Authority in Benjamin Rush's Travels through Life." *Texas Studies in Literature and Language* 34 (Summer): 284–300.

Butterfield, Lyman H. 1951. "Dr. Rush to Governor Henry on the Declaration of Independence and the Virginia Constitution." *Proceedings of the American Philosophical Society* 95 (June 12): 250–253.

D'Elia, Donald J. "Benjamin Rush: Philosopher of the American Revolution." *Transactions of the American Philosophical Society* 64: 1–113.

Doutrich, Paul. 1988. "From Revolution to Constitution: Pennsylvania's Path to Federalism." In *The Constitution and the States: The Role of the Original Thirteen in the Framing and Adoption of the Federal Constitution*, edited by Patrick T. Conley and John P. Kaminski, 37–54. Madison, WI: Madison House.

Grobel, Kendrick. 1943. "Charles Thomson, First American N.T. Translator: An Appraisal." *Journal of Bible and Religion* 11 (August): 145–151.

Grundfest, Jerry. 1982. *George Clymer: Philadelphia Revolutionary*. New York: Arno Press.

Hall, Mark David. 1997. *The Political and Legal Philosophy of James Wilson, 1742–1798*. Columbia: University of Missouri Press.

Isaacson, Walter. 2003. *Benjamin Franklin: An American Life*. New York: Simon and Schuster.

Miller, William B. 1958. "Presbyterian Signers of the Declaration of Independence." *Journal of the Presbyterian Historical Society* 36 (September): 139–179.

Mohr, Walter H. 1938. "George Clymer." *Pennsylvania History: A Journal of Mid-Atlantic Studies* 5 (October): 282–285.

Rappleye, Charles. 2010. *Robert Morris: Financier of the American Revolution*. New York: Simon and Schuster.

Rolater, Fred S. "Charles Thomson, 'Prime Minister' of the United States." *Pennsylvania Magazine of History and Biography* 101 (July): 322–348.

Schlenther, Boyd Stanley. 1990. *Charles Thomson: A Patriot's Pursuit*. Newark: University of Delaware Press.

Slaski, Eugene R. 1976. "Thomas Willing: A Study in Moderation, 1774–1778." *Pennsylvania Magazine of History and Biography* 100 (October): 491–506.

Smith, Charles Page. 1956. *James Wilson: Founding Father, 1742–1798*. Chapel Hill: University of North Carolina Press.

St. Paul's Burying Ground. www.oldchesterpa.com/cemeteries/stpcemetery.htm.

Stille, Charles J. 1889. "Pennsylvania and the Declaration of Independence." *Pennsylvania Magazine of History and Biography* 13 (January): 385–429.

Tiedemann, Joseph S. 2010. "A Tumultuous People: The Rage for Liberty and the Ambiance of Violence in the Middle Colonies in the Years Preceding the American Revolution." *Pennsylvania History: A Journal of Mid-Atlantic Studies* 77 (Autumn): 387–431.

Zimmerman, John J. 1958. "Charles Thomson, 'The Sam Adams of Philadelphia.'" *The Mississippi Valley Historical Review* 45 (December): 464–480.

PEOPLE

Fairly early in the document, the Declaration of Independence stated that the members of the 13 colonies had become a separate "people" from those in Great Britain. It further announced that it was therefore time "to dissolve the political bands which have connected them" to one another "and to assume among the powers of the earth, the separate and equal station to which the Laws of Nature and of Nature's God entitle them." Foreign translators have had difficulty in translating the word "people," in part because the Declaration is not always clear as to whether "'one people' already existed prior to July 4, 1776 . . . or whether the 'one people' were brought into being by the Declaration itself" (Thelen 2002, 197).

Randy Barnett asserts that the "one people" identified in the Declaration "is not a collective entity, but an aggregate of particular individuals" (2016, 36). He thus notes that "So 'they' not *it* should 'declare the causes which impel *them* to the separation' (2016, 36).

Three paragraphs from the end of the document, the Declaration says that "a prince whose character is thus marked by every act which may define a tyrant, is unfit to be the ruler of a free people." Although the king had not necessarily played the role of a tyrant within his own country, the authors of the Declaration believed that tyranny had characterized his relationship to the one-time 13 colonies, which now sought to rule themselves. They sought to make decisions that the king (and Parliament) had previously sought to make for them.

The penultimate paragraph of the Declaration pointed out that the colonies had not been "wanting [lacking] in attentions to our British brethren," whom it also identified as "our common kindred," and to whose ties of "consanguinity" (ties of blood) they had appealed. It went on to claim that the British inattention to colonial pleas had led to the necessity of holding them "as we hold the rest of mankind, enemies in war, in peace friends." Thomas Jefferson's original draft further said that it is necessary "to forget our former love for them [British brethren]," while noting that "we might have been a free & a great people together" (Maier, 1997, 240).

Today political scientists routinely distinguish between nations—whose people are bound together by such common ties as racial ancestry, history, language, literature, religion, and culture—and states, which represent geographical areas controlled by governments and may include one or more nations and/or ethnic groups. Further complicating, or clarifying, the situation, as the case may be, such states are often called nation-states, in part to distinguish them from entities, like the 50 states within the United States or those within other federal entities that are part of a larger sovereign whole. Under international law, nation-states have legal sovereignty, or control, over their own territories and meet one another as equals in the international arena. Over 190 such states are currently represented in the United Nations.

The final paragraph of the Declaration came closer to the usage of states than to that of people. After referring to "the good people of these colonies," this paragraph did not focus on the ties between the British and American people but on absolving "all allegiance to the British Crown." It further proclaimed that "all political connection between them and the state [Jefferson had originally referred to "parliament or people"] of Great Britain is & ought to be totally dissolved." Moreover, this paragraph proclaimed the right of the newly proclaimed "free & independent states" to "have full power to levy war, conclude peace, contract alliances, establish commerce, & to do all other acts and things which independent states may of right do."

Whether the ties that bind individuals within a nation or empire are stronger than those that lead them to separation is often a matter of perception. In the years leading up to the Declaration of Independence, the colonists had been claiming their rights as "Englishmen," therefore suggesting that they remained a single people, bound by common laws and by common allegiance to the king. In writing *Common Sense*, Thomas Paine noted that Britain had been a very poor "mother." Many people within Britain, however, asserted the sovereignty of the British Parliament (which the colonies had come to reject, particularly with respect to taxation) bound the two entities together. For Americans, breaking the tie to the monarch was the final demonstration that a people united were now separate, but from the English perspective, this break occurred when Americans renounced the authority of Parliament.

In an essay published in 1776, Josiah Tucker (1713–1799), who served as the dean of Gloucester from 1758 to 1799, asked whether Americans could remain tied to Britain, like the territory of Hanover (in today's northern Germany) without accepting parliamentary authority. Seeking to distinguish individuals in America from those in Hanover, he asked:

> Are Englishmen and Hanoverians the same People, or the same Nation? Are they the Subjects of the same Prince by one and the same Title? And do *Hanoverians* enjoy any one Privilege either at Home or Abroad, belonging to the *English* Nation? Certainly not: How then can these cases be pretended to be parallel? And to what Purpose are they brought, but to perplex the Cause, and to draw off the Attention of the Reader? To make the Cases parallel, we are to suppose an *American* to be as much an ALIEN, and to be as incapable by Law of enjoying any Honours, Places, or Preferments in their Realms, as an Hanoverian is. (1776, 54)

By contrast, in his call for reconciliation with the colonies that he gave on March 22, 1775, the British statesman and philosopher Edmund Burke expressed the view that feelings of nationalism would grow or diminish according to how they were treated:

> My hold of the Colonies is in the close affection which grows from common names, from kindred blood, from similar privileges, and equal protection. These are ties, which, though light as air, are as strong as links of iron. Let the colonists always keep the idea of their civil rights associated with your government;—they will cling and grapple to you; and no force under heaven will be of power to tear them from their allegiance. . . . Deny them this participation of freedom, and you will break that sole bond, which originally made, and must still preserve, the unity of the Empire. . . . It is the spirit of the English Constitution, which, infused through the might mass, pervades, feeds, unites invigorates, unifies every part of the empire, even down to the minutest member. (Savelle 1962, 902)

The British regarded colonists, as well as residents of Britain, to be "subjects" of the realm to which they were born. By contrast, Americans, borrowing from John Locke (see Vile 2016, 1–19), put far greater emphasis on the rights of individuals to choose their citizenship. The Declaration of Independence was essentially a collective renunciation of a common British citizenship for the embrace of a common American identity. Stephen Conway has demonstrated how the conflict led individuals within Britain, as well as in the colonies, to conclude that they were now two peoples (2002) despite what was often a common ethnic heritage.

Even within distinct peoples, there will be disagreements. During the American Revolution, some Loyalists went to Canada or Great Britain. Others accepted the majority will. Similarly, Americans had defenders, even among those who remained subjects of England or members of the British Parliament.

Even at the time of the American Revolution, the 13 colonies had distinct histories and consisted of multiple ethnic groups, including many slaves who had been imported from Africa. A passage that the Continental Congress had deleted, but was echoed in the provision, stated that the king "has excited domestic insurrections amongst us"; Jefferson had originally accused the king of bringing this "distant people" to America ("another hemisphere"), thus suggesting that they were separate from those who were declaring their independence (Ginsberg 1984, 38). Jefferson would later reinforce this theme in his *Notes on the State of Virginia*, where he proposed colonization of African Americans abroad as a solution to this problem (Onuf 1998b).

The Declaration's reference to "the merciless Indian savages, whose known rule of warfare is an undistinguished destruction of all ages, sexes & conditions," like Indian removal and reservation policies, indicates that white Americans also considered Native American Indians to be a distinct people. They appeared much like "the large armies of foreign mercenaries" that the Declaration also identified.

At the time of the U.S. Civil War (1861–1865), many Southerners believed that their own values (shaped to a large degree by the continuation of slavery) were distinct enough that they also constituted a separate people. Forrest A. Nabors has argued that the war was actually one between republican governments in the North, which recognized human equality, and oligarchic regimes in the South, which did not (Nabors 2017). Although one may question whether their governments were republican, Southern states thus associated their own attempt to secede with the earlier Revolution. In this conflict, as in the earlier Revolution, the question of continuing attachment was ultimately solved by force of arms.

In arguing for adoption of the U.S. Constitution in Federalist No. 2, John Jay observed that:

> Providence has been pleased to give this one connected country to one united people—a people descended from the same ancestors, speaking the same language, professing the same religion, attached to the same principles of government, very similar in their manners and customs, and who, by their joint counsels, arms, and efforts, fighting side by side throughout a long and bloody war, have nobly established their general liberty and independence. (Hamilton, Madison, and Jay [1787–1788] 1961, 38)

Although the 13 former colonies announced their independence in 1776, and fought another war with Britain beginning in 1812, the United States and Britain have been allied for most of the twentieth and twenty-first centuries. Although the "political bands" that once bound them together in a common empire have been severed, their history, commitment to forms of democratic government, and language undoubtedly facilitate this cordial relationship. Notably, English prime minister Winston Churchill wrote a multivolume work entitled *A History of the English-Speaking Peoples*.

Prior to the Revolution, many Americans had prized their relationship to Britain precisely because they believed it was committed to liberty. It is notable that the Declaration refers to Americans as "a free people," which, in a passage that Congress deleted, Jefferson had referred to as "a people fostered and fixed in principles of freedom," and that the last paragraph speaks "in the name and by authority of the good people of these colonies." One might make the association that one reason that the people can be called "good" is that they have due regard for the preservation of their own liberties.

Jeremy Rabkin has argued that the Declaration of Independence stands for the sovereignty of individual nations, each of which has the right to promote its own values and pursue its own destiny, apart from the dictation of super national organizations (2005, 233ff).

See also *Common Sense* (Paine); Native American Indians (Charge #27); Slavery; Transporting Large Armies of Foreign Mercenaries (Charge #25)

Further Reading

Baldwin, Simeon E. 1899. "The People of the United States." *Yale Law Journal* 8 (January): 159–167.

Barnett, Randy E. 2016. *Our Republican Constitution: Securing the Liberty and Sovereignty of We the People*. New York: Broadside Books.

Blassingame, John W. 1968. "American Nationalism and Other Loyalties in the Southern Colonies, 1763–1775." *Journal of Southern History* 334 (February): 50–75.

Conway, Stephen. 2002. "From Fellow-Nationals to Foreigners: British Perceptions of the Americans, circa 1739–1783." *William and Mary Quarterly* 59 (January): 65–100.

Ginsberg, Robert. 1984. "Suppose that Jefferson's Rough Draft of the Declaration of Independence Is a Work of Political Philosophy." *Eighteenth Century* 25 (Winter): 25–43.
Hamilton, Alexander, James Madison, and John Jay. (1787–1788). 1961 *The Federalist Papers*. New York: New American Library.
Jones, Howard Mumford. 1976. "The Declaration of Independence: A Critique." *Proceedings of the American Antiquarian Society*, pp. 55–72. www.americanantiquarian.org/proceedings/44498097.pdf.
Maier, Pauline. 1997. *American Scripture: Making the Declaration of Independence*. New York: Alfred A. Knopf.
Nabors, Forrest A. 2017. *From Oligarchy to Republicanism: The Great Task of Reconstruction*. Columbia: University of Missouri Press.
Onuf, Peter S. 1998a. "A Declaration of Independence for Diplomatic Historians." *Diplomatic History* 22 (Winter): 71–83.
Onuf, Peter S. 1998b. "'To Declare Them a Free and Independent People': Race, Slavery, and National Identity in Jefferson's Thought." *Journal of the Early Republic* 18 (Spring): 1–46.
Palmer, R. R. 2014. *The Age of the Democratic Revolution: A Political History of Europe and America, 1760–1800*. Princeton, NJ: Princeton University Press.
Pocock, J. G. A. 1987. "States, Republics, and Empires: The American Founding in Early Modern Perspective." *Social Science Quarterly* 68 (December): 703–723.
Rabkin, Jeremy A. 2005. *Law without Nations? American Independence and the Opinions of Mankind*. Princeton, NJ: Princeton University Press.
Savelle, Max. 1962. "Nationalism and Other Loyalties in the American Revolution." *American Historical Review* 67 (July): 901–923.
Thelen, David. 2002. "Reception of the Declaration of Independence." In *The Declaration of Independence Origins and Impact*, edited by Scott Douglas Gerber, 191–212. Washington, DC: CQ Press.
Tucker, Josiah. 1776. *A Series of Answers to Certain Popular Objections, Against Separating from the Rebellious Colonies and Discarding Them Entirely: Being the Concluding Tract of the Dean of Glocester on the Subject of American Affairs*. Gloucester, England: R. Raikes.
Vile, John R. 2016. *American Immigration and Citizenship: A Documentary History*. Lanham, MD: Rowman and Littlefield.
Wahrman, Dror. 2001. "The English Problem of Identity in the American Revolution." *American Historical Review* 107 (October): 1236–1261.

PETITION TO KING GEORGE III (1774)

One of the most important documents authored by the First Continental Congress that met in Carpenters' Hall in Philadelphia in 1774 was a Petition to George III. It remains significant as an early statement of grievances that the colonies had against the king, many of which are repeated in the Declaration of Independence. Moreover, the Declaration used the king's refusal to act on these grievances, as well as those later outlined in the Olive Branch Petition, as evidence that he was siding with the English Parliament against the colonies and that their time of petitioning had therefore come to an end.

The petition was the product of a committee consisting of Richard Henry Lee (the chair), John Adams, Thomas Johnson, Patrick Henry, and John Rutledge. The final document appears to be the primary product of John Dickinson (Wolf 1965).

Addressed to George III as "MOST GRACIOUS SOVEREIGN," it was from "We your majesty's faithful subjects" of the 12 colonies (all but Georgia) represented at the Congress.

The document consisted of 15 grievances, 2 of which were in multiple parts. The first grievance protested the presence of a "standing army" in the colonies, without their assent and partly for the purpose of collecting taxes. This was further tied to the next 2 grievances, which protested the supremacy of military commanders over civilian authorities and by the fact that the overall commander was appointed by a state governor.

The next grievance focused on the increase of "new, expensive, and oppressive officers" in the colonies.

The next set of grievances focused on issues connected to the judiciary. The document charged that "judges of admiralty and vice-admiralty courts" received their salaries and fees from confiscations that they leveled. The next was related to breaking and entering houses without civil approval or "legal information." The document further complained that common law judges had been made "entirely dependent on one part [of] the legislature for their salaries as well as for the duration of their commissions." This was followed by the charge, related to separation of powers, that "councilors, holding their commissions during pleasure, exercise legislative authority."

The next grievances focused on the rebuff of earlier petitions, disrespect to "agents of the people," and the resolving of legislative assemblies and "oppressive restrictions" on commerce.

Becoming much more specific, the document went on to list acts of Parliament that it traced respectively to "the fourth, fifth, sixth, seventh, and eighth years of your majesty's reign." These included the imposition of duties "for the purpose of raising a revenue," the extension of the jurisdiction of admiralty courts, abolition of the right to jury, "enormous forfeitures," favorable treatment of informers, and excessive security (bail?) required before allowing individuals "to defend their rights."

The petition further elaborated on parliamentary consent to allow Americans to be tried abroad before highlighting five acts of the last parliamentary sessions, all related to attempts to punish Massachusetts for the Boston Tea Party. These included acts blocking the Boston harbor, allowing the governor to send murder suspects abroad for trial, for altering the Massachusetts charter, for "extending the limits of Quebec," and restoring French laws and the Roman Catholic religion there, and for providing quarters for British troops in the colonies.

Whereas the Declaration of Independence would later articulate its philosophy in the first two paragraphs, the petition proclaimed that Americans had been "born the heirs of freedom and ever enjoyed our rights under the auspices of your royal ancestors" and stated their fear that they were being degraded from "freeman" to "servitude." The petition further expressed the hope that the king would express his "indignation" and his counselors, who were complicit in this attempt: "We ask but for peace, liberty, and safety. We wish not a diminution of the prerogative, nor do we solicit the grant of any new right in our favor." Appealing to "the magnanimity and justice of your majesty and Parliament," the petition appealed to God to establishing that the colonists were motivated by "no other motive than a dread of impending destruction" and appeals for the king's "interposition" on their behalf.

The document was signed under the name of Henry Middleton (who had replaced Peyton Randolph as president of the Congress after he had left) and by state delegates who recorded their names in two columns from right to left and from north to south.

See also Charges against the King and Others; George III, Proclamation of Rebellion (August 23, 1775)

Further Reading

"Petition to King George III." National Humanities Center, 2010/2013. America in Class. http://americainclass.org/sources/makingrevolution/crisis/text7/petitionkinggeorge3.pdf.

Wolf, Edwin. 1965. "The Authorship of the 1774 Address to the King Restudied." *William and Mary Quarterly* 22 (April): 189–224.

PETITIONS FOR REDRESS IGNORED (CHARGE #28)

The last charge that the Declaration of Independence lodged against the king noted that "In every stage of these oppressions, we have petitioned for redress in the most humble terms; our repeated petitions have been answered only by repeated injury." It thus draws the conclusion to all these charges by observing that "a prince whose character is thus marked by every act which may define a tyrant, is unfit to be the ruler of a free people." This final charge against the king thus reiterated the idea that the colonies had exercised patient prudence by petitioning for change before seeking dissolution of kingly rule. Perhaps thinking that Thomas Jefferson had gone a bit too far, Congress deleted his further elaboration that "future ages will scarce believe that the hardiness of one man, adventured within the short compass of twelve years only, on so many acts of tyranny without a mask, over a people fostered & fixed in principles of liberty."

Although the right to petition preceded the Magna Carta (1215) in England, the right actually developed more robustly in the colonies than it had in the mother country. In part this stemmed from the fact that colonial assemblies "were not solely legislative bodies but also served as judicial entities, to which appeals could be filed" (Krotoszynski 2012, 105). In Virginia alone, the legislature received an average of more than 200 petitions per legislative session (Krotoszynski 2012, 106). The right was especially valued because it was not limited to individuals who were eligible to vote (Krotoszynski 2012, 106–107). All nine states that adopted bills of rights between 1776 and 1789 provided for such a right (Krotoszynski 2012, 108).

The history of both Continental Congresses is a record of appeals to the king against what the colonists considered to be abuses, particularly on the part of Parliament, and against which the Congresses were hoping for the king to provide redress. The First Continental Congress thus sent a petition to George III in 1774 outlining a list of grievances that were similar to those that were repeated in the Declaration of Independence. Even after fighting had broken out at Lexington and Concord, the Second Continental Congress sent an Olive Branch Petition seeking to avert war. The mayor of London, who had special privileges to approach the king directly, had petitioned the king on behalf of his city beginning in April 1775 to protest what the mayor considered to be violations of colonial liberties (Knight 2017).

Because the king thought that the British Declaratory Act of 1766 had conclusively established the right of the British Parliament to legislate for (and tax) the colonies, he refused to read the petitions, making him appear arrogant to the colonists. For their part, the British thought the Americans were the arrogant ones. In responding to the Declaration, John Lind compared views on either side of the Atlantic: "*Here* Acts of Parliament are Acts of the Legislature, *acknowledged to be supreme*; *there* Acts only of *pretended* legislation, of *unacknowledged* individuals. *Here treason* is an offense of the most *atrocious* nature; *there* only a *pretended* offense. *Here* to deny the authority of Parliament is the utmost height of *audacity*; there it is the lowest pitch of *humility*" (1776, 111).

Paul Conkin observes that "the final colonial refuge in monarchy against Parliament makes up a strange interlude in our history. The numerous petitions to the king surely reflected, not realistic hopes of redress, but the great emotional trauma involved in making a final and complete separation" (1974, 46).

Such trauma was not forgotten. One of the rights, which the First Amendment, which was proposed in the first Congress under the U.S. Constitution and ratified in 1791, recognized provides for the right "to petition the Government for a redress of grievances."

See also Declaratory Act of 1766; George III, Speech to Parliament (October 31, 1776); Olive Branch Petition; Petition to King George III (1774); U.S. Constitution and the Declaration of Independence

Further Reading

Conkin, Paul K. 1974. *Self-Evident Truths: Being a Discourse on the Origins and Development of the First Principles of American Government—Popular Sovereignty, Natural Rights, and Balance & Separation of Powers*. Bloomington: Indiana University Press.

Knight, John. 2017. "King George III's Twitter War." *Journal of the American Revolution*. https://allthingsliberty.com/2017/07/king-george-iiis-twitter-war/

Krotoszynski, Ronald. 2012. *Reclaiming the Petition Clause: Sedition Libel, "Offensive," Protest, and the Right to Petition the Government for a Redress of Grievances*. New Haven, CT: Yale University Press.

Lind, John. 1776. *An Answer to the Declaration of the American Congress*. London: J. Walter, Charing-Cross and T. Sewell.

PHILADELPHIA

Philadelphia was the site of the Pennsylvania State House (Independence Hall), where the Second Continental Congress met (the first met in nearby Carpenters' Hall) and where the Declaration of Independence (1776), the Articles of Confederation, and the U.S. Constitution (1787) were all signed.

Located approximately midway in the 13 colonies, the city was accessible both by road and by sea. Originally settled by Swedes, William Penn, the Quaker proprietor, had laid out the "City of Brotherly Love" in an orderly manner. By 1776, it had about 40,000 residents and was the second largest city in the English-speaking world next to London, which probably had about three-quarters of a million.

Philadelphia was home to Benjamin Franklin, Robert Morris, James Wilson, and others who were to play vital roles in the Second Continental Congress and in the Revolutionary War. It was also home to the American Philosophical Society, the nation's first public library, and a medical school. The Pennsylvania legislature took a cautious approach to revolution and was eventually replaced by a popular convention, which pushed for revolution and for the most democratic constitution in the colonies, which would later be revised when the U.S. Constitution was written.

Had the Continental Congresses met in Boston, Massachusetts, or Williamsburg, Virginia, there might have been greater pressure to declare independence earlier, but it is also possible that such a body might have run so far ahead of public opinion in the colonies as a whole that it would not have received unanimous state approval, as the Declaration eventually did. Pennsylvania delegates were among the last to approve of the Declaration; indeed, the state's vote for independence appears to have occurred only after Robert Morris and John Dickinson either absented themselves or abstained from voting.

After the Declaration was read from a platform outside Independence Hall on July 8, 1776, the king's coat of arms was removed from the courtroom in the building and burned amid popular acclaim. When the city was occupied by the British between September 1776 and June 1778, however, a number of leading families who were Loyalists openly socialized with them, revealing that the sentiment for independence had been far from unanimous. Many Quaker families, who were traditionally pacifists, suffered from suspicions that they were unpatriotic.

Although the Congress under the Articles of Confederation moved out of Philadelphia on several occasions, after beginning in New York City, the Congress under the new government met there from 1790 to 1800.

As the birthplace of both the Declaration of Independence and the U.S. Constitution, Philadelphia remains at the symbolic center of the American experience. Independence Hall, a Constitution Center, a new museum of the American Revolution, and numerous historic and cultural attractions continue to draw tourists from throughout the country, and the city has been the site for numerous commemorations and celebrations of both documents. During centennial celebrations of the Declaration in 1876, the Declaration of Independence, which is displayed today in the National Archives, was returned to Philadelphia for display at Independence Hall (Stathis 1978).

See also Proclamation, Reading, and Reception of the Declaration of Independence

Further Reading

Irvin, Benjamin H. 2005. "The Streets of Philadelphia: Crowds, Congress, and the Political Culture of Revolution, 1774–1783. *Pennsylvania Magazine of History and Biography* 129 (January): 7–44.

Lucas, Stephen E. 1976. *Portents of Rebellion: Rhetoric and Revolution in Philadelphia, 1765–1776*. Philadelphia: Temple University Press.
Nash, Garb B. 2006. *First City: Philadelphia and the Forging of Historical Memory*. Philadelphia: University of Pennsylvania Press.
Raphael, Ray. "Revolutionary Philadelphia." https://www.gilderlehrman.org/history-by-era/war-for-independence/essays/revolutionary-philadelphia.
Stathis, Stephen W. 1978. "Returning the Declaration of Independence to Philadelphia: An Exercise in Centennial Politics." *Pennsylvania Magazine of History and Biography* 102 (April): 167–183.
Stille, Charles J. 1889. "Pennsylvania and the Declaration of Independence." *Pennsylvania Magazine of History and Biography* 13 (January): 385–429.
Wolf, Edwin II. 1975. *Philadelphia: Portrait of an American City*. Philadelphia: Wenchell.

PLUNDERED OUR SEAS (CHARGE #24)

The 24th accusation that the Declaration of Independence levels against the king, and the 2nd on its lists of war atrocities, is that "he has plundered our seas, ravaged our coasts, burnt our towns, & destroyed the lives of our people." The verbs used in this accusation are among the most intense in the Declaration and are more likely to evoke the image of piracy than of civilized warfare.

Once war starts, even unofficially, both sides are likely to be engaged in activities inimical and destructive to the welfare of the other. Over time, each side accumulates a list of deprecations and war atrocities, both on land and on sea. The British were a seafaring people, and Britain was known for its naval power, which the colonists could not match.

As the controversy between American and Britain intensified, some royal governors actually tried to govern from ships. Responding to fire upon his ships, Virginia's governor, Lord Dunmore, ordered the shelling of Norfolk. British sources were split as to whether their troops had inflicted the most damage or whether Patriots had used the occasion to burn down the houses of Loyalists (Parsons 1933), but there is considerable evidence for the latter (Charles 2008). Either action would likely lead to great personal hardships. The British had also burned Charlestown, Massachusetts, in June 1775 after the Battle of Bunker Hill. Similarly, in the autumn of 1775, royal cruisers had opened fire on the town of Stonington, Connecticut after pursuing a vessel that had sought shelter there (Lossing 1848, 300).

There is little doubt that a British bombardment on October 18, 1775, had leveled the town of Falmouth, today's Portland, Maine (Israel 2017, 39), with "red-hot cannon balls," although this was apparently in response to an attack by minutemen both on Captain Henry Mowatt and on his ships (Jones 1976, 18). The British, in turn, might also have pointed to the colonial burning of the HMS *Gaspee*, which was trying to enforce British customs, in Rhode Island on June 9, 1772.

In responding to this charge in the Declaration, John Lind sought to reverse the tables. He did so by comparing the colonists to pirates who were receiving their just desserts (1776, 95).

Some of America's most exciting victories in the Revolutionary War were naval victories, many led by John Paul Jones and Commodore John Barry, who is often designated as the father of the American navy. A statue on the south side of Independence Hall commemorates Barry.

See also Charges against the King and Others

Further Reading

Charles, Patrick J. 2008. *Irreconcilable Grievances: The Events That Shaped the Declaration of Independence*. Westminster, MD: Heritage Books.

Israel, Jonathan. 2017. *The Expanding Blaze: How the American Revolution Ignited the World, 1775–1848*. Princeton, NJ: Princeton University Press.

Jones, Howard Mumford. 1976. "The Declaration of Independence: A Critique." In *The Declaration of Independence: Two Essays by Howard Mumford Jones and Howard H. Peckham*, 3–20. Worcester, MA: American Antiquarian Society.

Lind, John. 1776. *An Answer to the Declaration of the American Congress*. London: J. Walter, Charing-Cross and T. Sewell.

Lossing, B. J. 1848. *Biographical Sketches of the Signers of the Declaration of American Independence; The Declaration Historical Considered; and a Sketch of the Leading Events Connected with the Adoption of the Articles of Confederation and of the Federal Constitution*. New York: George F. Cooledge and Brothers.

Parsons, H. S. "Contemporary English Accounts of the Destruction of Norfolk in 1776." *William and Mary Quarterly* 13 (October): 219–224.

PREAMBLE TO THE RESOLUTION OF VIRGINIA CONVENTION (MAY 15, 1776)

On May 15, 1776, the Virginia Convention, which had taken over legislative responsibilities for the state, adopted a resolution recommending that its delegates to the Continental Congress seek independence.

This resolution contained a preamble. It likely served as a template for some of the grievances outlined in the Declaration of Independence, especially those related to the king's reception of colonial receptions and those related to the king's war against the colonies.

As to the first, the preamble observed that after having petitioned the king for "a reunion with that people upon just and liberal terms," the colonies had been met with "increased insult, oppression, and a vigorous attempt to effect our total destruction" ("Preamble," 1776).

As to the second, the preamble delineated the following actions:

> By a late act all these Colonies are declared to be in rebellion, and out of the protection of the British Crown, our properties subjected to confiscation, our people, when captivated, compelled to join in the murder and plunder of their relations and countrymen, and all former rapine and oppression of Americans declared legal and just; fleets and armies are raised, and the aid of foreign troops engaged to assist these destructive purposes; the King's representative in this Colony hath not only withheld all the powers of Government from operating for our safety, but, having retired on board an armed ship, is carrying on a piratical and savage war against us, tempting our slaves by every artifice to resort to him, and training and employing them against their masters. ("Preamble," 1776)

The reference to "the King's representative in this Colony" is a reference to Lord Dunmore, who had transferred to a ship from where he was encouraging slaves to revolt.

Much as the Declaration later appealed "to the supreme judge of the world for the rectitude of our intentions," the Virginia Preamble invoked "the Searcher of hearts for the sincerity of former declarations expressing our desire to preserve the connection with that nation, and that we are driven from that inclination by their wicked councils, and the eternal law of self-preservation" ("Preamble" 1776). This was a way for the authors of both documents to indicate that they had sent earlier petitions in good faith.

See also Charges against the King and Others; Virginia and Its Signers

Further Reading

Morrison, Samuel Eliot. 1951. "Prelude to Independence: The Virginia Resolutions of May 15, 1776." *William and Mary Quarterly* 8 (October): 483–492.

"Preamble and Resolution of the Virginia Convention, May 15, 1776." Yale Law School. http://avalon.law.yale.edu/18th_century/const02.asp.

PRESERVING THE DECLARATION OF INDEPENDENCE

The signed parchment of the Declaration of Independence is now carefully preserved, along with the U.S. Constitution and the proposed Bill of Rights, at the National Archives in Washington, D.C., but it was not always the subject of such meticulous care. Indeed, one writer, noting that it "has very nearly been loved to death," calls it the "velveteen rabbit of America" (Phillips).

Originally entrusted to Charles Thomson, the secretary of the Continental Congress, the document was moved with Thomson and the Congress from Philadelphia, Pennsylvania, to Baltimore, Maryland, then to Lancaster and York, Pennsylvania, and back to Philadelphia, all before its second birthday (Malone 1954, 249). Kept for about five years at the State House (today's Independence Hall), the document then moved again with Congress to Princeton and Trenton, New Jersey, back to Annapolis, Maryland, and then to New York City, where it was kept in city hall.

The congressional secretary subsequently gave the document to George Washington, who entrusted it to John Jay and successive secretaries of state (including Thomas Jefferson), who eventually took it to the new capital in Washington, D.C., and deposited it in the War Office Building. Secretary of State James Monroe had the foresight to remove the document to Leesburg, Virginia, when the capitol was threatened during the War of 1812. After being stored at the house of a clergyman named Littlejohn, it was moved to the building housing the secretary of state. In 1841, Secretary of State Daniel Webster had the document moved to the new Patent Office building (Malone 1954, 257), and it was sent to Philadelphia for the Centennial in 1876 to be returned in 1877 for exhibit in the State Department, before being sealed between two glass plates and locked away.

In 1921, the document was removed to the Library of Congress, where by 1924, it was displayed on the second floor in a shrine designed by Francis H. Bacon, the brother of the architect of the Lincoln Memorial (Cole 1997). After the Japanese attacked Pearl Harbor, the document was moved to Ft. Knox in Kentucky for safekeeping but exhibited at the Jefferson Memorial from April 12 to 19, 1943 (Frieberg 1999), returned to Ft. Knox (Gawalt 1999, 10), and then returned to the Library of Congress for display on October 1, 1944. It remained there until December 15, 1952, when it was moved to the National Archives, along with the Constitution and the Bill of Rights (huge painted murals of the Declaration and the Constitution by Barry Faulkner flank the displays) where it remains today, after having been removed for about two years in 2001 to enhance its preservation.

The original ink on the document, called iron gall ink, would have included "tannic acid (from oak galls), iron (from nails or iron scraps), a binder (often gum arabic from acacia trees), and sometimes a colorant" (Bitzenthaler and Nicholson 2016). Much of this ink has been faded by sunlight or removed in the process of making facsimiles. The lower left corner of the front of the Declaration contains a handprint of unknown origin, which appears to have been made in the twentieth century. The back of the document contains an inscription that reads "Original Declaration of Independence dated 4th July 1776" for identification purposes (Ritzenthaler and Nicholson 2016). The plot of a popular movie, *National Treasure*, starring Nicolas Cage as Benjamin Franklin Gates, is based on the improbable premise that a clue to great treasure is written on the back of the Declaration in invisible ink.

See also Faulkner, Barry (Painting); Jefferson Memorial; Philadelphia

Further Reading

Cole, John Y. "The Library and the Declaration." Library of Congress. https://www.loc.gov/loc/lcib/9708/declare.html.

Freiberg, Malcolm. 1999. "All's Well That Ends Well: A Twentieth-Century Battle over the Declaration of Independence." *Massachusetts Historical Review* 1:127–134.

Gawalt, Gerald W. 1999. Preface. In Julian P. Boyd, *The Declaration of Independence: The Evolution of the Text*. Washington, DC, and Charlottesville, VA: The Library of Congress in association with the Thomas Jefferson Memorial Foundation.

Malone, Dumas. 1954. *The Story of the Declaration of Independence*. New York: Oxford University Press.

Phillips, Heather A. "Preserving Documents of Independence." Archiving Early America. https://www.varsitytutors.com/earlyamerica/early-america-review/volume-11/preserving-documents-of-independence.

Puleo, Stephen. 2016. *American Treasures: The Secret Efforts to Save the Declaration of Independence, the Constitution, and the Gettysburg Address*. New York: St. Martin's Press.

Ritzenthaler, Mary Lynn, and Catherine Nicholson. 2016. "The Declaration of Independence and the Hand of Time." *Prologue* 48 (2016). Accessed at https://www.archives.gov/publications/prologue/2016/fall/declaration.

PROCLAMATION, READING, AND RECEPTION OF THE DECLARATION OF INDEPENDENCE

The Declaration of Independence was designed to announce both to domestic and foreign audiences the reason that the one-time colonies had decided to sever their bonds with Great Britain. Almost immediately after the delegates approved of the Declaration, Congress commissioned John Dunlap to print copies. John Hancock sent these to the states and to state councils and committees of safety, with a recommendation that they hold public readings of the document.

Benjamin Towne, a Philadelphia printer, and later turncoat to the Patriot cause, was apparently the first of 30 publishers who printed the Declaration in newspapers, which he did in *The Pennsylvania Evening Post* on July 6, 1776 (Shields 2010). Robin Shields notes that the *Pennsylvania Gazette* printed the Declaration on July 10 on the first two columns, with column 3 ironically containing 2 of 14 advertisements offering rewards for those who returned slaves and indentured servants.

Professor Jay Fliegelman (1993) has emphasized the manner in which Thomas Jefferson wrote the Declaration, even marking pauses on his copy, so that it would be rhetorically suitable for such public readings. The Declaration proved to be an especially effective rallying point for Patriot troops in the field. Tory supporters of the king were undoubtedly more subdued.

Many of the descriptions of this event report the firing of cannon, three cheers, toasts (of which there were typically 13, one for each state), and—despite occasional destructions of symbols representing the king—reports that crowds were orderly. Cities and state celebrations were spread throughout the following month, largely depending on when they received the document.

The Declaration may or may not have been read in Philadelphia on the evening of July 4, 1776, but the weight of the current evidence (or lack of evidence) suggests that it was not. Stories originated by George Lippard in 1847 and subsequently repeated by others about a white-haired man waiting for word from "a flaxen haired" boy with blue eyes for word to ring the Liberty Bell are myths (Warren 1945, 248–254).

The Declaration is known to have been read from an observation platform that Dr. David Rittenhouse had constructed for observing the transit of Venus outside Independence Hall on July 8. According to Albert J. Beveridge, Colonel James Nixon, the son of an Irish immigrant, did the reading (1926, 296). After this reading, the king's coat of arms, which had adorned the courtroom in the building, was burned amid popular acclaim, a bonfire was lit, and houses were illumined (Desbler 1892, 166–167).

It seems likely to this author that a report in *The Scots Magazine* (reported in Desbler 1892, 167) that the group had placed a crown on a Bible and divided it into 13 parts was an interpretation based on a too-literal reading of Thomas Paine's *Common Sense*, which had argued that law should be the king in America. Another reading of the Declaration on July 8 took place in Easton, Pennsylvania, by Robert Levers, and was accompanied by drums and fifes (Desbler 1892, 168).

There were several known readings in New Jersey. The reading in Trenton occurred on July 8 and was met with "loud acclamations" (cited in Desbler 1893, 169). The reading at Princeton, the home of John Witherspoon, who had signed the document, occurred on July 9. It took place at Nassau Hall and was accompanied by musket fire and "universal acclamation for the prosperity of the United Colonies" (cited in Desbler 1892, 168). Another such reading occurred the same day in Sussex County, where Joseph Barton expressed gratefulness that having been previously caught between owing the king and fighting against him, his "heart and hand shall [now] move together" (cited in Desbler 1892, 169). A reading by Colonel John Neilson at the White Hall Tavern appears to have taken place in New Brunswick, New Jersey on either July 9 or 10, and was reportedly followed by loud cheering (Desbler 1892, 169). The reading at Bridgeton, New Jersey on August 7 was followed by a speech and by the burning of the king's coat of arms (Desbler 1892, 184).

When a copy of the Declaration arrived at Dover, Delaware, it was read from the courthouse. It was followed by cheers and accompanied by the burning of a picture of George III (Desbler 1892, 170).

When General George Washington received a copy in New York City on July 9, he ordered a parade and appeared on horseback as one of his aides read the document and soldiers cheered (Desbler 1892, 170). A mob subsequently tore down the gilded lead statute by Joseph Wilton of George III on a horse in a park in Bowling Green, Manhattan. In a type of tyrannicide, which a number of prints later commemorated (not always accurately), the lead body of George III was decapitated, and most of the remaining statute was melted into bullets for the Continental Army (Marks 1981). For their part, "British troops on Staten Island made effigies of Generals Washington, [Charles] Lee, and [Israel] Putnam and placed them in a line. Then they positioned before the generals an effigy of Witherspoon [the president of Princeton] with a copy of the Declaration in his hand" all of which were hanged from trees (Tucker 1979, 33).

The Provincial Congress meeting in White Plains, New York, also received its copy on July 9 and ordered that further printings of the document be distributed (Desbler 1892, 170–171). At a more formal celebration in New York City on July 25, the British coat of arms from the courthouse was burned to "repeated huzzas" and was ordered to be taken from all houses of worship (Desbler 1892, 173). One of the most sensational reactions to the Declaration took place at Huntington, Long Island, on July 22. After a parade and a reading of the Declaration, a flag that had liberty on one side and George III on the other was cut up and an effigy of George III in blackface (illustrative of Governor Lord Dunmore's willingness to free slaves who fought for Britain), constructed with a wooden crown of feathers (associating him with Native American Indians), was hung on gallows, exploded, and burned (Desbler 1892, 179). Colonel Arthur St. Clair read the Declaration at Ticonderoga, New York, on Sunday July 28 after worship, after which members of the army gave three cheers (Desbler 1892, 182).

When the Declaration arrived in Worchester, Massachusetts, on July 15, Patriots gathered on a green near a liberty pole, to the sounds of drums and bells, and read to huzzas, the firing of weapons, and bonfires. Patriots then assembled at what had previously been knowns as the King's Arms Tavern and commenced a series of toasts (Desbler 1892, 173–174). Boston held its reading on July 18 from the State House balcony, followed by huzzas, the firing of cannon, and toasts (Desbler 1892, 175–176). The Declaration was read from church pulpits in the city on August 15 (Desbler 1892, 175). Delayed by an outbreak of smallpox, the reading at Watertown, Massachusetts, took place on July 22, after which the king's arms in the town were defaced (Desbler 1892, 175).

Portsmouth, New Hampshire, apparently received the Declaration on July 18. It was read before troops and a general audience that responded with huzzas (Desbler 1892, 175–176).

The General Assembly of Rhode Island, meeting in Newport, adopted a resolution upon receipt of the Declaration on July 20, proclaiming that anyone praying for the king or his victory shall be guilty of a "high misdemeanor." It also mustered troops, fired cannon, and received applause from the crowd (Desbler 1892, 176). In East Greenwich, the Declaration was read on July 23, to gunfire, huzzas, and toasts. The Declaration was read in Providence, Rhode Island, on July 25, after which volleys were fired and celebrants went to Hacker's Hall to offer toasts (Desbler 1892, 181).

The provisional legislature in Connecticut received the Declaration on July 12. Perhaps because it was not a permanent body, it did not apparently commission a public reading.

At the state capitol in Williamsburg, the Virginia Council, which received the document on July 20, ordered the publication of the document. The *Virginia Gazette* published it on July 26, noting that it had been read the previous afternoon "at the Capitol, the Courthouse, and the Palace amidst the acclamations of the people, accompanied by firing cannons and musketry, the several regiments of continental troops having been paraded on that solemnity" (Shields 2010). The document was read to militiamen and other citizens in Richmond on August 5 to acclaim, followed by toasts and small arms fire and a large gathering that evening to drink toasts (Desbler 1892, 183). Apparently, the city of Williamsburg had previously paraded troops, discharged artillery, and illumined the town when members of its convention had voted on May 15 to send a petition to Congress petitioning for independence (Boyd 1999, 19).

The document arrived in Halifax, North Carolina, on July 22. It was ordered to be read at the courthouse on August 1.

In Baltimore, Maryland, the Declaration of Independence was read at the courthouse on July 30 and greeted with applause. That evening an effigy of George III was burned (Desbler 1892, 183).

In Charleston, South Carolina, the document was proclaimed by Major Bernard Elliott on August 5 to a large group gathered around a liberty tree and followed by an address (a common feature of later Independence Day celebrations) by Reverend William Percy of the Protestant Episcopal Church (Desbler 1891, 184). A foreigner, probably more alert to irony than the immediate audience, observed that a slave fanned Percy as he was delivering his address (Tsesis 2012, 31).

Savannah, Georgia, received its copy of the Declaration on August 10, where it was read before the Assembly House, and at the liberty pole, followed by the discharging of weapons, by toasts, and by illuminations. Participants parodied the Anglican Church's "Service for the Burial of the Dead." During this mock ceremony, the people committed King George's "political existences to the ground, corruption to corruption, tyranny to the grave, and oppression to eternal infamy" (Desbler 1892, 187).

It would appear that readings of the Declaration were thus generally received joyfully within the states. Not surprisingly, it was not always so well received overseas or in other colonies. In St. Augustine in east Florida, where Tories had fled, both John Hancock and Samuel Adams were burned in effigy (Peckham 1976, 22). In England, where the document appears to have been first printed under the date of August 16 (Peckham 1976, 24), Thomas Hutchinson and John Lind both attempted refutations of the document. Reporting on the Declaration the *Scots Magazine,* which was published in Edinburgh in August 1776 observed that "The Declaration is without doubt of the most extraordinary nature both with regard to sentiment and language; and considering that the motive of it is to assign some justifiable reasons of their separating themselves from G. Britain, unless it had been fraught with more truth and sense, [it] might well have been spared, as it reflects no honour upon either their erudition or their honesty (Hazelton [1905] 2015, 233; brackets in Hazelton).

By contrast, John Wilkes, a British parliamentarian who had long defended the American position, said that Americans "honor and value the blessings of liberty" (Hazelton [1905] 2015, 237).

The French were generally pleased with the Declaration because they believed it opened the opportunity for them to oppose Britain. Although the Declaration appears to have had some influence on the Declaration of the Rights of Man and the Citizen (Declaration des Droits de l'Homme et du Citoyen), it appears to have been more directly influenced by American state constitutions and bills of rights (Marienstras and Wulf 1999). In time, the Declaration served as a model for revolutions throughout the world, and especially for colonies that were seeking their independence (Armitage 2004, 63).

Many of the activities surrounding the original readings of the Declaration have been replicated at Independence Day celebrations, which typically also feature picnics and sports events. It appears more common publicly to read the Constitution on Constitution Day (September 17) than to read the Declaration on July 4, but this may largely stem from the fact that the readings of the Constitution often take place at colleges and universities, which are more likely to be in session during September than in July.

See also *An Answer to the Declaration of the American Colonies* (Lind); *Common Sense* (Paine); Dunlap Broadside Printing of the Declaration of Independence; Independence Day; *Strictures upon the Declaration of Independence* (Hutchinson)

Further Reading

Armitage, David. 2004. "The Declaration of Independence in World Context." *OAH Magazine of History* 18 (April): 61–66.

Beveridge, Albert J. 1926. "Sources of the Declaration of Independence." *Pennsylvania Magazine of History and Biography* 50:289–315.
Boyd, Julian P. 1999. *The Declaration of Independence: The Evolution of the Text*. Washington and Charlottesville: Library of Congress and Thomas Jefferson Memorial Foundation.
Desbler, Charles D. 1892. "How the Declaration Was Received in the Old Thirteen." *Harper's New Monthly Magazine* 85 (July): 165–187.
Fliegelman, Jay. 1993. *Declaring Independence: Jefferson, Natural Language, and the Culture of Performance*. Stanford, CA: Stanford University Press.
Hazelton, John H. (1905) 2015. *The Declaration of Independence: Its History*. Reprinted by Forgotten Books.
Irvin, Benjamin H. 2011. *Clothed in Robes of Sovereignty: The Continental Congress and the People Out of Doors*. New York: Oxford University Press.
Marienstras, Elise, and Naomi Wulf. "French Translations and Reception of the Declaration of Independence." *Journal of American History* 85 (March): 1299–1324.
Marks, Arthur S. 1981. "The Statute of King George III in New York and the Iconology of Regicide." *American Art Journal* 13 (Summer): 61–82.
Peckham, Howard H. 1976. *The Declaration of Independence: Two Essays by Howard Mumford Jones and Howard H. Peckham*, 21–37. Worcester, MA: American Antiquarian Society.
Shields, Robin. July 20, 2010. "Transcript of Publishing the Declaration of Independence." Journeys and Crossings, Library of Congress. https://www.loc.gov/rr/program/journey/declaration-transcript.html.
Tsesis, Alexander. 2012. *For Liberty and Equality: The Life and Times of the Declaration of Independence*. New York: Oxford University Press.
Tucker, Louis Leonard. 1979. "Centers of Sedition: Colonial Colleges and the American Revolution." *Proceedings of the Massachusetts Historical Society*, 3rd ser. 92:16–34.
Warren, Charles. 1945. "Fourth of July Myths." *William and Mary Quarterly* 2 (July): 237–272.

PROPERTY RIGHTS

The second paragraph of the Declaration of Independence lists as the primary purposes of government the protection of the rights to "life, liberty, and the pursuit of happiness." Although the third of these enumerated rights might well include the right to own property, omitting the term seemed to put some distance between the Declaration and the philosophy of John Locke, who considered the protection of property to be quite important. This may have been a way for the Continental Congress to indicate that, property being transferable, the right to property was not "unalienable. Alternatively, it may have been a way not to ensconce slavery (whose owners considered them to be property, subject to sale) into a Founding document (Blumrosen and Blumrosen 2005, 138).

The Founding Fathers, including Thomas Jefferson, the primary author of the Declaration of Independence, had relatively conservative views on property. Jefferson, who thought that independent farmers were the bedrock of a republic, was especially solicitous of the right to property in land (Katz 1976). Moreover, the Declaration levels a number of accusations against the king and others that relate to property rights.

At the heart of the dispute between the former colonies and Great Britain, of course, was the issue of whether Parliament had the right to tax the colonists, who were not physically represented in that body. Americans believed that the only bodies with the power to tax them were colonial legislatures where they were actually represented—a right that the third indictment against the king says is "a right inestimable to them, & formidable to tyrants only." British spokesmen tended to rely on the argument that all Englishmen, including those in the colonies, were virtually represented in Parliament, and the Declaratory Act of 1766 had made it clear that Parliament thought it had such power (McElroy 1919). By contrast, the Declaration of Independence considered such laws to be "acts of pretended legislation" and an attempt "for imposing taxes on us without our consent." Throughout the dispute with Britain, the colonists appeared far more concerned about the principle involved and the potential for future abuse than the actual amount of taxes that the British imposed.

In accusing the king of creating "a multitude of new offices," the Declaration suggested that they were in the colonies to "eat out their substance," which would certainly be considered to be an imposition on property rights. The Declaration also accused the king and Parliament for having "cut off our trade with all parts of the world" and of seeking to prevent immigration to the colonies, which would clearly have an adverse economic impact on them. Similarly, the charges that the king "has plundered our seas, ravaged our coasts, burnt our towns, & destroyed the lives of our people" indicated that the king no longer respected the lives or property of his subjects.

The U.S. Constitution later limited state laws impairing the obligation of contracts (Article I, Section 10); prohibited governmental deprivations of "life, liberty, or property, without due process of law" (Fifth and Fourteenth Amendments) and outlawed governmental takings of private property "without just compensation" (Fifth Amendment). Article III, Section 3 of the Constitution further limited forfeiture of property in cases of treason. In time, the Thirteenth Amendment (1865) abolished slavery, thus denying recognition to this form of "property" and refusing to provide compensation for former slave owners.

See also Charges against the King and Others; Declaratory Act of 1766; Life, Liberty, and the Pursuit of Happiness; Locke, John

Further Reading

Blumrosen, Alfred W, and Ruth G. Blumrosen. 2005. *Slave Nation: How Slavery United the Colonies and Sparked the American Revolution*. Naperville, IL: Sourcebooks, Inc.

Katz, Stanley N. 1976. "Thomas Jefferson and the Right to Property in Revolutionary America." *Journal of Law and Economics* 19 (October): 467–488.

McEloy, Robert McNutt. 1919. "The Representative Idea and the American Revolution." *Proceedings of the New York Historical Association* 17:44–55.

PROTECTING TROOPS BY MOCK TRIALS (CHARGE #15)

Immediately after accusing the king of having "combined with others" to quarter troops among the colonists, the Declaration accused the king and those with whom he was allied of "protecting them by a mock-trial from punishment for any murders which they should commit on the inhabitants of these states." The use of the word "murders" seems unusually provocative, much like the term "Boston Massacre," which was often used to describe the aftermath of a response by British troops to provocations against them. These troops, represented by John Adams, were acquitted, as were troops in Annapolis, Maryland, who had killed two citizens in 1768, and troops in North Carolina, who in 1771 had fired on a group of patriot "Regulators" after they failed to disperse (Lossing 1868, 287). Citizens of Boston, however, were quite upset that a customs officer, Ebenezer Richardson, had been pardoned after firing into a crowd that surrounded his house and killing an 11-year-old boy while Levi Adams, a burglar, had been executed for his offenses (Wilf 2000).

The accusation in the Declaration of Independence centers on the Administration of Justice Act, which Parliament adopted on May 20, 1774 ("Great Britain: Parliament," 1774). Pointing to the "disorder" occasioned by the Boston Tea Party and other acts of opposition to the collection of taxes, the law providing for moving the trial from Massachusetts to Great Britain or one of the other colonies in certain cases. These involved indictments against individuals "for murder, or other capital offenses" who were charged in connection with "the execution of his duty as a magistrate, for the suppression of riots, or in the support of the laws of revenue, or in acting in his duty as an officer of revenue, or in acting under the direction and order of any magistrate, for the suppression of riots, or for the carrying into effect the laws of revenue, or in aiding and assisting in any of the cases aforesaid."

This law was a clear sign of the rising tensions between Britain and the colonies, especially Massachusetts, and the obvious British fear that no individuals upholding laws that members of that colony opposed would be likely to receive a fair trial in the colony. Although the Declaration of Independence did not do so, Massachusetts could offer in its own defense the fact that John Adams had successfully helped defend Captain Thomas Preston and other soldiers who had been accused of murder in the so-called Boston Massacre and that he had done so in Massachusetts courts.

Thomas Jefferson had dwelled at length on the Administration of Justice Act in his *Summary View of the Rights of British America*, where he wondered how anyone "would cross the Atlantic for the sole purpose of bearing evidence to a fact?" or who would provide for the witness's family in the interim? (1774, 12). These questions reflected Jefferson's skepticism that anyone in Britain would ever convict a British soldier of murder, no matter what the evidence suggested.

Edward Dumbauld has observed that while Jefferson was particularly concerned about the trial of Americans abroad, it seems unlikely that Americans would have been charged for the offense of committing murder in an attempt to enforce British laws (1950, 129). This response, however, seems more appropriate for Jefferson's later accusation, accusing the king and his allies "for transporting us beyond seas to be tried for pretended offenses" than it does for this accusation, which specifically addresses the trial of British troops.

Modern laws permit lawyers to ask for a change of venue (location) for a trial where they believe that local juries might be unduly prejudiced. Not surprisingly, the English apologist John Lind observed that the law that Parliament adopted was intended to secure "*the impartial administration of justice*" (1776, 60). He further portrayed the act as less drastic than suspending existing courts of justice, establishing martial law, or similar remedies. He also said that the act was temporary, only designed to be in force for three years (1776, 62). In a similar vein, former Massachusetts governor Thomas Hutchinson observed that "the removal of trials for the sake of unprejudiced disinterested Juries, is altogether consistent with the spirit of our laws, and the practice of courts in changing the venue from one country to another" (1776, 21–22).

See also Adams, John; Charges against the King and Others; Quartering Troops (Charge #14)

Further Reading

Dumbauld, Edward. 1950. *The Declaration of Independence and What It Means Today*. Norman: University of Oklahoma Press.

"Great Britain: Parliament—The Administration of Justice Act; May 20, 1774." The Avalon Project. http://avalon.law.yale.edu/18th_century/admin_of_justice_act.asp.

Hutchinson, Thomas. 1776. "1776: Hutchinson, Strictures upon the Declaration of Independence." Online Library of Liberty. oll.libertyfund.org/pages/1776-hutchinson-strictures-upon-the-declaration-of-independence.

Jefferson, Thomas. 1774. *A Summary View of the Rights of British America*. Colonial Williamsburg. www.history.org/almanack/life/politics/sumview.cfm. Accessed July 8, 2017.

Lind, John. 1776 *An Answer to the Declaration of the American Congress*. London: J. Walter, Charing-Cross and T. Sewell.

Lossing, B. J. 1848. *Biographical Sketches of the Signers of the Declaration of American Independence; The Declaration Historical Considered; and a Sketch of the Leading Events Connected with the Adoption of the Articles of Confederation and of the Federal Constitution*. New York: George F. Cooledge and Brothers.

Sosin, Jack M. 1963. "The Massachusetts Acts of 1774: Coercive or Preventive?" *Huntington Library Quarterly* 26 (May): 235–252.

Wilf, Steven. 2000. "Placing Blame: Criminal Law and Constitutional Narratives in Revolutionary Boston." *Crime, History & Societies* 4:31–61.

PRUDENCE

Even though it advocated revolution against Great Britain, the Declaration of Independence observed that "Prudence, indeed, will dictate that Governments long established should not be changed for light and transient causes." It followed this normative principle with the psychological observation that "Mankind are more disposed to suffer, while Evils are sufferable, than to right themselves by abolishing the Forms to which they are accustomed." It so doing, the Declaration appeared to follow the lead of John Locke, who believed that revolution was appropriate, albeit only in the face of a long series of abuses.

Prudence is often associated with practical wisdom, which is in turn often associated with the best practical regime as opposed to the best city one might construct in speech. Along with fortitude, temperance, and justice, prudence was one of four classical virtues. Arguing for something imprudent is a bit like arguing for something foolhardy while ignoring possible negative consequences.

However this may be, persons of very timid dispositions might use prudence as an excuse to forestall needed action. Prior to the adoption of the resolution for independence and its subsequent justification, delegates to the Second Continental Congress were thus divided over whether the time was ripe for independence. John and Samuel Adams appear to have favored independence well over a year before Congress adopted it. Delegates like John Dickinson wanted to send petitions to the king and exercise all other possible remedies prior to taking such a step. Others wanted to wait on the progress of public opinion, believing that, whatever step the colonists took, they needed to do it unanimously, or as close to unanimity as possible.

It is thus noteworthy that in a letter to John Adams dated July 9, 1807, Dr. Benjamin Rush made the following observation:

> In one of your former letters you spoke in high terms of *prudence*. I neglected to reply to your encomiums upon it. General Lee used to call it a "rascally virtue." It certainly has more counterfeits than any other virtue, and when *real* it partakes very much of a selfish nature. It was this virtue that protected the property of most of the tories during the American Revolution. It never achieved anything great in human affairs. (Cited in Alkana 1992, 288)

In his portraits of individuals who signed the Constitution or were influential in the Revolution, however, Rush had criticized General Charles Lee's vices, among which he included that "He despised prudence and used to call it a rascally virtue" (Rush 1905, 119).

Because prudence involves application to individual situations, about which perspectives will vary, it does not provide the clear-cut calls to action that broad appeals to the rights of mankind or to such lofty goals as the preservation of life, liberty and the pursuit of happiness might in themselves do. The Declaration of Independence has often been praised for threading this conceptual needle by juxtaposing the two concepts (Diamond 1976). The Declaration sought to highlight its own "prudence" by citing it as commendable, by enumerating a long list of colonial grievances against the king, and by citing prior attempts to bring such grievances to the attention of "British Brethren."

See also Dissolution of Government; Human Nature and the Declaration of Independence; Locke, John; Moral Virtues in the Declaration of Independence; Revolution; Rush's (Benjamin) Characters of the Signers

Further Reading

Alkana, Joseph. 1992. "Spiritual and Rational Authority in Benjamin Rush's Travels through Life." *Texas Studies in Literature and Language* 34 (Summer): 284–300.

Diamond, Martin. 1976. "The Revolution of Sober Expectations." In *America's Continuing Revolution*, 23–40. Garden City, NY: Anchor Press.

Rush, Benjamin. 1905. *A Memorial Containing Travels through Life or Sundry Incidents in the Life of Dr. Benjamin Rush*. Lanoraie, QC: Louis Alexander Biddle.

PURSUIT OF HAPPINESS

See Life, Liberty, and the Pursuit of Happiness

Q

QUARTERING TROOPS (CHARGE #14)

Just after transitioning from the charges directed solely against the king to those in which "he has combined with others," namely the House of Commons and the House of Lords, the Declaration of Independence indicted them "for quartering large bodies of armed troops among us." In addition to sweeping Parliament in this indictment, this charge differed from the earlier indictment that "he has kept among us, in times of peace, standing armies without the consent of our legislatures" by complaining that the British were making colonists responsible for billeting them.

The Petition of Right, which Parliament had leveled against Charles I, contained very similar sentiments (Reid 1981, 85). Moreover, the Mutiny Act of 1689, which Parliament had annually renewed, had prohibited the quartering of troops in private homes without the owners' consent within Great Britain. At the time of the French and Indian War, it was not clear whether this act applied in the colonies, where public inns for such purposes were scarcer than in Britain, and thus potential demand for private homes was greater, especially during times of war. A number of British generals and governors had asserted their right to billet troops without the owners' consent, generally to colonial legislative opposition (Alan 1970 and Zimmerman 1967).

The 1765 reauthorization of the Mutiny Act had provided that all British troops billeted in the colonies should receive "fire, candles, vinegar, and salt, bedding, utensils for dressing their victuals, and small beer or cyder, not exceeding five pints, or half a pint of rum mixed with a quartet of water, to each man, without paying any thing for the same" ("Quartering Act," 1765). After the New York legislature refused to provide the vinegar, salt, and beer, Parliament suspended its legislature until it complied (Fisher 1907, 286).

The Quartering Act of 1774, which is often classed among the Coercive, or Intolerable, Acts, sought to provide for cases where colonies had not provided adequate barracks. It specified that when such barracks were unavailable, "it shall and may be lawful for the governor of the province to order and direct such and so many uninhabited houses, out-houses, barns, or other buildings, as he shall think necessary to be taken (making a reasonable allowance for the same) and make fit for the reception of such officers and soldiers, and to put and quarter such officers and soldiers therein, for such time as he shall think proper" ("Great Britain," 1774). This law clearly limited the quartering of troops to "unoccupied" buildings, although accounts of revolutionary grievances are rife with charges that the British had used private homes (Gerlach 1966).

In his critique of the Declaration, John Lind observed that "If troops may be stationed in America, quarters must be provided for them in America." He further argued that "One only body there is, whose controuling power superintends the whole of the empire; that body is Parliament" (1776, 58).

The Third Amendment to the U.S. Constitution specifies that "No Soldier shall, in time of peace be quartered in any house, without the consent of the Owner, nor in time of war, but in a manner to be prescribed by law."

See also Charges against the King and Others; He Has Combined with Others (Charge #13); Standing Armies (Charge #11)

Further Reading

Fisher, Sydney George. 1907. "The Twenty-Eight Charges against the King in the Declaration of Independence." *Pennsylvania Magazine of History and Biography* 31:157–303.

Gerlach, Don R. 1966. "A Note on the Quartering Act of 1774." *New England Quarterly* 39 (March): 80–88.

"Great Britain: Parliament—The Quartering Act; June 2, 1774." Avalon Project. avalon.law.yale.edu/18th_century/quartering_act_1774.asp.

Lind, John. 1776. *An Answer to the Declaration of the American Congress*. London: J. Walter, Charing-Cross and T. Sewell.

"The Quartering Act." 1765. America's Homepage. http://ahp.gatech.edu/quartering_act_1765.html.

Reid, John Phillip. 1981. "The Irrelevance of the Declaration." *Law in the American Revolution and the Revolution in the Law*, edited by Hendrik Hartog, 46–89. New York: New York University Press.

Rogers, J. Alan. 1970. "Colonial Opposition to the Quartering of Troops during the French and Indian War." *Military Affairs* 34 (February): 7–11.

Sosin, Jack M. 1963. "The Massachusetts Acts of 1774: Coercive or Preventive?" *Huntington Library Quarterly* 26 (May): 235–252.

Zimmerman, John J. 1967. "Governor Denny and the Quartering Act of 1756." *Pennsylvania Magazine of History and Biography* 91 (July): 266–281.

QUEBEC ACT OF 1774 (CHARGE #20)

One of the charges that the Declaration associates both with the king and "with others" (the English Parliament) focused on the unnamed Quebec Act of June 22, 1774. Although Parliament had adopted this law more as a way of assuring support from Canada than as a way of attacking the 13 colonies to its immediate south, the colonies associated the law with the contemporaneous Coercive, or Intolerable, Acts. Parliament had enacted these laws to punish the port of Boston and the colony of Massachusetts in the wake of the Boston Tea Party.

In a phrase that was added by the committee (perhaps at the request of John Adams, a delegate from Massachusetts), the Declaration criticized the king and his associates "For abolishing the free System of English Laws in a neighbouring Province, establishing therein an arbitrary Government, and enlarging its boundaries, so as to render it at once an Example and fit Instrument for introducing the same absolute Rule into these Colonies." It thus criticized the unnamed law for abolishing English laws in Canada, for establishing and enlarging an arbitrary government there, and for establishing a possible template for the colonies to the south. The last charge might be the most important in that one might otherwise wonder what concern the 13 colonies would have with administration in another colony.

John Phillip Reid has observed that the term "arbitrary" was widely used in English political thought to "sometimes as an adjective implying bad public policy, sometimes as the equivalent of 'unlawful,' of 'unjust,' or of 'slavery,' and sometimes as a way that today would imply 'unconstitutional'" (1977, 461–461). He further notes that one of the articles of treason that had been lodged against Edward Hyde, earl of Clarendon, before the Parliament in 1877 was that he had introduced "an arbitrary government in his majesty's foreign plantations" (1981, 85).

One fascinating, possibly anachronistic, feature of this set of charges is that it specifically references "English laws." Prior to the Declaration, the colonies had argued, as in the Declaration and Resolves of the First Continental Congress, in terms of "the immutable laws of nature, the principles of the English constitution, and the several charters or contracts" (Vile 2015, 77). Because the Declaration is renouncing ties to Britain and its constitution, it seems odd to blame the British for abolishing "English" laws, especially in a neighboring colony. This charge might thus more reasonably be understood to suggest that the authors of the Declaration regarded such laws as superior to those with which they were replaced.

It should be remembered that Canada had begun as a French colony that the English won as a result of the French and Indian (or Seven Years') War, in which the 13 colonies had joined Britain in fighting the French and their Native American allies. Whereas Great Britain acknowledged the Protestant Anglican Church of England, of which its monarch was the titular head, France had remained a Roman Catholic nation, and most Canadians were therefore members of this religion. Similarly, the French relied on a system of civil law rather than on the English common-law system, which was built on legal precedents rather than on an extensive legal code.

The Quebec Act had enlarged the boundaries of Quebec, much as had the Royal Proclamation of October 7, 1763, to which the Declaration had previously objected.

Recognizing that most Canadians were practicing Catholics, the Quebec Act had also provided that Canadian subjects "professing the Religion of the Church of Rome, of, and in the said Province of Quebec, may have, hold, and enjoy, the Free Exercise of the Religion of the church of Rome, subject to the King's Supremacy." It has also mandated that "the Clergy of the said Church may hold, receive, and enjoy their accustomed Dues and Rights, with respect to such Persons only as shall profess the said Religion" ("Quebec Act," 1774).

In describing this law, Arthur Lee had commented "a little Popery, a little arbitrary power, French law, French religion, French government, and in American only" (1775, 48). Despite widespread criticism within Great Britain itself that in approving the law, King George III had violated his coronation oath to uphold the Anglican Church (Creviston 2011) and that the law would be used to suppress the liberties of Protestants to the south (Sainsbury 1978, 432), the provision allowing Catholics to practice their religion was wise and generous. Indeed, it was similar to the free exercise clause of the First Amendment that Americans would ratify in 1791. By contrast, the idea of officially recognizing or "establishing" this religion would have been especially obnoxious to Thomas Jefferson, who listed the writing of the Virginia Statute of Religious Freedom as one of three accomplishments that he wanted his tombstone to record. No matter how either provision might thus have stirred fears among a largely Protestant population in the 13 states agreeing to the Declaration, the document did not indict either of them. Doing so might well have jeopardized the anticipated alliance with France to fight the British.

By contrast, in indicting the Quebec Act of 1774, the Declaration and Resolves of the First Continental Congress of October 14, 1774, had identified the law with "establishing the Roman Catholic religion, in the province of Canada" ("Declaration and Resolves," 1774). More consistent with the language of the Declaration of Independence, it had also indicted the law for "abolishing the equitable system of English laws, and erecting a tyranny there, to the great danger (from so total a dissimilarity of religion, law and government) of the neighboring British colonies, by the assistance of whose blood and treasure the said country was conquered from France."

Similarly, the Declaration of Independence highlighted the way in which the Quebec Act had abolished "the free system of English laws," thus laying the basis for "arbitrary government." Given the generally high regard that the colonists had for English common law, this may have referred to the provision of the Quebec Act that assured Canadians that they would retain the rights to their "Property and Possessions" under the preexisting rules, presumably civil law, that had been in place prior to British rule, much as the United States allows Louisiana, which was once a French and Spanish possession, to be largely governed by civil law. The force of such an objection, however, would seemingly have been blunted by the fact that the Quebec Act did assure Canadians "the Certainty and Lenity of the Criminal Law of England, and the Benefits and Advantages resulting from the Use of it" ("Quebec Act of 1774").

It thus seems more likely that the Declaration was expressing concern over the fact that the Quebec Act had decided to dispense with a Canadian representative body. Asserting that "it is at present inexpedient to call an Assembly," that law had provided that the king would "with the Advice of the Privy Council" "constitute and appoint a Council of the Province of Quebec, to consist of such Persons resident there, not exceeding twenty three, nor less than Seventeen, as His Majesty . . . shall be pleased to appoint" ("Quebec Act of 1774").

Analyzing the concerns of Whig critics both within the United States and Britain, Vernon P. Creviston noted that "their specific concerns centered on the Quebec governor's advisory council, which was appointed by the provincial governor (who was only answerable to the king) rather than chosen by its constituency" (2011, 467). Creviston further observed that "the council possessed no power to overrule the governor, all of which ran counter to long-held British traditions of popularly elected assemblies" (2011, 467).

The Declaration of Independence had already denounced the king for suspending and dissolving colonial assemblies, but the Quebec Act appeared to open the possibility that he might go farther and deny representative government in the colonies altogether. This might provide the answer to John Lind's question, "What have the revolted Colonies to do with his Majesty's government of another Colony?" (1776, 78).

Americans who hoped to add Canada to their Union either through voluntarily joining the colonial cause or through military conquest were disappointed (as they would be again during the War of 1812). It is noteworthy, however, that Article XI of the Articles of Confederation that the colonies adopted as their first government provided that Canada would be eligible to join the Union without the special approval otherwise required of nine of the states (Vile 2015, 123).

See also Declaration and Resolves of the First Continental Congress (1774); Endeavored to Prevent the Population (Charge #7); Jefferson's Epitaph; Representative (Republican) Government

Further Reading

Creviston, Vernon P. 2011. "'No King Unless it Be a Constitutional King': Rethinking the Place of the Quebec Act in the Coming of the American Revolution." *Historian* 73 (Fall): 463–479.

"Declaration and Resolves of the First Continental Congress." October 14, 1774. Avalon Project. http://avalon.law.yale.edu/18th_century/resolves.asp.

[Lee, Arthur]. 1775. *An Appeal to the Justice and Interests of the People of Great Britain in the Present Dispute with America. By an Old Member of Parliament.* 2nd ed. London: Printed for J. Almon.

Lind, John. 1776 *An Answer to the Declaration of the American Congress*. London: J. Walter, Charing-Cross and T. Sewell.

"Quebec Act of 1774 Text." https://www.landofthebrave.info/1774-quebec-act-text.htm.

Reid, John Phillip. 1977. "In Legitimate Stirps: The Concept of 'Arbitrary,' the Supremacy of Parliament, and the Coming of the American Revolution." *Hofstra Law Review* 5 (Spring): 459–499.

Reid, John Phillip. 1981. "The Irrelevance of the Declaration." In *Law in the American Revolution and the Revolution in the Law*, edited Hendrik Hartog, 46–89. New York: New York University Press.

Sainsbury, John. 1978. "The Pro-Americans of London, 1769 to 1782." *William and Mary Quarterly* 35 (July): 423–454.

Vile, John R. 2015. *Founding Documents of America: Documents Decoded*. Santa Barbara, CA: ABC-CLIO.

R

REASON

Although the Continental Congress voted for independence on July 2, it sought to persuade others of the justice of this decision in the Declaration of Independence, which it adopted on July 4. In so doing, it appealed to "the opinions of mankind," which it hoped to shape through reasoned argument and through cataloguing abuses that the colonists had already suffered (West 2002, 97).

In appealing to "the laws of nature and of nature's god," Congress was appealing to a reason implicit in human nature. Just as scientists like Galileo and Newton were using such reason to discern previously unknown laws of the physical universe, so too, the Founders thought that they could use the same reason to understand human nature and derive rules for human governance.

Thomas G. West observes, "Those laws are the discovery of human reason, the unaided intellect contemplating human nature as it is. Religion may confirm the discovery; tradition may embody it; but the principles of government are truths knowable to the human mind—in principle, any human mind—reflecting on the nature of man" (2002, 99). Those who believe that the Declaration of Independence may have been influenced by the Scottish Common Sense School of Philosophy may further argue that such reason is influenced by the common human possession of a "moral sense," akin to conscience, that aids in the perception of right and wrong (Wills 1978).

The theory of natural law and natural rights, with which the Declaration of Independence is often identified, rests on the idea that even individuals without access to divine revelation can come to an adequate understanding of how government should operate to create such systems for themselves. In later arguing for the adoption of the U.S. Constitution, Alexander Hamilton argued in Federalist No. 1 that "it seems to have been reserved to the people of this country, by their conduct and example, to decide the important question, whether societies of men are really capable or not of establishing good government from reflection and choice, or whether they are forever destined to depend for their political constitutions on accident and force" (Hamilton, Madison, and Jay [1787–1788] 1961, 33).

See also Equality; Human Nature and the Declaration of Independence; Laws of Nature and of Nature's God; Moral Virtues in the Declaration of Independence

Further Reading

Hamilton, Alexander, James Madison, and John Jay. (1787–1788) 1961. *The Federalist Papers*. New York: New American Library.

West, Thomas G. 2003. "The Political Theory of the Declaration of Independence." In *The American Founding and the Social Compact*, edited by Ronald J. Pestritto and Thomas G. West, 95–146. Lanham, MD: Lexington Books.

Wills, Garry. 1978. *Inventing America: Jefferson's Declaration of Independence*. Garden City, NY: Doubleday & Company, Inc.

REFERENCES TO KING GEORGE III IN THE DECLARATION OF INDEPENDENCE

One of the primary goals of the Declaration of Independence was that of establishing that George III, to whom the colonists had previously affirmed their allegiance, had forfeited the right to this trust. The Declaration never directly referred to him as George III; Indeed, in the long list of grievances that the Declaration cited, it referred to him simply as "He." It is unclear whether it did so with the understanding that his name did not deserve to be pronounced or as a way of making the attack less personal.

The Declaration's first reference to George III did not occur until close to the end of the second full paragraph, which referred to "this history of the present king of Great Britain" as "a history of repeated injuries and usurpations all having in direct object the establishment of an absolute tyranny over these states." According to Robert Ginsberg, John Adams originated this phrase in place of "his majesty," which would have had quite an ironic ring in light of the Declaration's accusations (1967, 225).

Classical political theorists often divided government into six types, depending on whether they were ruled by the one, the few, or the many, and according to whether they ruled on behalf of themselves or the people. It was standard thus to distinguish a kingdom from a tyranny, an aristocracy from an oligarchy, and the rule of the people from mob rule. The Declaration might have been indicating that although George III ruled as a king in Great Britain, where people were represented in Parliament, he was acting as a tyrant in the colonies, where the people were not so represented.

As noted above, the set of accusations all begin with the word "he," with the 13th accusation and those immediately following observing that "he has combined with others," an indirect reference to the two houses of Parliament, whose authority the colonies did not recognize in America. In describing how the colonists, whom the Declaration most frequently identifies as "we," had petitioned for redress of grievances, the Declaration shifted from king and back to tyrant by observing that "a prince whose character is thus marked by every act which may define a tyrant, is unfit to be the ruler of a free people." In previously accusing the king of refusing to provide adequate representation for the people in colonial legislatures, the Declaration had declared that such a right was "inestimable to them, & formidable to tyrants only."

In the paragraph that had immediately preceded, which had condemned the role of the English leader in introducing and perpetuating slavery, but which Congress had excised, Thomas Jefferson had somewhat ironically compared the "cruel war" that "the *Christian* king of Great Britain" had waged against Africans with the laws of warfare recognized by "*infidel* powers." In yet another passage that Congress excised after Jefferson's description of the petitions that the colonists had filed, he had referred to the fact that the colonists had initially recognized "one common king, thereby laying a foundation of perpetual league and amity" with the English people. In yet another passage that Congress excised, Jefferson referred to the king as the "chief magistrate."

The final paragraph of the Declaration merges the king, or tyrant, into "the British Crown," from whom it announced the dissolution of all further bonds.

In reflecting on the Declaration of Independence, John Adams had observed that "there were other expressions which I would not have inserted, if I had drawn it [the Declaration] up, particularly that which called the King a tyrant" (Zall 2004, 76). He went on to observe that he thought the expression was "too personal" and "too passionate . . . too much scolding, for so grave and solemn a document" (Zall 2004, 76). Perhaps seeking to explain why he had not struck it out, he further observed that "as [Benjamin] Franklin and [Roger] Sherman were to inspect it afterwards, I thought it would not become me to strike out. I consented to report it, and do not now remember that I made or suggested a single alteration" (Zall 2004, 76).

In his character sketches of signers of the Declaration of Independence, after noting that John Witherspoon was "free from the illiberality which sometimes accompanies zeal," Benjamin Rush observed that:

> In a report brought into Congress by a member from Virginia, George III was called the "tyrant of Britain." Dr. Witherspoon objected to the word "tyrant," and moved to substitute "king" in its room. He gave as reasons for his objection, "that the epithet was both *false* and *undignified.* It was *false*, because George 3d was not a *tyrant* in Great Britain; on the contrary he was beloved and respected by his subjects in Great Britain, and perhaps the more, for making war upon us. It was *undignified*, because it did not become one sovereign power to abuse or use harsh epithets, when it spoke of another." (1905, 110)

Rush further reports that Congress adopted Witherspoon's amendment.

Given that the unspecified manuscript to which Witherspoon had objected had been introduced by a Virginian, It is possible that Thomas Jefferson had sought to word the Declaration so as to prevent a similar objection. He therefore distinguished George III's kingly rule in Britain—where, however, he was not without harsh critics (Zaller 1993)—from his tyrannical rule in the colonies.

Although the Declaration identified the British king as a tyrant, at least with respect to his administration of the colonies, it appeared to indicate that the colonies would have been content to continue association with a true king who did not act tyrannically. By contrast, Thomas Paine's arguments in *Common Sense* indicted the whole monarchical system. In addition to focusing specifically on the evils of hereditary succession and the proclivity of kings to involve their subjects in war, Paine thus said that "monarchy in every instance is the popery of government" (1953, 14). In his judgment, "Of more worth is one honest man to society, and in the sight of God, than all the crowned ruffians that have ever lived" (1953, 18).

See also British Crown; *Common Sense* (Paine); Rush's (Benjamin) Characters of the Signers; Tyranny; "We" (First-Person Plural); Witherspoon, John

Further Reading

Ginsberg, Robert. 1967. "The Declaration as Rhetoric." In *A Casebook on the Declaration of Independence*, edited by Robert Ginsberg, 219–246. New York: Thomas Y. Crowell.

Paine, Thomas. 1953. *Common Sense and Other Political Writings.* Edited by Nelson F. Adkins. New York: Liberal Arts Press.

Rush, Benjamin. 1905. *A Memorial Containing Travels through Life or Sundry Incidents in the Life of Dr. Benjamin Rush.* Lanoraie, QC: Louis Alexander Biddle.

Zall, Paul M. 2004. *Adams on Adams.* Lexington: University Press of Kentucky.

Zaller, Robert. 1993. "The Figure of the Tyrant in English Revolutionary Thought." *Journal of the History of Ideas* 54 (October): 585–610.

REFUSED ASSENT TO COLONIAL LAWS (CHARGE #1)

The first accusation that the Declaration of Independence made against the king was that "He has refused his assent to laws the most wholesome and necessary for the public good." The terms "wholesome and necessary" clearly indicate that the Declaration was not averse to laws in general but only to laws that did not fulfill their proper purpose (Arnn 2012, 26).

In *A Summary View of the Rights of British America*, Thomas Jefferson had noted that it was "the great office of his majesty, to resume the exercise of his negative power, and to prevent the passage of laws by any one legislature of the empire, which might bear injuriously on the rights and interests of another" (1774). He had proceeded, however, to say that "this will not excuse the wanton exercise of this power which we have seen his majesty practice on the laws of the American legislatures," observing that "For the most trifling reasons, and sometimes for no conceivable reason at all, his majesty has rejected laws of the most salutary tendency" (1774). He had specifically mentioned the king's veto of state attempts to end the African slave trade.

In critiquing the charge within the Declaration of Independence, former Massachusetts governor Thomas Hutchinson observed that the charge "is of so general a nature, that it is not possible to conjecture to what laws or to what Colonies it refers" (1776). However, Hutchinson did suggest that it might have to do with laws that would have allowed colonies to issue "a fraudulent paper currency, and making it a legal tender" (on this subject, see Greene and Jellison 1961). A British critic, now known to be John Lind, observed that the law unfairly implied that the king had withheld authority from local legislatures to make laws on the spot, which the king usually approved, but that the king rightly retained the power to disallow laws that he believed to be contrary to the public good (1776, 15). Perhaps more importantly, Lind argued both that prior kings had exercised similar powers and that the power was recognized within colonial charters and commissions that the Declaration had otherwise favorably referenced (1776, 14).

Dr. Herbert Friedenwald associated this accusation with the increasingly minute supervision over colonial affairs that the colonists had exercised since the French and Indian War. Providing a more complete description of what the colonists might have had in mind, he said that all the states except Rhode Island, Connecticut, and Maryland had experienced such vetoes. He cited laws prohibiting governors from approving divorces; disallowing restrictions on the importation of slaves passed by South Carolina in 1760, New Jersey in 1763, and Virginia in 1772 (for further confirmation, see Pincus 2016, 128); state attempts in Virginia, Maryland, and Pennsylvania to restrict the immigration of convicts; and laws restricting the issuance of paper currency (Friedenwald, 1904, 214–217). Sydney George Fisher (1907, 163–164) largely cites the same examples while noting that the United States was during his day exercising similar authority over Puerto Rico (1907, 265). Edward Dumbauld observes that Virginia had been profoundly shocked when in 1752, the assembly learned that the king had disallowed so many of its laws that it had to publish a revised version (1950, 90).

In a letter that he wrote to Jedidiah Morse on November 29, 1815, John Adams, who was always jealous of his role and that of his state in the Revolution, said that the Revolution had begun "in the minds and hearts of the people, and in the union of the colonies" (Farrell 2006, 540). He had further credited James Otis with having lit the spark of revolution in his opposition to writs of assistance in Paxton's Case of 1761. Notably, the Massachusetts provincial legislature sought in the following year to require specific warrants, only to have the law vetoed by the governor (Marshall 2013, 2:748).

Unlike the modern presidential veto, which two-thirds majority of both houses can override, the royal veto, which was actually exercised by his Privy Council, which, in turn, often acted on recommendation of the Board of Trade, which had been established in 1696 (McGovney 1945, 65), was absolute. In part because of this, the royal veto of parliamentary legislation had fallen into disuse shortly after the beginning of the eighteenth century. By contrast, the king granted power to colonial assemblies through commission. The monarch and the Board of Trade had struck down nearly 400 colonial laws between 1696 and 1765 (Watson 1987, 404).

Memories of this use lingered. Although James Madison would later argue for vesting the U.S. Congress with a similar veto over state legislation, delegates meeting at the Constitutional Convention of 1787 rejected this proposal. New York's John Lansing observed that "Such a Negative would be more injurious than that of Great Britain heretofore was" (Farrand 1966, 1:337).

See also Charges against the King and Others; *A Summary View of the Rights of British America* (Jefferson)

Further Reading

Andrews, Charles M. 1914. "The Royal Disallowance." *American Antiquarian Society* 14 (October): 342–362.

Arnn, Larry P. 2012. *The Founders' Key: The Divine and Natural Connection between the Declaration and the Constitution and What We Risk by Losing It.* Nashville, TN: Thomas Nelson.

Dumbauld, Edward. 1950. *The Declaration of Independence and What It Means Today*. Norman: University of Oklahoma Press.

Farrand, Max. 1966. *The Records of the Federal Convention of 1787*. 4 vols. New Haven, CT: Yale University Press.

Farrell, James M. 2006. "The Writs of Assistance and Public Memory: John Adams and the Legacy of James Otis." *New England Quarterly* 79 (December): 533–556.

Fisher, Sydney George. 1907. "The Twenty-Eight Charges against the King in the Declaration of Independence." *Pennsylvania Magazine of History and Biography* 31:247–303.

Friedenwald, Herbert. 1904. *The Declaration of Independence: An Interpretation and an Analysis*. New York: Macmillan.

Greene, Evarts B. 1917. "American Opinion on the Imperial Review of Provincial Legislation, 1776–1787." *American Historical Review* 23 (October): 104–107

Greene, Jack P., and Richard M. Jellison. 1961. "The Currency Act of 1764 in Imperial-Colonial Relations, 1764–1776." *William and Mary Quarterly* 18 (October): 485–518.

Hutchinson, Thomas. 1776. "1776: Hutchinson, Strictures upon the Declaration of Independence." Online Library of Liberty. http://oll.libertyfund.org/pages/1776-hutchinson-strictures-upon-the-declaration-of-independence.

Jefferson, Thomas. 1774. *A Summary View of the Rights of British America*. Colonial Williamsburg. www.history.org/almanack/life/politics/sumview.cfm. Accessed July 8, 2017.

Lind, John. 1776 *An Answer to the Declaration of the American Congress*. London: J. Walter, Charing-Cross and T. Sewell.

Marshall, Christopher R. 2013. "Writs of Assistance." In *The Encyclopedia of the Fourth Amendment*, 2 vols., edited by John R. Vile and David L. Hudson Jr. Vol. 2., 747–748. Los Angeles: Sage Reference.

McGovney, Dudley Odell. 1945. "The British Privy Council's Power to Restrain the Legislatures of Colonial America: Power to Disallow Statutes: Power to Veto." *University of Pennsylvania Law Review* 94 (October): 59–93.

Pincus, Steve. 2016. *The Heart of the Declaration: The Founders' Case for an Activist Government*. New Haven, CT: Yale University Press.

Russell, E. B. 1915. *The Review of American Colonial Legislation by the King in Council*. New York: Columbia University Press.

Watson, Richard A. 1987. "Origins and Early Development of the Veto Power." *Presidential Studies Quarterly* 17 (Spring): 401–412.

REFUSED TO CAUSE OTHERS TO BE ELECTED (CHARGE #6)

One of the more verbose charges that the Declaration of Independence makes against the king states that "he has refused for a long time after such dissolutions to cause others to be elected whereby the legislative powers, incapable of annihilation, have returned to the people at large for their exercise, the state remaining in the meantime exposed to all the dangers of invasion from without, & convulsions within." This immediately follows the charge that the king had repeatedly "dissolved legislative houses."

While the second of these charges may appear overwrought, it arguably tied neatly back to the philosophy that the Declaration articulated in its second paragraph. Indeed, by referring to "the dangers of invasion from without, & convulsions within," it posed in even starker terms the need for governments to secure people's lives, liberties, and happiness. It is a reminder that the English philosopher Thomas Hobbes had described the stateless "state of nature" as a place where the life of man was "solitary, poore, nasty, brutish, and short" (1968, 186).

The passage further suggested that if the governments the people selected for these purposes fail, the people retain the power that they originally ceded to them. Notably, members of the Second Continental Congress had already authorized states whose governors had dissolved the legislatures to set up new governments to replace them (Friedenwald 1904, 34). Moreover, members of both Continental Congresses had essentially met in the absence of British approval.

This section of the Declaration is a reminder that, in declaring independence, the Declaration did not create a new government. That task would fall to the committee that created the Articles of Confederation and to the convention that later proposed the current U.S. Constitution (Vile 2016).

See also Charges against the King and Others; Dissolved Representative Houses (Charge #5)

Further Reading

Friedenwald, Herbert. 1904. *The Declaration of Independence: An Interpretation and an Analysis.* New York: Macmillan.

Hobbes, Thomas. (1651) 1968. *Leviathan.* Baltimore, MD: Penguin Books.

Vile, John R. 2016. *The Constitutional Convention of 1787: A Comprehensive Encyclopedia of America's Founding*, Rev. 2nd ed. Clark, NJ: Talbot Publishing.

REFUSED TO PASS OTHER LAWS (CHARGE #3)

The third accusation that the Declaration of Independence lodged against the king was that "he has refused to pass other laws for the accommodation of large districts of people, unless those people would relinquish the right of representation in the legislature; a right inestimable to them & formidable to tyrants only."

This accusation clearly pointed to the value that American revolutionaries placed on their own representative legislative institutions. This was highlighted by the fact that the Declaration classified "the right of representation" as "inestimable to them, & formidable to tyrants." Moreover, two paragraphs later, in accusing the king of improperly dissolving colonial legislatures, the Declaration described such actions "as invasions on the right of the people."

Herbert Friedenwald observes that the third accusation in the Declaration is "the first grievance in the list that meant much to the men of the days of the revolution, but which conveys no message to us" (1904, 222). He explains that as colonies expanded westward, these areas expected representation in colonial assemblies, but the king regarded this "as a prerogative of the sovereign, to be exercised in the colonies through the royal governors" (1904, 222–223). Friedenwald further traced discontentment over prior royal assent to such increased representation to New Hampshire, New York, New Jersey, and Virginia. Hans Eicholz notes that the popularly elected branch of the Massachusetts legislature grew from 84 in 1692 to more than 180 by 1776, whereas the Governor's Council remained at 28 (2001, 56). B. J. Lossing believes this complaint was tied to the Quebec Act and that its provisions for vesting the legislative powers in an unelected council was particularly resented in the English colonies bordering on Nova Scotia and aggravated by legislation related to Massachusetts (1858, 273).

Seeing Massachusetts Bay as the chief source of this complaint, former governor Thomas Hutchinson (1776) claimed that "No Governor ever refused to consent to a law for making a new town, even without a suspending clause, if provision was made that the inhabitants of the new town should continue to join with the old, or with any other town contiguous or near to it, in the choice of Representatives." He thus regarded this charge as "a willful misrepresentation."

In defending the king against this charge, John Lind further observed that within Britain itself the king had the right to refuse recognition to new boroughs (1776, 24). This argument would have been unlikely to impress most colonists.

By contrast, Sydney George Fisher observed that as the Patriot party gained strength after 1764, the king "became chary of allowing representatives from newly-created counties, because those representatives were very apt to be of the patriot or rebellious party" (1907, 272–273).

See also Charges against the King and Others; Quebec Act of 1774 (Charge #20); Representative (Republican) Government

Further Reading

Eicholz, Hans L. 2001. *Harmonizing Sentiments: The Declaration of Independence and the Jeffersonian Idea of Self-Government*. New York: Peter Lang.

Fisher, Sydney George. 1907. "The Twenty-Eight Charges against the King in the Declaration of Independence." *Pennsylvania Magazine of History and Biography* 31:257–303.

Friedenwald, Herbert. 1904. *The Declaration of Independence: An Interpretation and an Analysis*. New York: Macmillan.

Hutchinson, Thomas. 1776. "1776: Hutchinson, Strictures upon the Declaration of Independence." Online Library of Liberty. http://oll.libertyfund.org/pages/1776-hutchinson-strictures-upon-the-declaration-of-independence.

Lind, John. 1776 *An Answer to the Declaration of the American Congress*. London: J. Walter, Charing-Cross and T. Sewell.

Lossing, B. J. 1848. *Biographical Sketches of the Signers of the Declaration of American Independence; The Declaration Historical Considered; and a Sketch of the Leading Events Connected with the Adoption of the Articles of Confederation and of the Federal Constitution*. New York: George F. Cooledge and Brothers.

REMEMBER THE LADIES

The Declaration of Independence alternately referred to "human" events and to "mankind." One of its most famous statements asserted "that all men are created equal." Although there is general agreement that the term (like the word "mankind") was often used to embrace both males and females, the Declaration appears to have a masculine cast, as when it commends colonial assemblies for having resisted the king "with manly firmness." Moreover, Thomas Jefferson, its chief author, appeared uncomfortable with female participation in politics (Steele 2008).

Portrait of Abigail Adams, by Gilbert Stuart, ca. 1800–1815. Abigail Adams, the wife of President John Adams and the mother of President John Quincy Adams, was an ardent American patriot in her own right. She encouraged her husband to "remember the ladies" while securing equal rights for American men. (National Gallery of Art)

Even prior to the writing of the Declaration of Independence, Abigail Adams wrote to her husband on March 31, 1776, on hearing (apparently incorrectly) "that you have declared an independency." Looking to "the new code of laws which I suppose it will be necessary for you to make," she desired that her husband "would remember the ladies and be more generous and favorable to them than your ancestors." Asking that the Congress "not put such unlimited power into the hands of husbands," she reminded her husband that "all men would be tyrants if they could" (Vile 2015, 89). Showing her familiarity with the political rhetoric of the day, she observed that "If particular care and attention is not paid to the ladies, we are determined to foment a rebellion, and will not hold ourselves bound by any laws in which we have no voice or representation" (Vile 2015, 89–90; for later use of this argument, see Tutt 2010, 38, commenting in "Essay on Love and Marriage"). Although not referencing this specific letter, Norma Basch observes that an essay in the *Boston Magazine* in November 1783 would later repeat both the analogy of both men as tyrants and women as rebels (2003, 38).

It is often difficult to tease out the degree to which Abigail Adams intended for her letter to be serious and the degree to which she intended for it to be playful. John Adams's response on April 14, however, indicated that he was not unaware that the struggle for freedom from the king might well stir up questions about other forms of authority. Saying that he "cannot but laugh" at his wife's "extraordinary code of laws," John Adams observed that "we have been told that our struggle has loosened the bonds of government everywhere; that children and apprentices were disobedient; that schools and colleges were grown turbulent; that Indians slighted their guardians, and negroes grew insolent to their masters. But your letter was the first intimation that another tribe, more numerous and powerful than all the rest, were grown discontented" (Vile 2015, p. 90).

Observing that "we know better than to repeal our masculine systems," John Adams proceeded to argue that male dominance was more theoretical than real.

He noted that "We dare not exert our power in its full latitude," but keep the name of masters in order to prevent becoming subject "to the despotism of the petticoat" (Vile 2015, 90–91).

In a letter of May 26, 1776, to James Sullivan, however, John Adams engaged in further reflection on the meaning of the consent of the people and the implications of the revolutionary struggle. One of the questions Adams raised was, "Whence arises the Right of the Men to govern Women, without their Consent?" (Vile 2015, 92). Suggesting that women might be excluded on the basis that "their Delicacy renders them unfit for Practice and Experience, in the Great Business of Life, and the hardy Enterprises of War, as well as the arduous Cares of State" (Vile 2015, 92), Adams fretted that opening the franchise to individuals who did not own property would eventually open it to all, including women, who "will demand a Vote" (Vile 2015, 93).

In the meantime, Abigail wrote her husband on August 14, 1776, to argue that the "new constitution may be distinguished for learning and virtue" (Vile 2015, 91). She added that "If we mean to have heroes, statesmen and philosophers, we should have learned women" (Vile 2015, 91).

Over time, of course, the Revolution did have implications for a wide variety of social interactions, including the rights of women. Women meeting at Seneca Falls, New York, in 1848 drafted a Declaration of Sentiments, based on the Declaration of 1776, which asserted that "all men and women are created equal." After years of struggle, the Nineteenth Amendment finally prohibited discrimination in voting on the basis of sex in 1920.

See also Adams, John; Equality; Declaration of Sentiments (1848)

Further Reading

Basch, Norma. 2003. "Declarations of Independence: Women and Divorce in the Early Republic." In *Women and the U.S. Constitution*, 3rd ed., edited by Sibyl A. Schwarzenbach and Patricia Smith, 34–44. New York: Columbia University Press.

"An Essay on Love and Marriage." November 1783. *Boston Magazine*, 15–18.

Smith-Rosenberg. 2010. *This Violent Empire: The Birth of an American National Identify*. Greensboro: University of North Carolina Press.

Steele, Brian. 2008. "Thomas Jefferson's Gender Frontier." *Journal of American History* 95 (June): 17–42.

Tutt, Juliana. 2010. "'No Taxation without Representation' in the American Woman Suffrage Movement." *Stanford Law Review* 62 (May): 1473–1512.

Vile, John R. 2015. *Founding Documents of America: Documents Decoded*. Santa Barbara, CA: ABC-CLIO.

REPRESENTATIVE (REPUBLICAN) GOVERNMENT

The Declaration of Independence was not designed to create a new government but to clear the way to establish one by explaining why the one-time colonists were cutting their political ties to the mother country. The Declaration made it clear that it anticipated that the people would replace the old government with a new one, just as Congress had already authorized the states to do.

Although the Declaration addressed its primary complaints against the English king, it recognized that "he has combined with others"—namely, the House of Commons and the House of Lords of the British Parliament—in giving assent "to their acts of pretended legislation." This included "imposing taxes on us without our consent." The colonists had long argued that under principles established in the Magna Carta and other documents of liberty, the Parliament had no right to tax them because they had no representation there (Osgood 1898). Many colonists also thought that the system of representation within Great Britain itself (where suffrage was extremely limited and so-called rotten boroughs were ubiquitous) was defective, if not corrupt.

It seems likely that in the penultimate paragraph of the Declaration that described prior reminders that the colonists had made on behalf of colonial rights referred to documents, like the Declaration and Resolves of the First Congress, that representative bodies had authored on behalf of their constituents.

The first printing (the Dunlap Printing) described the document as "A Declaration by the Representatives of the UNITED STATES OF AMERICA in General Congress assembled." The engrossed copy that Congress commissioned after it had received the approval of New York was prefaced with the words "In Congress, July 4, 1776, The unanimous Declaration of the thirteen united States of America." Like the current Congress, the Congress that approved the Declaration was a representative body that had been elected by its constituents or their representatives.

Although the Declaration proclaimed that just governments rested on "the consent of the governed," it is likely that it expected that the people would primarily give such consent through the process of voting for representatives. Consistent with John Locke's insights that changes in the nature of representative bodies could serve as the basis for the dissolution of government, many of the charges that the Declaration lodged against the king focused on his interference with colonial legislatures.

In addition to the rights of "life, liberty, and the pursuit of happiness," the Declaration observed, in the course of lodging its complaints against the king, that "the right of representation in the legislature" was "a right inestimable to them, & formidable to tyrants only." It further connected the king's dissolution of representative houses with "his invasions on the rights of the people," and accused the British of "suspending our own legislatures, & declaring themselves invested with power to legislation for us in all cases whatsoever." In indicting the Quebec Act of 1774, which had substituted an appointed council in place of a representative assembly, the Declaration further accused the king of "combining with others" to render Canada "at once an example & fit instrument for introducing the same absolute rule into these states."

As if to repeat the importance of this link, the final paragraph of the Declaration began by saying that "We therefore the Representatives of the United states of America, in General Congress assembled . . . do in the name and by authority of the good people of these colonies" declare their independence of Britain.

Because each state had a single vote in the Continental Congress and under the Congress that was established under the Articles of Confederation, it shared some of the same flaws as did the British Parliament. The constitution that was written in the Convention of 1787 partially remedied this defect by basing representation in the House of Representatives on the basis of population. Article IV of the Constitution further sought "to guarantee to every State in this Union a Republican Form of Government." Future amendments prohibited governments from denying the vote on the basis of race, sex, or age above 18.

In Federalist No. 10, which he wrote to defend the new Constitution against its Anti-Federalist critics, James Madison distinguished the "republican," or representative, government under the new Constitution from the pure democracies of the past. He indicated both that the new government was a representative, rather than a direct democracy, and that, as a consequence, it could cover a larger territory that would include a greater number of factions and make it less likely that any one faction could dominate the government to the disadvantage of the others (Hamilton, Madison, and Jay, [1787–1788] 1961, 77–84).

The Declaration was generally phrased in the first-person plural. This arguably made it purposefully difficult to distinguish the views of the Congress adopting the Declaration from the views of their constituents. Ultimately, their own reception of the document, which had been debated and adopted in secret, and their own devotion to the revolutionary cause would be the test of whether the people were in accord with the representatives who professed to be speaking on their behalf.

See also Captions of the Declaration of Independence; Charges against the King and Others; Declaration and Resolves of the First Continental Congress (1774); Dissolution of Government; Dunlap Broadside Printing of the Declaration of Independence; Locke, John; People; Proclamation, Reading, and Reception of the Declaration of Independence; Quebec Act of 1774 (Charge #20); "We" (First-Person Plural)

Further Reading

Hamilton, Alexander, James Madison, and John Jay. (1787–1788) 1961. *The Federalist Papers*. New York: New American Library.

Osgood, Herbert L. 1898. "The American Revolution." *Political Science Quarterly* 13 (March): 41–59.

REPUTATION OF THE DECLARATION OF INDEPENDENCE

Today, the Declaration is proudly displayed at the National Archives along with the Constitution and the Bill of Rights. Every Fourth of July, the *New York Times* prints a copy of the document. When the British Museum commemorated the 800th anniversary of the Magna Carta in 2015, it also displayed a copy of the Declaration. Today, the document, and its chief author, are widely known, celebrated, and studied.

This was not always the case. Although the Declaration was widely read after its adoption by the Second Continental Congress, it then seemed to have fallen into relative obscurity. It was especially minimized by New England Federalists, who generally favored the British over the French, and who often associated the doctrines of the Declaration with those of Revolutionary France. They also had an incentive to minimize the role that Thomas Jefferson (the head of the Democratic-Republican Party) had in the American Revolution.

This attitude began to change with the demise of the Federalist Party and the death of most of the signers of the Declaration. Benjamin Owen Tyler and John Binns published engravings of the Declaration in 1818 and 1819, and Congress commissioned John Trumbull to do a painting of the Declaration for the Capitol Building in 1817. Whereas celebrations of Independence Day had often been highly partisan events during the contentions between Federalists and Democratic-Republicans, by 1817, the event began to take on a more bipartisan character (Detweiler 1962, 573). The role of the Declaration was highlighted with the simultaneous deaths of Jefferson and John Adams on July 4, 1826.

As the controversy over slavery increased, a number of Southerners, often guided by the philosophy of John C. Calhoun, took aim at the idea that individuals of different races were created equal, but Abraham Lincoln professed that he took his central principles from the document. As Americans respectively found themselves in the twentieth century battling autocracy, totalitarianism, and a philosophy that belittled private property, Americans increasingly found themselves seeking ideological support. The completion of the Jefferson Memorial in 1943, like Franklin Roosevelt's increasing invocations of the Bill of Rights, was designed to highlight American ideals in a world that threatened democratic values.

See also Calhoun, John C.; Equality; Independence Day; Lincoln, Abraham; Slavery

Further Reading

Detweiler, Philip F. 1962. "The Changing Reputation of the Declaration of Independence: The First Fifty Years." *William and Mary Quarterly* 19 (October): 557–574.

Maier, Pauline. 1997. *American Scripture: Making the Declaration of Independence*. New York: Alfred A. Knopf.

RESOLUTION ON INDEPENDENT GOVERNMENTS

See Creation of New State Governments

RESOLUTIONS INTRODUCED BY RICHARD HENRY LEE (JUNE 7, 1776)

On June 7, 1776, Richard Henry Lee of Virginia introduced the resolutions that initiated debates in the Second Continental Congress that eventually led to the writing and ratification of the Declaration of Independence. Lee had requested such instructions after telling the Virginia Convention that "Ages yet unborn and millions existing at present may rue or bless that assembly on which their happiness or misery will so eminently depend" (Hays 1898, 90–91).

The Virginia Convention then responded with a resolution dated May 15, 1776, in which delegates instructed their congressional delegates to introduce resolutions seeking independence, foreign alliances, and a confederation of the united colonies. Patrick Henry and Edmund Pendleton appear to have done much of the drafting, with Pendleton inserting a provision prohibiting Congress from dictating state governments (Selby 1988, 96–97).

Lee reworked this request into three resolutions (Hays 1898, 91). John Adams seconded Lee's resolution for independence (Maier 1997, 41).

Lee's three resolutions were as follows

> Resolved, That these United Colonies are, and of right ought to be, free and independent States, that they are absolved from all allegiance to the British Crown, and that all political connection between them and the State of Great Britain is, and ought to be, totally dissolved.
>
> That it is expedient forthwith to take the most effectual measures for forming foreign Alliances.
>
> That a plan of confederation be prepared and transmitted to the respective Colonies for their consideration and approbation. (Vile 2015, 95)

The first resolution, like the Declaration of Independence, focused on the British Crown (George III) because the colonies had already rejected the idea that Parliament had sovereignty, or power, over them, especially with respect to taxes. This was further grounded on the idea that the Magna Carta of 1215 and other British documents had denied that a body could tax people whom it did not represent. By this reasoning, the British Parliament had no right to tax the colonies because they were not seated in that body; by contrast, British spokesmen claimed that the Parliament "virtually" represented all Englishmen, including those in the American colonies. Lee's resolution directly contradicted the British Declaratory Act of 1766, which had asserted that the colonies "have been, are, and of right ought to be subordinate unto, and dependent upon the imperial crown and parliament of Great Britain" (Munves 1978, 9). A similar usage is found in the British Bill of Rights, where Parliament acknowledged that William and Mary "were, are, and of right ought to be" sovereigns (Dunning 1914, 83).

Lee's first resolution contains an ambiguity that arguably remained unsettled by the Declaration of Independence and that is further muddled by the fact that contemporary Americans still refer to fifty "states," whereas the term "state" is often used elsewhere to refer to distinct nations or nation-states. Notably, Lee's first resolution itself refers to "the State of Great Britain." Although Lee refers to the colonies as "United," one could also cite his document to stand for the principles that they are "free and independent states."

The second two resolutions that Lee introduced are inextricably linked to the first. In addition to its own troops, Britain was already recruiting troops from Germany to fight against the colonists. Foreign allies would more likely come to their aid if they were convinced that the split was permanent. They would be far less likely to participate in what was considered to be a civil war.

Colonies had already begun forming their own governments, but if these governments were to remain united in a common fight, it was clear that they would need some common direction. In 1777, Congress proposed the Articles of Confederation. Ratified by the last state in 1781, these articles, which perpetuated a unicameral Congress to control common affairs, lasted through 1789. They were then replaced by the Constitution proposed by the Constitutional Convention of 1787.

Lee is reputed to have given an address when he introduced his resolutions, and Charles Botta's *History of the War of the Independence of the United States* has included this alleged speech, which, whether authentic or not, "was in line with Lee's known views" (Chitwood 1967, 95). Arguing that necessity called for separation, the speech argued that the time was ripe for it; Lee said that "The eyes of Europe are fixed upon us; she demands of us a living example of freedom that may contrast by the felicity of her citizens with the very-increasing tyranny which desolates her polluted shores" (Shestokas 2017, 48). Lee went on to say that "If we are not this day wanting in our duty to our country, the names of the American legislators will be placed, by posterity, at the side of those of Theseus, of Lycurgus, of Romulus of Numa, of the three Williams of Nassau, and of all those whose memory has been and will be forever dear to virtuous men and good citizens" (Skestokas 2017, 49).

The last paragraph of the Declaration of Independence incorporated Lee's first resolution, using capital letters to emphasize the fact that the colonies were becoming "FREE AND INDEPENDENT STATES."

Lee's resolution for independence was too early for some. Edward Rutledge of South Carolina thus penned the following note to John Jay:

> The Congress sat till 7 o'clock this evening in consequence of a motion of R. H. Lee's rendering ourselves free and independent States. The sensible part of the House oppose the Motion—they had no objection to forming a Scheme of a Treaty which they would send to France by proper Persons and uniting this Continent by a Confederacy; they saw no Wisdom in a *Declaration* of Independence, nor any other purpose to be enforced by it, but placing ourselves in the Power of those with whom we mean to treat, giving our Enemy Notice of our Intentions before we had taken any steps to execute them and thereby enabling them to counteract us in our Intentions and rendering ourselves ridiculous in the eyes of foreign powers by attempting to bring them into an Union with us before we had united with each other. (Burnett 1964, 172)

On June 10, Congress accordingly tabled this motion for three weeks. During this time, however, a Committee of Five met to draft a document justifying the resolution, and support for independence grew. Congress finally voted for independence on July 2, 1776, and for the document explaining this action on July 4.

Richard Henry Lee had returned to Virginia to help with the writing of the Virginia Constitution. The Congress thus appointed Thomas Jefferson, a late arrival to the Congress, as Virginia's delegate on the committee. Lee did return by August 2 in time to sign the Declaration. When Jefferson sent his original draft to Lee, Lee commiserated with Jefferson's belief that the document had been "mangled," but observed that "the Thing is in its nature so good, that no Cookery can spoil the Dish for the palates of Freemen" (Chitwood 1967, 99).

See also Adams, John; Declaratory Act of 1766; Federalism; Jefferson, Thomas; Second Continental Congress; Virginia Declaration of Rights; Virginia Resolution of May 15, 1776

Further Reading

Burnett, Edmund C. 1964. *The Continental Congress*. New York: W. W. Norton.

Chitwood, Oliver Perry. 1967. *Richard Henry Lee: Statesman of the Revolution*. Morgantown: West Virginia University Library.

Cotter, Daniel A. June 19, 2017. "Richard Henry Lee and the first 'Declaration of Independence.'" *Chicago Daily Law Bulletin*, 5.

Dunning, William. 1903. "An Historical Phrase." *Annual Report of the American Historical Association for the Year 1902*. Vol. 1. Washington, DC: U.S. Government Printing Office.

Hays, Minis. 1898. "A Note on the History of the Jefferson Manuscript Draught of the Declaration of Independence in the Library of the American Philosophical Society." *Proceedings of the American Philosophical Society* 37 (January): 88–107.

Maier, Pauline. 1997. *American Scripture: Making the Declaration of Independence*. New York: Alfred A. Knopf.

Munves, James. 1978. *Thomas Jefferson and the Declaration of Independence: The Writing and Editing of the Document that Marked the Birth of the United States of America*. New York: Charles Scribner's Sons.

Selby, John E. 1988. *The Revolution in Virginia, 1775–1783*. Williamsburg, VA: Colonial Williamsburg Foundation.

Shestokas, David J. 2017. *Creating the Declaration of Independence*. Lemont, IL: Constitutionally Speaking.

Vile, John R. 2015. *Founding Documents of America: Documents Decoded*. Santa Barbara, CA: ABC-CLIO.

REVOLUTION

No document is more closely associated with the American Revolution than the Declaration of Independence. It sought to explain its decision for independence to both internal and external audiences. Curiously, although it laid the foundation for what is generally understood to be a right of revolution (at least in certain circumstances), it did not specifically use that word (Ginsberg 1984, 26), which did not come into widespread use to characterize the conflict against Britain until the 1780s (Rachum 1993, 81).

The first paragraph of the Declaration indicated that it had become "necessary for one people to dissolve the political bands which have connected them with another." After proclaiming that the purpose of government was to secure such rights as "life, liberty, and the pursuit of happiness," the second paragraph of the Declaration asserted that "whenever any form of government becomes destructive of these ends, it is the right of the people to alter or to abolish it." After indicating that "prudence indeed will dictate that governments long established should not be change for light & transient causes," the document further asserted that "when a long train of abuses and usurpations" indicate a desire of government to "reduce them under absolute despotism . . . it is their right, it is their duty, to throw off such government, & to provide new guards for their future security."

The Declaration's classification of the right to overturn despotic government as not simply a "right," but also a "duty" is especially fascinating. Theorists of rights often see them as correlative with duties. One who wants to speak or worship freely must be willing to accord the same rights to others. Whereas the king might stress the duty of obedience, the Declaration suggests, consistent with the views of John Locke as described below, that individuals have a duty to protect their unalienable rights. In serving on a congressional committee to recommend the Great Seal of the United States, Benjamin Franklin proposed a design picturing the Egyptians being swallowed by the Red Sea and surrounded by a motto saying, "Rebellion to Tyrants Is Obedience to God" (Sha'ban 2005, 59). Thomas Jefferson had, in turn, incorporated this motto on his personal seal.

There is general agreement that the philosophy embodied in these sentiments is similar to that which the English philosopher John Locke articulated in his *Second Treatise of Government.* This is especially true of in chapter 19, where he dealt with "the dissolution of governments." Because Locke believed that society preceded government, he thought that it was possible to dissolve the latter without dissolving the former, which would have thrust people back into the state of nature. For Locke, therefore, revolution did not necessitate anarchy. One indication that Congress shared this view was that it had already authorized states to draw up new constitutions to replace former British institutions.

Locke argued that government could be overthrown from without or dissolved from within. The latter occurred when the legislature was improperly altered, as when a ruler substituted his will for that of the legislature, when he hindered it from assembling, when he altered the elections, or when he delivered the people to the government of a foreign power (Locke [1690] 1924, 226). Government could also be dissolved when the king refused to enforce the law ([1690] 1924, 227) or when the legislature or executive acted contrary to their trust ([1690] 1924, 228). Notably, the charges that the Declaration leveled against the king and other British leaders included charges related to almost all of these.

Locke explained that "whenever the legislators endeavor to take away and destroy the property of the people, or to reduce them to slavery under arbitrary power, they put themselves into a state of war with the people, who are thereupon absolved from any farther obedience, and are left to the common refuge which God hath provided for all men against force and violence" ([1690] 1924, 229).

In defending himself against the charge that this analysis "lays a ferment for frequent rebellion" ([1690] 1924, 230), Locke made three arguments. First, he suggested that, theory or no theory, people would revolt when governments made them miserable. Second, in language that would be reflected in the Declaration of Independence, Locke observed that the people would not revolt over minor matters, "But if a long train of abuses, prevarications, and artifices, all tending the same way, make the design visible to the people . . . it is not to be wondered that they should then rouse themselves" ([1690] 1924, 231). Third, he suggested that his doctrine was, in fact, "the best fence against rebellion," because the true rebels are not people seeking to secure their rights but those "who, by force, break through, and, by force, justify their violation of them" ([1690] 1924, 231).

The Declaration's recognition that the people have the right "to alter or to abolish" destructive government suggested that they should attempt redress prior to rebellion. The penultimate paragraph of the Declaration thus indirectly referred to the Olive Branch Petition and other colonial publications and initiatives that had been designed to inform the British government and the British people of their grievances. When the English system thus showed itself incapable of peaceful legal change, the congressional delegates thought they had little choice but to use force of arms.

In a chapter asking, "Is There an American Right of Revolution?" Robert A. Goldwin argues that the term "right of revolution" does not appear until the mid-nineteenth century. Goldwin further attempts to distinguish the arguments of the Declaration from the right to revolution by suggesting (much as Locke had identified those who usurped government as the true rebels) that the only true governments are those based on consent. Because Goldwin does not believe the colonists had consented to British practices, there was no legitimate government left against which to revolt (1950, 46–54). The Declaration thus offered no general right of revolution, nor does it offer a general "right of national 'self-determination'" (Mansfield 1976, 152) but only the right to revolt against governments that were not based on the consent of the people.

Although the American Revolution was certainly an important event that stimulated internal examination of existing institutions that fell short of its ideals (Wood 1981; Bailyn 1967) as well as revolutionary sentiment elsewhere (Armitage 2007), many scholars agree with Martin Diamond's assessment that it was "the Revolution of Sober Expectations" (1976, 23). The primary goal that the Declaration of Independence announced was that of securing the rights to "life, liberty and the pursuit of happiness." The latter right suggests that individuals, rather than the state, would, within the limits of law, be responsible for securing their own happiness. American revolutionaries were not so much seeking to assert new rights as to secure rights that they thought they had previously exercised. In contrast to the French (1789) and Russian Revolutions (1917), there was no domestic king or noblemen to overthrow, the revolution resulted in little class warfare, and while states would in time disestablish state churches, those establishments that remained in 1776 were relatively mild (Kristol 1976; Malia 2006).

The American system of representative government seeks to keep leaders accountable to the people through a system of regular elections and attempts to secure individual rights through a written constitution enforceable in courts. Article V of the U.S. Constitution further established a way to alter the document through peaceful means, thus providing "an alternative to revolution" (Vile 1991, 173).

See also Charges against the King and Others; Dissolution of Government; Locke, John; Olive Branch Petition; State Constitutions and the Declaration of Independence

Further Reading

Armitage, David. 2007. *The Declaration of Independence: A Global History*. Cambridge, MA: Harvard University Press.

Bailyn, Bernard. 1967. *The Ideological Origins of the American Revolution*. Cambridge, MA: Belknap Press of Harvard University Press.

Diamond, Martin. 1976. "The Revolution of Sober Expectations." In *America's Continuing Revolution*, 23–40. Garden City, NY: Anchor Press.

Dipiero, Joseph. 2017. "The Common Law of Rebellion." *Georgetown Journal of International Law* 48 (Winter): 605–633.
Ginsberg, Robert. 1984. "Suppose that Jefferson's Rough Draft of the Declaration of Independence Is a Work of Political Philosophy." *Eighteenth Century* 25 (Winter): 25–43.
Goldwin, Robert A. 1990. *Why Blacks, Women, and Jews Are Not Mentioned in the Constitution, and Other Unorthodox Views*. Washington, DC: AEI Press.
Kristol, Irving. 1976. "The American Revolution as a Successful Revolution." In *America's Continuing Revolution*, 1–22. Garden City, NY: Anchor Press..
Locke, John. (1690) 1924. *Two Treatises of Government*. London: Dent, Everyman's Library.
Lynd, Staughton. 2009. *Intellectual Origins of American Radicalism*. New ed. New York: Cambridge University Press.
Malia, Martin. 2006. *History's Locomotives: Revolutions and the Making of the Modern World*. New Haven, CT: Yale University Press.
Mansfield, Harvey C., Jr. 1976. "The Right of Revolution." *Daedalus* 105 (Fall): 151–162.
Rachum, Illan. 1993. "From 'American Independence' to the 'American Revolution.'" *Journal of American Studies* 27 (April): 73–81.
Sha'ban, Fuad. 2005. *For Zion's Sake: The Judeo-Christian Tradition in American Culture*. Ann Arbor, MI: Pluto Press.
Vile, John R. 1992. *The Constitutional Amending Process in American Political Thought*. New York: Praeger.
Wood, Gordon S. 1991. *The Radicalism of the American Revolution*. New York: Vintage Books.

RHODE ISLAND AND ITS SIGNERS

The smallest of the thirteen colonies, Rhode Island was founded by Roger Williams and by other religious dissenters who had fled Massachusetts for religious liberty. In 1663, Charles II subsequently granted the colony a charter, to which it adhered until the 1840s. It was regarded as among the most democratic of the colonies.

Rhode Island was a leader among the eastern (northern) colonies in opposition to British policies. As a coastal colony, it was particularly concerned about British trade regulations. This had led in 1769 to the burning of the HMS *Liberty*, which the British had confiscated from John Hancock for alleged customs violations, and in 1772 to the burning of the HMS *Gaspee*, which was also involved in enforcing trade regulations. A commission appointed to look into the latter matter was unable to gather sufficient evidence to transport anyone to England for prosecution, a move that would undoubtedly have provoked even further alarm.

Closely influenced by events in nearby Massachusetts, the city of Providence had its own Tea Party on March 2, 1775. Rhode Island was the first to issue a call for a congress to protest the Coercive (Intolerable) Acts, and the first to appoint delegates to the anticipated meeting (Conley 1988, 271). Moreover, the state, which British troops occupied during the first three years of the war, had created an army of 1,500 men shortly after the fighting began at Lexington and Concord, and had already renounced its own allegiance to the king on May 4, 1776.

Both Rhode Island delegates to the Second Continental Congress voted for independence. William Ellery (1727–1820) was a lawyer and merchant who had graduated from Harvard but had been unable to study law until he was 40.

He had arrived at the Congress as a replacement for Samuel Ward, a former governor who had died from smallpox. Ellery may be best known for his observations at the signing of the Declaration: "I was determined to see how they all looked as they signed what might be their death warrant. I placed myself beside the secretary Charles Thomson and eyed each closely as he affixed his name to the document. Undaunted resolution was displayed in every countenance" (Kiernan and D'Agnese 2009, 47). Serving fairly continually in Congress for the next ten years, Ellery's home was partially burned during the war, but George Washington appointed him as customs collector of Newport in 1790, and he held this position for almost 30 years.

Ellery's colleague Stephen Hopkins (1707–1785) was a merchant and farmer who had served many terms as state governor as well as chief justice of the Superior Court, and a chancellor of Brown University. Hopkins is believed to be one of the figures in a satirical painting of frolicking ship captains in a painting by John Greenwood (Potvin 2011, 20). Hopkins is probably best known for his wide-brimmed hat (characteristic of Quakers of his day), for his love of Jamaican rum, for his good sense of humor, and for his wobbly signature, which appears to be the result of his age and of palsy. Although he introduced the first antislave legislation in Rhode Island, he owned a number of slaves, for which the Society of Friends expelled him. Hopkins's House, which was built around 1743, was moved in 1927 and remains a tourist site on the east side of Providence.

Although a leader in the movement for Independence, Rhode Island proved to be far less eager to accept the Constitution that delegates hammered out in the summer of 1787. Indeed, Rhode Island was the only state that did not send delegates to that convocation. Ever jealous of state power, the state did not ratify the Union until after the new government had already gone into effect.

See also Signers, Collective Profile

Further Reading

Conley, Patrick T. 1988. "First in War, Last in Peace: Rhode Island and the Constitution, 1786–1790." *The Constitution and the States: The Role of the Original Thirteen in the Framing and Adoption of the Federal Constitution*, edited by Patrick T. Conley and John P. Kaminski, 269–294. Madison, WI: Madison House.

Hall, David D. 2011. *A Reforming People: Puritanism and the Transformation of Public Life in New England*. Chapel Hill: University of North Carolina Press.

Kiernan, Denise, and Joseph D'Agnese. 2009. *Signing Their Lives Away: The Fame and Misfortune of the Men Who Signed the Declaration of Independence*. Philadelphia: Quirk Books.

Potvin, Ron M. 2011. "Washington Slept Here? Reinterpreting the Stephen Hopkins House," *History News* 66 (Spring): 17–20.

Rhode Island in the American Revolution. An Exhibition from the Library and Museum Collections of The Society of the Cincinnati. Washington, DC: October 17, 2000–April 14, 2001. http://www.societyofthecincinnati.org/pdf/downloads/exhibition_RhodeIsland.pdf.

THE RIGHTS OF GREAT BRITAIN ASSERTED AGAINST THE CLAIMS OF AMERICA (MACPHERSON)

The Scottish poet James Macpherson (1736–1796) anonymously authored a fascinating document entitled *The Rights of Great Britain Asserted against the Claims of America: Being an Answer to the Declaration of the General Congress* (1776). Although sometimes mistakenly taken to be an answer to the Declaration of Independence (Tyler 1896, 3), it was in fact, an answer to the Congress's earlier Declaration on the Necessity of Taking Up Arms. Although that Declaration was phrased in language that stressed the hope for reconciliation, Macpherson's answer clearly regarded it as the declaration of rebellion that the Declaration of Independence proved to be.

Accusing members of Congress of "willfully or ignorantly" misrepresenting the situation and of making deductions "from premises that have no foundation in truth" (1776, 2), Macpherson based his argument on the doctrine that "The Legislature [Parliament] is another name for the Constitution of the State; and, in fact, the State itself" (1776, 3). He further argued that "Representation never accompanied Taxation in any State" (1776, 4), pointing to numerous areas within Britain itself (to say nothing of the colonies) that had no parliamentary representation, but suggesting that had Americans actually sought such representation, it might have been given to them (1776, 8).

Macpherson did not believe that colonial charters exempted the colonies from taxation but indicated that even if they had, Parliament could revoke such an exemption. Scoffing at the idea that the colonists had settled America on their own, he pointed to large sums of money that the British government had expended on colonial support. In an interesting aside, he observed that "had Canada remained in the hands of the French, the Colonies would have remained dutiful subjects" (1776, 15), because they would have realized the precariousness of their situation.

Macpherson further showed that many colonial complaints had their origins in policies begun long before George III, citing examples of admiralty trials without benefit of jury, restrictions on colonial legislation, control over colonial manufacturing and commerce, and duties. Complaints relating to British actions with regard to Boston needed to be considered in relation to the rebellion that was breaking out there. As if anticipating the Declaration of Independence, Macpherson praised the king for viewing himself as "the Monarch of ONE great and free nation, rather than the Sovereign of a number of petty States, weakened by their own disunion" (1776, 55). He further accused the colonists of having engaged in even greater war atrocities than they were attributing to the king, including behaviors generally attributed to Native America Indians (1776, 65).

Macpherson stressed British power and American weakness and accused Americans of "Parricide" (1776, 70). Language that the Declaration of Independence appeared to echo Macpherson ended by observing that "the law of God and of Nature is on the side of an indulgent Parent, against an undutiful Child; and should necessary correction render him incapable of future offence, he has only his own obstinacy and folly to blame" (1776, 80).

See also Declaration on the Causes and Necessity of Taking Up Arms

Further Reading

Macpherson, James. 1776. *The Rights of Great Britain Asserted against the Claims of America: Being an Answer to the Declaration of the General Congress*. London: Printed for T. Cadell.

Tyler, Moses Coit. 1896. "The Declaration of Independence in the Light of Modern Criticism." *North American Review* 163 (July): 1–16.

RUSH'S (BENJAMIN) CHARACTERS OF THE SIGNERS

Although many of the delegates to the Second Continental Congress wrote letters in which they described fellow delegates and there have been many collections of the lives of the signers, only one of the delegates, Dr. Benjamin Rush, attempted to pen descriptions of each of the delegates who signed. Similarly, only one delegate, William Pierce, compiled biographies of most of the individuals who attended the Constitutional Convention of 1787 (Vile 2015).

Benjamin Rush served as a delegate from Pennsylvania in the Second Continental Congress and signed the Declaration of Independence. He was also briefly surgeon general of the Continental Army but had to resign in 1778 because of his association with Washington's critics in the Conway Cabal. Rush was an early opponent of slavery and a strong supporter of the Federal Constitution. Rush drafted short character sketches of most of the signers of the Declaration of Independence. (National Archives)

Pierce's account has the advantage that he wrote it either at the time of the Constitutional Convention or shortly thereafter. Rush did not complete his sketches until 1800 and reported that he had written them during the Revolutionary War and subsequently added to them (1905, 101). Like Pierce's later sketches (which had not been published at the time that Rush wrote), Rush's contain a fascinating mix of fact and opinion.

Rush's descriptions are found in an autobiography that he published "for the benefit of his Descendants." It is found in a chapter entitled "An Account of Political and Military Events and Observations," which detailed some of Rush's own interactions with fellow delegates. In one of the more interesting passages, Rush described how he helped Thomas Paine secure a publisher for *Common Sense*. He also explained how he met and married the daughter of Richard Stockton.

Rush divided Americans into Tories and Whigs, which he in turn divided into various subgroups while acknowledging that "There were besides these two classes of people, a great number of persons who were neither Whigs nor Tories" (1905, 89). Much like words that he would quote from Charles Thomson, Rush also opined that before giving too much credit to "Human wisdom" (1905, 89), individuals should know that "Not one man in a thousand contemplated or wished for the independence of our country in 1774, and but a few of those who assented to it foresaw the immense influence it would soon have upon the national and individual character of the Americans" (1905, 90). On a sadder note, he observed that: "I was surprised to observe how little of the spirit of that instrument [Declaration of Independence] actuated many of the members of Congress who had just before subscribed it" (1905, 90).

Rush, like Pierce, arranged his portraits by states from North to South. Most consisted of a single sentence or two. Thus his initial description of Josiah Bartlett simply refers to him as "a practitioner of physic, of excellent character and strongly attached to the liberties of his country" (1905, 101).

Rush knew some delegates far better than others, and he recognized that some delegates had contributed far more to the American Revolution and to the Declaration of Independence. Thus, he devoted considerably more attention to delegates like Samuel Adams, John Adams, Roger Sherman, John Witherspoon, Robert Morris, Benjamin Franklin, and Thomas Jefferson than to others. Rush generally began by identifying the occupation of each signer and then described one or more prominent character qualities.

Not all of Rush's comments were positive. He thus observed that Matthew Thornton "was ignorant of the world" (1905, 102) that Samuel Chase "possessed more learning than knowledge, and more of both than judgment" (1905, 113), that Robert Treat Paine had been labeled "the objection maker" (1905, 107), and that Thomas Stone "spoke well, but was sometimes mistaken upon plain subject" (1905, 114). Rush immediately followed this assessment by saying that "I once heard him say, 'he had never known a single instance of a negro being contented in slavery'" (1905, 114), but it is unclear whether Rush thereby intended to dismiss this statement as one that was similarly mistaken.

Rush took special efforts to identify individuals that he thought had a national perspective and those that he thought largely reflected the prejudices of their own state or region. Thus, he observed that Samuel Huntingdon of Connecticut was "wholly free from State prejudices" (1905, 109) while William Williams from the same state was "often misled by State prejudices" (1905, 109). Rush pinned a very succinct description of himself, writing only that "He aimed well" (1905, 111).

Rush's extensive description of John Adams identified him as "the first man of the house" (1905, 103) and emphasized his early advocacy of independence in that body as well as his own personal friendship with him. Rush's description of Samuel Adams further identified him as an early advocate of independence who "seldom spoke in Congress, but was active out of doors" (1905, 103). He said of Adams that even if 999 of 1,000 Americans had perished in the war, "he would vote for that war, rather than see his country enslaved" (1905, 102). Similarly, he reported that Stephen Hopkins had said that "The liberties of America would be a cheap purchase with the loss of 100,000 lives" (1905, 108). Rush emphasized Roger Sherman's piety and said that he "was so regular in business, and so democratic in his principles that he was called by one of his friends 'a republican machine'" (1905, 108).

Rush judged that John Witherspoon's "influence was less than might have been expected from his abilities and knowledge owing in part to his ecclesiastical character," but further noted that Witherspoon was "free from the illiberality which sometimes accompanies zeal" (1905, 110). On a more substantive issue, Rush said that Witherspoon had opposed a congressional resolution that called the English king a tyrant on the basis "that this epithet was both *false* and *undignified*" (1905, 110). He had explained that the king "was beloved and respected by his subjects in Great Britain, and perhaps the more, for making war upon us" (1905, 110).

Rush observed that Robert Morris "was opposed to the *time* (not the *act*) of the declaration of independence, but he yielded to no man in his exertions to support it and a year after it took place, he publicly acknowledged on the floor of Congress, that he had been mistaken in his former opinion as to its *time*, and said that it would have been better for our country had it been declared *sooner*" (1905, 111). Rush observed that Franklin had "treated kingly power at all times with ridicule and contempt and that "He early declared himself in favor of independence" (1905, 111). Rush identified Thomas Jefferson as "the penman of the declaration of independence" (1905, 114). Rush testified to having seen one of Jefferson's original copies of his Declaration that "contained a noble testimony against negro slavery which was struck out in its passage through Congress" (1905, 115).

Rush observed that "The act for renouncing the allegiance to the King of Great Britain by the declaration of independence has ever been considered as a very bold one. It was done in the face of a powerful army, with but slender resources for war, and without any assurance of foreign aid" (1905, 117). Rush further noted that New Hampshire, Massachusetts, Connecticut, Rhode Island, Virginia, and Georgia had been in the forefront of the movement for independence and that other states had followed their lead more reluctantly and that 34 of 54 signers of the Declaration had died before the year 1800 (1905, 117).

Rush went on to provide additional sketches of John Dickinson, Charles Thomson, Thomas Mifflin, General Charles Lee, General Horatio Gates, General Nathanael Greene, General Henry Knox, Lord Sterling, General Alexander McDougall, Commodore John Paul Jones, and General Benedict Arnold. Rush was quite generous to John Dickinson, observing that "Few men wrote, spoke and acted more for their country from the year 1764 to the establishment of the federal government, than Mr. Dickinson" (1905, 117). Much as in his description of Robert Morris, Rush observed that John Dickinson "was opposed to the declaration of independence at the time it took place, but concurred in supporting it" (1905, 118). Rush further observed that Charles Thomson, the secretary of the Second

Continental Congress, believed that the nation was less indebted to the men who proposed the Declaration than "to the agency of Providence for its successful issue" (1905, 118).

See also *Common Sense* (Paine); Signers, Collective Profile

Further Reading

Alkana, Joseph. 1992. "Spiritual and Rational Authority in Benjamin Rush's Travels through Life." *Texas Studies in Literature and Language* 34 (Summer): 284–300.

D'Elia, Donald J. 1974. "Benjamin Rush: Philosopher of the American Revolution." *Transactions of the American Philosophical Society* 64:1–113.

Lambert, Paul F. 1972. "Benjamin Rush and American Independence." *Pennsylvania History: A Journal of Mid-Atlantic Studies* 39 (October): 443–454.

Rush, Benjamin. 1905. *A Memorial containing Travels Through Life or Sundry Incidents in the Life of Dr. Benjamin Rush*. Lanoraie, QC: Louis Alexander Biddle. Note: For a condensed version that reorders the names and focuses only on those who signed the Declaration, see "Delegate Discussions: Benjamin Rush's Characters." Course of Human Events. https://declaration.fas.harvard.edu/blog/dd-rush.

Vile, John R. 2015. *The Wisest Council in the World: Restoring the Character Sketches by William Pierce of Georgia of the Delegates to the Constitutional Convention of 1787*. Athens: University of Georgia Press.

Vile, John R. 2019. *A Constellation of Great Men: Exploring the Character Sketches by Dr. Benjamin Rush of Pennsylvania of the Signers of the Declaration of Independence*. Clark, NJ: Talbot Publishing.

S

SCOTTISH ENLIGHTENMENT

Scholars continue to look for the philosophical underpinnings of the Declaration of Independence. This task is difficult because the Founders drank from many philosophic streams. Carl Becker, who has written one of the most influential interpretations of the Declaration ([1922] 1970), stressed the influence of the English philosopher John Locke, a classical liberal thinker whose natural rights philosophy is often accused of being excessively individualistic. Others have stressed more classical ideas of natural law or civic republicanism, which was sometimes mediated through Protestant theology.

In 1978, Garry Wills published a book in which he argued that the most important influence on the Declaration had not been John Locke but a group of philosophers from Scotland, who were known as Common Sense philosophers. They got this name because they tended to eschew abstract reasoning (especially about epistemology, or the theory of knowledge) and stress common sense, a term that Thomas Paine used for his work critiquing the institution of monarchy and calling for a Declaration of Independence. These philosophers were also known for their advocacy of the idea that all individuals possessed a "moral sense," akin to conscience, that essentially enabled them to make the kind of judgments that would be necessary in order to base government on consent. Wills noted that philosophers such as Adam Ferguson (1723–1816), David Hume (1711–1776), Francis Hutcheson (1694–1746), Lord Kames (1695–1782), and Adam Smith (1723–1790) were widely known and that they influenced teaching at American colleges through the colonies. They included such individuals as the following: William Small, who taught Thomas Jefferson at William and Mary; James Wilson, who would teach law at the University of Pennsylvania; and John Witherspoon, the president of the College of New Jersey, today's Princeton, who signed the Declaration of Independence (Noll 1989).

Professor Ronald Hamowy has written a critique of Wills (1979) that is generally accepted among scholars in which he points out that put side by side, the Declaration much more closely resembles the language of John Locke than it does of Francis Hutcheson (1979, 506–508). Hamowy observes that it is not surprising that there are also parallels to Hutcheson because "Hutcheson was closely acquainted with Locke's political writings, which were of enormous importance in determining the direction and structure of his own conclusions on politics and especially on the right of resistance" (1979, 508). He further concludes that Wills's history is "'impressionistic' intellectual history, where breadth of coverage substitutes for scholarly substance" (1979, 523). Hamowy acknowledges, however, that "future scholars may feel called upon to consult *Inventing America* when investigating Jefferson's intellectual roots, for completeness' sake if for no other reason" (1979, 523). Wills's forays into contemporary eighteenth-century writings, especially Jefferson's own *Notes on the State of Virginia*, are certainly provocative and thought-provoking.

See also *Common Sense* (Paine); Laws of Nature and of Nature's God; Locke, John

Further Reading

Becker, Carl. (1922) 1970. *The Declaration of Independence: A Study in the History of Political Ideas*. New York: Vintage Books.

Hamowy, Ronald. 1979. "Jefferson and the Scottish Enlightenment: A Critique of Garry Wills's *Inventing America: Jefferson's Declaration of Independence*." *William and Mary Quarterly* 36 (January): 503–523.

Kloppenberg, James T. 1987. "The Virtues of Liberalism: Christianity, Republicanism, and Ethics in Early American Political Discourse." *Journal of American History* 74 (June): 9–33.

Noll, Mark A. 1989. *Princeton and the Republic, 1768–1822: A Search for a Christian Enlightenment in the Era of Samuel Stanhope Smith*. Princeton, NJ: Princeton University Press.

Robinson, Daniel N. 2007. "The Scottish Enlightenment and the American Founding." *Monist* 90 (April): 170–181.

Wills, Garry. 1978. *Inventing America: Jefferson's Declaration of Independence*. Garden City, NY: Doubleday.

SECOND CONTINENTAL CONGRESS

Although Thomas Jefferson was the chief author of the Declaration of Independence, he was part of a Committee of Five that the Second Continental Congress chose to draft the document. It was subsequently debated within that Congress before eventually being approved on July 4 and later signed by 56 of its members.

Precedents for the Continental Congresses included the Albany Congress in 1754, in which seven states assembled to discuss defensive measures against the French, and the Stamp Act Congress in 1765, in which 12 states had met to protest a tax that the colonists found to be particularly obnoxious. The First Continental Congress met from September 5 to October 26, 1774, to protest the Coercive Acts, which the British had largely adopted in reaction to the Boston Tea Party. Its most significant achievement was the adoption of the Declaration and Resolves of 1774, which articulated colonial rights.

The term "Congress" had often been used to designate a temporary body, and James D. Drake observes that "when delegates converged in Philadelphia in the fall of 1774 to develop a response to the Coercive Acts, they had no expectation that their assembly would transform into a government" (2011, 162). Indeed, Drake believed that "the calling of a congress was itself a conciliatory gesture" (2011, 162) that had taken the place of implementing Boston's call for an immediate boycott of all trade with Great Britain. The delegates had variously been selected by state legislative bodies, by extralegal conventions, or by some combination of the two (Marsh 1941, 184). Moreover, although the convening of the Second Continental Congress in May 1775 came shortly after fighting between British and Americans had begun at Lexington and Concord, the date for the second Congress had been set by the previous one.

R. B. Bernstein believes that early congresses were constructed to blend two notions that were sometimes in tension with one another. What he calls the "Deliberative Model," which had been touted by Britain's Edmund Burke, stressed that elected representatives would meet, using parliamentary procedures, to deliberate on the people's behalf. By contrast, the "Representative Model" stressed that those who served were agents of the people and should be responsive to them. This model stressed the need for annual elections, rotation in office, and adherence to instructions by constituents (1999, 80–87).

The Congress faced many problems, with John Adams observing on July 24, 1775, that it seemed caught "between hawk and buzzard" (Pavlovsky 1977, 353). States often failed to pay delegates in a timely fashion, delegates found that they had to incur debts to pay living expenses, many delegates were absent for long periods, and those who remained had to bear heavy workloads. One-year terms resulted in constant turnover, which, while arguably keeping delegates responsive to their constituents, may specialization difficult. Deliberations were often desultory and trivial.

As the conflict escalated, the Continental Congress became the de facto government of the 13 colonies, particularly with respect to directing the war against Britain and with respect to foreign affairs in general. The Congress largely acted through committees, and, in a pattern that would be reflected in many state constitutions of the period, there was no independent executive or judicial branch. James D. Drake believes that the Congress, especially when designated as the "Continental Congress" ("General" was sometimes used in its place), helped to draw the colonists together, with their identity shaped in part by a common geography (2011).

Delegates to the Congress, in which all 13 states were represented, but in which each had a single vote, were divided by region—eastern (northern), middle, and southern. Often delegates from the same state were further divided among those who thought that the colonies should declare immediate independence and those who hoped either for delay or reconciliation. The adoption of the Olive Branch Petition of 1775 was one indication of this.

In May 1776, the Second Continental Congress authorized states to replace royal governments that were collapsing in the colonies. When Richard Henry Lee introduced three resolutions on June 7, 1776, they included not only a call for a declaration of independence but also calls for seeking foreign allies and for establishing a more permanent form of governance. Although not all delegates agreed, some thought that a Declaration was an essential element in getting foreign recognition and support. Still, Congress chose to delay discussion on the Declaration of Independence for three weeks, as delegates waited for instructions from their constituents authorizing or advising them to vote for independence.

John Dickinson had been appointed to replace an institution based on custom with a written constitution. Congress did not vote on this document until 1777, during which time the document was revised, and the last state (the document required that it be unanimously ratified) did not ratify until 1781. With respect to

Congress, this document largely formalized procedures that were already in place, including equal state representation. Delegates were to be elected by state legislatures and to serve one-year terms. States could have from two to seven delegates.

The Second Continental Congress transitioned to the Congress under the Articles of Confederation between May 1 and November 1, 1781. Despite some remarkable achievements, most notably negotiating an alliance with France (Kite 1928), successfully prosecuting the Revolutionary War, and adopting the Northwest Ordinance of 1787, this Congress was replaced by the Constitution created in a convention in Philadelphia in the summer of 1787. It replaced a unicameral body with one that was bicameral; based representation in one of the houses according to population; and vested Congress with increased powers, balanced against independent executive and judicial branches.

See also Committee Responsible for Writing the Declaration of Independence; Declaration and Resolves of the First Continental Congress (1774); International Law; Northwest Ordinance of 1787; Olive Branch Petition; Resolutions Introduced by Richard Henry Lee (June 7, 1776); U.S. Constitution and the Declaration of Independence

Further Reading

Bernstein, R. B. 1999. "Parliamentary Principles, American Realities: The Continental and Confederation Congresses, 1774–1789." In *Inventing Congress: Origins and Establishment of the First Federal Congress*, edited by Kenneth R. Bowling and Donald R. Kennon, 76–108. Athens: Ohio University Press.

Burnett, Edmund C. 1964. *The Continental Congress*. New York: W. W. Norton.

Charlton, Thomas Patrick. 2012. *The First American Republic, 1774–1789: The First Fourteen American Presidents before Washington*. Bloomington, IN: AuthorHouse.

Drake, James D. 2011. *The Nation's Nature: How Continental Presumptions Gave Rise to the United States of America*. Charlottesville: University of Virginia Press.

Garver, Frank Harmon. 1932. "The Transition from the Continental Congress to the Congress of the Confederation." *Pacific Historical Review* 1 (June): 221–234.

Irvin, Benjamin H. 2003. "The Attraction of the Continental Congress." *Pennsylvania Legacies* 3 (May): 28–29.

Irvin, Benjamin H. 2011. *Clothed in Robes of Sovereignty: The Continental Congress and the People Out of Doors*. New York: Oxford University Press.

Kite, Elizabeth S. 1928. "The Continental Congress and France: Secret Aid and the Alliance, 1776–1778." *Records of the American Catholic Historical Society of Philadelphia* 39 (June): 155–174.

Marsh, Esbon R. 1941. "The First Session of the Second Continental Congress." *Historian* 3 (Spring): 181–194.

Marston, Jerrilyn Greene. 1987. *King and Congress: The Transfer of Political Legitimacy, 1774–1776*. Princeton, NJ: Princeton University Press.

Pavlovsky, Arnold M. 1977. "'Between Hawk and Buzzard': Congress as Perceived by Its Members, 1775–1783." *Pennsylvania Magazine of History and Biography* 101 (July): 349–364.

Rakove, Jack N. 1979. *The Beginnings of National Politics: An Interpretative History of the Continental Congress*. New York: Alfred A. Knopf.

York, Neil. 1998. "The First Continental Congress and the Problem of American Rights." *Pennsylvania Magazine of History and Biography* 122 (October): 354–383.

SECRECY

On November 9, 1775, the Second Continental Congress adopted a resolution. It provided "That every member of this Congress considers himself under the ties of virtue, honour, and love of his country, not to divulge, directly or indirectly, any matter or thing agitated or debated in Congress, before the same shall have been determined, without leave of the Congress; nor any matter or thing determined in Congress, which a majority of the Congress shall order to be kept secret." It further specified that "if any member shall violate this agreement, he shall be expelled from this Congress, and deemed an enemy to the liberties of America, and liable to be treated as such; and that every member signify his consent to this agreement by signing the same" ("Resolution of Secrecy").

This resolution evidences the extremely delicate nature of what Congress was debating. It also highlights the possibility that publication of speeches could subject members to accusations of treason, which carried the death penalty.

Congress did keep journals, which, when published, provided key measures, but it did not always release them contemporaneously. Congress thus waited until news of American victories at Trenton and Princeton in January 1777 to release the names of the individuals who had signed the Declaration of Independence.

Eighteenth-century Americans had a high rate of literacy and were served by many newspapers. Given the variety of pamphlets that were published on all sides of the issue—most notably Thomas Jefferson's *Summary View of the Rights of British America* and Paine's *Common Sense*—and the resolutions that state delegations adopted urging or permitting their delegations to vote for independence, the public clearly knew that the prospect of independence was a key issue. While the public was far from completely unified, few could have been surprised when John Hancock sent copies of the Declaration to state leaders.

In addition to contemporaneously published pamphlets, modern scholars get much of their information from letters that congressional delegates wrote and received during this time as well as from their later recollections. Jefferson's pride in his original composition, which he mailed to a number of friends, also provide details about which parts Congress altered and which ones it did not.

The debates on the Declaration of Independence itself took place over a relatively short period (July 1 to July 4, 1776) and were held in a Committee of the Whole. Unfortunately, no one took notes of these debates as carefully as James Madison would take of the much longer deliberations over the U.S. Constitution in the Convention of 1787.

See also *Common Sense* (Paine); Goddard Printing of the Declaration of Independence; *A Summary View of the Rights of British America* (Jefferson); Treason

Further Reading

Friedenwald, Herbert. 1897. "The Journals and Papers of the Continental Congress." *Pennsylvania Magazine of History and Biography* 21:161–184.

"Resolution of Secrecy Adopted by the Continental Congress, November 9, 1775." http://avalon.law.yale.edu/18th_century/const01.asp.

SELF-EVIDENT TRUTHS

Thomas Jefferson's original draft of the second paragraph of the Declaration proclaimed that "We hold these truths to be sacred & undeniable." Sometime prior to congressional debates, he altered this to say that "We hold these truths to be self-evident." At least one commentator believes that that change not only made the terminology more succinct but that "Jefferson adapted a word from natural philosophy to politics and made the Law of Nature akin to the Law of Reason" (Hawke 1964, 155).

Even as amended, the expression is subject to criticism that it is naïve. It appears to reflect the more optimistic epistemological certainty of the Enlightenment, and of Whig political thought (See Darsey 1997, 35–60), which has been undermined both by subsequent studies both of the human mind and the way its grasp of truth may be distorted. Moreover, today's nature may seem less predictable than did the Newtonian perception of a well-ordered universe.

Modern thinkers are more likely to think that all beliefs are shaped by history and are therefore likely to question the idea of immutable truth, unless perhaps the truth that all is relative! The very fact that the Congress was setting forth a position at odds with that of the king and Parliament suggests that opinions would differ based on perspectives and that, in such matters, there might be no single "truth."

Mortimer J. Adler and William Gorman have set forth one plausible understanding of self-evident truths by relating the idea to "the sciences of logic and mathematics" (1975, 30). By this understanding, self-evident truths correspond to fundamental axioms, which then become the premises upon which other proofs are based. The classic example is the proposition that the whole is greater than any one of its part. Such an axiom, while not universally recognized, would be evident to anyone who understood the meaning of the terms. Notably, in his Gettysburg Address, President Abraham Lincoln said that the nation had been founded on the "*proposition* that all men are created equal."

Isaac Newton and other natural philosophers of his day used the term "natural laws" in a similar fashion. As I. Bernard Cohen has observed, "Every Newtonian was full convinced that Newton's three laws of motion were the incontestable foundation of any true understanding of nature, just as the Euclidean axioms are the incontestable foundation of geometry" (1995, 128).

The Declaration of Independence identifies five truths as self-evident. As Alan Grimes has observed, each is introduced by the word "that" (1976, 2). These respective truths are: "that all men are created equal"; that their Creator has endowed them "with certain unalienable rights"; that these include "life, Liberty, and the pursuit of happiness"; that governments are created to protect these rights and rest on "the consent of the governed"; and that people have the right to alter governments that do not secure such rights and create new ones.

In asserting the first of these truths, the Declaration was arguing that, as members of the same species, no individual or group of individuals could claim domination over another by right of birth or heredity, or what British kings might call "divine right." The Declaration further traced the idea of common humanity to the possession of common rights and proceeded, much as a geometric proof, to claim that people have the right both to secure such rights by dissolving governments and instituting new ones when existing governments do not accomplish this goal.

Adler and Gorman further argued that it is important to recognize that the term "self-evident" is not the same as "the obvious." As they explain, "Many statements may be accepted by many persons as obvious that, upon examination, are not in the strict logical sense self-evident" (1975, 30). They further argue that "the meanings of the term in some self-evident propositions may require prolonged reflection before they are adequately comprehended. The proposition here declared a self-evident truth—that all men are equal—is certainly less obvious than the axiom concerning the relation between a whole and its parts" (1976, 30).

Moreover, the words "we hold" are not so much designed to establish that everyone would adhere to such "self-evident truths," but that a majority of citizens in the former 13 colonies now did (Zuckert 1987, 322; Cohen 1995, 128). Christians, or other groups of believers, might assert what they believe when they repeat a creed, fully confident that what they are asserting is true, but recognizing that what largely sets them apart as believers is their adherence to such fundamentals. So too, the Declaration might affirm as self-evident, propositions, or truths, that others have not yet contemplated or comprehended but that, if they did, would lead them to the same conclusions. The doctrine of self-evidence in the Declaration might suggest, however, that its truths are purely a result of reason or intuition (Levinson 1979, 853) without necessarily meaning that they would thereby contradict divine revelation.

If so interpreted, the words suggest that for all individuals who accept the same premises as the Americans, then what they are doing is fully justified. If, by contrast, one believes that some individuals are born with royal blood or special privileges, that they are not therefore equal, that they do not have rights simply as a result of their status as humans, that government is created for a primary purpose other than to protect rights, or that any disobedience to established authority is therefore unwarranted or sinful, then they might embrace different conclusions.

Owen Anderson further explains that "for an idea or belief to be self-evident means that once the concepts are grasped, the truth of the belief is understood" (2017, 22). Illustrating with the laws of "identify, excluded middle, and noncontradiction," Anderson also observes that "people can disagree about what is self-evident" (2017, 22).

In arguing for ratification of the U.S. Constitution in *Federalist No. 31*, Alexander Hamilton argued that there were certain "primary truths, or first principles, upon which all subsequent reasonings must depend" (Hamilton, Madison, and Jay [1787–1788] 1961, 193). Some were built on "an internal evidence which, antecedent to all reflection or combination, commands the assent of the mind." Similarly, in the fields of "ethics and politics," there are truths "which, if they cannot pretend to rank in the class of axioms, are yet such direct inferences from them, and so obvious in themselves, and so agreeable to the natural and unsophisticated dictates of common sense that they challenge the assent of a sound and unbiased mind with a degree of force and conviction almost equally irresistible" ([1787–1788] 1961, 193).

The words introduced by these "self-evident truths" come as close as one can probably come to an American creed. Once accepted, the "truths" of this creed stand not only in potential judgment against a British king but against failures within current American government that betray these ideals. Reformers including abolitionists, suffragists, civil rights reformers, and advocates of gay rights have thus often used the "self-evident truths" of the Declaration to argue for still greater human equality.

See also Creed/Scriptures; Laws of Nature and of Nature's God; "We" (First-Person Plural)

Further Reading

Adler, Mortimer J., and William Gorman. 1975. *The American Testament*. New York: Praeger.

Anderson, Owen. 2017. *The Declaration of Independence and God: Self-Evident Truths in American Law*. New York: Cambridge University Press.

Cohen, I. Bernard. 1995. *Science and the Founding Fathers: Science in the Political Thought of Jefferson, Franklin, Adams, and Madison*. New York: W. W. Norton.

Darsey, James. 1997. *The Prophetic Tradition and Radical Rhetoric in America*. New York: New York University Press.

Grimes, Alan P. 1976. "Conservative Revolution and Liberal Rhetoric: The Declaration of Independence." *Journal of Politics* 28 (August): 1–19.

Hamilton, Alexander, James Madison, and John Jay. (1787–1788) 1961. *The Federalist Papers*. New York: New American Library.

Hawke, David Freeman. 1964. *A Transaction of Free Men: The Birth and Course of the Declaration of Independence*. New York: Charles Scribner's Sons.

Howell, Wilbur Samuel. 1961. "The Declaration of Independence and Eighteenth-Century Logic." *William and Mary Quarterly* 18 (October): 463–484.

Levinson, Sanford. 1979. "Self-Evident Truths in the Declaration of Independence." *Texas Law Review* 57:847–858.

White, Morton. 1978. *The Philosophy of the American Revolution*. New York: Oxford University Press.

Zuckert, Michael P. 1987. "Self-Evident Truth and the Declaration of Independence." *Review of Politics* 49 (Summer): 319–339.

SIGNERS, COLLECTIVE PROFILE

The Signers of the Declaration of Independence and the U.S. Constitution are often grouped together as "Founding Fathers," and some of those who have studied these groups have considered them together. Just as modern members of Congress are generally wealthier, better educated, and drawn primarily from white-collar occupations, so too were most members of the Second Continental Congress.

Altogether, 56 delegates to the Second Continental Congress signed the Declaration of Independence. In some cases—like Robert Morris, for example—individuals signed who had not originally cast their votes for the document. Because the signing of the engrossed Declaration did not take place until August 2, and days following, some individuals also signed who had not actually been there for the vote.

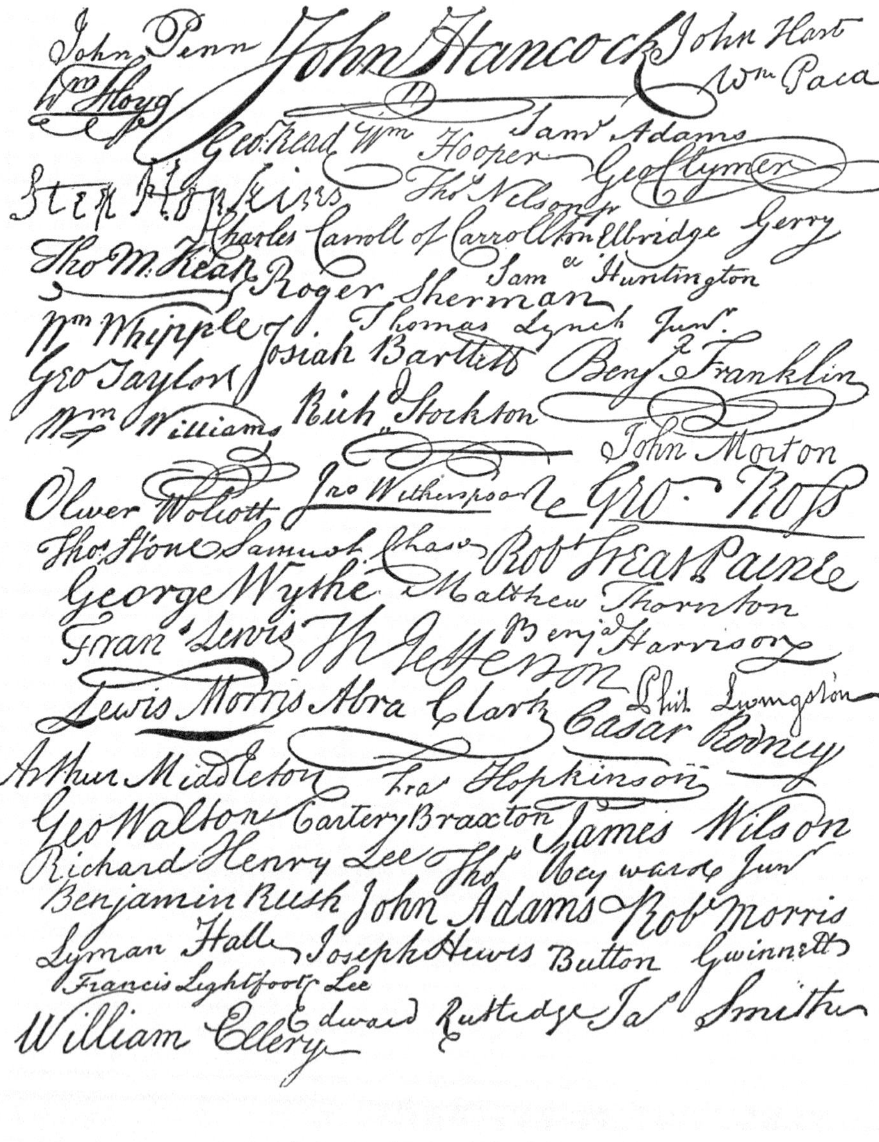

Reproduction of the signatures on the Declaration of Independence. (Universal History Archive/UIG via Getty Images)

Congressional rules called for the consent of nine states on key matters, but had states split, it would have sent a message or irresolution to the British. Each state had a single vote. When the vote on declaring independence took place on July 2, 1776, a majority of all state delegates present and voting favored independence. In the case of Pennsylvania, this was apparently achieved by the abstention of at least two delegates; in the case of Delaware, Caesar Rodney arrived on the second to break a tie. Delegates from New York had not received instructions on July 2 and accordingly abstained. When they received such approval, the vote then became unanimous.

Leadership in the Congress was highly decentralized. Like most other matters, Congress assigned the writing of the Declaration of Independence to a committee. The president of the Congress, John Hancock, like others who would follow, had relatively few powers (Wilson and Jillson 1989) other than that of facilitating discussion, at which he was quite adept.

Geographical Distribution and Slavery. It was common to divide the colonies into three sections—the northern, or eastern states, the middle states, and the southern states. By and large, the states in the north and south (with the notable exception of South Carolina) advocated independence earlier those in the middle states. Although slavery was concentrated in the south (and would become more so over time), a large majority of the delegates (41) owned or had owned slaves, including some from northern states ("How Many Signers . . .").

Origins. All the individuals who signed were white men (women did not yet have the franchise), and most had been born into families who had been in America for some time. Eight signers were born in the British Isles, with three (Matthew Thornton of New Hampshire and George Taylor and James Smith from Pennsylvania) from Ireland, one (Francis Lewis of New York) from Wales, two (James Wilson of Pennsylvania and John Witherspoon from New Jersey) from Scotland, and two (Robert Morris from Pennsylvania and Button Gwinnett from Georgia) from England (Robbins 1977, 78–79). Two delegates, Richard Henry Lee and Francis Lightfoot Lee, from Virginia, were brothers. Benjamin Rush was the son-in-law of New Jersey's Richard Stockton.

Ages. The oldest delegate (b. in 1706) was Benjamin Franklin, who was also the oldest at the Constitutional Convention of 1787. The youngest was Edward Rutledge of South Carolina, who was born in 1749. The average age was 45 (Brown 1976, 469). The last surviving member of the Congress was Charles Carroll of Carrollton, who died on November 14, 1832.

Education. Twenty-eight of the signers of the Declaration were college graduates (Tourtellot 1962). Although the University of New Jersey (today's Princeton) would produce the most college graduates at the Constitutional Convention, Harvard had this distinction in the Second Continental Congress. Eight of the signers, most from Massachusetts, were from Harvard; four were from Yale; four were from William and Mary; two were from Princeton; and two were from the College of Philadelphia (Brown, 80–81). Several had also studied abroad, three in Scotland. Six, including all four South Carolina delegates, were members of the Middle Temple in England, which educated barristers (lawyers) (Gregory, 1948, 875).

Studies have shown that "the vast majority of the British-Americans trained at the colleges in the two-decade period prior to the war became hard-core patriots" with approximately five of every six graduates supporting the Revolution (Tucker 1979, 17). Most college presidents of the day were Whigs, but even colleges like King's (today's Columbia), where the president was a Tory, ended up producing many who favored the revolutionary cause (Tucker 1979, 29–30). Most contemporary curricula, which were largely classical in nature, devoted significant attention to history and to Whig political thought.

Occupations. Twenty-two or more of the 56 signers were lawyers, including four of five men—all but Franklin—appointed to the Committee to write the Document. This made them the best-represented profession at the Congress. Many had read law under other lawyers (Thomas Jefferson, for example, had studied under George Wythe) at a time before official law schools had been established in the colonies, and others had studied at London's Middle Temple (Lambeth 1976).

Five signers (Josiah Bartlett, Lyman Hall, Benjamin Rush, Matthew Thornton, and Oliver Wolcott) were physicians (Spillane 1976), and one was a surveyor. Jefferson and Franklin were men of science (Cattell 1927). Two signers (Robert Treat Paine and Lyman Hall) had spent time as ministers, although neither had the reputation of Princeton's John Witherspoon. Richard D. Brown has labeled others as "landowners, planters, farmers, and surveyors" (1976, 82). There were also a fair number of what Brown calls "merchants, bankers, and manufacturers" (1976, 83).

Prior Governmental Service. Most of the delegates had been colonial legislators and/or judges prior to serving in the Continental Congress. John Adams and Thomas Jefferson would go on to serve as presidents of the United States. Three others were to become vice presidents, 2 would become Supreme Court justices, 4 would become U.S. senators, 4 would become ambassadors, 17 would become state governors, and they would fill many other posts (Tourtellot 19761).

Military Service. Prior to the official outbreak of the Revolutionary War, far fewer would have had the opportunity for military service than would those who would later serve in the Constitutional Convention of 1787. According to Arthur Tourtellot, 17 of the signers "saw military service, and twelve of these were actively in the field during the Revolution" (1962).

Families. All but 2 of the delegates were married, and, according to Tourtellot, 14 were married twice (1962). Although, like later delegates to the Convention, they tended to marry latter and have smaller families, they averaged six children (Tourtellot 1961). Consistent with greater cosmopolitanism, more of the delegates would have spouses from other states than would members of the general population (Brown 1976, 470).

Religion. Although some, like Jefferson and Franklin, are generally classified as Deists, all but Charles Carroll of Maryland (a Roman Catholic) who were officially identified with religious faith were Protestants. Of these, more than half were members of the Episcopalian (Anglican) Church—southern Anglicans were more likely to be Patriots than their northern counterparts (Holmes 1978), who often felt bound to the king because he headed the church, which they had taken an oath to uphold (Pennington 1939). Just over 23 percent of the delegates, most from the northeast states, were Congregationalists, just over 21 percent were Presbyterians, and at least two, Pennsylvania's Benjamin Rush and New Jersey's Richard Stockton, while probably best classified as Presbyterians, had some Quaker affiliations (Peltson 2012, 61; Jenkins 1929). Affiliations differed from state to state. Thus, all but one of the signers from New Jersey, who included cleric John Witherspoon, were Presbyterians. Religious delegates sometimes assigned apocalyptic significance to the struggle with Britain (McKenna 2007).

Although some alleged that the number is much higher, eight of the signers have been documented as members of the Masons. They were Benjamin Franklin, John Hancock, Joseph Hewes, William Hooper, Robert Treat Paine, Richard Stockton, George Walton, and William Whipple.

Other. Several members of the Second Continental Congress, namely Benjamin Franklin, Robert Morris, John Dickinson, Elbridge Gerry, Roger Sherman, James Wilson, George Clymer, George Wythe, and George Read, later served at the Constitutional Convention of 1787, and all of them (one by proxy) except Gerry (who was an Anti-Federalist) and Wythe (who had gone home to take care of his wife) would sign the resulting document. Scholars believe that many of the Founders were motivated by the desire for fame, the love of which "encourages a man to make history, to leave the mark of his deeds and his ideals on the world" thus "transforming egotism and self-aggrandizing impulses into public service" (Adair 1976, 11, 8).

See also Signing of the Declaration of Independence; Slavery

Special Note: For individual signers, please check the entry connected to the state that they represented in Congress.

Further Reading

Adair, Douglass 1974. "Fame and the Founding Fathers." In *Fame and the Founding Fathers: Essays*, edited by Trevor Colbourn, 3–26. New York: Norton.

Brown, Richard D. 1976. "The Founding Fathers of 1776 and 1787: A Collective View." *William and Mary Quarterly* 33 (July): 465–480.

Cain, Aine. July 3, 2017. "Who Signed the Declaration of Independence?" http://www.businessinsider.com/who-signed-the-declaration-of-independence-2017-6#elbridge-gerry-25.

Cattell, J. McKeen. 1927. "Science, the Declaration, Democracy." *Scientific Monthly* 24 (March): 200–205.

Gregory, Tappan. 1948. "The Annual Address: 'Our Lives, Our Fortunes, and Our Sacred Honor." *American Bar Association Journal* 34 (October): 874–876, 969–974.

Holmes, David L. 1978. "The Episcopal Church and the American Revolution." *Historical Magazine of the Protestant Episcopal Church* 47 (September): 261–291.

"How Many of the Signers of the Declaration of Independence Owned Slaves?" http://www.mrheintz.com/how-many-signers-of-the-declaration-of-independence-owned-slaves.html.

Jenkins, Charles F. 1929. "The Two Quaker Signers." *Bulletin of Friends Historical Association* 18 (Spring): 1–32.

Lambeth, Harry J. 1976. "The Lawyers Who Signed the Declaration of Independence." *American Bar Association Journal* 62 (July): 868–873, 876–880.

McKenna, George. 2007. *The Puritan Origins of American Patriotism.* New Haven, CT: Yale University Press.

Miller, William B. 1958. "Presbyterian Signers of the Declaration of Independence." *Journal of the Presbyterian Historical Society* 36 (September): 139–179.

Pelton, Robert W. 2012. *Men of Destiny! Signers of Our Declaration of Independence and Our Constitution.* Knoxville, TN: Freedom and Liberty Foundation Press.

Pennington, Edgar Legare. 1939. "The Anglican Clergy of Pennsylvania in the American Revolution." *Pennsylvania Magazine of History and Biography* 63 (October): 401–439.

Robbins, Caroline. 1977. "Decision in '76: Reflections on the 56 Signers." *Proceedings of the Massachusetts Historical Society*, 3rd ser. 89:72–87.
"Signers of the Declaration of Independence." National Archives. https://www.archives.gov/founding-docs/signers-factsheet.
Spillane, J. D. 1976. "Doctors of 1776. *British Medical Journal* 1, no. 6025 (June 16): 1571–1574.
Tourtellot, Arthur Bernon. 1962. "We Mutually Pledge to Each Other Our Lives, Our Fortunes, and Our Sacred Honor." *American Heritage*. https://www.americanheritage.com/content/we-mutually-pledge-each-other-our-lives-our-fortunes-and-our-sacred-honor.
Tucker, Louis Leonard. 1979. "Centers of Sedition: Colonial Colleges and the American Revolution." *Proceedings of the Massachusetts Historical Society*, 3rd ser. 92:16–34.
Wilson, Rick K., and Calvin Jillson. 1989. "Leadership Patterns in the Continental Congress, 1774–1789." *Legislative Studies Quarterly* 14 (February): 5–37.

SIGNING OF THE DECLARATION OF INDEPENDENCE

The Declaration of Independence is only one of only a few documents that members of the Continental Congress individually signed. The others were the Petition of October 1774, the Olive Branch Petition, and the Articles of Confederation. Delegates to the U.S. Constitutional Convention would later do the same.

Congress voted for Richard Henry Lee's resolution for independence on July 2 and adopted the Declaration of Independence two days later. John Dunlap then printed the document, with only two names (both printed), those of John Hancock, the president of the Congress, and Charles Thomson, the secretary. It was titled "In CONGRESS, JULY 4, 1776, A DECLARATION BY THE REPRESENTATIVES OF THE UNITED STATES OF AMERICA, IN GENERAL CONGRESS ASSEMBLED." In the bottom in very small print, are the words "Philadelphia, Printed by John Dunlap." Although some delegates later recalled signing a document on July 4, and at least one scholar believes they were correct (Ritz 1986), no such document has been found, and the majority of historians believe it was not signed until later ("Unsullied by Falsehood," 2016).

After the New York delegation gave its consent to the Declaration on July 18, 1776, it was then engrossed in script (the only prior documents that the Congress had engrossed in script, albeit prior to printing, were "the Plan of Association, the Petition to the King, and the Olive Branch Petition" (Starr, 2002, 153), after which it was signed beginning on August 2 and apparently continuing for some time. It was headed with the words 'IN CONGRESS, JULY 4, 1776. THE UNANIMOUS DECLARATION OF THE THIRTEEN UNITED STATES OF AMERICA."

Delegates signed at the bottom in groups beginning with the northernmost state on the far right and continuing in six columns to the far left. John Hancock's bold signature was centered in the middle. Thomas Jefferson's was included with other signers from Virginia. Although delegates signed by states, in contrast to the Articles of Confederation and the Constitution, the individual states were not listed.

A total of 56 individuals signed the document.

A number of printings and engravings of the Document, included the recently discovered Sussex Declaration, have scrambled the names, possibly for the purpose of emphasizing the role of individuals rather than states in its formation. The Goddard printing of the Declaration in early 1777 read the names from right to left and thus reordered the signers' names while adding the names of the states that they represented.

Congress did not order copies of the Declaration of Independence that included the names of the signers until January 18, 1777, after revolutionary forces had captured Trenton and Princeton, New Jersey. John Hancock composed a circular letter to accompany these documents, which he sent to state legislatures. He observed that "As there is not a more distinguished event in the history of America, than the Declaration of her Independence,—nor any, that in all probability, will so much excite the attention of future ages, it is highly proper, that the memory of that transactions together with the causes that gave rise to it should be preserved in the most careful manner that can be devised" (Hancock 1777). He therefore transmitted the document and signatures to the legislatures and asked that they put them in their records as "a lasting testimony of your approbation of that necessary and important measure."

Thomas McKean of Delaware, the last signer of the Declaration, was under the impression that the Continental Congress had adopted a secret resolution requiring all incoming members to sign the Declaration as a way "to prevent traitors or spies from worming themselves amongst us" (Burnett 1921, 535). If he were correct, this would imply that adherence to the principles of the Declaration served for a time much like the current Constitution, to which all federal officers must pledge adherence before assuming office.

See also Captions of the Declaration of Independence; Dunlap Broadside Printing of the Declaration of Independence; Goddard Printing of the Declaration of Independence; Hancock's Letters Accompanying the Declaration of Independence; Sussex Declaration

Further Reading

Burnett, Edmund C., ed. 1921. *Letters of Members of the Continental Congress*, Vol. 1, *August 29, 1774 to July 4, 1776*. Washington, DC: Carnegie Institute.

Hancock, John. January 31, 1777. "Circular Letter from John Hancock to the State Legislatures." http://www.docsouth.unc.edu/csr/index.html/document/csr11-0249.

Malone, Dumas. 1954. *The Story of the Declaration of Independence*. New York: Oxford University Press.

Ritz, Wilfred J. 1986. "The Authentication of the Engrossed Declaration of Independence on July 4, 1776." *Law and History Review* 4 (Spring): 179–204.

Starr, Thomas. 2002. "Separated at Birth: Text and Context of the Declaration of Independence." *Proceedings of the American Antiquarian Society*. http://www.americanantiquarian.org/proceedings/44539508.pdf.

"Unsullied by Falsehood: The Signing." Course of Human Events. https://declaration.fas.harvard.edu/blog/signing.

SLAVERY

Of all the ills of the colonial world, none is likely to occupy a more prominent spot in modern consciousness than that of slavery. Although many Europeans

TO BE SOLD, on board the Ship *Bance-Iſland*, on tueſday the 6th of *May* next, at *Aſhley-Ferry*; a choice cargo of about 250 fine healthy

NEGROES,

juſt arrived from the Windward & Rice Coaſt. —The utmoſt care has already been taken, and ſhall be continued, to keep them free from the leaſt danger of being infected with the SMALL-POX, no boat having been on board, and all other communication with people from *Charles-Town* prevented.

Auſtin, Laurens, & Appleby.

N. B. Full one Half of the above Negroes have had the SMALL-POX in their own Country.

A notice from the 1780s advertising slaves for sale at Ashley Ferry outside of Charleston, South Carolina. Slavery in America began in the early 17th century and ended with the adoption of the Thirteenth Amendment in 1865. (Library of Congress)

willingly immigrated to North America (sometimes as indentured servants), most Africans who arrived did so on slave ships, which were notorious for their inhumane conditions and high death rates. Even those who found justification for slavery in the Bible or elsewhere often looked disdainfully on those who trafficked in slaves.

On its face, few documents appear more antislavery than the Declaration of Independence, which proclaims in its opening paragraph that "all men are created equal" and "endowed by their Creator with certain unalienable rights," which include "life, liberty, and the pursuit of happiness." Those who look behind this rhetoric, however, know that Thomas Jefferson, the primary author of the document, held numerous slaves. Indeed, some have even charged that he would not have later won the presidency had it not been for the three-fifths compromise, which provided extra Electoral College votes for slave states (Wills 2003). Further adding to the apparent hypocrisy is the evidence that Jefferson apparently kept one of his slaves, Sally Hemings, the half-sister of his wife who had died, as a mistress (Gordon-Reed, 2009). This irony is heightened by the fact that the disability of slavery passed from one generation to another, much like the privileges of hereditary succession determined accession to kingship within Great Britain.

Edwin Gittleman is among those who has noted that the Declaration of Independence resembles a slave narrative (1974), while Stephen Lucas observes that prior writers had expressed fears that Britain was attempting to enslave the colonies (1976, 102–104). It thus seeks to portray King George III of Great Britain as "having in direct object the establishment of an absolute tyranny over these states." T. H. Breen has observed that much of the rhetoric leading up to the American Revolution was phrased in terms of Americans being unwilling to be treated as slaves (1997, 32–33). In a speech to Jean Baptiste Ducoigne, the chief of the Kaskaskia nation, Jefferson later told him that the dispute with Great Britain had arisen because the British "at length began to say we were their slaves, and should do whatever they ordered us" (Jefferson 1781). Samuel Johnson, a Tory spokesman in Great Britain, rhetorically asked, "how is it that we hear the loudest yelps for liberty among the drivers of negroes?" (Kaplan 1976, 253).

Jefferson agonized as fellow delegates to the Second Continental Congress edited his draft of the Declaration. Its most extensive deletion was, in fact, a strong denunciation of the king for failing to stop the further introduction of slaves into the colonies *and* for encouraging them to revolt against their masters. This paragraph was to be the last of the Declaration's descriptions of war atrocities against the colonies and is as follows:

> He has waged cruel war against human nature itself, violating it's most sacred rights of life & liberty in the persons of a distant people, who never offended him, captivating and carrying them into slavery in another hemisphere, or to incur miserable death in their transportation thither. This piratical warfare, the opprobrium of *infidel* powers, is the warfare of the *Christian* king of Great Britain. determined to keep open a market where MEN should be bought & sold, he has prostituted his negative for suppressing every legislative attempt to prohibit or to restrain this execrable commerce: and that this assemblage of horrors might want to fact of distinguished die, he now is exciting these very people to rise in arms among us, and to purchase that liberty of which *he* has deprived them, by murdering the people upon whom *he* also obtruded them: thus paying off former crimes committed against the *liberties* of one people, with crimes which he urges them to commit against the *lives* of another. (Maier 1997, 239)

The first part of Jefferson's charge was likely meant to relate directly to the actions of Virginia governor Lord Dunmore. After seeking shelter in a ship, on November 7, 1775, he had issued an order proclaiming that "I do hereby further declare all indentured servants, Negroes, or others, (appertaining to Rebels,) free, that are able and willing to bear arms, they joining His Majesty's Troops, as soon as may be, for the more speedily reducing the Colony to a proper sense of their duty, to His Majesty's crown and dignity" (Quarles 1958, 494; David 2013, 105–108). The British would pursue a similar strategy, condemned in one of the verses of "The Star-Spangled Banner," during the War of 1812.

Jefferson said that his criticism of the slave trade had been "struck out in complaisance to S. Carolina & Georgia, who had never attempted to restrain the importation of slaves & who on the contrary still wished to continue it" (Boyd 1999, 37). Somewhat spreading the blame, however, he also observed that "our northern brethren also, I believe, felt a little tender under those censures; for tho' their people have very few slaves themselves, yet they had been pretty considerable carriers of them to others" (Body 1999, 37). While their sentiments may have played a role, other delegates may well have thought that it was hypocritical both to condemn the king for an institution with which many colonists had been comfortable while simultaneously criticizing him for encouraging them to pursue the rights that the Declaration was proclaiming to be unalienable!

It is notable that Jefferson refers to slaves as "MEN" (Richardson 1984, 452; Yarbrough 1991). However, in his *Notes on the State of Virginia*, Jefferson, while advocating a plan for emancipation, had also proposed sending freedman to foreign colonies because "Deep-rooted prejudices entertained by the whites; ten thousand recollections, by the blacks, of the injuries they have sustained; the provocations; the real distinctions which nature has made, and many other circumstances, will divide us into parties, and produce convulsions, which will probably [otherwise] never end but in the extermination of the one or the other race" ([1785] 1964, 132–133).

Jefferson doubted that whites and blacks could live peacefully together if the latter were freed. He appeared to view them, much like the British from whom the colonists were separating, as a distinct "people" rather than as part of the people who were revolting against the mother country.

Jefferson's characterization of the king's behavior as reflecting the practice of "*infidel*" (pagan) powers, like his emphasis on how such behavior is inconsistent with that of a "Christian king," is fascinating given Jefferson's relatively scarce references to the Deity in his original manuscript—the references other than to "nature and of nature's god" were added by the Congress. This passage also showed an awareness of the Barbary pirates, against whom the nations would war during Jefferson's presidency (Hitchens 2005, 28).

Steve Pincus is among those who believe that Jefferson's charge that the king had "prostituted his negative for suppressing every legislative attempt to prohibit or to restrain this execrable commerce," may be partially reflected in the charge that "He [the king] has refused his assent to laws the most wholesome and necessary for the public good" (2016, 128). Pincus observes that this "was language frequently deployed by Patriot critics of slavery and the slave trade" (2016, 128; see also Eicholz 2001, 523).

More directly, although it eliminated Jefferson's long condemnation of the king's role in importing slaves and encouraging them to revolt, the Congress inserted a provision, tied to the king's employment of Native American Indians, that "he has excited domestic insurrections amongst us." This passage almost surely was intended to echo the second part of Jefferson's original charge in somewhat more succinct and oblique terms (Kaplan 1976).

There is evidence that the colonial quest for independence and the document that justified it stirred concerns about slavery (Bailyn 1967, 232–246). While the institution continued to lose ground in Northern states, however, it continued in the South. When delegates drafted a constitution in Philadelphia in 1787 to replace the Articles of Confederation, they did not use the word "slavery," but they did not eliminate the institution. Instead, they permitted slave importation until 1808, provided for the return of those who were attempting to escape their servitude, and rewarded slaveholding states by counting slaves as three-fifths of a person for purposes of representation in the House of Representation and the Electoral College.

Abolitionists would use the language of the Declaration of Independence to question the institution of slavery (Bay 2006). Abraham Lincoln, who opposed the expansion of slavery into the territories, would later identify the Civil War with the cause of insuring that "all men are created equal." The war resulted in the adoption of the Thirteenth Amendment (1865). The Fourteenth Amendment (1868) subsequently guaranteed the "equal protection of the laws" to all persons.

See also Abolitionism; Charges against the King and Others; Jefferson, Thomas; Lincoln, Abraham; Native American Indians; People; Refused Assent to Colonial Laws (Charge #1)

Further Reading

Bailyn, Bernard. 1967. *The Ideological Origins of the American Revolution*. Cambridge, MA: Belknap Press of Harvard University Press.

Bay, Mia. 2006. "See Your Declaration Americans!!! Abolitionism, Americanism, and the Revolutionary Tradition in Free Black Politics." In *Americanism: New Perspectives on the History of an Ideal*, ed. Michael Kazin, and Joseph A. McCartin, 25–52. Chapel Hill: University of North Carolina Press.

Boyd, Julian P. 1999. *The Declaration of Independence: The Evolution of the Text*. Washington and Charlottesville: The Library of Congress in association with the Thomas Jefferson Memorial Foundation, Inc.

Breen, T. H. 1997. "Ideology and Nationalism on the Eve of the American Revolution: Revisions Once More in Need of Revising." *Journal of American History* 84 (June): 13–39.

David, James Corbett. 2013. *Dunmore's New World*. Charlottesville: University of Virginia Press.

Eicholz, Hans L. 2001. *Harmonizing Sentiments: The Declaration of Independence and the Jeffersonian Idea of Self-Government*. New York: Peter Lang.

Finkelman, Paul. 1996. *Slavery and the Founders: Race and Liberty in the Age of Jefferson*. Armonk, NY: M. E. Sharpe.

Freehling, William W. 1972. "The Founding Fathers and Slavery." *American Historical Review* 77 (February): 81–93.

Gittleman, Edwin. 1974. "Jefferson's 'Slave Narrative': The Declaration of Independence as a Literary Text." *Early American Literature* 8 (Winter): 239–256.

Gordon-Reed, Annette. 2009. *The Hemingses of Monticello: An American Family*. New York: W. W. Norton.

Hitchens, Christopher. 2005. *Thomas Jefferson: Author of America*. New York: Atlas Books.

Jefferson, Thomas. 1781, June. "Speech to Jean Baptiste Ducoigne [CA.1]. Founders Online. https://founders/archives.gov/documents/Jefferson/01-06-02-0059.

Jefferson, Thomas. (1785) 1964. *Notes on the State of Virginia*. New York: Harper and Row.

Kaplan, Sidney. 1976. "The 'Domestic Insurrections' of the Declaration of Independence." *Journal of Negro History* 61 (July): 243–255.

Lucas, Stephen E. 1976. *Portents of Rebellion: Rhetoric and Revolution in Philadelphia, 1765–1776*. Philadelphia: Temple University Press.

Lynd, Staughton, and David Waldstreicher. 2011. "Free Trade, Sovereignty, and Slavery: Toward an Economic Interpretation of American Independence." *William and Mary Quarterly* 68 (October) 597–630.

Maier, Pauline. 1997. *American Scripture: Making the Declaration of Independence*. New York: Alfred A. Knopf.

Onuf, Peter S. 1998. "'To Declare Them a Free and Independent People': Race, Slavery, and National Identity in Jefferson's Thought." *Journal of the Early Republic* 18 (Spring): 1–46.

Parkinson, Robert G. 2016. *The Common Cause: Creating Race and Nation in the American Revolution*. Chapel Hill: University of North Carolina Press.

Pincus, Steve. 2016. *The Heart of the Declaration: The Founders' Case for an Activist Government*. New Haven, CT: Yale University Press.

Quarles, Benjamin. 1958. "Lord Dunmore as Liberator." *William and Mary Quarterly* 14 (October): 494–507.

Richardson, William D. 1984. "Thomas Jefferson and Race: The Declaration and Notes on the State of Virginia." *Polity* 16 (Spring): 447–466.

Waldstreicher, David. 2010. *Slavery's Constitution: From Revolution to Ratification*. New York: Hill and Wang.

Wills, Garry. 2003. *"Negro President": Jefferson and the Slave Power*. Boston: Houghton Mifflin.
Yarbrough, Jean. 1991. "Race and the Moral Foundations of the American Republic: Another Look at the Declaration and the Notes on Virginia." *Journal of Politics* 53 (February): 90–105.

SOUTH CAROLINA AND ITS SIGNERS

As the wealthiest of the southern states, with the eastern part of the state (the low country) with monied elites, often pitted against less-represented frontiersmen from the West (the backcountry), South Carolina delegates to the Second Continental Congress were among those moderates who sought reconciliation prior to supporting independence. The state delegation voted against independence when acting as part a Committee of the Whole on July 1, but, when the vote came to the full Congress, Edward Rutledge asked to postpone the vote for another day where he correctly predicted that he thought his colleagues "would then join in for the sake of unanimity" (Haw 1993, 249). The roster of South Carolinians who signed the document consisted of Thomas Heyward Jr., Thomas Lynch Jr., Arthur Middleton, and Edward Rutledge. Lynch, Middleton, and Rutledge had all also attended the First Continental Congress, where Christopher Gadsden had joined them.

Of the delegates to the First Continental Congress, none appears to have been more adamant for independence than Christopher Gadsden (1724–1805). Gadsden was a merchant and plantation owner who had served in the British navy. He had attended the Stamp Act Congress, where he expressed strong opposition to British taxes and a sense of emerging American nationhood: "there ought to be no New England men, no New Yorker, etc., known on the Continent, but all of us Americans" (Blassingame 1968, 65). He served as a brigadier general during the Revolutionary War, during which he became a prisoner of war. Gadsden is often associated with the so-called Gadsden flag that portrays a coiled rattlesnake with the words "Don't Tread on Me" against a solid yellow background. In the First Continental Congress, Gadsden had been the only delegate who had fully supported the Continental Association, which provided first for nonimportation and then for no-importation with Britain. After the other delegates walked out, they were able to get a compromise that exempted rice (they had also sought one for indigo) (Ryan 1959).

Thomas Heyward Jr. (1746–1809) was a lawyer who had studied in London and signed not only the Declaration of Independence but also the Articles of Confederation. Heyward served as a captain in the Revolutionary War and was wounded, captured, and imprisoned, where he may or may not have written the song "God Save the Thirteen States" (Kiernan and D'Agnese 2009, 217).

Thomas Lynch Jr. (1749–1779) had also studied law in London and was selected to the Continental Congress after his father had a stroke (and who died before being able to sign the Declaration). Lynch and his wife died when their ship went down in 1779, making him the signer who died at the youngest age.

Arthur Middleton (1742–1787) was the son of Henry Middleton, who had served as president of the First Continental Congress. Arthur studied law at Britain's Middle Temple and was quite active in the movement for independence. He did not make a very favorable impression on John Adams, however, who observed that "He had little information and less argument; in rudeness and sarcasm his forte lay, and he played off his artillery without reserve" (Kiernan and D'Agnese 2009, 210). Middleton was captured during the siege of Charleston and served for a time under British house arrest. He later returned to Congress but spent time restoring his house, which had been trashed and looted.

Edward Rutledge Jr. (1749–1800) is often paired in discussions of the Continental Congress with his older brother, John Rutledge (1739–1800), who left prior to the vote for independence in order to serve as president (later governor) of his home state. John would later serve as a delegate to the Constitutional Convention of 1787 and as a U.S. Supreme Court justice. Sons of a physician who had immigrated from Ireland, both Rutledges were educated in the law in England; Arthur Middleton was Edward's father-in-law.

Although Edward's rhetoric was more radical than that of his brother, their political stances were similar (Haw 1993, 234), joining more moderate delegates who sought reconciliation with Britain rather than early rebellion. Edward had argued for exempting both rice and indigo from the continental embargo, but he had supported the creation of an American navy in December 1775. Edward Rutledge apparently had some concern over whether adoption the Declaration would give the British "Notice of our Intentions before we had taken any Steps to execute them" (Haw 1998, 246–247) and he was responsible for introducing the motion to postpone actual debate on the Declaration for almost a month and the actual vote on independence from July 1 to July 2, when South Carolina joined other states in calling for independence. Like other members of the South Carolina delegation, Edward expressed suspicion of the New England delegates, who in turn considered most of the young Carolinians to be dandies. Rutledge also feared that John Dickinson's initial version of the Articles of Confederation did not sufficiently recognize state sovereignty, a theme that persisted into the firing on Fort Sumter that provoked the Civil War in 1861.

South Carolina's delegates were among those who insisted on deleting Thomas Jefferson's references within the Declaration that condemned the king for introducing slaves into the colonies and for failing to block their further importation. Some northern merchants who had participated in this notorious trade might also have shared this sentiment. South Carolina fought hard at the Constitutional Convention of 1787 for the three-fifths clause and for a provision permitting the importation of slaves for another 20 years. Long associated with a strong states' rights movement, South Carolina's desire to perpetuate slavery ultimately led them to become the first state to engage federal troops to star the Civil War (1861–1865) which led to the demise of this institution.

See also Signers, Collective Profile; Signing of the Declaration of Independence; Slavery

Further Reading

Blassingame, John W. 1968. "American Nationalism and Other Loyalties in the Southern Colonies, 1763–1775." *Journal of Southern History* 334 (February): 50–75.

Gould, Christopher. 1986. "The South Carolina and Continental Associations: Prelude to Revolution." *South Carolina Historical Magazine* 87 (January): 30–48.
Haw, James. 1993. "The Rutledges, the Continental Congress, and Independence." *South Carolina Historical Magazine* 94 (October): 232–251.
Head, John M. 1968. *A Time to Rend: An Essay on the Decision for American Independence*. Madison: State Historical Society of Wisconsin.
Kiernan, Denise, and Joseph D'Agnese. 2009. *Signing Their Lives Away: The Fame and Misfortune of the Men Who Signed the Declaration of Independence*. Philadelphia: Quirk Books.
Ryan, Frank W., Jr. 1959. "The Role of South Carolina in the First Continental Congress." *South Carolina Historical Magazine* 60 (July): 147–153.
Salley, A. S. 1927. *Delegates to the Continental Congress from South Carolina, 1774–1779, with Sketches of the Four Who Signed the Declaration of Independence*. Columbia, SC: State Company.
Webber, Mabel I. 1930. "Dr. John Rutledge and His Descendants." *South Carolina Historical and Genealogical Magazine* 31 (January): 7–25.

SOVEREIGNTY

See International Law

STANDING ARMIES (CHARGE #11)

Just after accusing the king of erecting new offices among the people, the Declaration of Independence also charged him as follows: "he has kept among us, in time of peace, standing armies without the consent of our legislatures." Immediately after the word "armies," Thomas Jefferson's original version had also included the words "and ships of war," but Congress deleted this phrase. It may have done so because it recognized that ships could serve the purpose of protecting the continent from pirates and foreign enemies and in the belief that ships did not, per se, constitute as great a threat to liberty as did standing armies.

The Declaration and Resolves of the First Continental Congress had previously charged that "keeping a standing army in several of these colonies, in time of peace, without the consent of the legislature of that colony, in which such army is kept, is against the law" ("Declaration and Resolves," 79). Josiah Quincy Jr., a Boston lawyer, had further criticized such an army in his observation on the Boston Port Bill (1774, 30–35). In a related charge, the Declaration of Independence would further accuse the king and Parliament of "quartering large bodies of armed troops among us."

Most nations need armies to protect themselves, especially during times of war. Philosophers in what was known as the civic republican tradition, which was reflected in Whig political thought, however, preferred defense on the part of citizen militiamen, who would be far more likely to defend their land and families than to be interested in deposing the existing government or seizing power for their own advantage. Long before Jefferson charged George III with keeping standing armies among the people, English philosophers had expressed concern that prior kings were doing this in England. One of the charges that the English Declaration of Rights of 1689 articulated was that James II had tried to subvert English laws, in among other ways, "By raising and keeping a standing army within this kingdom in time of peace without consent of Parliament, and quartering soldiers contrary to law." When King William subsequently asked for a standing army, there was a pamphlet war, which, while not rejecting the request, limited its size so as to protect civil liberties. One of those who argued against such a standing army was John Trenchard (Schwoerer 1965) who, along with Thomas Gordon, authored *Cato's Letters*, a series of essays that were highly influential in shaping political thought in the colonies.

With France having been defeated in the French and Indian War and Britain controlling Canada, colonists viewed English troops not as protectors but as enforcers of British taxes and other laws designed to penalize the colonists. Indeed, the British had increased the number of troops after rioting over the Stamp Act and in anticipation of trouble over enforcing the Townshend Acts (Friedenwald, 1904, 238). The so-called Boston Massacre in March 1770 illustrated the tensions that arose when British troops were garrisoned in the colonies (Archer 2010).

From the British standpoint, the colonies had asked for help during the French and Indian Wars, and Parliament had sent troops. From the colonial perspective, the only legislative bodies with authority to raise and quarter such troops were their own colonial legislatures. Jefferson had expressed this view in *A Summary View of the Rights of British America,* when he had indicated "That in order to enforce the arbitrary measures before complained of, his majesty has from time to time sent among us large bodies of armed forces, not made up of the people here, nor raised by the authority of our laws." Jefferson had gone on to ask, "Did his majesty possess such a right as this, it might swallow up all our other rights whenever he should think proper" and to observe that "his majesty has no right to land a single armed man on our shores, and those whom he sends here are liable to our laws made for the suppression and punishment of riots, routs, and unlawful assemblies; or are hostile bodies, invading us in defiance of law."

In answering this accusation, John Lind observed that Parliament had recognized the right of the monarch to send troops to any part of the empire that he deemed necessary (1776, 51–52). He further noted that Britain had originally sent troops to America to protect them from the French but that dangers from Native American Indians remained (1776, 54).

Experience during the Revolutionary War demonstrated that professionally trained soldiers were typically better disciplined than militiamen, but at war's end, the national military shrank, and some opponents to the Constitution that was written in Philadelphia in 1787 sought to add a provision to the Constitution prohibiting or limiting standing armies, as many state constitutions had done (Fields and Hardy 1991, 418). Although Federalists beat back attempts to impose such limits, the Third Amendment did prohibit the quartering of soldiers in private homes in peacetime without the owner's consent or in times of war except according to law. In vesting Congress with the power "to raise and support Armies," Article I, Section 8 of the U.S. Constitution further provided that "no Appropriation of Money to that Use shall be for a longer Term than two Years."

Modern arguments over the military have tended to focus on whether it is better to have an all-volunteer force (the current U.S. model) or whether compulsory service results in a more representative force.

See also Charges against the King and Others; English Declaration of Rights; Quartering Troops (Charge #14); *A Summary View of the Rights of British America* (Jefferson)

Further Reading

Archer, Richard. 2010. *As If an Enemy's Country: The British Occupation of Boston and the Origins of Revolution*. New York: Oxford University Press.

"Declaration and Resolves of the First Continental Congress." 2015. In *Founding Document of America: Documents Decoded*, edited by John R. Vile, 75–80. Santa Barbara, CA: ABC-CLIO.

Fields, William S., and David T. Hardy. 1991. "The Third Amendment and the Issue of the Maintenance of Standing Armies: A Legal History." *American Journal of Legal History* 35 (October): 393–431.

Friedenwald, Herbert. 1904. *The Declaration of Independence: An Interpretation and an Analysis*. New York: Macmillan.

Lind, John. 1776 *An Answer to the Declaration of the American Congress*. London: J. Walter, Charing-Cross and T. Sewell.

Quincy, Josiah, Jr. 1774. *Observations on the Act of Parliament, Commonly Called the Boston Port-Bill; with Thoughts on Civil Society and Standing Armies*. Boston: N.E. Printed.

Schwoerer, Lois G. 1965. "The Literature of the Standing Army Controversy, 1697–1699." *Huntington Library Quarterly* 28 (May): 187–212.

STATE CONSTITUTIONS AND THE DECLARATION OF INDEPENDENCE

State and local bodies issued many declarations prior to the Declaration of Independence (Maier 1997), and Thomas Jefferson may have drawn from some of these in writing the document. The most influential was probably the Virginia Declaration of Rights, which George Mason chiefly authored.

Just as the Declaration drew from state documents, so too, the principles of the Declaration have been embodied in subsequent state constitutions, which were all based on a system of representative government. Many of them specifically mentioned and sought to protect natural rights; Vermont and New Hampshire even outlawed slavery based on principles of the Declaration, while New York did so gradually (Tsesis 2012, 41–43). Like the Declaration, almost all recognized that government was based on consent. Such consent to the documents themselves was increasingly affirmed through state conventions or state referenda. Continuing consent was formalized in regularized elections.

Many state constitutions also incorporated statements about human equality, with some southern states limiting this principle to "freeman" or members of the social contract, thus seeking to exclude African American slaves. Significantly, the Northwest Ordinance sought to promote the principle of human equality by excluding slavery from the territories. Consistent with the language of the Declaration, this law further provided "that the States so formed shall be distinct republican States, and admitted members of the Federal Union, having the same rights of sovereignty, freedom, and independence as the other States" (Eastman 2002, 102–103). These two principles were sometimes in conflict. Most of the states (like Tennessee, Kentucky, Mississippi, and Alabama) that were formed from prior slave states continued to perpetuate this institution, while most new states in the north did not.

After the Civil War, even state constitutions in the South specifically recognized the equality of all citizens. A number of states modified provisions that had been interpreted to allow for secession as a way of protecting the right to "property" in slaves (Eastman 2002, 113–114). The enabling acts from the admission of Nevada on March 21, 1864, to the present (Park 1960, 410) required that the constitutions of new states "shall be republican, and not repugnant to the Constitution of the United States and the principles in the Declaration of Independence" (Eastman 2002, 114).

See also Northwest Ordinance of 1787; Slavery; U.S. Constitution and the Declaration of Independence; Virginia Declaration of Rights

Further Reading

Eastman, John C. 2002. "The Declaration of Independence as Viewed from the States." In *The Declaration of Independence: Origins and Impact*, edited by Scott Douglas Gerber, 97–117. Washington, DC: CQ Press.

Maier, Pauline. 1997. *American Scripture: Making the Declaration of Independence*. New York: Alfred A. Knopf.

Park, Lawrence N. 1960. "Admission of States and the Declaration of Independence." *Temple Law Quarterly* 33:403–418.

"State Constitutions, Enabling Acts, Admission Acts, and Presidential Proclamations of Admission." In *The Declaration of Independence: Origins and Impact*, edited by Scott Douglas Gerber, 267–296, Washington, DC: CQ Press.

Surrency, Erwin C. 2004. "The Transition from Colonialism to Independence." *American Journal of Legal History* 46 (January): 55–81.

Tsesis, Alexander. 2012. *For Liberty and Equality: The Life and Times of the Declaration of Independence*. New York: Oxford University Press.

STATUE OF LIBERTY

One of America's most iconic symbols is the Statue of Liberty (Liberty Enlightening the World), which was completed in 1886. The statue, which stands on Ellis Island in the New York Harbor, was given to the United States by France as a symbol of friendship and to commemorate the end of slavery. Frédéric Auguste Bartholdi designed the statute, which was built by Gustave Eiffel, whose company would build an equally famous landmark in Paris. The statue holds a torch in her right hand and a table in her left. The tablet has the date, which says JULY IV MDCCLXXVI (July 4, 1776), thus pointing to the day that the Declaration of Independence was adopted and to the ideals of liberty for which it stood.

The Declaration of Independence had accused the king of trying to block immigration to America. Many immigrants later arrived in the United States through

The Statue of Liberty (official name: Liberty Enlightening the World) on Ellis Island in New York Harbor was a gift of the French government to America. It was completed in 1886 to commemorate the end of slavery. The tablet in Lady Liberty's hand contains the date on which Congress adopted the Declaration of Independence. (Ang Wee Heng John/Dreamstime.com)

processing facilities at Ellis Island. The statute was one of the most prominent landmarks that many immigrants would connect to this experience.

Emma Lazarus (1849–1887), a New York poet from a family that had immigrated to the United States from Portugal, penned lines, now inscribed on a bronze plaque at the base of the Statue. It contrasted this statue to the Colossus of Rhodes, which stood for military victory, with the Statue of Liberty, which she associated with welcome:

> Give me your tired, your poor,
> Your huddled masses yearning to breathe free,
> The wretched refuse of your teeming shore.
> Send these, the homeless, tempest-tost to me,
> I lift my lamp beside the golden door!

See also Endeavored to Prevent the Population (Charge #7); Slavery

Further Reading

Ha, Thu-Huong. February 1, 2017. "The Story behind the Statue of Liberty's Unexpected Transformation into a Beacon for Refugees and Immigrants." https://qz.com/898486/give-me-your-tired-your-poor-the-statue-of-libertys-unexpected-transformation-into-a-beacon-for-refugees-and-immigrants/.

Statue of Liberty—Ellis Island Foundation, Inc. n.d. "Statue History." https://www.libertyellisfoundation.org/statue-history.

STONE ENGRAVING OF THE DECLARATION OF INDEPENDENCE

One reason for the popularity of the Declaration of Independence has been that it is short enough to be displayed on a single sheet. More often than not, such copies mimic the calligraphy text that Congress commissioned Timothy Matlack to copy onto a vellum sheet on July 19, 1776, and that contains the names of signers who began adding their names on August 2, 1776 and thereafter rather than the original printed manuscript that John Dunlap printed on the evening of July 4.

The Matlack manuscript, now displayed at the National Archives, followed Congress in its early transfers from city to city and had begun to fade during its first 50 years, during most of which it was rolled up.

In 1820, Secretary of State (later president) John Quincy Adams commissioned William J. Stone of Washington, D.C., to engrave the Matlack manuscript on copperplate and then on calfskin vellum. Stone worked on this project for about three years, after which Daniel Brent of the Department of State requested that he print 200 facsimile copies and return the copper plate; Stone apparently copied a number of proofs on paper and kept one for himself ("The Declaration of Independence"). Congress sent copies to the three remaining signers (Thomas Jefferson, John Adams, and Charles Carroll), to the president and vice president, to James Madison, to the Marquis de Lafayette, to the House and Senate, the Supreme Court, to state governors, and to some universities.

The original 201 facsimiles are imprinted at the top "engraved by W. I. Stone, for the Dept. of State, by order of J. Q. Adams, Sect. of State, July 4th, 1823" ("Declaration of Independence"). In subsequent imprints, Stone's notation at the top was replace at the bottom by "W.J. Stone Sc Washn."

In 2006, a visitor to a thrift shop in Nashville, Tennessee, bought a document, later authenticated as one of these Stone reprints, for $2.48 and was later able to sell it at auction for $477,000. The individual who donated it had purchased it at a flea market for $10 a decade earlier.

Scholars remain uncertain whether Stone used a "wet-press copy" process that may have resulted in further deterioration of the Matlack manuscript or whether he meticulously copied it (Puleo, 2016, 241–242).

See also Dunlap Broadside Printing of the Declaration of Independence; Engravings and Printings of the Declaration of Independence; Preserving the Declaration of Independence

Further Reading

"The Declaration of Independence—William J. Stone Engraving," Seth Kaller, Inc. https://www.sethkaller.com/declaration-of-independence/william-stone/.

Puleo, Stephen. 2016. *American Treasures: The Secret Efforts to Save the Declaration of Independence, the Constitution, and the Gettysburg Address*. New York: St. Martin's Press.

STRICTURES UPON THE DECLARATION OF INDEPENDENCE (HUTCHINSON)

Thomas Hutchinson (1711–1780), the former governor of Massachusetts who had served from 1758 to 1774 during both the Stamp Act Crisis and the Boston Massacre, published a pamphlet in London in 1776 designed to refute the Declaration of Independence. Written in the form of a letter to an English lord, the work is most notable for charging that the accusations against the king are both vague and untrue. Hutchinson also used the work to express his fairly conspiratorial view that even if Parliament had yielded to the colonists' insistence that they cease taxing them, "other pretences would have been found for exception to the authority of Parliament."

Thomas Hutchinson was the colonial governor of Massachusetts at the outbreak of the American Revolution. Between 1765 and 1774, he came to symbolize those loyal to Britain in Massachusetts and authored a contemporary critique of the Declaration of Independence. (New York Public Library)

Claiming that the colonists could find no other basis than "the natural rights of mankind to chuse their own forms of Government, and change them when they please," he claimed that "Some grievances, real or imaginary, were therefore necessary." Noting initial opposition to the courts of admiralty and writs of assistance, he claimed that Massachusetts had been the first to oppose the Stamp Act but thought that its suggestion for colonial representation in Parliament "was only intended to amuse the authority in England."

In examining the opening paragraphs of the Declaration of Independence, Hutchinson denied that "The Colonies, *politically* considered" ever "were a *distinct* people from the kingdom." He further identified Parliament as "the Supreme Legislative Authority, which hath essential right, and is indispensably bound to keep all parts of the Empire entire." As to the Declaration's claims that all men were created equal and were endowed with certain unalienable rights, Hutchinson "could wish to ask the Delegates of Maryland, Virginia, and the Carolinas, how their Constituents justify the depriving more than an hundred thousand Africans of their rights to liberty, and *the pursuit of happiness*, and in some degree to their lives, if these rights are so absolutely unalienable."

Hutchinson said that the claim that the king had refused to assent to colonial laws "is of so general a nature, that it is not possible to conjecture to what laws or to what Colonies it refers." The only such law Hutchinson could remember was one preventing a colony from "issuing a fraudulent paper currency, and making it a legal tender." He further denied that there was anything extraordinary about the king disallowing unjust or unwise laws.

Hutchinson recognized that a number of the accusations arose from Massachusetts, but he thought that most were at best half-truths. He thought that dissolutions of colonial legislatures had been relatively rare and had been justified by good reasons.

As to claims that judges were dependent on the Crown, he noted that this was the rule "when the Colonies were planted." Moreover, he asserted that such salaries were fixed. Hutchinson considered charges that the king had sent "Swarms of officers" to the colonies was highly exaggerated.

Any troops that the king had sent to the colonies, he had sent with the consent of Parliament, which was sufficient authorization. Hutchinson further thought that Parliament had the right to move trials to fair venues and to tax as it chose. He essentially defended parliamentary sovereignty over the New World as in Britain.

Hutchinson thought that colonial complaints about how Britain chose to govern and trade with Canada were essentially none of their business since it was beyond their own territory.

Turning to the accusations that the king was making war against the colonies, he observed that "These, my Lord, would be weighty charges from a *loyal and dutiful* people against an *unprovoked* Sovereign." In the Declaration of Independence, they were "consummate effrontery" since "The Acts of a *justly incensed* Sovereign for suppressing a most *unnatural, unprovoked* Rebellion, are here assigned as the *causes* of this Rebellion."

Probably because England had, after adoption of the Declaration Act of 1766, refused to accept any petitions that rejected parliamentary supremacy (Chaffin, 1974, 18), Hutchinson denied that the colonists had ever properly petitioned the king. He took particular umbrage that the Declaration had declared the king to be a tyrant. He rhetorically asked, "Have these men given an instance of any one Act in which the king has exceeded the just Powers of the Crown as limited by the English Constitution?"

Condemning the colonists for their ingratitude, Hutchinson concluded his essay by say that despite appealing to mankind, "the real design was to reconcile the people of American to that Independence, which always before, they had been made to believe was not intended."

See also Charges against the King and Others; Declaratory Act of 1766; Massachusetts and Its Signers

Further Reading

Bailyn, Bernard. 1976. *The Ordeal of Thomas Hutchinson*. Cambridge, MA: Belknap Press of Harvard University Press.

Chaffin, Robert J. 1974. "The Declaratory Act of 1766: A Reappraisal." *Historian* 37 (November): 5–25.

Hutchinson, Thomas. 1776. "1776: Hutchinson, Strictures upon the Declaration of Independence." Online Library of Liberty. http://oll.libertyfund.org/pages/1776-hutchinson-strictures-upon-the-declaration-of-independence.

Peckham, Howard H. 1976. "Independence: The View from Britain." www.americanantiquarian.org/proceedings/44498108.pdf.

Reck, Andrew J. 1977. "The Declaration of Independence as an 'Expression of the American Mind.'" *Revue Internationale de Philosophie* 31:404–437.

STYLE OF THE DECLARATION OF INDEPENDENCE

Although scholars have sometimes disputed propositions within the Declaration of Independence, there is general consensus among scholars from a variety of fields that the style of the Declaration of Independence places it among the most felicitously written documents in U.S. history.

One of the reason that committee members, most notably John Adams, assigned the primary task of writing the document to Thomas Jefferson was that, although he was not a strong speaker, he was already known for his felicitous written documents. Although Jefferson was trained under George Wythe as a lawyer, and the Declaration followed a number of earlier governmental documents, including British Deposition Apologias and other documents labeled Declarations, it is remarkably free of legalese, thus beginning with a simple "when" rather than the more characteristic "whereas" of other legal documents.

Although analyses of the Declaration's style most frequently focus on the initial two paragraphs of the Declaration, which are particularly known for the succinctness with which they attempt to place American grievances within a larger philosophical context that logically builds from premises of equal rights and the purposes of government to the right of revolution, the entire document rose to the rhetorical occasion. Commenting specifically on the first paragraph of the Declaration, Dumas Malone observes that "it is hard to see how Jefferson could have combined in such compass a larger number of important ideas or could have better imparted the tone of dignity, solemnity, respectful firmness, and injured virtue which the circumstances required" (1948, 223). Christopher Hitchens has likewise observed that the style "allied the plain language of Thomas Paine to the loftier expositions of John Locke" (2005, 25).

After announcing the purpose of the Declaration in the first paragraph and the philosophy that motivated it in the second, the Declaration proceeded to list 28 grievances that the colonies had against King George III, who was nowhere mentioned by name but was rather referred to as "He." Eschewing specific dates, Jefferson gathered grievances from all of the colonies. Jefferson designed them collectively to show that the king was attempting "the establishment of an absolute tyranny over these states."

Historians of the period from the end of the French and Indian War in 1763 to the proclamation of independence in 1776 generally identify the primary bone of contention between the one-time colonies and Great Britain as whether the British Parliament could exercise sovereignty in America. Colonists were particularly adamant that Parliament could not tax them without their consent, although some early colonial spokesmen had suggested that it might have authority over external, as opposed to internal, taxes. Colonists had initially recognized themselves bound to the British by charters and other agreements through their loyalty to a common king. They had held out hope, reflected in a number of petitions that they submitted to him, that the king would intervene on their behalf. Having previously renounced parliamentary authority, all that remained for the Declaration of Independence to do was to renounce this remaining loyalty to the king.

Because of this history, however, Jefferson subtly moved about halfway through his charges against the king (the first of which largely focused on legislative matters) to the accusation that "he [the king] has combined with others." These "others" clearly included Parliament as well as mercenaries, slaves, and Native American Indians that the king had sought to enlist on his side.

In revising the Declaration, the Second Continental Congress made a number of changes, which mostly consisted of excising large swaths of Jefferson's accusations. These included a section, undoubtedly regarded as hypocritical, in which the Document had accused the king of failing to stop the slave trade. The delegates also excised a section in which Jefferson had claimed that the colonists had settled America without British help and another which specifically singled out the king's use of Scottish mercenaries.

Jefferson found listening to such debates extremely painful and mailed copies of his own version to friends in hopes that his friends would accept his judgment that his original had been better. There is, however, consensus that most of these changes actually strengthened the document.

The Congress arguably expanded the reach of the document in the popular mind by inserting a number of references to God, as in "appealing to the supreme judge of the world for the rectitude of our intentions" and in affirming "a firm reliance on the protection of divine providence." The Congress also strengthened the document by specifically using the words of Richard Henry Lee's original resolution for Independence in the final paragraph. It wisely retained, however, Jefferson's memorable closing reference to the delegates' mutual pledge of "our lives, our fortunes, and our sacred honor."

One of the most remarkable aspects of the Declaration is the manner in which it has been linked to so many contemporary philosophical movements. Consistent with Jefferson's comment that he intended for the document "to be an expression of the American mind" (Smith n.d.), advocates of natural law thinking, classical liberalism, social contract thinking, Scottish Common Sense philosophy, scientific enlightenment, religious faith, and many others could find elements within the Declaration that resonated with them. Similarly, Jefferson's list of grievances embraced complaints from each of the colonies.

It is significant that much of the rhetorical power of the opening lines of Abraham Lincoln's Gettysburg Address, which proclaimed that "our fathers brought forth on this continent, a new nation, conceived in Liberty, and dedicated to the proposition that all men are created equal" derived from its rhetorically seamless evocation of the doctrine of equality articulated within the earlier Declaration.

See also Adams, John; British Deposition Apologias; Charges against the King and Others; Declaration (Meaning of Term); Equality; God; Jefferson, Thomas; Lincoln, Abraham; Originality of the Declaration of Independence; Resolutions Introduced by Richard Henry Lee (June 7, 1776); Slavery

Further Reading

Becker, Carl. (1922) 1970. *The Declaration of Independence: A Study in the History of Political Ideas*. New York: Vintage Books.

Hitchens, Christopher. 2005. *Thomas Jefferson: Author of America*. New York: Atlas Books.
Lucas, Stephen M. 1998. "The Rhetorical Ancestry of the Declaration of Independence." *Rhetoric and Public Affairs* 1 (Summer): 143–184.
Malone, Dumas. 1948. *Jefferson the Virginian*. Vol. 1 of *Jefferson and His Time*. Boston: Little, Brown.
Mon Droit. [Richard Ely Selden]. 1846. *Criticism on the Declaration of Independence as a Literary Document*. New York: For Sale at the News Offices.
Smith, George H. n.d. "Was Thomas Jefferson a Plagiarist?" Libertanism.org. https://www.libertarianism.org/publications/essays/excursions/was-thomas-jefferson-plagiarist.

SUFFOLK RESOLVES OF 1774

On September 17, 1774, almost a full month prior to adopting its Declaration and Resolves, the First Continental Congress adopted a series of resolution from the county of Suffolk in Massachusetts. The Suffolk Resolves were largely harsher in tone that the Declaration and Resolves. Like them, they could also have served as a source of grievances for Jefferson when he wrote the Declaration of Independence.

One obvious difference is that the Suffolk Resolves began with a statement in which it "cheerfully acknowledge[d] the said George the Third" (Webster and Morris 1973, 23). Like the Declaration of Independence, the Resolves described the need to maintain rights as a "duty" (Webster and Morris 1973, 23).

Most of the Resolves focus chiefly on the Coercive Acts. They thus objected to blocking the Boston Harbor, to changing the tenure of judicial officers, contrary to the Massachusetts Charter, and to the construction of military fortifications on Boston Neck. The Suffolk Resolves also objected to the British law recognizing the Roman Catholic Religion and French laws (these would have been civil laws rather than English common law) in Canada. The Resolves further pledged to withhold "all commercial intercourse with Great Britain, Ireland, and the West-Indies, and abstain from the consumption of British merchandise and manufacturers, and especially of East-India teas" (Webster and Morris 1973, 31). Opposing "any routs, riots, or licentious attacks upon the properties of any person" as "being subversive to all order and government," the Resolves called for "a steady, manly, uniform, and persevering opposition" to other British invasions of rights.

Jerrilyn Marston believes that the fact that the British learned of the adoption of these Resolves before they learned of the more measured and conciliatory Olive Branch Petition, accounts in large part for the king's belief that the colonists were rebels and that he accordingly needed to respond with strong measures (1987, 44).

See also Declaration and Resolves of the First Continental Congress (1774)

Further Reading

Marston, Jerrilyn Greene. 1987. *King and Congress: The Transfer of Political Legitimacy, 1774–1776*. Princeton, NJ: Princeton University Press.
Webster, Mary Phillips, and Charles R. Morris. 1973. *The Story of the Suffolk Resolves*. Milton: Massachusetts Historical Commission.

A SUMMARY VIEW OF THE RIGHTS OF BRITISH AMERICA (JEFFERSON)

One of the reasons that the committee of the Second Continental Congress selected Thomas Jefferson to write the Declaration of Independence was that he had already established a reputation for defending the colonial cause in writing. His most important writing prior to 1776 was the essay that he originally titled "Draft of Instructions to the Virginia Delegates in the Continental Congress" (Hedges 1987, 166), which was later printed as a pamphlet under the title *A Summary View of the Rights of British America*. Although he was a member of the House of Burgesses (the Virginia state legislature), which was tasked with choosing delegates to the Continental Congress, illness prevented him from attending (Hedges, 167).

Robert Webking says that the *Summary View* "is the first major work by a major American political thinker of the period to concentrate upon the king and not merely upon Parliament" (1988, 96). In addition to explaining Jefferson's literary reputation, the document also shows that Jefferson did not invent the sentiments in the Declaration of Independence in 1776 but that they followed consistently from his earlier views. The primary difference is that while Jefferson acknowledged the authority of George III over the colonies in 1774, in 1776 he no longer did so. By that time, he thought that the king had forfeited his authority by failing to redress the colonists' valid arguments against parliamentary sovereignty.

Much of Jefferson's argument in the *Summary View* stemmed from his understanding of colonial origins. He believed that nature gave individuals the right "of departing from the country in which chance, not choice, has placed them, of going in quest of new habitations, and of there establishing new societies, under such laws and regulations as to them shall seem most likely to promote public happiness." He believed that English Saxon forebears had exercised this right by migrating from the "woods in the north of Europe" to Great Britain. Jefferson argued that Americans, like these Saxons, had settled and "conquered" the new land with their own blood and treasure, content however, to submit themselves "to the same common sovereign, who was thereby made the central link connecting the several parts of the empire thus newly multiplied." British "princes" had improperly divided the settlers into independent governments and sought to regulate their trade, such actions being particularly prominent during the reigns of Charles I and II. Parliament had subsequently furthered such offenses by prohibiting colonists from making hats from the fur that they had gathered or from manufacturing their own iron.

As he would later do in the Declaration of Independence, Jefferson distinguished "Single acts of tyranny" from "a series of oppressions" that demonstrated "a deliberate and systematical plan of reducing us to slavery." At this point, he cited various acts of taxation that the British Parliament had sought to levy from the time of the French and Indian War. He also cited the act suspending the New York legislature, which had the potential of reducing its people "to a state of nature." Why, he asked, should 160,000 electors in Britain [suffrage was tightly restricted there] govern four million Americans?

Referring to the Boston Tea Party as one of those "extraordinary situations which require extraordinary interposition," Jefferson said that Parliament's Coercive Acts failed to distinguish the innocent from the guilty. He further called into question plans to try Americans in Britain. He earnestly entreated the king, "as yet the only mediatory power between the several states of the British empire, to recommend to his parliament of Great Britain the total revocation of these acts."

Jefferson proceeded to accuse the king of using a heavy hand in refusing to agree to colonial laws. As he would later seek to do in the Declaration of Independence, he also accused the king of refusing colonial request to abolish "domestic slavery."

Jefferson further questioned the king's right under Saxon common law, which he thought the colonists had brought with them to America, as a feudal landlord. Acknowledging that American ancestors had been "farmers, not lawyers," who had sometimes accepted such claims, he feared this assumed power was now being used to stop American expansion westward.

Jefferson said that "his majesty has no right to land a single armed man on our shores, and those whom he sends here are liable to our laws made for the suppression and punishment of riots, routs, and unlawful assemblies." Granting the king's right to exercise "the executive power of the laws of every state," he did not think this gave the king the right to exercise the powers of the British Parliament over Americans.

Asserting that he was merely "asserting the right of human nature," Jefferson proclaimed "that kings are the servants, not the proprietors of the people." He further thought that the king's duty was to pursue right over wrong. Asserting that "It is neither our wish, nor our interest, to separate" from Britain, he invoked "the God who gave us liberty," in hopes that the king would "interpose with that efficacy which your earnest endeavours may ensure to procure redress of these our great grievances, to quiet the minds of your subjects in British America, against any apprehensions of future encroachment."

In writing the Declaration of Independence, Jefferson would move from his indictments of Parliament to indictment of the king.

See also Jefferson, Thomas; Laws of Nature and of Nature's God

Further Reading

Colburn, Trevor. 1998. *The Lamp of Experience: Whig History and the Intellectual Origins of the American Revolution*. Indianapolis: Liberty Fund.

Hedges, William L. 1987. "Telling Off the King: Jefferson's 'Summary View' as American Fantasy. Special issue, *Early American Literature: Politics as Art, Art as Politics: Literature of the Early Republic, 1760–1820* 22, no. 2 (Fall): 166–174.

Jefferson, Thomas. 1774. *A Summary View of the Rights of British America*. Williamsburg, VA: Clementina Rind. Reprint, with an introduction by Paul Leicester Ford. New York: Historical Printing Club. 1892.

Lewis, Anthony M. 1948. "Jefferson's Summary View as a Chart of Political Union." *William and Mary Quarterly* 5 (January): 34–51.

Lynd, Staughton, and David Waldstreicher. 2011. "Free Trade, Sovereignty, and Slavery: Toward an Economic Interpretation of American Independence." *William and Mary Quarterly* 68 (October) 597–630.

Webking, Robert H. 1988. *The American Revolution and the Politics of Liberty*. Baton Rouge: Louisiana State University Press.

SUPREME COURT AND THE DECLARATION OF INDEPENDENCE

Although there is general agreement that the Declaration of Independence is not enforceable in court, it can be argued that the central purpose of the Constitution was to secure the rights that the Declaration had announced. Moreover, U.S. Supreme Court justices regularly refer to the Declaration for guidance as to how to interpret the Constitution.

Mark David Hall discovered that by the end of the 2000 term of the Supreme Court, "justices had explicitly invoked the Declaration in 184 opinions (106 majority, 54 dissenting, and 24 concurring or other type of opinion)" (2002, 142). In examining these references, Hall finds that justices have uniformly cited the date the formal document was adopted (July 4) rather than the date that Congress voted for independence (July 2). By contrast, Charles H. Cosgrove does not believe that some of the justices actually distinguished between the two dates (1998, 110–111).

Hall finds that justices often interpret the Constitution through the lens of the Declaration. He observed that Justice David Brewer noted in an 1897 case (*Gulf, Colorado and Santa Fe Railway v. Ellis*) that "it is always safe to read the letter of the Constitution in the spirit of the Declaration of Independence" (2002, 145). Hall notes that there has been some ambiguity through history (largely ended with the Civil War) as to whether the Declaration declared the independence of a single nation or of 13 individual states. He finds that justices sometimes pick out individual accusations against the king to question certain exercises of executive power (2002, 148). Many justices have similarly relied upon the Declaration in interpreting provisions of the Bill of Rights. Interestingly, the Court upheld the exclusion of George Anastaplo from the Illinois Bar after he cited the principle of revolution as articulated in the Declaration. A number of justices have cited the religious language of the Declaration to indicate that the United States is a religious nation.

In the notorious *Dred Scott* decision of 1857, Chief Justice Roger Taney read the Declaration of Independence as being limited to protecting the rights of white men, but the Fourteenth Amendment overruled this decision and extended citizenship to all persons born or naturalized within the United States. Other justices, however, have followed Taney's understanding that the Framers of the Declaration were at the very least hypocritical when they announced that all men were created equal while allowing slavery to continue. A number of prominent justices during the postbellum era used the provisions of the Fourteenth Amendment to defend property rights, which they considered to be among the Declaration's "unalienable rights." In recent years, justices have applied the principles of the Declaration differently in cases involving affirmative action (Cosgrove 1998, 152–161).

Hall found that justices who are associated both with judicial activism and those associated with judicial restraint have cited the Declaration. He concluded that "the justices' use of the Declaration has generally fallen within the boundaries of mainstream scholarship, however, and no instances can be cited in which they have used the Declaration in a patently misleading manner" (2002, 158).

See also Interpreting the Declaration of Independence; U.S. Constitution and the Declaration of Independence

Further Reading

Cosgrove, Charles H. 1998. "The Declaration of Independence in Constitutional Interpretation: A Selective History and Analysis." *University of Richmond Law Review* 32 (January): 107–164.

Hall, Mark David. 2002. "The Declaration of Independence in the Supreme Court." *The Declaration of Independence Origins and Impact*, edited by Scott Douglas Gerber, 142–160. Washington, DC: CQ Press. For a list of Supreme Court decisions that cite the Declaration, see "Supreme Court Cases That Invoke the Declaration of Independence" in the same volume, pp. 303–314.

SUSPENDING LEGISLATURES (CHARGE #22)

At the heart of the conflict between Great Britain and the 13 colonies was the issue of legislation. Parliament thought that it was as sovereign in the colonies as in Britain, and patriotic colonists thought that only their own legislatures could tax them. The 22nd charge that the Declaration of Independence lodged against the king was that he had "combined with others . . . for suspending our own legislatures, & declaring themselves invested with power to legislate for us in all cases whatsoever."

In the draft that Thomas Jefferson, in the Declaration of the Causes and Necessity for Taking Up Arms that he presented to the congressional committee in 1775, he had similarly observed that "by one act they have suspended the powers of one American legislature, & by another have declared they may legislate for themselves in all cases whatsoever" (Jefferson 1776, 1:200). Perhaps even more importantly, he had followed this accusation with the observation that "these two acts alone form a basis broad enough whereon to erect a despotism of unlimited extend, and what is to secure us against this dreaded evil?" (1776, 200–201).

The Declaration of Independence's accusation overlaps with its earlier charge accusing the king of having "dissolved Representative houses repeatedly." The charge of suspending legislatures applies primarily to Parliament rather than the king and appears primarily related to the New York Suspending Act of 1767. The act punished New York for failing to provide barracks and supplies for British troops by prohibiting:

> the governor, lieutenant governor, or person presiding or acting as governor of commander in chief, or for the council for the time being, within the colony, plantation, or province of New York in America, to pass, or give his or their assent to, or concurrence in, the making or passing any act of assembly; or his or their assent to any order, resolution or vote, in concurrence with the house of representatives for the time being within the said colony, plantation, or province; or for the said house of representatives to pass or make any bill, order, resolution, whatsoever. . . before and until provision shall have been made for supplying his Majesty's troops with necessaries. ("The New York Suspending Act")

The charge that the British had declared themselves "invested with Power to legislate for us in all Cases whatsoever" appears to be a reference to the Declaratory Act of

1766, in which Parliament had reasserted in sovereignty over American affairs, which the colonists had consistently questioned on the basis of the principle of no taxation without representation.

See also Declaration on the Causes and Necessity of Taking Up Arms; Declaratory Act of 1766; He Has Combined with Others (Charge #13)

Further Reading

"The New York Suspending Act." July 2, 1767. TeachingAmericanHistory.org. http://teachingamericanhistory.org/library/document/the-new-york-suspending-act/.

Varga, Nicholas. "The New York Restraining Act: Its Passage and Some Effects, 1766–1768." *New York History* 37 (July): 233–258.

SUSSEX DECLARATION

Early copies of the Declaration of Independence are both rare and highly prized, so discoveries of such documents raise public interest and can sometimes contribute to public understandings. Such is the case of the so-called Sussex Declaration, a parchment manuscript found in the West Sussex Records Office in Chichester, West Sussex, England. Deposited there by Leslie Holdon of Chichester, the document was part of a trove of documents from a law firm for which he worked. These were apparently from the dukes of Richmond, one of whom, Charles Lennon, had spoken in the House of Lords on behalf of the American cause. Aside from the parchment that is housed in the National Archives, this is the only other contemporary copy on parchment (Allen and Sneff 2017, 3).

One of the most unusual aspects of the document is that it is in what would be called landscape (horizontal) rather than portrait (vertical) style. Moreover, facsimiles of the signers' signatures are not arranged, as on the original, by states but in an order that is not immediately apparent. The Sussex Declaration is approximately 24 inches tall and 30.5 inches wide. This is similar in size to the parchment in the National Archives but much larger than most contemporary copies. This suggests that it was originally made for public display.

The two scholars who have done the most investigation of the manuscript have concluded through an analysis of handwriting styles, punctuation, spelling, and other evidence, that the Document dates sometime from 1777 to 1792, most likely between 1783 and 1790 (Allen and Sneff 2017, 43–44). Their research further suggests that the document, or another like it, served as a source for some popular early 19th-century engravings. They believe the piece was likely commissioned by Pennsylvania's James Wilson.

See also Engravings and Printings of the Declaration of Independence; Signing of the Declaration of Independence

Further Reading

Allen, Danielle, and Emily Sneff. 2017. "The Sussex Declaration: Dating the Parchment Manuscript of the Declaration of Independence Held at the West Sussex Record Office (Chichester, UK)." Under final revision and preparation for publication at *Papers of the Bibliographic Society of America*.

Dreier, Natalie. 2017. "Copy of Declaration of Independence found in unlikely location." https://www.ajc.com/news/national/copy-declaration-independence-found-unlikely-location/0WX2mdlhbNvkF5oEnf0J6M/.

Ruell, Peter. 2017. "A Hidden Declaration." *Harvard Gazette*. http://news.harvard.edu/gazette/story/2017/04/declaration-different-from-any-copy-we-had-seen/.

SYNG INKSTAND

Although Independence Hall remains an exciting place to visit, all but two items in the room where the Declaration of Independence was approved and where the U.S. Constitution was later drafted have been replaced. The two items known to be original are a Chippendale chair, where George Washington sat during the Constitutional Convention, and a silver inkstand that served as the reservoir in which delegates dipped their pens for the signing of both documents.

This inkwell, which has been reproduced, was designed by Philip Syng Jr. (1703–1789), of Philadelphia. An immigrant from Ireland, he was a friend of Benjamin Franklin and part of his so-called Junto. Moved to Harrisburg when the state capital relocated there, the stand was returned to Philadelphia during the centennial of the signing of the Declaration of Independence in 1876.

Made by Philip Syng in 1752, this silver inkstand is believed to be the one the Founding Fathers used to sign the Declaration of Independence and the U.S. Constitution. (Independence National Historical Park/National Park Service)

Syng's grave marker was found in 2003 on the grounds of Christ Church in Philadelphia, where he served as a vestryman.

In 1918, Thomas Masuryk, who had just drafted the Declaration of Independence of the Czechoslovak Nation, symbolically used the Syng inkwell to sign the Declaration of Independence of the Mid-European Union in Philadelphia (Armitage 2007, 133).

One relic associated with the Declaration of Independence (but not with the Constitution) is Thomas Jefferson's Writing Desk, which is displayed in the National Museum of American History in Washington, D.C.

See also Declaration of Independence Desk; Independence Hall

Further Reading

Armitage, David. 2007. *The Declaration of Independence: A Global History*. Cambridge, MA: Harvard University Press.

"Penn Biographies: Philip Syng (1703–1789)." Penn University Archives & Records Center. http://www.archives.upenn.edu/people/1700s/syng_phil.html.

Stoiber, Julie. 2003. "Discovery of Stone Uncovers Syng Plot." *Philadelphia Inquirer*, May 18, 2003. https://www.fireback.com/Drphysick.com/syngplot.html.

T

TAKING AWAY OUR CHARTERS (CHARGE #21)

It is common for political scientists to contrast America's written constitution to Britain's unwritten constitution, but neither description is completely accurate. Although the U.S. Constitution may be paramount, it is but one of many laws that govern, and while Britain does not have a single equivalent document, it relies on many statements and restatements of principle throughout its history.

When the Declaration accused the king of having combined with parliament "For taking away our Charters, abolishing our most valuable Laws, and altering fundamentally the Forms of our Governments," however, it might have been anticipating the higher sanctity with which Americans regarded written outlines of government by comparison to their British counterparts.

Most colonies were authorized by charters, sometimes to companies and other times to proprietors such as William Penn or Lord Baltimore. Beginning at about 1675, the Crown sought to centralize colonial administration, often based on what it considered to be colonial violations of customs and other laws. Although this effort took decades to effect and was not limited to the 13 colonies, it is easy to see how colonists might have thought that such alterations threatened their freedoms (Haffenden 1958a,b). Edmund Burke was among English members of Parliament who was sympathetic. In an address to America in January 1777, he observed that:

> We also reason and feel as you do on the invasion of your charters. Because the charters comprehend the essential forms by which you enjoy your liberties, we regard them as most sacred, and by no means to be taken away or altered without process, without examination, and without hearing, as they have lately been. We even think that they ought by no means to be altered at all but at the desire of the greater part of the people who live under them. (Burke, 1966, 164)

Edward Dumbauld believes that the Declaration was likely focusing chiefly on the Massachusetts Government Act of 1774, which changed selection of the council from election by the House to appointment by the Crown (1950, 138). This could also have provoked alarm in other states, which may have been the reason that George III had opposed such a change when it had been proposed in 1769 (Thomas 1985, 26). Benjamin Rush thus reported that Roger Sherman, who served on the committee to write the Declaration, had told Patrick Henry that the people of Connecticut were especially devoted to liberty "because we have more to lose than any of them." Asked by Henry to explain, Sherman had responded with a reference to "Our beloved charter" ("Delegate Discussions 2016).

From the British perspective, such a change had been necessitated by violence in Massachusetts (Sosin 1963). Thomas Hutchinson, the former royal governor of Massachusetts, observed that Britain's alteration of the colony's charter, which had been enacted by Parliament, simply aligned its government with that of others in America (Hutchinson 1776). John Lind argued that Britain had shown forbearance by not altering the charter even more radically than it did. He further observed that charters were not sacrosanct but had been altered many times previously (1776, 81–82).

When Americans later drew up their own constitutions, they provided that they could only be changed by supermajorities that they hoped would express the popular will.

See also Covenants and Compacts

Further Reading

Burke, Edmund. 1966. *On the American Revolution: Selected Speeches and Letters*. Edited by Elliott Robert Barkan. New York: Harper and Row.

Crittendon, Charles Christopher. 1924. "The Surrender of the Charter of Carolina." *North Carolina Historical Review* 1 (October): 383–402.

"Delegate Discussions: Benjamin Rush's Characters," Course of Human Events. https://declaration.fas.harvard.edu/blog/dd-rush.

Dumbauld, Edward. 1950. *The Declaration of Independence and What It Means Today*. Norman: University of Oklahoma Press.

Haffenden, Philip S. 1958a. "The Crown and the Colonial Charters, 1675–1688: Part I." *William and Mary Quarterly* 15 (July): 297–311.

Haffenden, Philip S. 1958b. "The Crown and the Colonial Charters, 1675–1688: Part II." *William and Mary Quarterly* 15 (October): 452–466.

Hutchinson, Thomas. 1776. "1776: Hutchinson, Strictures upon the Declaration of Independence." Online Library of Liberty. http://oll.libertyfund.org/pages/1776-hutchinson-strictures-upon-the-declaration-of-independence.

Kellogg, Louise Phelps. 1904. *The American Colonial Charter*. Washington, DC: U.S. Government Printing Office.

Lind, John. 1776 *An Answer to the Declaration of the American Congress*. London: J. Walter, Charing-Cross and T. Sewell.

Sosin, Jack M. "The Massachusetts Acts of 1774: Coercive or Preventive?" *Huntington Library Quarterly* 26 (May): 235–252.

Thomas, P. D. G. 1985. "George III and the American Revolution." *History* 70 (February): 16–31.

TAXES (CHARGE #17)

If the Revolutionary War is associated with one principle, it is that there should be "no taxation without representation." Americans traced this principle all the way to the Magna Carta of 1215, which had laid the foundation for the creation of Parliament, but the doctrine had also been expressed in the English Declaration of Rights (1689) and other documents.

It is thus someone unusual to see the charge that the king "has combined with others" (the two houses of Parliament) "for imposing taxes on us without our consent" as the 17th of 28 separate charges against the king and his allies rather than at the forefront of the Declaration. Part of the reason that the accusation comes so late in the document is that the first 12 charges were specifically directed against the king, who had no power on his own authority to levy taxes.

Steve Pincus has persuasively argued that the imposition of taxes on the colonies was part of a larger British project to regard the colonists more as producers rather than as consumers (2016). Initially, the colonists had accepted the idea that Britain might levy duties on trade. Thus, when the Parliament asked Benjamin Franklin about colonial attitudes toward Parliamentary rule, he had responded that "I never heard any objection to the right of laying duties to regulate commerce, but a right to lay internal taxes was never supposed to be in Parliament, as we are not represented there" (Bergen 1897, 27).

The imposition of the Stamp Act in 1765 had led to the Stamp Act Congress. On October 19, 1765, it had proclaimed "that it is inseparably essential to the freedom of a people, and the undoubted rights of Englishmen, that no taxes should be imposed on them, but with their own consent, given personally, or by their representatives" (Dumbauld 1950, 131). Although Parliament repealed this tax, it accompanied the repeal with the Declaratory Act, which asserted its authority over the colonies in all matters whatsoever. This led to a series of taxes including the Townshend Duties and the tax on tea. This in turn led to the Boston Tea Party and the Coercive Acts against Boston and Massachusetts that further united the colonies and led in turn to the Continental Congresses from which the Declaration of Independence emerged.

In responding to the accusation that Parliament was taxing the colonists without their consent, John Lind argued that the colonies were making much ado about nothing. He observed that they could not claim that the taxes had been exorbitant, that the mode by which they had been imposed was unusual, or that the uses to which the taxes raised had been improper (1776, 68–69). Asking the nature of the colonial grievance, he said that "it existed in imagination only" (1776, 70). A later critic observed that "Those who rebelled in good faith did so because they feared that the power of Parliament to tax them moderately to raise money for their own defense might be used some time in the future for a less worthy purpose, and then they would all be 'slaves'" (Gergen 1898, 47).

In the American constitutional system, Congress is the only body that can levy taxes. Because voting representation is apportioned only to states, residents of the nation's capital, who have no voting members in Congress, have often complained that they are also victims of "taxation without representation."

See also Charges against the King and Others; Declaratory Act of 1766; He Has Combined with Others (Charge #13)

Further Reading

Bergen, Frank. 1898. *The Other Side of the Declaration of Independences*. Newark, NJ: Baker Printing Co.

Dumbauld, Edward. 1950. *The Declaration of Independence and What It Means Today*. Norman: University of Oklahoma Press.

Lind, John. 1776 *An Answer to the Declaration of the American Congress*. London: J. Walter, Charing-Cross and T. Sewell.

Pincus, Steve. 2016. *The Heart of the Declaration: The Founders' Case for an Activist Government*. New Haven, CT: Yale University Press.

TEMPERATURE ON JULY 4, 1776

As July 4, 1776, has become enshrined as the day on which Congress adopted the Declaration of Independence, legends have grown surrounding the trials that members of the Continental Congress faced.

Many writers have logically assumed that, coming in midsummer, the day must have been quite hot. In the process of editing letters from delegates to the convention, however, Paul H. Smith has discovered that this was not the case. This evidence comes from two sources: Thomas Jefferson and Robert Treat Paine. Smith notes that Jefferson's readings, which were relatively low, had led some to suspect either "that Jefferson's thermometer was not properly calibrated or that it had been placed in an unusual location" (1776, 297). He recorded that it was 68 degrees at 6:00 a.m., 72 degrees at 9:00 a.m., and 76 degrees at 1:00 p.m. (Strauss 2012). Smith finds however, that while Paine had recorded a temperature of 95 degrees Fahrenheit on June 28, he had recorded that showers had brought relief on July 1 and that he had recorded the following three days all as "cool" (1776, 298).

See also Jefferson, Thomas

Further Reading

Smith, Paul H. 1976. "Time and Temperature: Philadelphia, July 4, 1776." *Quarterly Journal of the Library of Congress* 33 (October): 294–299.

Strauss, Valerie. "How Hot Was It on July 4, 1776?" *Washington Post*. July 4, 2012. https://www.washingtonpost.com/blogs/answer-sheet/post/how-hot-was-july-4-1776-thanks-to-jefferson-we-know/2012/07/04/gJQAPnjPNW_blog.html?utm_term=.9b4bb89b669d.

TIMING OF THE DECLARATION OF INDEPENDENCE

Not long after the end of the French and Indian War (1754–1763), the British ended their prior policy of "salutary neglect" and began exercising greater control over the American colonies. The imposition of the Stamp Act led the colonists to convene the Stamp Act Congress of 1765. Parliament combined the repeal of the Stamp Act with the Declaratory Act of 1766, asserting its power to enact further taxes, and it attempted to do so over the next decade. Its attempt to tax tea ultimately resulted in the so-called Boston Tea Party on December 16, 1773. This in turn led to Coercive Acts, which the colonists dubbed the Intolerable Acts, and the quartering of even more British troops in America. Fighting broke out at Lexington and Concord in April 1775, and the Continental Congress recruited military forces and appointed George Washington as commander in chief while still waiting more than another year before proclaiming independence.

This leads to the question of why Congress decided to act when it did. The Declaration of Independence provides one answer when it suggested in the second paragraph that "mankind are more disposed to suffer, while evils are sufferable, than to right themselves by abolishing the forms to which they are accustomed." It argued that the colonists had exercised "patient sufferance" until necessity compelled them to exercise their duty of replacing a government at war with their liberties with one that would provide for their future safety and happiness. It further suggested that one reason for the colonists' forbearance was that they had long regarded Englishmen as "our common kindred."

It is important to remember that each of the colonies had its own separate history and administration and that it was common opposition to English policies, as expressed in committees of correspondence and continental congresses, that effectively led to the development of a continental union. Just as the unwritten English constitution had taken hundreds of years to develop, so too, it took more than a decade for leading American thinkers to explain how they believed they had the rights of Englishmen without thereby acknowledging the right of the English Parliament to tax them (a process during which some of them had initially distinguished between internal and external taxes). Anticipating a connection similar to Commonwealth status, most colonists continued to hope that the king would intervene against Parliament on their behalf even though in England itself, the king had increasingly lost power vis-à-vis this body.

George III's rejection of the Olive Branch Petition, his Proclamation of Rebellion on August 23, 1775, and his speech to Parliament of October 17, 1775, declaring that the colonies were now outside of his protection, were the background against which Thomas Paine published *Common Sense*. Whereas most previous colonial writings had questioned the authority of Parliament, this publication specifically questioned the monarchy, associating kingship with war and corruption, and opening the doctrine of hereditary succession to ridicule. Thomas Paine further argued in *Common Sense* that the time was ripe for a declaration of independence.

As many members of Congress continued to seek reconciliation, the Battle of Bunker Hill provided a point of continental pride and gave hope for military success. Many leaders anticipated that such success might ultimately hinge on whether the colonists could attract allies in their fight against Great Britain. When Richard Henry Lee introduced the resolution for independence on June 7, 1776, he also called for creating a new confederation and for seeking foreign allies.

France and Spain had been traditional rivals to Great Britain, so there was some hope for securing their help against it. This was, however balanced by fears that European empires might also band together and seek to divide the Americas among them, much as Russia, Prussian, and Austria had partitioned Poland in 1772 and much as Genoa had transferred the island of Corsica to France in 1768. This fear was furthered by rumors, which began to circulate shortly after the publication of Paine's *Common Sense*, and might have been planted by the British, to the effect that Britain was considering an arrangement in which it might give Canada back to France and Florida to Spain in exchange for help in quelling rebellion in the thirteen colonies and that the French were sending additional troops to its colonies in the Caribbean (Hutson 1972). A partition would be far less likely if the colonies had already declared their separation.

Even under such threats, a number of moderate delegates who had been hoping for reconciliation had to absent themselves in order to get 12 states to approve the resolution for independence on July 2, 1776, and it took until July 18 before New York was able to add its consent to make state approval unanimous. Had more radical delegates prevailed a year or two earlier, it seems likely that colonies would have been far less united in their opposition than when they finally voted for it. John Adams, who was one of the earliest advocates for independence, noted that "The complete accomplishment of it [independence] in so short a time and by such simple means was perhaps a singular example in the history of mankind. Thirteen clocks were made to strike together, a perfection of mechanism which no artist had ever before effected" (Warner 2009, 145). The Declaration made several direct references to time. It noted that the king had waited "a long time" before calling colonial legislatures back in session. It observed that the king was "at this time" transporting armies to America. It further noted that the colonies had "from time to time" warned "our British brethren" "of attempts by their legislature to extend an unwarrantable jurisdiction over us."

See also Adams, John; *Common Sense* (Paine); Declaratory Act of 1766; George III, Proclamation of Rebellion (August 23, 1775); George III, Speech to Parliament (October 27, 1775); Jefferson's Notes on Debates over Declaration; Olive Branch Petition; Resolutions Introduced by Richard Henry Lee (June 7, 1776); When in the Course of Human Events

Further Reading

Hutson, James H. 1971. "The Partition Treaty and the Declaration of American Independence." *Journal of American History* 58 (March): 877–896.

Warner, William B. 2009. "The Invention of a Public Machine for Revolutionary Sentiment: The Boston Committee of Correspondence." *Eighteenth Century* 50 (Summer/Fall): 145–164.

TORIES

One of the accusations that the Second Continental Congress deleted from Jefferson's draft of the Declaration of Independence was that "he has incited treasonable insurrections of our fellow citizens, with the allurements of forfeiture & confiscation of property." The decision to delete this charge was arguably a wise decision.

In effect, this charge, being made by individuals who were subject to trial for treason under British law, accused the king of encouraging the Tories who remained loyal to him to commit "treasonable insurrections" against Patriots who were rebelling against him! One could hardly have expected the king to do otherwise. Moreover, Robert Parkinson observes that "it made practical political sense to leave the tories out of the Declaration; castigating and condemning the loyalists might engender antipathy toward the common cause among those on the fence and, worse, prove an obstacle for incorporating those people into the polity in the future" (2016, 253).

Patriots often agreed on common principles while disagreeing about what to do about them. Max Savelle has thus observed that "the American Whigs stood for the maintenance of the old loyalty to the British national ideals, as they understood them, *against* the policies and actions of what they took to be a series of misguided ministries; the Tories clung to the old loyalty *despite* the policies of those same ministries, however misguided" (1962, 904).

Estimates of Tory strength vary, with some individuals inadvertently attributing a quotation by John Adams about one-third of Americans opposing, one-third favoring, and another one-third as lukewarm toward the French Revolution as applying to the Revolution (Schellhammer 2013). Paul H. Smith believes that approximately 19,000 loyalists served with British forces and estimates that Loyalists constituted approximately 16 percent of those who lived in America and 19.8 percent of whites (1968, 269).

In point of fact, revolutionary forces did confiscate Tory property during the revolution. A study of such confiscations in Georgia indicates that such confiscations were not only designed to punish Tories but also to provide funds to prosecute the revolution (Lambert 1963, 80).

See also Charges against the King and Others; Treason; Whig Political Thought

Further Reading

Chopra, Ruma. 2011. *Unnatural Rebellion: Loyalists in New York City during the Revolution.* Charlottesville: University of Virginia Press.

Lambert, Robert S. "The Confiscation of Loyalist Property in Georgia, 1782–1786." *William and Mary Quarterly* 20 (January): 80–94.

Parkinson, Robert G. 2016. *The Common Cause.* Chapel Hill: University of North Carolina Press.

Savelle, Max. 1962. "Nationalism and Other Loyalties in the American Revolution." *American Historical Review* 67 (July): 901–923.

Schellhammer, Michael. February 11, 2013. "John Adams's Rule of Thirds." Nhttps://allthingsliberty.com/2013/02/john-adamss-rule-of-thirds/.

Smith, Paul H. 1968. "The American Loyalists: Notes on Their Organization and Numerical Strength." *William and Mary Quarterly* 35 (April): 259–277.

TRADE (CHARGE #16)

The 4th of 10 charges that the Declaration accused the king of having "combined with others" to effect is that of "cutting off our trade with all parts of the world."

Unlike many of the colonists' other concerns, this one appears to precede changes in policy usually associated with the end of the French and Indian War. Indeed, Edward Dumbauld says that there were approximately 50 acts from the Navigation Act of 1660 to the Revolution that were designed to monopolize trade between the colonies and Britain (1950, 129).

In the early stages of the dispute with Britain, colonists had suggested that while the king and Parliament might have power to regulate external matters, like trade, they did not have authority to enact internal taxes (Morgan 1968, 151). While appreciating the mutual benefits of trade with Britain, the colonists may well have thought that restrictions on such trade already constituted due recompense for any benefits association with the motherland might have brought.

As English sought to impose new taxes on the colonies, they also began to tighten trade regulations. Prior to this, they had often turned a blind eye to colonial evasions of such regulations, often in an attempt to gain hard currency, which was otherwise largely flowing to Britain. In cataloguing trade restrictions that the British had imposed on England, Arthur Lee had pointed to prohibitions on making steel or erecting steel furnaces, obligating them to accept Spanish and Portuguese wines, forbidding the manufacture of hats, limiting the construction of mills, prohibiting the transport of wool from one colony to another, and limiting the export of logwood prior to taking it to British ports (1775, 56–57). Thomas Jefferson had referenced some of these in his *Summary View of the Rights of British America.*

The most direct focus of complaints about trade probably focused on the Restraining Acts of 1775 (indeed Dickerson 1951, 133, believes these referred only to "the Boston port Bill and the New England Restraining Act"), which Parliament enacted in response to increasing acts of civil disobedience in Massachusetts and other New England colonies. The New England Trade and Fisheries Act, which was adopted on March 30, 1775, and applied to this area, limited both trade and fishing rights. The later Trade Act of April 15, 1775, imposed similar limitations on most southern states. Like the earlier Coercive, or Intolerable Acts, these could be considered equivalent to war measures, which were as much an indication of the pending rupture between the colonies and Britain as it was the cause of it.

John Lind thus observed that the colonists had previously declared their own boycotts against Britain and that if they returned "to their allegiance," the acts of 1775 would cease (1776, 64).

Significantly, the last paragraph of the Declaration of Independence announced that "as free & independent states," the former colonies would "have full power" not only to "levy war, conclude peace, [and] contract alliances," but also to "establish commerce."

See also Charges against the King and Others; He Has Combined with Others (Charge #13); International Law; *A Summary View of the Rights of British America* (Jefferson)

Further Reading

Dickerson, Oliver M. 1951. *The Navigation Acts and the American Revolution*. Philadelphia: University of Pennsylvania Press.

Dumbauld, Edward. 1950. *The Declaration of Independence and What It Means Today*. Norman: University of Oklahoma Press.

[Lee, Arthur]. 1775. *An Appeal to the Justice and Interests of the People of Great Britain in the Present Dispute with America. By an Old Member of Parliament*. 2nd ed. London: Printed for J. Almon.

Lind, John. 1776 *An Answer to the Declaration of the American Congress*. London: J. Walter, Charing-Cross and T. Sewell.

Morgan, Edmund S. 1968. "Colonial Ideas of Parliamentary Power, 1764–1766." In *The Reinterpretation of the American Revolution, 1763–1789*, edited by Jack P. Greene, 151–180. New York: Harper and Row.

TRANSLATIONS OF THE DECLARATION OF INDEPENDENCE

The Declaration of Independence was intended both to rally patriots within the colonies and to appeal to foreign governments who could provide aid against the British. David Armitage has demonstrated how the Document has served as a model for declaration in such widely disparate nations as Flanders (1790), Haiti (1804), Venezuela (1811), New Zealand (1835), the Republic of Texas (1826), Liberia (1847), the Czechoslovak Nation (1918), the Democratic Republic of Vietnam (1945), Israel (1948) and Southern Rhodesia (1965) (Armitage 2007, 187–248).

David Thelen has written an essay in which he describes how foreign translations of the document have often presented individuals with interpretative issues that help enlighten the meaning of the document itself. Thelen observes that the first such translation was in German and was published in the *Pennsylvanischer Staatsbote* even before the document was sent abroad (2002, 192).

Thelan notes that it has been particularly difficult for translators to come up with a synonym for "people." Some, like one whom Thelan describes as "a Japanese champion of the Meiji enlightenment in the 1860s," used the term to refer to "a 'kin group of people'" (2002, 176), whereas German translators have variously alternated "between place of residence and shared cultural pasts" (2002, 197).

A Japanese translator managed to convert the "prudence" of the Declaration into "timid conservatives[s]" (2002, 199), while a Nazi translator interpreted the American people according to blood and soil (2002, 199). Some translations have managed to put distance between their own situations and those of 1776 by specifically identifying the "we" of the Declaration with "the Americans" (2002, 199).

Thelen finds that translators have sometimes been puzzled by the word "unalienable" (2002, 200). Some—Sun Yat-sen, for example—simply did not believe that the Declaration's principles accorded with "the 'common sense' of Chinese experience." Others found the idea simply incomprehensible or untranslatable, and still others wanted to expand the negative rights of the Declaration into more positive social rights (2002, 201). Some have further tried to associate human rights with the rights of a particular people, like the Jews or others (2002, 202).

The "pursuit of happiness" has proven to be another interpretive conundrum. French translators have alternated "between *bonheur* (happiness) and *bien-etre* (well-being)" and "its quest as a *recherché* (pursuit) and a *desir* (desire)" (2002, 203). Some Buddhists regard "the pursuit of happiness" as "both futile and a human vanity," while some Catholic theologians believe happiness is attainable only in the afterlife (2002, 203).

Not surprisingly, foreign interpreters have detected the same disparities between the aspirations of the Declaration and day-to-day practice in the areas of race, imperialism, and the rights of women. Americans have followed similar paths in the years leading up to the Civil War and those surrounding the U.S. acquisition of foreign colonies as a result of the Spanish-American War.

Given the challenges, teachers of foreign language might well find it productive to have their students seek to translate the Declaration into the language they are teaching.

See also Life, Liberty, and the Pursuit of Happiness; People; Prudence; Unalienable Rights; "We" (First-Person Plural)

Further Reading

Adams, William Paul. 1999. "German Translations of the American Declaration of Independence." *Journal of American History* 85 (March): 1325–1349.

Armitage, David. 2007. *The Declaration of Independence: A Global History*. Cambridge, MA: Harvard University Press.

Eoyang, Eugene. 1999. "Life, Liberty, and the Pursuit of Linguistic Parity: Multilingual Perspectives on the Declaration of Independence." *Journal of American History* 85 (March): 1449–1454.

Marienstras, Elise, and Naomi Wulf. 1999. "French Translations and Reception of the Declaration of Independence." *Journal of American History* 85 (March): 1299–1324.

Thelen, David. 2002. "Reception of the Declaration of Independence." In *The Declaration of Independence: Origins and Impact*, edited by Scott Douglas Gerber, 191–212. Washington, DC: CQ Press.

Vlasova, Marina A. 1999. "The American Declaration of Independence in Russian: The History of Translation and the Translation of History." *Journal of American History* 85 (March): 1399–1408.

TRANSPORTING LARGE ARMIES OF FOREIGN MERCENARIES (CHARGE #25)

The 25th accusation that the Declaration of Independence lodged against the king was that "he is at this time transporting large armies of foreign mercenaries, to compleat the works of death, desolation & tyranny, already begun with circumstances of Cruelty & Perfidy scarcely paralleled in the most barbarous ages and totally unworthy the head of a civilized nation." This is the third of five charges that related to war atrocities that had taken place since the first shots were fired at Lexington and Concord. In Thomas Jefferson's original draft of the Declaration, he had observed that "British brethren" were "permitting their chief magistrate to send over not only soldiers of our common blood, but Scotch and foreign mercenaries to invade and destroy us."

Because Britain was an island nation and its citizens were averse to standing armies, they tended to wage most of their land wars with mercenaries, or hired soldiers. In defending the king's use of mercenaries, John Lind had observed that "So small is the ordinary establishment of the British army, that there has not been a war, *foreign* or *domestic*, within the memory of us or our fathers, where foreign troops have not been employed" (1776, 96).

About 30,000 Germans fought in the American Revolution. Although George III had employed some soldiers from the Scottish Highlands, both the Dutch and Catherine the Great of Russia had rebuffed his request for mercenaries (Fetter 1980, 510), and he ended up relying mostly on soldiers from Germany, from which the king's family had originated. Many came from the Hesse and were thus known as Hessians. There was some criticism within Germany of this practice (Schmidt 1958). In contrast to most American fighters, the German mercenaries, or auxiliaries, had little ideological motivation, and their native language kept most from fully appreciating American motivations for the war.

The colonies, especially Pennsylvania, had a fair number of German citizens, but early in the war, American soldiers had exaggerated notions of German military prowess. George Washington successfully undermined these conceptions in his victory on Christmas Day 1776 at the Battle of Trenton (Mauch 2003, 416). Although most Hessians eventually returned to their homes after the war, some deserted and married American women (Mauch 2003).

The Declaration's reference to "foreign" mercenaries further highlights its emphasis on distinct peoples. It undoubtedly raised further questions about why a king did not, or could not, employ his own people to fight his wars. In accusing the king of being "barbarous" and uncivilized, the Declaration further suggested the idea, consistent with Enlightenment thought, that although they may have settled an uncivilized land, Americans might have progressed beyond the behavior of their former British monarch. Notably, the charge against the employment of mercenaries immediately precedes the Declaration's accusation that the king employed the "merciless Indian savages."

See also Charges against the King and Others; People; Standing Armies (Charge #11)

Further Reading

Atwood, Rodney. 2002. *The Hessians: Mercenaries from Hesse-Kassel in the American Revolution*. New York: Cambridge University Press.

Charles, Patrick J. 2008. *Irreconcilable Grievances: The Events That Shaped the Declaration of Independence*. Westminster, MD: Heritage Books.

Fetter, Frank Whitson. 1980. "Who Were the Foreign Mercenaries of the Declaration of Independence?" *Pennsylvania Magazine of History and Biography* 104 (October): 508–513.

Krebs, Daniel. 2015. *A Generous and Merciful Enemy: Life for German Prisoners of War during the American Revolution*. Norman: University of Oklahoma Press.

Lind, John. 1776 *An Answer to the Declaration of the American Congress*. London: J. Walter, Charing-Cross and T. Sewell.

Mauch, Christof. 2003. "Images of America—Political Myths—Historiography: Hessians in the War of Independence." *Amerikastudien / American Studies* 48:411–423.

Schmidt, H. D. 1958. "The Hessian Mercenaries: The Career of a Political Cliché." *History* 43:207–212.

Wilhelmy, Jean-Pierre. 2009. *Soldiers for Sale: German 'Mercenaries' with the British in Canada during the American Revolution, 1776–1783*. Montreal: Baraka Books.

TRANSPORTING US BEYOND SEAS (CHARGE #19)

The 19th accusation that the Declaration of Independence lodged against the king (and "others") was "for transporting us beyond Seas to be tried for pretended Offenses."

This accusation highlighted a law adopted during the reign of Henry VIII. It permitted the trial of individuals for treason outside the realm to be transported to England for this purpose (Fisher 1907, 133). Such a trial could be especially consequential since treason was considered to be a capital offense (Hurst 1944).

Parliament reminded the king of this statute in 1769, but he appeared to have agreed with Constantine Phipps, who observed in Parliament that "these measures are more calculated to promote rather than to prevent rebellion" (York. 2011, 659). There is thus no example of an American being transported to England for such a treason trial.

Similarly, Parliament adopted another law that coincided with (but slightly preceded) the burning of the HMS *Gaspee on* June 9–10, 1772, on the Providence River in Rhode Island (Leslie 1952). Although it would have permitted the trial in England of those who burned British ships, the investigation bogged down and stirred up colonial resistance, and no American was actually transported to England for this purpose.

This does not mean that the possibility had not stirred discontent. On May 16, 1769, the Virginia House of Burgesses met in secret session to adopt the Virginia Resolves of 1769. In addition to contesting Parliament's right to tax the colony, the resolution also opposed trials in England in the following language:

> Resolved, That it is the Opinion of this Committee, that all Trials for Treason, Misprison of Treason, or for any Felony or Crime whatsoever, committed and done in this his Majesty's said Colony and dominion, by any Person or Persons, residing in this Colony, suspected of any crime whatsoever, committed therein, and sending such Person, or Persons, to Places beyond the Sea, to be tried, is highly derogatory of the rights of *British* Subjects; as thereby the inestimable Privilege of being tried by a Jury from the Vicinage, as well as the Liberty of summoning and producing Witnesses on such Trial, will be taken away from the Party accused. ("The Virginia Resolves of 1769")

The Declaration was thus technically correct. It did not accuse the king of actually transporting individuals from American to England for trial but of "giving his assent to their [Parliament's] pretended legislation . . . for transporting us beyond seas to be tried for pretended offenses." This double use of "pretended" is designed to indicate both that Parliament had no power to legislate for the colonies and that allegations of treason against people who were merely asserting their rights were unwarranted.

It is noteworthy that six accusations later, the Declaration indicted the same king of "transporting large armies of foreign mercenaries" to America to make war on its people. Congress deleted a later charge that Thomas Jefferson had originally penned, accusing the king of having "incited treasonable insurrections of our fellow citizens, with the allurements of forfeiture & confiscation of property." It is reasonable to surmise that the delegates realized that the king would consider their own declaration to be treasonable and thought it a bit too ironic to be accusing the king of inciting his Loyalist subjects within the colonies.

See also Charges against the King and Others; He Has Combined with Others (Charge #13)

Further Reading

Fisher, Sydney George. 1907. "The Twenty-Eight Charges against the King in the Declaration of Independence." *Pennsylvania Magazine of History and Biography* 31:247–303.

Hurst, Willard. 1944. "Treason in the United States? I. Treason down to the Constitution." *Harvard Law Review* 58 (December): 226–272.

Leslie, William R. 1952. "The *Gaspee* Affair: A Study of Its Constitutional Significance." *Mississippi Valley Historical Review* 39 (September): 233–256.

"The Virginia Resolves of 1769." TeachingAmericanHistory.org. http://teachingamerican-history.org/library/document/the-virginia-resolves-of-1769/.

York, Neil L. 2011. "Imperial Impotence: Treason in 1774 Massachusetts." *Law and History Review* 29 (August): 657–701.

TREASON

Writing to John Adams in 1811, Benjamin Rush asked, "Do you not recollect the pensive and awful silence which pervaded the house when we were called up, one after another, to the table of the President of the Congress to subscribe what was believed by many at the time to be our own death warrants?" (Kennedy 1999, abstract).

After the signing of the Declaration of Independence, Benjamin Franklin was alleged to have said, "We must, indeed, all hang together or, most assuredly, we shall all hang separately" ("Franklin's Contributions"). Whether spoken or not, his words may well have expressed the concerns of many of the delegates who signed the Declaration. Benjamin Harrison and Elbridge Gerry apparently engaged in gallows humor when Harrison addressed Gerry by saying, "I shall have a great advantage over you, Mr. Gerry, when we are hung for what we are doing. From the size and weight of my body I shall die in a few minutes, but from the lightness of your body you will dance in the air an hour or two before you are dead" (Billias 1990, 68).

Although the delegates gathered at the Second Continental Congress dubbed themselves as patriots, and declared that they were a separate "people," they were not seeking to exit the empire with the consent of the king but in the face of his opposition. In his view, the Declaration, like prior preparations for combat, was an act of high treason, meriting the death penalty.

The offense of treason had been outlined in a statute from the reign of Edward III, which was adopted in 1350. In addition to applying to anyone who "doeth compass or imagine the death of our Lord the King" or his top associates, the law applied to any man who sought to "levy war against our said Lord the King in his realm, or be adherent to the enemies of our Lords the King in the realm, giving to them aid and support in his realm or elsewhere" (Hurst 1944, 226). In a move ridiculed by Edmund Burke, Parliament had sought to put further teeth into this measure by voting in 1769 to permit the transportation of individuals accused to treason to England (Unger 2000, 132–133).

There were attempts to use treason to punish those who had been responsible for the burning of the HMS *Gaspee* in Rhode Island, but it failed for lack of reliable evidence (York 2011, 667). Threats to try individuals for a capital offense were more likely to stir additional opposition to tyranny than to stifle dissent. Referring to the charge that the king had combined with others "for transporting us beyond seas to be tried for pretended offenses," Willard Hurst observed that "the clearest complaint of the Declaration of Independence . . . was with reference to oppressive trial practice regarding treason, rather than to the breadth of the crime" (1944, 256).

On June 24, 1776, faced with a Tory plot in New York, the Continental Congress adopted a set of resolutions. The first was as follows:

> That all persons abiding within any of the United Colonies, and deriving protection from the laws of the same, owe allegiance to the said laws, and are members of such colony; and that all persons passing through, visiting, or make [*sic*] a temporary stay in any of the said colonies, being entitled to the protection of the laws during the time of such passage, visitation or temporary stay, owe, during the same time, allegiance thereto. (*Journals*, 5:475)

Congress proceeded to specify that any such individuals "who shall levy war against any of the said colonies within the same, or be adherent to the king of Great Britain, or others the enemies of the said colonies, or any of them, within the same, giving to him or them aid and comfort, are guilty of treason against such colony" (*Journals*, 5:475). Brian F. Carso says these resolutions constituted "a de facto declaration of independence" and cites a letter that Elbridge Gerry wrote the next day referencing the law and noting that "I think we are in a fair way to a speedy Declaration of Independency, confederating, and other measures" (2006, 59).

Congress decided to delete a provision in Thomas Jefferson's Declaration that had accused the king of having "incited treasonable insurrections of our fellow citizens," perhaps recognizing that the king regarded the delegates' own actions as treasonous.

In writing the U.S. Constitution, the Framers incorporated provisions of English law by defining treason in Article III, Section 3 as "levying War against them [the United States], giving them Aid and Comfort." It further provided that no individual could be convicted "unless on the Testimony of two Witnesses to the same overt Act or on Confession in open Court" and that although Congress could proscribe the penalties, "no Attainder of Treason shall work Corruption of Blood, or forfeiture except during the Life of the Person attainted."

See also People; Tories; Transporting Us beyond Seas (Charge #19)

Further Reading

Billias, George Athan. 1990. "Elbridge Gerry." *This Constitution* 2 (Spring–Summer): 68–73.

Carso, Brian F., Jr. 2006. *"Whom Can We Trust Now?" The Meaning of Treason in the United States, from the Revolution through the Civil War.* Lanham, MD: Lexington Books.

"Franklin's Contributions to the American Revolution as a Diplomat in France." Historic Valley Forge. www.ushistory.org/valleyforge/history/franklin.html.

Hurst, Willard. 1944. "Treason in the United States? I. Treason down to the Constitution." *Harvard Law Review* 58 (December): 226–272.

Journals of the Continental Congress, 1774–1789. 1906. Vol. 5, *1776, June 5–October 8*. Washington, DC: Government Printing Office.

Kennedy, Jennifer Tiercel. 1999. "Signing History: The Memoirs of Benjamin Franklin, Benjamin Rush, John Adams, and Thomas Jefferson." PhD diss., Yale University.

Unger, Harlow Giles. 2000. *John Hancock: Merchant King and American Patriot*. New York: John Wiley and Sons.

York, Neil L. 2011. "Imperial Impotence: Treason in 1774 Massachusetts." *Law and History Review* 29 (August): 657–701.

TRIAL BY JURY (CHARGE #18)

One of the fundamental elements of the English common law system of justice was that of providing a jury of one's peers. The Declaration's 18th charge against the king accused him of having "combined with others . . . for depriving us in many cases of the benefits of trial by jury." The phrase "in many cases," which arguably reduced the force of the accusation while increasing its accuracy, was not in Thomas Jefferson's original manuscript and appears to have been added during congressional debates.

This accusation, like the one that follows accusing the king of "transporting us beyond Seas to be tried for pretended Offenses," refers to trials before admiralty courts, which had never provided for jury trials. These courts had been granted authority to enforce the Sugar Act of 1764, which colonists had sought to evade through smuggling.

If they were tried in their own colony by a jury of their peers, who themselves would likely profit from reduced customs duties, it is unlikely that individuals accused of smuggling would be convicted. If tried in a court whose judges were appointed by the Crown, however, conviction seemed much more likely.

Admiralty courts within Britain, like those in America, did not provide for jury trials. Moreover, while Britain had sought to increase colonial taxes after the French and Indian War, they had provided as early as the reign of William III (from 1689 to 1702) that individuals who had cut down tall white pine trees that had been designated as masts for the British Navy would be tried in such juryless courts (Fisher 1907, 289). Similar provisions had been made for pirates (Fisher 1907, 289), a comparison that would not likely have made such trials very palatable to the colonists. This accusation thus highlighted the manner in which the interests of the mother country and her colonies had become so disparate that the former no longer trusted the latter to carry out its laws on their own.

Because admiralty courts in America had far greater authority than those in Britain, the differences in treatment further highlighted the inequality between the rights of individuals living in Britain and those living in America. David S. Lovejoy points out these differences:

> The act of 1696 gave a larger jurisdiction to admiralty courts in America than had ever been given to the same courts in England, thus distinguishing between Americans and Englishmen in matters of justice. His Majesty's courts at Westminster, that is common-law courts with juries, enforced the acts of trade in England, while admiralty courts, which proceeded under the civil law without juries, could enforce some, if not all, of the same acts in America. (Lovejoy 1959, 462)

Lovejoy further points out that this was a long-standing grievance that was mentioned in resolutions of the Stamp Act Congress and in writings of James Otis, John Dickinson, and John Adams (1959, 466–467). Stephen Hopkins had also complained about the possibility that someone could be transported 1,500 miles, tried before individuals who did not know him, and be bankrupt by the expenses even if exonerated (1776, 29–30). The British launched highly political and highly publicized suits in admiralty courts against Henry Laurens in South Carolina and against John Hancock in Massachusetts that had further highlighted colonial grievances both against the taxes being levied and the methods used to collect them. The First Continental Congresses had objected to the jurisdiction of the admiralty courts in its Declaration and Resolves of 1774.

See also Charges against the King and Others; Declaration and Resolves of the First Continental Congress (1774); He Has Combined with Others (Charge #13)

Further Reading

Burgess, Douglas R., Jr. 2014. *The Politics of Piracy: Crime and Civil Disobedience in Colonial America*. Lebanon, NH: ForeEdge, an imprint of University Press of New England.

Fisher, Sydney George. 1907. "The Twenty-Eight Charges against the King in the Declaration of Independence." *Pennsylvania Magazine of History and Biography* 31:257–303.

Hopkins, Stephen. 1766. *The Grievances of the American Colonies Candidly Examined*. Providence, RI, and Salem, MA: New England & Virginia Col, Historical Reproductions and Reprints.

Lovejoy, David S. 1959. "Rights Imply Equality: The Case against Admiralty Jurisdiction in America, 1764–1776." *William and Mary Quarterly* 16 (October): 459–484.

Owen, David R., and Michael C. Tolley. 1995. *Courts of Admiralty in Colonial America: The Maryland Experience, 1634–1776*. Durham, NC: Carolina Academic Press.

TRUMBULL, JOHN (PAINTINGS)

One of the most iconic images associated with the Declaration of Independence is that painted by John Trumbull (1765–1743). Born to a prominent Connecticut family (Trumbull's father served as governor), Trumbull was educated at Harvard before serving as an aide-de-camp to George Washington and later being named a colonel by Major General Horatio Gates.

A strong patriot, Trumbull nonetheless traveled to London in order to study art under Benjamin West and other artists. Because of his outspoken views and known association with Benjamin Franklin, Trumbull was arrested and imprisoned for eight months before being deported to America. Trumbull was determined to capture the heroism that American Patriots had displayed during the Revolutionary War, and to this end, he painted five paintings that focused on famous battles. They were as follows: *The Death of General Warren at the Battle of Bunker's Hill, June 17, 1776*; *The Death of General Montgomery in the Attack on Quebec, December 31, 1776*; *The Death of General Mercer at the Battle of Princeton, January 3, 1777*; *The Capture of the Hessians at Trenton, December 26, 1777*; and *The Surrender of Lord Cornwallis at Yorktown, October 19, 1781* (Zymont).

American artist John Trumbull's *The Declaration of Independence* was painted in the decades after the American Revolution. One version of this painting hangs in the rotunda of the U.S. Capitol Building. This version portrays committee members presenting the Declaration to John Hancock, the president of the Second Continental Congress. (Corel)

Trumbull was inspired to paint *The Declaration of Independence* after visiting Thomas Jefferson in London in 1785. Jefferson subsequently invited him to view art with him in France the following year, where Trumbull began the first of three canvases on the subject that would occupy him for the next 34 years. The first, consisting of a 20-by-30-inch canvas, is now at the Yale University Art Gallery. His second such painting is one of four 12-by-18-foot life-size canvases commissioned by Congress for the Capitol Buildings. The other scenes in this series, for each of which Congress paid Trumbull $8,000, depicted the British surrenders at Saratoga and Yorktown, and George Washington's resignation at Annapolis (Tigner 1993, 89). In 1832, Trumbull painted yet a third 6-by-9-foot painting for the Wadsworth Atheneum in Hartford, Connecticut.

Trumbull drew most of the men he depicted in the Declaration of Independence either from real life or from other paintings that had portrayed them. He patterned the design of the room based on a description that Thomas Jefferson had provided him. Trumbull's largest version portrayed 47 portraits, leaving out 13 of the signers and including 5 nonsigners (Tigner, 1993, 90).

Although Trumbull assigned the date of July 4, 1776, to the painting that he made for the Capitol Rotunda, which is sometimes incorrectly titled *The Signing of the Declaration of Independence*, this painting actually depicts the presentation of the draft of the Declaration by the Committee of Five that took place on June 28, 1776. In the painting, committee members stand before John Hancock. Charles Thomson, the secretary of the Second Continental Congress, is standing just behind him. Benjamin Harrison, who presided over the Committee of the Whole that debated the Declaration, and Richard Henry Lee, who offered the resolution for independence that was incorporated into the document, also had prominent positions in the painting.

Trumbull exhibited his work in New York, Boston, Philadelphia, and Baltimore, in what Pohrt describes as "the first large-scale, multi-city exhibition of a painting in America" (2013, 117) prior to taking it to the Capitol. He managed to get John Adams to come to the viewing at Faneuil Hall in Boston (Pohrt 2013, 118).

Howard Mumford Jones notes that the painting contains a number of historical inaccuracies. He observes that the committee chair rather than the entire committee would have presented the report; Hancock would not have been presiding because the committee made its presentation to the Committee of the Whole; and, in parliamentary procedure, "voting to lay a report on a table does not require a table" like the one pictured (1976, 58).

Trumbull's painting, although largely a static image featuring a lot of what contemporaries might call "dead white males," has been one of the most popular images associated with the Declaration and has been featured on postage stamps and on the back of a hundred-dollar bank note and the two-dollar bill. It is also the model for an engraving by John Francis Paramino, which was commissioned for the sesquicentennial of Independence, and is located on the Boston Common, on Tremont Street Mall just above an image of a copy of the engrossed Declaration modeled on that of Timothy Matlack (Boston Art Commission). Largely because Trumbull's painting is sometimes referred to as *The Signing of the Declaration of Independence*, it is sometimes falsely associated with the congressional adoption of the document, which took place on July 4, and the signing, which began on August 2. Thomas Jefferson displayed an engraving of Trumbull's work in the entrance hall at Monticello ("Declaration of Independence by Tyler").

In addition to Trumbull's works, the U.S. Capitol contains what Francis V. O'Connor describes as "a painted frieze of illusionistic sculpture showing historical scenes with an impressive array of life-size figures in sepia grisaille fresco" (1998, 149). The 14th of 20 such chronologically arranged scenes, ultimately painted by Filippo Costaggini, presents an idealized depiction of John Adams, Thomas Jefferson, and Benjamin Franklin reading the Declaration on the steps of what is otherwise an outdoor setting.

See also Coins and Stamps Depicting the Declaration of Independence; Jefferson, Thomas; Signing of the Declaration of Independence

Further Reading

Boston Art Commission. "Declaration of Independence Tablet." http://97.74.183.147/content/declaration-independence-tablet.

"Declaration of Independence by Tyler (Engraving)." Thomas Jefferson's Monticello. https://www.monticello.org/site/research-and-collections/declaration-independence-tyler-engraving.

Mulcahy, James M. 1956. "Congress Voting Independence. The Trumbull and Pine-Savage Paintings." *Pennsylvania Magazine of History and Biography* 80 (January): 74–91.

Jones, Howard Mumford. 1976. "The Declaration of Independence: A Critique." *Proceedings of the American Antiquarian Society*, pp. 55–72. www.americanantiquarian.org/proceedings/44498097.pdf.

O'Connor, Francis V. 1998. "Symbolism in the Rotunda." In *Constantino Brumidi: Artist of the Capitol*, edited by Barbara A. Wolanin, 141–155. Washington, DC: U.S. Congress.

Pohrt, Tanya. 2013. "Reception and Meaning in John Trumbull's 'Declaration of Independence.'" Teaching with Art. *Yale University Art Gallery Bulletin*, 116–119.

Sumrell, Morgan. January 28, 2013. "John Trumbull: Art and Politics in the Revolution." *Journal of the American Revelation*. https://allthingsliberty.com/2013/01/john-trumbull-art-and-politics-in-the-revolution.

Tigner, Steven S. 1993. "Didactic Images and the Declaration of Independence." *Journal of Education* 175:85–104.

Wills, Garry. 1978. *Inventing America: Jefferson's Declaration of Independence*. Garden City, NY: Doubleday.

Zygmont, Bryan. "John Trumbull, The Declaration of Independence." Khan Academy. https://www.khanacademy.org/humanities/art-americas/british-colonies/early-republic/a/trumbull-declaration-of-independence.

TYLER ENGRAVING OF THE DECLARATION OF INDEPENDENCE

On July 4, 1776, the Second Continental Congress commissioned John Dunlap to print a one-page broadside of the Declaration of Independence. Later that month, it commissioned Timothy Matlack to prepare an engrossed (handwritten) copy on parchment, which the delegates signed beginning on August 2. In January 1777, Mary Katherine Goddard subsequently published the first printing of the document with the signers' names, but they were in italics rather than facsimiles, and she scrambled the order of names on the original.

In the 1810s, two engravers, Benjamin Owen Tyler and John Binns, sought to be the first to publish facsimiles of the engrossed manuscript. Tyler (b. 1789) was the first to accomplish the task, producing a 31-by-27-inch copy, adorned only by an arched heading, in which his capitalization and bolding differed from the Matlack engrossment, which he used as a model (Allen and Sneff 2017, 36), but which was complete with full-size facsimiles of the Framers' signatures as originally placed (Puleo 2016, 239). He dedicated the engraving to Thomas Jefferson, who accepted the honor, while noting that he was "but a fellow signer" ("Declaration of Independence by Tyler [Engraving]"). Tyler subsequently presented Jefferson with a parchment copy and visited Monticello.

Tyler solicited Richard Rush, the acting secretary of state and son of Benjamin Rush, who was one of the original signers, to validate the accuracy of the work. Tyler recorded Rush's validation on the bottom left-hand corner of his print just above the seal of the secretary of state's office:

> The foregoing copy of the Declaration of Independence has been collated with the original instrument and found correct. I have myself examined the signature to each. Those executed by Mr. Tyler are curiously exact imitations, so much so that it would be difficult, if not impossible, for the closest scrutiny to distinguish them, were it not for the hand of time, from the originals. (Puleo 2016, 240)

The work of both Binns and Tyler was overshadowed by a print by William J. Stone, which then–secretary of state John Quincy Adams commissioned in 1820 and which was completed in 1823 and was considered to be the "official" copy.

See also Dunlap Broadside Printing of the Declaration of Independence; Goddard Printing of the Declaration of Independence; Stone Engraving of the Declaration of Independence

Further Reading

Allen, Danielle, and Emily Sneff. 2017."The Sussex Declaration: Dating the Parchment Manuscript of the Declaration of Independence Held at the West Sussex Record Office (Chichester, UK). Under final revision and preparation for publication at *Papers of the Bibliographic Society of America*.

"Declaration of Independence by Tyler (Engraving)." Thomas Jefferson's Monticello. https://www.monticello.org/site/research-and-collections/declaration-independence-tyler-engraving.

Puleo, Stephen. 2016. *American Treasures: The Secret Efforts to Save the Declaration of Independence, the Constitution, and the Gettysburg Address*. New York: St. Martin's Press.

TYRANNY

One of the aspects of the Declaration of Independence that may undermine its persuasiveness was its reference to the king as a tyrant. The Declaration's third charge against the king thus said that in refusing legislative representation in some colonies, the king was interfering with "a right inestimable to them, and formidable to tyrants alone." Similarly, in explaining how the colonies had unsuccessfully petitioned for redress of grievances, the Declaration proclaimed that "A prince whose character is thus marked by every act which may define a tyrant, is unfit to be the ruler of a free people."

In introducing the accusations against the king, the Declaration charged that "The history of the present king of Great Britain is a history of repeated injuries and usurpations all having in direct object the establishment of an absolute tyranny over these states." Although this charge is fairly categorical, it omits a phrase "among which appears no solitary fact to contradict the uniform tenor of the rest," which Jefferson had included in his draft but which Congress deleted. In detailing war atrocities, the Declaration further indicted the king for "transporting large armies of foreign mercenaries to complete the works of death, desolation, and tyranny." Jefferson's original draft had further charged that "future ages will scarce believe that the hardiness of one man, adventured within the short compass of twelve years only, on so many acts of tyranny without a mask, over a people fostered & fixed in principles of liberty." Similarly, the second paragraph of the Declaration justified independence on the basis that the colonies have endured "a long train of abuses and usurpations, pursuing invariably the same object" and evincing a design to reduce them under absolute despotism." This term "despotism" is essentially a synonym for tyranny.

A tyrant is a single ruler who rules oppressively for his own benefit rather than for the benefit of his people. Given the constraints of the British constitution, which embodied a mixed form of government in which the king shared power with the

House of Commons and the House of Lords, few would have characterized George III as a tyrant, especially prior to the publication of Thomas Paine's *Common Sense.* Even that provocative writing focused not so much on the abuses of George III in particular but on those of kings in general. Moreover, as monarchs go, George III does not seem to fit the bill as a tyrant. Howard Mumford Jones thus observes that:

> George III never attempted to govern either Great Britain without a parliament as Charles I had done, nor corrupted the judiciary as James II did; during his long reign, so long as he was sane, George III governed his realm according to then-existent parliamentary formulae. He was neither a Turkish sultan nor a Moorish despot; he led a most exemplary private life; and since words like "despot" and "tyrant" bring to our minds names like that of Napoleon or Hitler, we are at a loss whether Jefferson really meant what he said. (1976, 17–18)

This criticism is not new. Benjamin Rush thus reports that John Witherspoon had objected to an earlier use of the word "tyrant" to describe the king on the basis "that the epithet was both *false* and *undignified.* It was *false*, because George 3d was not a tyrant in Great Britain; on the contrary he was beloved and respected by his subjects in Great Britain, and perhaps the more, for making war upon us. It was *undignified*, because it did not become one sovereign power to abuse or use harsh epithets, when it spoke of another" (1905, 110).

If the colonies were not already in what George III considered to be open revolt, the charges that he was already warring against the colonies might be considered tyrannical, but by the time of the Declaration, both sides had reason to charge the other with such atrocities. Moreover, the fact that the Declaration accused the king of having "combined with others," an indirect reference to the two houses of Parliament, would indicate that he was acting in conjunction, rather than in opposition, to other institutions within the British government. From this perspective, it is relatively easy to dismiss the charges as an example of hyperbole or outright propaganda.

A closer examination of the charges, however, reveals that the Declaration was focusing not so much on the king's motives as on his behavior; it was not so much trying to prove that he was a bad man but that he was engaging in conduct that was bad for Americans. Moreover, the Declaration was not accusing the king of being a tyrant at home in Great Britain but of acting like a tyrant with respect to the colonies. History reveals many examples of republics that treated colonies in an arbitrary, or tyrannical, fashion. In his classic treatment of the Peloponnesian War, for example, Thucydides revealed that Athens, which was a democracy, engaged in such behavior (1951, 147–172). Moreover, later opponents of American imperialism essentially made the same charge against its policies with respect to its foreign territories in the aftermath of the Spanish-American War (Kinzer 2017).

In urging her husband to "Remember the Ladies," Abigail Adams observed that "all men would be tyrants if they could" (Vile 2015, 89). Rather obviously, she was not saying that all men tyrannized over other men, but simply that they did so over women.

Under the colonial view, their legislatures were entitled to equal respect with parliament. The king, as head of the empire, should adjudicate fairly between them. When he invariably sided with Parliament, this indicated a joint tyrannical posture toward them.

Although the opening paragraphs of the Declaration speak eloquently of the rights of men, it is important to remember that the paramount purpose of the Document was to declare the equal station of the American people. If the British people, led by the king and any others, were treating them tyrannically, then Americans certainly had the right to claim their "separate and equal station" with other nations.

In this respect, the argument against tyranny is similar to the argument that colonists had been making with respect to Britain's attempts to enslave the colonies (Gittleman 1974; Lucas 1976). While they might not literally be in chains, assertions of British authority posed sufficient danger for them to be wary of the loss of their liberties. This view was articulated by Chief Justice John Marshall in a letter that he sent to Edward Everett on August 2, 1826. After commending Everett for an address on the American Revolution and the Declaration, Marshall observed that:

> Our resistance was not made to actual oppression. Americans were not pressed down to the earth by the weight of their chains, nor goaded to resistance by actual suffering. "They were not slaves rising in desperation from beneath the agonies of the lash; but freemen snuffing from afar 'the tainted gale of tyranny.'" This view of the subject is not only more consistent with the fact, but is more honorable to the intelligence of those virtuous patriots and sensible men who dared to lead us into the mighty conflict. The long list of tyrannical acts which is found in our declaration of independence, and which swells the papers of the day, was judiciously inserted as tending to produce unanimity, and was justified by the irritated feelings of the moment; but the time is arrived when the truth may be declared, and it is most honorable to our ancestors to declare it. The war was a war of principle, against a system hostile to political liberty, from which oppression was to be dreaded, not against actual oppression. (Quoted by Walsh 2015)

Although Marshall, as a former Federalist, has probably overstated his arguments with respect to a document authored by Jefferson (a Democratic-Republican)—the British had, after all, taken some steps, including military actions, which had dire actual effects on the colonists—his overall point is that the colonists were just as concerned about potential future abuses as about current grievances. As A. W. Clason would later describe the Founders, "it seemed to them, as it undoubtedly is, more wise, and equally safe, to fight upon the first aggression. Submission makes a precedent for future encroachment" (1885, 445).

In *Common Sense*, Thomas Paine had essentially argued that all hereditary monarchs were tyrants. The Declaration makes a more modest argument, opposing tyranny, or what Harvey Mansfield calls an "absolute monarchy," while leaving open the possibility of a "limited monarchy," so long as it had the consent of the people (Mansfield 1983, 27).

See also British Constitution; Charges against the King and Others; *Common Sense* (Paine); He Has Combined with Others (Charge #13); References to King George III in the Declaration of Independence; Slavery

Further Reading

Clason, A. W. 1885. "The Fallacy of 1776." *Magazine of American History* 13 (May): 445–456.

Gittleman, Edwin. 1974. "Jefferson's 'Slave Narrative': The Declaration of Independence as a Literary Text." *Early American Literature* 8 (Winter): 239–256.

Jones, Howard Mumford. 1976. "The Declaration of Independence: A Critique." In *The Declaration of Independence: Two Essays by Howard Mumford Jones and Howard H. Peckham*, 3–20. Worcester, MA: American Antiquarian Society.

Kinzer, Stephen. 2017. *The True Flag: Theodore Roosevelt, Mark Twain, and the Birth of American Empire*. New York: Henry Holt.

Lucas, Stephen E. 1976. *Portents of Rebellion: Rhetoric and Revolution in Philadelphia, 1765–1776*. Philadelphia: Temple University Press.

Mansfield, Harvey C., Jr. 1983. "Thomas Jefferson." In *American Political Thought: The Philosophic Dimension of American Statesmanship*, edited by Morton J. Frisch and Richard G. Stevens, 23–50. Itasca, IL: F. E. Peacock.

Rush, Benjamin. 1905. *A Memorial Containing Travels through Life or Sundry Incidents in the Life of Dr. Benjamin Rush*. Lanoraie, QC: Louis Alexander Biddle.

Thucydides. 1951. *The Peloponnesian War*. New York: Modern Library.

Vile, John R. 2015. *Founding Documents of America: Documents Decoded*. Santa Barbara, CA: ABC-CLIO.

Walsh, Kevin C. March 10, 2015. "Marshall on Political Liberty, the Declaration of Independence, and Jefferson's 1801 Inaugural Address." http://mirrorofjustice.blogs.com/mirrorofjustice/2015/03/marshall-on-political-liberty-the-declaration-of-independence-and-jeffersons-1801-inaugural-address.html.

U

UNALIENABLE RIGHTS

One of the most controversial assertions in the Declaration of Independence is contained in the second paragraph, which proclaims that all men are "created equal" and that they are endowed by their Creator with certain inalienable rights." Thomas Jefferson's "inalienable" became "unalienable" when John Dunlap printed the Document, perhaps at the insistence of John Adams, or whoever else might have been there for that process. The change was inconsequential because the words are synonyms (Smith 2017, 113–114).

Jefferson's initial draft had referred to "inherent and inalienable rights." The word "inherent" suggests something intrinsic to, or implicit in the nature of, something. Similarly, something that is unalienable cannot be willingly transferred to another. Although it is possible that one can conceive of humans as rights-bearing individuals from a nontheological perspective, the Declaration specifically indicated that they have been "endowed by their Creator," much as Scriptures teach that human beings are uniquely created "in the image of God." Basic rights are not the gift of the state but of God, who is the author of life, liberty, and the means to pursue happiness. As John Alvis expresses it, "the rights here mentioned are entitlements neither conferred by Britain nor deduced from nature (even if Jefferson believed Britain had once so conferred them and that the nature of the human species so requires them)" (1998, 384). As Jefferson noted in his Bill for Establishing Religious Freedom in Virginia, "Almighty God hath created the mind free, and manifested his supreme will that free it shall remain by making it altogether insusceptible of restraint" (Jefferson 1779).

John E. Smith notes that the Declaration ties rights to the proposition that "all men are created equal." He observes that many early Americans regarded their continent as "a new Promised Land whose inhabitants were to be forever free of the encumbrances, injustices, and tyrannies which were associated not only with European civilization, but with the entire previous history of the world" (Smith 1977, 365). He further notes that this led to the belief that "as bearers of a common humanity" individuals "enter the world on an equal footing so that each individual is seen as entitled to the same respect as any other" (1977, 365).

Rights are often tied to duties. God grants individuals life not simply for their own good but for that of others; they cannot invest their lives in others if they are subjected as slaves to the will of another. As the corresponding right of revolution suggests, individuals have not only the right, but arguably the duty, to defend their right to worship. Humans have the right not only to seek their own happiness but that of the communities of which they are a part.

One of the most frequent criticisms of unalienable rights is based on the erroneous notion that such rights must therefore be absolute. It seems clear, however, that the rights the Declaration defends do not exempt individuals who run roughshod over the rights of others from punishments that could involve forfeiture of either life or liberty. B. A. Richards thus notes that "it is characteristic of constitutions of this period that they begin with categorical declarations of rights and follow them with qualifying articles" (1969, 394). Somewhat departing from the trilogy of rights listed in the Declaration of Independence, Thomas G. West acknowledges that "the government has authority to order its citizens to risk their *lives* fighting the enemies of the country, to limit their *liberty* by doing whatever the law orders them to do, and to give up some of their *property* in taxes" (West 2003, 118). He further asserts that "as long as government promotes the common good of the society, by protecting the life, liberty, and property of the people, its constraints on liberty in fact enhance the actual liberty we enjoy" (2003, 119).

See also Equality; God; Life, Liberty and the Pursuit of Happiness

Further Reading

Alvis, John. 1998. "Milton and the Declaration of Independence." *Interpretation* 25 (Spring): 367–405.

Jefferson, Thomas. June 18, 1779. "A Bill for Establishing Religious Freedom." Founders Online. https://founders.archives.gov/documents/Jefferson/01-02-02-0132-0004-0082.

Richards, B. A. 1969. "Inalienable Rights: Recent Criticism and Old Doctrine." *Philosophy and Phenomenological Research* 29 (March): 391–404.

Smith, George H. 2017. *The American Revolution and the Declaration of Independence*. Washington, DC: Cato Institute.

Smith, John E. 1977. "Philosophical Ideas behind the 'Declaration of Independence.'" *Revue Internationale de Philosophie* 31:360–376.

West, Thomas G. 2003. "The Political Theory of the Declaration of Independence." In *The American Founding and the Social Compact*, edited by Ronald J. Pestritto and Thomas G. West, 95–146. Lanham, MD: Lexington Books.

UNITED STATES OF AMERICA (NAME)

The closing paragraph of the Declaration of Independence is written in the name of "the Representatives of the United states of America." Both the original Dunlap printing of the Declaration of Independence and the subsequent embossed copy on parchment identify themselves as being from the United States of America (with the latter, however, adding the word "thirteen" and leaving the word "united" uncapitalized).

The term "Americans" apparently came into use in the New World at about the time of the British conquest of Quebec in the fall of 1759 (Varg 1964, 170). Daniel Dulany further used the term "American" in reference to all the colonies in his *Considerations on the Propriety of Imposing Taxes in the British Colonies, for the Purpose of Raising a Revenue, by an Act of Parliament*, which he published in 1765 (Varg 1964, 179). An increasing sense of American nationalism followed, and somewhat mimicked, the development of British nationalism (Varg 1964).

A newspaper letter signed "Republicus" and dated June 29, 1776, proposed that Americans call themselves "the *United States of America*" (Maier 1999, 44). Similarly, on June 24, 1776, the day that Congress adopted resolutions designed to address Tory opposition in New York, John Hancock, the president of the Congress, issued an army commission to Antoine-Félix Wuibert in which he used the expression "United States" three different times (Nettels 1946, 36). Moreover, the very next day, Elbridge Gerry wrote a letter in which he referred to "enemies of the United States of America" (Nettels 1946, 44).

It appears as though the Declaration of Independence was the first governmental document that used the full terminology of the United States of America. This would stand to reason. Prior to this time, the American entities involved were colonies. Moreover, a central point of the Declaration was to declare that they were no longer so but that they were assuming their right "as free & independent states" with "full power to levy war, conclude peace, contract alliances, establish commerce, & to do all other acts and things which independent states may of right do."

Prior to the Declaration, the collective name used was typically "the United Colonies," sometimes prefaced with the specific number of colonies involved. Other variations included "United Colonies," "United English Colonies of North America," "United Colonies in Congress," or "The United States of North America." Edmund Burnett observed (1925) that the term "The United States of North America," was initially used in the treaty that was signed with France. J. G. A. Pocock observes that, based on the predominate terminology of 1776, the former colonists could have referred "'the United Commonwealths,' or even 'the United Republics,' instead of 'the United States'" (1987, 705).

See also Captions of the Declaration of Independence

Further Reading

Burnett, Edmund D. 1925. "The Name 'United States of America.'" *American Historical Review* 31 (October): 79–81.

Maier, Pauline. 1997. *American Scripture: Making the Declaration of Independence*. New York: Alfred A. Knopf.

Nettels, Curtis P. 1946. "A Link in the Chain of Events Leading to American Independence." *William and Mary Quarterly* 3 (January): 36–47.

Pocock, J. G. A. 1987. "States, Republics, and Empires: The American Founding in Early Modern Perspective." *Social Science Quarterly* 68 (December): 703–723.

Varg, Paul A. 1964. "The Advent of Nationalism, 1758–1776." *American Quarterly* 16 (Summer): 169–181.

U.S. CONSTITUTION AND THE DECLARATION OF INDEPENDENCE

Because both documents are so seminal, it is common for citizens to confuse the Declaration of Independence and the Constitution. Their purposes were quite different. The Declaration of Independence, some of the principles of which states' bills of rights had previously articulated, attempted to justify the decision that members of the Second Continental Congress had made two days earlier to declare their independence of British rule in the hope of rallying both internal and external support. In reporting the Declaration to the states, John Hancock proclaimed that it could be considered "as the Ground and Foundation of a Future Government" (Mahoney 1987, 55).

The primary purpose of the Constitution was to effectuate the protection of the natural rights that the Declaration had declared. It sought to do so by outlining governmental structures and restrictions that would better secure these goals than the existing government under the Articles of Confederation which preceded it.

The Declaration of Independence grew out of differing views of how the unwritten British constitution operated. The British Parliament asserted that it exercised sovereignty (including the power of taxation) throughout the empire. Americans initially felt tied to the English homeland through loyalty to the king but declared an end to that loyalty when the king rebuffed colonial petitions and continued to support the authority of Parliament (Greene 2011).

Clues as to the Kinds of Government Americans Desired

Although the primary goal of the Declaration of Independence was to declare the purposes for separation from Great Britain, the Declaration left many clues about the kind of government that the former colonists were seeking. The second paragraph of the Declaration had asserted that individuals were "created equal." This was in clear contrast to ideas that one bloodline of people was superior to others by birth, enough to justify that one would rule and the other would be ruled. Although not necessarily disavowing the idea of an elected king, the principles of the Declaration would appear to oppose one who was hereditary, unless the monarch's role was purely symbolic.

This paragraph further specified that people instituted government to secure the rights to "life, liberty, and the pursuit of happiness," that government rested upon "the consent of the governed," and that the people had the right to remove and replace governments that did not secure such rights and that were not so established. This clearly envisioned a government from the grass roots up rather than imposed from the top down. The Constitution provided for an amending process by which the people could seek peaceful change in the document if the government it created proved to be oppressive.

In critiquing the rule of the British king and his association with "others" (the two houses of the British Parliament), the Declaration further provided numerous principles by which to judge future governments.

With regard to laws, the Declaration stated that "the right of representation in the legislature" was "a right inestimable to them, & formidable to tyrants only." Identifying such representation as an "inestimable" right seemed to place this on a par with the rights of "life, liberty, and the pursuit of happiness." Linking the first several charges against the king to abuses of legislative authority further highlighted the commitment of the document to representative government. Notably, the colonists had protested from the beginning against parliamentary taxation without representation, and the Continental Congress had already authorized states to replace royal governments with those more accountable to the people.

Although phrasing the grievances in the Declaration against the king might suggest that the Declaration opposed strong executive power, it is notable that, especially in the part of the document that accuses the king of having "combined with others," the Declaration excoriates the king for failing to protect his people's rights. The document appears to recognize the need for an executive power to deal with foreign affairs, while expressing disappointment that the current king had not adequately provided for the naturalization of foreigners and had warred against his people.

A number of the accusations against the king deal with the judiciary. The Declaration accused the king of "refusing his assent to laws for establishing judiciary powers," for making "judges dependent on his will alone, for the tenure of their offices," for subjecting Americans to "foreign jurisdictions," for protecting lawbreakers through "mock-trial from punishment," for depriving Americans of "trial by Jury," and transporting them abroad for trials. Such accusations would set the expectation that the former colonies would provide for judicial independence, trials in suspects' communities, and trial by jury.

In addition to highlighting the need for protection of life, liberty, the pursuit of happiness, and legislative representation, the Declaration clearly valued the right of the people to petition the king. This right was later enshrined within the First Amendment.

The Declaration showed its regard for the rule of law by indicting the king "for taking away our charters abolishing our most valuable laws, and altering fundamentally the forms of our government." The Declaration further evidenced its support of civilian control of the military when it accused the king of having "affected to render the military independent of, & superior to, the civil power." The U.S. Constitution entrusted the president, an elected official, with the power of serving as commander-in-chief of the military.

Creation of New Governments

One of the other two resolutions that Richard Henry Lee had introduced along with the Declaration of Independence had called for the creation of a new government. Congress subsequently approved the Articles of Confederation, which the last state did not ratify, and which therefore did not go into effect, until 1781. It had provided for a single branch of the government (a unicameral Congress) in which states were equally represented. This government did not have the power to act directly on individual citizens because primary sovereignty rested with the states, which had vested primary powers in their legislatures. It was later replaced with a constitution that provided greater national powers.

Some revolutionaries, among them Thomas Paine, may have had exaggerated ideas of the way that direct popular government would protect the individual rights that the Declaration of Independence had highlighted. During government under the Articles of Confederation, weak governors and judges were often unable to block unjust state legislation, and the national government proved unable to provide adequate security for state republican governments (Wood 1969; Van Cleve 2017).

Faced with such problems, leading statesmen eventually met in Philadelphia at the Constitutional Convention of 1787 to draw up a new government.

The Declaration was not the subject of much debate there but was mentioned in discussions on June 19–20 of the relationship between the states and the national government. On the 19th, Maryland's Luther Martin, who would become an Anti-Federalist, claimed "that the separation from G. B. placed the 13 States in a state of nature towards each other" and that they had entered the Articles "on the footing of equality" (Farrand 1966, 1:324). By contrast, James Wilson, who had been a delegate to the Second Continental Congress, observed that he did not think the states had ever been independent: "He read the declaration of Independence, observing thereon that the United Colonies were declared to be free & independent States; and inferring that they were independent, not Individually but Unitedly and that they were confederated as they were independent, States" (Farrand 1966, 1:324). Alexander Hamilton agreed with Wilson's analysis, which Martin, however, reaffirmed on the following day (Farrand 1966, 1:340–41).

The U.S. Constitution

The Declaration had called for a government based on consent; the opening words of the Constitution, which had been ratified in special conventions within each of the states, was "We the People." The preamble further listed the goals of this new constitution "to form a more perfect Union, establish Justice, insure domestic Tranquility, provide for the common defence, promote the general Welfare, and secure the Blessings of Liberty to ourselves and our Posterity."

To secure these ends, the Framers created a strengthened national government, against whose abuses it sought to protect by dividing Congress into two houses, one of which (the House of Representatives, which was apportioned according to population) was especially close to the people, who elected all its members every two years. It further balanced this branch against an executive who was chosen indirectly through the Electoral College by the people. The Constitution also provided for a federal judiciary whose members were appointed by the president with the advice and consent of the senate and who served "during good behavior," thus freeing them from control by the two elected branches.

Although it increased the power of the national government, the new constitution continued to divide powers between the national government and the states. This largely rested on the notion that some matters were better left to local authorities and partly on the idea that the two levels of government would serve as checks on one another. Consistent with the Declaration's emphasis on representative assemblies, Article IV, Section 4 of the Constitution guaranteed to each state a "republican" form of government. By contrast, the Constitution embodied a number of compromises related to representation in the House of Representatives, the importation of slaves, and the return of runaways that fell short of providing the equality of rights that the Declaration had sought.

In addition to vesting each branch with specific powers, the Constitution provided protections against both Congress (Article I, Section 9) and the states

(Article I, Section 10). It limited suspensions of habeas corpus, prevented ex post facto laws and bills of attainder, prohibited titles of nobility (which would produce inequality), and prohibited states from abridging freedom of contracts.

Apart from the preamble, the Constitution largely lacked the ringing phrases of the Declaration of Independence. Many states constitutions that had begun with declaration of rights, which had affirmed natural rights, had lacked institutional structures to effectuate such freedoms. When the Convention sent the Constitution to the states for ratification, Anti-Federalist opponents complained that the new Constitution lacked such a bill of rights. In time, leading Federalists, most notably James Madison, promised to work for a bill of rights once the constitution was ratified.

The Bill of Rights

Partly as a way of avoiding another Convention that might overturn the work of the first, Madison led the fight for what became the first ten amendments in the very first Congress (Goldwin 1997; Labunski 2006). These amendments both prohibited the government from interfering with certain key rights such as the free exercise of religion, speech, press, peaceable assembly, and petition, which were listed in the First Amendment, and provided procedural protections for individuals like those found in the Fourth through Eighth Amendments. Substituting the word "property" for "the pursuit of happiness" that had been employed in the Declaration of Independence, the Fifth Amendment provided that the government could not deprive individuals of "life, liberty, or property" without due process of law. The Fifth Amendment also guaranteed the right to indictment by grand juries while the Sixth Amendment, arguably thinking of some of the abuses that the Declaration had mentioned, further provided that "the accused shall enjoy the right to a speedy and public trial, by an impartial jury of the state and district wherein the crime shall have been committed."

Subsequent Amendments

The Constitution did not protect the rights of American slaves, who were counted as three-fifths of a person for purposes of taxation and representation within the U.S. House of Representatives. In time, Abraham Lincoln argued that the Constitution should effectuate the equality that was mentioned within the Declaration of Independence and that it could not adequately do so if it remained half free and half slave.

At the end of the Civil War, the Thirteenth Amendment (1865) freed the slaves, and, in a clear echo of the Declaration, the Fourteenth Amendment (1868) declared that all persons should be accorded "equal protection of the laws." Shortly thereafter the Fifteenth Amendment (1870) outlawed voting discrimination on the basis of race. The Nineteenth Amendment (1920) would more effectively extend similar protections to women, thus more clearly including them in the phrase that "all men are created equal."

Over time, individuals have critiqued some of the compromises (like equal state representation in the U.S. Senate and the Electoral College) that, while making the Constitution possible, also made the document less democratic (Levinson 2006). Some historians of the Progressive Era were particularly critical of the document, which they regarded as a betrayal of the principles of the Declaration (See Vile 2016, 1:235). It is important to recognize, however, that notable figures including Benjamin Franklin, Robert Morris, John Dickinson, Elbridge Gerry, and others attended both bodies and that the authors of the Constitution dated their own work in relation to the Declaration. Once ratified, the Constitution stood for the principle articulated in the Declaration that had recognized the right of the people to create new governments as necessary.

Continuing Issues

There are continuing issues involving the degree to which the Declaration of Independence can be considered to be national law and the degree to which the principles of the Declaration, and especially its doctrine of natural rights, should be used to interpret the Constitution. This largely pits those who want justices to engage in such interpretations (Gerber 1995; Sandefur 2014) against those who fear that this will encourage undue judicial activism and therefore undermine democracy. Lee Strang has argued that "the Declaration of Independence is one of many sources of the Constitution's original meaning" (2006, 414) while denying that its placement at the beginning of the U.S. Code (which also includes the Articles of Confederation and the Northwest Ordinance) thereby make it an actual part of the Constitution.

In 1976, Republican Representative Robert Michel of Illinois introduced a constitutional amendment to incorporate some of the principles of the Declaration of Independence into the preamble to the U.S. Constitution (Vile 2015, 1:139).

See also Attestation Clauses; *Common Sense* (Paine); Creation of New State Governments; Hancock's Letters Accompanying the Declaration of Independence; Representative (Republican) Government; Resolutions Introduced by Richard Henry Lee (June 7, 1776)

Further Reading

Arnn, Larry P. 2012. *The Founders' Key: The Divine and Natural Connection between the Declaration and the Constitution and What We Risk by Losing It*. Nashville, TN: Thomas Nelson.

Billias, George Athan. 1985. "The Declaration of Independence: A Constitutional Document." *This Constitution*, no. 6 (Spring): 47–52.

Cosgrove, Charles H. 1998. "The Declaration of Independence in Constitutional Interpretation: A Selective History and Analysis." *University of Richmond Law Review* 32 (January): 107–164.

Farrand, Max, ed. 1966. *The Records of the Federal Convention of 1787*. 4 vols. New Haven, CT: Yale University Press.

Gerber, Scott Douglas. 1995. *To Secure These Rights: The Declaration of Independence and Constitutional Interpretation*. New York: New York University Press.

Goldwin, Robert A. 1997. *From Parchment to Power: How James Madison Used the Bill of Rights to Save the Constitution*. Washington, DC: AEI Press.

Greene, Jack P. 2011. *The Constitutional Origins of the American Revolution*. New York: Cambridge University Press.

Himmelfarb, Dan. 1990. "The Constitutional Relevance of the Second Sentence of the Declaration of Independence." *Yale Law Journal* 100 (October): 169–187.

Labunski, Richard. 2006. *James Madison and the Struggle for the Bill of Rights*. New York: Oxford University Press.

Levinson. Sanford. 2006. *Our Undemocratic Constitution: Where the Constitution Goes Wrong (and How We the People Can Correct It)*. New York: Oxford University Press.

Lutz, Donald S. 1989. "The Declaration of Independence as Part of an American National Compact." *Publius* 19 (Winter): 41–58.

Mahoney, Dennis J. 1987. "The Declaration of Independence as a Constitutional Document." In *The Framing and Ratification of the Constitution*, edited by Leonard W. Levy and Dennis J. Mahoney, 54–68. New York: Macmillan.

Nicol, Gene R. 1985. "Children of Distant Fathers: Sketching an Ethos of Constitutional Liberty." *Wisconsin Law Review* 1985 (November/December): 1305–1356.

Reinstein, Robert. 1993. "Completing the Constitution: The Declaration of Independence, Bill of Rights and Fourteenth Amendment." *Temple Law Review* 66 (Summer): 361–418.

Sandefur, Timothy. 2014. *The Conscience of the Constitution: The Declaration of Independence and the Right to Liberty*. Washington, DC: Cato Institute.

Snow, Alpheus Henry. 1921. "The Declaration of Independence as the Fundamental Constitution of the United States." In *The American Philosophy of Government*, 35–66. New York: G. P. Putnam's Sons.

Strang, Lee J. 2006. "Originalism, the Declaration of Independence, and the Constitution: A Unique Role in Constitutional Interpretation?" *Penn State Law Review* 111 (Fall): 413–479.

Tsesis, Alexander. 2012. "Self-Government and the Declaration of Independence." *Cornell Law Review* 97 (May): 693–751.

Tsesis, Alexander. 2016. "The Declaration of Independence as Introduction to the Constitution." *Southern California Law Review* 89 (March): 359–367.

Van Cleve, George William. 2017. *We Have Not a Government: The Articles of Confederation and the Road to the Constitution*. Chicago: University of Chicago Press.

Vile, John R. 2015. *Encyclopedia of Constitutional Amendments, Proposed Amendments, and Amending Issues, 1789–2015*, 4th ed., 2 vols. Santa Barbara, CA: ABC-CLIO.

Vile, John R. 2016. *The Constitutional Convention of 1787: A Comprehensive Encyclopedia of America's Founding*. Rev. 2nd edition. 2 vols. Clark, NJ: Talbot Publishing.

West, Thomas G. 2002a. "The Declaration of Independence, the U.S. Constitution, and the Bill of Rights." In *The Declaration of Independence Origins and Impact*, edited by Scott Douglas Gerber, 72–95. Washington, DC: CQ Press.

West, Thomas G. 2002b. "*Jaffa versus Mansfield*: Does American Have a Constitutional or a 'Declaration of Independence' Soul?" *Perspectives on Political Science* 31 (Fall): 235–246.

Wood, Gordon S. 1969. *The Creation of the American Republic, 1776–1787*. Chapel Hill: University of North Carolina Press.

Wright, Benjamin Fletcher. 1958. "Consensus and Continuity, 1776–1787." *Boston University Law Review* 38 (Winter): 1–52.

V

VIRGINIA AND ITS SIGNERS

Virginia was the oldest, largest (at the time it included present-day West Virginia and Kentucky), and the most populous of the 13 English colonies in America. It was a royal colony but had a long history. Its legislature, the House of Burgesses, dated back to 1619. Williamsburg served as its colonial capital and was the site of the College of William and Mary, which was originally established as an Anglican Institution (James Madison and Thomas Jefferson would later be among those who sought to disestablish this church in the state) and would educate a number of revolutionary leaders, including Jefferson. Virginia politics were dominated by large plantation owners in the Tidewater, many with palatial estates that depended heavily upon slave labor.

Along with Massachusetts, the state was an early leader in the movement for independence. Patrick Henry (1736–1799) had become especially noted for his speech in opposition to the Stamp Act of 1765, in which he had placed the desire for liberty over life. Reacting to the Townshend Duties, Virginia had subsequently initiated the boycott of British goods, and the First Continental Congress had chosen Virginia's Peyton Randolph as its president. On June 19, 1775, Congress had further appointed Virginia's George Washington (1732–1799), who had experience fighting alongside the British during the French and Indian War, as commander in chief, partly because of his prior military experience, but also in the hope that he would bring support from the southern colonies.

Much like Massachusetts, Virginia had engaged in military conflict with the British prior to the Declaration of Independence. Lord Dunmore, the colonial governor, had fled to a ship from which he tried to enlist slaves with promises of emancipation. Further concerns that the British would enlist Native American Indians, stirred considerable fear within the colony (Pierce 1972, 447). Virginia had originated the resolution for independence, which Richard Henry Lee had introduced in Congress on June 7, 1776. The Virginia Declaration of Rights, largely authored by George Mason (1724–1792), played a major role in articulating republican principles, and the Virginia Constitution would serve as a guide to other states.

Seven Virginians signed the Declaration. They were as follows: Carter Braxton, Benjamin Harrison, Thomas Jefferson, Francis Lightfoot Lee, Richard Henry Lee, Thomas Nelson Jr., and George Wythe.

Carter Braxton (1736–1797), a planter and merchant, had been educated at William and Mary. He served in the Virginia House of Burgesses and helped negotiate a temporary peace after Governor Dunmore seized colonial gunpowder. Initially tepid toward independence and especially suspicious of the delegates from New England, he was elected to the Continental Congress to replace Peyton Randolph, who had died. Braxton not only voted for independence but signed the Declaration. Braxton was no friend to democracy, as he demonstrated in *An Address to the Convention of the Colony and Ancient Dominion of Virginia*, a pamphlet, which he published in 1776 disputing John Adams's *Thoughts on Government.*

Benjamin Harrison V (1726–1791) was another wealthy Virginia planter who attended William and Mary but had to drop out after his father died. A large man, Harrison was selected a president of the Committee of the Whole in the Second Continental Congress and was thus responsible for presiding over the debates over the Declaration and, later, the Articles of Confederation. Harrison was the father of William Henry Harrison and great grandfather of Benjamin Harrison, both of whom would become U.S. presidents.

Thomas Jefferson (1743–1826), who is described in greater detail in a separate essay in this encyclopedia, had been educated at the College of William and Mary and studied law under George Wythe before serving in the House of Burgesses and establishing his reputation by his writings, which included his *Summary View of the Rights of British America.* The only Virginian on the Committee of Five appointed to write the Declaration, he took the lead, either because he was chair or (if Adams remembered correctly) at the urging of John Adams. Jefferson was not a good public speaker and he remained silent during the debate over the Declaration, long believing that his original draft was better than the one that Congress finally adopted. During the Revolutionary War, Jefferson would serve as governor of Virginia and as an ambassador to France. He was not present for the Constitutional Convention of 1787, but supported it, albeit with the addition of a Bill of Rights. He subsequently served as George Washington's secretary of state, as John Adams's vice president, and as third president, during whose terms the United States purchased the Louisiana Territory. Jefferson and Madison founded the Democratic-Republican Party and wrote the Virginia and Kentucky Resolutions in opposition to the Alien and Sedition Acts. Jefferson most wanted to be remembered for writing the Declaration of Independence, authoring the Virginia Statute for Religious Liberty, and Founding the University of Virginia. He and John Adams, with whom he had resumed correspondence in his later years, both died on the fiftieth anniversary of the adoption of the Declaration. Writing to Roger C. Weightman, the mayor of Washington, D.C., shortly before his death, Jefferson echoed words of a former English revolutionary by citing the "palpable truth, that the mass of mankind has not been born with saddles on their backs, nor a favored few booted and spurred, ready to ride them legitimately, by the grace of God."

Francis Lightfoot Lee (1734–1797) was a younger brother of Richard Henry Lee. Educated at home, Lee was an early opponent of British taxation. Lee was a member of the House of Burgesses, a delegate to the Virginia Convention, and served in the Continental Congress from 1774 to 1779. While there, he signed both the Declaration of Independence and the Articles of Confederation. He would later serve in the Virginia Senate. In contrast to his brother, Francis was strongly in favor of ratification of the Constitution of 1787.

Richard Henry Lee (1732 or 1733–1794) is probably best known for introducing the resolution in the Continental Congress for Independence. The older brother of Francis Lightfoot, Richard was both tutored at home and spent time studying in England. He served as a justice of the peace and was elected to the Virginia House of Burgesses, where he established a friendship with Patrick Henry and helped create the Committees of Correspondence. Lee was a gifted orator (whose presence was probably enhanced by a black silk scarf that he used to hide the fact that he had lost four fingers on one hand in a hunting accident) and an influential member of the Continental Congress (he would serve as its president in 1785). Although he signed the Declaration, he was in Virginia working on the Virginia Constitution during debates about it (Selby 1976). Although he had opposed ratification of the U.S. Constitution because it originally lacked a bill of rights, he served as one of Virginia's first two senators under the government that it created.

Thomas Nelson Jr. (1738–1789) was born to a wealthy Virginia family and educated at Cambridge University before coming becoming a planter and merchant. Nelson was elected to the Virginia House of Burgesses and became a member of the Virginia Provincial Convention before being elected to the Continental Congress. Nelson led the Virginia militia during the Revolutionary War and had the reputation of ordering troops to fire on his own house at Yorktown that the British were occupying. He followed Thomas Jefferson as governor of Virginia. Nelson suffered asthma for much of his life.

George Wythe (ca. 1726–1806) was largely educated at home and in the law offices of his uncle Stephen Dewey. He served in a variety of public posts, including acting attorney general, mayor, vestryman, and clerk for the Virginia House of Burgesses. A strong proponent of colonial rights, he had protested against the Stamp Act. He became the first professor of law in America, and in this role at William and Mary, he taught many leading Americans, including Thomas Jefferson, John Marshall, St. George Tucker, and Henry Clay. Wythe left the Continental Congress in order to help draft the Virginia Constitution but returned to sign the Declaration. He later served as a prominent state judge and as a delegate to the Constitutional Convention of 1787 but left early in the convention because of his wife's illness. Wythe lived to an old age but died tragically after a nephew poisoned him.

Virginia delegates played a major role at the Constitutional Convention of 1787. That convention selected George Washington to preside. Virginia took the lead in introducing the Virginia Plan of government, which dominated early debate. James Madison played a major role both in participating in and in recording debates. Four of the first five presidents (Washington, Jefferson, Madison, and Monroe) were from Virginia.

See also Committee Responsible for Writing the Declaration of Independence; Jefferson, Thomas; Preamble to the Resolution of Virginia Convention (May 15, 1776); *A Summary View of the Rights of British America* (Jefferson); Virginia Constitution of 1776; Virginia Declaration of Rights; Virginia Resolution of May 15, 1776

Further Reading

Briceland, Alan V. "Virginia: The Cement of the Union." In *The Constitution and the States: The Role of the Original Thirteen in the Framing and Adoption of the Federal Constitution*, edited by Patrick T. Conley and John P. Kaminski, 201–223. Madison, WI: Madison House.

Brown, Imogene E. 1982. *American Aristides: A Biography of George Wythe*. Madison, NJ: Fairleigh Dickinson University Press.

Chitwood, Oliver Perry. 1967. *Richard Henry Lee: Statesman of the Revolution*. Morgantown: West Virginia University Library.

Dill, Alonzo Thomas. 1983. *Carter Braxton: Virginia Signer; A Conservative in Revolt*. Lanham, MD: University Press of America.

Lee, Nell Moore. 1988. *Patriot above Profit: A Portrait of Thomas Nelson, Jr., Who Supported the American Revolution with His Purse and Sword*. Nashville, TN: Rutledge Hill Press.

McGaughy, J. Kent. 2004. *Richard Henry Lee of Virginia: A Portrait of an American Revolutionary*. Lanham, MD: Rowman and Littlefield.

Morison, Samuel Eliot. 1951. "Prelude to Independence: The Virginia Resolutions of May 15, 1776." *William and Mary Quarterly* 8 (October): 483–492.

Nagel, Paul C. 2006. *The Lees of Virginia: Seven Generations of an American Family*. New York: Oxford University Press.

Pierce, Michael D. 1972. "The Independence Movement in Virginia, 1775–1776." *Virginia Magazine of History and Biography* 80 (October): 442–452.

Selby, John E. 1976. "Richard Henry Lee, John Adams, and the Virginia Constitution of 1776." *Virginia Magazine of History and Biography* 84 (October): 387–400.

Selby, John E. 1988. *The Revolution in Virginia, 1775–1783*. Williamsburg, VA: Colonial Williamsburg Foundation.

Unger, Harlow Giles. 2017. *First Founding Father: Richard Henry Lee and the Call to Independence*. New York: Da Capo Press.

VIRGINIA CONSTITUTION OF 1776

On May 14, 1776, the Second Continental Congress encouraged states to adopt new governing structures to replace British rule.

On June 29, 1776, the convention called in Virginia responded with its constitution, which, like the accompanying Declaration of Rights, appears largely to have been the work of George Mason (Selby 1976, 387). It opened with a statement, contributed from Philadelphia by Thomas Jefferson, that he modeled on the British Declaration of Rights of 1689. As in the later Declaration of Independence, this document accused George III of having "endeavored to pervert the same into a detestable and insupportable Tyranny."

The document followed with a series of examples, which closely resemble the indictments that Jefferson later listed in the Declaration of Independence. The indictments in the Virginia Constitution included the king's exercise of his veto over colonial laws; his refusal to allow governors to pass other laws; dissolving colonial assemblies; obstructing naturalization; keeping a standing army; failing to provide civilian control over the military; subjecting Americans to foreign trials; cutting off trade; imposing taxes; denying trial by jury; making war on the colonies and prompting insurrections among slaves; using mercenaries; and refusing colonial petitions.

The document ended by proclaiming that by the "several acts of misrule" that it had cited, "the government of this country, as formerly exercised under the crown of *Great Britain*, is TOTALLY DISSOLVED."

See also Charges against the King and Others; Jefferson, Thomas; Virginia and Its Signers

Further Reading

Selby, John E. "Richard Henry Lee, John Adams, and the Virginia Constitution of 1776." *Virginia Magazine of History and Biography* 84 (October): 387–400.

"Virginia Constitution" June 20, 1776. Jefferson Papers 1:377–83, The Founders' Constitution. http://press-pubs.uchicago.edu/founders/documents/v1ch1s4.html.

VIRGINIA DECLARATION OF RIGHTS

A Virginia convention ratified its Declaration of Rights on June 12, 1776. Written by a committee headed by George Mason, this document, about which the Second Continental Congress knew before adopting the Declaration of Independence, would have helped shaped that document, especially as Thomas Jefferson was from the same state.

Professor David Armitage has observed that the Declaration of Independence has three parts: the declaration (found at the beginning and end of the document); a declaration of rights, chiefly the second paragraph; and the manifesto, which largely consist of the list of grievances (2007, 14). Of these, the second portion is both the most discussed and most influenced by the Virginia Declaration.

Section 1 of the Virginia Declaration, stated:

> That all men are by nature equally free and independent and have certain inherent rights, of which, when they enter into a state of society, they cannot, by any compact, deprive or divest their posterity; namely, the enjoyment of life and liberty, with the means of acquiring and possessing property, and pursuing and obtaining happiness and safety. (Vile 2015, 96)

Like paragraph 2 of the Declaration of Independence, this paragraph references the natural equality of men; the idea that they have rights; and life, liberty, and happiness. The Declaration of Rights seems to be based on the social contract theory of John Locke (Dana 1900, 328). In contrast to the Declaration of Independence, the Virginia Declaration more closely linked happiness to property and safety. The phrase in the "when they enter into a state of society" within the Virginia Declaration of Rights was not the original (which Jefferson had likely read in the *Pennsylvania Gazette*) but was added in deference to slaveholders, who would have excluded slaves from such society (Beeman 2013, 396).

Section 2 of the Virginia Declaration asserted "That all power is vested in, and consequently derived from, the people" and is accountable to them, while section 3 further asserts that when government fails to secure the "happiness and safety" of the people, a majority "hath an indubitable, inalienable, and indefeasible right to reform, alter, or abolish it" (Vile 2015, 97). This is clearly similar to the right of revolution that Jefferson asserted in the Declaration of Independence.

Section 4 of the Virginia Declaration went somewhat beyond the Declaration in condemning the principle of hereditary succession rather than a specific king. Whereas the manifesto section of the Declaration of Independence pointed to areas where British rule has been oppressive, the Virginia Declaration proceeded to outline specific principles that all governments should incorporate. These include separation of powers (section 5); principles of election (section 6); limitation of executive vetoes (section 7); rights of criminal defendants (section 8); concerns over excessive bail and fines and cruel and unusual punishments (section 9); concern over general warrants (section 10); the right to a jury trial (section 11); concern for freedom of the press (section 12); support for local militia (section 13); the right to uniform government (section 14); the necessity for republican virtues like "justice, moderation, temperance, frugality, and virtue"; and support for the "free exercise" of religion (section 16). The provision upholding free exercise was inserted at the insistence of James Madison, who later incorporated similar language into the First Amendment (Holland 2007, 94).

George Mason was the primary author of the Virginia Declaration of Rights, which influenced both the Declaration of Independence, subsequent state bills of rights, and the first 10 amendments to the U.S. Constitution. Although he served as a prominent delegate to the Constitutional Convention of 1787, he did not sign because it initially lacked a bill of rights. (New York Public Library)

Randy Barnett observes that "Mason's words would become even more canonical than Jefferson's more succinct version in the Declaration of Independence, as variations were incorporated into several state constitutions, and they would be echoed in the Ninth Amendment, and much later in the Privileges or Immunities Clause of the Fourteenth Amendment" (2016, 33–34). George Mason was one of three remaining delegates at the Constitutional Convention of 1787 who did not sign the document in part because he thought it should include a bill, or declaration, of rights, and his opposition stirred adoption of the first ten amendments.

See also Equality; Laws of Nature and of Nature's God; U.S. Constitution and the Declaration of Independence; Virginia and Its Signers

Further Reading

Armitage, David. 2007. *The Declaration of Independence: A Global History*. Cambridge, MA: Harvard University Press.

Barnett, Randy E. 2016. *Our Republican Constitution: Securing the Liberty and Sovereignty of We the People*. New York: Broadside Books.

Beeman, Richard R. 2013. *Our Lives, Our Fortunes and Our Sacred Honors: The Forging of American Independence, 1776–1776*. New York: Basic Books.

Broadwater, Jeff. 2006. *George Mason: Forgotten Founder*. Chapel Hill: University of North Carolina Press.

Dana, William E. 1900. "The Declaration of Independence." *Harvard Law Review* 13 (January): 319–343.

Holland, Matthew S. 2007. *Bonds of Affection: Civic Charity and the Making of America—Winthrop, Jefferson, and Lincoln*. Washington, DC: Georgetown University Press.

Vile, John R. 2015. *Founding Documents of America: Documents Decoded*. Santa Barbara, CA: ABC-CLIO.

VIRGINIA RESOLUTION OF MAY 15, 1776

As the state of Virginia was drafting its constitution, it also adopted a resolution instructing its delegates at the Second Continental Congress to "Propose to that respectable body to declare the united colonies free and independent states" ("Virginia Resolution") Richard Henry Lee subsequently introduced three resolutions on June 7, 1776, that led to the Declaration of Independence.

There are fascinating parallels between the language of the Virginia Resolution and this latter document. The Virginia Resolution begins with sentiments expressed near the end of the latter document by noting that instead of bringing about reconciliation, colonial petitions have "produced, from an imperious and vindictive Administration, increased insult, oppression, and a vigorous attempt to effect our total destruction." The resolution detailed British attempts to wage war on the colonies and the Virginia governor's retreat to a ship from which he "is carrying on a piratical and savage war against us." As in Thomas Jefferson's original draft of the Declaration, Virginia specifically mentioned "that the Governor was training and employing" slaves to rise "against their masters." Calling for "a total separation from the Crown and Government of Great Britain," the resolution expressed the hope for alliances with other nations and appealed, much like the Declaration "to the Searcher of hearts for the sincerity of former declarations" (Virginia Resolution, May 15, 1776).

This resolution ended with instructions to the state's representatives in Congress "to declare the United Colonies free and independent States, absolved from all allegiance to, or dependence upon, the Crown or Parliament of Great Britain." The resolution further assented to efforts to secure "foreign alliance, and a Confederation of the Colonies," with, however, "the regulations of the internal concerns of each Colony" to "be left to the respective Colonial Legislatures."

See also Resolutions Introduced by Richard Henry Lee (June 7, 1776); Slavery; Virginia and Its Signers

Further Reading

Pierce, Michael D. 1972. "The Independence Movement in Virginia, 1775–1776." *Virginia Magazine of History and Biography* 80 (October): 442–452.
"Virginia Resolution—May 15, 1776." http://www.revolutionary-war-and-beyond.com/virginia-resolution-proposing-independence.html.

VIRTUE

See Moral Virtues in the Declaration of Independence

VOTE FOR INDEPENDENCE

Although fighting between the colonists and Great Britain began at Lexington and Concord, Massachusetts, on April 19, 1775, the Continental Congress did not vote for independence until July 2, 1776, and did not adopt the Declaration of Independence until two days later.

Between these events, Congress adopted the Olive Branch Petition on July 8, 1775. John Dickinson was the chief author of this petition. It was based on hopes that King George III might side with them against the Parliament. The king refused to receive it because he believed that the Declaratory Act had settled the issue of parliamentary authority. Indeed, on August 23, 1775, the king proclaimed the colonies to be in rebellion, and in a speech to Parliament on October 27, 1775, which the Second Continental Congress received on January 8, 1776, he reiterated this point.

Even as some colonial governments were crumbling, representatives to the Second Continental Congress remained divided. Indeed, much of the drama portrayed in the musical *1776* stemmed from conflicts between delegates like John Adams and Samuel Adams, of Massachusetts, and Thomas Jefferson, from Virginia, who favored independence from a fairly early date, and delegates like Edward Rutledge of South Carolina and John Dickinson of Pennsylvania, who took a much more cautious approach.

Voting in Congress was done on the basis of state equality, and many of the colonies exercised the right to instruct their delegates on how they should vote on important issues, including independence. These instructions eventually generated the momentum necessary for the positive vote on independence on July 2 and on the Declaration on July 4.

Richard Beeman has traced the progress of these votes in his book on American Independence, which this essay will attempt to simplify by highlighting key dates within each state. Beeman notes that while the Massachusetts General Court (the name of its legislature) had, with its election of Elbridge Gerry, given proindependence delegates a majority in the election of December 15, 1775, it never formally endorsed independence prior to congressional action (2013, 358–359). The Georgia legislature had voted on April 5, 1776, to allow its delegates to exercise their judgment on the matter, but it took some time for delegates that it had elected on February 2 to arrive at the Second Continental Congress (2013, 356). Beeman further identifies the North Carolina Provincial Congress as the first to endorse, without requiring its delegates to vote for, independence on April 12, 1776 (2013, 355–56). Rhode Island authorized its delegates to support independence on May 4 but chose not to use that word for fear that it might unduly frighten the people (2013, 357).

On May 15, 1776, the Virginia Convention voted on the resolution for independence, which Richard Henry Lee formally introduced in Congress on Friday, June 7, 1776. After an exhausting day of debate on June 8 in which Edward Rutledge and John Dickinson were particularly adamant about the need to exercise prudence before taking a vote, the Congress voted on June 10 to postpone consideration on the resolution until July 1.

On June 14, the Connecticut legislature instructed its delegates to vote for independence, and on June 15, New Hampshire, answering a query that their delegates had sent on May 28, instructed their delegates to do the same (2013, 359). The Provincial Conference of Pennsylvania, which had supplanted the state legislature, gave its endorsement to independence on June 24, without thereby persuading a majority of its delegates that it was yet time to act.

New Jersey had voted on June 10 to condemn Governor William Franklin and form a new government rather than remain "in a state of nature" (Beeman 2013, 362), thereby implicitly endorsing independence. On July 1, the day when debate was to resume on Richard Henry Lee's resolution for independence, an express rider arrived from Maryland's Provincial Congress, which had previously been on the fence, instructing its delegates to vote for independence. This appears to be the day on which Thomas McKean of Delaware sent word to his fellow delegate Caesar Rodney, who was in Dover, that he needed to come in order to provide a majority for independence (2013, 377).

Meeting as a Committee of the Whole, on July 1, nine states at the Continental Congress voted in favor of Lee's Resolution for Independence. Pennsylvania and South Carolina voted against it, Delaware was divided, and New York, whose delegates were still awaiting instructions, abstained. Beeman believes, however, that a majority of South Carolina delegates may have favored independence but voted no out of respect for Rutledge, who, according to Thomas Jefferson, had hinted that his state might vote differently on the following day (2013, 376). Although nine votes were sufficient to carry the measure had Congress been in full session, rather than meeting as a committee of the whole, it would have sent a strong signal of disunity that the British would undoubtedly have been able to exploit.

When the final vote was taken on July 2, all 12 states that voted approved of independence. Delaware achieved its majority with the arrival of Caesar Rodney. South Carolina voted unanimously for independence. Pennsylvania mustered a bare majority for independence after James Wilson voted for independence out of respect for the people's wishes, and Robert Morris and John Dickinson, who were both holding out hopes for reconciliation, apparently decided not to vote.

New York delegates were still awaiting instructions. They finally arrived on July 9, after which Congress designated the document, which it ordered to be engrossed, the Unanimous Declaration of the thirteen states of the United States of America.

Although the nation now celebrates July 4, the day on which the Declaration of Independence was adopted, as Independence Day, John Adams was among those who anticipated, in a letter to his wife, that the nation would celebrate on July 2. Although he got the date of the celebration wrong, his description of the occasion was fairly prophetic.

> The Second Day of July 1776 will be the most memorable Epocha, in the history of America. I am apt to believe that it will be celebrated, by succeeding Generations, as the great anniversary Festival. It ought to be commemorated, as the Day of Deliverance by solemn Acts of Devotion to God Almighty. It ought to be solemnized with Pomp and Parade, with Shews, Games, Sports, Guns, Bells, Bonfires, and Illuminations from one End of this Continent to the other from this Time forward forever more. (Beeman 2013, 382)

Although Adams was among those who had expressed frustration over how long the process had taken, the time and deliberation that this took, as well as the petitions that it had allowed Congress to send to the king, highlighted the arguments in the Declaration of Independence that the colonists had acted not "for light and transient causes," but prudently after enduring "a long train of abuses."

See also Adams, John; Captions of the Declaration of Independence; Declaratory Act of 1766; George III, Proclamation of Rebellion (August 23, 1775); George III, Speech to Parliament (October 27, 1775); Independence Day; Olive Branch Petition; Resolutions Introduced by Richard Henry Lee (June 7, 1776)

Note: Further developments within states that led to their votes are described in entries under their names.

Further Reading

Beeman, Richard R. 2013. *Our Lives, Our Fortunes, and Our Sacred Honor: The Forging of American Independence, 1774–1776*. New York: Basic Books.

Strauss, Valerie. 2012. "Why July 2 Is Really America's Independence Day." *Washington Post*, July 2, 2012.

W

"WE" (FIRST-PERSON PLURAL)

Thomas Jefferson's primary authorship of the Declaration of Independence was not widely known until the publication of a sermon by Ezra Stiles, the president of Yale, in the form of a pamphlet in 1783 (McDonald 1999, 171). The most prominent signature on the Declaration was the bold signature of John Hancock, the president of the Second Continental Congress, rather than of Jefferson, but the document would be signed by 56 delegates from all 13 states. Moreover, a document authored and signed by one man, expressing disfavor with English policies, would have had little consequence.

It was therefore appropriate that when the Declaration referred directly to its authors, and to the American people, rather than using third person, as in "he [the king] has" (Mortensen 1961, 122), it used the first-person plural. Robert McDonald observes that "'We' appears thirteen times in Jefferson's draft and ten times in the Declaration as altered by Congress" (1999, 172). Its most notable usages are probably the statements in paragraph two that "We hold these truths to be self-evident" and in the concluding sentence where the delegates announce that "we mutually pledge to each other our Lives, our Fortunes and our sacred Honor." Stephen E. Lucas further notes 26 uses of the word "our" in the Declaration and 11 uses of the word "us" (1990).

Although the document was approved by a Congress, it is possible to read many of the first-person-plural usages within the Declaration not as the view of the delegates alone, but as their role as representatives of the individual states or the nation as a whole. The first interpretation is furthered by the first printed parchment copy of the Declaration, printed after the New York delegation was finally authorized to give its consent, which is titled "The unanimous Declaration of the thirteen united States of America." Elsewhere, however, the document often refers specifically to "these States," "Free and Independent States," and the like (Larson 2001, 729). The interpretation of the first plural to represent Americans as a whole stems from the association of the "we" in the Declaration with its proclamation of a new "people" (Larson 2001, 733–734).

The most famous use of the first-person plural in a political document in the United States occurs in the preamble to the U.S. Constitution, which begins with the words "We the People." It therefore affirms the principle stated in the Declaration that governments are to be based on "the consent of the governed."

McDonald observes that "the sublimation of self was also commonplace within eighteenth-century texts" (1999, 175). He further observes that the Declaration's "depersonalized voice enabled it to sound disinterested at the same time that it aired the colonies' grievances" (1999, 177). Many political documents of the day, most notably the Federalist Papers, were written under pseudonyms.

The Declaration is not altogether clear about the composition of people that it identifies as rebelling against England. The accusation that links the king to exciting "domestic insurrections amongst us" and accusing him of endeavoring to recruit "the merciless Indian savages," suggests however, that the latter groups remained (with foreign mercenaries) among the enemies, rather than the friends, of America (Parkinson 1016, 255).

See also Hancock's Letters Accompanying the Declaration of Independence; Signing of the Declaration of Independence

Further Reading

Larson, Carlton F. W. 2001. "The Declaration of Independence: A 225th Anniversary Re-Interpretation," *Washington Law Review* 76 (July): 701–791.

Lucas, Stephen E. 1990. "The Stylistic Artistry of the Declaration of Independence." *Prologue: Quarterly of the National Archives and Records Administration*. https://www.archives.gov/founding-docs/stylistic-artistry-of-the-declaration.

McDonald, Robert M. S. 1999. "Thomas Jefferson's Changing Reputation as Author of the Declaration of Independence: The First Fifty Years." *Journal of the Early Republic* 19 (Summer): 169–195.

Mortensen, Louise H. 1961. "Idea Inventory." *Elementary English* 38 (February): 122–124.

Parkinson, Robert G. 2016. *The Common Cause*. Chapel Hill: University of North Carolina Press.

WE HAVE APPEALED TO THEIR NATIVE JUSTICE & MAGNANIMITY

After having ended all the accusations against the king with one accusing him of having ignored colonial petitions, the penultimate paragraph of the Declaration of Independence had described how the colonists had not "been wanting [lacking] in attentions to our British brethren."

After the Declaration explained the colonists' view that the British legislature had no authority over them and reminded them of "the circumstances of our emigration and settlement here" while deleting Thomas Jefferson's more detailed explanation of what this meant and how the colonists had to this point considered themselves bound to Britain only by a common king, the Declaration continued. It thus noted that "we have appealed to their native justice & magnanimity, and we have conjured them by the tyes [*sic*] of our common kindred, to disavow these usurpations, which would inevitably interrupt our connections & correspondence" while noting that the British people had not responded positively.

The Second Continental Congress, however, decided to delete Jefferson's most bathetic charges against the people, constituting its longest deletion apart from Jefferson's attack on slavery, which it had also deleted.

The words that the Congress deleted followed the charge that the British "have been deaf to the voice of justice and of consanguinity." Jefferson then said:

> And when occasions have been given them, by the regular course of their laws, of removing from their councils the disturbers of our harmony, they have by their free election re-established them in power. At this very time too, they are permitting their chief magistrate to send over not only soldiers of our common blood, but Scotch and foreign mercenaries to invade and destroy us. These facts have given the last stab to agonizing affection; and manly spirit bids us to renounce forever these unfelling brethren. [We must therefore] endeavor to forget our former love for them, and to hold them, as we hold the rest of mankind, enemies in war, in peace friends. We might have been a free & a great people together; but a communication of grandeur and of freedom, it seems, is below their dignity. Be it so, since they will have it. The road to happiness and to glory is open to us too; we will claim it apart from them. (Maier 1997, 240–241)

Robert Middlekauff is among scholars (probably not a majority) who believe that "the Jeffersonian draft is a much more powerful statement than the one finally approved by Congress (2005, 336). Middlekauff likes the deleted passage because of the way that it so effectively conveyed "a sense of betrayal, a sense that the Americans had been abandoned by their own kind, by their own blood, by brethren who had lost their capacity to honor justice and ties of affection, who had indeed become 'unfeeling brethren'" (2005, 336).

Jefferson explained the deletion by observing that "the pusillanimous idea that we had friends in England worth keeping terms which still haunted the minds of many," and that therefore "those passages which conveyed censures on the people of England were struck out lest they should give them offense" (Boyd 1999, 37).

Just as most American presidents have subsequently chosen to wage wars against foreign regimes, rather than against foreign peoples, however, Jefferson's language arguably unduly accused both British supporters and opponents of the American cause (and there were plenty of Whigs within Britain who sympathized with America's grievances) and was therefore arguably impolitic. Moreover, one could argue that Jefferson's reference to "the last stab to agonizing affection," was melodramatic, more appropriate for a lover's quarrel than for a dispute between an empire and her colonies.

Moreover, as colonial criticism of rotten boroughs and of kingly corruption of Parliament reveals, it might have been unfair to blame British voters for the policy of British ministers and their king, the latter of which they certainly had not elected.

Jefferson's criticism of the king's use of Scottish mercenaries, while undoubtedly heightening his sense of betrayal, would not have been well received by delegates like John Witherspoon, Thomas McKean, and James Wilson, who had immigrated to America from Scotland. Although modern Americans are more likely to identify the mercenaries in the Revolution with those whom the king had recruited in Germany (so-called Hessians), they had not yet arrived in July 1776, whereas some 3,000 Scottish Highlanders had arrived including nearly 500 who were taken prisoners in early June (Fetter 1980, 510).

Jefferson's surmise that "we might have been a free & a great people together," and that the nation would climb on its own "to happiness and to glory," while arguably prophetic, may have fed into the English narrative that revolutionary leaders were seeking their own glory rather than their nation's true happiness.

See also Charges against the King and Others; Nor Have We Been Wanting in Attention to our Foreign Brethren; Slavery; Transporting Large Armies of Foreign Mercenaries (Charge #25); We Have Appealed to Their Native Justice & Magnanimity

Further Reading

Boyd, Julian P. 1999. *The Declaration of Independence: The Evolution of the Text.* Washington, DC, and Charlottesville, VA: The Library of Congress in association with the Thomas Jefferson Memorial Foundation.

Fetter, Frank Whitson. 1980. "Who Were the Foreign Mercenaries of the Declaration of Independence?" *Pennsylvania Magazine of History and Biography* 104 (October): 508–513.

Maier, Pauline. 1997. *American Scripture: Making the Declaration of Independence.* New York: Alfred A. Knopf.

Middlekauff, Robert. 2005. *The Glorious Cause: The American Revolution, 1763–1789.* New York: Oxford University Press.

WHEN IN THE COURSE OF HUMAN EVENTS

The opening word of the Declaration of Independence, as well as those that surround it, focused on timing. They stated that "When in the course of human events it becomes necessary" for one people to separate from another and claim their equal status as a nation, they should "declare the causes which impel them to the separation." Undoubtedly unwilling to admit that they had ever been subordinate to Britain (Hawke 1964, 146), Congress had altered the original statement, which had declared that the American people were ready "to advance from that subordination in which they have hitherto remained."

American colonial leaders had been protesting against parliamentary taxation and other perceived abuses of their rights since the end of the French and Indian War, but even after fighting broke out at Lexington and Concord in April 1775, Congress continued to petition the king, and some delegates resisted officially declaring colonial independence. Thomas Jefferson's notes of the debates indicate that while many delegates to the Second Continental Congress were convinced that separation from Britain was inevitable, the members' primary concerns centered on whether the delegates were outpacing sentiments within the colonies, especially the Middle Colonies. In part because they recognized the formidable military power of the British, the delegates knew that it was important to achieve a consensus so that Britain could not pit one colony or set of colonies against the others.

In addition to striking a blow against hereditary succession, Thomas Paine's *Common Sense*, which he published in January 1776, had suggested that that the colonists were now in a position to declare their independence. Paine's work appears to have done much to persuade colonists that the time for independence had now arrived.

By starting with the word "when," Jefferson was putting his finger on the question of timing. Initially indicating that independence was now a matter of necessity, Jefferson devoted the major portion of his manuscript to demonstrating that the colonists had not jumped the gun but that they had hesitantly come to their decision only after a "long train of abuses & usurpations" that demonstrated the king's intention to "reduce them under absolute despotism."

This sentiment was similar to a secondhand account of a speech that delegate John Witherspoon reputedly gave to the Congress. He had reportedly said that "There is a tide in the affairs of men—a nick of time. We perceive it now before us. To hesitate, is to consent to slavery" (Mailer 2017, 276).

See also Jefferson's Notes on Debates over Independence; Necessity; Timing of the Declaration of Independence

Further Reading

Allen, Danielle. 2014. *Our Declaration: A Reading of the Declaration of Independence in Defense of Equality*. New York: W. W. Norton.

Hawke, David Freeman. 1964. *A Transaction of Free Men: The Birth and Course of the Declaration of Independence*. New York: Charles Scribner's Sons.

Mailer, Gideon. 2017. *John Witherspoon's American Revolution: Enlightenment and Religion from the Creation of Britain to the Founding of the United States*. Chapel Hill: University of North Carolina Press.

Spahn, Hannah. 2011. *Thomas Jefferson: Time, and History*. Charlottesville: University of Virginia Press.

WHIG POLITICAL THOUGHT

It is common to find references to Whig political thought in discussions of the Declaration of Independence and its supporters. The Whigs designated members of the political party within the English Parliament who had resisted Charles I and James II. The first had been beheaded under parliamentary authority in 1649, and the second had fled and been replaced by William and Mary in the Glorious Revolution of 1688, which had provided a model for a revolution designed to restore and secure threatened rights. The king's defenders, like American Loyalists, were called Tories.

Whigs traced English liberties back to the Saxons and early documents like the Magna Carta of 1215. They favored republican principles, which in Great Britain meant that they usually upheld the powers of the Parliament, which the colonists resisted, at least with respect to themselves. American Revolutionaries drew heavily from Whig Republican arguments that the king had "corrupted" Parliament. Essays entitled *Cato's Letters*, by John Trenchard and Thomas Gordon, were particularly effective means of transmitting republican thought in America. Staughton Lynd has further identified "James Burgh, Richard Price, Joseph Priestley, John Wilkes, John Cartwright, Granville Sharpe, Catharine Macaulay, and Thomas Paine" as "the principal members of a group of English publicists whose writing cleared the ground for revolution" (2009, 24). Bernard Bailyn has further pointed to individuals like John Milton, Bishop Benjamin Hoadly, Richard Baron, Algernon Sidney, and others (1967, 34–42). John Locke wrote his famed *Second Treatise on Government* as justification for the Glorious Revolution of 1788.

Allen Guelzo has described the primary principles of Whig ideology as follows:

1. Liberty is natural, and cannot be a gift of a monarch.
2. Liberty, however, can be destroyed, normally by the corrupt elite, who strive to concentrate power in themselves and corrupt others.
3. Liberty, therefore requires an alliance with virtue for protection from corruption and power, whether in the form of the natural virtues (like modesty, productive work, or self restraint), or religious ones (such as would be found in strict Protestant moralism).
4. Because Whigs prefer virtue to power, they are most often the "country" party, and are found outside the centers of power. (Guelzo 2001, 197)

As this description should make clear, Whig thought often overlapped with both classical liberalism and republicanism. Thomas Jefferson's articulation of natural rights, his concern over the king's interference in colonial legislative affairs, and his opposition to the occupation of standing armies in the colonies would all have resonated with Whigs.

In April 1775, the lord mayor of London sent a petition to George III referring to "the oppression of our fellow subjects in America." In language quite close to that later echoed in the Declaration of Independence, the mayor had charged that the "real purpose" of the king's policy has been "to establish arbitrary power over all America" (Knight 2017). Although some supported the government, Durward T. Stokes observes that some British clergymen, particularly Presbyterians, "were openly critical of the crown, and made their sentiments known through sermons which they preached to their congregations" (1973, 131).

See also Laws of Nature and of Nature's God; Locke, John; Standing Armies (Charge #11); Tories

Further Reading

Bailyn, Bernard. 1967. *The Ideological Origins of the American Revolution*. Cambridge, MA: Belknap Press of Harvard University Press.

Bradley, James E. 1975. "Whigs and Nonconformists: 'Slumbering Radicalism' in English Politics, 1739–1789." *Eighteenth Century Studies* 9 (Autumn): 1–27.

Colburn, H. Trevor. 1965. *The Lamp of Experience: Whig History and the Intellectual Origins of the American Revolution*. Chapel Hill: University of North Carolina Press.

Dickinson, Harry T., ed. 2007. *British Pamphlets on the American Revolution, 1763–1785*. Part I, 4 vols. New York: Routledge.

Guelzo, Allen C. 2001. "Whig Ideology." In *The Encyclopedia of American Cultural and Intellectual History*, Vol. 1, edited by Mary K. Cayton and Peter W. Williams, 197–204. New York: Charles Scribner's Sons.

Knight, John. July 11, 2017. "King George III's Twitter War." Journal of the American Revolution. https://allthingsliberty.com/2017/07/king-george-iiis-twitter-war/.

Lokken, Roy N. 1974. "The Political Theory of the American Revolution: Changing Interpretations." *History Teacher* 8 (November): 81–95.

Lynd, Staughton. 2009. *Intellectual Origins of American Radicalism*. New ed. New York: Cambridge University Press.

Reich, Jerome R. 2015. *British Friends of the American Revolution*. New York: Routledge.

Stokes, Durward T. 1973. "British Sermons Favorable to the American Revolution." *Social Science* 58 (Summer): 131–141.

Trenchard, John, and Thomas Gordon. (1755) 1995. *Cato's Letters or Essays on Liberty, Civil and Religious, and Other Important Subjects*, ed. Ronald Hamowy. 2 vols. Indianapolis, IN: Liberty Fund.

WHITNEY, PETER (SERMON)

Although there are two fairly well known critiques of the Declaration from the Loyalist and British perspectives, most notably Thomas Hutchinson's *Strictures upon the Declaration of Independence* and John Lind's *An Answer to the Declaration of the American Colonies*, apart from official documents delineating colonial grievances against the king, there are relatively few contemporary defenses of the Declaration of Independence. One, which scholars have largely ignored (albeit see Bell 1983) is a sermon that Peter Whitney (1744–1816), pastor of the Church of Christ in Northborough, Massachusetts, delivered on September 12, 1776.

The sermon is important in explaining how evangelical Christians of the day would have found themselves on the same side as Deists and others who favored separation from Britain. However differently they may have understood God, both groups saw the colonial cause as divinely ordained and as consistent with rights of covenant and contract.

Whitney dedicated his sermon to John Hancock, and he chose as his text 2 Kings 17:16, which described how the 10 northern tribes of Israel split from the tribes of Judah after King Solomon's son, Rehoboam, refused to heed their petitions and promised to tax them even more harshly than his father. Noting that Rehoboam, like George III, was the third successive king, Whitney accused him of following in Rehoboam's footsteps by turning aside the prudent counsels of older men for the rash counsels of those who were younger.

Whitney listed all the charges within the Declaration against the king. Attempting to refute charges that the colonists had "by our abusive treatment of the kings' servants, provoked government to treat us with such unexampled severity" (1777, 21), Whitney said that the colonists had submitted to British regulations until 1764. Although colonial actions had sometimes exceeded the bounds of propriety, the English had in turn punished "the innocent with the guilty" and deprived "a whole province of its chartered rights, for the follies and freaks of individuals" (1777, 22). Whitney further thought that Britain had exaggerated and misrepresented colonial actions as being more serious than they were.

Whitney pointed out that the colonists had attempted to petition the king lawfully, but that in some cases these petitions lacked complete legal form because the king and his ministers had closed down the bodies that sent them. As Whitney viewed the situation, the colonists had been forced either to accept "abject slavery and wretchedness" or assert their liberties (1777, 29). Like Thomas Jefferson, Whitney pointed to "a long train of abuses, and usurpations, pursuing invariably the same object . . . to reduce us under absolute despotism" (1777, 30).

Like the Declaration, Whitney's sermon said that the people "have adopted independence of necessity, not of choice" (1777, 33). Whitney further invoked the "covenant" between the people and the king, which gave them the right to revolt "when rulers, by leaping the bounds of constitution, violate the covenant or compact, between them, and the people" (1777, 39). The opponents of the revolutionary cause had been able to point out any "other way wherein to look for, or expect relief" (1777, 41).

Drawing in part from the arguments that Thomas Paine had made in *Common Sense*, Whitney further cited Old Testament passages that indicated that God did not approve of monarchy and hereditary succession (King 2013, 167).

Attempting to rally people to the revolutionary cause, Whitney argued "that Independence is, in every view, the interest of America" (1777, 47). He further pointed to the need to build proper forms of civil government to take the place of kingly rule. He favored legislative assemblies, frequently elected, and providing "free and full liberty of conscience, in religious matters, to all sects, parties and denominations, to whom it can be allowed, consistent with the safety of the State" (1777, 50). Whitney further likened America to Israel and foresaw peace and prosperity for the American cause.

In interpreting Whitney's sermon, Barry Bell argues that it "reminds us that the Declaration was a political document, not a philosophical treatise" (1983, 73). As he further explains, "the significance of Whitney's sermon lies not in the foolish inference that Jefferson himself was a secret Evangelical, but rather in the implication that both the Declaration's success and its longevity stemmed from its simultaneous appeal to various, and often conflicting, traditions in American thought, that is, from the protean qualities of its text that allowed diverse and even divergent interpretations" (1983, 73). Citing arguments that the Declaration was a form of "Slave Narrative," Bell observed that Whitney's sermon revealed fears of "religious" or "ecclesiastical" slavery (1783, 78).

See also *An Answer to the Declaration of the American Colonies* (Lind); *Common Sense* (Paine); Covenants and Compacts; *Strictures upon the Declaration of Independence* (Hutchinson)

Further Reading

Bell, Barry. 1983. "Reading and 'Misreading' the Declaration of Independence." *Early American Literature* 18 (Spring): 71–83.

King, William Casey. 2013. *Ambition: A History from Vice to Virtue*. New Haven, CT: Yale University Press.

Whitney, Peter. 1777. *A Sermon Delivered September 12, 1776. At a Lecture Appointed for Publishing the Declaration of Independence Passed July 4, 1776. By the Representatives of the United States of America in General Congress Assembled*. Boston, Massachusetts Bay: E. Draper.

WRITING THE DECLARATION OF INDEPENDENCE (J. L. G. FERRIS PAINTING)

Although the most famous paintings of the Declaration of Independence, most notably those of John Trumbull and Edward Savage, depict numerous delegates, a painting by Jean Leon Gerome Ferris (1863–1930) focuses instead on the three men most responsible for the original draft. They were Thomas Jefferson, whom Ferris depicts standing to the right of a desk, at which two other members, Benjamin Franklin on the left and John Adams in the middle, are sitting. Ferris designed the painting to depict the room in what is today known as the Declaration of Independence House, where Jefferson was staying. In the painting, Franklin is examining a document at the table, while Jefferson is holding one in his left hand. There are numerous crumpled papers on the floor, suggesting extensive rewriting.

Benjamin Franklin, John Adams, and Thomas Jefferson, at Jefferson's lodgings on the corner of 7th and Market streets in Philadelphia, Pennsylvania, to review a draft of the Declaration of Independence, in 1776. (Library of Congress)

The painter executed a series of 78 colorful and idealized paintings entitled *The Pageant of a Nation,* which were exhibited for a time in Independence Hall and Congress Hall. Although the artist kept the paintings together during his lifetime, he allowed publishers to print reproductions, which added to their popular recognition

See also *Congress Voting Independence* (Painting by Savage); Declaration House; Trumbull, John (Paintings)

Further Reading

Ferris, J. L. G. 1932. "Writing the Declaration of Independence, 1776." Library of Congress, http://www.loc.gov/pictures/item/2002719535/.

Constitution Facts. n.d. "Independence Artwork: Famous Pieces Inspired by United States Constitutional History." https://www.constitutionfacts.com/founders-library/independence-artwork/.

Appendix A: Thomas Jefferson's Rough Draft of the Declaration of Independence

Historian Dumas Malone believes that Thomas Jefferson likely copied his "original" four-page draft of the Declaration from prior fragments, sometime before June 28, 1776 (Malone 1954, 72), and then recorded changes as they were made. Although fellow committee members made only modest stylistic changes, Congress subjected the document to paragraph-by-paragraph scrutiny, during debates that Jefferson found to be excruciating.

One of the most fascinating changes on the first page was the substitution of the words "self-evident" for "sacred and undeniable" truths. Although both Jefferson and Congress referred to "inalienable" rights, the printer apparently transposed "inalienable" into "unalienable" when he converted the handwritten document into print.

Congress largely deleted Jefferson's passionate denunciation of the "Christian" king for introducing slavery into the New World on page 3, which Jefferson accordingly placed within brackets. On page 4, Congress further shortened Jefferson's theory of colonial rights. Mindful of continuing personal ties between Americans and Britain, Congress also deleted Jefferson's criticism of the British people's inaction against the king's encroachment on colonial rights and Jefferson's reference to "Scottish" mercenaries on page 4. Although Jefferson continued to believe that his original was stronger than its revisions, most historians believe that these revisions actually strengthened the Declaration by making it less abstract and (especially with respect to slavery) less subject to criticisms that it was hypocritical.

Reference

Malone, Dumas. 1954. *The Story of the Declaration of Independence*. New York: Oxford University Press.

A Declaration by the Representatives of the UNITED STATES OF AMERICA, in General Congress assembled.

When in the course of human events it becomes necessary for one people to dissolve the political bands which have connected them with another, and to assume among the powers of the earth the separate and equal station to which the laws of nature & of nature's god entitle them, a decent respect to the opinions of mankind requires that they should declare the causes which impel them to the separation.

We hold these truths to be self-evident; that all men are created equal; that they are endowed by their creator with [inherent &] inalienable rights; that among these are life, liberty, & the pursuit of happiness; that to secure these rights, governments are instituted among men, deriving their just powers from the consent of the governed; that whenever any form of government becomes destructive of these ends, it is the right of the people to alter or to abolish it, & to institute new government, laying it's foundation on such principles & organising it's powers in such form, as to them shall seem most likely to effect their safety & happiness. prudence indeed will dictate that governments long established should not be changed for light & transient causes: and accordingly all experience hath shewn that mankind are more disposed to suffer while evils are sufferable, than to right themselves by abolishing the forms to which they are accustomed. but when a long train of abuses & usurpations [begun at a distinguished period, &] pursuing invariably the same object, evinces a design to reduce them under absolute Despotism, it is their right, it is their duty, to throw off such government & to provide new guards for their future security. such has been the patient sufferance of these colonies; & such is now the necessity which constrains them to [expunge] their former systems of government. the history of the present King of Great Britain is a history of [unremitting] injuries and usurpations, [among which appears no solitary fact to contradict the uniform tenor of the rest, but all have] in direct object the establishment of an absolute tyranny over these states. to prove this, let facts be submitted to a candid world [for the truth of which we pledge a faith yet unsullied by falsehood]

Dr. Franklin's handwriting

Mr. Adams' hand

he has refused his assent to laws the most wholesome and necessary for the pub-
-lic good:

he has forbidden his governors to pass laws of immediate & pressing importance, unless suspended in their operation till his assent should be obtained; and when so suspended, he has utterly neglected utterly to attend to them.

he has refused to pass other laws for the accomodation of large districts of people unless those people would relinquish the right of representation in the legislature, a right inestimable to them, & formidable to tyrants alone:

he called together legislative bodies at places unusual, unco[illegible] the depository of their public records for the sole purpose of fat[illegible] with [illegible] measures:

[illegible] he has refused for a long space of time time after such dissolutions to cause others to be elected, whereby the legislative powers, incapable of annihilation, have returned to the people at large for their exercise, the state remaining in the mean time exposed to all the dangers of invasion from without, & convulsions within:

has endeavored to prevent the population of these states; for that purpose obstructing the laws for naturalization of foreigners; refusing to pass others to encourage their migrations hither; & raising the conditions of new ap-
-propriations of lands:

he has [suffered the] [illegible]ministration of justice [totally to cease in some of these states] refusing his assent to laws for establishing judiciary powers:

he has made [our] judges dependant on his will alone, for the tenure of their offices, and the † & payment amount of their salaries:

† Dr. Franklin

he has erected a multitude of new offices [by a self-assumed power,] & sent hi-
-ther swarms of officers to harrass our people & eat out their substance:

he has kept among us in times of peace standing armies [& ships of war] without the consent of our legislatures:

he has affected to render the military, independent of & superior to the civil power:

he has combined with others to subject us to a [illegible] jurisdiction foreign to our constitu-
-tions and unacknoleged by our laws; giving his assent to their acts of pretended acts of legislation, for quartering large bodies of armed troops among us;

for protecting them by a mock-trial from punishment for any murders which they should commit on the inhabitants of these states;

for cutting off our trade with all parts of the world;

for imposing taxes on us without our consent;

for depriving us in many cases of the benefits of trial by jury;

for transporting us beyond seas to be tried for pretended offences:

for abolishing the free system of English laws in a neighboring province, establishing therein an a[illegible] government and enlarging it's boundaries so as to render it at once an example & fit instrument for introducing the [illegible] [illegible] these colonies [illegible]

+ Dr. Franklin +abolishing our most ~~important~~ valuable laws

for taking away our charters ^& altering fundamentally the forms of our governments;

for suspending our own legislatures & declaring themselves invested with power to legislate for us in all cases whatsoever:

he has abdicated government here, [~~withdrawing his governors, & declaring us out of his allegiance & protection:~~] by declaring us out of his protection & waging war against us.

he has plundered our seas, ravaged our coasts, burnt our towns & destroyed the lives of our people:

he is at this time transporting large armies of Scotch and other foreign mercenaries to compleat the works of death, desolation & tyranny already begun with circumstances of cruelty & perfidy scarcely paralleled in the most barbarous ages, & totally unworthy the head of a civilised nation:

× he has excited domestic insurrections amongst us, and has

he has endeavored to bring on the inhabitants of our frontiers the merciless Indian savages, whose known rule of warfare is an undistinguished destruction of all ages, sexes, & conditions [of existence:]

[he has incited treasonable insurrections of our fellow-citizens, with the ~~allurements of forfeiture & confiscation of our property:~~

× he has constrained others taken captives on the high seas to bear arms against their country, to become the executioners of their friends & brethren, or to fall themselves by their hands.

he has waged cruel war against human nature itself, violating it's most sacred rights of life & liberty in the persons of a distant people who never offended him, captivating & carrying them into slavery in another hemisphere, or to incur miserable death in their transportation thither. this piratical warfare, the opprobrium of infidel powers, is the warfare of the Christian king of Great Britain. determined to keep open a market where MEN should be bought & sold, he has prostituted his negative for suppressing every legislative attempt to prohibit or to restrain this ~~determining to keep open a market where MEN should be bought & sold~~: execrable commerce ^: and that this assemblage of horrors might want no fact of distinguished die, he is now exciting those very people to rise in arms among us, and to purchase that liberty of which he has deprived them, by murdering the people upon whom he also obtruded them: thus paying off former crimes committed against the liberties of one people, with crimes which he urges them to commit against the lives of another.]

+ Dr. Franklin

in every stage of these oppressions we have petitioned for redress in the most humble terms; our repeated petitions have been answered ^only by repeated injuries. a prince whose character is thus marked by every act which may define a tyrant, is unfit to be the ruler of a ^free people [who mean to be free. future ages will scarce believe that the hardiness of one man adventured within the short compass of twelve years only, to ~~lay~~ build a foundation so broad & undisguised for tyranny ~~[illegible]~~, over a people fostered & fixed in principles of ~~liberty~~ freedom.]

Nor have we been wanting in attentions to our British brethren. we have warned them from time to time of attempts by their legislature to extend ^an unwarrantable^ a jurisdiction over [these our states]. we have reminded them of the circumstances of our emigration & settlement here, [no one of which could warrant so strange a pretension: that these were effected at the expence of our own blood & treasure, unassisted by the wealth or the strength of Great Britain: that in constituting indeed our several forms of government, we had adopted one common king, thereby laying a foundation for perpetual league & amity with them: but that submission to their [illegible] credited: and] we appealed to their native justice & magnanimity [as well as to] the ties of our common kindred to disavow these usurpations which [were likely to] interrupt our ^connection &^ correspondence ~~& connection~~. they too have been deaf to the voice of justice & of consanguinity, [& when occasions have been given them, by the regular course of their laws, of removing from their councils the disturbers of our harmony, they have by their free election re-established them in power. at this very time too they are permitting their chief magistrate to send over not only soldiers of our common blood, but Scotch & foreign mercenaries to invade & destroy us. these facts have given the last stab to agonizing affection and manly spirit bids us to renounce for ever these unfeeling brethren. we must endeavor to forget our former love for them, and to hold them as we hold the rest of mankind, enemies in war, in peace friends. we might have been a free & a great people together; but a communication of grandeur & of freedom it seems is below their dignity. be it so, since they will have it: the road to ~~glory &~~ happiness ^& to glory^ is open to us too; we ~~will climb~~ ^must tread^ it ~~in separate state~~ ^apart from them^, and] acquiesce in the necessity which ~~pro~~ ^de^nounces our ~~everlasting Adieu!~~ [eternal] separation!

We therefore the representatives of the United States of America in General Congress assembled, do, in the name & by authority of the good people of these [states,] ^colonies^ reject & renounce all allegiance & subjection to the kings of Great Britain & all others who may hereafter claim by, through, or under them; we utterly dissolve ~~& break off~~ all political connection which may ~~have~~ heretofore ^have^ subsisted between us & the people or parliament of Great Britain; and finally we do assert and declare these colonies to be free and independant states, and that as free & independant states they ~~shall hereafter~~ have ^full^ power to levy war, conclude peace, contract alliances, establish commerce, & to do all other acts and things which independant states may of right do. And for the support of this declaration] we mutually pledge to each other our lives, our fortunes, & our sacred honour.

Appendix B: Declaration of Independence (1776)[1]

July 4, 1776[2]

The Unanimous Declaration[3] of The Thirteen United States of America

When in the Course of human events,[4] it becomes necessary[5] for one people[6] to dissolve the political bands which have connected them with another,[7] and to assume among the Powers of the earth,[8] the separate and equal station[9] to which the Laws of Nature and of Nature's God[10] entitle them, a decent respect to the opinions of mankind[11] requires that they should declare the causes which impel them to the separation.[12] We[13] hold these truths to be self-evident,[14] that all men[15] are created equal,[16] that they are endowed by their Creator[17] with certain

1. Footnotes reference corresponding entries in this book. The notes will not include all entries that are listed in the table of contents, since some focus on aspects of the Declaration other than the specific language of the document.
2. *See* Dunlap Broadside Printing of the Declaration of Independence; Independence Day; Timing of the Declaration of Independence; Vote for Declaration.
3. *See* Declaration (Meaning of Term); Declaration and Resolves of the First Continental Congress (1774); Declaration of Sentiments (1848); Declaration on the Causes and Necessity of Taking Up Arms.
4. *See* Timing of the Declaration of Independence; When in the Course of Human Events.
5. *See* Necessity.
6. *See* People.
7. *See* Dissolution of Government.
8. *See* Ambition.
9. *See* International Law.
10. *See* Laws of Nature and of Nature's God.
11. *See* Audiences for the Declaration of Independence; Reason.
12. *See* Charges against the King.
13. *See* "We" (First-Person Plural).
14. *See* Self-Evident Truths.
15. *See* Declaration of Sentiments (1848); Remember the Ladies.
16. *See* Calhoun, John C.; Equality; Human Nature and the Declaration of Independence; Lincoln, Abraham; Slavery.
17. *See* God.

unalienable Rights,[18] that among these are Life, Liberty and the pursuit of Happiness.[19] That to secure these rights, Governments are instituted among Men,[20] deriving their just powers from the consent of the governed,[21] That whenever any Form of Government becomes destructive of these ends, it is the Right of the People to alter or to abolish it,[22] and to institute new Government,[23] laying its foundation on such principles and organizing its powers in such form, as to them shall seem most likely to effect their Safety and Happiness.[24] Prudence,[25] indeed, will dictate that Governments long established should not be changed for light and transient causes;[26] and accordingly all experience hath shown, that mankind are more disposed to suffer, while evils are sufferable, than to right themselves by abolishing the forms to which they are accustomed.[27] But when a long train of abuses and usurpations, pursuing invariably the same Object evinces a design to reduce them under absolute Despotism,[28] it is their right, it is their duty,[29] to throw off such Government, and to provide new Guards for their future security.[30]—Such has been the patient sufferance of these Colonies; and such is now the necessity[31] which constrains them to alter their former Systems of Government. The history of the present King of Great Britain[32] is a history of repeated injuries and usurpations,[33] all having in direct object the establishment of an absolute Tyranny over these States.[34] To prove this, let Facts be submitted to a candid world.[35]

He has refused his Assent to Laws, the most wholesome and necessary for the public good.[36]

---

18. *See* Unalienable Rights.
19. *See* George III, Speech to Parliament (October 31, 1776); Life, Liberty, and the Pursuit of Happiness; Property Rights.
20. *See* U.S. Constitution and the Declaration of Independence.
21. *See* Consent of the Governed.
22. *See* Revolution.
23. *See* Creation of New State Governments.
24. *See* Life, Liberty, and the Pursuit of Happiness.
25. *See* Prudence.
26. *See* Revolution.
27. *See* Human Nature and the Declaration of Independence.
28. *See* Conspiracy.
29. *See* Moral Virtues in the Declaration of Independence.
30. *See* Life, Liberty, and the Pursuit of Happiness.
31. *See* Necessity.
32. *See* Kingship.
33. *See* Charges against the King and Others.
34. *See* Tyranny.
35. *See* Audiences for the Declaration of Independence; British Deposition Apologias; Legal Form of the Declaration of Independence.
36. *See* Refused Assent to Colonial Laws (Charge #1).

He has forbidden his Governors to pass Laws of immediate and pressing importance, unless suspended in their operation till his Assent should be obtained; and when so suspended, he has utterly neglected to attend to them.[37]

He has refused to pass other Laws for the accommodation of large districts of people,[38] unless those people would relinquish the right of Representation in the Legislature,[39] a right inestimable to them and formidable to tyrants only.[40]

He has called together legislative bodies[41] at places unusual, uncomfortable, and distant from the depository or their public Records, for the sole purpose of fatiguing them into compliance with his measures.[42]

He has dissolved Representative Houses repeatedly,[43] for opposing with manly firmness[44] his invasions on the rights of the people.

He has refused for a long time, after such dissolutions, to cause others to be elected; whereby the Legislative powers,[45] incapable of Annihilation, have returned to the People at large for their exercise;[46] the State remaining in the mean time exposed to all the dangers of invasion from without, and convulsions within.[47]

He has endeavoured to prevent the population of these States;[48] for that purpose obstructing the Laws for Naturalization of Foreigners; refusing to pass others to encourage their migration hither, and raising the conditions of new Appropriations of Lands.[49]

He has obstructed the Administration of Justice, by refusing his Assent to Laws for establishing Judiciary powers.[50]

He has made Judges dependent on his Will alone, for the tenure of their offices, and the amount and payment of their salaries.[51]

---

37. *See* Forbidding Governors from Passing Laws (Charge #2).
38. *See* Refused to Pass Other Laws (Charge #3).
39. *See* Representative (Republican) Government.
40. *See* Tyranny.
41. *See* Representative (Republican) Government.
42. *See* Called Together Legislative Bodies Unusually (Charge #4).
43. *See* Dissolved Representative Houses (Charge #5).
44. *See* Moral Virtues in the Declaration of Independence.
45. *See* Representative (Republican) Government.
46. *See* Locke, John.
47. *See* Refused to Cause Others to be Elected (Charge #6).
48. *See* Endeavored to Prevent the Population (Charge #7).
49. *See* Native American Indians (Charge #27).
50. *See* Obstructed the Administration of Justice (Charge #8).
51. *See* Made Judges Dependent on His Will (Charge #9).

He has erected a multitude of New Offices, and sent hither swarms of Officers to harass our people, and eat out their substance.[52]

He has kept among us, in times of peace, Standing Armies,[53] without the Consent of our legislatures.[54]

He has affected to render the Military independent of and superior to the Civil power.[55]

He has combined with others to subject us to a jurisdiction foreign to our constitution, and unacknowledged by our laws; giving his Assent to their Acts of pretended Legislation:[56]

For quartering large bodies of armed troops among us:[57]

For protecting them, by a mock Trial, from Punishment for any Murders which they should commit on the Inhabitants of these States:[58]

For cutting off our Trade with all parts of the world:[59]

For imposing Taxes on us without our Consent:[60]

For depriving us in many cases, of the benefits of Trial by Jury:[61]

For transporting us beyond Seas to be tried for pretended offenses:[62]

For abolishing the free System of English Laws in a neighboring Province,[63] establishing therein an Arbitrary government, and enlarging its Boundaries so as to render it at once an example and fit instrument for introducing the same absolute rule into these Colonies:

---

52. *See* Erected a Multitude of New Offices (Charge #10).
53. *See* Standing Armies (Charge #11).
54. *See* Consent of the Governed; Representative (Republican) Government.
55. *See* Civilian Control of the Military (Charge #12).
56. *See* He Has Combined with Others (Charge #13).
57. *See* Standing Armies (Charge #11).
58. *See* Protecting Troops by Mock Trial (Charge #15).
59. *See* Trade (Charge #16).
60. *See* Consent of the Governed; Taxes (Charge #17).
61. *See* Trial by Jury (Charge #18).
62. *See* Transporting Us beyond Seas (Charge #19).
63. *See* Quebec Act of 1774 (Charge #20).

For taking away our Charters, abolishing our most valuable Laws, and altering fundamentally the Forms of our Governments: [64]

For suspending our own Legislatures, and declaring themselves invested with power to legislate for us in all cases whatsoever.[65]

He has abdicated Government here, by declaring us out of his Protection and waging War against us.[66]

He has plundered our seas, ravaged our Coasts, burnt our towns, and destroyed the lives of our people.[67]

He is at this time transporting large Armies of foreign Mercenaries[68] to compleat the works of death, desolation and tyranny,[69] already begun with circumstances of Cruelty & perfidy scarcely paralleled in the most barbarous ages, and totally unworthy the Head of a civilized nation.

He has constrained our fellow Citizens taken Captive on the high Seas to bear Arms against their Country, to become the executioners of their friends and Brethren,[70] or to fall themselves by their Hands.[71]

He has excited domestic insurrections amongst us,[72] and has endeavoured to bring on the inhabitants of our frontiers, the merciless Indian Savages, whose known rule of warfare, is an undistinguished destruction of all ages, sexes and conditions.[73]

In every state of these Oppressions We have Petitioned for Redress in the most humble terms: Our repeated Petitions have been answered only by repeated injury.[74] A Prince, whose character is thus marked by every act which may define a Tyrant,[75] is unfit to be the ruler of a free people.[76]

---

64. *See* Covenant and Contracts; Taking Away Our Charters (Charge #21).
65. *See* Suspending Legislatures (Charge #22).
66. *See* Abdication of Government (Charge #23); George III, Speech to Parliament (October 27, 1775).
67. *See* Plundered Our Seas (Charge #24).
68. *See* Transporting Large Armies of Foreign Mercenaries (Charge #25).
69. *See* Tyranny.
70. *See* Friends and Enemies.
71. *See* Constrained Our Fellow Citizens Taken Captive on the High Seas (Charge #26).
72. *See* Slavery.
73. *See* Native American Indians (Charge #27).
74. *See* Olive Branch Petition; Petitions for Redress Ignored (Charge #28); Petition to King George III (1774).
75. *See* Tyranny.
76. *See* People.

Nor have We been wanting in attentions to our British brethren.[77] We have warned them from time to time of attempts by their legislature to extend an unwarrantable jurisdiction over us. We have reminded them of the circumstances of our emigration and settlement here.[78] We have appealed to their native justice and magnanimity, and we have conjured them by the ties of our common kindred to disavow these usurpations, which, would inevitably interrupt our connections and correspondence. They too have been deaf to the voice of justice and of consanguinity. We must, therefore, acquiesce in the necessity,[79] which denounces our Separation, and hold them, as we hold the rest of mankind, Enemies in War, in Peace Friends.[80]

We,[81] Therefore, the Representatives[82] of the United States of America,[83] in General Congress, Assembled,[84] appealing to the Supreme Judge of the world[85] for the rectitude of our intentions,[86] do, in the Name, and by Authority of the good People of these Colonies,[87] solemnly publish and declare, That these United Colonies are, and of Right ought to be[88] Free and Independent States;[89] that they are Absolved from all Allegiance to the British Crown,[90] and that all political connection between them and the State of Great Britain, is and ought to be totally dissolved;[91] and that as Free and Independent States, they have full Power to levy War, conclude Peace, contract Alliances, establish Commerce, and to do all other Acts and Things which Independent States may of right do.[92] And for the support of this Declaration,[93] with a firm reliance on the protection of Divine Providence,[94] we[95] mutually pledge to each other our Lives, our Fortunes and our sacred Honor.[96]

---

77. Nor Have We Been Wanting in Attention to Our British Brethren.
78. *See A Summary View of the Rights of British America* (Jefferson).
79. *See* Necessity.
80. See Friends and Enemies.
81. *See* "We" (First-Person Plural).
82. *See* Representative (Republican) Government.
83. *See* United States of America (Name).
84. *See* Second Continental Congress.
85. *See* God.
86. *See* Moral Virtues in the Declaration of Independence.
87. *See* People.
88. *See* Declaratory Act of 1766.
89. *See* Federalism.
90. *See* British Crown.
91. *See* Resolutions Introduced by Richard Henry Lee (June 7, 1776).
92. *See* International Law.
93. *See* Declaration (Meaning of Term); Preamble to the Resolution of Virginia Convention (May 15, 1776)
94. *See* God.
95. *See* "We" (First-Person Plural).
96. *See* Attestation Clauses; Moral Virtues in the Declaration of Independence; Our Lives, Our Fortunes, and Our Sacred Honor.

[Signators][97]

John Adams, Samuel Adams, Josiah Bartlett, Carter Braxton, Charles Carroll, Samuel Chase, Abraham Clark, George Clymer, William Ellery, William Floyd, Benjamin Franklin, Elbridge Gerry, Button Gwinnett, Lyman Hall, John Hancock, Benjamin Harrison, John Hart, Richard Henry Lee, Joseph Hewes, Thomas Heyward, Jr., William Hooper, Stephen Hopkins, Fras. Hopkinson, Samuel Huntington, Thomas Jefferson, Frans. Lewis, Francis Lightfoot Lee, Phil. Livingston, Thomas Lynch, Jr., Thomas M'Kean, Arthur Middleton, Lewis Morris, Robert Morris, John Morton, Thomas Nelson, Jr., William Paca, John Penn, George Read, Caesar Rodney, George Ross, Benjamin Rush, Edward Rutledge, Roger Sherman, Jason Smith, Richard Stockton, Thomas Stone, George Taylor, Matthew Thornton, Robert Treat Paine, George Walton, William Whipple, William Williams, James Wilson, Johnothan Witherspoon, Oliver Wolcott, George Wythe.

Source: *In Congress, July 4, 1776. A Declaration By the Representatives of the United States of America, In General Congress Assembled.* Philadelphia: John Dunlap, July 4, 1776. Available at the Library of Congress, https://memory.loc.gov/cgi-bin/ampage?collId=lljc&fileName=005/lljc005.db&recNum=94.

97. *See* Signers, Collective Profile.

Appendix C: Signers by State from North to South[1]

New Hampshire[2]

Josiah Bartlett
Matthew Thornton
William Whipple

Massachusetts[3]

John Adams[4]
Samuel Adams
Elbridge Gerry
John Hancock[5]
Robert Treat Paine

Rhode Island[6]

William Ellery
Stephen Hopkins

Connecticut[7]

Samuel Huntington
Roger Sherman
William Williams
Oliver Wolcott

---

1. *See* Signers, Collective Profile.
2. *See* New Hampshire and Its Signers.
3. *See* Massachusetts and Its Signers; Suffolk Resolves of 1774.
4. *See* Adams, John.
5. *See* Hancock's Letters Accompanying the Declaration of Independence.
6. *See* Rhode Island and Its Signers.
7. *See* Connecticut and Its Signers.

New York[8]

William Floyd
Francis Lewis
Philip Livingston
Lewis Morris

New Jersey[9]

Abraham Clark
John Hart
Francis Hopkinson
Richard Stockton
John Witherspoon

Pennsylvania[10]

George Clymer
Benjamin Franklin[11]
Robert Morris
John Morton
George Ross
Benjamin Rush[12]
James Smith
George Taylor
James Wilson[13]

Delaware[14]

Thomas McKean
George Read
Caesar Rodney

---

8. *See* New York and Its Signers.
9. *See* New Jersey and Its Signers.
10. *See* Pennsylvania and Its Signers.
11. *See* Franklin, Benjamin.
12. *See* Rush's (Benjamin) Characters of the Signers.
13. *See Considerations on the Nature and Extent of Legislative Authority of the British Parliament* (Wilson).
14. *See* Delaware and Its Signers.

Maryland[15]

Charles Carroll of Carrollton
Samuel Chase
William Paca
Thomas Stone

Virginia[16]

Carter Braxton
Benjamin Harrison
Thomas Jefferson[17]
Francis Lightfoot Lee
Richard Henry Lee[18]
Thomas Nelson Jr.
George Wythe

North Carolina[19]

Joseph Hewes
William Hooper
John Penn

South Carolina[20]

Thomas Heyward Jr.
Thomas Lynch Jr.
Arthur Middleton
Edward Rutledge

Georgia[21]

Button Gwinnett
Lyman Hall
George Walton

---

15. *See* Maryland and Its Signers.
16. *See* Virginia and Its Signers; Virginia Constitution of 1776; Virginia Declaration of Rights; Virginia Resolution of May 15, 1776.
17. *See* Jefferson, Thomas.
18. *See* Resolutions Introduced by Richard Henry Lee (June 7, 1776)
19. *See* North Carolina and Its Signers.
20. *See* South Carolina and Its Signers.
21. *See* Georgia and Its Signers.

Glossary

Abdicated

Abandoned or renounced. When the Declaration of Independence said that the king "has abdicated government here," it meant that he had substituted force for use of routine methods of government. Kings who resign their posts rather than continuing to govern are also said to have abdicated.

Abolish

Eliminate. The Declaration says the people have the right to "alter or abolish" unjust government and accuses the king and his allies "for abolishing the free system of English laws" in Canada.

Absolute rule

Rule without proper legal boundaries, as in an absolutist, or authoritarian, government

Absolved

Free from. The Declaration of Independence announced that the former colonies were now "absolved from all allegiance to the British Crown."

Abuses

Wrongs or mistreatments.

Accommodation

Convenience or benefit. The Declaration notes that the British king has "refused to pass other Laws for the Accommodation of large District of People."

Acquiesce

Agree or accede. The Declaration says that it is necessary to "acquiesce in the necessity" of parting with the British.

Actual representation

The idea that for its interests to be fairly represented, representatives from the American colonies would have to have been seated in Parliament so that those who wrote the laws would also be affected by them.

Administration

Institutions and processes for carrying out a function.

Affected

Sought. When the Declaration accuses the king of having "affected to render the Military independent of and superior to the Civil Power," it means he has sought to do so.

Allegiance

Loyalty. The Declaration of Independence announced in its final paragraph that the former colonists were "absolved from all allegiance to the British Crown." Those who repeat the pledge to the U.S. flag pledge their "allegiance to the flag, and to the republic for which it stands."

Alliances

Partnerships, often for mutual defense, typically entered into with other nations by means of treaties.

Alter

Change.

Annihilation

Total destruction. The Declaration asserted that legislative (lawmaking powers) were incapable of annihilation.

Appealing

Making a plea to.

Appropriations

Grants of money or land by the government. The Declaration accused George III of "raising the Conditions of new appropriations of Lands."

Arbitrary

Capricious. In accusing the king of establishing an "arbitrary government" in Canada, the Declaration was accusing him of ignoring established procedures of due process.

Aristocracy

Rule by an elite on behalf of the common good.

Assembled

Gathered together.

Assent

Approval. The Declaration accuses the king of refusing his "assent" to good laws for the colonies.

Assume

Undertake. The Declaration proclaims that the colonies are ready "to assume" their "separate and equal station" with other nations.

Attend

Take care of; direct attention or effort toward something.

Attest

Witness or validate.

Authority

Authorization. When the Declaration says that it is declaring independence "in the name and by authority of the good people of these colonies," it is indicating that it is acting on their behalf. Political scientists often distinguish the exercise of authority, which implies political consent, from mere force or power.

Bands

Ties. The Declaration was describing why the colonies were dissolving the "political bands" that had bound them to Britain.

Barbarous

Uncivilized. The word, which is the root of "barbarity," is also often associated with savagery and violence.

Brethren

Brothers or others who are closely bound by kinship or other ties. Prior to the Revolution, Americans would have considered the British to be brethren.

British Crown

A reference to the British monarchy, headed in 1776 by King George III, and, more generally, to the British government of which it was the symbolic head.

Broadside

A large piece of paper printed only on one side and used to display advertisements and documents. John Dunlap of Philadelphia printed the first broadside of the Declaration of Independence to be sent throughout the former colonies.

Candid

Honest or impartial. In appealing to a "candid world," the Declaration of Independence was appealing to those who took an honest, or unbiased, view of the situation.

Captive

Involuntarily held in the custody of another.

Charters

Legal authorizations. Many of those who settled in the American colonies did so under authority of grants, or charters issued by the king.

Civilian or Civil power

Nonmilitary.

Civilian control of the military

Vesting ultimate control of the military in elected branches of government. The U.S. Constitution attempts to do this by vesting the power to declare war in Congress and making the president the commander in chief of the armed forces.

Civilized

Cultured or refined, often used by European governments to distinguish themselves from more barbarous nations.

Colony

A territory that has been settled by and/or is now dependent upon another. Most of the 13 colonies south of Canada and north of Mexico began as, or became, colonies of Great Britain. The Declaration of Independence was designed to announce that the colonies no longer considered themselves to be bound by British rule.

Commerce

Trade, exchange, and intercourse. The Declaration anticipated that the one-time colonies as independent states would be able to "establish commerce."

Committee of the Whole

A parliamentary mechanism that allows representative bodies to debate bills with a lower quorum and with relaxed rules. Such a committee was used to debate the Declaration of Independence. There are consequently no official notes of these proceedings.

Common law

The system of law, developed in Britain and transported to America, in which judicial interpretations are used to ascertain the law and how it is applied to day-to-day situations.

Compliance

Conformity or submission. The Declaration accuses the British king of seeking to fatigue colonists "into Compliance with his Measures" by calling legislatures in inconvenient places.

Congress

A formal gathering of delegates to deliberate and, in the case of legislative bodies, to adopt laws. The Congress that adopted the Declaration eventually assumed such legislative responsibilities. A *general* congress is one with a broad agenda.

Conjure

Call upon. The Declaration of Independence says that the colonies have "conjured" the British on the basis of their common heritage.

Consanguinity

Ancestral and familial ties. The Declaration of Independence accused the British of being "deaf to the voice of justice and of consanguinity."

Consent

Agreement or approval. In arguing for government "by the consent of the governed," the Declaration was opposing the idea that kingly authority was created directly by God.

Constitution

The configuration of power within a nation or state. The British had an established way of governing that the colonies thought they were violating. In overthrowing British rule, Americans settled on a written constitution, which defined governmental powers and individual liberties rather than relying, as had the British, on an "unwritten constitution," in which Parliament was sovereign.

Constrained

Forced, compelled, or limited.

Contract

Enter into agreements, often called contracts. The Declaration says Americans will have full power to "contract alliances," which would typically be done through treaties.

Convulsions

Ordinarily used to describe an uncontrollable body movement caused by a seizure, the term is used in the Declaration to refer to domestic disturbances within the body politic.

Course

Path or direction as in a river's course to the sea. The Declaration of Independence referred to the "course" of human affairs with the understanding that this course pointed in a particular direction that was discernable to astute observers.

Creator

Maker. The Declaration refers to mankind as having been "created" equal.

Crown

Symbol of rule, generally connected to a king or queen. By renouncing allegiance to the "British Crown," the Declaration is proclaiming that it is no longer bound to it.

Decent

Appropriate or fitting. The Declaration is written out of "a decent respect to the opinions of mankind."

Declaration

An announcement, typically formal, often by a representative body such as a parliament or a Congress.

Democracy

Rule by the people. In the United States, such rule is mediated through elected representatives.

Denounces

In the next to the last paragraph, the Declaration of Independence, says that it "denounces our separation" from the British. Instead of abjuring or renouncing such a separation (which would be the most common current usage), the document was announcing the end to a relationship, a term that was sometimes used to indicate the ending of a treaty.

Depository

A place where records, especially public records, are stored.

Depriving

Withholding.

Deriving

Stemming from. The Declaration affirms that governments derive their just powers from popular consent.

Design

A pattern or intent. The Declaration said that the actions of the British king showed "A Design to reduce the colonies under an absolute Despotism."

Desolation

Destruction. The Declaration accused the king of sending mercenaries to "compleat the works of death, desolation and tyranny."

Despotism

Arbitrary rule, often by a single ruler, or tyrant.

Dictate

Require or guide. The Declaration says that prudence "will dictate" against changing governments "for light and transient causes."

Direct object

Intended purpose. The Declaration says that the King's actions have the "direct object" of establishing tyranny over the colonies.

Disavow

Renounce or repudiate.

Disposed

Inclined. The Declaration said that individuals were generally more "disposed to suffer" than to seek changes in their forms of government.

Dissolve

End. The Declaration declared that the political connection between Great Britain and the one-time American colonies had been dissolved.

Divine right of kings

The idea, contrary to the social contract thinking reflected in the Declaration of Independence, that kings were created by God and were accountable only to him rather than resting on the consent of the people.

Domestic

Internal. When the Declaration refers to "domestic insurrections," it is referring to insurrections within the colonies.

Duty

Obligation.

Emigration

The act of leaving one country for another. Emigrants from one country become immigrants to another. The Declaration of Independence reminded the British "of the circumstances of our emigration and settlement here."

Endeavor

To attempt through effort. The Declaration said that the king had "endeavored to prevent the population of these States."

Endowed

That with which one is enriched or gifted. The Declaration claimed that the Creator had endowed human beings with certain rights. Classical Christian thinkers had believed that men were created in the image of God, with attributes that reflected rationality and other godlike characteristics.

Entitle

Vest. The Declaration claims that the Laws of Nature and of Nature's God entitle Americans to equal status among other nations.

Equal

Having the same status as others. The Declaration said that men were "created equal," in that all had the same rights as others.

Erected

Created or built. The Declaration accused the king of having "erected a multitude of new offices" in the colonies.

Evinces

Shows evidence of an intent.

Executioner

One who purposely kills, or is forced to kill, another.

Facts

Things that are known. Facts may also refer to occurrences. The law sometimes describes crimes as facts. Just before describing the king's mistreatment of the colonies, the Declaration of Independence states that it will "let facts be submitted to a candid world."

Fatiguing

Wearying or tiring. The Declaration accused the British king of moving the places where legislatures met as a way of "fatiguing them into Compliance with his Measures."

Foreign

Alien, or from another country.

Form

Structure or shape. At the time of the writing of the Declaration of Independence, commentaries generally identified governments according to their forms. Governments could be classified according to whether they were ruled by the one, the few, or the many, or by how they divided powers between the central authority and various subunits. The Declaration asserted that the people had the right to configure governments in such form as to be conducive to their happiness.

Formidable

So large, important, or weighty as to inspire fear.

Fortunes

Although typically thought to involve a lot of money, as used in the Declaration, the term applies to one's financial means, whatever their amount. It may also refer to a common fate.

Foundation

That upon which something is built.

Frontiers

The outer edges or borders of advancing civilizations, where there is most likely to be violent conflict with native peoples. The Declaration accused the king of encouraging "Indian Savages" on the frontiers to make war on the colonists.

God

The divine power referred to in the Declaration as Creator and Supreme Judge of human intentions.

Governed

Those subject to legitimate authority.

Government

Rule and the institutions that carry out such rule.

Great Britain

The island nation, separated from Western Europe by the English Channel. It was formed by the union of England and Scotland (first through a common king in 1603 and then by a common parliament in 1707), and in 1801, by Ireland against which the former 13 North American colonies declared their independence.

Happiness

Philosophers generally identify happiness with contentment and fulfillment toward which all human beings are believed to strive. The Declaration of Independence identified the "pursuit of happiness" as a basic human right, which government was bound to preserve. Happiness was often associated with the right to own property. Utilitarianism identified happiness with pleasure.

Harass

To assail or bully.

Hereditary succession

The method by which authority passes in some monarchical societies from the king or queen to his children after the monarch's passing.

High seas

The open ocean, which is not within the jurisdiction of any single nation.

Hither

Antiquated word for "here."

Hold

To maintain or believe dearly, as in "we hold these truths to be self-evident."

Honor

Both classical and Christian thinkers associated individuals of virtue with honor. Individuals were deemed to act with regard for their reputations. Just as individuals might honor a handshake or contract, so too they pledged this "sacred honor" to one another in the last sentence of the Declaration of Independence.

Impel

To drive or force. In describing the necessity of independence, the Declaration of Independence states its intention of declaring "the causes which impel them to the separation."

Independence

Freedom. The Declaration of Independence announced that colonies, once dependent on Great Britain as colonies, now intended to run their own affairs.

Inestimable

Priceless. Of great value. The Declaration of Independence refers to the right to legislative representation as "inestimable."

Inevitably

Invariably bound to happen in due course

Inhabitant

An individual who lives in a particular geographical area. An inhabitant may or not be a citizen, with accompanying rights.

Injury

Snub or slight. When the Declaration says that the king has answered colonial petitions "by repeated injury," it is accusing him of having ignored, or snubbed, them.

Instituted

Created or established. The Declaration says that "governments are instituted among men."

Insurrections

Revolts. The Declaration of Independence accused the King of having "excited domestic insurrections among us." There is a certain redundancy in this claim since domestic (internal) insurrections are often distinguished between foreign wars.

Invariably

Without variation. The Declaration said that the king's actions were "invariably" pursuing a design to subject the colonies to despotism.

Invasion

Physical incursions (invasions or attacks), typically at the hands of a foreign foe.

Invested

Vested or authorized

Judiciary powers

Those involving courts.

Jurisdiction

Authority. The Declaration observes that Americans had warned Britons "of attempts by their legislature to extend an unwarrantable jurisdiction over us."

Jury

A group of fellow citizens called upon to decide whether a person should be charged with a crime (grand jury) or convicted of it (petit jury).

Justice

Fairness. The Declaration refers to just powers and says that Americans had previously appealed to the "native justice & magnanimity" of "our British brethren."

Just powers

Those which are fairly and legitimately exercised. The Declaration associates such powers with "the consent of the governed."

Kindred

Individuals who are related, typically through blood. Similar to the term "brethren."

King

A single ruler of a nation. A king (or queen) may be largely symbolic (head of state) or wield independent power (head of government).

Laws of nature

Principles of human behavior ascertainable by unaided human reason, which should, if adhered to, produce good government.

Legislation

Laws. When the Declaration refers to acts of "pretended legislation," it is questioning the right of the English Parliament to make laws for the colonies.

Legislature

Body entrusted with law-making.

Levy

To impose, wage, or conduct. The Declaration of Independence claimed the right of Americans, as "free & independent states," to "levy war."

Liberty

The rightful exercise of freedom.

Magna Carta

A document signed by King John I in 1215, and subsequently reaffirmed by succeeding kings, to which the colonies traced the principle of "no taxation without representation." The document also contained a phrase that is the predecessor to modern notions of due process.

Magnanimity

Greatness of spirit, often displayed through kindness and generosity. The Declaration of Independence said that the colonists had unsuccessfully appealed to the "native Justice & magnanimity" of the British people.

Manly

Associated with resolve or strength, which was in turn associated with manliness, as when the Declaration says that legislative assemblies have opposed tyrannical acts with "manly firmness."

Men

Adult male human beings. This term may, however, sometimes be used in the sense of "mankind" (another term used within the Declaration) to refer to all adult human beings. It seems likely that the authors of the Declaration believed that all human beings had the right to life, liberty, and the pursuit of happiness without thinking that women and children would necessarily have an equality of political rights like voting or serving on juries.

Mercenaries

Hired troops, sometimes from foreign lands. The colonies were incensed that George III had hired mercenaries from Germany and elsewhere to fight against them.

Migration

Moving from one area or country to another. American colonies were founded by migrants from Great Britain and other nations.

Mock trial

One that cannot be considered fair. Provisions allowing British soldiers accused of misbehavior in the colonies to be tried in Britain, while arguably designed to shield them from local prejudice, was criticized in the Declaration as a way of helping them avoid just punishment.

Monarchy

Rule by a king. In constitutional monarchies, the king or queen is largely a figurehead with the prime minister, or premier, typically leading the government.

Multitude

Large number.

Mutually

Collectively.

Native

Innate, as when the Declaration says that Americans have appealed to the "native justice & magnanimity" of "our English brethren. A native may also refer to an individual who has been born in a particular place.

Nature's God

Associated with creation. Christians associate the Creator-God with active intervention in human affairs. Deists tended to believe that God largely left humankind to look after their own affairs.

Natural law

A concept dating back to classical philosophy stressing that certain actions are proper because they accord with nature. The idea was in time further connected to the idea that individuals had certain natural rights, which stemmed from their status as human beings.

Natural rights

The idea that individuals have certain common rights, which they share as a result of common humanity. While the Declaration of Independence listed "life, liberty, and the pursuit of happiness," as being "among these rights," the word "among" indicates that the list was not complete.

Naturalization

The process by which a foreigner becomes a citizen.

Necessary

Incumbent upon. The Declaration argued that the time had come when it was "necessary" for the American people to separate themselves from the British people.

Necessity

Mandated by circumstances. The Declaration of Independence argued that separation from Great Britain was necessitated, or "impelled," much in the same way as natural laws of the universe.

No taxation without representation

The idea, which American Revolutionaries traced to the Magna Carta (1215), that Parliament had no right to tax areas, like the colonies, whose representatives were not seated in that body.

Obstruct

To serve as an obstacle. The Declaration accused the king of having "obstructed the administration of justice."

Offenses

Crimes or wrongdoings.

Oppressions

Arbitrary actions contrary to the people's liberties.

Parliament

The chief legislative body in Great Britain and in other parliamentary democracies. It is a bicameral body (two houses) that consists of a House of Commons and a House of Lords. The British perceived that the Parliament was sovereign with legal power to do everything that was not naturally impossible. The colonies did not think that Parliament had the power to tax them.

Parliamentary sovereignty

The idea, prominent in Britain, that the Parliament had the legal authority, as representative of the people, to do anything that was not naturally impossible. By contrast, American revolutionaries questioned parliamentary sovereignty over colonial affairs, thinking that such affairs should be governed by locally elected legislative bodies.

Patriots

The name given to those in the United States who supported the revolutionary cause.

People

A distinct group. Today, the more common descriptor is probably that of a nation. The Declaration of Independence announced that the American people now considered themselves to be distinct from those of the mother country in Britain.

Perfidy

Treachery or duplicity. The Declaration of Independence says that the king's acts in sending troops to the colonies were acts of "cruelty & perfidy."

Petition

A formal request. The Declaration of Independence accused the king of ignoring colonial petitions. The First Amendment to the U.S. Constitution guarantees the right to petition.

Pledge

Promise. Signers of the Declaration made a mutual pledge to support one another.

Plundered

Taken items as booty. The Declaration accused the king of having "plundered our seas."

Powers of the Earth

A reference to other sovereign nation states, which the United States sought to join by declaring its independence from Great Britain.

Preamble

The opening two paragraphs of both the Declaration of Independence and the opening paragraph of the U.S. Constitution are known as the preamble. The preambles to both announce the purposes of the documents. In addition, the preamble to the Declaration outlines a right to revolution against oppressive governments. Pressing: Urgent or critical.

Pretended

Imagined or falsely asserted. In accusing the king of "giving his assent to their acts of pretended legislation," the Declaration was questioning the right of Parliament to enact laws (especially those related to taxes) for the colonies who did not elect representatives to this body. Similarly, in accusing the King of transporting Americans for "pretended offenses," the Declaration was indicating that accusations of such offenses were fabricated.

Prevent

Stop, reduce, or check.

Prince

Although this term is more commonly used today to denote a son of a king or queen and putative heir, it is used in the Declaration of Independence to mean "king."

Principles

Fundamental truths or precepts.

Providence

God's protective care.

Province

Administrative subdivision. In referring to "a neighboring province," the Declaration is referring to Canada, which had been won from France by Great Britain.

Prudence

Practical wisdom. One of the four cardinal virtues that also included fortitude, temperance, and justice. The Declaration declared that "prudence indeed will dictate that governments long established should not be changed for light & transient causes."

Pursuit

Quest.

Quartering

The act of housing, especially by the military. The Declaration accused the British king of "quartering large Bodies of Armed Troops" among the colonists.

Ravage

Raid or pillage. The Declaration accused the king of having "ravaged our Coasts."

Rebel

Someone who is fighting against established authority. Although King George III considered American patriots to be rebels, they believed that he was the real rebel in that he had attempted to suppress their legitimate rights. By proclaiming that they were a separate "people," the former colonists proclaimed that America was the juridical equal to Britain.

Rectitude

Morally correct behavior. The final paragraph of the Declaration of Independence appeals to "the supreme judge of the world for the rectitude of our intentions."

Redress

Correction or amelioration. The Declaration of Independence states that "we have petitioned for redress in the most humble terms."

Reliance

Dependence.

Relinquish

Give up. The Declaration asserted that the people had been unwilling to relinquish their right of representation.

Render

To cause or make.

Representative

Reflecting popular will through individuals or institutions. A representative may also be the name of a delegate in a representative body.

Representation

Having a voice through a spokesperson.

Republic

A government in which people elect officials who make and enforce the laws. Such a representative government is also called a republican (small "r") government.

Respect

Regard or Consideration. The opening paragraph of the Declaration refers to "a decent Respect to the Opinions of Mankind."

Revolution

A term, taken from astronomy, and designed to emphasis a change. The theory of revolution, which the Declaration of Independence announced, was relatively mild (an attempt to return to what the colonies understood to be a previous legal relationship) rather than an attempt to make all things new.

Rights

Legitimate claims. The Declaration of Independence proclaimed that individuals had the right to "life, liberty, and the pursuit of happiness" and that they formed governments to protect these rights. The Document further tied such rights to human equality, which was based on Creation.

Sacred

Holy or deserving veneration. The concluding sentence of the Declaration of Independence ties the delegates' commitment of their "sacred honor" with that of their "lives" and "fortunes."

Savages

People who were considered to be cruel, primitive, or uncivilized.

Sea

Although commonly used today to describe a large body of water (as in an "inland sea") it is used in the Declaration to describe the ocean.

Secure

To safeguard, as in "to secure these rights."

Self-evident

A "self-evident truth" is one, such as the affirmation that humans are equal because they share a common humanity, which is evident without further demonstration.

Social contract

The idea, which is correlative to the idea of government by consent and articulated in the philosophy of John Locke, that individuals contract with one another, first to leave the state of nature and join society, and then to institute government to protect their rights.

Solemnly

Seriously.

Sovereignty

Ultimate power. Nations exercise sovereign authority within their jurisdictions. Within Great Britain, Parliament claimed to be sovereign. American colonists argued that this sovereignty did not extend to the New World, particularly with respect to the power of taxation.

Standing armies

Permanent professional armies, which were suspect in the eyes of colonists who thought their liberties would be better preserved by local militias consisting of able-bodied male citizens. The Declaration of Independence accused the king of maintaining standing armies in the colonies without their consent.

State of nature

A hypothesized prepolitical condition in which there is no government and thus little security of life, liberty, or property.

Station

Status. The Declaration says that it is time for the united colonies to assume their "separate and equal station" with other nations.

Submitted

Offered. The Declaration precedes its list of grievances with the words "let facts be submitted to a candid world."

Sufferable

Capable of being endured. The Declaration says that men are inclined to suffer, when conditions are sufferable, than to revolt.

Sufferance

Patient endurance. The Declaration refers to "the patient sufferance of these Colonies" and stresses that they are revolting only after a long series of abuses.

Suspend

Prevent implementation. On several occasions, royal governors had suspended colonial legislatures.

Suspending clause

Regulations that prevented colonial laws from going into effect until royal assent was attained. The second charge that the Declaration leveled against the king cited this as a grievance.

Swarms

Large numbers, often of insects. The Declaration accused the King of sending "Swarms of Officers to harass our People."

Tenure

Duration or security. The Declaration of Independence accused the king of making judges "dependent on his will alone, for the tenure of their offices."

Tories

Those both in Great Britain and the colonies who supported the king.

Train

Series, as in "a long train of abuses."

Transient

Passing or temporary. The Declaration of Independence asserted that the colonists were not revolting from Britain "for light [insignificant] and transient causes."

Transporting

Carrying.

Trial by jury

One conducted by one's peers. Although developed in Britain, Americans had an even greater attachment to this institution, which they considered to be essential to due process.

Tyranny

A government ruled by a single individual on behalf of his own interests. The Declaration charged that the king of Great Britain had acted as a tyrant with respect to the 13 American colonies.

Tyrant

A single ruler who governs arbitrarily on behalf of his own interests. Although the Declaration of Independence described George III in such a fashion; instead of simply enforcing his own will, he was seeking to uphold the authority of the Parliament (proclaimed in the Declaratory Act of 1765) over the colonists.

Unalienable

Inalienable. Something (specifically rights in the Declaration of Independence) that is so essential to the flourishing of human personhood that it cannot be renounced or restricted.

Unanimous

In one accord. After ratification by New York in mid-July, the Founders referred to the unanimous declaration of the states. This did not mean that every delegate to the Continental Congress had voted for independence but that a majority of every state delegation (each state had an equal vote) had done so.

Undistinguished

Without making distinctions. When the Declaration refers to Indian warfare as resulting in "an undistinguished destruction of all ages, sexes & conditions," it essentially means that the natives fought without distinguishing, as would European powers, between military and civilian personnel.

Unwarrantable

Unjustified. The Declaration accused the Parliament of attempting to "extend an unwarrantable jurisdiction over us."

Usurpations

Unjust claims of authority. In the eyes of American revolutionaries, the British had engaged in "a long train of abuses and usurpations" when, largely after the end of the French and Indian War, they began to tax the colonies.

Virtual representation

The idea, propounded in Great Britain, that since the Parliament represented the interests of all Englishmen, it was not necessary for representatives of the colonies to be physically represented in Parliament (the theory of actual representation) for that body to adopt legislation on their behalf.

Wanting

Lacking. The Declaration proclaimed that Americans had not "been wanting in attentions to our British Brethren."

Whigs

A British political party that was generally more sympathetic to the American cause than Tory supporters of the King. American Patriots drew much of their own political thought from English Whig thinkers, particularly the "Old Whigs," who had not adopted the theory of parliamentary sovereignty.

Further Reading

"The Declaration of Independence." Vocabulary.com. https://www.vocabulary.com/lists/406061.

Lucas, Stephen E. "The Stylistic Artistry of the Declaration of Independence." National Archives. https://www.archives.gov/founding-docs/stylistic-artistry-of-the-declaration.

Bibliography

Articles, Chapters, and Essays

Abbott, Philip. 1997. "The Declaration of Independence: From Philadelphia to Gettysburg to Birmingham." *Amerikastudien / American Studies* 42:451–469.

"The Act of Abjuration and the Declaration of Independence." 2018. https://www.newnetherlandinstitute.org/history-and-heritage/additional-resources/dutch-treats/the-act-of-abjuration/.

Adair, Douglass. 1952. "Rumbold's Dying Speech, 1685, and Jefferson's Last Words on Democracy, 1826." *William and Mary Quarterly* 9 (October):521–531.

Adair, Douglass. 1974. "Fame and the Founding Fathers." In *Fame and the Founding Fathers: Essays*, edited by Trevor Colbourn, 3–26. New York: Norton.

Adams, John. 1776. John Adams to Abigail Adams. July 3. "Had a Declaration . . ." Adams Family Papers: An Electronic Archive. Massachusetts Historical Society. http://www.masshist.org/digitaladams/.

"Address to the People of Great Britain." *American Archives.* 4th ser., 1:917–921. http://amarch.lib.niu.edu/islandora/object/niu-amarch%3A97565.

Agresto, John T. 1977. "Liberty, Virtue, and Republicanism, 1776–1787." *Review of Politics* 39 (October): 473–504.

Alkana, Joseph. 1992. "Spiritual and Rational Authority in Benjamin Rush's Travels through Life." *Texas Studies in Literature and Language* 34 (Summer): 284–300.

Allen, Danielle, and Emily Sneff. 2017. "The Sussex Declaration: Dating the Parchment Manuscript of the Declaration of Independence Held at the West Sussex Record Office (Chichester, UK)." Under final revision and preparation for publication at *Papers of the Bibliographic Society of America.*

Alvis, John. 1998. "Milton and the Declaration of Independence." *Interpretation* 25 (Spring): 367–405.

Andrews, Charles M. 1914. "The Royal Disallowance." Pt. 2. *Proceedings of the American Antiquarian Society* 24 (October): 342–362.

Anthony, Robert W. 1924. "Philip Livingston—A Tribute." *Quarterly Journal of the New York State Historical Association* 5: (October): 311–316.

Armitage, David. 2002. "The Declaration of Independence and International Law." *William and Mary Quarterly* 59:9 (January): 39–64.

Armitage, David. 2004. "The Declaration of Independence in World Context." *OAH Magazine of History* 18 (April): 61–66.

"Assembly Room of Independence Hall." https://www.nps.gov/inde/learn/historyculture/places-independencehall-assemblyroom.htm.

Avery, Margaret. 1978. "Toryism in the Age of the American Revolution: John Lind and John Shebbeare." *Historical Studies* 18:24–36.

Azerrad, David. 2017. "The Declaration of Independence and the American Creed." July 3. The Heritage Foundation. https://www.heritage.org/political-process/commentary/the-declaration-independence-and-the-american-creed.

Bailyn, Bernard. 1976. "1776: A Year of Challenge—A World Transformed." *Journal of Law and Economics* 19:437–466.

Baldwin, Simeon E. 1899. "The People of the United States." *Yale Law Journal* 8:159–167.

Balkin, J. M. "The Declaration and the Promise of a Democratic Culture." *Widener Law Symposium Journal* 4:167–180.

Basch, Norma. 2003. "Declarations of Independence: Women and Divorce in the Early Republic." In *Women and the U.S. Constitution*, 3rd ed., edited by Sibyl A. Schwarzenbach and Patricia Smith, 34–44. New York: Columbia University Press.

Baxter, Maurice. 1987. "The Northwest Ordinance—Our First National Bill of Rights." *OAH Magazine of History* 2 (Fall): 13–14, 18.

Bay, Mia. 2006. "See Your Declaration Americans!!! Abolitionism, Americanism, and the Revolutionary Tradition in Free Black Politics." In *Americanism: New Perspectives on the History of an Ideal*, edited by Michael Kazin and Joseph A. McCartin, 25–52. Chapel Hill: University of North Carolina Press.

Becker, Carl. 1903a. "Election of Delegates from New York to the Second Continental Congress." *American Historical Review* 9 (October): 66–85.

Becker, Carl. 1903b. "The Nomination and Election of Delegates from New York to the First Continental Congress, 1774." *Political Science Quarterly* 18 (March): 17–46.

Belfigio, Valentine J. 1976. "Italians and the American Revolution." *Italian Americana* 3 (Autumn): 1–17.

Bell, Barry. 1983. "Reading, and 'Misreading,' the Declaration of Independence." *Early American Literature* 18 (Spring): 71–83.

Belz, Herman. 1988. "Abraham Lincoln and American Constitutionalism." *Review of Politics* 50 (Spring): 169–197.

[Bentham, Jeremy]. 1776. "Short Review of the Declaration." In *An Answer to the Declaration of the American Congress*, John Lind, 119–132. London: J. Walter, Charingcross and T. Sewell.

Bernstein, R. B. 1999. "Parliamentary Principles, American Realities: The Continental and Confederation Congresses, 1774–1789." In *Inventing Congress: Origins and Establishment of the First Federal Congress*, edited by Kenneth R. Bowling and Donald R. Kennon, 76–108. Athens: Ohio University Press.

Beveridge, Albert J. 1926. "Sources of the Declaration of Independence." *Pennsylvania Magazine of History and Biography* 50:289–315.

Billias, George Athan. 1990. "Elbridge Gerry." *This Constitution* 2 (Spring–Summer): 68–73.

Blasi, Laura, and John K. Lee. 2001. "From the Quill to the Keyboard: Technology and Literacy as Seen through the Declaration of Independence." *English Journal* 90 (May): 123–126.

Blassingame, John W. 1968. "American Nationalism and Other Loyalties in the Southern Colonies, 1763–1775." *Journal of Southern History* 334 (February): 50–75.

Blau, Eleanor. June 14, 1991. "Declaration of Independence Sells for $2.4 Million." *New York Times*. http://www.nytimes.com/1991/06/14/arts/declaration-of-independence-sells-for-2.4-million.html.

Bogin, Ruth. "New Jersey's True Policy: The Radical Republican Vision of Abraham Clark." *William and Mary Quarterly* 35 (January): 100–109.

Boston Committee of Correspondence. 1772. Document known as the "Boston Pamphlet." http://americainclass.org/sources/makingrevolution/crisis/text6/bostonpamphlet.pdf.

Boyd, Julian P. 1932. "Roger Sherman: Portrait of a Cordwainer Statesman." *New England Quarterly* 5 (April): 221–236.

Boyd, Julian P. 1950. "The Disputed Authorship of the *Declaration on the Causes and Necessity of Taking up Arms*, 1774." *Pennsylvania Magazine of History and Biography* 74 (January): 51–73.

Boyd, Julian P. 1976. "The Declaration of Independence: The Mystery of the Lost Original." *Pennsylvania Magazine of History and Biography* 100 (October): 438–467.

Bradley, James E. 1975. "Whigs and Nonconformists: 'Slumbering Radicalism' in English Politics, 1739–1789." *Eighteenth Century Studies* 9 (Autumn): 1–27.

Bradsher, Greg. 2006. "A Founding Father in Dissent." *Prologue* 38 (Spring): 30–35.

Breen, T. H. 1997. "Ideology and Nationalism on the Eve of the American Revolution: Revisions Once More in Need of Revising." *Journal of American History* 84 (June): 13–39.

Briceland, Alan V. "Virginia: The Cement of the Union." In *The Constitution and the States: The Role of the Original Thirteen in the Framing and Adoption of the Federal Constitution*, edited by Patrick T. Conley and John P. Kaminski, 201–223. Madison, WI: Madison House.

Brown, Richard D. 1976. "The Founding Fathers of 1776 and 1787: A Collective View." *William and Mary Quarterly* 33 (July): 465–480.

Buffett, E. P. 1877. "Abraham Clark." *Pennsylvania Magazine of History and Biography* 1:445–448.

Burnett, Edmund C. 1925. "The Name 'United States of America.'" *American Historical Review* 31 (October): 79–81.

Burt, John. 2009. "Lincoln's Dred Scott: Contesting the Declaration of Independence." *American Literary History* 21 (Winter): 730–751.

Butterfield, Lyman H. 1951. "Dr. Rush to Governor Henry on the Declaration of Independence and the Virginia Constitution." *Proceedings of the American Philosophical Society* 95 (June 12): 250–253.

Butterfield, Lyman H. 1953. "The Jubilee of Independence, July 4, 1826." *Virginia Magazine of History and Biography* 61 (April): 119–140.

Cain, Aine. 2017. "Who Signed the Declaration of Independence?" (July 3). http://www.businessinsider.com/who-signed-the-declaration-of-independence-2017-6#elbridge-gerry-25.

Calhoun, John C. (1848, June 27) 1992. "Speech on the Oregon Bill." TeachingAmericanHistory.org/ http://teachingamericanhistory.org/library/document/oregon-bill-speech/. In *Union and Liberty: The Political Philosophy of John C. Calhoun*, edited by Ross M. Lence. Indianapolis: Liberty Fund.

Carpenter, A. H. 1904. "Naturalization in England and the American Colonies." *American Historical Review* 9 (January): 288–303.

Cassinelli, C. W. 1959. "The 'Consent' of the Governed." *Western Political Quarterly* 12 (June): 391–409.

Cattell, J. McKeen. 1927. "Science, the Declaration, Democracy." *Scientific Monthly* 24 (March): 200–205.

Chaffin, Robert J. 1974. "The Declaratory Act of 1766: A Reappraisal." *Historian* 37 (November): 5–25.

Champagne, Roger J. 1964. "New York's Radicals and the Coming of Independence." *Journal of American History* 51 (June): 21–40.

Clason, A. W. 1885. "The Fallacy of 1776." *Magazine of American History* 13 (May): 445–456.

"Coat of Arms." Thomas Jefferson's Monticello. https://www.monticello.org/site/research-and-collections/coat-arms.

Coenen, Michael. 2010. "The Significance of the Signatures: Why the Framers Signed the Constitution and What They Meant by Doing So." *Yale Law Journal* 119 (March): 966–1010.

Colburn, H. Trevor. 1959. "John Dickinson, Historical Revolutionary." *Pennsylvania Magazine of History and Biography* 83 (July): 271–292.

Cole, John Y. 1997. "The Library and the Declaration." The Library of Congress. https://www.loc.gov/loc/lcib/9708/declare.html.

Collier, Christopher. 1988. "Sovereignty Finessed: Roger Sherman, Oliver Ellsworth, and the Ratification of the Constitution in Connecticut." In *The Constitution and the States: The Role of the Original Thirteen in the Framing and Adoption of the Federal Constitution*, edited by Patrick T. Conley and John P. Kaminski, 93–112. Madison, WI: Madison House.

Conley, Patrick T. 1988. "First in War, Last in Peace: Rhode Island and the Constitution, 1786–1790." In *The Constitution and the States: The Role of the Original Thirteen in the Framing and Adoption of the Federal Constitution*, edited by Patrick T. Conley and John P. Kaminski, 269–294. Madison, WI: Madison House.

Conway, Stephen. 2002. "From Fellow-Nationals to Foreigners: British Perceptions of the Americans, circa 1739–1783." *William and Mary Quarterly* 59 (January): 65–100.

Cosgrove, Charles H. 1998. "The Declaration of Independence in Constitutional Interpretation: A Selective History and Analysis." *University of Richmond Law Review* 32 (January): 107–164.

Cotter, Daniel A. 2017. "Richard Henry Lee and the first 'Declaration of Independence.'" *Chicago Daily Law Bulletin*, 19 (June): 5.

Creviston, Vernon P. 2011. "'No King unless It Be a Constitutional King': Rethinking the Place of the Quebec Act in the Coming of the American Revolution." *Historian* 73 (Fall): 463–479.

Crittendon, Charles Christopher. 1924. "The Surrender of the Charter of Carolina." *North Carolina Historical Review* 1 (October): 383–402.

Current, Richard N. 1977. "That Other Declaration: May 20, 1775–May 20, 1975." *North Carolina Historical Review* 54 (April): 169–191.

Dana, William E. 1900. "The Declaration of Independence." *Harvard Law Review* 13 (January): 319–343.

Daniell, Jere. 1988. "Ideology and Hardball: Ratification of the Federal Constitution in New Hampshire." In *The Constitution and the States: The Role of the Original Thirteen in the Framing and Adoption of the Federal Constitution*, edited by Patrick T. Conley and John P. Kaminski. Madison, WI: Madison House.

"Declaration and Resolves of the First Continental Congress." 1774 (October 14). Avalon Project. http://avalon.law.yale.edu/18th_century/resolves.asp.

"Declaration House—An Exact Replica of Where Thomas Jefferson Stayed in 1776." http://www.enjoyingphiladelphia.com/declaration_house.html.

"The Declaration of Independence." Vocabulary.com. https://www.vocabulary.com/lists/406061.

"Declaration of Independence by Binns (Engraving)." Thomas Jefferson's Monticello. https://www.monticello.org/site/house-and-gardens/declaration-indepedence-binns-engraving.

"Declaration of Independence Desk." http://americanhistory.si.edu/collections/search/object/nmah_513641. Accessed August 20, 2017.

"The Declaration of Independence in Modern English." 2008. Surfnetkids. Feldman Publishing. May 28, 2008. Web. November 4, 2018. https://www.surfnetkids.com/independenceday/267/the-declaration-of-independence-in-modern-english/.

"Declaration of Independence Paper." *Thomas Jefferson Encyclopedia*. https://www.monticello.org/site/jefferson/declaration-independence-paper.

"Declaration on Taking Arms." (July 6, 1775) 2014. In *The Declaration of Independence in Historical Context: American State Papers, Petitions, Proclamations, and Letters of the Delegates to the First National Congresses*, compiled and edited by Barry Alan Shain, 277–282. Indianapolis: Liberty Fund.

"Delegate Discussions: Benjamin Rush's Characters." Course of Human Events, August 26, 2016. https://declaration.fas.harvard.edu/blog/dd-rush.

D'Elia, Donald J. 1974. "Benjamin Rush: Philosopher of the American Revolution." *Transactions of the American Philosophical Society* 64:1–113.

Desbler, Charles D. 1892. "How the Declaration Was Received in the Old Thirteen." *Harper's New Monthly Magazine* 85 (July): 165–187.

Detweiler, Philip F. 1958. "Congressional Debate on Slavery and the Declaration of Independence, 1819–1821." *American Historical Review* 63:598–616.

Detweiler, Philip F. 1962. "The Changing Reputation of the Declaration of Independence: The First Fifty Years." *William and Mary Quarterly*, 3rd ser. 29: 557–574.

Diamond, Martin. 1976a. "The American Idea of Equality: The View from the Founding." *Review of Politics* 38 (July): 313–331.

Diamond, Martin. 1976b. "The Revolution of Sober Expectations." In *America's Continuing Revolution*, 23–40. Garden City, NY: Anchor Press.

Diggins, Patrick. 1995. "The Pursuit of Whining." *New York Times*, September 25, A15.

Dipiero, Joseph 2017. "The Common Law of Rebellion." *Georgetown Journal of International Law* 48 (Winter): 605–633.

Doutrich, Paul. 1988. "From Revolution to Constitution: Pennsylvania's Path to Federalism." In *The Constitution and the States: The Role of the Original Thirteen in the Framing and Adoption of the Federal Constitution*, edited by Patrick T. Conley and John P. Kaminski, 37–54. Madison, WI: Madison House.

Downes, Paul. 2012. "Does the Declaration of Independence Declare a State of Emergency?" *Canadian Review of American Studies* 42:7–20.

Drayton, William Henry. 1776. "Judge Drayton's Charge to the Grand Jury of Charleston." American Archives, Documents of the American Revolutionary Period, 1774–1776. 2:1047–1058. http://amarch.lib.niu.edu/islandora/object/niu-amarch%3A100837.

Dreier, Natalie. 2017. "Copy of Declaration of Independence Found in Unlikely Location." April 25. https://www.ajc.com/news/national/copy-declaration-independence-found-unlikely-location/0WX2mdlhbNvkF5oEnf0J6m/

Duff, Stella F. 1949. "The Case against the King: The Virginia Gazettes Indict George III." *William and Mary Quarterly* 6 (July): 383–397.

Dunham, William Huse, Jr., and Charles T. Wood. 1976. "The Right to Rule in England: Depositions and the Kingdom's Authority, 1327–1485." *American Historical Review* 81 (October): 738–761.

Dunn, John. 1967. "Consent in the Political Theory of John Locke." *Historical Journal* 10:153–182.

Dunning, William A. "An Historic Phrase." Part 2. *Proceedings of the American Antiquarian Society*, 24 (October): 82–85.

Eastman, John C. 2002. "The Declaration of Independence as Viewed from the States." In *The Declaration of Independence: Origins and Impact*, edited by Scott Douglas Gerber, 97–117. Washington, DC: CQ Press.

Eltringham, Mark. 2016. "How Thomas Jefferson Came to Invent the Swivel Chair and Laptop." http://workplaceinsight.net/thomas-jefferson-came-invent-swivel-chair/laptop/.

"An Englishman." 1776. Notes accompanying printing of the Declaration of Independence. *Scots Magazine* 38 (August): 433—434.

Eoyang, Eugene. 1999. "Life, Liberty, and the Pursuit of Linguistic Parity: Multilingual Perspectives on the Declaration of Independence." *Journal of American History* 85 (March): 1449–1454.

"An Essay on Love and Marriage." November 1783. *Boston Magazine*, 15–18.

Fairbanks, Rick. 1994–1995. "The Laws of Nature and of Nature's God: The Role of Theological Claims in the Argument of the Declaration of Independence." *Journal of Law and Religion* 11:551–589.

Farrell, James M. 2006. "The Writs of Assistance and Public Memory: John Adams and the Legacy of James Otis." *New England Quarterly* 79 (December): 533–556.

Faulkner, Ronnie W. "Mecklenburg Declaration of Independence." *Encyclopedia of North Carolina*. http://www.ncpedia.org/mecklenburg-declaration.

Fellman, David. 1947. "The American Creed." *Prairie Schooner* 21 (Summer): 231–243.

Ferling, John. 2011. "'The Character of a Fine Writer': Thomas Jefferson and the Drafting of the Declaration of Independence." In *Independence: The Struggle to Set America Free,* 294–317. New York: Bloomsbury Press.

Fetter, Frank Whitson. 1974. "The Revision of the Declaration of Independence in 1941." *William and Mary Quarterly* 31 (January): 133–138.

Fetter, Frank Whitson. 1980. "Who Were the Foreign Mercenaries of the Declaration of Independence?" *Pennsylvania Magazine of History and Biography* 104 (October): 508–513.

Fields, William S., and David T. Hardy. 1991. "The Third Amendment and the Issue of the Maintenance of Standing Armies: A Legal History." *American Journal of Legal History* 35 (October): 393–431.

Fisher, Sydney George. 1907. "The Twenty-Eight Charges against the King in the Declaration of Independence." *Pennsylvania Magazine of History and Biography* 31:247–303.

Ford, John C. 1951. "Natural Law and the Pursuit of Happiness." *Notre Dame Law Review* 26:429–461.

Freehling, William W. 1972. "The Founding Fathers and Slavery." *American Historical Review* 77 (February): 81–93.

Freiberg, Malcolm. 1999. "All's Well That Ends Well: A Twentieth-Century Battle over the Declaration of Independence." *Massachusetts Historical Review* 1:127–134.

"Fresh Takes on the Declaration of Independence." 2017. Edited by Emily Sneff. Harvard University: Declaration Resources Project. https://declaration.fas.harvard.edu/files/declaration/files/fresh_takes.pdf.

Friedenwald, Herbert. 1897. "The Journals and Papers of the Continental Congress." *Pennsylvania Magazine of History and Biography* 21:161–184.

Friedenwald, Herbert. 1904. *The Declaration of Independence: An Interpretation and an Analysis*. New York: Macmillan. www.history.org/almanack/life/politics/sumview.cfm. Accessed July 8, 2017.

Ganter, Herbert Lawrence. 1936. "Jefferson's 'Pursuit of Happiness' and Some Forgotten Men." *William and Mary Quarterly* 16 (July): 422–434.

Garver, Frank Harmon. 1932. "The Transition from the Continental Congress to the Congress of the Confederation." *Pacific Historical Review* 1 (June): 221–234.

George III. 1775. "His Majesty's Most Gracious Speech to Both Houses of Parliament, on Friday, October 27, 1775." Philadelphia. Library of Congress. http://www.loc.gov/resource/rbpe.1440150a.

Gerber, Scott D. 1993. "Whatever Happened to the Declaration of Independence? A Commentary on the Republican Revisionism in the Political Thought of the American Revolution. *Polity* 26 (Winter): 207–231.

Gerlach, Don R. 1966. "A Note on the Quartering Act of 1774." *New England Quarterly* 39 (March): 80–88.

Ginsberg, Robert. 1967. "The Declaration as Rhetoric." In *A Casebook on the Declaration of Independence*, edited by Robert Ginsberg, 219–246. New York: Thomas Y. Crowell Company.

Ginsberg, Robert. 1984. "Suppose that Jefferson's Rough Draft of the Declaration of Independence Is a Work of Political Philosophy." *Eighteenth Century* 25 (Winter): 25–43.

Gipson, Lawrence H. 1931. "Connecticut Taxation and Parliamentary Aid Preceding the Revolutionary War." *American Historical Review* 36 (July): 721–739.

Gittleman, Edwin. 1974. "Jefferson's 'Slave Narrative': The Declaration of Independence as a Literary Text." *Early American Literature* 8 (Winter): 239–256.

Goff, Frederick R. 1947. "A Contemporary Broadside Printing of the Declaration of Independence." *Quarterly Journal of Current Acquisitions* 5 (November): 12–16.

Gorelic, Lester S. 2014: "Depicting the Creation of a Nation: The Story behind the Murals about Our Founding Documents." *Prologue* (Spring): 44–54.

Gould, Christopher. 1986. "The South Carolina and Continental Associations: Prelude to Revolution." *South Carolina Historical Magazine* 87 (January): 30–48.

"Great Britain: Parliament—The Administration of Justice Act; May 20, 1774." The Avalon Project. http://avalon.law.yale.edu/18th_century/admin_of_justice_act.asp.

"Great Britain: Parliament—The Quartering Act; June 2, 1774." Avalon Project. avalon.law .yale.edu/18th_century/quartering_act_1774.asp.

Greene, Evarts B. 1917. "American Opinion on the Imperial Review of Provincial Legislation, 1776–1787." *American Historical Review* 23 (October): 104–107.

Greene, Evarts B. 1936. "Jefferson's 'Pursuit of Happiness' and Some Forgotten Men." *William and Mary Quarterly* 16 (October): 558–585.

Greene, Jack P. 1976. "The Alienation of Benjamin Franklin—British American." *Journal of the Royal Society of Arts* 124 (January): 52–73.

Greene, Jack P. 2000. "The American Revolution." *American Historical Review* 105 (February): 93–102.

Greene, Jack P., and Richard M. Jellison. 1961. "The Currency Act of 1764 in Imperial -Colonial Relations, 1764–1776." *William and Mary Quarterly* 18 (October): 485–518.

Gregory, Tappan. 1948. "The Annual Address: 'Our Lives, Our Fortunes, and Our Sacred Honor.'" *American Bar Association Journal* 34 (October): 874–876, 969–974.

Grey, Thomas C. 1978. "Origins of the Unwritten Constitution: Fundamental Law in American Revolutionary Thought." *Stanford Law Review* 30 (May): 843–893.

Grimes, Alan P. 1976. "Conservative Revolution and Liberal Rhetoric: The Declaration of Independence." *Journal of Politics* 28 (August): 1–19.

Guelzo, Allen C. 2001. "Whig Ideology." In *The Encyclopedia of American Cultural & Intellectual History*, edited by Mary K. Cayton and Peter W. Williams, 197–204. New York: Charles Scribner's Sons.

Ha, Thu-Huong. February 1, 2017. "The Story behind the Statue of Liberty's Unexpected Transformation into a Beacon for Refugees and Immigrants." https://qz.com/898486 /give-me-your-tired-your-poor-the-statue-of-libertys-unexpected-transformation-into -a-beacon-for-refugees-and immigrants/.

Haffenden, Philip S. 1958a. "The Crown and the Colonial Charters, 1675–1688: Part I." *William and Mary Quarterly* 15 (July): 297–311.

Haffenden, Philip S. 1958b. "The Crown and the Colonial Charters, 1675–1688: Part II." *William and Mary Quarterly* 15 (October): 452–466.

Hall, Mark David. 2009. "Roger Sherman: An Old Puritan in a New Nation." In *The Forgotten Founders on Religion and Public Life*, edited by Daniel L. Dreisbach, Mark David Hall, and Jeffrey H. Morrison, 248–277. Notre Dame, IN: University of Notre Dame Press.

Hall, Mark David. 2011. "Did American Have a Christian Founding?" *Faculty Publications—Department of History, Politics, and International Studies*. Paper 53. http//digitalcommons.georgefox.edu/hist_fac/53.

Hamburger, Philip A. 1993. "Natural Rights, Natural Law, and the American Constitutions." *Yale Law Journal* 102 (January): 907–960.

Hamer, Phillip M. 1930. "John Stuart's Indian Policy during the Early Months of the American Revolution." *Mississippi Valley Historical Review* 17 (December): 351–366.

Hamowy, Ronald. 1979. "Jefferson and the Scottish Enlightenment: A Critique of Garry Wills's *Inventing America: Jefferson's Declaration of Independence*." *William and Mary Quarterly* 36 (January): 503–523.

Hancock, John. "To George Washington from John Hancock, 6 July 1776." Founders Online. https://founders.archives.gov/documents/Washington/03-05-02-0153.

Hancock, John. January 31, 1777. "Circular Letter from John Hancock to the State Legislatures." http://;www.docsouth.unc.edu/csr/index.html/document/crs11-0249.

Hancock, John. 1865. "A Relic of the Revolution; Letter from John Hancock to the Convention of North Carolina." http://www.nytimes.com/1865/08/13/archives/a-relic-of-the-revolution-letter-from-john-hancock-to-the.html.

Hart, Charles Henry. 1905. "'*The Congress Voting Independence*. A Painting by Robert Edge Pine and Edward Savage in the Hall of the Historical Society of Pennsylvania." *Pennsylvania Magazine of History and Biography* 29:1–14.

Haw, James. 1993. "The Rutledges, the Continental Congress, and Independence." *South Carolina Historical Magazine* 94 (October): 232–251.

Hays, Minis. 1898. "A Note on the History of the Jefferson Manuscript Draught of the Declaration of Independence in the Library of the American Philosophical Society." *Proceedings of the American Philosophical Society* 37 (January): 88–107.

Hays, Minis. 1900. "A Contribution to the Bibliography of the Declaration of Independence." *Proceedings of the American Philosophical Society* 39 (January): 69–78.

Hedges, William L. 1987. "Telling off the King: Jefferson's 'Summary View' as American Fantasy. Early American Literature." *Politics as Art, Art as Politics: Literature of the Early Republic, 1760–1820* 22 (Fall): 166–174.

Higginbotham, Don. 1994. "Fomenters of Revolution: Massachusetts and South Carolina." *Journal of the Early Republic* 14 (Spring): 1–33.

Hill, Robert S. 1988. "Federalism, Republicanism, and the Northwest Ordinance." *Publius* 18 (Autumn): 41–52.

Himmelfarb, Dan. 1990. "The Constitutional Relevance of the Second Sentence of the Declaration of Independence." *Yale Law Journal* 100 (October): 169–187.

Hoffer, Peter Charles. 1989. "The Declaration of Independence as a Bill in Equity." In *The Law in America, 1607–1861*, edited by William Pencak and Wythe W. Holt Jr., 186–209. New York: New York Historical Society.

Holmes, David L. 1978. "The Episcopal Church and the American Revolution." *Historical Magazine of the Protestant Episcopal Church* 47 (September): 261–291.

Honig, B. 1991. "Declarations of Independence: Arendt and Derrida on the Problem of Founding a Republic." *American Political Science Review* 85 (March): 97–113.

Howell, Wilbur Samuel. 1961. "The Declaration of Independence and Eighteenth-Century Logic." *William and Mary Quarterly* 18 (October): 463–484.

Howell, William Huntting. 2007. "A More Perfect Copy: David Rittenhouse and the Reproduction of Republican Virtue." *William and Mary Quarterly*, 3rd ser. 64 (October): 757–790.

Humphreys, R. A. 1934. "Lord Shelburne and the Proclamation of 1763." *English Historical Review* 49 (April): 241–264.

Hurst, Willard. 1944. "Treason in the United States? I. Treason down to the Constitution." *Harvard Law Review* 58 (December): 226–272.

Hutson, James H. 1972. "The Partition Treaty and the Declaration of Independence." *Journal of American History* 58 (March): 877–896.

Hutchinson, Thomas. 1776. "1776: Hutchinson, Strictures upon the Declaration of Independence." Online Library of Liberty. http://oll.libertyfund.org/pages/1776-hutchinson-strictures-upon-the-declaration-of-independence.

Ingersoll, Robert G. 1924. Declaration of Independence." In *Forty-four Complete Lectures*. Chicago: M. A. Donohue. Accessible at https://lectures-by-ingersoll.blogspot.com/2012/04/declaration-of-independence.html.

Irvin, Benjamin H. 2003. "The Attraction of the Continental Congress." *Pennsylvania Legacies* 3 (May): 28–29.

Irvin, Benjamin H. 2005. "The Streets of Philadelphia: Crowds, Congress, and the Political Culture of Revolution, 1774–1783. *Pennsylvania Magazine of History and Biography* 129 (January): 7–44.

"Jefferson, Franklin, and Adams." http://www.nhd.uscourts.gov/sites/default/files/ci/exhibits/tour/floor-three-exhibits/jefferson-franklin-and-adams.aspx. Accessed August 21, 2017.

Jefferson, Thomas. June 18, 1779. "A Bill for Establishing Religious Freedom." Founders Online. https://founders.archives.gov/documents/Jefferson/01-02-02-0132-0004-0082.

Jefferson, Thomas. "Speech to Jean Baptiste Ducoigne [CA.1] June 1781. Founders Online. https://founders.archives.gov/documents/Jefferson/01-06-02-0059.

Jefferson, Thomas. 1774. *A Summary View of the Rights of British America*. Colonial Williamsburg. Reprint, with an introduction by Paul Leicester Ford. New York: Historical Printing Club, 1892.

Jenkins, Charles F. 1929. "The Two Quaker Signers." *Bulletin of Friends Historical Association* 18 (Spring): 1–32.

Jezierski, John V. 1971. "Parliament or People: James Wilson and Blackstone on the Nature and Location of Sovereignty." *Journal of the History of Ideas* 32 (January–March): 95–106.

Johnson, Amanda. 1932. "Georgia: From Colony to Commonwealth, 1774–1774." *Georgia Historical Quarterly* 16 (December): 253–273.

Jones, Howard Mumford. 1976. "The Declaration of Independence: A Critique." *Proceedings of the American Antiquarian Society*, 55–72. www.americanantiquarian.org/proceedings/4449897.pdf.

Jordan, Winthrop D. 1973. "Familial Politics: Thomas Paine and the Killing of the King, 1776." *Journal of American History* 60 (September): 294–308.

Kahn, Eve M. October 5, 2017. "Newly Discovered Copy of Declaration of Independence Will Be Auctioned." *New York Times*. https://www.nytimes.com/2017/10/05/arts/design/declaration-of-independence-holt-broadside-auction.html.

Kammen, Michael. 2003. "Commemoration and Contestation in American Culture: Historical Perspectives." *Amerikastudien/American Studies* 48:2: 185–205.

Kaplan, Sidney. 1976. "The 'Domestic Insurrections' of the Declaration of Independence." *Journal of Negro History* 61 (July): 243–255.

Karsch, Carl G. n.d. "The First Continental Congress: A Dangerous Journey Begins." Carpenters' Hall. https://web.archive.org/web/20120118024728/http://www.ushistory.org:80/carpentershall/history/congress.htm.

Katz, Stanley N. 1976. "Thomas Jefferson and the Right to Property in Revolutionary America." *Journal of Law & Economics* 29 (October): 467–488.

Kaufman, Irving R. 1980. "The Essence of Judicial Independence." *Columbia Law Review* 80 (May): 671–701.

Kauper, Paul G. 1976. "The Higher Law and the Rights of Man in a Revolutionary Society." In *American's Continuing Revolution,* 41–68. New York: Anchor Press.

Kenyon, Cecelia M. 1951. "Where Paine Went Wrong." *American Political Science Review* 45 (December): 1086–1099.

Kenyon, Cecelia M. 1973. "The Declaration of Independence." *Fundamental Testaments of the American Revolution,* 25–47. Washington, DC: Library of Congress.

Kimball, Roger. November 2006. "The Forgotten Founder: John Witherspoon." *New Criterion.* https://www.newcriterion.com/issues/2006/6/the-forgotten-founder-john-witherspoon.

King, Martin Luther, Jr. "I Have a Dream. . . ." https://www.archives.gov/files/press/exhibits/dream-speech.pdf.

King, Willard L., and Allan Nevins. 1959. "The Constitution and Declaration of Independence as Issues in the Lincoln-Douglas Debates." *Journal of the Illinois State Historical Society* 52 (Spring): 7–32.

Kite, Elizabeth S. 1928. "The Continental Congress and France: Secret Aid and the Alliance, 1776–1778." *Records of the American Catholic Historical Society of Philadelphia* 39 (June): 155–174.

Klein, Milton M. 2000. "John Jay and the Revolution." *New York History* 81 (January): 19–30.

Kloppenberg, James T. 1987. "The Virtues of Liberalism: Christianity, Republicanism, and Ethics in Early American Political Discourse." *Journal of American History* 74 (June): 9–33.

Kmiec, Douglas W. 2005. "The Human Nature of Freedom and Identity—We Hold More than Random Thoughts." *Harvard Journal of Law & Public Policy* 29:33–52.

Knight, John. July 11, 2017. "King George III's Twitter War." *Journal of the American Revolution.* https://allthingsliberty.com/2017/07/king-george-iiis-twitter-war/

Knollenberg, Bernhard. 1963. "John Dickinson vs. John Adams, 1774–1776." *Proceedings of the American Philosophical Society* 107 (April 15): 138–144.

Kristol, Irving. 1976. "The American Revolution as a Successful Revolution." In *America's Continuing Revolution,* 1–22. Garden City, NY: Anchor Press.

Kromkowski, Charles A. 2002. "The Declaration of Independence, Congress, and Presidents of the United States." In *The Declaration of Independence: Origins and Impact*, edited by Scott Douglas Gerber, 118–141. Washington, DC: CQ Press.

Labaree, Benjamin W. 1970. "The Idea of American Independence: The British View, 1774–1776." *Proceedings of the Massachusetts Historical Society*, 3rd Ser. 83: 3–20.

Lambert, Paul F. 1972. "Benjamin Rush and American Independence." *Pennsylvania History: A Journal of Mid-Atlantic Studies* 39 (October): 443–454.

Lambert, Robert S. "The Confiscation of Loyalist Property in Georgia, 1782–1786." *William and Mary Quarterly* 20 (January): 80–94.

Lambeth, Harry J. 1976. "The Lawyers Who Signed the Declaration of Independence." *American Bar Association Journal* 62 (July): 868–873, 876–880.

Lamplugh, George R. 1981. "George Walton, Chief Justice of Georgia, 1783–1785." *Georgia Historical Quarterly*. 65 (Summer): 82–91.

Larson, Carlton F. W. 2001. "The Declaration of Independence: A 225th Anniversary Re-Interpretation," *Washington Law Review* 76 (July): 701–791.

Leffmann, Henry. 1923. "The Real Declaration of Independence: A Study in Colonial History under a Modern Theory." *Pennsylvania Magazine of History and Biography* 47:281–297.

Lence, Ross. 1976. "Thomas Jefferson and the American Declaration of Independence: The Power and Natural Rights of a Free People." *Political Science Reviewer* 6 (Fall): 1–31.

Lence, Ross. 1986. "The American Declaration of Independence: The Majority and the Right of Political Power." In *Founding Principles of American Government: Two Hundred Years of Democracy on Trial,* rev. ed., edited by George J. Graham Jr. and Scarlett G. Graham. Chatham, NJ: Chatham House Publishers.

Lerner, Ralph. "Calhoun's New Science of Politics." *American Political Science Review* 57 (December): 918–932.

Leslie, William R. 1952. "The Gaspee Affair: A Study of Its Constitutional Significance." *Mississippi Valley Historical Review* 39 (September): 233–256.

Levin, David. 1977. "Cotton Mather's Declaration of Gentlemen and Thomas Jefferson's Declaration of Independence." *New England Quarterly* 50 (September): 509–514.

Levinson, Sanford. 1979. "Self-Evident Truths in the Declaration of Independence." *Texas Law Review* 57:847–858.

Lewis, Anthony M. 1948. "Jefferson's Summary View as a Chart of Political Union." *William and Mary Quarterly* 5 (January): 34–51.

Liddle, William D. 1979. "'A Patriot King or None': Lord Bolingbroke and the American Renunciation of George III." *Journal of American History* 65 (March): 951–970.

Lightner, David. 1982. "Abraham Lincoln and the Ideal of Equality." *Journal of the Illinois State Historical Society* 75 (Winter): 289–308.

Lokken, Roy N. 1974. "The Political Theory of the American Revolution: Changing Interpretations." *History Teacher* 8 (November): 81–95.

Looney, J. Jefferson. 2004. "Thomas Jefferson's Last Letter." *Virginia Magazine of History and Biography* 112:178–184.

Lord, Donald C., and Robert M. Calhoon. 1969. "The Removal of the Massachusetts General Court from Boston, 1769–1772." *Journal of American History* 55 (March): 735–755.

Lovejoy, David S. 1959. "Rights Imply Equality: The Case against Admiralty Jurisdiction in America, 1764–1776." *William and Mary Quarterly* 16 (October): 459–484.

Lucas, Stephen E. 1990. "The Stylistic Artistry of the Declaration of Independence." *Prologue: Quarterly of the National Archives and Records Administration.* https://www.archives.gov/founding-docs/stylistic-artistry-of-the-declaration.

Lucas, Stephen E. 1998. "The Rhetorical Ancestry of the Declaration of Independence." *Rhetoric and Public Affairs* 1 (Summer): 143–184.

Lukacs, John. 1987. "Unexpected Philadelphia." *American Heritage* (May/June): 72–81.

Lutz, Donald S. 1989. "The Declaration of Independence as Part of an American National Compact." *Publius* 19 (Winter): 41–58.

Lutz, Donald S. 1990. "The Declaration of Independence, 1776, Commentary." In *Roots of the Republic: American Founding Documents Interpreted*, edited by Stephen L. Schechter, 1138–1145. Madison, WI: Madison House.

Lynd, Straughton, and David Waldstreicher. 2011. "Free Trade, Sovereignty, and Slavery: Toward an Economic Interpretation of American Independence." *William and Mary Quarterly* 68 (October) 597–630.

Mahoney, Dennis J. 1987. "The Declaration of Independence as a Constitutional Document." In *The Framing and Ratification of the Constitution*, edited by Leonard W. Levy and Dennis J. Mahoney, 54–68. New York: Macmillan.

Maier, Pauline. 1976. "Coming to Terms with Samuel Adams." *American Historical Review* 81 (February): 12–37.

Maier, Pauline. 1999. "The Strange History of 'All Men Are Created Equal.'" *Washington and Lee Law Review* 56 (Summer): 873–888.

Maier, Pauline. 2017. "The Strange History of the Bill of Rights." *Georgetown Journal of Law and Public Policy* 15 (Summer): 497–511.

Manca, Joseph. 2003. "Cicero in America: Civic Duty and Private Happiness in Charles Willson Peale's Portrait of 'William Paca.'" *American Art* 17 (Spring): 68–89.

Mansfield, Harvey C., Jr. 1976. "The Right of Revolution." *Daedalus* 105 (Fall): 151–162.

Mansfield, Harvey C., Jr. 1983. "Thomas Jefferson." In *American Political Thought: The Philosophic Dimension of American Statesmanship*, edited by Morton J. Frisch and Richard G. Stevens, 23–50. Itasca, IL: F. E. Peacock.

"March Highlight: Mary Katherine Goddard. Declaration Resource Project. https://declaration.fas.harvard.edu/blog/march-goddard.

Marienstras, Elise, and Naomi Wulf. "French Translations and Reception of the Declaration of Independence." *Journal of American History* 85 (March): 1299–1324.

Marks, Arthur S. 1981. "The Statute of King George III in New York and the Iconology of Regicide." *American Art Journal* 13 (Summer): 61–82.

Marsh, Esbon R. 1941. "The First Session of the Second Continental Congress." *Historian* 3 (Spring): 181–194.

Martinez, Albert J., Jr. 2008–2010. "The Palatinate Clause of the Maryland Charter, 1632–1776: From Independent Jurisdiction to Independence." *American Journal of Legal History* 50 (July): 305–325.

"Massachusetts Circular Letter to the Colonial Legislatures, February 11, 1768." Avalon Project. http://avalon.law.yale.edu/18th_century/mass_circ_let_1768.asp.

Masters, Roger D. 1967. "The Lockean Tradition in American Foreign Policy." *Journal of International Affairs* 21: 253–277.

Matthews, L. L. 1914. "Benjamin Franklin's Plans for a Colonial Union, 1750–1775." *American Political Science Review* 8 (August): 393–412.

Mauch, Christof. 2003. "Images of America—Political Myths—Historiography: 'Hessians' in the War of Independence." *Amerikastudien / American Studies* 48: 411–423.

McCurry, Allan J. 1963. "Joseph Hewes and Independence: A Suggestion." *North Carolina Office of Archives and History* 40 (October): 455–464.

McDonald, Robert M. S. 1999. "Thomas Jefferson's Changing Reputation as Author of the Declaration of Independence: The First Fifty Years." *Journal of the Early Republic* 19 (Summer): 169–195.

McEloy, Robert McNutt. 1919. "The Representative Idea and the American Revolution." *Proceedings of the New York Historical Association* 17:44–55.

McGlone, Robert. 1998. "Deciphering Memory: John Adams and the Authorship of the Declaration of Independence." *Journal of American History* 85 (September): 411–438.

McGovney, Dudley Odell. 1945. "The British Privy Council's Power to Restrain the Legislatures of Colonial America: Power to Disallow Statutes; Power to Veto." *University of Pennsylvania Law Review* 94 (October): 59–93.

McHan, George L. 1978. "The Self-Evident Truths of the Declaration of Independence." *Journal of Thought* 13 (July): 168–175.

McKee, Mary. 2017. "British Reaction to America's Declaration of Independence." British Newspaper Archive, https://blog.britishnewspaperarchive.co.uk/2017/07/04/british-reaction-to-americas-declaration-of-independence/.

McMahon, Darrin M. 2004. "From the Happiness of Virtue to the Virtue of Happiness: 400 B.C.–A.D. 1780." 133 *Daedalus* (Spring): 5–17.

McMahon, Darrin M. 2005. "The Quest for Happiness." *Wilson Quarterly* 29 (Winter): 62–71.

Memmott, Mark. July 4, 2015. "Just a Few Important Words about the Declaration of Independence." NPR. http://www.npr.org/sections/thetwo-way/2015/07/04/419243874/just-a-few-important-words-about-the-declaration-of-independence.

Miller, William B. 1958. "Presbyterian Signers of the Declaration of Independence." *Journal of the Presbyterian Historical Society* 36 (September): 139–179.

Mintage World: Online Museum and Collectorspedia. "American Declaration of Independence." https://www.mintageworld.com/blog/american-declaration-of-independence/.

Mires, Charlene. 1999. "In the Shadow of Independence Hall: Vernacular Activities and the Meanings of Historic Places." *Public Historian* 21 (Spring): 49–64.

Mishra, Pramod K. 2002. "'[A]ll the World Was America': The Transatlantic (Post) Coloniality of John Locke, William Bartram, and the Declaration of Independence." *New Centennial Review* 2 (Spring): 213–258.

Mohr, Walter H. 1938. "George Clymer." *Pennsylvania History: A Journal of Mid-Atlantic Studies* 5 (October): 282–285.

Morgan, David T., and William J. Schmidt. 1975. "From Economic Sanctions to Political Separation: The North Carolina Delegation to the Continental Congress, 1774–1776." *North Carolina Historical Review* 52 (July): 215–234.

Morgan, Edmund S. 1968. "Colonial Ideas of Parliamentary Power, 1764–1766." In *The Reinterpretation of the American Revolution, 1763–1789*, edited by Jack P. Greene, 151–180. New York: Harper and Row.

Morison, Samuel Eliot. 1929. "Elbridge Gerry, Gentleman-Democrat." *New England Quarterly* 2 (January): 6033.

Morison, Samuel Eliot. 1951. "Prelude to Independence: The Virginia Resolutions of May 15, 1776." *William and Mary Quarterly* 8 (October): 483–492.

Mortensen, Louise H. 1961. "Idea Inventory." *Elementary English* 38 (February): 122–124.

Mulcahy, J. T., and James M. Mulcahy. 1956. "*Congress Voting Independence*: The Trumbull and Pine-Savage Paintings." *Pennsylvania Magazine of History and Biography* 80 (January): 74–91.

Munroe, John A. 1952. "Nonresident Representation in the Continental Congress: The Delaware Delegation of 1782." *William and Mary Quarterly*, 3rd ser. 9 (April): 166–190.

Nettels, Curtis P. 1946. "A Link in the Chain of Events Leading to American Independence." *William and Mary Quarterly* 3 (January): 36–47.

New England Historical Society. "The Faulkner Murals Come to Life after Three Long Years." October 5, 2016. http://www.newenglandhistoricalsociety.com/faulkner-murals-come-life-three-long-years/.

"The New York Suspending Act." July 2, 1767. TeachingAmericanHistory.org. http://teachingamericanhistory.org/library/document/the-new-york-suspending-act/.

Nicgorski, Walter. 1976. "The Significance of the Non-Lockean Heritage of the Declaration of Independence." *American Journal of Jurisprudence* 21:156–177.

Nicol, Gene R. 1985. "Children of Distant Fathers: Sketching an Ethos of Constitutional Liberty." *Wisconsin Law Review* 1985 (November/December): 1305–1356.

O'Connor, Francis V. 1998. "Symbolism in the Rotunda." In *Constantino Brumidi: Artist of the Capitol*," edited by Barbara A. Wolanin, 141–155. Washington, DC: U.S. Congress.

Olson, Alison Gilbert. 1960. "The British Government and Colonial Union, 1754." *William and Mary Quarterly*, 3rd ser. 17 (January): 22–34.

Onuf, Peter S. 1998. "A Declaration of Independence for Diplomatic Historians," *Diplomatic History* 22 (Winter): 71–83.

Onuf, Peter S. 1999. "'We Shall All Be Americans': Thomas Jefferson and the Indians." *Indiana Magazine of History* 95 (June): 103–141.

Osgood, Herbert L. 1898. "The American Revolution." *Political Science Quarterly* 13 (March): 41–59.

Paine, Thomas. *Common Sense*. (1776) 2007. In *Classics of American Political & Constitutional Thought: Origins through the Civil War*, edited by Scott J. Hammond, Kevin R. Hardwick, and Howard L. Lubert, 1:267–280. Indianapolis, IN: Hackett.

Papa, Eugene M. Del 1975. "The Royal Proclamation of 1763: Its Effect upon Virginia Land Companies." *Virginia Magazine of History and Biography* 83 (October): 406–411.

Park, Lawrence N. 1960. "Admission of States and the Declaration of Independence." *Temple Law Quarterly* 33: 403–418.

Parker, Geoffrey. 1981. "July 26, 1581: The Dutch 'Declaration of Independence.'" *History Today* 31 (July): 3–6.

Parsons, H. S. "Contemporary English Accounts of the Destruction of Norfolk in 1776." *William and Mary Quarterly* 13 (October): 219–224.

Patrick, Charles J. 2011. "Restoring 'Life, Liberty, and the Pursuit of Happiness' in our Constitutional Jurisprudence: An Exercise in Legal History." *William and Mary Bill of Rights Journal* 20 (December) 457–532.

Pavlovsky, Arnold M. 1977. "'Between Hawk and Buzzard': Congress as Perceived by Its Members, 1775–1783." *Pennsylvania Magazine of History and Biography* 101 (July): 349–364.

Peckham, Howard H. 1976. "Independence: The View from Britain." *Proceedings of the American Antiquarian Society* 85, pt. 2: 387–403. www.americanantiquarian.org/proceedings/44498108.pdf.

Pencak, William. 1990. "The Declaration of Independence: Changing Interpretations and a New Hypothesis." *Pennsylvania History: A Journal of Mid-Atlantic Studies* 57 (July): 225–235.

Penn Biographies. Philip Syng (1703–1789), Penn University Archives & Records Center.http://www.archives.upenn.edu/people/1700s/syng_phil.html.

Pennington, Edgar Legare. "The Anglican Clergy of Pennsylvania in the American Revolution." *Pennsylvania Magazine of History and Biography* 63 (October): 401–439.

Perkins, Eunice Ross. 1933. "The Progress of the Revolution in Georgia." *Georgia Historical Quarterly* 17 (December): 259–275.

Perry, Ralph Barton. 1956. "The Declaration of Independence." In *The Declaration of Independence and the Constitution*, edited by Earl Latham, 108. Boston: D.C. Heath.

"Petition to the King, July 8, 1775." Journals of the Continental Congress. avalon.law.yale.edu/18th_century/con tcong_07-08-75.asp.

Phillips, Heather A. "Preserving Documents of Independence." Archiving Early America. https://www.varsitytutors.com/earlyamerica/early-america-review/volume-11/preserving-documents-of-independence.

Pierce, Michael D. 1972. "The Independence Movement in Virginia, 1775–1776." *Virginia Magazine of History and Biography* 80 (October): 442–452.

Pincus, Steve. September 22, 2016. "America's Declaration of Independence was Pro-immigrant." Aeon Ideas. https://aeon.co/ideas/america-s-declaration-of-independence-was-pro-immigrant.

Pocock, J. G. A. 1987. "States, Republics, and Empires: The American Founding in Early Modern Perspective." *Social Science Quarterly* 68 (December): 703–723.

Pohrt, Tanya. 2013. "Reception and Meaning in John Trumbull's 'Declaration of Independence.'" *Yale University Art Gallery Bulletin*. Teaching with Art: 116–119.

Potvin, Ron M. 2011. "Washington Slept Here? Reinterpreting the Stephen Hopkins House," *History News* 66 (Spring): 17–20.

Powell, John H. 1941. "Notes and Documents, Speech of John Dickinson Opposing the Declaration of Independence, 1 July 1776." *Pennsylvania Magazine of History and Biography* 65 (October): 458–481.

Powell, John H. 1950. "The Debate on American Independence: July 1, 1776." *Delaware Notes* 23:37–62.

"Preamble and Resolution of the Virginia Convention, May 15, 1776." Yale Law School. http://avalon.law.yale.edu/18th_century/const02.asp.

"Preamble to Resolution on Independent Governments, 15 May 1776," Founders Online. https://founders.archives.gov/documents/Adams/06-04-02-0001-0006.

Proctor, Donald J. 1977. "John Hancock: New Soundings on an Old Barrel." *Journal of American History* 64 (December): 652–677.

Quarles, Benjamin. 1958. "Lord Dunmore as Liberator." *William and Mary Quarterly* 14 (October): 494–507.

"The Quartering Act." 1765. America's Homepage. http://ahp.gatech.edu/quartering_act_1765.html.

"Quebec Act of 1774 Text." https://www.landofthebrave.info/1774-quebec-act-text.htm.

Rachum, Illan. 1993. "From 'American Independence' to the 'American Revolution.'" *Journal of American Studies* 27 (April): 73–81.

Rakove, Jack. June 3, 2010. "The Patriot Who Refused to Sign the Declaration of Independence." http://www.historynet.com/the-patriot-who-refused-to-sign-the-declaration-of-independence.htm.

Randall, David A. 1962. "'Duketon Large Enough': III. Thomas Jefferson and the Declaration of Independence." *Papers of the Bibliographical Society of America* 45:472–480.

Raphael, Ray. "Revolutionary Philadelphia." https://www.gilderlehrman.org/history-by-ear/war-for-independence/essays/revolutionary-philadelphia.

Reck, Andrew J. 1977. "The Declaration of Independence as an 'Expression of the American Mind,'" *Revue Internationale de Philosophie* 31:404–437.

Reck, Andrew J. 1991."The Enlightenment in American Law I: The Declaration of Independence." *Review of Metaphysics* 44 (March): 549–573.

Reid, John Phillip. 1977. "In Legitimate Stirps: The Concept of 'Arbitrary,' the Supremacy of Parliament, and the Coming of the American Revolution. *Hofstra Law Review* 5 (Spring): 459–499.

Reid, John Phillip. 1981. "The Irrelevance of the Declaration." *Law in the American Revolution and the Revolution in the Law*, edited by Hendrik Hartog. New York: New York University Press.

Reinstein, Robert. 1993. "Completing the Constitution: The Declaration of Independence, Bill of Rights and Fourteenth Amendment." *Temple Law Review* 66 (Summer): 361–418.

Remini, Robert V. 1988. "The Northwest Ordinance of 1787: Bulwark of the Republic." *Indiana Magazine of History* 84 (March): 15–24.

Renker, Elizabeth M. 1989. "'Declaration-Men' and the Rhetoric of Self-Presentation." *Early American Literature* 24:129–134.

"Resolution of Secrecy Adopted by the Continental Congress, November 9, 1775." http://avalon.law.yale.edu/18th_century/const01.asp.

"Resolutions of Congress on Lord North's Conciliatory Proposal." 1775. The Avalon Project. http://avalon.law.yale.edu/18th_century/jeffnort.asp. Accessed March 19, 2018.

Richards, B. A. 1969. "Inalienable Rights: Recent Criticism and Old Doctrine." *Philosophy and Phenomenological Research* 29 (March): 391–404.

Richardson, William D. 1984. "Thomas Jefferson and Race: The Declaration and Notes on the State of Virginia." *Polity* 16 (Spring): 447–466.

Riker, William H. 1957. "Dutch and American Federalism." *Journal of the History of Ideas* 18 (October): 495–521.

Riley, Edward M. 1953. "The Independence Hall Group." *Transactions of the American Philosophical Society* 43: 7–42.

Ritz, Wilfred J. 1986. "The Authentication of the Engrossed Declaration of Independence on July 4, 1776." *Law and History Review* 4 (Spring): 179–204.

Ritz, Wilfred J. 1992. "From the Here of Jefferson's Handwritten Rough Draft of the Declaration of Independence to the There of the Printed Dunlap Broadside." *Pennsylvania Magazine of History and Biography* 116 (October): 499–512.

Ritzenthaler, Mary Lynn, and Catherine Nicholson. 2016. "The Declaration of Independence and the Hand of Time." *Prologue* 48 (2016). Accessed at https://www.archives.gov/publications/prologue/2016/fall/declaration.

Robbins, Caroline. 1976. "The Pursuit of Happiness." In *America's Continuing Revolution: Eighteen Distinguished Americans Discuss Our Revolutionary Heritage,* edited by Irving Kristol, 115–136. New York: Anchor Press.

Robbins, Caroline. 1977. "Decision in '76: Reflections on the 56 Signers." *Proceedings of the Massachusetts Historical Society*, 3rd ser. 89: 72–87.

Robertson, William J. 1946. "Rare Button Gwinnett." *Georgia Historical Quarterly* 30 (December): 297–307.

Robinson, Daniel N. 2007. "The Scottish Enlightenment and the American Founding." *Monist* 90 (April): 170–181.

Rodney, Caesar A., and Thomas McKean. 1915. "Caesar Rodney's Ride, July 1776." *Pennsylvania Magazine of History and Biography* 39:254–461.

Rogers, J. Alan. 1970. "Colonial Opposition to the Quartering of Troops during the French and Indian War." *Military Affairs* 34 (February): 7–11.

Rolater, Fred S. "Charles Thomson, 'Prime Minister' of the United States." *Pennsylvania Magazine of History and Biography* 101 (July): 322–348.

Rosenfeld, Sophia. 2008. "Tom Paine's Common Sense and Ours," *William and Mary Quarterly*, 3rd Ser. 65 (October): 633–668.

Ross, Jesse. 2012. "'Done in Convention': The Attestation Clause and the Declaration of Independence." *Yale Law Journal* 121 (March): 1236–1249.

Rowe, G. S. 1971. "A Valuable Acquisition in Congress: Thomas McKean, Delegate from Delaware to the Continental Congress, 1774–1783." *Pennsylvania History: A Journal of Mid-Atlantic Studies* 38 (July): 225–264.

"The Royal Proclamation—October 7, 1763," Avalon Project. http://avalon.law.yale.edu/18th_century/proc1763.asp.

Ruell, Peter. April 21, 2017. "A Hidden Declaration." Harvard Gazette. http://news.harvard.edu/gazette/story/2017/04/declaration-different-from-any-copy-we-had-seen/.

Ryan, Frank W., Jr. 1959. "The Role of South Carolina in the First Continental Congress." *South Carolina Historical Magazine* 60 (July): 147–153.

Sacks, Jonathan. 2017. "2017 Irving Kristol Award recipient Rabbi Lord Jonathan Sacks' remarks." ADI. https://www.aei.org/publication/2017-irving-kristol-award-recipient-rabbi-lord-jonathan-sacks-remarks/.

Sadler, Sarah. 2012. "Prelude to the American Revolution? The War of Regulation: A Revolutionary Reaction for Reform." *History Teacher* 46 (November): 97–126.

Sainsbury, John. 1978. "The Pro-Americans of London, 1769 to 1782." *William and Mary Quarterly* 35 (July): 423–454.

Savelle, Max. 1962. "Nationalism and Other Loyalties in the American Revolution." *American Historical Review* 67 (July): 901–923.

Schellhammer, Michael. February 11, 2013. "John Adam's Rule of Thirds." Nhttps://allthingsliberty.com/2013/02/john-adamss-rule-of-thirds/.

Schlesinger, Arthur M. 1964. "The Lost Meaning of 'The Pursuit of Happiness.'" *William and Mary Quarterly* 21 (July): 325–327.

Schmidt, H. D. 1958. "The Hessian Mercenaries: The Career of a Political Cliché." *History* 43:207–212.

Schuessler, Jennifer. 2014. "If Only Thomas Jefferson Could Settle the Issue." *New York Times*, July 2. https://www.nytimes.com/2014/07/03/us/politics/a-period-is-questioned-in-the-declaration-of-independence.html?_r=0.

Schwoerer, Lois G. 1965. "The Literature of the Standing Army Controversy, 1697–1699." *Huntington Library Quarterly* 28 (May): 187–212.

Seagrave, Adam. 2011. "Darwin and the Declaration." *Politics and the Life Sciences* 30 (Spring) 2–16.

Selby, John E. "Richard Henry Lee, John Adams, and the Virginia Constitution of 1776." *Virginia Magazine of History and Biography* 84 (October): 387–400.

Sellers, Charles Coleman, and Charles Willson Peale. 1952. "Portraits and Miniatures by Charles Willson Peale." *Transactions of the American Philosophical Society* 42:1–369.

Shields, Robin. 2010. "Transcript of Publishing the Declaration of Independence." Journeys & Crossings, Library of Congress, July 20. https://www.loc.gov/rr/program/journey/declaration-transcript.html.

"Signers of the Declaration of Independence." National Archives. https://www.archives.gov/founding-docs/signers-factsheet.

Slaski, Eugene R. 1976. "Thomas Willing: A Study in Moderation, 1774–1778." *Pennsylvania Magazine of History and Biography* 100 (October): 491–506.

Smelser, Marshall. 1970. "The Glorious Fourth—or, Glorious Second? Or Eighth?" *History Teacher* 3 (January): 25–30.

Smith, George H. "Was Thomas Jefferson a Plagiarist?" Libertanism.org. https://www.libertarianism.org/publications/essays/excursions/was-thomas-jefferson-plagiarist.

Smith, John E. 1977. "Philosophical Ideas behind the 'Declaration of Independence." *Revue Internationale de Philosophie* 31:360–376.

Smith, Paul H. 1968. "The American Loyalists: Notes on Their Organization and Numerical Strength." *William and Mary Quarterly* 35 (April): 259–277.

Smith, Paul H. 1976. "Time and Temperature: Philadelphia, July 4, 1776." *Quarterly Journal of the Library of Congress* 33 (October): 294–299.

Smith, Richard. 1896. "Diary of Richard Smith in the Continental Congress, 1775–1776." *American Historical Review* 1 (January): 288–310 and 1 (April): 493–516.

Smith, William Raymond. 1965. "The Rhetoric of the Declaration of Independence." *College English* 26 (January): 306–309.

Snow, Alpheus Henry. 1921. "The Declaration of Independence as the Fundamental Constitution of the United States." In *The American Philosophy of Government*, 35–66. New York: G. P. Putnam's Sons.

Sosin, Jack M. 1963. "The Massachusetts Acts of 1774: Coercive or Preventive?" *Huntington Library Quarterly* 26 (May): 235–252.

Spillane, J. D. 1976. "Doctors of 1776." *British Medical Journal* 1, no. 6025 (June 16): 1571–1574.

"Stamp for Independence: A Brief Philatelic Tour of the Declaration of Independence." http://blogs.bl.uk/americas/2017/06/stamp-for-independence-a-brief-philatelic-tour-of-the-declaration-of-independence.html.

Starr, Thomas. 2002. "Separated at Birth: Text and Context of the Declaration of Independence." *Proceedings of the American Antiquarian Society*. http://www.americanantiquarian.org/proceedings/44539508.pdf.

"The States and the Congress Move toward Independence, 1775–1776." *Publius* 6 (Winter): 135–143.

Stathis, Stephen W. 1978. "Returning the Declaration of Independence to Philadelphia: An Exercise in Centennial Politics." *Pennsylvania Magazine of History and Biography* 102 (April): 167–183.

Steele, Brian. 2008. "Thomas Jefferson's Gender Frontier." *Journal of American History* 95 (June): 17–42.

Stille, Charles J. 2890. "Pennsylvania and the Declaration of Independence." *Pennsylvania Magazine of History and Biography* 13 (January): 385–429.

Stoiber, Julie. 2003. Discovery of Stone Uncovers Syng Plot." *Philadelphia Inquirer*, May 18: B01.

Stokes, Durward T. 1973. "British Sermons Favorable to the American Revolution." *Social Science* 58 (Summer): 131–141.

Stoner, James R., Jr. 2011. "The Declaration of Independence." http://www.nlnrac.org/american/declaration-of-independence.

Stoner, James R., Jr. 2005. "Is There a Political Philosophy in the Declaration of Independence?" https://home.isi.org/there-political-philosophy-declaration-independence.

Strang, Lee J. 2006. "Originalism, the Declaration of Independence, and the Constitution: A Unique Role in Constitutional Interpretation?" *Penn State Law Review* 111 (Fall): 413–479.

Strauss, Valerie. "How Hot Was It on July 4, 1776?" *Washington Post*. July 4, 2012. https://www.washingtonpost.com/blogs/answer-sheet/post/how-hot-was-july-4-1776-thanks-to-jefferson-we-know/2012/07/04/gJQAPnjPNW_blog.html?utm_term=.9b4bb89b669d.

Surrency, Erwin C. 2004. "The Transition from Colonialism to Independence." *American Journal of Legal History* 46 (January): 55–81.

Taylor, Robert J. 1977. "John Adams: Legalist as Revolutionist." *Proceedings of the Massachusetts Historical Society*, 3rd Ser. 89:55–71.

Thelen, David. 2002. "Reception of the Declaration of Independence." In *The Declaration of Independence: Origins and Impact*, edited by Scott Douglas Gerber, 191–212. Washington, DC: CQ Press.

Thomas, P. D. G. 1985. "George III and the American Revolution." *History* 70 (February): 16–31.

Tiedemann, Joseph S. 2009. "Interconnected Communities: The Middle Colonies on the Eve of the American Revolution." *Pennsylvania History: A Journal of Mid-Atlantic Studies* 76 (Winter): 1–41.

Tiedemann, Joseph S. 2010. "A Tumultuous People: The Rage for Liberty and the Ambiance of Violence in the Middle Colonies in the Years Preceding the American Revolution." *Pennsylvania History: A Journal of Mid-Atlantic Studies* 77 (Autumn): 387–431.

Totten, Robbie. 2008. "National Security and U.S. Immigration Policy, 1776–1790." *Journal of Interdisciplinary History* 39 (Summer): 37–64.

Tourtellot, Arthur Bernon. 1962. "We Mutually Pledge to Each Other Our Lives, Our Fortunes and Our Sacred Honor." *American Heritage*. https://www.americanheritage.com/content/we-mutually-pledge-each-other-our-lives-our-fortunes-and-our-sacred-honor.

Trujillo, Joaquin. 2011. "The American Appropriation of God in Select Foundational Documents of the United States." *Analecta Hermeneutica* 3:1–15.

Tsesis, Alexander. 2012. "Self-Government and the Declaration of Independence." *Cornell Law Review* 97 (May): 693–751.

Tsesis, Alexander. 2016. "The Declaration of Independence as Introduction to the Constitution." *Southern California Law Review* 89 (March): 359–367.

Tucker, Louis Leonard. 1979. "Centers of Sedition: Colonial Colleges and the American Revolution." *Proceedings of the Massachusetts Historical Society*, 3rd ser. 92:16–34.

Tutt, Juliana. 2010. "'No Taxation without Representation' in the American Woman Suffrage Movement." *Stanford Law Review* 62 (May): 1473–1512.

Tyler, Moses Coit. 1896. "The Declaration of Independence in the Light of Modern Criticism." *North American Review* 163 (July): 1–16.

"Unsullied by Falsehood: The Signing." Course of Human Events. https://declaration.fas.harvard.edu/blog/signing.

Van Tyne, Claude H. 1907. "Sovereignty in the American Revolution: An Historical Study." *American Historical Review* 12 (April): 529–545.

Varg, Paul A. 1964. "The Advent of Nationalism, 1758–1776." *American Quarterly* 16 (Summer): 169–181.

Varga, Nicholas. "The New York Restraining Act: Its Passage and Some Effects, 1766–1768." *New York History* 37 (July): 233–258.

"Virginia Resolution—May 15, 1776." http://www.revolutionary-war-and-beyond.com/virginia-resolution-proposing-independence.html.

"Virginia Resolutions on Lord North's Conciliatory Proposal, 10 June 1775." Founders Online. https://founders.archives.gov/documents/Jefferson/01-01-02-0106.

"The Virginia Resolves of 1769," TeachingAmericanHistory.org. http://teachingamericanhistory.org/library/document/the-virginia-resolves-of-1769/.

"Virginia Stamp Act Resolutions." Colonial Williamsburg. http://www.history.org/history/teaching/tchcrvar.cfm.

Wahrman, Dror. 2001. "The English Problem of Identity in the American Revolution." *American Historical Review* 107 (October): 1236–1261.

Walker, Gay. 1987. "Women Printers in Early American Printing History." *Yale University Library Gazette* 61 (April): 116–124.

Walsh, Kevin C. March 10, 2015. "Marshall on Political Liberty, the Declaration of Independence, and Jefferson's 1801 Inaugural Address." http://mirrorofjustice.blogs.com/mirrorofjustice/2015/023/marshall-on-political-liberty-the-declaration-of-independence-and-jeffersons-1801-inaugural-address.html.

Wang, Amy B. 2017. "Some Trump Supporters Thought NPR Tweeted 'Propaganda.' It was the Declaration of Independence." *Washington Post*, July 5.

Warner, William B. 2009. "The Invention of a Public Machine for Revolutionary Sentiment: The Boston Committee of Correspondence." *Eighteenth Century* 40 (Summer/Fall): 145–164.

Warren, Charles. 1945. "Fourth of July Myths." *William and Mary Quarterly* 2 (July): 237–272.

Washington, George. June 8, 1783. "Washington's Circular Letter of Farewell to the Army." http://www.loc.govve/teachers/classroommaterials/presentationsandactivities/presentations/timeline/amrev/peace/circular.html.

Watson, Alan D. 1996. "The Committees of Safety and the Coming of the American Revolution in North Carolina, 1776–1776." *North Carolina Historical Review* 73 (April): 131–155.

Watson, Richard A. 1987. "Origins and Early Development of the Veto Power," *Presidential Studies Quarterly* 17 (Spring): 401–412.

Webber, Mabel I. 1930. "Dr. John Rutledge and His Descendants." *South Carolina Historical and Genealogical Magazine* 31 (January): 7–25.

Wendorf, Richard. 2014. "Declaring, Drafting, and Composing American Independence." *Bibliographical Society of America* 108:307–324.

West, Thomas G. 2002a. "The Declaration of Independence, the U.S. Constitution, and the Bill of Rights." In *The Declaration of Independence Origins and Impact*, edited by Scott Douglas Gerber, 72–95. Washington, DC: CQ Press.

West, Thomas G. 2002b. "*Jaffa versus Mansfield*: Does America Have a Constitutional or a 'Declaration of Independence' Soul?" *Perspectives on Political Science* 32 (Fall): 235–246.

West, Thomas G. 2003. "The Political Theory of the Declaration of Independence." In *The American Founding and the Social Compact*, edited by Ronald J. Pestritto and Thomas G. West, 95–146. Lanham, MD: Lexington Books.

Wilf, Steven. 2000. "Placing Blame: Criminal Law and Constitutional Narratives in Revolutionary Boston." *Crime, History & Societies* 4:31–61.

Wilhoite, Fred H., Jr. 1965. "'The Consent of the Governed' in Two Traditions of Political Thought." *Southwestern Social Science Quarterly* 46 (June): 59–66.

Wilkinson, Norman B. 1941. "Francis Hopkinson: Humor Propagandist of the American Revolution." *Historian* 4 (Autumn): 5–33.

Wilson, James. 2007. "Considerations on the Nature and Extent of the Legislative Authority of the British Parliament, 1774." In *Collected Works of James Wilson*, Vol. 1, edited by Kermit L. Hall and Mark David Hall, 3–30. 2 vols. Indianapolis, IN: Liberty Fund.

Wilson, Rick K., and Calvin Jillson. 1989. "Leadership Patterns in the Continental Congress, 1774–1789." *Legislative Studies Quarterly* 14 (February): 5–37.

Wilson, Woodrow. 1907. "The Author and Signers of the Declaration of Independence." *North American Review* 186 (September): 22–33.

Wishy, Bernard. 1958. "John Locke and the Spirit of '76." *Political Science Quarterly*. 73 (September): 413–425.

Wolfe, Christopher. 2004. "Thomistic Natural Law and the American Natural Law Tradition." In *St. Thomas Aquinas and the Natural Law Tradition: Contemporary Perspectives*, edited by John Gotette et al. Washington, DC: Catholic University of America Press.

Wood, Gordon S. 2011. "The Problem of Sovereignty." *William and Mary Quarterly* 68 (October): 573–577.

Wrenn, Tony P. 1969. "The Honest Man—Matthew Thornton of New Hampshire." *Pioneer America* 1 (July): 30–39.

Wright, Benjamin Fletcher. 1958. "Consensus and Continuity, 1776–1787." *Boston University Law Review* 38 (Winter): 1–52.

"Writing the Declaration of Independence, 1776 / J. L. G. Ferris." Library of Congress. https://www.loc.gov/item/2002719535/.

Wunder, John R. 2000/2001. "'Merciless Indian Savages' and the Declaration of Independence: Native Americans Translate the Ecunnaunuxulgee Document." *American Indian Law Review* 25: 65–92.

Yarbrough, Jean. 1991. "Race and the Moral Foundations of the American Republic: Another Look at the Declaration and the Notes on Virginia." *Journal of Politics* 53 (February): 90–105.

York, Neil L. 1998. "The First Continental Congress and the Problem of American Rights." *Pennsylvania Magazine of History and Biography* 122 (October): 353–383.

York, Neil L. 2009. "George III, Tyrant: 'The Crisis' as Critics of Empire, 1775–1776," *History* 94 (October): 434–460.

York, Neil L. 2011. "Imperial Impotence: Treason in 1774 Massachusetts." *Law and History Review* 29 (August): 657–701.

York, Neil L. 2017. "Natural Rights Dissected and Rejected: John Lind's Counter to the Declaration of Independence." *Law and History Review* 35 (August): 563–593.

Zall, Paul M. 2004. *Adams on Adams*. Lexington: University Press of Kentucky.

Zaller, Robert. 1993. "The Figure of the Tyrant in English Revolutionary Thought." *Journal of the History of Ideas* 54 (October): 585–610.

Zetterberg, Hans L. 2010. "A Vocabulary Justifying Revolutions." *Sociologisk Forskning* 47:75–81.

Zimmerman, John J. 1958. "Charles Thomson: 'The Sam Adams of Philadelphia.'" *Mississippi Valley Historical Review* 45 (December): 464–480.

Zimmerman, John J. 1967. "Governor Denny and the Quartering Act of 1756." *Pennsylvania Magazine of History and Biography* 91 (July): 266–281.

Zuckert, Michael P. 1987. "Self-Evident Truth and the Declaration of Independence." *Review of Politics* 49 (Summer): 319–339.

Zucker, Michael P. 2004. "Natural Rights and Protestant Politics." In *Protestantism and the American Founding*, edited by Thomas S. Engeman and Michael P. Zuckert, 21–76. Notre Dame, IN: University of Notre Dame Press.

Books

Adams, John. 1979. *Papers of John Adams*. Vol. 4, *February–August 1776*. Edited by Robert J. Taylor. Cambridge, MA: Belknap Press of Harvard University Press.

Adams, Samuel. *The Writings of Samuel Adams*. Vol. 3, *1773–1777*. Edited by Harry Alonzo Cushing. New York: G. P. Putnam's Sons.

Adams, William Paul. 2001. *The First American Constitutions: Republican Ideology and the Making of the State Constitutions in the Revolutionary Era*. Lanham, MD: Rowman and Littlefield.

Adler, Mortimer J., and William Gorman. 1975. *The American Testament*. New York: Praeger.

Allen, Danielle. 2014. *Our Declaration: A Reading of the Declaration of Independence in Defense of Equality*. New York: W. W. Norton

Amar, Akhil Reed. 1998. *The Bill of Rights: Creation and Reconstruction*. New Haven, CT: Yale University Press.

Ammerman, David. 1974. *In the Common Cause: American Response to the Coercive Acts of 1775*. Charlottesville: University Press of Virginia.

Amos, Gary T. 1989. *Defending the Declaration: How the Bible and Christianity Influenced the Writing of the Declaration of Independence*. Charlottesville, VA: Providence Foundation.

Anastaplo, George. 2007. *Reflections on Freedom of Speech and the First Amendment*. Lexington: University Press of Kentucky.

Anderson, Owen. 2015. *The Declaration of Independence and God: Self-Evident Truths in American Law*. New York: Cambridge University Press.

Andrlik, Todd. 2012. *Reporting the Revolutionary War: Before it Was History, It Was News*. Naperville, IL: Sourcebooks.

Archer, Richard. 2010. *As If an Enemy's Country: The British Occupation of Boston and the Origins of Revolution*. New York: Oxford University Press.

Armitage, David. 2007. *The Declaration of Independence: A Global History*. Cambridge, MA: Harvard University Press.

Arnn, Larry P. 2012. *The Founders' Key: The Divine and Natural Connection between the Declaration and the Constitution and What We Risk by Losing It*. Nashville, TN: Thomas Nelson.

Atwood, Rodney. 2002. *The Hessians: Mercenaries from Hesse-Kassel in the American Revolution*. New York: Cambridge University Press.

Bailyn, Bernard. 1967. *The Ideological Origins of the American Revolution*. Cambridge, MA: Belknap Press of Harvard University Press.

Bailyn, Bernard. 1976. *The Ordeal of Thomas Hutchinson*. Cambridge, MA: Belknap Press of Harvard University Press.

Burnett, Edmund C., ed. 1921. *Letters of Members of the Continental Congress*. Washington, DC: Carnegie Institution of Washington.

Barnett, Randy E. 2016. *Our Republican Constitution: Securing the Liberty and Sovereignty of We the People*. New York: Broadside Books.

Barone, Michael. 2007. *Our First Revolution: The Remarkable British Upheaval That Inspired America's Founding Fathers*. New York: Crown Publishers.

Bean, Jonathan, ed. 2009. *Race and Liberty in America: The Essential Reader*. Lexington: University Press of Kentucky.

Becker, Carl. (1922) 1970. *The Declaration of Independence: A Study in the History of Political Ideas*. New York: Vintage Books.

Bedini, Silvio A. 1981. *Declaration of Independence Desk: Relic of Revolution*. Washington, DC: Smithsonian Institution Press.

Beeman, Richard R. 2013. *Our Lives, Our Fortunes, and Our Sacred Honors: The Forging of American Independence, 1774–1776*. New York: Basic Books.

Bergen, Frank. 1898. *The Other Side of the Declaration of Independences*. Newark, NJ: Baker Printing Co.

Bernhard, Virginia, and Elizabeth Fox-Genovese, eds. 1995. *The Birth of American Feminism: The Seneca Falls Woman's Convention of 1848*. St. James, NY: Brandywine Press.

Billias, George Athan. 1976. *Elbridge Gerry: Founding Father and Republican Statesman*. New York: McGraw-Hill.

Birzer, Bradley J. 2010. *American Cicero: The Life of Charles Carroll*. Wilmington, DE: ISI Books.

Black, Jeremy. 2006. *George III: America's Last King*. New Haven, CT: Yale University Press.

Blumrosen, Alfred W., and Ruth G. Blumrosen. 2005. *Slave Nation: How Slavery United the Colonies and Sparked the American Revolution*. Naperville, IL: Sourcebooks, Inc.

Bolla, Peter de. 2007. *The Fourth of July and the Founding of America*. Woodstock, NY: Overlook Press.

Bowen, Catherine Drinker. 1950. *John Adams and the American Revolution*. Boston: Little, Brown.

Boyd, Julian P. 1999. *The Declaration of Independence: The Evolution of the Text*. Washington, DC: Library of Congress in association with the Thomas Jefferson Memorial Foundation, Inc.

Boyer, William W., and Edward C. Ratledge. 2009. *Delaware Politics and Government*. Lincoln: University of Nebraska Press.

Bradburn, Douglas. 2009. *The Citizenship Revolution: Politics and the Creation of the American Union, 1774–1804*. Charlottesville: University of Virginia Press.

Bradford, M. E. 1979. *A Better Guide Than Reason: Studies in the American Revolution*. La Salle, IL: Sherwood Sugden.

Broadwater, Jeff. 2006. *George Mason: Forgotten Founder*. Chapel Hill: University of North Carolina Press.

Brookhiser, Richard. 2003. *Gentleman Revolutionary: Gouverneur Morris, The Rake Who Wrote the Constitution*. New York: Free Press.

Brown, Imogene E. 1982. *American Aristides: A Biography of George Wythe*. Madison, NJ: Fairleigh Dickinson University Press.

Brown, Richard D. 2017. *Self-Evident Truths: Contesting Equal Rights from the Revolution to the Civil War.* New Haven, CT: Yale University Press.

Bruckberger, R. L. 1959. *Image of America*. New York: Viking Press.

Brunsman, Denver. 2013. *The Evil Necessity: British Naval Impressment in the Eighteenth-Century Atlantic World*. Charlottesville: University of Virginia Press.

Burgess, Douglas R., Jr. 2014. *The Politics of Piracy: Crime and Civil Disobedience in Colonial America*. Lebanon, NH: ForeEdge, an imprint of University Press of New England.

Burke, Edmund. 1966. *On the American Revolution: Selected Speeches and Letters*. Edited by Elliott Robert Barkan. New York: Harper and Row.

Burnett, Edmund C. 1964. *The Continental Congress*. New York: W. W. Norton.

Burstein, Andrew. 2001. *America's Jubilee: How in 1826 a Generation Remembered Fifty Years of Independence*. New York: Alfred A. Knopf.

Calhoun, John C. 1854. *The Works of John C. Calhoun*. Vol. 4. New York: D. Appleton.

Calvert, Jane E. 2008. *Quaker Constitutionalism and the Political Thought of John Dickinson*. Cambridge: Cambridge University Press.

Candidus [James Chalmers]. 1776. *Plain Truth: Addressed to the Inhabitants of American, Containing Remarks on a late Pamphlet, intitled Common Sense. . . .* 2nd ed. Philadelphia: R. Bell.

Capansky, Trisha. 2011. "The Declaration of Independence: A New Genre in Political Discourse or Mixed Genres in an Unlikely Medium?" PhD diss., East Carolina University.

Carso, Brian F., Jr. 2006. *"Whom Can We Trust Now?" The Meaning of Treason in the United States, from the Revolution through the Civil War*. Lanham, MD: Lexington Books.

Cassel, Melissa. 2011. *Abraham Clark*. Conshohocken, PA: Infinity Publishing.

Charles, Patrick J. 2008. *Irreconcilable Grievances: The Events That Shaped the Declaration of Independence*. Westminster, MD: Heritage Books.

Charlton, Thomas Patrick. 2012. *The First American Republic, 1774–1789: The First Fourteen American Presidents before Washington*. Bloomington, IN: AuthorHouse.

Chernow, Ron. 2004. *Alexander Hamilton*. New York: Penguin Press.

Chitwood, Oliver Perry. 1967. *Richard Henry Lee: Statesman of the Revolution*. Morgantown: West Virginia University Library.

Chopra, Ruma. 2011. *Unnatural Rebellion: Loyalists in New York City during the Revolution*. Charlottesville: University of Virginia Press.

Coelho, Chris. 2013. *Timothy Matlack: Scribe of the Declaration of Independence*. Jefferson, NC: McFarland.

Cogliano, Francis D. 2006. *Thomas Jefferson: Reputation and Legacy*. Edinburgh: Edinburgh University Press.

Cohen, I. Bernard. 1995. *Science and the Founding Fathers: Science in the Political Thought of Jefferson, Franklin, Adams, and Madison*. New York: W. W. Norton.

Colburn, Trevor. 1998. *The Lamp of Experience: Whig History and the Intellectual Origins of the American Revolution*. Indianapolis: Liberty Fund.

Coleman, Kenneth. 1958. *The American Revolution in Georgia, 1763–1789*. Athens: University of Georgia Press.

Corn, Ira G., Jr. 1977. *The Story of the Declaration of Independence, Illustrated and Documented*. Los Angeles: Corwin Books.

Cunningham, Noble E. 1987. *The Pursuit of Reason: The Life of Thomas Jefferson*. Baton Rouge: Louisiana State University Press.

Curran, Robert Emmett. 2014. *Papist Devils*. Washington, DC: Catholic University of America Press.

Darsey, James. 1997. *The Prophetic Tradition and Radical Rhetoric in America*. New York: New York University Press.

David, James Corbett. 2013. *Dunmore's New World*. Charlottesville: University of Virginia Press.

Davidson, James West, and Mark Hamilton Lytle. 1982. *After the Fact: The Art of Historical Detection*. New York: Alfred A. Knopf.

Davis, Derek H. 2000. *Religion and the Continental Congress, 1774–1789: Contributions to Original Intent*. New York: Oxford University Press.

Deloria, Vine, Jr. 1985. *Behind the Trail of Broken Treaties: An Indian Declaration of Independence*. El Paso: University of Texas Press.

Dershowitz, Alan. 2003. *America Declares Independence*. Hoboken, NJ: John Wiley and Sons.

Dickerson, Oliver M. 1951. *The Navigation Acts and the American Revolution*. Philadelphia: University of Pennsylvania Press.

Dickinson, Harry T., ed. *British Pamphlets on the American Revolution, 1763—1785*. 4 vols. New York: Routledge.

Donaldson, Thomas. 1898. *The House in Which Thomas Jefferson Wrote the Declaration of Independence*. Philadelphia: Avil Printing Company.

Drake, James D. 2011. *The Nation's Nature: How Continental Presumptions Gave Rise to the United States of America*. Charlottesville: University of Virginia Press.

Dumbauld, Edward. 1950. *The Declaration of Independence and What It Means Today*. Norman: University of Oklahoma Press.

Eicholz, Hans L. 2001. *Harmonizing Sentiments: The Declaration of Independence and the Jeffersonian Idea of Self-Government*. New York: Peter Lang.

Eidelberg, Paul. 1974. *A Discourse on Statesmanship: The Design and Transformation of the American Polity*. Urbana: University of Illinois Press.

Eidelberg, Paul. 1976. *On the Silence of the Declaration of Independence*. Amherst: University of Massachusetts Press.

Ellis, Joseph J. 1993. *Passionate Sage: The Character and Legacy of John Adams*. New York: W. W. Norton.

Ellis, Joseph J. 2007. *American Creation: Triumphs and Tragedies at the Founding of the Republic*. New York: Alfred A. Knopf.

Engels, Jeremy. 2010. *Enemyship: Democracy and Counter-Revolution in the Early Republic*. East Lansing: Michigan State University Press.

Farrand, Max, ed. 1966. *The Records of the Federal Convention of 1787*. 4 vols. New Haven, CT: Yale University Press.

Ferling, John. 1992. *John Adams: A Life*. New York: Henry Holt.

Ferris, Robert G., ed. 1975. *Signers of the Declaration: Historical Places Commemorating the Signing of the Declaration of Independence*. Rev. ed. Washington, DC: U.S. Department of the Interior, National Park Service.

Finkelman, Paul. 1996. *Slavery and the Founders: Race and Liberty in the Age of Jefferson*. Armonk, NY: M. E. Sharpe.

Finnis, John. 2011. *Natural Law and Natural Rights*. New York: Oxford University Press.

Fitcher, James R. 2010. *So Great a Profit*. Cambridge, MA: Harvard University Press.

Fliegelman, Jay. 1993. *Declaring Independence: Jefferson, Natural Language, and the Culture of Performance*. Stanford, CA: Stanford University Press.

Ford, Paul Leicester, ed. 1893. *The Writings of Thomas Jefferson*. Vol. 2, 1776–1781. New York: G. P. Putnam's Sons.

Forman, Samuel A. 2011. *Dr. Joseph Warren: The Boston Tea Party, Bunker Hill, and the Birth of American Liberty*. Gretna, LA: Pelican Publishing.

Friedenwald, Herbert. 1904. *The Declaration of Independence: An Interpretation and an Analysis*. New York: Macmillan.

Galloway, Joseph. 1775. *A Candid Examination of the Mutual Claims of Great-Britain and the Colonies, with a Plan of Accommodation, on Constitutional Principles*. New York: James Rivington.

Gerber, Scott Douglas. 1995. *To Secure These Rights: The Declaration of Independence and Constitutional Interpretation*. New York: New York University Press.

Gerber, Scott Douglas, ed. 2002. *The Declaration of Independence: Origins and Impact*. Washington, DC: CQ Press.

Ginsberg, Robert, ed. 1967. *A Casebook on the Declaration of Independence*. New York: Thomas Y. Crowell.

Goff, Frederick R. 1976. *The John Dunlap Broadside: The First Printing of the Declaration of Independence*. Washington, DC: Library of Congress.

Goldwin, Robert A. 1990. *Why Blacks, Women, and Jews Are Not Mentioned in the Constitution, and Other Unorthodox Views*. Washington, DC: AEI Press.

Goldwin, Robert A. 1997. *From Parchment to Power: How James Madison Used the Bill of Rights to Save the Constitution*. Washington, DC: AEI Press.

Gordon-Reed, Annette. 2009. *The Hemingses of Monticello: An American Family*. New York: W. W. Norton.

Greene, Jack P. 2011. *The Constitutional Origins of the American Revolution*. New York: Cambridge University Press.

Grossman, Mark. 2015. *Encyclopedia of the Continental Congresses*. 2 vols. Amenia, NY: Grey House Publishing.

Grudin, Robert. 2010. *Design and Truth*. New Haven, CT: Yale University Press.

Grundfest, Jerry. 1982. *George Clymer. Philadelphia Revolutionary*. New York: Arno.

Hall, David. 1997. *The Political and Legal Philosophy of James Wilson, 1742–1798*. Columbia: University of Missouri Press.

Hall, David. 2011. *A Reforming People: Puritanism and the Transformation of Public Life in New England*. Chapel Hill: University of North Carolina Press.

Hamilton, Alexander, James Madison, and John Jay. (1787–1788) 1961. *The Federalist Papers*. New York: New American Library.

Hammond, Cleon E. 1977. *John Hart: The Biography of a Signer of the Declaration of Independence*. Newfane, VT: Pioneer.

Hastings, George E. 1926. *The Life and Work of Francis Hopkinson*. Chicago: University of Chicago Press.

Hawke, David Freeman. 1964. *A Transaction of Free Men: The Birth and Course of the Declaration of Independence*. New York: Charles Scribner's Sons.

Hawke, David Freeman. 1976. *Honorable Treason: The Declaration of Independence and the Men Who Signed It*. New York: Viking Press.

Hazelton, John H. (1905) 2015. *The Declaration of Independence: Its History*. London: Forgotten Books.

Head, John M. 1968. *A Time to Rend: An Essay on the Decision for American Independence.* Madison: State Historical Society of Wisconsin.

Hess, Stephen. 2016. *America's Political Dynasties.* Washington, DC: Brookings Institution Press.

Hitchens, Christopher. 2005. *Thomas Jefferson: Author of America.* New York: Atlas Books.

Hobbes, Thomas. (1651) 1968. *Leviathan.* Baltimore, MD: Penguin Books.

Holland, Matthew S. 2007. *Bonds of Affection: Civic Charity and the Making of America—Winthrop, Jefferson, and Lincoln.* Washington, DC: Georgetown University Press.

[Hopkins, Stephen]. 1764. *The Grievances of the American Colonies Candidly Examined.* Providence, RI: William Goddard.

Huston, James L. *The American and British Debate over Equality, 1776–1920.* Baton Rouge: Louisiana State University Press.

Irvin, Benjamin H. 2011. *Clothed in Robes of Sovereignty: The Continental Congress and the People Out of Doors.* New York: Oxford University Press.

Isaacson, Walter. 2003. *Benjamin Franklin: An American Life.* New York: Simon and Schuster.

Israel, Jonathan. 2017. *The Expanding Blaze: How the American Revolution Ignited the World, 1775–1849.* Princeton, NJ: Princeton University Press.

Jacobsohn, Gary Jeffrey. 1993. *Apple of Gold: Constitutionalism in Israel and the United States.* Princeton, NJ: Princeton University Press.

Jayne, Allen. 1998. *Jefferson's Declaration of Independence.* Lexington: University Press of Kentucky.

Jefferson, Thomas. (1785) 1964. *Notes on the State of Virginia.* New York: Harper and Row.

Jefferson, Thomas. 1893. *The Writings of Thomas Jefferson.* Vol. 2. Edited by Paul Leicester Ford. New York: Putnam's.

Jefferson, Thomas. 1950. *The Papers of Thomas Jefferson.* Edited by Julian P. Boyd. Vol. 1, *1760–1776.* Princeton, NJ: Princeton University Press.

Jefferson, Thomas. 1974. *Thomas Jefferson: A Biography in His Own Words.* 2 vols. New York: Newsweek.

Jillson, Cal. 2016. *The American Dream: In History, Politics, and Fiction.* Lawrence: University Press of Kansas.

Jones, Howard Mumford. 1953. *The Pursuit of Happiness.* Ithaca, NY: Cornell University Press.

Jones, Howard Mumford, and Howard H. Peckham. 1976. *The Declaration of Independence: Two Essays.* Worcester, MA: American Antiquarian Society.

Journals of the Continental Congress, 1774–1789. 1906a. Vol. 4, *January 1–June 4, 1776.* Washington, DC: Government Printing Office.

Journals of the Continental Congress, 1774–1789. 1906b. Vol. 5, *June 5–October 8, 1776.* Washington, DC: Government Printing Office.

Kellogg, Louise Phelps. 1904. *The American Colonial Charter.* Washington, DC: U.S. Government Printing Office.

Kendall, Willmoore, and George W. Carey. 1970. *The Basic Symbols of the American Political Tradition.* Baton Rouge: Louisiana State University Press.

Kennedy, Jennifer Tiercel. 1999. "Signing History: The Memoirs of Benjamin Franklin, Benjamin Rush, John Adams, and Thomas Jefferson." PhD diss., Yale University.

Kiernan, Denise, and Joseph D'Agnese. 2009. *Signing Their Lives Away: The Fame and Misfortune of the Men Who Signed the Declaration of Independence.* Philadelphia: Quirk Books.

King, William Casey. 2013. *Ambition, a History: From Vice to Virtue*. New Haven, CT: Yale University Press.

Kinzer, Stephen. 2017. *The True Flag: Theodore Roosevelt, Mark Twain, and the Birth of American Empire*. New York: Henry Holt.

Koch, Adrienne. 1950. *Jefferson and Madison: The Great Collaboration*. New York: Oxford University Press.

Krebs, Daniel. 2015. *A Generous and Merciful Enemy: Life for German Prisoners of War during the American Revolution*. Norman: University of Oklahoma Press.

Krotoszynski, Ronald. 2012. *Reclaiming the Petition Clause: Sedition Libel, "Offensive" Protest, and the Right to Petition the Government for a Redress of Grievances*. New Haven, CT: Yale University Press.

Labunski, Richard. 2006. *James Madison and the Struggle for the Bill of Rights*. New York: Oxford University Press.

Lawler, Peter Augustine. 2010. *Modern and American Dignity: Who We Are as Persons, and What That Means for Our Future*. Wilmington, DE: ISI Books.

Lealock, John. 1776. *The Fall of British Tyranny; or, American Liberty Triumphant, The First Campaign*. Philadelphia: Styner and Cist. Pla.

[Lee, Arthur]. 1775. *An Appeal to the Justice and Interests of the People of Great Britain in the Present Dispute with America. By an Old Member of Parliament*. 2nd ed. London: Printed for J. Almon.

Lee, Nell Moore. 1988. *Patriot above Profit: A Portrait of Thomas Nelson Jr., Who Supported the American Revolution with His Purse and Sword*. Nashville, TN: Rutledge Hill Press.

Lengyel, Cornel. 1958. *Four Days in July*. Garden City, NY: Doubleday.

Letters of Members of the Continental Congress. Edited by Edmund C. Burnett. Vol. 1, *August 29, 1774, to July 4, 1776*. Washington, DC: Carnegie Institute.

Levinson. Sanford. 2006. *Our UnDemocratic Constitution: Where the Constitution Goes Wrong (and How We the People Can Correct It)*. New York: Oxford University Press.

Lewis, Joseph. *Thomas Paine, Author of the Declaration of Independence*. New York: Freethought Press Association.

Lincoln, Abraham. 1953. *The Collected Works of Abraham Lincoln*. Edited by Roy P. Basler. 9 vols. New Brunswick, NJ: Rutgers University Press.

Lind, John. 1776. *An Answer to the Declaration of the American Congress*. London: J. Walter, Charingcross and T. Sewell.

Litke, Justin B. 2013. *Twilight of the Republic*. Lexington: University Press of Kentucky.

Locke, John. (1690) 1924. *Two Treatises of Government*. London: Dent, Everyman's Library.

Lossing, B. J. 1848. *Biographical Sketches of the Signers of the Declaration of American Independence; The Declaration Historical Considered; and a Sketch of the Leading Events Connected with the Adoption of the Articles of Confederation and of the Federal Constitution*. New York: George F. Cooledge and Brothers.

Lucas, Stephen E. 1976. *Portents of Rebellion: Rhetoric and Revolution in Philadelphia, 1765–1776*. Philadelphia: Temple University Press.

Lynd, Staughton. 2009. *Intellectual Origins of American Radicalism*. New ed. New York: Cambridge University Press.

[Macpherson, James.] (1775). 1776 *The Rights of Great Britain Asserted against the Claims of America: Being an Answer to the Declaration of the General Congress*. London: Printed for T. Cadell.

Magliocca, Gerard N. 2018. *The Heart of the Constitution: How the Bill of Rights Became the Bill of Rights*. New York: Oxford University Press.

Maier, Pauline. 1997. *American Scripture: Making the Declaration of Independence*. New York: Alfred A. Knopf.

Mailer, Gideon. 2017. *John Witherspoon's American Revolution: Enlightenment and Religion from the Creation of Britain to the Founding of the United States*. Chapel Hill: University of North Carolina Press.

Malia, Martin. 2006. *History's Locomotives: Revolutions and the Making of the Modern World*. New Haven, CT: Yale University Press.

Malone, Dumas. 1948. *Jefferson the Virginian*. Vol 1 of *Jefferson and His Time*. Boston: Little, Brown.

Malone, Dumas. 1954. *The Story of the Declaration of Independence*. New York: Oxford University Press.

Marston, Jerrilyn Greene. 1987. *King and Congress: The Transfer of Political Legitimacy, 1774–1776*. Princeton, NJ: Princeton University Press.

Mayer, David N. 1994. *The Constitutional Thought of Thomas Jefferson*. Charlottesville: University Press of Virginia.

McClellan, James. 2000. *Liberty, Order, and Justice: An Introduction to the Constitutional Principles of American Government*. 3rd ed. Indianapolis: Liberty Fund.

McCullough, David. 2002. *John Adams*. New York: Simon and Schuster.

McGaughy, J. Kent. 2004. *Richard Henry Lee of Virginia: A Portrait of an American Revolutionary*. Lanham, MD: Rowman and Littlefield.

McKenna, George. 2007. *The Puritan Origins of American Patriotism*. New Haven, CT: Yale University Press.

Meacham, Jon. 2012. *Thomas Jefferson: The Art of Power*. New York: Random House.

Michael, William H. 1904. *The Declaration of Independence: Illustrated Story of Its Adoption with the Biographies and Portraits of the Signers and of the Secretary of the Congress*. Washington, DC: Government Printing Office.

Middlekauff, Robert. 2005. *The Glorious Cause: The American Revolution, 1763–1789*. New York: Oxford University Press.

Miller, Thomas P., ed. 2015. *The Selected Writings of John Witherspoon*. Carbondale: Southern Illinois University Press, Landmarks in Rhetoric and Public Address.

Mires, Charlene. 2013. *Independence Hall in American Memory*. Philadelphia: University of Pennsylvania Press.

Mon Droit [Selden, Richard Ely]. 1846. *Criticism on the Declaration of Independence as a Literary Document*. New York: For Sale at the News Offices.

Morgan, David T., and William J. Schmidt. 1976. *North Carolinians in the Continental Congress*. Winston-Salem, NC: John F. Blair Publisher.

Morgan, Edmund S. 1976. *The Meaning of Independence: John Adams, Thomas Jefferson, George Washington*. New York: W. W. Norton.

Morrison, Jeffry H. 2007. *John Witherspoon and the Founding of the American Republic*. Notre Dame, IN: University of Notre Dame Press.

Munves, James. 1978. *Thomas Jefferson and the Declaration of Independence: The Writing and Editing of the Document That Marked the Birth of the United States of America*. New York: Charles Scribner's Sons.

Myers, Henry Alonzo. 1955. *Are Men Equal? An Inquiry into the Meaning of American Democracy*. Ithaca, NY: Great Seal Books of Cornell University Press.

Nabors, Forrest A. 2017. *From Oligarchy to Republicanism: The Great Task of Reconstruction*. Columbia: University of Missouri Press.

Nagel, Paul C. 2006. *The Lees of Virginia: Seven Generations of an American Family*. New York: Oxford University Press.

Nash, Garb B. 2006. *First City: Philadelphia and the Forging of Historical Memory*. Philadelphia: University of Pennsylvania Press.

Nelson, Eric. 2014. *The Royalist Revolution: Monarchy and the American Founding*. Cambridge, MA: Harvard University Press.

Noll, Mark A. 1989. *Princeton and the Republic, 1768–1822: A Search for a Christian Enlightenment in the Era of Samuel Stanhope Smith*. Princeton, NJ: Princeton University Press.

Nordholt, J. W. Schulte. 1982. *The Dutch Republican and American Independence*. Translated by Herbert H. Rowen. Chapel Hill: University of North Carolina Press.

O'Leary, Cecilia Elizabeth. 1999. *To Die For: The Paradox of American Patriotism*. Princeton, NJ: Princeton University Press.

Ostwald, Martin. 2009. *Language and History in Ancient Greek Culture*. Philadelphia: University of Pennsylvania Press.

Owen, David R., and Michael C. Tolley. 1995. *Courts of Admiralty in Colonial America: The Maryland Experience, 1634–1776*. Durham, NC: Carolina Academic Press.

Paine, Thomas. 1953. *Common Sense and Other Political Writings*. Edited by Nelson F. Adkins. New York: Liberal Arts Press.

Palmer, R. R. 2014. *The Age of the Democratic Revolution: A Political History of Europe and America, 1760–1800*. Princeton, NJ: Princeton University Press.

Pangle, Thomas L. 1988. *The Spirit of Modern Republicanism: The Moral Vision of the American Founders and the Philosophy of Locke*. Chicago: University of Chicago Press.

Parkinson, Robert G. 2016. *The Common Cause: Creating Race and Nation in the American Revolution*. Chapel Hill: University of North Carolina Press.

Patrick, Tim. 2017. *Self-Evident: Discovering the Ideas and Events that Made the Declaration of Independence Possible*. Seattle: Owani Press.

Pelton, Robert W. 2012. *Men of Destiny! Signers of Our Declaration of Independence and Our Constitution*. Knoxville, TN: Freedom and Liberty Foundation Press.

Penegar, Kenneth Lawing. 2011. *The Political Trial of Benjamin Franklin: A Prelude to the American Revolution*. New York: Algora Publishing.

Peters, Ronald M., Jr. 1978. *The Massachusetts Constitution of 1780: A Social Compact*. Amherst: University of Massachusetts Press.

Pincus, Steve. 2016. *The Heart of the Declaration: The Founders' Case for an Activist Government*. New Haven, CT: Yale University Press.

Pole, J. R. 1975. *The Decision for American Independence*. Edited by Harold M. Hyman. Philadelphia: J. B. Lippincott.

Puleo, Stephen. 2016. *American Treasures: The Secret Efforts to Save the Declaration of Independence, the Constitution, and the Gettysburg Address*. New York: St. Martin's.

Quincy, Josiah, Jr. 1774. *Observations on the Act of Parliament, Commonly Called the Boston Port-Bill; with Thoughts on Civil Society and Standing Armies*. Boston: Edes and Gill.

Rabkin, Jeremy A. 2005. *Law without Nations? American Independence and the Opinions of Mankind*. Princeton, NJ: Princeton University Press.

Rakove, Jack N. 1979. *The Beginnings of National Politics: An Interpretive History of the Continental Congress*. New York: Alfred A. Knopf.

Raphael, Ray. 2004. *Founding Myths: Stories That Hide Our Patriotic Past*. New York: MJF Books.

Rappleye, Charles. 2010. *Robert Morris: Financier of the American Revolution*. New York: Simon and Schuster.

Reich, Jerome R. 2015. *British Friends of the American Revolution*. New York: Routledge.

Reid, John Philip. 1991. *Constitutional History of the American Revolution: The Authority to Legislate*. Madison: University of Wisconsin Press.

Rhode Island in the American Revolution. An Exhibition from the Library and Museum Collections of the Society of the Cincinnati. Washington, DC: October 17, 2000–April 14, 2001. http://www.societyofthecincinnati.org/pdf/downloads/exhibition_RhodeIsland.pdf.

Rosenfeld, Sophia. 2011. *Common Sense*. Cambridge, MA: Harvard University Press.

Rubin, Dan, ed. 2013. *Words on Plays: Insight into the Play, the Playwright, and the Production: 1776, a Musical Play*. San Francisco: American Conservatory Theatre.

Rush, Benjamin. 1905. *A Memorial containing Travels through Life or Sundry Incidents in the Life of Dr. Benjamin Rush*. Lanoraie, QC: Louis Alexander Biddle.

Russell, E. B. 1915. *The Review of American Colonial Legislation by the King in Council*. New York: Columbia University Press.

Sadosky, Leonard J. 2009. *Revolutionary Negotiations: Indians, Empires, and Diplomats in the Founding of America*. Charlottesville: University of Virginia Press.

Salley, A. S. *Delegates to the Continental Congress from South Carolina, 1774–1779, with Sketches of the Four Who Signed the Declaration of Independence*. 1927. Columbia, SC: State Company.

Sandefur, Timothy. 2014. *The Conscience of the Constitution: The Declaration of Independence and the Right to Liberty*. Washington, DC: Cato Institute.

Schlenther, Boyd Stanley. 1990. *Charles Thomson: A Patriot's Pursuit*. Newark: University of Delaware Press.

Schwoerer, Lois G. 1981. *The Declaration of Rights, 1689*. Baltimore, MD: Johns Hopkins University Press.

Selby, John E. 1988. *The Revolution in Virginia, 1775–1783*. Williamsburg, VA: Colonial Williamsburg Foundation.

Sha'ban, Fuad. 2005. *For Zion's Sake: The Judeo-Christian Tradition in American Culture*. Ann Arbor, MI: Pluto Press.

Shain, Barry Alan, ed. 2014. *The Declaration of Independence in Historical Context*. Indianapolis: Liberty Fund.

Shalev, Eran. 2009. *Rome Reborn on Western Shores*. Charlottesville: University of Virginia Press.

Sheldon, Garrett Ward. 1991. *The Political Philosophy of Thomas Jefferson*. Baltimore, MD: Johns Hopkins University Press.

Shestokas, David J. 2017. *Creating the Declaration of Independence*. Lemont, IL: Constitutionally Speaking.

Sims, Kevin F. 1991. "The Defense of American Sovereignty: The Declaration of Independence as a Foreign Policy Statements." PhD diss., Claremont Graduate School.

Smith, Charles Page. 1956. *James Wilson: Founding Father, 1742–1798*. Chapel Hill: University of North Carolina Press.

Smith, George H. 2017. *The American Revolution and the Declaration of Independence*. Washington, DC: Cato Institute.

Smith, Herbert C., and John T. Willis. 2012. *Maryland Politics and Government*. Lincoln: University of Nebraska Press.

Smith-Rosenberg, Carroll. 2010. *This Violent Empire: The Birth of an American National Identify*. Greensboro: University of North Carolina Press.

Spalding, Matthew. 2009. *We Still Hold These Truths: Rediscovering Our Principles, Reclaiming Our Future*. Wilmington, DE: ISI Books.

Stahr, Walter. 2005. *John Jay: Founding Father*. New York: Bloomsbury.

Stewart, Matthew. 2014. *Nature's God: The Heretical Origins of the American Republic*. New York: W. W. Norton.

Stoll, Ira. 2008. *Samuel Adams: A Life*. New York: Free Press.

Strauss, Leo. 1999. *Natural Rights and History*. Rev. ed. Chicago: University of Chicago Press.

Taylor, Alan. 2016. *American Revolutions: A Continental History, 1750–1804*. New York: W. W. Norton.

Tetrault, Lisa. 2014. *The Myth of Seneca Falls: Memory and the Woman's Suffrage Movement, 1848–1898*. Chapel Hill: University of North Carolina Press.

Thomson, Keith. 2012. *Jefferson's Shadow: The Story of His Science*. New Haven, CT: Yale University Press.

Thucydides. 1951. *The Peloponnesian War*. New York: Modern Library.

Traves, Len. 1997. *Celebrating the Fourth: Independence Day and the Rites of Nationalism in the Early Republic*. Amherst: University of Massachusetts Press.

Trenchard, John, and Thomas Gordon. (1755) 1995. *Cato's Letters or Essays on Liberty, Civil and Religious, and Other Important Subjects*. Edited by Ronald Hamowy. 2 vols. Indianapolis, IN: Liberty Fund.

Tsesis, Alexander. 2012. *For Liberty and Equality: The Life and Times of The Declaration of Independence*. New York: Oxford University Press.

[Tucker, Josiah]. 1776. *A Series of Answers to Certain Popular Objections, Against Separating from the Rebellious Colonies and Discarding Them Entirely: Being the Concluding Tract of the Dean of Glocester on the Subject of American Affairs*. Gloucester: R. Raikes.

Unger, Harlow Giles. 2000. *John Hancock: Merchant King and American Patriot*. New York: John Wiley and Sons.

Unger, Harlow Giles. 2017. *First Founding Father: Richard Henry Lee and the Call to Independence*. New York: Da Capo Press.

Valsania, Maurizio. 2013. *Nature's Man: Thomas Jefferson's Philosophical Anthropology*. Charlottesville: University of Virginia Press.

Van Cleve, George William. 2017. *We Have Not a Government: The Articles of Confederation and the Road to the Constitution*. Chicago: University of Chicago Press.

Vile, John R. 1992. *The Constitutional Amending Process in American Political Thought*. New York: Praeger.

Vile, John R. 2015a. *A Companion to the United States Constitution and Its Amendments*. 6th ed. Santa Barbara, CA: Praeger.

Vile, John R. 2015b. *Encyclopedia of Constitutional Amendments, Proposed Amendments, and Amending Issues, 1789–2015*, 4th ed. 2 vols. Santa Barbara, CA: ABC-CLIO.

Vile, John R. 2015c. *Founding Documents of America: Documents Decoded*. Santa Barbara, CA: ABC-CLIO.

Vile, John R. 2015d. *The Wisest Council in the World: Restoring the Character Sketches by William Pierce of Georgia of the Delegates to the Constitutional Convention of 1787*. Athens: University of Georgia Press.

Vile, John R. 2016. *American Immigration and Citizenship: A Documentary History*. Lanham, MD: Rowman and Littlefield.

Vile, John R. 2017. *The Jacksonian and Antebellum Eras: Documents Decoded*. Santa Barbara, CA: ABC-CLIO.

Waites, Alfred. 1903. *A Brief Account of John Milton and His Declaration of Independence*. Worcester, MA: Gilbert G. Davis.

Waldman, Steven. 2008. *Founding Faith: Providence, Politics, and the Birth of Religious Freedom in America*. New York: Random House.

Waldstreicher, David. 2010. *Slavery's Constitution: From Revolution to Ratification*. New York: Hill and Wang.

Webking, Robert H. 1988. *The American Revolution and the Politics of Liberty*. Baton Rouge: Louisiana State University Press.

West, Thomas G. 2017. *The Political Theory of the American Founding: Natural Rights, Public Policy, and the Moral Conditions of Freedom*. New York: Cambridge University Press.

White, Morton. 1978. *The Philosophy of the American Revolution*. New York: Oxford University Press.

Whitney, Peter. 1777. *A Sermon Delivered September 12, 1776. At a Lecture Appointed for Publishing the Declaration of Independence Passed July 4, 1776. By the Representatives of the United States of America in General Congress Assembled*. Boston: E. Draper.

Wilhelmy, Jean-Pierre. 2009. *Soldiers for Sale: German "Mercenaries" with the British in Canada during the American Revolution, 1776–1783*. Montreal: Baraka Books.

Wills, Garry. 1978. *Inventing America: Jefferson's Declaration of Independence*. Garden City, NY: Doubleday.

Wills, Garry. 2003. *"Negro President": Jefferson and the Slave Power*. Boston: Houghton Mifflin.

Wolf, Edwin II. 1975. *Philadelphia: Portrait of an American City*. Philadelphia: Wenchell.

Wood, Gordon S. 1969. *The Creation of the American Republic, 1776–1787*. Chapel Hill: University of North Carolina Press.

Wood, Gordon S. 2004. *The Americanization of Benjamin Franklin*. New York: Penguin Press.

Yolton, John W., ed. 1969. *John Locke: Problems and Perspectives*. Cambridge: University Press.

Young, Ralph. 2015. *Dissent: The History of an American Ideal*. New York: New York University Press.

Index

Page numbers in **bold** indicate the location of main entries; page numbers in *italics* indicate photos.

About the Author

John R. Vile, PhD, is professor of political science and dean of the University Honors College at Middle Tennessee State University. He has written and edited a variety of books on legal issues, the U.S. Constitution, and the American Founding period. They include the following: *The American Flag: An Encyclopedia of the Stars and Stripes in U.S. History, Culture, and Law* (2018); *Essential Supreme Court Decisions*, 17th ed (2018); *Constitutional Law in Contemporary America*, 2 vols. (2017); *The Constitutional Convention of 1787: A Comprehensive Encyclopedia of America's Founding*, 2 vols., 2nd ed. (2016); *Conventional Wisdom: The Alternative Article V Mechanism for Proposing Amendments to the U.S. Constitution* (2016); *The Civil War and Reconstruction Eras* (2018); *The Jacksonian and Antebellum Eras* (2017); *The Early Republic* (2016); *Founding Documents of America: Documents Decoded* (2015); *American Immigration and Citizenship* (2016); *Encyclopedia of Constitutional Amendments, Proposed Amendments, and Amending Issues, 1789–2015*, 4th ed. (2015); *The United States Constitution: One Document, Many Choices* (2015); *A Companion to the United States Constitution and Its Amendments*, 6th ed. (2015); *The Wisest Council in the World: Restoring the Character Sketches by William Pierce of Georgia of the Delegates to the Constitutional Convention of 1787* (2015); *Re-Framers: 170 Eccentric, Visionary, and Patriotic Proposals to Rewrite the U.S. Constitution* (2014); *The Men Who Made the Constitution: Lives of the Delegates to the Constitutional Convention of 1787* (2013); *Encyclopedia of the Fourth Amendment* (2013); *The Writing and Ratification of the U.S. Constitution: Practical Virtue in Action* (2012); *Encyclopedia of the First Amendment*, rev. online ed. (2017); *James Madison: Founder, Philosopher, Founder and Statesman* (2008); *The Encyclopedia of Civil Liberties in America* (2005); *Great American Judges: An Encyclopedia* (2003); *Great American Lawyers: An Encyclopedia* (2002); *Tennessee Government and Politics* (1998); *Constitutional Change in the United States* (1994); *The Theory and Practice of Constitutional Change in America* (1993); *Contemporary Questions Surrounding the Constitutional Amending Process* (1993); *The Constitutional Amending Process in American Political Thought* (1992); *Rewriting the United States Constitution* (1991); and *History of the American Legal System: Interactive Encyclopedia* (CD-ROM, 2000).